Education and Development:
Latin America and the Caribbean

Latin American Studies Series
Volume 18

Education and Development: Latin America and the Caribbean

Edited by Thomas J. La Belle

Latin American Center · University of California · Los Angeles · 1972

Acknowledgments

I wish to express my appreciation to Johannes Wilbert, Director of the Latin American Center at UCLA, whose encouragement promoted the publication of this book through the Center's facilities. I also wish to thank Jan Van Orman, a graduate student in comparative education at UCLA, who aided in finding all of the articles originally considered for inclusion through diligent searching in the libraries. In addition I owe considerable gratitude to Janina Ely, publications editor in the Latin American Center, whose administrative, editorial, and secretarial skills aided greatly in the preparation of this book.

This anthology was developed with the financial support of the Agency for International Development. The information and conclusions contained herein do not necessarily reflect the position of A.I.D. or the U.S. Government.

T. J. L.

Minor editing has been done mainly to assure greater stylistic uniformity; e.g., endnotes were converted into footnotes, the rhetorical "we" of several selections (1, 2, 7, 11, 12, 14, and 27) was changed to "I," capitalization, italicization, and use of quotes were simplified, and all tables set up to fit one format. It is hoped that these editorial measures have enhanced the overall appeal of the book.

Preface

The professional educator's desire to better comprehend the variability in human behavior corresponds to his interest in the promotion of experiences which lead to changes in that behavior. Although the educator has increasingly been attracted to other institutional and noninstitutional settings, the school remains his, as well as society's, primary center for promoting cognitive, affective, and psychomotor growth or change in learners. The school's role in guiding these behavioral changes toward the fulfillment of a nation's collective goals often corresponds to the learner's desire for a different and improved life style as a reward for successful mastery of the schooling process. Although the peoples of Latin America and the Caribbean along with their counterparts in much of the world generally support the schools for meeting such individual and collective goals, the evidence suggests that they are often frustrated in their use of the school to achieve the better life.

This book is addressed to the complexities inherent in meeting both individual and national goals through schooling. The problems and issues surrounding the role and function of schools in this development process are most often multifaceted and thus require complicated and difficult modes of inquiry. How, for example, does the scholar measure the economic and social return on an investment to a particular type or level of schooling? Of what importance are the social, cultural, political, and economic contexts in which schooling takes place? The answers to such questions will emerge only through reliance on multidisciplinary conceptualizations and methodological approaches. Thus, this book contains contributions by both educators and social scientists who attempt to reveal the myths about schooling as well as its abilities and potentials in the development process.

Although this is not the first book of data on the relationship between education and development, it is the first educational anthology which is devoted to the issue in the context of Latin America and the Caribbean. Since the schooling process can only reflect the environment in which it exists, its structure and orientation must be viewed in terms of its referent culture. The culture in turn sets limits on the possible strategies for resolving the issues and problems. This volume seeks to clarify some of these problems. It does not go far enough in this respect, however, since Latin America and the Caribbean, even separately, are not culturally, politically, economically, or socially homogeneous environments. In this sense, the scope of the book is too broad. On the other hand, the availability of research and scholarly literature obviates any narrower approach.

This dearth of material is the major reason why such a book has not been published before. In the introduction to his annotated bibliography on education in Latin America and the Caribbean, Gordon C. Ruscoe provides some substance for this reasoning. He states:

> The Scholar of Latin American Education, particularly if his bent is toward empirical research, will continue to be disappointed in the materials available. Polemical and oratorical works, on the one hand, and sterile collections of ill-organized and unanalyzed statistical and historical information. on the other, continue to prevail. There have been some attempts to explore empirical data and to develop theoretical frameworks in which to maximize the use of such data but most of these are marred by claims about Latin American education which are unsubstantiated, stemming in part from a paucity of evidence and in part from inadequate conceptualization. In either case the empirical studies, although certainly welcomed, remain limited in usefulness and scope.[1]

Although one is almost forced to concur with Ruscoe's observations on the state of knowledge about education in these geographical areas, it would be inaccurate to suggest that considerable progress has not been made. For example, several substantial studies have been completed during recent years.[2] In addition, empirical data have been published in periodicals and

---

[1] Ruscoe, Gordon C., "Latin America (except Brazil)," in Henry E. Adams (ed.), Handbook of Latin American Studies (Social Sciences), 31 (1968), p. 310. University of Florida Press, Gainesville, Florida.

Roscoe's review of the literature on Latin America and the Caribbean and Agnes Toward's adjoining article reviewing the literature on education in Brazil are among the most complete bibliographic sources available and follow a special issue of the Latin American Research Review devoted to education (Latin American Research Review, III, no. 1 [Fall, 1967], University of Texas, Austin).

[2] Among these recent studies, the following are noteworthy contributions: Havighurst, Robert J., and Aparecida J. Gouveia, Brazilian Secondary Education and Socio-Economic Development (New York: Praeger Publishers, 1969); Benveniste, Guy, Bureaucracy and National Planning: A Sociological Case Study in Mexico (New York: Praeger Publishers, 1970); McGinn, Noel F., and Russell G. Davis, Build a Mill, Build a City, Build a School (Cambridge, Mass.: Massachusetts Institute of Technology Press, 1970).

elsewhere which, although relatively isolated conceptually, provide a base line from which other studies might be generated. Unfortunately, these data are not readily available to students and scholars. It is from these latter studies that the present text has emerged.[3]

It is the intent of this book to provide: (1) several theoretical frameworks on the relationship between education and development in Latin America and the Caribbean, (2) empirical studies which supply some indication of what is known about this relationship in Latin America and the Caribbean, and (3) a reservoir of methodological approaches which may be employed in testing hypotheses and answering basic questions about the relationship. The articles included, therefore, have been chosen because they evidence scholarly research or creative thinking by the respective authors and because they are felt to be appropriate as either prototypic investigations or theoretical frameworks to which further attention might be directed.

The book is primarily a classroom text for the study of education in Latin America and the Caribbean and for the study of comparative and development education. It is suitable as a supplemental textbook for courses which focus on the development process and for courses in Latin American studies. Each section of the book is preceded by a relatively brief summary of its articles, thus enabling the reader to judge their respective relevance to his own concerns.

The organization of the 37 articles into eight sections emerged after the articles had been selected. Although it might have been preferable to devise the categories and subsequently search out the articles, the nature of the literature available necessitated the opposite approach. Section One attempts to ascertain how well Latin American countries are meeting their identified needs through schooling and whether schools should be the primary institutions for achieving these ends. Section Two deals with some of the perspectives used in conceptualizing the area of education and development and draws upon the fields of sociology, political science, and economics in defining these orientations. In Section Three the articles relate to educational structural differentiation, administrative organization, teacher composition and perception, and the distribution of enrollments. In Section Four, the essays concern the orientation of educational institutions in their role and function as catalysts, supporters, or obstacles to the development process. Section Five concentrates on studies of secondary school students in Panama, Costa Rica, Brazil, Guatemala, and Venezuela. Section Six is primarily concerned with rural education at the elementary level and includes studies on rural Brazil, Mexico, Guatemala, and Colombia. Section Seven shifts to studies on Puerto Rico and Paraguay, where more than one

---

[3]The contributions to this volume were selected from the relevant literature available as of January, 1971.

linguistic code has confounded the problems of education in the development process, and to Colombia, where literacy is investigated in terms of a number of indicators of modernization. The final article in this section discusses one possible interventionist strategy in promoting literacy. Section Eight concerns the interests, aspirations, and attitudes of university students in Colombia, Argentina, and Chile as well as the history of reform and autonomy in Latin American universities.

Table of Contents

Section 1:
Progress in Meeting National Needs

Introduction to Section 1

In the first article, J. Roberto Moreira proposes a number of topics and issues which he suggests are in need of study and research. In assessing school programs, he indicates that 65.5 per cent of those seven to 14 years old are able to be educated; only 5 per cent of these actually receive eight years of schooling. Dropouts and repeaters account for the disparity, which the author suggests results from institutional examination and promotional procedures as well as from a series of socioeconomic status variables. In his second section, Moreira views the impact of urbanization on school utilization and suggests that although educational programs interact with all forms of this phenomena, urbanization is not a sufficient indicator of such utilization unless concomitant changes in technology and the economy accompany urban growth. Viewing educational investment, the author questions how quality of instructional programs at the primary levels can be sustained while costs per pupil are lowered and whether Latin America is overly concerned with establishing vocational and technical institutions, when the skills they teach are learned through on-the-job training and apprenticeship programs. In addition, Moreira presents data on the proportion of secondary schools and universities to primary schools and compares these actual ratios with those hypothesized for national development. He finds that Latin America as a region has not satisfied its needs at the primary level and is failing to develop secondary and higher education in proportion to its primary increases. In his concluding remarks Moreira suggests that Latin America does not possess the economic and technical resources to meet its needs and calls upon planners to base educational investment decisions on systematic investigations of education problems.

In the second selection, Michel Debeauvais discusses the progress which has been made in Latin America in meeting regional goals established since 1960. He asserts that there is reason to assume that regional conferences in the areas which propose aims are worthwhile since they tend to establish bench marks for measuring progress. The data presented by Debeauvais indicate that the expansion of schooling at the primary, secondary, and higher levels actually preceded the Santiago Plan of 1961 and the priority project of UNESCO in 1958. Secondary and higher education have developed more rapidly than primary education in this period, and the targets established for primary education at Santiago have been surpassed. The author turns to discussions of efficiency at the primary level, differential effects of education between the sexes and between urban and rural areas, and measures to decrease wastage rates. The reorganization at the secondary level now underway in many countries, separating a basic from an advanced, specialized cycle, is criticized by the author because students who complete secondary education seldom enter the economy but instead go directly on to universities. Thus, the incorporation of specialized tracks into the advanced cycle of the secondary school may not fulfill expectations because of the insufficient number of individuals who have completed secondary and higher education in the region. Debeauvais also notes the considerable recent increases both in educational expenditures and in the proportion of national income allocated to education. With increasing enrollments expected at all levels in the future, the author asks whether education will continue to be singled out as a priority over other social services presently in need of increased support.

The third paper, by Ivan Illich, is a radical departure from normal concerns in the development of educational institutions in Latin America. The author asks that the assumptions underlying the support of schools be challenged. Schools are singled out as institutions which effectively produce two distinct social classes: one encompassing those individuals who have successfully completed schooling and the other encompassing the failures. Thus schools are viewed as institutions which prevent, rather than encourage, social integration because they represent the only legitimate path to participation in society. Universal schooling, as suggested by Illich, is not a viable target for Latin America. It cannot be afforded by the limited resources available as retention rates increase and qualitative improvements become more costly. The author asserts that: "Everywhere in Latin America more money for schools means more privilege for a few at the cost of most, and this patronage of an elite is explained as a political ideal." Professor Illich suggests that radical alternatives are needed to existing institutions, alternatives which encompass imagination and ingenuity yet fulfill the natural desire of individuals to pursue knowledge.

Original Sources for Selections

Moreira, J. Roberto. "Education and Development in Latin America," *in* Egbert de Vries and José Medina Echavarria, eds., *Social Aspects of Economic Development in Latin America*, Vol. I. Paris: UNESCO, 1963. Pp. 308-344.

Debeauvais, Michel. "The Development of Education in Latin America since the Santiago Plan," in *The World Year Book of Education 1967* (Educational Planning). London: Evans Brothers, Ltd., Publishers, 1967. Pp. 358-374.

Illich, Ivan. "The Futility of Schooling in Latin America," *Saturday Review*, 51 (April 20, 1968), pp. 57-59, 74-75.

Education and Development in Latin America

J. ROBERTO MOREIRA

Assessment of Basic Schooling

Taken as a whole, and leaving the socioeconomic situation out of account, the educational institutions of Latin America are inadequate both quantitatively and qualitatively. Schools are few, the types of education are very limited, and the schooling received is brief and poor.

A single pointer is enough to make this quite clear. To receive the minimum education required to cope with the exigencies of a modern society, children need to attend school from seven to 14 years of age. None of the Latin American countries reaches this minimum standard.

One can divide these countries into four groups: (a) those in which over 80 per cent of the seven-to-14 age group attend primary and junior secondary schools, and which can be deemed to be in a fair way to overcoming the essential problems of schooling at an early date (within 20 years); (b) those in which more than 60 per cent but less than 80 per cent of the same age group attend school, and which can be regarded as likely to solve the problems of formal education before the end of the century (within 40 years); (c) those in which over 40 per cent and significantly less than 60 per cent attend school and which can be rated as educationally backward; (d) lastly those in which under 40 per cent of the seven-to-14 age group attend school and the prospects of an improvement in education are very bad.

If one takes into consideration the fact that seven-to-14 age-group enrollments are partly in primary schools with a four- to six-year curriculum and

From *Social Aspects of Economic Development in Latin America,* vol. I, 1963 – Reproduced with the permission of UNESCO.

partly in secondary schools with a five- to seven-year curriculum, a fraction of the secondary school enrollment must also be added to the primary school figures, to include under-14's already in secondary schools. Rough calculations on these lines have been made for 17 Latin American countries, using figures from UNESCO's *World Survey of Education: II—Primary Education* (1960), the Pan American Union's two-volume *Demographic Structure of the American Nations* (1960) and various scattered items from publications in a number of countries.

On the basis of these calculations, the 17 countries break down, according to the percentages of their estimated seven-to-14 age groups enrolled annually in primary and secondary schools over the period 1953–1958, into the following groups: *Group 1*—Argentina 89.0 per cent, Panama 86.5 per cent, Chile 84.2 per cent; *Group 2*—Costa Rica 77.0 per cent, Uruguay 69.0 per cent, Cuba 64.2 per cent, Brazil[1] 63.3 per cent; *Group 3*—Ecuador 61.5 per cent, Mexico 59.6 per cent, Peru 59.0 per cent, Venezuela 59.0 per cent, Paraguay 59.0 per cent; and *Group 4*—Colombia 52.6 per cent, Salvador 50.5 per cent, Bolivia 43.7 per cent, Guatemala 35.5 per cent, Haiti 32.0 per cent.

A feature of the Latin American countries is their low national income per capita, involving a low upper limit to government taxation of the national product for public services, including institutionalized education. There is thus a natural financial limit to the expansion of education services, in view of the urgent need for government investment in public works such as highways, power stations, heavy industries and financing production in general, to promote development.

As for the differences between one area and another in regard to enrollment possibilities, it is beyond doubt that the urban areas offer greater facilities: the schools opened there are immediately filled, besides being better equipped and staffed with better-qualified teachers. In the rural areas, however, with low standards of living and practically no production surplus, no need is felt for schools, and schooling has no meaning as a preparation for work and life.

The combined seven-to-14 age group for the 17 countries of the sample totals approximately 31,268,000, while total enrollments in the first eight school grades (primary and junior secondary) make a combined figure of 20,502,000. I can therefore say that Latin America, considered as a whole, is equipped to provide approximately 65 per cent of its population between seven and 14 with basic schooling (eight years).

---

[1]According to the provisionally computed data of the 1960 census there were about 13,700,000 children between the ages of seven and 14 in Brazil in 1960. As the total real enrollment in elementary schools and first cycle of secondary schools (junior) amounted to 7,071,000, it follows that only 51.6 per cent of this age group were attending school. The discrepancy between this percentage and the percentage given above is no doubt due to underestimation of population growth.

However, it does not necessarily follow that this percentage is in fact attending school for eight years, but merely that it could. While the 17 countries I am considering have 20,502,000 children enrolled in the first eight school grades (primary and secondary), it does not follow that all of them complete the eight-year course.

In South America, a large proportion of the children enrolling in school stop attending during their second, third, fourth, or fifth year. In the 14 Latin American countries for which enough data are available, the number of pupils taking the last grade of the primary course in 1950 ranged from 1.7 per cent to 18.1 per cent of the first-year enrollments. In some countries more than half the primary school attendance consisted of first-grade (first-year) pupils.[1]

In view of this, the real meaning of the x per cent given as the proportion of seven- to 14-year olds attending school needs to be checked. Of the total x per cent, xa per cent will be in first grade, a smaller proportion, xb per cent, in second grade, etc. In the following year, only part of the xa per cent will move up to the second grade; of the remainder, part will repeat the first year and the rest will leave school, and so on for every grade in turn.

Only by looking at the enrollments per grade, shall we be able to get an idea of the real situation in regard to elementary education in Latin America. Thus the figures above show Cuba, for example, as having the equivalent of 64.2 per cent of its seven- to 14-year olds in school. However, the actual breakdown of this percentage for the first eight school grades is as follows:

Table 1. Cuba: Breakdown of School Enrollment

School Grade	Town	Country
	%	%
I	30.6	45.3
II	20.7	24.8
III	16.4	15.0
IV	12.7	9.2
V	9.2	4.2
VI	6.1	1.5
VII	2.9	—
VIII	1.4	—

In Brazil, the percentage breakdown of the 1958 total enrollment in the eight school years or grades under consideration was as follows: I, 41 per cent; II, 21; III, 15; IV, 10; V, 5; VI, 4; VII, 2.5; and VIII, 1.5.

[1] United Nations, "Education," in *Preliminary Report on the World Social Situation*, chap. VI (1952), p. 65.

Thus, although enrollments in the first eight school grades represent the equivalent of 65.6 per cent of all Latin American children seven to 14 years old, a large proportion, probably 40 per cent, are in the first grade[1] and only about 1.5 per cent in the eighth. It follows that the first grade is not confined to seven-year olds but contains children eight, nine, and 10 years and older; while the second grade includes older children as well as its normal eight-year olds and so on.

If this irregular enrollment pattern merely reflected a progressive and increased interest in schooling causing a massive first-grade intake each year, the situation would be gradually corrected as the years passed so that the body of the enrollment pyramid would be gradually flattened out.

However, judging by Brazil, this is happening only slowly if at all. In 1948, 10 years prior to the date of the above percentages, the situation was as follows: Grade I, 46.2 per cent; II, 17.3; III, 15.4; IV, 9.5; V, 4.2; VI, 3.5; VII, 2.7; and VIII, 1.2.

Although the 1948 percentages are slightly higher for the first grade and lower for the second, they hardly differ at all for the other grades, which goes to show that any shift in pupil distribution between grades is an extremely slow process.

The inference to be drawn from the situation described is that, although Latin America considered as a unit may already have the means to educate 65.5 per cent of its seven- to 14-year olds properly, it is not using them and seems to be letting a variety of circumstances force a large proportion of its children and young people to stick in the first two or three grades and never get higher.

The average schooling of each new generation is under four years instead of the eight it should be, and probably a third of the numbers never get beyond the second grade.

This sets us a problem for analysis: when eight years' schooling could be given to at least 65 per cent of each new generation why is it only given to less than 5 per cent? Why is the average length of schooling for each new intake under four years and why is it two years or less for from 33 per cent to 51 per cent of them?

A number of considerations can be suggested in explanation, each bearing on one possible facet of the situation.

(a)   The low average length of schooling is partly due to the system itself holding pupils back by restrictive examination and promotion norms.

---

[1] In the writer's belief, the Brazil averages can serve for the whole of Latin America; within limits, Brazil can reproduce every disparity and contrast in Latin America. Thus, taking each region separately, I find that the percentages of children seven to 14 years old in the first eight grades range from 81 per cent in the South to 66 per cent in the East and 57 per cent in the Western Central and North to 48 per cent in the Northeast.

When this occurs, the school is no longer an agency for building personality and training for life, but for selection and discrimination. Such a situation may be due to any of a number of causes or factors; for instance, an obvious one is the primary school being geared to preparing pupils for secondary school, the latter in turn for higher education and the last for training the nation's leaders; in this case common elementary education would cease to have purpose in itself and would become a means of class discrimination for the selection and training of an elite.

(b) For children of the poorer and more backward classes, initial enrollment in a school presents more difficulties for a number of reasons. They may live further away from any school, and have to delay enrollment until they are over seven, in which case they reach working age (14 or 15) before completing the basic course; the normal physical development of children, and consequently school enrollment, may be retarded by endemic diseases; enrollment at the right age may be overlooked because the need for schooling is not properly appreciated; parents may experience difficulty in outfitting the child for enrollment and attendance; etc.

(c) There are also a number of reasons making it more difficult for the lower classes to persist in attendance: disparity in wealth and status between the pupil's family and those of the rest of the school (and also the teacher, who is generally middle class); more dropping out because of illness, domestic chores, indifference to education or failure to keep up with the class; lack of money for the minimum equipment needed for attendance; less ability to persist in the face of failure so that the pupil gives up school because he is required to repeat a grade; irrelevance of the school curriculum to the interests of the lower classes; etc.

All these factors probably operate concurrently and synergically and all of them are conditioned by the social, economic and cultural situation of each country and each of its zones or regions. Hence, in studying them one needs to verify their specific social frames of reference, how far they are products of removable residual traits and how far they are inherent in the economic and social structure of the nation or region.

Without an accurate understanding and appraisal of the observed abnormalities of Latin American school attendance as functions of social, economic and cultural factors and situations determined by the socioeconomic structures of specific countries or regions, it will not be possible to devise any program for fuller and wider schooling with serious prospects of implementation.

Given a school system already able to accommodate over 60 per cent of the seven- to 14-year olds for a full eight-grade course but actually retaining that percentage for an average of four years' schooling or less, one must see the situation in its whole context of antecedents and consequences in order to assess the extent to which the anomaly can be put to rights.

This would seem to be question number one and the careful and comprehensive study it requires would be a complex research task since it would involve recourse to sociological, economic, anthropological and educational techniques.

With this problem duly elucidated, the investigation of others of no less importance would be eased.

Urbanization as a Factor in School Attendance

It is conceded fairly generally—and specifically in a number of UNESCO technical reports—that, in underdeveloped countries, urbanization can be reckoned a prime factor in getting more children to attend school, and the assumption does, in fact, seem to be confirmed by certain general data from Brazil.

In 1956 the primary schools reported a total real attendance of 5.1 million, of whom no less than three million were in schools located in the municipal administrative towns or cities (2.5 million) and in the administrative villages[1] of districts (0.5 million). As the total population of these at the time could not have been above 23 million, one gets a school enrollment quota of 130 per 1,000 population. Concurrently, enrollments in primary schools outside those towns or cities and villages totaled 2.1 million, but this was for a population of about 37 million, giving a quota of 57 children in school per 1,000 population, or less than half that for the urbanized or semiurbanized areas.

It seems logical to assume that a country's difficulties in putting its people through school would diminish in direct proportion to the speed with which it became urbanized. I consider it necessary to study this hypothesis in this part of the work with a view to elucidating other educational problems of Latin America.

With five types of data, although they are rather out of date since they relate to 1950, I think it possible to establish in broad outlines the problems of the relationship between urbanization and school attendance.

These data relate to the following points: (a) number of inhabitants per primary school; (b) number of inhabitants per serving primary teacher; (c) population density; (d) percentage of the population living in towns of 20,000 inhabitants and over; and (e) per capita income.

---

[1] Every *municipium,* the minor administrative and political unit in Brazil, has an administrative town or city, and no more than one. The *municipium* is divided into districts, each one with a main village.

As the sources[1] used do not yield the full range of data above for some countries, I must confine this examination to 13 only—Argentina, Brazil, Chile, Colombia, Cuba, Ecuador, Honduras, Mexico, Panama, Paraguay, Peru, Uruguay and Venezuela.

In terms of per capita national income the 1950 ranking of these countries was as follows: Argentina and Venezuela over U.S. $400; Chile, Cuba, and Uruguay $301–400; Brazil, Colombia, Mexico, and Panama $201–300; and Ecuador, Honduras, Paraguay, and Peru $101–200.

In terms of percentages of population resident in cities of 20,000 inhabitants and over in 1950, the situation was as follows: Argentina, 41–50 per cent; Chile, Venezuela, Uruguay, Cuba, 31–40 per cent; Brazil, Mexico, Panama, Colombia, 21–30 per cent; Ecuador, Paraguay, Peru, Honduras, 11–20 per cent.

In terms of population density per square kilometer, the ranking was as follows: Paraguay, under 6; Argentina, Brazil, Chile, Peru, and Venezuela, 6–10; Colombia, Ecuador, Honduras, Panama, and Uruguay, 11–15; Mexico, 16–20; and Cuba, over 21.

As regards the ratio of existing primary schools to population the order was as follows: Brazil, Cuba, Honduras, Peru, and Venezuela, 601–800; Colombia, Ecuador, Mexico, Panama, and Paraguay, 801–1,000; Uruguay and Chile, 1,001–1,200; and Argentina, 1,201–1,400.

Finally, for my purposes, the number of inhabitants per serving primary school teacher is an important consideration and the order was: Argentina, 100–200; Chile, Cuba, Mexico, Panama, and Uruguay, 201–300; Brazil, Ecuador, Honduras, Peru, and Venezuela, 301–400; and Colombia, over 400.

It is easy to see from the above figures that those countries which have a relatively high per capita income are also those with the largest percentage of their population resident in cities of 20,000 inhabitants or over. In Argentina, with a per capita income of over $400, more than 41 per cent of the population lived in cities of this size, including about 33 per cent in Buenos Aires and its suburbs. In Venezuela, with a per capita income of over $500, the urban population did not reach 40 per cent since the high per capita income comes from oilfield operation for which intensive urbanization is not essential.

Chile, Cuba and Uruguay had per capita incomes above $300, and over 31 per cent of their populations were urbanized in the sense defined. Chile had a mechanized extraction industry, coupled with some processing, insignificant primary industries but an extremely vigorous range of tertiary

[1] For the extraction of the data indicated the following sources were used: *World Survey of Education*, UNESCO, Paris, 1955; *Statistical Abstract of Latin America for 1957*, University of California, Los Angeles; *Report on the World Social Situation*, United Nations, New York, 1957; *Demographic Yearbook*, United Nations, New York, 1957.

activities. The basis of the Uruguayan economy is primary industry—mechanized, however—without much secondary industry but with a large tertiary sector; some data used by Professor Gino Germani, in lectures given at the University of Chicago, lead me to suspect that Uruguay may well have the highest proportion of office workers of any country in Latin America. In Cuba, as the production of sugar is the country's economic basis, I can infer a very vigorous and more or less organized primary industry and secondary industry (processing) to scale, plus a tertiary sector kept permanently flourishing by tourism and gambling.

Brazil and Mexico are countries in the typical phase of economic transformation: Brazil is taking the decisive first steps to develop a heavy industry while Mexico is endeavoring to nationalize its primary and to increase its processing industries. In 1950 both had high percentages of nonurban population and barely more than 20 per cent in cities of 20,000 inhabitants and above. The per capita income was roughly between $240 and $260. It should be pointed out that almost 70 per cent of the population contributed approximately 30 per cent of the national income per inhabitant, while the urbanized population (roughly 30 per cent, engaged in tertiary and secondary activities) contributed the remaining 70 per cent. In both countries urbanization is proceeding apace and it is probable that in 1960 approximately 40 per cent of the population in either country was located in urbanized communities of 5,000 inhabitants or over. In both countries, too, there appear to be three reasons for the move to the cities: industrialization, the nationalization of primary production in some areas or its decay in others. Hence the existence of underemployed "misfit" populations in many urban areas, mainly in cities with 100,000 inhabitants or over.

Colombia and Panama, with per capita incomes approximately the same in the year of reference as those of Brazil and Mexico, appear to represent the two extremes of a situation: Panama has a predominance of tertiary activities as a result of its geographical position and the existence of the Panama Canal, while in Colombia primary activities predominate and there are indications of extensive unemployment among the urban lower classes.

Ecuador, Honduras, Paraguay and Peru all have low urbanization indices and per capita incomes and are probably among the countries where the process of economic development and urbanization will present the greatest difficulties. Population densities are also low—under 15 per square kilometer in all and falling to under 10 in Peru and under five in Paraguay.

It should, however, be noted that Argentina combines the highest urbanization index in Latin America with a low population density. This means an excessive concentration of population in cities and a largely depopulated countryside; Brazil, with a lower urbanization index, has the same population density as Argentina (seven per square kilometer).

Another special case is Cuba, where an intermediate urbanization index (over 30 per cent and less than 40 per cent) is coupled with a high population density (51 per square kilometer). Economically, it ranked relatively high among the 13 countries of the sample with a per capita income of over $300 ($315).

I will now show how these respective situations are reflected in the primary schooling levels in the 13 countries.

Argentina, Chile and Uruguay, three countries with per capita incomes of more than $301, partly industrialized and partly having semirationalized and semimechanized primary industries with from 31–50 per cent of their populations living in towns of 20,000 inhabitants or over, had the highest number of inhabitants per primary school (over 1,001) and also the lowest number per serving primary teacher.

This means that, in these countries, schools were mostly large units (hence the higher number of inhabitants per school) and amply staffed (hence the lower number of inhabitants per teacher). At the same time they are among the most urbanized countries, with primary activities rationalized, secondary already appreciable and tertiary extremely vigorous. In these conditions the extension of schooling is easier and it becomes possible to establish large school units.

Cuba, with an urbanization index of over 30 per cent and under 40 per cent, a per capita income of over $300, primary industries organized (until recently) on a plantation basis, a sugar processing industry and well-developed tertiary activities, ranks with the first three countries except for a lower ratio of inhabitants per school. However, since the ratio of inhabitants per teacher is practically the same, it seems that the peculiar conditions of the social and economic life in Cuba are responsible for the existence of large numbers of small schools sparsely staffed (two teachers on average) instead of large units with large staffs. Although reliable documentary data are not available I believe, nevertheless, that the relative rationalization of capitalist production of sugar results in a demographic structure in the form of nuclei, that is, that it does not lead to a dispersal of the rural population but to the formation of rural towns or agglomerations, as is evidenced in part by the high population density of the country.

Although the multiplication of small school units may be expensive, it is a possible solution. Culturally, however, the results are inferior to those of the large units where more teaching equipment and technically superior instructional facilities can be provided.

From the data above it would seem that a similar policy is pursued in Mexico. Though much lower than in Cuba, population density is higher than in any of the other sample countries. However, reports of a number of sample surveys I have read indicate that the process of the structuralization of the agricultural population in the form of nuclei is less decisive in Mexico than in Cuba. For this reason I believe that Mexico's efforts to educate its people are outstanding and are probably unequaled in the whole of Latin America.

Brazil, too, is above average in this respect. Even at the date of reference it compared very favorably with the other sample countries in numbers of primary schools and it had the smallest number of inhabitants (615) per school of any of the 13. However the number per teacher in service was high (376), which means an average of under two teachers per school. Population density was seven per square kilometer and the proportion of the population urbanized was still low, in spite of the extreme speed at which the process was going on.

Colombia had the lowest school attendance index of all the 13 countries, with one active teacher for over 800 inhabitants.[1]

In the remaining countries one finds a situation similar to that in Brazil, with rates approximating to those obtained in Brazil, indicating a real effort in Latin America to provide for the primary education of the population despite low per capita income, a low level of urbanization, scanty industrialization and the primitive state of the primary economic activities.

Thus the available data show that the areas with the most developed economies as a result either of industrialization and consequent urbanization or of the more rationalized organization of their primary activities and consequent structuralization of the rural population in nuclei, accompanied in either case by a substantial increase in tertiary activities, are also those achieving the best indices of school attendance simply because it is easier for them to manage it.

Compared with these countries, those not so privileged have to make much greater efforts and still fail to secure comparable results in more extended schooling and better-organized school units.

The tables nevertheless show some discrepancies between attendance and urbanization indices. Supposing them to be really trying to tackle the question of primary education, the countries with the lowest urbanization indices should also have the smallest numbers of inhabitants per school and the highest per teacher. Thus, Brazil, with 21 per cent of its population in cities of 20,000 and over—a low index of urbanization in 1950 compared with other Latin American countries—clearly had many schools as the average number of inhabitants served by each was 700, but the fact that proportion of teachers to population was about one to 350 shows that they were small schools. In Mexico, with a slightly better urbanization index than Brazil, there were more people per school and fewer per teacher. But Venezuela, with over 31 per cent of the population in cities, upsets the correlation, having had the same numbers of inhabitants per school and per

---

[1]Colombia's situation is improving very rapidly. According to data published in 1960 (United Nations *Statistical Yearbook*), Colombia had, in 1958, 760 inhabitants per elementary school, and 354 per serving teacher.

teacher as Brazil whereas, going by the urbanization indices, it should have shown more people per school and fewer per teacher than Brazil by developing a school system using larger units. This last, however, may have been difficult for social and economic reasons. Despite Venezuela's being more urbanized than many other countries in Latin America, it may have suburban areas larger than the cities, and the populations even of the latter may include a significant proportion of economically marginal elements. In this case its relatively high per capita income (compared with the remaining Latin American countries) might mean that a large proportion of the national income was being concentrated in the hands of a small minority with a resultant maldistribution of wealth. This, however, is mere conjecture since the data quoted do not permit of any valid conclusions being drawn on the matter.

The point I want to make is that urbanization by itself cannot be taken as the key to more intensive and fuller schooling. In Rio de Janeiro itself, the average length of schooling of the economically semimarginal population of the suburban shanty towns is two years against an average of about five years for the rest of the city's population, according to calculations made in the manner described in the first section of this paper.

It is the normal practice, both for census and for statistical purposes, to count the inhabitants of the shanty towns as urban population, as that is, in fact, what they are. It is therefore essential to examine the various kinds of urbanization in order to estimate how far the process does or does not contribute to educational development.

When urbanization is due to increasing industrialization and consequent transformation of the economic structure, it will have characteristic repercussions on the educational situation. Industrialization attracts labor from the country to the cities. The resulting manpower shortage in the rural areas encourages the progressive modernization of agricultural and extractive production, and this in turn makes it possible to do without the rural manpower absorbed by urban development. In these conditions the changeover brings with it a rise in per capita income and this, in turn, removes the need for children and adolescents to work for their living. The new generations can thus afford more time for study or schooling and above all are obliged to give thought to getting proper training for future employment.

If, however, urbanization is due to a rise in the numbers of town dwellers as a result of a drift to the cities not prompted by industrialization and the modernization of agricultural and extractive production, it can mean both an excessive growth of population in the country as a whole and an insufficient development of agricultural and extractive production, which is unable to absorb the extra manpower made available by such population growth. An example of this is in northeastern Brazil, where a number of cities— e.g., Recife, which must now have reached a million mark—are growing at a spectacular rate without having jobs available for everyone and with no increase in their share of the national income. Although it had 23.8 per cent of the total population of Brazil in 1957, the Northeast accounted for barely 11.5 per cent of the national income, and reckoning the 1957 per capita income of south Brazil as 100, that of the Northeast would not reach 29. Thus in these cases there is the paradox of urbanization meaning impoverishment and although the young could get to school they do not go, partly through lack of incentives and partly through lack of funds for investment in education, due to the nonexistence of any surplus above bare subsistence income.

Again a movement to the towns sometimes develops as a result neither of industrialization nor of excessive population increase, but of factors diminishing the productivity of agriculture and the extraction industries, such as exhaustion of the soil, cattle plague, drought, exhaustion of natural raw materials, etc. Here again urbanization is not a stride forward economically but constitutes a social and economic problem and its effect on institutionalized education is as detrimental as that of the preceding type.

Finally, all these types of influence may operate concomitantly to produce an anomalous urbanization pattern of concurrent economic upgrading and downgrading, with city populations subdivided into fully employed, partially employed, and unemployed segments. The schooling situation will then also be anomalous: with high percentage and extended enrollment by some groups and others, even in the rural areas, educated poorly or hardly at all.

It seems probable that, as in Brazil, so in the rest of Latin America, we are likely to find examples of various types of urbanization and hence various forms and degrees of development of primary schooling. While it seems to be clear that the nature of the urbanization process in a given area will shape the educational structure in that area, it also seems no less clear that the educational structure and the processes of education can be deliberately improved so as to influence the nature of the urbanization process. At the very least, educational progress can help to smooth the process of transition to the more complex urban situation.

It is therefore essential to study the forms of urbanization existing in our countries in order to understand the educational problems which they raise. Every aspect of the economic, social and cultural adjustment of recent arrivals in urban areas demands study and research for the purposes of educational planning, and so, conversely, does everything relating to the greater or lesser ability of urban areas to absorb labor put at their disposal by internal immigration, since these questions strictly condition the newcomers' adjustment and hence the whole educational process.

Finally, both in those country areas where the modernization and mechanization of productive activities release a certain amount of manpower and in areas where overpopulation compels people to move away, a whole process of training is needed to make resettlement in the cities, or alternatively in other agricultural areas, as easy as possible and to prevent the growth of pauper nuclei.

Thus, there is every indication that in the urbanization process, whether its aspect is negative or positive, education plays a role—likewise negative or positive—which must be thoroughly studied in order to be able to plan the modifications and reforms which will make it more adequate for the economic, social and cultural purposes it is to serve.

Thus the phenomenon of urbanization in Latin America offers a vast field of study and research all of which is essential for any objective planning of educational development.

Primary Education and Its Financing

For the purposes of these suggestions on lines of study and research, it is proposed to discuss four Latin American countries on which I possess some of the essential data. They are Argentina, Brazil, Colombia and Peru.

Assuming, the suppositions set out below to be valid for Latin America, we can make an assessment, with some possibility of being right, of the real educational needs of each of our countries and the possibilities of meeting them. These suppositions are as follows:

(a) *The whole seven- to 11-year-old age group of the population should be attending school (five-year course).* This supposition agrees with the fact that most of the Latin American countries have an elementary school of four or five grades (school years). But in most of these countries this schooling is not for all; the number of enrollments is smaller than the number of people between the ages of six and 10 or of seven and 11. Hence the high percentage of illiteracy among the population. Thus, as a matter of socioeconomic need as well as of social justice and democracy, it is absolutely necessary that all people should have this minimum of schooling.

(b) *A percentage of the 12- to 16-year-old age group, equal to the percentage of the total working population employed in the secondary and tertiary sectors, should be attending school (technical or humanistic studies at secondary level).* This supposition is based mainly on the consideration that production and consequently the nation's wealth are dependent on the number and the capacity of the semiskilled and skilled workers who constitute most of the secondary and tertiary sectors of the national labor force. I take this to be a minimum condition. The democratic ideal would be to have the great majority of the 12- to 16-year-old age group attending secondary schools. The purpose of the supposition is to establish a preliminary goal in this matter for the underdeveloped Latin American

countries. I assume that there must be a numerical correlation between those two sectors and secondary school enrollment. I shall
attempt to explain this hypothesis in subsequent pages.

(c) *Not less than 20 per cent of the population who have been or are
enrolled in secondary schools must go on to higher education if the
problem of training scientists, senior experts in technology, and
senior leaders for the country is to be dealt with satisfactorily.* As
I assume that Brazil, with its contradictions of underdeveloped and
progressive modern and archaic areas, is more or less representative
of all Latin America I have based the above proposition on the
Brazilian situation. An analysis of the labor market, carried out by
the Commission for Training and Improving Higher Level Personnel (CAPES), led me to the conclusion that at least 20 per cent of
the people enrolled in secondary schools must go on to higher
schools or universities. At the present time the proportion is less
than 8 per cent, and in some other Latin American countries lower
still.

(d) *It is difficult to set aside more than 3.5 per cent of the national income for formal education,* in view of the need to invest money in
other sectors for social and economic development, and also in view
of the very limited reserves which the Latin American countries,
individually and collectively, have at their disposal.

In his book *Les Deux Brésils*, Jacques Lambert notes that for
every 1 per cent increase in population a corresponding 4 per cent
increase in national income is required to offset the new generation's
needs with respect to medical care, clothing, housing, food, education, etc. Since the annual rate of population increase in Latin America is about 2.5 per cent, one must then postulate an average annual
increase of about 10 per cent in national income to meet these needs.
Moreover, when one considers the problems of housing and of food
and sanitation individually, each appears to be just as important as
the problem of education, which would mean that only a part of
the hypothetical 10 per cent increase could be earmarked for education alone. The actual figures, however, show no such increase.
The annual percentage increase in national income in Brazil, for the
years 1948 to 1957, was in fact 5.4 per cent—and few other Latin
American countries were able to equal even this. Thus, instead of
the 4:1 ratio indicated by Lambert, there is a ratio of only 2.16:1
in Brazil and of less still in other Latin American countries.

Besides these considerations one must keep in mind the fact that
the provision of education, food, housing, sanitation, clothes, etc.
for the new generation calls for improvements in the means and
methods of production, expansion of the network of roads, railways,

etc.—all of which entail considerable financial investment. As Brazil is already spending about 2.2 per cent and a group of other Latin American countries are spending from 2 to 2.5 per cent of their national income on education, I believe that it is very difficult for them to increase their expenditure on education to more than 3.5 per cent of the national income. This would mean a ratio of 1.4:1 in terms of percentage of national income to percentage of population increase, for the sole purpose of education. Note that Mexico spent 1.12 per cent of the national income on education in 1956, Argentina 3.15 per cent in 1954, Brazil 2.2 per cent in 1960, Chile 2.02 per cent in 1956, Colombia 1.88 per cent in 1957, Peru 3.10 per cent in 1955, and Venezuela 1.01 per cent in 1957.[1]

(e) Countries with a sustained rapid increase in population (as is the case in Latin America) have an abnormally large group of children between the ages of seven and 14 and their need for educational facilities will thus be exceptionally great. *It may well be that in these circumstances 4.5 to 5 per cent of the national income must be devoted to educational investment, which represents indeed a heavy burden on the resources of these countries in view of all their other needs.*

This proposition seems to contradict the preceding one. Nevertheless, it represents what I suppose to be necessary while the preceding one represents what is possible. The contradiction, in fact, illustrates the problem of financing educational progress in Latin America. If an increase of 10 per cent in the national income is needed to provide for the housing, feeding, sanitation, clothing, education, etc. of the new generations, in a population that increases at the rate of 2.5 per cent per year, I believe that, education being a part of these needs, about 2.5 per cent (i.e., one fourth of the total income increase) must be devoted to it. As the majority of the Latin American countries are already spending 2 to 2.5 per cent, if the percentage needed to provide for the increase in population is added, there is a minimum 4.5 to 5 per cent required for educational expenses.

It is known that a few countries, both developed and underdeveloped, are spending more than that. Japan for instance spent about 5.5 per cent in 1957–1958. Addis Ababa targets set for all Africa were 4 per cent by 1965 and 6 per cent by 1980. Cuba spent 4.13 per cent in 1956.

Nevertheless for underdeveloped countries "it would be unsound to use limited resources disproportionately to eliminate present evils at the expense of failing to increase national productivity and thus dooming the population to continued low levels of living." But it is obvious that, "on

---

[1] Data from *Statistical Abstract of Latin America: 1960* (Latin American Center, University of California, Los Angeles).

the other hand, it is difficult to resist the appeal for social investment represented by the dire needs of the mass population, for example, investments in education and certain minimum standards of sanitation and housing."[1]

As the maximum possible investment by the Latin American countries is about 3.5 per cent of the national income, and the minimum needed is about 4.5 to 5 per cent, there is a vast field for international cooperation in education in Latin America.

Given these premises, I can formulate, on the basis of the data at my disposal, the needs of the four countries under review in relation to their respective population and employment situations. Furthermore, taking into account the economic and financial situation represented by the per capita income reckoned in international units, I shall be able to estimate the possibilities of meeting these needs. I shall thus show how a series of problems relating to education can be investigated.

In or around 1955, the seven-to-11 age groups numbered 1,900,000 (9.7 per cent of the population) in Argentina, 7,800,000 (11.2 per cent of the population) in Brazil,[2] 1,500,000 (13.4 per cent of the population) in Colombia and 1,240,000 (13.5 per cent of the population) in Peru.

These data already confirm my premise, that a rapid population increase affects the percentage of children in the school-going age group.

Argentina then had a six-grade primary course for children between six and 11 years of age. The numbers attending school at this level were equivalent to 11.5 per cent of the population though the entire age group only accounted for 11.2 per cent. There is thus little doubt that, at least numerically, Argentina was already making full provision for the population of primary school age. The problems, if any, of this category of schooling, would relate to the quality of the instruction or the administration of education.

In Brazil there was a five-grade primary course and the total enrollment (4,600,000) was equivalent to 6.6 per cent of the population. However, since the seven-to-11 age groups amounted to 11.2 per cent of the population, it might be inferred that around 41 per cent (3,200,000) of the children in this group remained without the minimum educational provisions indicated. Nevertheless, a knowledge of the situation in Brazil enables me to assert that this is not the case, because not all of the children (only about 55 per cent) enter primary school at seven years of age—a good number of beginners being over 10 years old—and others take more than five years to complete the course. This means a larger "deficit," and the

---

[1] Quoted and adapted from *Report on the World Social Situation,* United Nations, 1952.

[2] The figures for Brazil for 1955 have been estimated from the 1950 census data and the preliminary synopsis of the 1960 census; according to this last census the population of Brazil is a little over 70 million. Data for Argentina, Colombia and Peru have been obtained from the 1957 *Demographic Yearbook* and from the 1960 *Statistical Yearbook,* both published by the United Nations.

same thing probably happens in other Latin American countries.

If one takes the three Brazilian regions referred to earlier, one finds that 56 per cent of the children of school age in the Northeast, 29 per cent in the East and 4.5 per cent in the South do not attend school. (The bases on which these percentages are calculated are the same as those described earlier both for Brazil and for other countries and do not take into account the age dispersal of children in all elementary grades.) Only in the state of São Paulo, is there a situation comparable to that in Argentina, i.e., about 1.3 million children in primary school (99 per cent of a seven-to-11 age group about 1.313 million strong) for a 1958 population of roughly 13 million.

Colombia[1] has a system of four-grade primary schools in the rural areas and five-grade primary schools in the urban areas. In 1956 a total of 907,000 pupils were enrolled in primary schools, whereas the seven-to-11 age group numbered 1,500,000. Consequently, at least 32.9 per cent of the children were not attending school.

Peru too has five-grade primary schools and in 1955 the total number of children attending was about 990,000 out of a total of 1,240,000 in the seven-to-11 age group. Thus, at least 20.2 per cent of children of school age were not attending school. (In 1958 the total number of children in elementary school was over 1.3 million.)

To sum up what has been said above concerning primary education, it appears that whereas Argentina has probably to solve only problems relating to the quality of primary education, Brazil will, in addition, have to expand its system by more than 41 per cent if it is to provide for all the children in the seven-to-11 age group; Colombia will have to expand its system by more than 32.9 per cent; and Peru by more than 20.2 per cent. It is, of course, difficult to assess expansion requirements with any exactitude. It is true that the figures in Table 1 of this paper might lead one to think differently. Nevertheless, it is both easier and safer to mention only an incontestable lower limit with the certainty that such expansion as is needed must be larger than it.

I will take the cost of primary education per pupil per year as my unit; the cost per pupil per year at the secondary level will then be five units, and at the university level 20 units.[2]

Now, by 1955–1956 the total population of the four countries under

---

[1] Primary school enrollment in Colombia has since improved considerably; in 1958 the total was over 1.4 million.

[2] The above proportions are calculated on the basis of the average Brazilian expenditure on education in 1958, when an elementary pupil cost 2,216 cruzeiros, a secondary pupil about 11,500 cruzeiros, and a university student a little more than 44,500 cruzeiros. I have no information on other Latin American countries in this respect. My assumption that these Brazilian data can be considered representative of Latin America as a whole may be completely wrong, but since I have no other hypothesis, I must use the only one available. It may be that in Argentina, Uruguay, Chile and Costa Rica the ratio is very different, because these are countries which have a satisfactory

consideration was estimated to be around 100.2 million, the employed population around 34.1 million, and the employees in the secondary and tertiary sectors 16.2 million. At the same time, the 12-to-16 age group for the four countries totaled 12.1 million and the seven-to-11 group 12.4 million.

According to the above-mentioned assumption (a), 12.4 million children should have been enrolled in primary schools; according to assumption (b), 47.5 per cent of the 12-to-16 age group should have been enrolled in secondary schools (about 5.7 million pupils), and 20 per cent of the same should have been in higher schools or universities (about 1.14 million).

On the basis of these figures, if one has to spend five times more money for a secondary pupil and 20 times more for a university-level student than for a primary school pupil, it follows that the expenses for education in Latin America should be divided in the following proportions: 19.5 per cent of the resources for primary education, 44.7 per cent for secondary, and 35.8 per cent for higher.

Brazilian experts in education do not agree with this conclusion; they believe that the ratio 1: 5: 20 (primary: secondary: higher) as a basis for apportioning the national budget for education is indicative of a complete misconception of the social and economic importance of both primary and secondary education.

During the discussion in the national Congress of the draft law on the principles and basis of the Brazilian system of education, the evident trend was toward the equalization of expenses for primary and secondary education (70 per cent for both out of the total budget), only 30 per cent being reserved for higher education. Nevertheless because of the already existing disproportion the figures approved were 1 per cent for the administration of education, 2 per cent for the improvement of private schools (primary, secondary, and higher), 3 per cent for primary education, 3 per cent for secondary and 3 per cent for higher, of the total tax revenue of the federal government. This means that 12 per cent of the federal budget has to be set aside for education. As the states and *municipia* each have to allot 20 per cent of their budgets for the same purpose, the sum of these three amounts is approximately equivalent to 3.1 per cent of the national income (estimation based on the budgets and national income from 1955 to 1959).

At the request of a group of members of the Chamber of Deputies, the author of this paper prepared a report based on an analysis of the federal expenditure for education. The recommendations of the report were that, if unproductive investments in sumptuous buildings, furniture and equipment were excluded, (a) the nation, states, *municipia,* and private organizations should be encouraged to increase their efforts to bring the national expenditure for education up to at least 3.5 per cent of the national income;

elementary school enrollment, more or less balanced by proportionate figures for secondary and higher educational enrollment.

(b) 36 per cent of the financial resources available for education should be devoted to primary schooling, 36 per cent to secondary and 28 per cent to higher education; (c) the preliminary target should be 20 secondary and four university-level students for every 100 primary school pupils; and (d) the ratio of this target should be raised to 100: 50: 25 before 1975.

I shall retain the percentage ratio of 36 : 36 : 28 (primary: secondary: higher) for the allotment of educational expenditure as being possibly suited to conditions in Latin America today.

That being so, and given the premise that no more than 3.5 per cent of the national income can be used for education, I reach the conclusion that none of the countries under consideration can spend more than 1.26 per cent of its national income on primary, 1.26 per cent on secondary, and 0.98 per cent on higher education.

I estimate that the cost per pupil per annum in primary schools would need to be at least 48.5 Colin Clark international units for the teachers to have adequate minimum salaries and for the indispensable minimum of equipment to be provided. Brazil, however, spent the equivalent of only 29.0 international units per pupil in 1958–1959, a rate of expenditure which has been more or less constant since 1950 (see footnote on the following page).

On that basis the cost to Argentina of providing schooling for 1,900,000 children in the seven-to-11 age group (in 1955–1956) would have been 92.15 million international units per annum representing 1.32 per cent of the national income (at the time), whereas I have just calculated that the maximum expenditure on primary education for any Latin American country would be 1.26 per cent of the national income. In fact, Argentina had over 1,900,000 children going through its six-grade primary school system during the period mentioned and its actual expenditure on primary education was 75.8 million international units or 1.08 per cent of the national income.[1]

The number of children Brazil should have had in primary school in 1955 was 7.8 million, which would have meant a minimum expenditure of 378.30 million international units per annum. Thus, as the Brazilian national income in 1955 was 12,154 million international units, 3.11 per cent of the national income would have been needed merely in order to solve the problem of primary education. In fact, Brazil had about 4.6 million children in its primary schools in 1952, which should have meant an annual expenditure of 203.7 million international units (1.67 per cent of the national income). Since the actual expenditure was 135.24 million international units (1.11 per cent of the national income), financially speaking, the Brazilian school system could obviously and immediately have been expanded to the permissible limit. However, Brazil was then, as it is today,

---

[1] Estimation based on figures from *Statistical Abstract of Latin America: 1960*, published by the Latin American Center, University of California, Los Angeles.

more concerned with industrialization than with social welfare. I am sincerely convinced that if this country were to decide to make the provision for primary education of which it is capable, the number of pupils in the schools could be increased satisfactorily, even though I cannot but recognize that in order to achieve an acceptable level of quality it is necessary to spend 48.5 international units per pupil per annum, which in 1955[1] would have been equivalent to 2,199 cruzeiros.

At the period referred to (1955–1956), Colombia had 907,000 children in primary schools out of a total of 1.5 million in the seven-to-11 age group, and at 48.5 international units per head, this would have cost a total of 43.99 million international units per annum. As the Colombia national income was no more than 1,400 million international units at the time, this would have meant devoting 3.14 per cent of it to primary education alone to make the minimum acceptable provision for the children already enrolled, and 5.2 per cent (72.7 million international units) to educate all the children in the seven-to-11 age group.

Peru had 1.24 million children of primary school age in 1955, 990,000 of whom were attending school; to provide the minimum acceptable conditions for the number attending school would have called for 48.0 million international units per annum or 4 per cent of the national income (1,237 million international units). To cater for all the children in the age group (1.24 million), the expenditure would have had to be 60.14 million international units, or around 4.9 per cent of the national income.

I shall now estimate, on the basis of the period 1955–1956, what each of the four countries can spend per year, without prejudice to other needed investment, in order to determine the possibilities of solving the problem of providing five-grade primary education conforming to the minimum acceptable standards—starting from the following assumptions: (a) that all four countries in the sample are already spending around 1.26 per cent of their respective national incomes on primary education; and (b) that

---

[1] In 1958 Brazil spent 2,216 cruzeiros per pupil per annum, when it should have spent 3,706 cruzeiros, if, while maintaining the rate of 48.5 international units per pupil per annum, one establishes the relation of the cruzeiro to the international unit by taking into account the annual depreciation of the currency by about 11 per cent up to 1954 and by about 19 per cent each year thereafter.

The postulated rate of 48.5 international units per pupil per year is based on the following reasoning. Let us accept the number of 35 pupils per classroom and per teacher as reasonable. This would mean 1,697.5 international units per classroom per year. The mean annual salary for a teacher, according to the average standards for middle class white-collar workers in Rio de Janeiro, Buenos Aires, Bogotá and Lima, should be 1,164 international units (97 per month). Administration, teaching material, and other permanent expenses would amount to about 533.5 international units per year, according to current rates in Rio de Janeiro. Besides this criterion I also used the one that is explained on page 25. Nevertheless, the hypothesis is not sufficiently well founded. I recognize that it is only a tentative approximation to a method. The purpose of this paper is to draw attention to the research and studies required to provide a sound basis for the planning of those changes in the educational system that must accompany social and economic development.

(although this may not be quite so in fact) all children attending school are receiving an education in conformity with this minimum acceptable level and that, consequently, the average of 48.5 international units per pupil per annum applies only to those who have still to receive their education and to the new generations that are to attend school.

The results will be fairly optimistic, however, owing to the erroneous supposition made under (b) above. Table 2 shows the calculation concerned.

Table 2. Possibilities of Extending Primary Schooling, Relationship between National Income, Population, and Expenditure on Primary Education

	A			B				C			D			E
	a	b	c	a	b	c	d	a	b	c	a	b	c	
Argentina	4,053	6,974	4.0	1.90	1.9	0.00	0.00	000	0.00	0	—	—	—	—
Brazil	5,787	12,154	5.4	7.80	3.0	3.20	41.02	155	1.27	9	23.8	115.43	0.33	11
Colombia	779	1,398	4.0	1.50	2.6	0.59	39.33	29	2.07	14	6.47	31.38	0.68	20
Peru	697	1,235	4.2	1.24	2.6	0.25	20.16	12	0.97	7	2.44	11.83	0.26	9

Key to Table:

Aa. 1942 national income in millions of Colin Clark international units.
Ab. 1955 national income in millions of Colin Clark international units.
Ac. Average percentage of annual increase of national income from 1942 to 1955.
Ba. Population of primary school age (over seven and under 14) in 1955 (millions of pupils).
Bb. Average of annual increase per centum in population of primary school age.
Bc. Population of school age not attending primary schools in 1955 (millions of children).
Bd. Percentage of children not attending school.
Ca. Minimum expenditure required to make good the primary schooling deficit shown in *Bc* and *Bd,* expressed in millions of international units at the rate of 48.5 international units per pupil per annum.
Cb. Percentage of the 1955 national income represented by the minimum expenditure indicated in *Ca.*
Cc. Years required to extend primary schooling to the children that were not yet receiving it in 1955, on the assumption that each country can devote an additional 0.15 per cent per annum of the national income to primary education alone.
Da. Primary school accommodation deficit represented by the excess, in hundred thousands, of children reaching school age after 1955 and between the ages of seven and 11 at the end of the period given in *Cc* over the estimated numbers in school at that date.
Db. Amounts needed to make good the deficit shown in *Da,* reckoned in millions of international units at the rate of 48.5 international units per pupil per annum.
Dc. Amounts shown under *Db* expressed as percentages of the probable national incomes at the end of the period indicated in *Ca* (national incomes estimated on the basis of the data shown under *Ab* and *Ac*).
E. Probable minimum number of years required to extend primary schooling to all children from seven to 12 years old, provided that the primary education budget continues to increase annually by about 0.15 per cent of the national income, and at a rate of expenditure of 48.5 international units per pupil per annum.

Obviously the prospects indicated in column *E* of the table are not really so optimistic, since I have not taken into account the fact that if the sums spent by the other three countries (Argentina excepted) are converted into international units and divided by 48.5 (assumed minimum cost per pupil per annum) the quotients obtained will be much lower than the figures representing the primary school enrollments of each country. This, according to my previous hypothesis, should mean stinted and inadequate primary education. In spite of that hypothesis or assumption, I am finding out that in Peru, Bolivia, Colombia, Venezuela, Paraguay and other Latin American countries the enrollment of children in primary schools is increasing at a higher percentage rate than expenditure for primary education. In Venezuela, enrollments have more than doubled over the last four years, but expenditure has not doubled.

Therefore one may assume that Latin America is attempting to offer the opportunity of primary education to all at low cost. The inability to provide qualitatively good schooling, however, only serves to expand the poor systems already in existence.

Next, no country in Latin America, except Argentina and perhaps Uruguay and Chile, will be able to provide qualitatively good primary schooling for all children of the appropriate age in less than 11 years and some of them will require more than 20 years (barring disproportionate expenditure involving cuts in investments in other social and economic sectors which are also important for Latin American development), and this is without taking into account the incidence of repetition of courses and premature school leaving which we discussed in the first section of this chapter.

Against the whole line of argument so far propounded it may, however, be objected that the figure of 48.5 international units per pupil per annum is a minimum for developed countries. According to Colin Clark's criteria an international unit corresponds to a defined amount of goods and services needed for a human being in social life. It is an abstraction representing that amount. The value in national currencies of an international unit may vary, but not the amount of goods and services to which it refers.[1]

Our calculation of 48.5 international units per pupil per annum has had two bases: (a) what is needed to give, in Brazil, good schooling to a group of 35 children, in one classroom with one teacher; and (b) an investigation of the situation in Brazil. Representative schools were selected in Santa Catarina, São Paulo, Minas Gerais, Bahia and Pernambuco and the average cost per pupil in 1956 (the year of reference) was calculated for each. The average cost per pupil for the five schools together was then calculated. By using Colin Clark's criteria I reduced the average cost to international units and the result came to about 48.5.

---

[1] Nevertheless one must bear in mind the fact that Colin Clark himself pointed out that "conversion of national income to international units by means of ideal index numbers ... is a system which works satisfactorily in comparing economically advanced countries, and as we go down to lower real incomes ... we find that the international unit becomes less satisfactory ... because the whole scale of relative values alters."

Since Brazilian urban schools are just acceptable as regards equipment and quality of schooling, they seemed a suitable yardstick for assessing the situation in Latin America. However, Brazil also has schools much inferior in equipment and quality of schooling to the five selected for the calculation, and the same situation is to be expected in the other countries.

While the ideal cost per pupil per annum, based on the five schools in question, was 2,601 cruzeiros in 1956, the real cost, based on public primary schools in Brazil, was 1,538 (about 29 international units). If, then, there are schools for which the calculated cost of 48.5 international units per pupil per annum is valid but if the average cost for the whole country is below this, it follows that there must necessarily be various levels in the quality of primary schooling and, consequently, various costs per pupil per annum.

This is the situation, to a greater or lesser degree, in all South American countries, since it is a characteristic of underdeveloped countries that the inconsistencies and inequalities of their institutions and financing are also found in education in respect to premises and equipment, teachers' qualifications and earnings, school administration machinery and funds, teaching materials, etc.

Accordingly, if one establishes the reasonable average cost per pupil per annum at 48.5 international units and also finds that in one country at least—Brazil, which represents all the inconsistencies and inequalities of the whole of Latin America—the real average cost is about 29 international units per pupil per annum, it will not be possible for the time being to raise this real average cost to 48.5 international units, the figure that is considered reasonable.

Under these conditions, the calculation in the table of primary school extension prospects represents at one and the same time a minimum and a maximum, the former in respect to the number of years necessary to extend primary education to all children of school age and the latter in respect to the cost of satisfactory primary schooling. Consequently, the minimum indicated can be achieved without undertaking the maximum expenditure, and this seems to be happening in Latin America.

In other words, it is financially possible to get the whole school-age population to receive primary education within a short time, provided that low-cost—and hence, stinted and inadequate—education is given.

If we abandon the objective of 48.5 international units per pupil per annum for a lower one, say 25 international units, it will be possible to get more children into school within a briefer time.

However, I consider that it would be good policy in our underdeveloped countries to extend the school system as far as possible and at the same time progressively improve the quality of schooling. In financial terms this would involve a double program: on the one hand, the establishment of more and more primary schools within the approximate limit of 1.26 per cent of the national income, subject to not reducing the cost per pupil per annum in the new schools below a certain minimum, for instance 25 international units; on the other hand, progressive improvement of the present school system, so as to do away with the old schools where the cost per pupil per annum is below 25 international units and replace them by better ones. In other words, we should have one part of the budget for expansion and one part for improvement of the system.

For this, however, it is necessary to have adequate and precise knowledge of the differences in quality of the schools within the existing school systems and of their respective costs. Hence the need for a financial survey of the primary schools of Latin America with a view to evaluating the possibilities of improvements from the standpoint of financing and investments.

Planning educational reforms is not enough; more than the needs, the possibilities of meeting them have also to be taken into account.

Here then one has another field of study and research which needs proper exploration to facilitate determination of what can be done to improve and expand the school systems.

Some Problems of Secondary Education

For the purpose of this research proposal I shall again use the four Latin American countries: Argentina, Brazil, Colombia and Peru—for which I have the main data.

In Brazil's case, in addition to considering the country as a whole, I will deal especially with three of its regions: the Northeast, the East and the South. The 1950 census shows population densities of over 15 per square kilometer for all these, but they are at contrasting levels of social and economic development. The South is at about the level of the most developed areas of Latin America and is comparable with Argentina; the East is perhaps on a level with Mexico, and the Northeast can probably be compared to certain countries of Central America and certain areas of Andean America. As already suggested, Brazil as a whole is comparable to the whole of "non-Portuguese" Latin America, that is, it can serve to represent the Latin American socioeconomic composite of areas in the course of development, areas almost static and backward, and areas still in process of settlement by human beings.

Consequently, if I add to the sample the data relating to Argentina, Colombia and Peru, this group of countries may perhaps be sufficient to provide a general idea of the problem arising in Latin America as a whole. At the same time, I shall refer as far as possible to other Latin American countries as well, whenever any known fact enables me to do so.

Within the group of four countries, Argentina is the one with the highest proportion of people in employment: 29 per cent of the total population, or one person employed to 1.5 not employed. Brazil follows next with 33 per cent (one employed for two not employed); then Colombia with 32 per cent and Peru with 32 per cent. Argentina is practically at the United States (40 per cent) level of economically active population, while Brazil, considered as a whole, and Colombia and Peru are closely similar (32 per cent to 33 per cent). Mexico, Venezuela and Cuba are in the same category, with over 30 per cent and under 34 per cent. Paradoxically, Ecuador and Bolivia have high percentages (38 per cent and 39 per cent respectively), possibly as a result of more-extensive recording of female and child labor in rural areas. In Bolivia, 401,500 women are employed in primary activities, as against 313,800 men, while in Ecuador the proportion is 169,700 women to 153,700 men.

If one considers the three regions of Brazil I have selected, one finds that, whereas the South approximates to the Argentinian situation with 36 per cent of its population in gainful employment, the East approaches the Brazilian average with 32.2 per cent, while the Northeast falls below this average with only 31.5 per cent.

Obviously, in comparing these percentages one should bear in mind the criteria used in collecting and tabulating the data. The use of different census criteria may lessen the comparability of the results. In Brazil itself there is an example of this, because if one compares the results of the 1940 census with those of the 1950 census one gets the impression that the number of women in employment has decreased, whereas what happened in fact was a modification of the criterion whereby many of the women in rural areas were rated as employed.

In the absence of other information, I have adopted the hypothesis that the data are comparable, bearing in mind that they all come from censuses conducted more or less at the same time, that is, in or around 1950. In this matter of employed population, estimations based on census data are always uncertain because of the fact that urbanization and industrialization, which are particular to some areas, can change the whole structure of employment in a few years.

The next consideration is how the employed population is distributed among the three major sectors of activity—primary, secondary and tertiary—in the four countries.

In Argentina 21 per cent of the employed population was engaged in primary activities (agriculture, stock raising and extraction industries), 30 per cent in secondary activities (industry, civil engineering and public utilities) and 49 per cent in tertiary activities (commerce, transportation, communications, public service, miscellaneous services, etc.).

Brazil as a whole had 61 per cent of its employed population in primary activities, 13 per cent in secondary activities and 26 per cent in tertiary activities.

In south Brazil, however, the distribution was: primary 50.6 per cent, secondary 20.3 per cent and tertiary 29.1 per cent. The position in São Paulo State, with 41.6 per cent employed in primary activities, 25.4 per cent in secondary and 33 per cent in tertiary, is worthy of note.

In east Brazil the employment pattern approximated closely to the national average: 56.9 per cent in primary activities, 12.9 per cent in secondary and 30.2 per cent in tertiary. In the Northeast, with relatively high population density, the percentages were respectively 74.7, 7.4 and 17.9. In Colombia and Peru the percentages approximated to the Brazilian average, with primary activities accounting respectively for 56 per cent and 60 per cent, secondary for 16 per cent and 14 per cent, and tertiary for 28 per cent and 26 per cent. Thus, while the percentages for Colombia and Peru indicate a higher degree of industrialization than in the Brazilian east and north-east regions, they do not equal those for the southern region, especially those for São Paulo which approximate to the percentages in Argentina.

I believe, however, that a more rigorous definition of manufacturing activities (processing industries) was applied in Brazil than in other countries and that accordingly the position as regards tertiary activities, which, economically, are largely the result of urbanization and the secondary activities, may indicate a better development. One needs only to reflect that world statistics show Bolivia and Ecuador, both notoriously poor and nonindustrialized countries, as having higher percentages of secondary activities than Brazil and a number of other more developed Latin American countries—18 per cent for Bolivia and 25 per cent for Ecuador. I believe this is mainly the result of counting in small home industries and the same circumstance would go some way towards explaining the higher percentage of employment in these two countries (which almost equals that in the United States), while the per capita income, at about 100 Colin Clark international units, is very low. The per capita income in Brazil is almost double this (190 international units in 1952), almost 50 per cent higher in Peru (145 international units in 1951), three times as much in Argentina (363 international units in 1951) and slightly higher in Colombia (118 international units in 1951); but it is worth noting that the per capita income of the combined southern states of Brazil (São Paulo, Paraná, Santa Catarina, and Rio Grande do Sul) was close to that of Argentina: in fact, taking into account that in 1952 a Colin Clark international unit was equal to 30.77 cruzeiros, I find that the per capita income in these states as a whole was, on an average, 300 international units.

Furthermore, as a counterbalance to the relatively high percentage of population employed in secondary activities in Bolivia and Ecuador, one needs to recall that over 40 per cent of their gross national income comes from farming and extraction industries against only 24 per cent from primary activities in Argentina, 20 per cent in Brazil, 39 per cent in Colombia and 34 per cent in Peru.

Two more facts should be noted, in addition to what has already been said. First, except in Argentina, there is a highly significant disproportion between the percentage of the working population engaged in primary activities and the percentage of the national income represented by the product of primary activities, which is indicative of a very poor rural population with low per capita productivity and hence insufficient means to provide for the education of their children. Secondly, the relatively high percentage of the working population engaged in tertiary activities does not mean that all these people belong to the middle class simply because tertiary activities include employments in commerce, transport, communication, services, etc. The category "services" includes not only public civil service but also the work done by servants, and this group, in towns and cities, includes a large number of unskilled people who have no other alternative but to accept humble positions as servants. Even in Argentina this is true. I estimate roughly that perhaps 5.9 per cent of the economically active population in this country, 9.8 per cent in Brazil, 8.9 per cent in Colombia and 9.1 per cent in Peru occupy such low rank in the tertiary sector.

To sum up, Table 3 shows the comparative position in the four countries under consideration.

I shall now consider, in relation to the population in employment, the needs of each country in respect to secondary education. Then, bearing in mind the economic and financial possibilities, I shall ascertain how far these needs can be met.

I shall assume that secondary education must be given to a percentage of the 12-to-16 age group equal to the percentage of the working population in secondary and tertiary activities combined,[1] if the society or country in question wants to have the right kind of manpower for development on modern technological lines.

In 1950–1951, the total 12-to-18 age group numbered approximately 1.6 million in Argentina, 5.9 million in Brazil, 1.4 million in Colombia, and 1.1 million in Peru.

---

[1] If x is the number of persons engaged in secondary activities, and y the number in tertiary activities, and t the total number in employment, the percentage of young people over 12 and under 16 who should be in secondary school will be $\frac{100\,(x+y)}{t}$.

This is a rule of thumb proportion suggested by the tables given in the United Nations *Statistical Yearbook* for 1957 and by those in *America's Resources of Specialized Talent* by Dael Wolfie, *The American High School Today* by James B. Conant, and *Technical Education and Social Change* by Stephen F. Cotogreve.

For the United States $\frac{100\,(x+y)}{t}$ works out at 74, compared with 88 per cent of the 12-to-16 age group in junior or senior high schools. For England the equation gives 93 compared with 93 per cent in school, for France 61 compared with 67 per cent and for Italy 59 compared with 48 per cent.

Table 3. Employed Population and per Capita Income in Latin America

Country or Region[1]	Total Population	Working Population in Primary Activities	Working Population in Secondary Activities	Working Population in Tertiary Activities Excluding Servants	Per Capita Income in International Units	National Income Represented by Product of Primary Activities
	%	%	%	%		%
Argentina	39.0	21	30	43	363	24
Brazil	33.0	61	13	16	190	29
Colombia	32.6	56	16	19	118	39
Peru	32.0	60	14	17	145	34
Brazil						
South region	36.0	51	20	22	300	27
East region	32.2	57	13	20	180	32
Northeast region	31.5	75	7	12	80	43

[1]The data in the above table do not all relate to the same year, some being for 1950, some for 1951, and some for 1952, with the exception of the data for Argentina, which relate to 1947. It is considered that where the data relate to any one of these three consecutive years, their comparability is not seriously prejudiced thereby.

Concurrently, 73 per cent of the Argentine working population, 29 per cent of the Brazilian, 35 per cent of the Colombian and 31 per cent of the Peruvian were employed in the secondary and tertiary sectors. Accordingly, the numbers in secondary school should have been 1,168,000 in Argentina, 1,711,000 in Brazil, 490,000 in Colombia and 341,000 in Peru.

As I have already shown, the cost of secondary schooling per pupil per annum in Brazil should be approximately five times the cost of primary schooling; at the rate of 48.5 international units per primary school pupil this would amount to 242.5 international units, which would be too much for Latin America, and even for Brazil. Accepting the second supposition, that is, the rate of 25 international units per primary school pupil, I arrive at 125 international units per secondary school pupil.

At this rate, Argentina would have to spend about 146 million international units, Brazil 214 million, Colombia 61.25 million and Peru 42.62 million.

At 1952 values, this would have meant Argentina allocating 2.4 per cent of its national income to secondary education, Brazil 2.06 per cent, Colombia 5.12 per cent and Peru 3.9 per cent, and arguments have already been adduced to show that it would be difficult for the Latin American countries to devote more than 1.26 per cent of the national income to secondary education, without endangering other essential investments. Thus, in 1952, Argentina could have spent on this category of education only 63.5 million international units, Brazil 101 million, Colombia 11.9 million and Peru 10.7 million.

On this basis Argentina, at the date of reference, could have had about 508,000 pupils in secondary schools of all types, Brazil some 808,000, Colombia about 95,200 and Peru 85,600.

In actual fact the Argentine secondary school population at the date concerned was around 167,000, that of Brazil 417,000, that of Colombia 49,000 and that of Peru 44,000. Hence, even Argentina was doing less than it could have done and I find the only country in Latin America (except probably Uruguay) with universal primary schooling nevertheless showing a considerable "deficit" in secondary schooling, with numbers representing less than 33 per cent of those who could be provided for and less than 16 per cent of the country's probable needs according to its possible skilled and semiskilled manpower requirements for a rising rate of development.

While the remaining countries are not meeting the real requirements for their technological development, they are doing all they can in this sector of education.

It has been possible to work out rule-of-thumb ratios between the numbers in secondary-level technical and vocational schools and the working population for the following developed countries: United States, United Kingdom, France and Italy.

In this respect, I have assumed that the percentage of the total secondary school population which should be in technical schools should be equivalent to the percentage of the number of persons employed in secondary and tertiary activities combined represented by the number employed in the secondary sector alone.[1]

In France the numbers employed in secondary and tertiary activities together were 13.25 million and in secondary activities alone 6.10 million, giving the equation $\dfrac{6.10 \times 100}{13.25} = 46$. Against this the total of enrollments in secondary technical schools was 0.398 million and the total enrollment in all secondary schools was 1.40 million; thus we have $\dfrac{0.398 \times 100}{1.40} = 28.4$.

In the United States the ratio is harder to calculate because of the way the secondary schools are organized. However, if one examines the high school and its curriculum one finds that the numbers electing technical-

---

[1] If x is the number employed in secondary occupations, and y the number in tertiary occupations, r the enrollment in technical secondary schools and s the enrollments in all secondary schools, then $\dfrac{100x}{x+y} = \dfrac{100r}{s}$.

scientific and vocational subjects represent 40 per cent of the total high school enrollments while the population employed in secondary activities represents 40.6 per cent of the total population employed in secondary and tertiary activities together.

In the United Kingdom, if one considers the modern secondary schools, the technical schools and special studies at secondary level, one finds that the percentage of technical and scientific enrollments is 48.2 per cent of the total of secondary school enrollments while the population employed in secondary activities is equivalent to 49.5 per cent of the total population employed in secondary and tertiary activities.

In France there has always been some prejudice against technical and vocational education at the secondary level, reflected even in the laws which considered it unworthy of the *baccalauréat*. Even so, the proportion of enrollments in this branch to the total numbers in secondary education is appreciable, being 28.4 per cent.

In Italy, the total employment in secondary and tertiary activities was 12.2 million, of which secondary activities accounted for 51 per cent. The total enrollments in all technical-vocational, academic and secondary schools were 1.48 million, of which 55 per cent were in technical-vocational schools, suggesting that Italy was training a slight surplus of specialist manpower.

In the light of the foregoing, my rule-of-thumb criterion for assessing technical education requirements at secondary level from the total secondary school enrollments and total employment in secondary and tertiary activities shows itself as not completely explained by the facts. Nevertheless, it is only a working hypothesis for the moment.

As regards the purely practical justification of this criterion, I consider that as things stand at present primary school education is a sufficient qualification for activities in the primary sector, since the need for skilled specialist labor in this sector depends on economic development. Such development, of course, with increasing mechanization, would result in a reduction of the numbers employed in primary activities: the greater the number of workers in the primary sector, the poorer the economy and the more primitive the working methods.

As the numbers employed in tertiary and secondary activities increase, the greater becomes the need for specialist vocational training, both at the secondary and the higher levels. Nevertheless, there is a multitude of non-primary employments for which social and intellectual knowledge and training, not technical qualifications, are needed. The ratio between the two categories of secondary education (technical and nontechnical) should correspond to that between the numbers employed in industry (secondary sector) and those employed in commerce, transportation, administration, etc. (tertiary sector).

I have thus given reasons for the criterion adopted; Table 4 shows how it applies to secondary school enrollments in the four Latin American countries I am studying.

Table 4. Working Population and Secondary School Enrollments

Country	*Secondary Activities*	*Tertiary Activities Excluding Servants*	*Total (a) + (b)*	$100 \times \dfrac{(a)}{(c)}$	*Pupils in Technical Schools*	*Pupils in All Secondary Schools*	$100 \times \dfrac{(e)}{(f)}$	$(g) - (d)$
	(a)	(b)	(c)	(d)	(e)	(f)	(g)	(h)
	(000)	(000)	(000)		(000)	(000)		
Argentina	1,795.4	2,652.0	4,447.4	40	35.0	167	21	−19
Brazil	2,231.0	4,073.0	6,304.0	35	109.0	615	18	−17
Colombia	604.4	971.9	1,576.3	38	7.5	72	10	−28
Peru	568.2	884.7	1,452.9	39	11.9	69	17	−22

Column *(h)* of Table 4 shows that, according to the rule-of-thumb criterion adopted, the country with the heaviest deficit in technical and vocational education is Colombia and that with the smallest,[1] though still a heavy one, is Brazil.

From the foregoing it can be asserted that secondary school technical and vocational training is unquestionably extremely inadequate in Latin America in terms of the skilled and semiskilled manpower likely to be needed for economic development.

Nevertheless, examination of what is happening in Brazil leads me to believe that most of the needed specialist or industrial training is being carried out in a noninstitutionalized manner, that is to say outside the schools. Up to a point, the great majority of the workers in Brazil's modern automobile industry, already over 100,000 in number, got their training "on the job," by learning as workers in the factories. According to Stephen F. Cotogreve's *Technical Education and Social Change* the same kind of thing went on in England from the eighteenth to the beginning of the present century. It was only between 1882 and 1905 that technical and vocational training began to develop satisfactorily in England and became able to meet some of the needs of industry and technological progress.

This suggests that technical secondary education is not an absolute prerequisite for economic and technological development. Table 4 is only a

---

[1] In the above calculations, by reason of the ratio established between secondary activities and the total of nonprimary activities, only enrollments in industrial training schools, trade schools and craft schools are taken into account for the purposes of column (e). The figures in column (f) show all enrollments in middle-level schools.

device for crude measuring; it does not say definitely that secondary technical education is a necessary step on the way to industrial development.

It seems that Brazil and other Latin American countries may possibly be overconcerned with this kind of education, which may perhaps mean some waste of money. It is possible to learn to operate very complex machines without understanding their scientific principles. Recently I had a very amusing example of this in Brazil. An electronic computer was bought by a government agency, and five electronic engineers (with higher educational and specialized qualifications) were selected to operate it. But the experts, who came from the United States to give them the operating instructions, were not graduates; they had only had secondary education.

University Education and Its Problems

Latin American universities publish little information about their organization, courses of study, conditions for admission and enrollment, requirements for intermediate and final examinations, etc. I wrote to 100 state or independent universities asking them to send publications explaining their organization, and the courses and curricula available. Only five responded and even so did not supply full information. Hence it is difficult to discuss the merits and defects of the universities.

Nevertheless, I do know roughly that university education in Latin America is more academic than technical and scientific, thus retaining an out-of-date orientation peculiar to the eighteenth and nineteenth centuries when culture was the distinguishing mark of a small ruling elite of more or less aristocratic nature, and technology and science were private hobbies of visionaries or persistent and almost heroic men intent on dominating nature for the benefit of human society.

Over the same period, however, the social and economic development of the bourgeoisie and its perpetual search for means to enable them to achieve social and economic power did result in scientists and inventors receiving some support and encouragement in their independent activities. For all practical purposes the evolution of science and technology over this period took place outside the universities.

From his birth in poverty at Newington, Surrey, to his election to the Royal Society, Faraday did no university work. The young Pascal, with his invention of a calculating machine as an aid to public administration, his mathematical studies and analyses and his proof of Torricelli's theory that nature does not abhor a vacuum, was never to reach a university at all. While Newton did graduate at Trinity College, Cambridge, his great discoveries in physics and mathematics were made away from the university and with no help from it. There is no need to continue the tale of the great scientists and inventors of the past centuries. Edison and Bell are recent examples of scientific and technological individualism.

However, in that age, economic, social and political conditions left room for this kind of individualism and up to a point required and imposed it. In our day technology and science are no longer one-man undertakings but are becoming increasingly dependent on teamwork, substantial investment, public support and government backing. Their proper place is the universities with their research institutes and postgraduate schools.

In most South American countries one does not find the economic, social and political conditions which permitted the survival of technological and scientific individualism in Europe and the United States as late as the dawn of the present century. Today science and technology have reached a stage where this individualism is no longer possible either in underdeveloped or in developed societies.

The era of the anchorite in science and technology has already passed away. It seems as though everything that could be discovered by the individual genius, working patiently and assiduously in isolation, has already been discovered. It is not that personal talent and ability have ceased to be valuable but that, without laboratories and equipment, assistants and supporting teams, it is no longer possible for the brilliant individual to do all the study and research required for further progress in science and technology.

Both the existence of research institutes, within or outside the universities, and the development of individual talent are directly dependent on the economic and technological potential of each national society. The equipment required for research is extremely expensive to import and difficult and complicated to manufacture locally, which means that an appreciable economic potential is necessary to start with, that the standards for specialists must be higher and that social and economic prospects must also be good.

In the present state of affairs, the local development of science and technology is no longer an essential preliminary for, but an outcome of, social and economic development. To meet their needs, developing countries now have practically no alternative but to import the science and technology they require.

These present-day circumstances largely explain the antiquated complexion of the universities of Latin America, which are not yet provided with scientific and technological research institutes and concentrate almost entirely on studies of an academic nature. Some improvements have been introduced these last two years, which may lead one to suppose that the old system is losing ground.

Industrialization and progressive urbanization are contributing to new perspectives. One can see now in Brazil that the middle and upper sections of the lower classes are asking for education. This means, of course, change and diminished influence for the old aristocracy.

I believe that these, broadly speaking, are the economic and social conditions of higher education in Latin America. Naturally changes are already beginning to take place. In Brazil the process is plain to see and in Mexico, Chile, Venezuela and Argentina it is also discernible from the current data and documents it has been possible to procure.

The evaluation of Latin American systems of higher education is nevertheless a task which still remains to be done. I shall set out below a number of criteria which, together with the data available, will enable me to make some observations on the situation.

As long ago as the achievement of independence, if not earlier, institutes were established all over South America for the training of doctors. As a result we ought, today, to have satisfactory medical services, but in fact that is not how things have turned out, the reasons being social and economic.

Table 5. Enrollments in University-Level Medical Schools

Country	Year	Enrollment	Inhabitants per Student
Argentina	1950	20,446	870
Brazil	1957	17,591	3,400
Colombia	1957	4,615	2,400
Cuba	1952	4,364	1,350
Ecuador	1951	1,471	2,200
El Salvador	1953	366	5,600
Guatemala	1951	691	4,050
Honduras	1953	307	5,100
Mexico	1950	5,663	4,900
Panama	1950	170	4,700
Paraguay	1950	581	2,300
Peru	1951	3,792	2,400
Dominican Republic	1952	989	2,300
Venezuela	1950	2,944	1,700
Nicaragua	1958	392	3,500

Turning to the statistics available one finds that in the most highly developed countries, between 1953 and 1956, there was one graduate physician to every 600–900 inhabitants (790 in the United States in 1955, and concurrently 620 in Austria, 820 in Italy, 850 in Norway, 700 in Switzerland, 610 in the U.S.S.R., etc.).

The countries of Latin America can be grouped as follows in this respect: Argentina and Uruguay, 800–999 persons per physician; Chile, Cuba and Venezuela, 1,000–1,999; Colombia, Costa Rica, Brazil, Mexico, Nicaragua and Paraguay, 2,000–2,999; Panama, Peru and Ecuador, 3,000–3,999;

Bolivia and Honduras, 4,000–4,999; and Dominican Republic, El Salvador, Guatemala and Haiti, over 5,000.

I shall now look at the ratio between enrollments in the various institutes of higher education and the number of inhabitants, in order to ascertain the importance attached to each type of education.

Of the eight Latin American countries for which I have data, Argentina has the most university students in proportion to population. It also has the highest number of students in medicine, law and social sciences, engineering, architecture, physical and mathematical sciences, agronomy, and in economics, commerce and business management. The only subjects in which it is outdistanced by any of the other countries are chemistry and pharmacology, philosophy and letters and fine arts.

Table 6. Number of Inhabitants per Student Enrolled
in Institutes of Higher Education

School or Course	Argentina	Brazil	Colombia	Mexico	Peru	Venezuela	Cuba	Ecuador
Law and social science	1,025	2,830	4,310	10,600	5,850	5,300	2,850	3,120
Medicine	870	3,400	2,400	4,900	2,400	1,700	1,350	2,200
Chemistry and pharmacology	11,420	35,400	38,000	21,400	11,400	10,800	4,300	13,100
Engineering, architecture, physical and mathematical sciences	1,100	5,800	2,640	8,750	3,730	3,360	3,100	6,060
Philosophy and letters	4,660	3,900	1,220	25,800	3,190	9,950	1,290	11,300
Agronomics	8,900	42,000	31,000	–	–	16,650	14,700	22,400
Economics, commerce and business management	880	9,130	23,600	10,700	2,100	18,700	2,620	14,000
Fine arts	46,000	26,600	–	50,500	–	–	–	–
Others	–	39,800	130,000	62,000	300,000	–	–	170,000
Total for all courses and schools	214	720	915	1,550	685	725	1,435	3,220

In Brazil one finds several university-level specialist courses not classifiable under the headings of the table. There are more such courses in Brazil than in any other country in the sample and probably in the whole of Latin America, but the numbers taking them are low, of the order of one student per 39,800 inhabitants. The other courses call for no particular comment apart from the percentages of enrollments in law, philosophy and letters (47 per cent) and in technical and scientific courses (44 per cent) respectively being practically equal.

With respect to the proportion of total numbers in higher education to population, Brazil is left far behind by Argentina and is only third in the sample, the country with the least proportion of students to population being Ecuador.

Thus Argentina is the only country in the sample in a similar position to that of the developed countries of Europe, which have from 227 to 356 inhabitants per university student (Italy 227, France 284, Switzerland 286, Belgium 307, Netherlands 326, Sweden 336, Denmark 356, United Kingdom 745, and U.S.S.R. 905).

I have already postulated that, to train the manpower needed for national development in Brazil, as a probable first goal, the numbers receiving primary, secondary and higher education respectively need to be in the proportions of 100 : 20 : 4. I shall now take a look at the situation in the countries of Latin America, supposing that such a goal, as a preliminary achievement, is perhaps valid for all of them. It is a supposition or, at most, a hypothesis to be tested, not a scientifically established proposition. I believe that it is really a first goal for Brazil, not for all Latin American countries. Nevertheless it allows me to draw certain comparisons that demonstrate the magnitude of our educational problems.

Table 7 thus shows that the countries with the highest proportions of secondary to primary school numbers are Panama, Uruguay and Brazil,[1] but that not even in these countries is the desired level of 20 per cent attained.

As regards higher education, the proportion of 4 per cent of primary school enrollments is exceeded only in Argentina and Uruguay, while in Cuba the proportion is 3 per cent. In Brazil, Costa Rica and Peru it is 1.5 per cent. All the rest have under 1.5 per cent and six, including Mexico, under 1 per cent.

In general, it can be said that Latin America, which has not yet satisfied its minimum needs in primary education, is not developing secondary and higher education proportionately to its existing primary education. I believe that countries like Brazil, Mexico, Venezuela, Argentina, and Colombia can improve the situation and for them perhaps my hypothesis may be valid.

However, both to ascertain the real terms of these problems and to find out how far the secondary schools and institutes of higher education are catering for the real needs of our countries, we need to investigate not only the social, economic and cultural factors affecting attendance at educational establishments but also the latter as such, their equipment, curricula, teaching staffs and functioning. In addition to that, an objective analysis

---

[1]The calculation covers both academic and technical vocational secondary schoools.

Table 7. Secondary Schools and Universities
Compared to Primary Schools

Country	Primary	Secondary	Higher
	%	%	%
Argentina	100	15.6	5.5
Bolivia	100	14.4	–
Brazil	100	17.3	1.5
Chile	100	15.4	–
Colombia	100	10.5	1.1
Costa Rica	100	10.4	1.5
Cuba	100	8.7	3.0
Dominican Republic	100	13.0	0.7
Ecuador	100	9.7	1.3
Guatemala	100	8.8	0.5
Haiti	100	8.9	0.4
Honduras	100	6.1	0.7
Mexico	100	4.5	0.8
Nicaragua	100	6.5	0.9
Panama	100	18.4	1.4
Paraguay	100	9.7	1.0
Peru	100	9.8	1.5
El Salvador	100	6.6	0.9
Uruguay	100	17.4	4.3
Venezuela	100	6.1	1.2

of requirements in manpower of secondary school and university levels, specialized or not, is needed to see how far it is necessary to diversify these categories of education and how far they will have to be expanded and the numbers of students increased. The calculations and rough measurements set out in this study will not suffice for this purpose: here I have simply tried to call attention to the problem and to approach a possible method to be developed in practice.

Finally, it will be necessary to determine the financial and technical possibilities (staff and equipment) for implementing an objective plan drawn up under these conditions.

Some Preliminary Conclusions: International Cooperation

Obviously, the data and indices I have used as a basis for my comments are inconclusive and inadequate, including those on the subject of finance, and I must emphasize this.

What they do enable me to assert unequivocably, however, is that we are not providing at any level the education our peoples need and that, in general terms, our countries do not possess the financial and technical resources to meet these needs completely and satisfactorily.

However, what has emerged also makes it clear that changes are taking place in our educational systems and that up to a point we are contriving to solve our educational problems.

If, once the necessary investigations have been carried out, we succeed in drawing up national schemes of educational development coupled with plans for inter-American cooperation and technical assistance, it will be possible to direct the attempts at reform already in progress along practical and functional lines, with due regard to our real needs.

The plans can, it is felt, be allocated realistic priorities, in view of the limitations of our financial and technical potential due to underdevelopment, so as to enable us to devote the greatest effort to what is of most immediate importance.

In present-day Brazil—and probably in other Latin American countries—we are witnessing an important expansion of educational projects which follow no coordinated national and regional plan. Nevertheless, I believe that after the conference of Punta del Este, UNESCO, the Organization of American States, the International Co-operation Administration and other international organizations will be able to develop a coordinated program of education at all levels: primary, secondary and higher education.

Merely trying to cater for needs without prior study may lead to the adoption of conflicting solutions which will make our educational problems worse still.

International cooperation and technical assistance must be considered from this standpoint. In Brazil the independent programs of many international organizations are not yet fully coordinated to meet the problems on an integrated basis.

I believe that education, although it relies on specialists for planning and for advice as to how to put such plans into effect, is a responsibility which must be undertaken by all for all.

Hence the need for a comprehensive understanding of the problems of education and of their economic and social context as a basis on which to work out a national education policy. It would then be in accordance with this comprehensive understanding and this national policy that particular projects, both as components and as consequences thereof, should be proposed and implemented.

It is obvious that international cooperation will have to take these various aspects of educational study and planning into account; otherwise they will become obstacles and hindrances to the development of our countries.

The Development of Education in Latin America since the Santiago Plan

MICHEL DEBEAUVAIS

One of the three projects to which UNESCO gave priority in 1958 was universal primary education in Latin America. In 1963, the Conference of Latin American Ministers of Education adopted the Santiago Plan which established targets for all levels of schooling up to 1970. One year later, the Conference of Bogotá revised these objectives, reducing the calculated figures by one third, which in practice amounts to postponing universal primary education until 1975. The Conference of Ministers of Education at Buenos Aires in June 1966 did not significantly change this orientation of general policy. This paper[1] provides a quantitative analysis of the developments in Latin American education since 1960, as compared with the forecasts made a few years ago, using UNESCO data and statistical data from various other sources. This analysis suggests a number of observations on the value of educational planning at the regional level. There may be differences of opinion on regional forecasting and planning, but the experience of the last few years shows that in fact these regional meetings, involving as they do interregional comparisons of statistics, aims, and policies in education, do exercise a positive influence on the countries taking part. The recommendations they adopt, the targets which they explicitly or implicitly approve, and the methods of forecasting which they employ at the regional level serve later as a standard of reference for national plans.

Reproduced from *The World Year Book of Education 1967* (Educational Planning), pp. 358–374, 1967, with the permission of Evans Brothers, Ltd., Publishers (London).

[1] The author is indebted to M. Sylvain Lourié for many of the ideas expressed here. Moreover, most of the figures have been collected and discussed within a study group at the École Pratique des Hautes Études.

The Objects of the Santiago Plan

What is known as the Santiago Plan is, in fact, a collection of preparatory documents and recommendations which were adopted by the Conference of Ministers of Education held at Santiago in March 1963, under the auspices of UNESCO, the Economic Commission of Latin America, and the Organization of American States.[1] The quantitative aims appear chiefly in an appended document compiled by a study group during the conference;[2] this expresses in numbers of pupils and in total educational expenditure certain of the aims adopted in plenary session, notably that of universal primary education by 1970.

The forecasts were largely concerned with enrollment targets for 1965 and 1970, with the countries divided into three groups according to their enrollment rates at the secondary level. Universal primary schooling was to be reached by 1965 in the two leading groups, and by 1970 in the third. With regard to secondary education, the targets called for the provision of schooling for one third of the young people by 1970 throughout the region. As the groupings of countries seem rather arbitrary, only the total objectives at the regional level[3] will be examined here.

Table 1 indicates the enrollment rates obtained in 1955 and 1960, as well as the objectives proposed for 1965 and 1970.

Table 1. Enrollment Rates in Latin America

	Actual Rates*		Objectives of Santiago for the Entire Region	
	1955	1960	1965	1970
Primary	64	78	91	100
Secondary	10	15	22	34
Higher	2	3.1	3.4	4

*Values observed, according to the educational statistics and the population data available at the time. Source: Cedes.

These percentages can be converted into numbers of pupils by means of estimates of the population in five-year age groups. The estimated increase in pupils from 1960 determines the number of new places to be provided, and this figure can be used to estimate the expenditure required, by applying given figures for the costs per new place.[4] A similar estimate of current

[1] Most of the documents were published in the review, *Proyecto Principal de Educación*, 14 (June, 1962).
[2] Cedes, Anexo 4 published in the above review.
[3] A questionable index of secondary schooling was taken as a criterion for the division of the countries into three groups.
[4] Costs for the provision of one new place: primary, $65; secondary, $300; and higher, $1,200.

costs per pupil makes it possible to arrive at the figure for total expenditure which would correspond to the stated aims. The total expenditure for each five-year period is as follows (in billion U.S. dollars): $13.9 for 1960–1965 and $20.6 for 1965–1970.[1]

I have elsewhere criticized this method of presenting the expenditure as a lump sum.[2] It has several serious disadvantages: (a) it is not possible to calculate the amount of educational expenditure in any one year and especially in the last year, 1970; (b) it is impossible to verify whether the share of the national resources devoted to education is or is not compatible with the targets laid down in the Santiago Plan; and (c) it is impossible to estimate the rate of increase in educational expenditure over the 10-year period. It is therefore necessary to present the forecasts for educational expenditure in a form which permits a comparison with the developments that are actually observed. The method of calculation adopted here has been set out in the paper just cited: it is assumed that total educational expenditure increases at a regular geometric rate; and the annual rate of increase is estimated by successive approximations. Educational expenditure for the whole of Latin America in 1960 has been estimated at $1.32 billion according to the national figures. To reach the comprehensive total of $34.5 billion, the annual rate of increase in educational expenditure would have to be 16.4 per cent, or three times as much as the rate of increase of national income forecast by the Decade of Development and the Alliance for Progress. At this rate, educational expenditures would increase by 355 per cent, reaching $6 billion in 1970, or 6.4 per cent of the gross national product, on the assumption that the Decade's objective for economic expansion will be realized.

I shall not undertake an internal criticism of the Santiago targets. It would in fact be easy to arrive at more-likely figures by starting with a higher estimate of the educational expenditure for 1960.[3] It must also be mentioned that the 1970 targets of the Santiago Plan have been postponed to 1975.[4] In order to judge the implications and the feasibility of the 10-year

---

[1] *Ibid.*, p. 160.

[2] See M. Debeauvais, *A Study on Regional Planning: Examples of the Karachi Plan*, IEDES, to be published by UNESCO, 1967.

[3] For example if the total expenditure on education was estimated at $1.7 billion, increasing the preceding amounts by 29 per cent to allow for omissions, and taking into account expenditure on private education, the annual rate of increase in educational expenditure would be brought up to 11.6 per cent and the expenditure for 1970 would be $5.1 billion, or 5.4 per cent of GNP. These figures are close to the forecasts recently worked out by the Division of Statistics of UNESCO for Latin America in 1970: $4.94 billion or 5.25 per cent of GNP.

[4] A study prepared by the Task Force of the Organization of American States and approved by the Conference of Ministers at Bogotá, *Perspectivas de desarrollo de la educación en América Latina* (IEDES, PAU, Washington, 1963). The assumption with regard to educational expenditure was an increase of about 10 per cent per year calculated on the basis of expenditure observed in 1960, and not on standard costs as was the case in the Santiago Plan.

financial forecasts on the regional scale, it is necessary to know the present
level of educational expenditure. Taking the first two estimates as an example, if the total is $1.3 billion or $1.7 billion, the total cost in 1970 will
be respectively $3.37 billion or $4.4 billion, given an annual rate of increase of 10 per cent. These calculations show the importance for any attempts at forecasting of better knowledge of the present level of expenditure
on education.

In the past, attention has been directed primarily to the targets of pupils
to be educated, rather than studies of costs and finance. What is important
for comparing forecasts with outcomes is not so much the figures themselves as the rates of increase. Furthermore, the totals for educational expenditure are systematically underestimated, owing to the failure to take
account of either the expenditures of local communities or private education. It is the annual rates of increase, therefore, which we shall use to
analyze the forecasts of the Santiago Plan. For enrollments, there are acceptable statistics for 1950–1965 for the whole of Latin America. For educational expenditure, the last data available refer to the years 1960 and
1961. An inquiry has been undertaken by UNESCO on this subject, but we
shall have to wait several months yet before knowing the complete results.
So it is possible to analyze the development of expenditures only in the
case of certain countries.

The Growth in Enrollments

Table 2 presents the rates of increase in the number of pupils at each educational level in five-year periods.

Table 2. Annual Rates of Increase in Enrolled Pupils

	Actual Rates			Forecasts of Santiago		Corrected Forecasts
	1950–55 (b)	1955–60 (b)	1960–65 (c)	1960–65 (a)	1965–70 (a)	1965–70 (d)
Primary	6.9	5.7	5.4	5.4	4.75	4.6
Secondary	13.3	7.87	11.5	10.9	10.9	13.0
Higher	12.8	7.7	8.15	5.67	7.3	6.3

Sources: (a) Cedes, *Proyecto Principal,* Anexo 4, Cuadro 12; (b) *UNESCO Statistical Year
Book, 1963;* (c) UNESCO, *Evaluación del Proyecto Principal,* Minedeca 5 (mimeo.), 1966; (d)
UNESCO, *Education, Science and Communication in the UN Development Decade* (Paris, 1966).

It is obvious that the expansion of schooling preceded rather than followed the Santiago Plan (1961) and even preceded the adoption of the priority project of UNESCO for universal primary education in Latin America
(1958). Already by 1955, the expansion had reached a very high rate, and

it would be interesting to analyze the determining factors; whether the cause was the attitude of individuals, of social groups, or of governments towards education, a change has been produced during the last few years with spectacular results. Contrary to an often-repeated assertion, primary education has not been given priority at the expense of secondary and higher education; the latter are in fact developing much more rapidly. If one allows for the fact that, at these two levels, the cost per pupil is much higher than at the primary level, one can see that an increasing share of educational expenditure is being devoted to secondary and higher education. The enrollment targets of the Santiago Plan, which many experts thought too ambitious, have been reached and, indeed, surpassed.

In order to analyze this development more precisely, I shall examine the three levels of education in turn, mentioning only those national results which differ radically from the development of the whole region.

PRIMARY EDUCATION

Indices of Primary School Enrollments

Table 3 shows that the ratio of 100 per cent for primary school enrollments has been reached and passed in most countries in the region. There are now only four countries where the ratio is lower than 85 per cent, and the regional average is around 100 per cent. The apparent paradox of enrollment ratios in excess of 100 per cent is due to the difference between the actual ages of pupils and the theoretical age group chosen for the calculation. It is worthwhile making this point clear as the attainment of 100 per cent enrollment has usually been considered an ultimate objective of educational planning. The problem is that of measuring the actual attendance among children of school age in primary education. UNESCO attempts to standardize the calculation by relating the number of pupils at primary schools to the age group which corresponds to the number of grades at the primary level; but this definition does not correspond to reality in Latin America, as the pupils in one grade are often of different ages. Certain pupils spend several years in the same grade, and, furthermore, legal ages for compulsory schooling do not exactly correspond with actual ages. For example the 1963–1964 enrollment ratios for Uruguay take on very different values according to which method of calculation is employed.[1] The primary cycle consists of six years of study, and the UNESCO method, comparing six tenths of the 402,000 children aged between five and 14 years with the 319,512 pupils in primary schools, gives an enrollment ratio of 132 per cent. But the six-to-11 age group which is nearer to the actual age of pupils is, according to population statistics, 292,300, which gives a ratio of 109 per cent. Furthermore, 10 per cent of the children between six and 11

---

[1] Ministerio de Instrucción Pública, *Plan de desarrollo educativo,* Table I (Montevideo, 1965).

years are not at school, whereas 10 per cent of the pupils in primary education are under six years old or over 12, and from the age of 11 quite a large number of children are at secondary schools.

So as to allow for the spread in the ages of pupils, an index of schooling has recently been prepared which relates the numbers enrolled in primary education to the seven-to-14 age group.[1] But this procedure has the drawback of not taking account of differences in the number of years of study allotted to the primary cycle in some of the countries. I have therefore calculated an index using, as far as possible, the method recommended by UNESCO, but taking into account the respective duration of primary schooling in each country.

It is evident that enrollment ratios are too ambiguous to serve as objectives of educational planning; they would be more useful in international comparisons if the number of years of study at each educational level were identical in all countries, but that is not the case. The difficulty can to some extent be overcome by taking into account the numbers in schools during similar numbers of years of study, but this method, employed in some studies, is only an expedient which does not solve the problems of comparison.

Education Efficiency

Since the enrollment ratio in primary education is no longer the main problem, educational plans now being formulated in almost all the Latin American countries are giving attention to "educational efficiency." This notion may be looked at in different ways. The grouping of pupils according to years of study may conceal a faulty distribution. Thus over the whole region, more than one third of the pupils in the primary cycle are in the first grade and represent a number twice as great as the total number of children seven years of age. The index most widely used at present is a wastage rate which is obtained by the "cohort method";[2] that is, the number of pupils in the first year of study is compared with the number six years later in the sixth grade (if the primary cycle consists of six years of study). Wastage rates have been calculated by this method for each country in the region, and range from less than 10 per cent (in Nicaragua and the Dominican

---

[1] UNESCO, *Progress Report of the Priority Project,* Minedecal 5 (May 1966), p. 46. Mimeo.

[2] The word "cohort" refers to a group of pupils enrolled in the same year, for the first time in that cycle, in the first grade, whatever their age. This notion is therefore different from that of the population cohort, which includes all children born in the same year whether at school or not. As for the notion of cohort employed in the usual method of reckoning scholastic wastage, it does not follow the same pupils throughout their school career because some have to repeat their courses, some pupils leaving the group of children who started school the same year and others joining them in the course of their school career. Therefore six years later the initial group is noticeably altered.

Table 3. Index of Primary School Enrollment in 1965

	Length of Primary Cycle (years)	Number in Age Group 7-14 Years (millions)	Number in Primary Schools (millions)	Gross Enrollment Ratio %	Adjusted Enrollment Ratio %
Argentina	7	3.500	3.170	91	103.5
Bolivia	6	1.040	.547	53	70
Brazil	5	17.853	9.878	55	88.5
Colombia	5	3.550	2.330	66	105
Costa Rica	6	1.280	.279	100	133
Cuba	6	1.417	1.324	93	125
Chile	6	1.600	1.378	86	115
Ecuador	6	1.025	.752	73	98
Salvador	6	.599	.387	65	86
Guatemala	6	.864	.405	47	62.5
Haiti	6	.810	.274	34	45
Honduras	6	.400	.284	71	95
Mexico	6	8.370	6.916	83	110
Nicaragua	6	.360	.227	63	84
Panama	6	.243	.199	82	109
Paraguay	6	.415	.365	88	117
Peru	5	2.412	1.927	80	128
Dominican Republic	6	.710	.518	73	97.4
Uruguay	6	.390	.359	93	124
Venezuela	6	1.715	1.397	81	108.5
Total		47.550	32.915	69	92

Sources: The age groups are taken from Appendix A of the *Progress Report of the Priority Project*, UNESCO, p. 8, and the primary school enrollment from Table 14, p. 16.

Note: The adjusted indices are calculated on the basis of the fraction of the age group corresponding to the number of years of the primary cycle, which is six years for most of the countries (but seven years for Argentina, and five years for three other countries). The gross ratios are those indicated in the *Progress Report of the Priority Project*, UNESCO, p. 46.

Republic) to 50 per cent (in Uruguay and Panama). Wastage rates are now available for each country for the past five years and in each case there has been a progressive reduction in the ratios, that is, an improvement in educational efficiency. According to these indices it does not seem that the increased number of pupils causes a deterioration in returns; quality and quantity are no doubt linked together, but in a much more complex way than is often claimed when one is directly set against the other.

The notion of school wastage is not exact enough, for it only registers the net result of repeats and dropouts. At the end of a scholastic year, pupils can be in only one of three situations: being promoted, repeating the course, or leaving, and to know the number of enrolled repeaters in each year of study is all that is necessary to reconstitute the scholastic cycle. A system of linear equations based on this principle has recently been applied in Argentina[1] to the statistics on primary education; it shows that the wastage ratio obtained by the cohort method (60 per cent) overestimates the number who leave school (50 per cent) before completing the cycle. On the other hand, only 21 per cent of the pupils who started school seven years earlier finish their school career in the normal period; 17 per cent finish it in eight years, and 12 per cent in nine years or more; moreover the number repeating the course reaches 25 per cent of the pupils in the first year of study. A similar calculation done in Ecuador showed that out of 1,000 pupils beginning secondary studies, 470 finished the cycle (six years of study), of whom 224 took the normal time of six years and 153 took seven years. It can also be shown that those who leave do so chiefly in the first year of study (204 pupils) and during the third year (114 pupils); in all, 4,769 school years have been given to a cohort of 1,000 pupils, which has produced 470 certificated school leavers. But these certificated leavers received only 3,240 years of study, or on an average 6.8 years each; the remaining 1,159 years of study were given to pupils who left during the cycle. In terms of educational efficiency, one may therefore say that 4,769 school years were needed to produce 470 school leavers instead of the 2,820 necessary in theory, that is, 1.7 times as much. Of these extra expenses 22 per cent are due to repeaters and 78 per cent to dropouts. It must be added that in an educational system with neither repeaters nor dropouts, the "cost price" of a certificated school leaver would be reduced by 70 per cent but educational provision for the whole cohort would require 6,000 school years, or an increase of 25 per cent in the total cost of education. These notions, based on the numbers of those finishing the course, are much more exact and significant than those based on wastage, which in this case give a return of 37 per cent for the cohort 1956–1961. A superficial interpretation of the statistics for the year 1962–1963 would be equally false; 17 per cent of the pupils are counted as repeating a course and 10.3 per cent as leaving early during the year, but that does not mean, as shown earlier, a scholastic yield of 73 per cent.

One can see that an analysis based on data concerning repeaters by grades does allow the development of education to be formulated with fair accuracy, and several criteria of "efficiency" emerge from it. It is thus possible to understand the weak points of a scholastic system, and to forecast the consequence of an improvement in efficiency.

Disparities

The data quoted above are national averages and do not take into account all the disparities within one country. The educational inequalities within the whole region are considerable, but lie outside the framework of this

---

[1] The calculations have been carried out at the National Development Council (CONADE). They will shortly be published by OECD. [This note was written in 1967.–Ed.]

survey. The differences between boys and girls are less and less pronounced, and, taking the countries as a whole, are barely noticeable outside higher education. On the other hand the greatest disparity remains between town and country. Incomplete schools are still very common in rural districts, and in three countries (Colombia, Honduras, and the Dominican Republic) the primary cycle is of shorter legal duration in rural schools than town schools. Although half the population of the region still lives in rural districts, the proportion of rural pupils and teachers has remained at 40 per cent of the total during the last 10 years. But this situation is improving rapidly, since the increase in pupils is the same as in the towns (5.7 per cent per year on an average) while the population increase is very different (1.4 as against 5.75 per cent per year in urban districts). Judging from these overall figures, it appears that schooling in rural districts is increasing four times as quickly as in the towns.

The data show that the problems in primary education are henceforth of a qualitative nature: reducing age disparities, repeats and dropouts. Among the appropriate measures, the most important is without doubt the training of qualified teachers. While the total number of teachers has increased as fast as that of pupils, rising from 635,000 in 1957 to 989,000 in 1965, the proportion of unqualified teachers has fallen during the same period from 53 to 37 per cent. The net annual increase in the number of qualified teachers has therefore been on an average 9.1 per cent while the number of diploma students from the training colleges has only increased by 6.5 per cent. The difference is explained by the change in category of many unqualified teachers after a course of further training. These promotions have the effect of increasing total teachers' salaries but are not always linked with a corresponding rise in the levels of qualification. In any case, the shortage of qualified teachers no longer constitutes a limiting factor in the development of primary education. The number of student teachers in the training colleges is at present growing twice as fast (8.9 per cent) as that of pupils in school; in 1965 it reached the figure of 570,000 student teachers, or more than half of the total number of teachers in the profession. In many countries in the region, those at training colleges (for the most part women) already far exceed the capacity of the educational system to absorb them; in Argentina, it is thought that the number of diploma students from the training colleges is five times higher than requirements; in Venezuela the number of admissions to public training colleges has been drastically reduced, but private colleges have continued to increase their intake. It seems that one of the most urgent problems is to adapt the training of teachers to the schools' requirements in the framework of national plans for education.

The major issue in Latin American primary education is no longer that of universal schooling; the complete attainment of this is in sight, despite

the doubts expressed by many experts at the time of the adoption of the
Santiago Plan. Priority must now be given to qualitative improvements in
primary education, and to solving the far-reaching economic and social
problems which will be raised by the burgeoning educated generation suc-
ceeding a largely illiterate one; neither the labor market, nor society in general, is adequately prepared for this transition.

SECONDARY AND HIGHER EDUCATION

Although the statistics are less exact than those for primary education, all
the available data show a spectacular increase in the number of pupils in
secondary and higher education in the last few years. This phenomenon
does not appear to be closely related either to the rise in the standard of
living or to any other obvious indicator of economic expansion. The lowest
rates observed, namely those in Argentina and Chile, are about 6 per cent
per annum, nevertheless an appreciable rate of growth; in the continent as
a whole, secondary and higher education has been expanding at 10 per cent
per annum.

The distribution of pupils among the different types of education is a
much-discussed issue in Latin America. The high proportion of academic-
type secondary education and the low priority assigned to professional and
technical education is frequently deplored. These observations may be relevant at the country level, but not for the region as a whole. Overall statistics
do not always allow for the distinction between technical and commercial
education, and the latter is often a substitute for general education. Moreover, in many countries attention is drawn to the mediocre quality of the
training given in the technical industrial schools, and the prevalent tendency now is to set up autonomous centers of professional training which
employ another mode of recruitment and very different methods of training. In addition, the training colleges in many countries play the part of
schools for general training in the case of girls (notably in Argentina); nowhere does a diploma from the training colleges give access to the teaching
profession directly; this absence of coordination between training and employment is particularly serious because in several countries the output of
training colleges has already exceeded requirements for teaching staff.

Statistics on the distribution of pupils among the different types of secondary schools thus provide very little information about the quality of
secondary education. But educationists are unanimous in emphasizing the
urgent necessity of reforming the curricula, and the structure of the secondary schools. A common tendency in the suggested reforms is the creation of two distinct secondary stages: the first, lasting two to three years,
would provide general education for all children; the second cycle of three
years would consist of technical and professional preparation, or a long
academic course leading to the university. But, gradually, the equivalence

of technical courses and the general secondary course is being recognized and there is reason to think that a large number of certificated secondary leavers will seek to pursue their studies in higher education rather than to take up work immediately.

One of the main problems is that there is no clearly defined educational pyramid in these countries. There is considerable wastage during the early years of a cycle, but pupils who do reach the last year of study nearly all go on to the higher cycle. Every increase in the number of leaving certificates at one level therefore has repercussions on the others; thus, improvements in the efficiency of primary education, which I have already noted, explain the disproportionate increase in secondary education. Perhaps the most serious deficiency is the absence of a body of teachers with adequate training and regular employment. Although the standard of teachers in secondary schools varies from one country to another, it is unsatisfactory almost everywhere in that there are too few full-time teachers who have received adequate training, and most of them teach in several establishments.

In higher education the increase in the number of students was greatly underestimated in the Santiago Plan, apparently because of the erroneous statistics of past developments then available. But the trend in numbers now shows great year by year instability, due no doubt to the creation of new universities; in several countries (Colombia and Peru) new universities have appeared at an inordinate rate; in others (Argentina, Venezuela, Chile, Brazil, Ecuador, and Mexico) measures have been taken by the universities to control the admission of students or to eliminate repeaters. These measures seem hardly to have reduced the pressure of the secondary school leavers seeking to enter higher education. The very rapid growth in the number of students has been accompanied by considerable efforts to increase the supply of equipment, especially in engineering schools and faculties of science, and by a noticeable increase in the number of full-time teaching posts. But in spite of this progress, the structure of university education in most of the countries seems ill adapted to present needs for research and student training. It is not only a question of the pronounced emphasis on "traditional" disciplines in contrast to science and technology, but other causes of educational malaise in most Latin American universities, of which the most dramatic manifestation is numerous and prolonged student strikes. It would require sociological analysis to explore this difficult problem which has made its appearance at the same time and with the same frequency in countries otherwise very different.

Several inquiries undertaken recently in the four principal Argentine universities provide some evidence of this situation: 40–60 per cent of enrolled students follow a profession, most full-time; only one third of the students claim to pursue their studies regularly; a large number of students enrolled in 1964 (40–70 per cent) have passed no examinations for four years; 80

per cent of the students came from families which had never had a university education, and 40 per cent of the parents have not gone further than primary school; the number of graduates is much smaller than the number of first-class students, and it is increasing three times less quickly.[1]

FINANCING AND COSTS

One may wonder how such an increase in the number of pupils and teachers has been paid for; I have shown that the financial forecasts of the Santiago Plan seemed a priori difficult to implement, whereas the enrollment targets were fully attained. It is much more difficult to measure the cost of education than the number of pupils in spite of improvements in statistical information which have taken place in recent years. Provincial expenditures and, in certain cases, local expenditures were included in the budgets of the ministers of education a few years ago, but these figures hide much double counting due to subsidies of local communities by the central government. Where one finds estimates of expenditures on private education, one is seldom told whether this refers to the amount of public subsidies, plus student fees, or to an estimate arrived at by multiplying per pupil costs by the number of pupils.

With these reservations in mind, two complete series of costs of education in Latin America for the years 1960–1961 are available. Official exchange rates were used to convert the 1960 figures into dollars, and purchasing-power parity rates for the 1961 figures. In 1960, the total cost of education in Latin America is estimated at $1.32 billion, or 2.3 per cent of the GNP for the region. For 1961, the total is $1.76 billion, or 3 per cent of GNP; the differences between the two years not only represent an increase in expenditure but also a more precise analysis which reevaluates the expenditures for the most important countries (Brazil, Mexico, Argentina, etc.). By taking the financial targets of Santiago, namely, 4 per cent of GNP in 1965 as a basis, and combining it with the targets of the Decade for Development, i.e., a GNP growth rate of 5 per cent per annum, one should arrive at an expenditure on education of $2.88 billion in 1965, that is, an annual increase of 13.3 per cent.

It is not possible at present to verify this hypothesis directly. Using an indirect method, however, one may analyze the relation between the cost of education and national income for all the countries of Latin America for the same year, or one may investigate the relation between the cost of education and per capita GNP. Table 4 shows regression equations derived from these data. Although the figures for 1960 and 1961 are quite different, and although the mode of conversion into dollars is not the same, the results are fairly close and the correlations obtained appear very satisfactory.

---

[1] The figures here quoted are taken from various studies of G. Germani and from inquiries undertaken in 1965 on the initiative of the National Council of Development (CONADE).

If one uses these equations to forecast educational expenditure in relation to the expected increase of national income or income per head of the population, one would conclude that the increase should be roughly proportional, as the elasticity coefficient is only slightly in excess of unity. Such an interpretation would contradict the very rapid growth of educational expenditure over the last few years, while GNP over the same period has hardly increased more than 5 per cent per year on an average, and per capita GNP by only 2.5 per cent per year. It is therefore preferable to use time series for individual countries where they are available in spite of their imperfections and omissions.

One may derive some insight from the fragmentary historical series which are available for certain countries (Table 5). In all the countries there are considerable increases in educational expenditure, as well as in the proportion of national income devoted to education (see column 7); four countries at least reach 5 per cent (Costa Rica, Panama, Peru, and Venezuela), which is comparable to the proportion found in the most highly developed industrialized countries.

The educational expenditures of the 11 countries have been expressed in constant prices, using a cost-of-living index as a deflator; the rates of increase shown are annual averages worked out from the first and last years of the series. Notice the very high rates of increase in public expenditures for education (column 1): about 20 per cent in Peru, Ecuador, and Mexico, and above 10 per cent in three other countries. In all cases (except Brazil, for which information is rather sketchy), growth of educational expenditure greatly exceeds growth of the GNP. These spectacular increases are not limited to the 1960–1965 period, for similar calculations worked out previously over the period 1955–1960 show comparable rates; six countries out of nine had increases above 10 per cent per year. The rise in national resources devoted to education (column 7) is partly explained by an increase in the size of the whole public sector. But among the items of public expenditure, it is education which seems to increase its relative share almost everywhere to the detriment of the other social services. Can this privileged situation continue? It seems unlikely that such increases can be maintained for long. A country which increases its educational budget at the exceptional rate of 10 per cent per year would double its expenditure in just over seven years, and quadruple it in about 13 years. Educational and financial objectives as ambitious as those of the Santiago Plan can only be considered as exceptional and temporary. The process of leveling off seems to be imminent in countries such as Costa Rica, Panama, Peru, and Venezuela, which have already reached very high levels of educational expenditure. Brazil, Mexico and Argentina, however, are still far from devoting to education a fraction of income comparable to the former countries.

So far as cost components are concerned, enrollment targets have up to

Table 4. Educational Expenditure and National Income for 20 Countries of Latin America

	Equations of Regression	Coefficient of Correlation	Coefficient of Elasticity	Margin of Error for Coefficients of Elasticity at 5% Level of Significance
Data for 1960 according to official rates of exchange (1)	$\log E = 1.032 \log R - 1.749$	$r = 0.973$	1.03	0.91–1.115
Ditto (2)	$\log \frac{E}{P} = 1.303 \log \frac{R}{P} - 2.379$	$r = 0.936$	1.3	1.06–1.55
Data for 1961 according to purchasing power parity rates (3)	$\log \frac{E}{P} = \underset{(0.158)}{1.42} \log \frac{R}{P} - \underset{(0.373)}{2.561}$	$r = 0.898$	1.42	1.104–1.736

Key to Table: E = Expenditure on Education, P = Population, R = GNP.

Source: D. Blot and M. Debeauvais, "Expenditure on Education in the Developing Regions: Some Statistical Aspects," OECD Conference on Financing Education, 1964.

Table 5. Latin America: Relationships between Rates of Growth of Educational Expenditures and Other Indices of Economic Growth

	Period	Rate of Increase of Public Expenditure on Education (1)	Rate of Increase of Private Education (2)	Rate of Increase of Government Budget (3)	Rate of Increase of per Capita GNP 1961–1965 (4)	Rate of Increase GNP (5)	Ratio of Public Expenditure on Education to the Total Government Budget (6)	Ratio of Public Expenditure on Education to GNP (7)
Argentina	1959–1964	6.68	11.2	2.62	0.1	2.62	17.2–20.5 (e)	2.1–2.7
Brazil	1959–1963	2.0			0.2	1.4		2.20–2.48 (e)
Guatemala	1958–1964	7.2 (a)	14.6 (b)		3.9	4.9		
Honduras	1960–1965	12.3			1.6		16.9–20.7	1.4–2.4 (f)
Peru	1960–1965	21.5	17.8	17.8	2.9	6.3	15.0–15.3	2.6–4.9
Venezuela	1960–1965	8.6		2.1	4.2 (c)	1.2	11.3–17.4	3.57–4.74
Ecuador	1961–1965	20.0		9	1.4			1.7–2.76
Chile	1958–1965	7.1	1.5	11.9	1.7	4.0	15.6–11.5	3.2–3.7 (d)
Costa Rica	1960–1964	7.4		5.7	1.7	4.0	28.4–30.7	4.8–5.2
Colombia	1960–1964	11.3			1.6	4.2 (g)	11.9–14 (d)	
Salvador	1960–1964	10.1		4.4	4.5	7.8	19.4–24	2.22–2.25
Mexico	1960–1965	17.3			3.4	5.9	13.7–25.5	1.7–2.5

Key to Table: (a) 1962–1964, (b) 1958–1964, (c) 1958–1962, (d) 1963–1965, (e) the two figures indicated in columns 6 and 7 are the percentages relative to the first and last years of the period considered, (f) 1957–1963, (g) 1959–1963, and (h) current prices have been deflated by an index of retail prices (columns 1, 2 and 3) or parity rates (column 5).

Sources: Replies to a questionnaire of UNESCO on the cost of education in Latin America, and various other sources.

now been considered the most important. In primary education, one may surmise that the rate of expansion will shortly slow down and approach the rate of population increase.[1] In secondary and higher education, there are no signs of a slackening of the growth rates of recent years. If the costs per pupil remain the same, the increase in numbers forecast by the Santiago Plan will bring about an increase in educational expenditure of about 10 per cent per year between 1965 and 1970. This estimate ought to be considerably increased, because of two important factors which seem to have been neglected in previous forecasts: the low levels of capital expenditure can hardly be maintained; also, costs per pupil are rapidly increasing, due to large increases in expenditure on staff.

An analysis of the unit costs of each educational level emphasizes this phenomenon. The available data are not entirely satisfactory, but a comparison of the rate of increase in unit costs with the rate of increase of pupils and teachers shows that in several countries the rise in current expenditures is much greater than the increase in numbers of teachers and pupils. One may expect the salaries of teachers to rise with the rise of income per head, but in addition one often finds sudden developments in educational costs which reflect administrative increases in teacher salary scales. In Ecuador, for example, teachers' salaries were increased by 33 per cent in 1960, and a similar decision was put in force in Peru in 1965. In countries with severe inflation, such as Chile, Argentina, and Brazil, these increases follow periods in which salaries actually fell in real terms. As teachers' salaries represent the largest part of educational expenditures, unit costs rise rapidly but irregularly. In Ecuador, the annual increases per pupil costs for primary, secondary, and higher education have gone up by 12, 14, and 18 per cent per year respectively, since 1960, compared with increases of only 0.8 to 1.75 per cent per year between 1950 and 1960.

Up to now, the educational plans of all the countries of Latin America have been able to reconcile enrollment targets with the spontaneous growth in the demand for schooling. At the same time, the shortage of skilled labor has justified expansion on manpower-forecasting grounds. In the future, however, educational planning in Latin America will have to face up to choices between conflicting social and financial objectives. This emphasizes the importance of long-term forecasts of manpower requirements which several Latin American countries are now undertaking (Argentina, Peru, Mexico, Chile and Ecuador). This is likely to prove the best way of considering, at one and the same time, the foreseeable consequences of the development of the educational system, of the number of school leavers looking for jobs and of the requirements of the labor market.

---

[1] The rapid growth of the urban population will however generate an additional demand for primary schooling.

The Futility of Schooling in Latin America

IVAN ILLICH

For the past two decades, demographic considerations have colored all discussion about development in Latin America. In 1950, some 200 million people occupied the area extending from Mexico to Chile. Of these, 120 million lived directly or indirectly on primitive agriculture. Assuming both effective population controls and the most favorable possible results from programs aimed at the increase of agriculture, by 1985 40,000,000 people will produce most of the food for a total population of 360 million. The remaining 320 million will be either marginal to the economy or will have to be incorporated somehow into urban living and agricultural production.

During these same past 20 years, both Latin American governments and foreign technical assistance agencies have come to rely increasingly on the capacity of grammar, trade, and high schools to lead the nonrural majority out of its marginality in shanty towns and subsistence farms, into the type of factory, market, and public forum which corresponds to modern technology. It was assumed that schooling would eventually produce a broad middle class with values resembling those of highly industrialized nations, despite the economy of continued scarcity.

Ivan Illich is a founder of the Centro Intercultural de Documentación (CIDOC) in Cuernavaca, Mexico, an organization of scholars engaged in the study, analysis, and publication of sociocultural information about Latin America. Monsignor Illich was formerly vice president of the Catholic University of Puerto Rico and on the Commonwealth Board of Higher Education involved in educational planning for Puerto Rico. This article is based on discussions conducted at CIDOC during the past year.

A slightly altered version of this article appeared as a chapter in Ivan D. Illich's book, *Celebration of Awareness: A Call for Institutional Revolution*, published by Doubleday & Company, Inc.

Accumulating evidence now indicates that schooling does not and cannot produce the expected results. Seven years ago the governments of the Americas joined in an Alliance for Progress, which has, in practice, served mainly the progress of the middle classes in the Latin nations. In most countries, the Alliance has encouraged the replacement of a closed, feudal, hereditary elite by one which is supposedly "meritocratic" and open to the few who manage to finish school. Concomitantly, the urban service proletariat has grown at several times the rate of the traditional landless rural mass and has replaced it in importance. The marginal majority and the schooled minority grow ever further apart. One old feudal society has brought forth two classes, separate and unequal.

This development has led to educational research focused on the improvement of the learning process in schools and on the adaptations of schools themselves to the special circumstances prevailing in underdeveloped societies. But logic would seem to require that we do not stop with an effort to improve schools, rather, that we question the assumption on which the school system itself is based. We must not exclude the possibility that the emerging nations cannot be schooled, that schooling is not a viable answer to their need for universal education. Perhaps this type of insight is needed to clear the way for a futuristic scenario in which schools as we know them today would disappear.

The social distance between the growing urban mass and the new elite is a new phenomenon, unlike the traditional forms of discrimination known in Latin America. This new discrimination is not a transitory thing which can be overcome by schooling. On the contrary: I submit that one of the reasons for the awakening frustration in the majorities is the progressive acceptance of the "liberal myth," the assumption that schooling is an assurance of social integration.

The solidarity of all citizens based on their common graduation from school has been an inalienable part of the modern, Western self-image. Colonization has not succeeded in implanting this myth equally in all countries, but everywhere schooling has become the prerequisite for membership in a managerial middle class. The constitutional history of Latin America since its independence has made the masses of this continent particularly susceptible to the conviction that all citizens have a right to enter—and, therefore, have some possibility of entering—their society through the door of a school.

More than elsewhere, in Latin America the teacher as missionary for the school-gospel has found adherents at the grassroots. Only a few years ago many of us were happy when finally the Latin American school system was singled out as the area of privileged investment for international assistance funds. In fact, during the past years, both national budgets and private investment have been stimulated to increase educational allocations. But a second look reveals that this school system has built a narrow bridge across a widening social gap. As the only legitimate passage to the middle class, the school restricts all unconventional crossings and leaves the underachiever to bear the blame for his marginality.

This statement is difficult for Americans to understand. In the United States, the nineteenth-century persuasion that free schooling insures all citizens equality in the economy and effective participation in the society survives. It is by no means certain that the result of schooling ever measured up to this expectation, but the schools certainly played a more prominent role in this process some hundred years ago.

In the United States of the midnineteenth century, six years of schooling frequently made a young man the educational superior of his boss. In a society largely dominated by unschooled achievers, the little red schoolhouse was an effective road to social equality. A few years in school for all brought most extremes together. Those who achieved power and money without schooling had to accept a degree of equality with those who achieved literacy and did not strike it rich. Computers, television, and airplanes have changed this. Today in Latin America, in the midst of modern technology, three times as many years of schooling and 20 times as much money as was then spent on grammar schools will not produce the same social result. The dropout from the sixth grade is unable to find a job even as a punchcard operator or a railroad engineer.

Contemporary Latin America needs school systems no more than it needs railroad tracks. Both—spanning continents—served to speed the now-rich and established nations into the industrial age. Both, if now handled with care, are harmless heirlooms from the Victorian period. But neither is relevant to countries emerging from primitive agriculture directly into the jet age. Latin America cannot afford to maintain outmoded social institutions amid modern technological processes.

By "school," of course, I do not mean all organized formal education. I use the terms "school" and "schooling" here to designate a form of childcare and a *rite de passage* which we take for granted. We forget that this institution and the corresponding creed appeared on the scene only with the growth of the industrial state. Comprehensive schooling today involves year-round, obligatory, and universal classroom attendance in small groups for several hours each day. It is imposed on all citizens for a period of 10 to 18 years. School divides life into two segments, which are increasingly of comparable length. As much as anything else, schooling implies custodial care for persons who are declared undesirable elsewhere by the simple fact that a school has been built to serve them. The school is supposed to take the excess population from the street, the family, or the labor force. Teachers are given the power to invent new criteria according to which new segments of the population may be committed to a school. This restraint on healthy, productive, and potentially independent human beings is performed by schools with an economy which only labor camps could rival.

Schooling also involves a process of accepted ritual certification for all members of a "schooled" society. Schools select those who are bound to succeed and send them on their way with a badge marking them fit. Once universal schooling has been accepted as the hallmark for the in-members of a society, fitness is measured by the amount of time and money spent on formal education in youth rather than by ability acquired independently from an "accredited'' curriculum.

A first important step toward radical educational reform in Latin America will be taken when the educational system of the United States is accepted for what it is: a recent, imaginative social invention perfected since World War II and rooted in the American frontier. The creation of the all-pervasive school establishment, tied into industry, government, and the military, is an invention no less original than the guild-centered apprenticeship of the Middle Ages, or the *doctrina de los indios* and the *Reducción* of Spanish missionaries in Mexico and Paraguay, respectively, or the *lycée* and *les grandes ecoles* in France. Each one of these systems was produced by its society to give stability to an achievement, each has been heavily pervaded by ritual to which society bowed, and each has been rationalized into an all-embracing persuasion, religion, or ideology. The United States is not the first nation which has been willing to pay a high price to have its educational system exported by missionaries to all corners of the world. The colonization of Latin America by the catechism is certainly a noteworthy precedent.

It is difficult now to challenge the school as a system because we are so used to it. Our industrial categories tend to define results as products of specialized institutions and instruments. Armies produce defense for countries. Churches procure salvation in an afterlife. Binet defined intelligence as that which his tests test. Why not, then, conceive of education as the product of schools? Once this tag has been accepted, unschooled education gives the impression of something spurious, illegitimate, and certainly unaccredited.

For some generations, education has been based on massive schooling, just as security was based on massive retaliation and, at least in the United States, transportation on the family car. The United States, because it industrialized earlier, is rich enough to afford schools, the Strategic Air Command, and the car—no matter what the toll. Most nations of the world are not that rich; they behave, however, as if they were. The example of nations which "made it" leads Brazilians to pursue the ideal of the family car—just for a few. It compels Peruvians to squander on Mirage bombers—just for a show. And it drives every government in Latin America to spend up to two fifths of its total budget on schools, and to do so unchallenged.

Let us insist, for a moment, on this analogy between the school system and the system of transportation based on the family car. Ownership of a car is now rapidly becoming the ideal in Latin America—at least among those who have a voice in formulating national goals. During the past 20 years, roads, parking facilities, and services for private automobiles have been immensely improved. These improvements benefit overwhelmingly those who have their own cars—that is, a tiny percentage. The bias of the budget allocated for transportation thus discriminates against the best transportation for the greatest number—and the huge capital investments in this area insure that this bias is here to stay. In some countries, articulate minorities now challenge the family car as the fundamental unit of transportation in emerging societies. But everywhere in Latin America it would be political suicide to advocate radical limitations on the multiplication of schools. Opposition parties may challenge at times the need for superhighways or the need for weapons which will see active duty only in a parade. But what man in his right mind would challenge the need to provide every child with a chance to go to high school?

Before poor nations could reach this point of universal schooling, however, their ability to educate would be exhausted. Even 10 or 12 years of schooling are beyond 85 per cent of all men of our century if they happen to live outside the tiny islands where capital accumulates. Nowhere in Latin America do 27 per cent of any age group get beyond the sixth grade, nor do more than 1 per cent graduate from a university. Yet no government spends less than 18 per cent of its budget on schools, and many spend more than 30 per cent. Universal schooling, as this concept has been defined recently in industrial societies, is obviously beyond their means. The annual cost of schooling a United States citizen between the ages of 12 and 24 costs as much as most Latin Americans earn in two to three years.

Schools will stay beyond the means of the developing nations: Neither radical population control nor maximum reallocations of government budgets nor unprecedented foreign aid would end the present unfeasibility of school systems aimed at 12 years of schooling for all. Population control needs time to become effective when the total population is as young as that of tropical America. The percentage of the world's resources invested in schooling cannot be raised beyond certain levels, nor can this budget grow beyond foreseeable maximal rates. Finally, foreign aid would have to increase to 30 per cent of the receiving nation's national budget to provide effectively for schooling, a goal not to be anticipated.

Furthermore, the per capita cost of schooling itself is rising everywhere as schools accept those who are difficult to teach, as retention rates rise, and as the quality of schooling itself improves. This rise in cost neutralizes much of the new investments. Schools do not come cheaper by the dozen.

In view of all these factors, increases in school budgets must usually be defended by arguments which imply default. In fact, however, schools are untouchable because they are vital to the status quo. Schools have the effect of tempering the subversive potential of education in an alienated society because, if education is confined to schools, only those who have been schooled into compliance on a lower grade are admitted to its higher reaches. In capital-starved societies not rich enough to purchase unlimited schooling, the majority is schooled not only into compliance but also into subservience.

Since Latin American constitutions were written with an eye on the United States, the ideal of universal schooling was a creative utopia. It was a condition necessary to create the Latin American nineteenth-century bourgeoisie. Without the pretense that every citizen has a right to go to school, the liberal bourgeoisie could never have developed; neither could the middle-class masses of present-day Europe, the United States, and Russia, nor the managerial middle elite of their cultural colonies in South America. But the same school which worked in the last century to overcome feudalism has now become an oppressive idol which protects those who are already schooled. Schools grade and, therefore, they degrade. They make the degraded accept his own submission. Social seniority is bestowed according to the level of schooling achieved. Everywhere in Latin America more money for schools means more privilege for a few at the cost of most, and this patronage of an elite is explained as a political ideal. This ideal is written into laws which state the patently impossible: equal scholastic opportunities for all.

The number of satisfied clients who graduate from schools every year is much smaller than the number of frustrated dropouts who are conveniently graded by their failure for use in a marginal labor pool. The resulting steep educational pyramid defines a rationale for the corresponding levels of social status. Citizens are "schooled" into their places. This results in politically acceptable forms of discrimination which benefit the relatively few achievers.

The move from the farm to the city in Latin America still frequently means a move from a world where status is explained as a result of inheritance into a world where it is explained as a result of schooling. Schools allow a head start to be rationalized as an achievement. They give to privilege not only the appearance of equality but also of generosity: Should somebody who missed out on early schooling be dissatisfied with the status he holds, he can always be referred to a night or trade school. If he does not take advantage of such recognized remedies, his exclusion from privilege can be explained as his own fault. Schools temper the frustrations they provoke.

The school system also inculcates its own universal acceptance. Some schooling is not necessarily more educational than none, especially in a country where every year a few more people can get all the schooling they want while most people never complete the sixth grade. But much less than six years seems to be sufficient to inculcate in the child the acceptance of the ideology which goes with the school grade. The child learns only about the superior status and unquestioned authority of those who have more schooling than he has.

Any discussion of radical alternatives to school-centered formal education upsets our notions of society. No matter how inefficient schools are in educating a majority, no matter how effective schools are in limiting the access to the elite, no matter how liberally schools shower their noneducational benefits on the members of this elite, schools do increase the national income. They qualify their graduates for more economic production. In an economy on the lower rungs of development toward United States-type industrialization, a school graduate is enormously more productive than a dropout. Schools are part and parcel of a society in which a minority is on the way to becoming so productive that the majority must be schooled into disciplined consumption. Schooling therefore—under the best of circumstances—helps to divide society into two groups: those so productive that their expectation of annual rise in personal income lies far beyond the national average, and the overwhelming majority, whose income also rises, but at a rate clearly below the former's. These rates, of course, are compounded and lead the two groups further apart.

Radical innovation in formal education presupposes radical political changes, radical changes in the organization of production, and radical changes in man's image of himself as an animal which needs school. This is often forgotten when sweeping reforms of the schools are proposed and fail because of the societal framework we accept. For instance, the trade school is sometimes advocated as a cure-all for mass schooling. Yet it is doubtful that the products of trade schools would find employment in a continuously changing, ever more automated economy. Moreover, the capital and operating costs of trade schools, as we know them today, are several times as high as those for a standard school on the same grade. Also, trade schools usually take in sixth graders, who, as we have seen, are already the exception. They pretend to educate by creating a spurious facsimile of the factory within a school building.

Instead of the trade school, we should think of a subsidized transformation of the industrial plant. It should be possible to make it obligatory for factories to serve as training centers during off hours, for managers to spend part of their time planning and supervising this training, and for the industrial process to be so redesigned that it has educational value. If the expenditures for present schools were partly allocated to sponsor this kind of educational exploitation of existing resources, then the final results—both economic and educational—might be incomparably greater. If, further, such subsidized apprenticeship were offered to all who ask for it, irrespective of age, and not only to those who are destined to be employees in the particular plant, industry would have begun to assume an important role now played by school. We would be on the way to disabuse ourselves of the idea that manpower qualification must precede employment, that schooling must precede productive work. There is no reason for us to continue the medieval tradition in which men are prepared for the "secular world" by incarceration in a sacred precinct, be it monastery, synagogue, or school.

A second, frequently discussed, remedy for the failure of schools is fundamental, or adult, education. It has been proved by Paolo Freire in Brazil that those adults who can be interested in political issues of their community can be made literate within six weeks of evening classes. The program teaching such reading and writing skills, of course, must be built around the emotion-loaded key words of their political vocabulary. Understandably, this fact has gotten his program into trouble. It has been equally suggested that the dollar-cost of 10 separate months of adult education is equal to one year of early schooling, and can be incomparably more effective than schooling at its best.

Unfortunately, "adult education" now is conceived principaliy as a device to give the "underprivileged" a palliative for the schooling he lacks. The situation would have to be reversed if we wanted to conceive of all education as an exercise in adulthood. We should consider a radical reduction of the length of the formal obligatory school sessions to only two months each year—but spread this type of formal schooling over the first 20 or 30 years of a man's life.

While various forms of in-service apprenticeship in factories and programed math and language teaching could assume a large proportion of what we have previously called "instruction," two months a year of formal schooling should be considered ample time for what the Greeks meant by *schole*—leisure for the pursuit of insight. No wonder we find it nearly impossible to conceive of comprehensive social changes in which the educational functions of schools would be thus redistributed in new patterns among institutions we do not now envisage. We find it equally difficult to indicate concrete ways in which the noneducational functions of a vanishing school system would be redistributed. We do not know what to do with those whom we now label "children" or "students" and commit to school.

It is difficult to foresee the political consequences of changes as fundamental as those proposed, not to mention the international consequences. How should a school-reared society coexist with one which has gone "off the school standard," and whose industry, commerce, advertising, and participation in politics is different as a matter of principle? Areas which develop outside the universal school standard would lack the common language and criteria for respectful coexistence with the schooled. Two such worlds, such as China and the United States, might almost have to seal themselves off from each other.

Rashly, the school-bred mind abhors the educational devices available to these worlds. It is difficult mentally to "accredit" Mao's party as an educational institution which might prove more effective than the schools are at their best—at least when it comes to inculcating citizenship. Guerrilla warfare in Latin America is another educational device much more frequently misused or misunderstood than applied. Che Guevara, for instance, clearly saw it as a last educational resort to teach a people about the illegitimacy of their political system. Especially in unschooled countries, where the transistor radio has come to every village, we must never underrate the educational functions of great charismatic dissidents like Dom Helder Camara in Brazil or Camilo Torres in Colombia. Castro described his early charismatic harangues as teaching sessions.

The schooled mind perceives these processes exclusively as political indoctrination, and their educational purpose eludes its grasp. The legitimation of education by schools tends to render all nonschool education an accident, if not an outright misdemeanor. And yet, it is surprising with what difficulty the school-bred mind perceives the rigor with which schools inculcate their own presumed necessity, and with it the supposed inevitability of the system they sponsor. Schools indoctrinate the child into the acceptance of the political system his teachers represent, despite the claim that teaching is nonpolitical.

Ultimately, the cult of schooling will lead to violence. The establishment of any religion has led to it. To permit the gospel of universal schooling to spread, the military's ability to repress insurgency in Latin America must grow. Only force will ultimately control the insurgency inspired by the frustrated expectations which the propagation of the school myth enkindles. The maintenance of the present school system may turn out to be an important step on the way to Latin American fascism. Only fanaticism inspired by idolatry of a system can ultimately rationalize the massive discrimination which will result from another 20 years of grading a capital-starved society with school marks.

The time has come to recognize the real burden of the schools in the emerging nations, so that we may become free to envisage change in the social structure which now makes schools a necessity. I do not advocate a sweeping utopia like the Chinese commune for Latin America. But I do suggest that we plunge our imagination into the construction of scenarios which would allow a bold reallocation of educational functions among industry, politics, short scholastic retreats, and intensive preparation of parents for early childhood education. The cost of schools must be measured not only in economic, social and educational terms, but in political terms as well. Schools, in an economy of scarcity invaded by automation, accentuate and rationalize the coexistence of two societies, one a colony of the other.

Once it is understood that the cost of schooling is not inferior to the cost of chaos, we might be on the brink of courageously costly compromise. Today it is as dangerous in Latin America to question the myth of social salvation through schooling as it was dangerous 300 years ago to question the divine rights of the Catholic kings.

Section 2:
Social, Political, and Economic Goals

Introduction to Section 2

The following articles deal with the questions which normally surround the areas of "development" and "modernization" and discuss the functions of formal and informal education in meeting such goals.

In the first selection, Seymour Martin Lipset analyzes the value structure of Latin American cultures, which he suggests effectively militates against the development process. Borrowing from Talcott Parsons, Lipset suggests that Latin American values are characterized as particularistic and ascriptive rather than universal and achievement-oriented, the latter being the combination most closely associated with the emergence of an industrial society. Turning to an analysis of entrepreneurial behavior, Lipset asserts that much of the existing economic growth which has occurred in Latin America can be traced to those deviant entrepreneurs who are most receptive to innovation, who are carriers of "modern" values and thus more likely to reject the traditional elite. Lipset offers several suggestions for moving toward a "modern" system which need not involve a rejection of a nation's basic values. He feels education can play an important part in fostering entrepreneurial elites through expanding and broadening the educational enterprise in order to provide the skills, values, and aspirations which sustain modern occupational structures.

The second article, by W. Raymond Duncan, analyzes the role of education in altering the "culture of politics" or the underlying attitudes toward authority and leadership. The author indicates that although literacy has been shown to be associated with increased interest in election campaigns, with an increased feeling of potency in influencing governmental decisions, and with skills which propel individuals to become associated with special interest groups, thus diversifying the structure of action in the political arena, there is little evidence to indicate that literacy is related to changes in attitudes toward authority. Citing examples of past research, the author asserts that the highly educated populations in Latin America continue to support traditional values related to political action by adhering to extreme individualism and to a deep respect for authority. Thus, Duncan hypothesizes that the structure of politics changes more rapidly than the culture of politics and that education is associated with the former but not necessarily with the latter. The final section of the paper discusses an investigation undertaken by the author on political attitudes in Mexico City. The results indicate that increasing levels of education do not relate significantly to decreasing authoritarian attitudes or "modern" political perceptions.

The third selection, by James V. Cornehls, presents an analysis of manpower planning as a framework for educational research and development. Through a case study of Peru, the author focuses on the kind and amount of training needed to obtain the greatest impact on economic and social development. Cornehls presents the assumptions underlying the approach, describes the steps taken to study the Peruvian economy, projects needs through 1980, and translates these manpower requirements into their educational equivalents. Because of the population growth rates, the author suggests that 64 per cent of the 1980 labor force will be composed of new entrants, potentially enabling Peru to upgrade the economically active population but at the same time placing great strain on the educational system.

The need for scientific and technically trained personnel in Peru demands increased efficiency within the educational system, a closer relationship between training received and actual job skills needed, cost/benefit analyses of educational expenditures, and the training of high-level teachers in science and technology. The author remarks that a major constraint in meeting target goals rests within the area of wages and salaries of the teaching staff, which constituted 93.5 per cent of Peruvian educational expenditures in 1965.

The fourth article, by Martin Carnoy, is an original contribution to this volume. The author argues that, irrespective of a society being ruled by "modern" or "traditional" elites, the outcome is retention of the status quo, leaving power with the ruling group, which acts in its own best interests rather than in the interests of other population sectors. In directing his attention to societies already committed to development through "modern" elites, Carnoy remarks: "A dilemma for the elite is how to satisfy the social demand for more and more schooling *without* giving away economic and policy-making power." Carnoy suggests that this is accomplished by restricting access to schools to those who already have elite status; those not characterized as elites, and who inevitably fail to adequately deal with the educational system, accept their failures as personal inadequacies rather than as inadequacies of the system. Following the analysis, the author discusses evidence indicating that elites as opposed to nonelites receive differential rates of return for the investment at the same level of education.

Carnoy presents a model of rates of return to schooling based on an elite design. He remarks that: "The model explains how a monopoly rent to investment in schooling shifts over time to higher and higher levels of schooling and is eliminated when nonelites dominate the enrollment of any schooling level." Thus, in accord with different periods of development, the model shows how increasing enrollment of an age cohort at various schooling levels changes the role of the school at any given level from achievement to socialization and from elite formation to nonelite formation. It is necessary, as Carnoy suggests, to correct rates of return to the various levels of schooling since unadjusted rates do not allow for these changes in the function of schooling and fail to take into account either the increase of human relative to physical capital in the economy or the changes in the background and ability of students as the function of schooling is altered.

In order to overcome the inequities in a schooling system which is oriented toward elites, Carnoy argues that per pupil expenditures should be adjusted for students from different family backgrounds, thus assuming that such differential financing can alleviate elite-nonelite differences in performance. In the final part of the article the author suggests that most educational planners assume limited roles in decision making since they are constrained by elite control of policy to make schooling more efficient. Recognizing this often-limited impact on policy, Carnoy feels that more local control of the schooling enterprise is needed and that: "Any meaningful concept of development must include a specific theory of distribution of economic and social gains."

Original Sources for Selections

Lipset, Seymour Martin. "Values, Education, and Entrepreneurship," *in* Seymour M. Lipset and Aldo Solari, eds., *Elites in Latin America.* New York: Oxford University Press, 1967. Pp. 3–60.

Duncan, W. Raymond. "Education and Political Development: The Latin American Case," *The Journal of Developing Areas,* 2 (January, 1968), pp. 187–210.

Cornehls, James V. "Forecasting Manpower and Education Requirements for Economic and Social Development in Peru," *Comparative Education Review,* 12 (February, 1968), pp. 1–27.

Carnoy, Martin. "The Political Economy of Education." Original article.

Values, Education, and Entrepreneurship

SEYMOUR MARTIN LIPSET

Discussions of the requisites of economic development have been concerned with the relative importance of the appropriate economic conditions, rather than the presumed effects on varying rates of economic growth of diverse value systems. Much of the analysis which stems from economic thought has tended to see value orientations as derivative from economic factors. Most sociological analysts, on the other hand, following in the tradition of Max Weber, have placed a major independent role on the effect of values in fostering economic development.[1]

Although the evaluation of the causal significance of economic factors and value orientations has often taken the form of a debate pitting one against the other, increasingly more people have come to accept the premise that both sets of variables are relevant. Many economists now discuss the role of "noneconomic" factors in economic growth, and some have attempted to include concepts developed in sociology and psychology into their overall frame of analysis. Sociologists, from Weber on, have rarely argued that value analysis could account for economic growth. Rather the thesis suggested by Weber is that, given the economic conditions for the

I am extremely indebted to Ivan Vallier and Neil Smelser for detailed critiques of the earlier draft of this chapter. I would also like to express my appreciation to Elsa Turner for research assistance. [S.M.L.]

Reproduced from *Elites in Latin America,* pp. 3–60, 1967, with the permission of Oxford University Press (New York).

[1] For an excellent general discussion of the relationships between values and economic behavior written in a Latin American context see Thomas C. Cochran, "Cultural Factors in Economic Growth," *Journal of Economic History,* 20 (1960), 515–530; see also John Gillin, "Ethos Components in Modern Latin American Culture," *American Anthropologist,* 57 (1955), 488–500.

emergence of a system of rational capital accumulation, whether or not such growth occurred in a systematic fashion would be determined by the values present. Structural conditions make development possible; cultural factors determine whether the possibility becomes an actuality. And Weber sought to prove that capitalism and industrialization emerged in Western Europe and North America because value elements inherent in or derivative from the Protestant ethic fostered the necessary kinds of behavior by those who had access to capital; while conversely during other periods in other cultures, the social and religious ethics inhibited a systematic rational emphasis on growth.[1]

The general Weberian approach has been applied to many of the contemporary underdeveloped countries. It has been argued that these countries not only lack the economic prerequisites for growth, but that many of them preserve values which foster behavior antithetical to the systematic accumulation of capital. The relative failure of Latin American countries to develop on a scale comparable to those of North America or Australasia has been seen as, in some part, a consequence of variations in value systems dominating these two areas. The overseas offspring of Great Britain seemingly had the advantage of values derivative in part from the Protestant ethic and from the formation of new societies in which feudal ascriptive elements were missing.[2] Since Latin America, on the other hand, is Catholic, it has been dominated for long centuries by ruling elites who created a social structure congruent with feudal social values.

Perhaps the most impressive comparative evidence bearing on the significance of value orientations for economic development may be found in the work of David McClelland and his colleagues, who have undertaken detailed content analyses of folk tales in primitive cultures and of children's story books in literate ones, seeking to correlate degrees of emphasis on achievement values in these books with rates of economic development.[3]

Among the primitive tribes, those which were classified as high in achievement orientation on the basis of the content of their folk tales were much more likely to contain full-time business entrepreneurs (persons engaged in a market economy) than those which were low. To measure the relationships in literate societies, McClelland and his co-workers analyzed the content of children's stories read by early primary school children during two time periods, 1925 and 1950, in many nations. Statistically significant correlations were found between this measure of achievement level for 1925

---

[1] Max Weber, *The Protestant Ethic and the Spirit of Capitalism* (New York: Scribner's, 1935).

[2] See Louis Hartz, *The Founding of New Societies. Studies in the History of the United States, Latin America, South Africa, Canada, and Australia* (New York: Harcourt, Brace and World, 1964).

[3] David C. McClelland, *The Achieving Society* (Princeton: Van Nostrand, 1961), pp. 70–79; McClelland, "The Achievement Motive in Economic Growth," *in* Bert Hoselitz and Wilbert Moore, eds., *Industrialization and Society* (Paris: UNESCO-Mouton, 1963), pp. 79–81.

and the extent to which the increase in use of electrical energy (a measure of development) was higher or lower than the expected rate of growth for the period from 1925 and 1950, for a group of 23 countries. Similar findings are reported for 40 countries for the period 1952 to 1958. As McClelland comments, the latter "finding is more striking than the earlier one, because many Communist and underdeveloped countries are included in the sample. Apparently N Achievement [his term for the achievement orientation] is a precursor of economic growth—and not only in the Western style type of capitalism . . . but also in economies controlled and fostered largely by the state."[1] These findings are reinforced by two historical studies of thematic content of various types of literature in England between 1400 and 1800, and in Spain between 1200 and 1700. In both countries, the "quantitative evidence is clear cut and a rise and fall of the n Ach level *preceded in time* the rise and fall of economic development."[2]

Striking differences have been found by McClelland and his collaborators in the value orientations of comparable samples of populations in less-developed as compared with more-developed countries. Thus, research in Brazil and the United States analyzing the achievement motivations of students aged nine to 12, with the Brazilian sample drawn from São Paulo and Rio Claro, and the North American one from four northeastern states, reports that "Brazilian boys on the average have lower achievement motivation than their American peers . . . [that] upper, middle, and lower class Brazilians tend to have lower achievement motivation scores than Americans of a comparable class. *What is more startling is the finding that the mean score of Brazilian boys in any social class is lower than the motivation score of the Americans . . . whatever their class may be.*"[3]

On a theoretical level, the systematic analysis of the relations of value systems to the conditions for economic development requires concepts which permit one to contrast the relative strength of different values. Thus far, the most useful concepts for this purpose are Talcott Parsons' pattern variables. These refer to basic orientations toward human action, and are sufficiently comprehensive to encompass the norms affecting behavior within all social systems, both total societies and their subsystems, such as the family or the university.[4]

---

[1] McClelland, "The Achievement Motive in Economic Growth," p. 79.

[2] Juan B. Cortés, "The Achievement Motive in the Spanish Economy between the 13th and 18th Centuries," *Economic Development and Cultural Change,* 9 (1961), pp. 159, 144–163; Norman N. Bradburn and David E. Berlew, "Need for Achievement and English Industrial Growth," *Economic Development and Cultural Change,* 10 (1961), pp. 8–20.

[3] Bernard Rosen, "The Achievement Syndrome and Economic Growth in Brazil," *Social Forces,* 42 (1964), pp. 345–346 (emphasis in original).

[4] See Talcott Parsons, *The Social System* (Glencoe: The Free Press, 1951), pp. 58–67 and *passim;* "Pattern Variables Revisited," *American Sociological Review,* 25 (1960), pp. 467–483; and "The Point of View of the Author," *in* Max Black, ed., *The Social Theories of Talcott Parsons* (Englewood

Distinctions which seem particularly useful for analyzing the relation between values and the conditions for development are achievement-ascription, universalism-particularism, specificity-diffuseness, and equalitarianism-elitism. (The latter is not one of Parsons' distinctions, but rather one which I have added.) A society's value system may emphasize that a person in his orientation to others treats them in terms of their abilities and performances (achievement) or in terms of inherited qualities (ascription); applies a general standard (universalism) or responds to some personal attribute or relationship (particularism); or deals with them in terms of the specific positions which they happen to occupy (specificity) or in general terms as individual members of the collectivity (diffuseness).

Concepts such as these are most appropriately used in a comparative context. Thus the claim that the United States is achievement-oriented, or that it is equalitarian, obviously does not refer to these characteristics in any absolute sense. The statement that a national value system is equalitarian clearly does not imply the absence of great differences in power, income, wealth, or status. It means rather that from a comparative perspective nations defined as equalitarian tend to place more emphasis than elitist nations on universalistic criteria in interpersonal judgments, and that they tend to de-emphasize behavior patterns which stress hierarchical differences. No society is equalitarian, ascriptive, or universalistic in any total sense; all systems about which we have knowledge are characterized by values and behavior which reflect both ends of any given polarity, e.g., all systems have some mobility and some inheritance of position.

In his original presentation of the pattern variables, Parsons linked combinations of two of them, achievement-ascription and universalism-particularism, to different forms of existing societies. Thus the combination of universalism-achievement may be exemplified by the United States. It is the combination most favorable to the emergence of an industrial society since it encourages respect or deference toward others on the basis of merit and places an emphasis on achievement. It is typically linked with a stress on specificity, the judging of individuals and institutions in terms of their individual roles, rather than generally.[1] The Soviet system expresses many of the same values as the United States in its ideals. One important difference, of course, is in the position of the Communist party. Membership in the party conveys particularistic rights and obligations. Otherwise both systems resemble each other in value terms with reference to the original pattern variables. Both denigrate extended kinship ties, view ethnic subdivisions as a strain, emphasize individual success, but at the same time insist that

---

Cliffs, N.J.: Prentice-Hall, 1961), pp. 319–320, 329–336. I have discussed the pattern variables and attempted to use them in an analysis of differences among the four major English-speaking nations. See S. M. Lipset, *The First New Nation* (New York: Basic Books, 1963), pp. 207–273.

[1] See Parsons, *The Social System*, pp. 182–191.

inequality should be reduced, and that the norms inherent in equalitarian-ism should govern social relationships. The two systems, North American and Communist, diverge, however, with respect to another key pattern-variable polarity, self-orientation versus collectivity-orientation—the emphasis that a collectivity has a claim on its individual units to conform to the defined interests of the larger group, as opposed to the legitimacy of actions reflecting the perceived needs of the individual unit.

Conceptualization at such an abstract level is not very useful unless it serves to specify hypotheses about the differences in norms and behavior inherent in different value emphases.[1] Such work would clearly have utility for the effort to understand the varying relationships between levels of economic development and social values.[2]

The Latin American system has been identified by Parsons as an example of the particularistic-ascriptive pattern. Such a system tends to be focused around kinship and local community, and to de-emphasize the need for powerful and legitimate larger centers of authority such as the state. Given a weak achievement orientation, such systems see work as a necessary evil. Morality converges around the traditionalistic acceptance of received standards and arrangements. There is an emphasis on expressive rather than instrumental behavior. There is little concern with the behavior of external authority so long as it does not interfere with expressive freedom. Such systems also tend to emphasize diffuseness and elitism. The status conferred by one position tends to be accorded in all situations. Thus if one plays one elite role, he is respected generally.[3]

---

[1] A comprehensive specification of the norms and behavior involved in concepts of political, social, economic, and intellectual modernization may be found in John Whitney Hall, "Changing Conceptions of the Modernization of Japan," *in* Marius B. Jansen, ed., *Changing Japanese Attitudes toward Modernization* (Princeton: Princeton University Press, 1965), pp. 20–23 and footnote 19.

[2] The pattern variables have been applied in various discussions of social and economic development. For examples, see Fred W. Riggs, "Agraria and Industria—Toward a Typology of Comparative Administration," *in* William J. Siffin, ed., *Toward the Comparative Study of Public Administration* (Bloomington: Indiana University Press, 1959), pp. 23–116; Joseph J. Spengler, "Social Structure, the State, and Economic Growth," *in* Simon Kuznets, Wilbert E. Moore and Joseph J. Spengler, eds., *Economic Growth: Brazil, India, Japan* (Durham: Duke University Press, 1955), especially pp. 379–384; Bert F. Hoselitz, *Sociological Aspects of Economic Growth* (New York: The Free Press, 1960), pp. 29–42, 59–60; David C. McClelland, *The Achieving Society*, pp. 172–188; G. A. Theodorson, "Acceptance of Industrialization and Its Attendant Consequences for the Social Patterns of Non-Western Societies," *American Sociological Review*, 18 (1958), pp. 437–484.

[3] Parsons, *The Social System*, pp. 198–200. For a comparative social-psychological study of the orientations of comparable samples of adolescents in Buenos Aires and Chicago where the findings are congruent with Parsons's assumptions about differences between North American and Latin American values, see R. J. Havighurst, Maria Eugenia Dubois, M. Csikszentmihalyi, and R. Doll, *A Cross-National Study of Buenos Aires and Chicago Adolescents* (Basel: S. Karger, 1965). The authors report that the Chicago group differs from the Buenos Aires one in being "more self-assertive and autonomous . . . more resistive to authority . . . more instrumental . . . the Buenos Aires group are more expressive in their orientation to the world" (p. 79).

Although the various Latin American countries obviously differ considerably—a point which will be elaborated later—it is interesting to note that a recent analysis of the social structure of the most developed nation, Uruguay, describes the contemporary situation there in much the same terms as Parsons does for the area as a whole. Aldo Solari has summed up some of his findings about his own country:

> It is clear that particularism is a very important phenomenon in Uruguayan society and it prevails over universalism. A great number of facts support this. It is well known that the prevailing system of selection for government employees is based on kinship, on membership in a certain club or political faction, on friendship, etc. These are all particularistic criteria. A similar phenomenon is present in private enterprise where selection of personnel on the basis of particularistic relations is very common. The use of universalistic criteria, such as the use of standardized examinations is exceptional. Quite frequently when such universalistic criteria seem operative, they are applied to candidates who have been previously selected on the basis of personal relationships.[1]

Ascriptive ties are also quite strong in Uruguay, linked in large part to the importance of the family in the system. Concern with fulfilling family obligations and maintaining family prestige leads propertied Uruguayans to avoid risking the economic base of the family position. The concerns of the middle class which tend to affect the expectations and norms of the whole society are for "security, moderation, lack of risk, and prestige."[2]

The sources of Latin American values have been generally credited to the institutions and norms of the Iberian nations, as practiced by an Iberian-born elite during the three centuries of colonial rule. Those sent over from Spain or Portugal held the predominant positions, and in the colonies "ostentatiously proclaimed their lack of association with manual, productive labor or any kind of vile employment."[3] And Spain and Portugal, prior to colonizing the Americas, had been engaged for eight centuries in conflict with the Moors, resulting in the glorification of the roles of soldier and priest, and in the denigration of commercial and banking activities, often in the hands of Jews and Moslems. Iberian values and institutions were transferred to the American continent. To establish them securely, there were constant efforts by the "Church militant" to Christianize heathen population, the need to justify morally Spanish and Portuguese rule over "inferior"

---

[1] Aldo E. Solari, *Estudios sobre la sociedad uruguaya* (Montevideo: Arca, 1964), p. 162.

[2] *Ibid.*, p. 171.

[3] Frederick B. Pike, *Chile and the United States, 1880–1962* (Notre Dame: University of Notre Dame Press, 1962), p. 78. The strength of these values may be seen in the fact that for much of the colonial period, at the University of San Gregorio in Quito, "Applicants for entrance had to establish by a detailed legal process 'the purity of their blood,' and *prove that none of their ancestors had engaged in trade."* Harold Benjamin, *Higher Education in the American Republics* (New York: McGraw-Hill, 1965), p. 16 (my italics).

peoples, Indians, and imported Africans, and the fostering of a "get rich quick mentality" introduced by the *conquistadores,* but reinforced by efforts to locate valuable minerals or mine the land, and most significantly by the establishment of the *latifundia* (large-scale plantations) as the predominant form of economic, social, and political organization.[1] Almost everywhere in Latin America, the original upper class was composed of the owners of *latifundia,* and these set the model for elite behavior to which lesser classes, including the businessmen of the towns, sought to adapt.

And as Ronald Dore points out, in *arielismo,* the Latin American scorn for pragmatism and materialism, now usually identified with the United States, "there is an element that can only be explained by the existence of a traditional, landed upper class."[2] The period of the predominance of *latifundia* social structure is far from over. In most Latin American nations (Mexico, Bolivia, and Cuba are perhaps the major exceptions), agriculture is still dominated by *latifundia.* Thus farms of 1,000 hectares or more, which constitute 1.5 per cent of all farms in Latin America, possess 65 per cent of the total farm acreage. *Minifundia* (small farms of under 20 hectares) constitute 73 per cent of all farms, but less than 4 per cent of the acreage.[3] The high-status social clubs of most major cities are still controlled or highly influenced by men whose families derived their original wealth and status from *latifundia.* In spite of repeated demands for land reform, little has been done to reduce the economic source of the influence of *latifundia* families.[4] Hence the continuation of preindustrial values in much of Latin America can be linked in large part to the persistence of the rural social structure which originally fostered these values.[5] Even in Uruguay, which

---

[1] For a collection of papers dealing with the social structure of *latifundia* in different parts of the Americas, see Division of Science Development (Social Sciences), Pan American Union, *Plantation Systems of the New World* (Washington: Pan American Union, 1959), and Charles Wagley and Marvin Harris, "A Typology of Latin American Subcultures," *American Anthropologist,* 57 (1955), pp. 433–437.

[2] R. P. Dore, "Latin America and Japan Compared," *in* John J. Johnson, ed., *Continuity and Change in Latin America* (Stanford: Stanford University Press, 1964), p. 245. He indicates also that the absence of such attitudes in Japan is related to "the attenuation of the ties that had bound the feudal aristocracy and gentry began at the end of the sixteenth century and was completed in 1870." For a discussion of the concept of *arielismo,* see Kalman H. Silvert, *The Conflict Society: Reaction and Revolution in Latin America* (New Orleans: Hauser Press, 1961), pp. 144–161.

[3] United Nations Economic and Social Council. Economic Commission for Latin America, *Provisional Report on the Conference on Education and Economic and Social Development in Latin America* (Mar del Plata, Argentina: 1963, E/CN.12/639), p. 250.

[4] Thomas F. Carroll, "Land Reform as an Explosive Force in Latin America," *in* John J. Tepaske and Sidney N. Fisher, eds., *Explosive Forces in Latin America* (Columbus: Ohio State University Press, 1964), pp. 81–125.

[5] Wagley and Harris, "A Typology of Latin American Subcultures," pp. 439–441; Frank Tannenbaum, "Toward an Appreciation of Latin America," *in* Herbert L. Matthews, ed., *The United States and Latin America* (Englewood Cliffs, N.J.: Prentice-Hall, 1963), pp. 32–41; José Medina Echavarría, "A Sociologist's View," *in* José Medina Echavarría and B. Higgins, eds., *Social Aspects of Economic Development in Latin America,* Vol. II (Paris: UNESCO, 1963), pp. 33–39; Gino Germani, "The

has long been dominated by the metropolis of Montevideo, one finds that
much of the upper social class of the city is composed of members of powerful old land-owning families. Many of those involved in commercial and
banking activities have close kinship ties with the large cattle raisers and
estancieros. And the upper rural class maintains considerable influence on
the society as a whole through its control over the main agricultural organizations, and the continued strength of a widespread ideology which states
that the wealth of the country depends on land, and on the activities of
those who farm it.[1]

In many countries the prestige attaching to land ownership still leads
many businessmen to invest the moneys they have made in industry in
farms.[2] A study of the Argentinian elite indicates that similar emphases are
important there also, in spite of the influence of its cosmopolitan, six-
million-strong capital city Buenos Aires:

> Insofar as the entrepreneurial bourgeoisie moved up in the social scale, they
> were absorbed by the old upper classes. They lost their dynamic power and with-
> out the ability to create a new ideology of their own, they accepted the existing
> scale of social prestige, the values and system of stratification of the traditional
> rural sectors. When they could they bought *estancias* [ranches] not only for eco-
> nomic reasons, but for prestige, and became cattle raisers, themselves.[3]

In Chile, too, many analysts have suggested that much of the behavior
and values of the urban bourgeoisie reflect their effort to imitate and gain
acceptance from an extremely conservative land-based upper class. Less
than 10 per cent of the landowners own close to 90 per cent of the arable
land; this group show little interest in efficient productivity and sustain
semifeudal relations with their workers.[4] One possible superficial advantage of the close identification of the urban middle class with that of the
old aristocracy has been suggested by a North American commentator.
"Because this group has in its political, social, and economic thinking so
closely reflected the attitudes of the aristocracy, there has been almost no
disruption as middle sectors have won increasing power in Chilean politics."

Strategy of Fostering Social Mobility," *in* Egbert de Vries and José Medina Echavarría, eds., *Social
Aspects of Economic Development in Latin America,* Vol. I (Paris: UNESCO, 1963), pp. 222–229;
Charles Wagley, *Race and Class in Rural Brazil* (Paris: UNESCO, 1952), pp. 144–145; Bernard J.
Siegel, "Social Structure and Economic Change in Brazil," *in* Kuznets, Moore, and Spengler, eds.,
Economic Growth, pp. 405–408.

[1] Solari, *Estudios sobre la sociedad uruguaya,* pp. 113–122, 127–129.

[2] J. Richard Powell, "Notes on Latin American Industrialization," *Inter-American Economic Affairs,* 6 (Winter, 1952), p. 83.

[3] José Luis de Imaz, *Los que mandan* (Buenos Aires: Editorial Universitaria de Buenos Aires,
1964), p. 160.

[4] Pike, *Chile and the United States,* pp. 280–283.

But he notes that, while producing political stability, this role "may also have contributed to economic and social stagnation."[1]

Similar patterns have been described by many students of Brazilian society to account for the strong emphasis on family particularism within industrial life there. Brazil, of course, as the last major country to retain slavery, as a former empire which ennobled its leading citizens, and as the most rural of South America's major countries, can be expected to retain many of the value emphases of an elitist traditional culture, even among the successful "new classes" of its relatively highly developed southern regions.

Rather than considering themselves a new "middle class," these newly successful groups have come to share, with the descendants of the old landed gentry, an aristocratic set of ideals and patterns of behavior which they have inherited from the nobility of the Brazilian empire. . . .

One of these aristocratic values relevant to economic change is what Gilberto Freyre has called a "Gentleman complex"—a dispraisal of manual labor in every form. . . . Just as in the past when manual labor was the lot of slaves in Brazil, it is considered today to be the work of the lower classes. . . .

[S]emi feudal relationships continue to dominate the social and economic relations of the simple rural worker. . . . The traditional relationships between this small upper [landed] class and the rural peasant and the growing class of urban workers are important factors in economic growth. The institutions and the value system of this upper class affect the ideology of change, the entry of foreign capital into the country, the encouragement and development of appropriate skills, and other acts facilitating economic growth. To a large extent it is their "aristocratic" values and ideal which provide many of the life expectations and incentives. . . .[2]

The stress on values as a key source of differences in the rate of development of economic and political institutions has been countered by some students of Latin America; they will point to the southern states of the American union as an example of a subculture which has been relatively underdeveloped economically, which has lacked a stable democratic political system, and which has placed a greater emphasis on violence and law

---

[1] *Ibid.,* p. 287. This book was published in 1962, before the victory of the left-wing Christian Democrats.

[2] Siegel, "Social Structure and Economic Change in Brazil," pp. 406–411. See also Charles Wagley, *An Introduction to Brazil* (New York: Columbia University Press, 1963), pp. 126–131. A summary of a detailed study of Brazilian industrialists reports that other than European immigrants and their offspring, "Most of the new industrialists were simply large landowners diversifying into manufacturing. Those who did not actually retain their plantations, retained strong links with the land. Their style of life hardly changed; their social attitudes changed not at all." See Emanuel de Kadt, "The Brazilian Impasse," *Encounter,* 25 (September, 1965), p. 57. He is reporting on the findings in Fernando Henrique Cardoso, *Empresário industrial e desenvolvimento econômico no Brasil* (São Paulo: Difusão Européia do Livro, 1964).

violation to attain political ends than the rest of the country. And as these scholars point out, the white South is the most purely Anglo-Saxon and Protestant part of the United States.

The American South resembles much of Latin America, including Brazil, in having an institutional structure and value system erected around a plantation (or *latifundia*) economy, which employed large numbers of slaves, and which after the abolition of slavery developed a stratification hierarchy correlated with variations in racial background. From this point of view, the clue to understanding the economic backwardness and political instability of Brazil and much of Spanish America lies in their structural similarities with the American South, rather than in those values which stem from Iberian or Catholic origins.[1] This argument is strengthened by analyses of the differences between southern and northern Brazil. The southern part of the country, which was much less involved in large-scale slave labor agriculture, differs from the northern part in much the same way as the United States North varies from its South. Southern Brazil and the northern United States are much more developed economically, and they place more emphasis on the "modern" value system—achievement, universalism, and the like—than the warmer regions of their countries.

There are certain similarities in another American country, Canada, and its internal cultural and economic differentiation. French Canada, historically, has been less developed than English Canada. Much of its economic development has been dominated by entrepreneurs from English-speaking backgrounds.[2] A recent analysis of French-Canadian businessmen, based on interviews, reports their economic value orientations in terms very reminiscent of the studies of Latin American entrepreneurs.[3] Though not as unstable politically as the southern United States or most of Latin America, Quebec has long exhibited symptoms of political instability (an opposition party system is perhaps less institutionalized there than in any other populous province); charges of political corruption, illegal tactics in campaigns, violations of civil liberties, and the like seem much more common in Quebec than in the English-speaking provinces.[4] Quebec is certainly Latin and

---

[1] See Sanford Mosk, "Latin America versus the United States," *American Economic Association, Papers and Proceedings,* 40 (1950), pp. 367–383. See also Gilberto Freyre, *New World in the Tropics. The Culture of Modern Brazil* (New York: Vintage Books, 1963), pp. 71–72, 82–87, 193–195.

[2] See Bernard Blishen, "The Construction and Use of an Occupational Class Scale," *Canadian Journal of Economics and Political Science,* 24 (1958), pp. 519–531; Yves de Jocas and Guy Rocher, "Inter-Generational Occupational Mobility in the Province of Quebec," *Canadian Journal of Economics and Political Science,* 23 (1957), pp. 377–394; John Porter, *The Vertical Mosaic: An Analysis of Social Class and Power in Canada* (Toronto: University of Toronto Press, 1965), pp. 91–98, passim.

[3] Norman W. Taylor, "The French-Canadian Industrial Entrepreneur and His Social Environment," in Marcel Rioux and Yves Martin, eds., *French-Canadian Society,* Vol. I (Toronto: McClelland and Stewart, 1964), pp. 271–295.

[4] One French Canadian analyst has argued recently that "historically French-Canadians have not

Catholic (if these terms have any general analytic or descriptive meaning), but it obviously has had no plantation culture, nor a significant racial minority, though it could be argued that the English-French relationships resemble those of white-Negro, or white-Indian, in other countries of the Americas.

Various analyses of the weakness of democracy in Quebec do argue that religious-linked factors are relevant. As Pierre Trudeau has put it: "French Canadians are Catholics; and Catholic nations have not always been ardent supporters of democracy. They are authoritarian in spiritual matters; and since the dividing line between the spiritual and the temporal may be very fine or even confused, they are often disinclined to seek solutions in temporal affairs through the mere counting of heads."[1] And many have pointed to the differences in the economic development of the two Canadas as evidence that Catholic values and social organization are much less favorable to economic development than Protestant ones have been. As S. D. Clark has reasoned, "in nineteenth century Quebec religion was organized in terms of a hierarchy of social classes which had little relation to the much more fluid class system of capitalism, and sharp separation from the outside capitalist world was maintained through an emphasis upon ethnic and religious differences and through geographic isolation."[2]

These comparisons between the United States North and South, and English and French Canada, show that structure and values are clearly interrelated. Structure such as a plantation system combined with a racially based hierarchy is functionally tied to a given set of aristocratic values, and antipathetic to an emphasis on achievement, universalism, and hard work. But any value system derived from given sets of historical experience institutionalized in religious systems, family structures, class relations, and education will affect the pace and even direction and content of social and economic change.

If we now turn to studies focusing directly on the relationship between values and entrepreneurial behavior, the available materials from many Latin American countries seem to agree that the predominant values which

---

really believed in democracy for themselves." He suggests "that they have never achieved any sense of obligation towards the general welfare, including the welfare of the French-Canadians on non-racial issues," Pierre Elliot Trudeau, "Some Obstacles to Democracy in Quebec," *in* Mason Wade, ed., *Canadian Dualism* (Toronto: University of Toronto Press, 1960), pp. 241–259. On the general problems of, and weakness of, democracy in Quebec see Herbert Quinn, *The Union Nationale* (Toronto: University of Toronto Press, 1963), especially pp. 3–19, 23, 65–67, 126–129, 131–151; Gerard Dion and Louis O'Neill, *Political Immorality in the Province of Quebec* (Montreal: Civic Action League, 1956); Arthur Maheux, "French Canadians and Democracy," *in* Douglas Grant, ed., *Quebec Today* (Toronto: University of Toronto Press, 1960), pp. 341–351; Frank R. Scott, "Canada et Canada Français," *Esprit,* 20 (1952), pp. 178–189; and Michael Oliver, "Quebec and Canadian Democracy," *Canadian Journal of Economics and Political Science,* 23 (1957), pp. 504–515.

[1] Trudeau, "Some Obstacles to Democracy," p. 245; see also Quinn, *The Union Nationale,* pp. 17–18.

[2] S. D. Clark, *The Canadian Community* (Toronto: University of Toronto Press, 1962), p. 161.

continue to inform the behavior of the elite stem from the continued and combined strength of ascription, particularism, and diffuseness. Thomas Cochran has examined the literature from various American cultures, as well as from his own empirical research, and has conjectured that Latin American businessmen differ from North American ones in being:

> 1) more interested in inner worth and justification by standards of personal feeling than they are in the opinion of peer groups; 2) disinclined to sacrifice personal authority to group decisions; 3) disliking impersonal as opposed to personal arrangements, and generally preferring family relations to those with outsiders; 4) inclined to prefer social prestige to money; and 5) somewhat aloof from and disinterested in science and technology.[1]

Somewhat similar conclusions are reported in various surveys of managerial attitudes in various Latin American countries. These indicate that role specificity, i.e., separation of managerial from other activities, is relatively less common there than in more-developed areas. A Latin American manager "is quite likely to devote part of his office hours to politics or family affairs."[2] Bureaucratic and competitive norms are comparatively weak. Personal characteristics are valued more than technical or organizational ability.[3]

Family particularism is much more common among Latin American business executives than among their counterparts in more-developed nations. "Managers are frequently selected on the basis of family links, rather than specialized training." The entire managerial group often came from one family, and the "great majority of managers interviewed either considered this to be an appropriate arrangement under the conditions of their country, or had not thought of alternatives."[4] In Brazil, even the growth of large industries and corporate forms of ownership has not drastically changed the pattern. In many companies the modal pattern seems to involve an adjustment between family control and the rational demands of running a big business. Either the children or the in-laws of the old patriarch are technically trained, or the company involves a mixed system of family members working closely with technically educated nonfamily executives. However, the type of managers employed by family groups are known as *hombres de*

---

[1] Thomas C. Cochran, *The Puerto Rican Businessman* (Philadelphia: University of Pennsylvania Press, 1959), p. 131; see also pp. 151–154 and Cochran, "Cultural Factors in Economic Growth."

[2] Albert Lauterbach, "Managerial Attitudes and Economic Growth," *Kyklos,* 15 (1962), p. 384. This study is based on interviews with managers in eight countries.

[3] Eduardo A. Zalduendo, *El empresario industrial en América Latina: Argentina* (Mar del Plata, Argentina: Naciones Unidas, Comisión Económica para América Latina, 1963. E/CN/12/642/Add. I), p. 46.

[4] Albert Lauterbach, "Government and Development: Managerial Attitudes in Latin America," *Journal of Inter-American Studies,* 7 (1965), pp. 202–203; see also L. C. Bresser Pereira, "The Rise of Middle Class and Middle Management in Brazil," *Journal of Inter-American Studies,* 4 (1962), pp. 322–323.

confianza (men who can be trusted), and have been selected more for this quality than for their expertise.[1]

Most analysts of Latin American business behavior agree that a principal concern of the typical entrepreneur is to maintain family prestige; thus he is reluctant to give up the family-owned and -managed type of corporation. Outsiders are distrusted, for the entrepreneur "is acutely aware that any advantage that may be given to somebody outside his family is necessarily at the expense of himself and his own family."[2] From this evolves an unwillingness to cooperate with others outside of one's firm, and a defensiveness toward subordinates, as well as toward creditors, distributors, and others. Such assumptions about the behavior of others are, of course, self-maintaining, since people tend to behave as significant others define them, thus reinforcing a mutual state of distrust. In the family-dominated firms which constitute such a large proportion of Latin American business, non-family, middle-management personnel will often be untrustworthy and inefficient, since they will lack identification with firms in which "the 'road upward' is blocked by family barriers," and they are given limited responsibility.[3] This fear of dealing with outsiders even extends to reluctance to permit investment in the firm. For many Brazilian "industrialists, the sale of stocks to the public seems to involve . . . a loss of property. . . ." A Brazilian market research survey reported that 93 per cent of entrepreneurs interviewed stated "that they had never thought of selling stock in their enterprise."[4] As Emilio Willems points out, "such a typically modern institution as the stock-market in large metropolitan centers failed to develop because the most important joint-stock companies are owned by kin-groups which handle transfer of stock as a purely domestic matter."[5]

Although not statistically typical of Brazilian entrepreneurial behavior, some of the practices of the largest Brazilian firm, the United Industries, which in 1952 employed 30,000 workers in 367 plants, indicate the way in which family particularism and other traditional practices can continue within a massive industrial complex. In spite of its size, it is owned largely

---

[1] Fernando H. Cardoso, *El empresario industrial en América Latina: Brasil* (Mar del Plata, Argentina: Naciones Unidas, Comisión Económica para América Latina, 1963. E/CN/12/642/Add. 2), pp. 25–26; for a description of the way in which *hombres de confianza* were incorporated into a major Argentinian industrial complex see Thomas C. Cochran and Ruben E. Reina, *Entrepreneurship in Argentine Culture. Torcuato Di Tella and S.I.A.M.* (Philadelphia: University of Pennsylvania Press, 1962), pp. 266–268; see also de Kadt, "The Brazilian Impasse," p. 57, for a summary of Brazilian evidence on this point.

[2] Tomás Roberto Fillol, *Social Factors in Economic Development. The Argentine Case* (Cambridge: M.I.T. Press, 1961), pp. 13–14.

[3] *Ibid.*, p. 61.

[4] Cardoso, *El empresario industrial en América Latina: Brasil*, p. 31; Siegel, "Social Structure and Economic Change in Brazil," pp. 405–408. Robert J. Alexander, *Labor Relations in Argentina, Brazil, Chile* (New York: McGraw-Hill, 1962), pp. 48–49.

[5] Emilio Willems, "The Structure of the Brazilian Family," *Social Forces*, 31 (1953), p. 343.

by the son of the founder, Francisco Matarazzo, Jr., and various family members. "The bleak and impeccably dressed Francisco, Jr., controls his empire from a pigskin-paneled office that is fitted with a buzzer system to summon top executives, who, on leaving, *must bow their way backward from his presence.*"[1]

The managers of foreign-owned companies, whether Brazilian or foreign, are different in their behavior. They tend to emphasize a high degree of rationalization and bureaucratic practice in running their firms. Although they are interested in securing personal loyalty from subordinates, it is not the basic requirement for employment. The executive personnel are ambitious and competent employees, concerned with their personal success, and valuing ambition in themselves and others.[2]

The lack of a concern with national interests or institutional development among Latin American entrepreneurs has been related by Albert Hirschman to what he calls an "ego-focussed image of change," characteristic of badly integrated underdeveloped societies. Individuals in nations dominated by such an image, "not indentifying with society," will view new developments or experiences simply as opportunities for self-aggrandizement. Although seemingly reflecting a desire to get ahead, this orientation, which inhibits efforts to advance by cooperation with others, "is inimical to economic development, [since]. . . success is conceived not as a result of systematic application of effort and creative energy, combined perhaps with 'a little bit of luck,' but as due either to sheer luck or to the outwitting of others through careful scheming." And Hirschman, like other analysts of Latin America, sees the inability to trust and work with others as antithetical to effective entrepreneurship.[3]

A 1960–1961 analysis of the "technological decisions" of Mexican and Puerto Rican entrepreneurs, compared with foreign-born managers of subsidiaries of international companies, supports these interpretations. "Differences among foreign and national enterprises in ways of attracting capital, handling labor relations, arranging technical flexibility, channeling information internally and externally (and even willingness to respond to impertinent interview questions) are all consistent with an interpretation that the native entrepreneurs view society as probably malevolent and that the foreigners would have stayed home if they agreed [with this view of society]."[4]

Attitudes to money similar to those frequently reported as characteristic

---

[1] Richard M. Morse, *From Community to Metropolis. A Biography of São Paulo, Brazil* (Gainesville: University of Florida Press, 1958), p. 229 (my italics).

[2] Cardoso, *El empresario industrial en América Latina: Brasil,* pp. 35–39.

[3] Albert Hirschman, *The Strategy of Economic Development* (New Haven: Yale University Press, 1958), pp. 14–19.

[4] W. Paul Strassmann, "The Industrialist," *in* Johnson, ed., *Continuity and Change in Latin America,* pp. 173–174.

of a nonindustrial, traditional population have been reported in studies of Latin American business leaders. A short-range rather than a long-range orientation is common: make money now "and then to live happily—that is, idly—ever after."[1] This means that entrepreneurs frequently prefer to make a high profit quickly, often by charging a high price to a small market, rather than to maximize long-range profits by seeking to cut costs and prices, which would take more effort.[2] Although the concept of immediate profit "in industrial enterprises usually meant within one year or else after paying back initial loans," this does not reflect a Schumpeterian assumption about the reward or encouragement necessary to entrepreneurial risk-taking. Rather, the overwhelming majority of the Latin American businessmen interviewed argued that risk is to be avoided, and that "when there is risk there will not be new investment," that investment risk is a luxury which only those in wealthy countries can afford.[3] Reluctance to take risks may be related to the strong concern with family integrity, with viewing business property much like a family estate. "Where bankruptcy might disgrace one's family, managers will be more cautious than where it is regarded impersonally as expedient corporate strategy."[4]

It is important to note that these generalizations about the attitudes and behavior of Latin American entrepreneurs are all made in a comparative context. Those who stress their commitment to particularistic and diffuse values are generally comparing them to North Americans, or to a model of rational, bureaucratic, competitive enterprise. However, as contrasted with other groups within their societies, Latin American entrepreneurs, particularly those involved in large-scale enterprise, tend to be the carriers of "modern" values. Thus one analysis of Colombian businessmen points out: "They are urban people in a rural country. In a relatively traditionally oriented society, their values are rational and modern."[5]

The impact of Latin American orientations to entrepreneurial behavior has been summed up in the following terms:

---

[1] Lauterbach, "Managerial Attitudes and Economic Growth," p. 379; Fillol, *Social Factors in Economic Development,* pp. 13–14.

[2] One report on Panama comments that "their business philosophy . . . is that of the gambler or plunger. . . . They prefer low volume and high markup; they want quick, large profits on small investment. They cannot think in pennies," John Biesanz, "The Economy of Panama," *Inter-American Economic Affairs,* 6 (Summer, 1952), p. 10.

[3] Lauterbach, "Government and Development," pp. 209–210. J. Richard Powell, "Latin American Industrialization," pp. 82–83.

[4] Strassmann, "The Industrialist," p. 173.

[5] Aarón Lipman, *El empresario industrial en América Latina: Colombia* (Mar del Plata, Argentina: Naciones Unidas, Comisión para América Latina, 1963. E/CN/12/642/Add. 4), p. 30; Guillermo Briones, *El empresario industrial en América Latina: Chile* (Mar del Plata, Argentina: Naciones Unidas, Comisión para América Latina, 1963. E/CN/12/642/Add. 3), p. 35. It should be noted that most of the above generalizations about Latin American entrepreneurs are based on interview data. And as Fernando Cardoso points out, such data may tend to variance with actual behavior. Many of those interviewed are well educated and aware of the nature of a modern entrepreneurial outlook.

Comparatively the Latin American complex: 1) sacrifices rigorous economically directed effort, or profit maximization, to family interests; 2) places social and personal emotional interests ahead of business obligations; 3) impedes mergers and other changes in ownership desirable for higher levels of technological efficiency and better adjustments to markets; 4) fosters nepotism to a degree harmful to continuously able top-management; 5) hinders the building up of a supply of competent and cooperative middle managers; 6) makes managers and workers less amenable to constructive criticism; 7) creates barriers of disinterest in the flow of technological communication; and 8) lessens the urge for expansion and risk-taking.[1]

The emphases on the value orientations of entrepreneurs as a major factor in limiting economic development in Latin America may be criticized for de-emphasizing the extent to which the values themselves are a product of, or sustained by, so-called structural or economic factors. Thus, it has been suggested that the unwillingness to delegate responsibility to nonfamily members reflects the objective dangers of operating in unstable political and economic environments. Such conditions dictate extreme caution and the need to be certain that one can quickly change company policy so as to avoid major losses or bankruptcy as a result of government policy changes, change in foreign exchange rates, and the like. An outsider presumably will not have as much interest in the finances of the firm, or the authority to react quickly. Rapid inflation, high interest rates, and other instability factors would all seem to inhibit long-range planning and encourage a quick and high profit. There can be little doubt that such structural factors help to preserve many of the traditionalistic practices. And such a conclusion would imply the need for deliberate government policies to create a stable environment, such as planned investment policies, regulation of inflation, and restrictions on the export of capital.

But if the existence of interacting supportive mechanisms, which will inhibit economic support, is admitted, the fact remains that similar generalizations have been made about the effect of values on attitudes and behavior of other groups and institutions. For example, an analysis of Argentine politics points to the effect of these values in preventing stable political life. "Argentina's class-bound politics assume that no public measure can be good for almost everybody, that the benefit of one group is the automatic loss of all others."[2] Although Argentina is, after Uruguay, socially the most developed nation in Latin America, highly literate and urbanized, its citizens still do not accept the notion of, nor do they show loyalty to, a national

---

Cardoso suggests that the actual behavior of those interviewed is much less modern and rational than would be suggested by the interviews. Cardoso, *Empresario industrial en América Latina: Brasil*, pp. 47–48, 59.

[1] Cochran, "Cultural Factors in Economic Growth," pp. 529–530.

[2] Kalman H. Silvert, "The Costs of Anti-Nationalism: Argentina," *in* Silvert, ed., *Expectant Peoples: Nationalism and Development* (New York: Random House, 1963), p. 350.

state which acts universalistically. Argentina is instead characterized by the "survival or [sic] localistic, sub-national views and loyalties archetypical of the traditional society...."[1] Similarly in the largest country in Latin America, it "is a well known fact that local government, party politics, and bureaucracy in Brazil still largely reflect family interests which are of course at variance with the principles of objective management as dictated by democratic rule."[2]

Efforts to "modernize" values and behavior are not solely, or even primarily, located in the economic or political spheres. Rather, those professionally concerned with ideas and values, the intellectuals, may play a decisive role in resisting or facilitating social change. As John Friedmann has pointed out, the intellectual in developing countries has three essential tasks to fulfill, "each of which is essential to the process of cultural transformation: he mediates new values, he formulates an effective ideology, and he creates an adequate, collective (national) self-image."[3] In Latin America, however, the large body of literature concerning the values of the extremely prestigious *pensadores* or intellectuals, whether creative artists or academics, agrees that they continue to reject the values of industrial society, which they often identify with the United States. A survey of the writings of Latin American intellectuals points up this conclusion: "There is no school of literature in Latin America ... which argues that technology and technological change represent values which should be adopted, cherished, and used as a means to a more meaningful life."[4] Even when modern technology is accepted as a necessary precondition for social betterment, it is often described as a threat to the traditional values of the society.[5]

Some of the factors which sustain these attitudes, even in the face of the recognized need of the nations of Latin America to change to get out of the "humiliating" status of being considered "underdeveloped" or even backward, have been suggested in an interesting comparison of the different ways in which Japan and Latin America reacted to similar concerns.

When seeking to define a national self-image in a nationalistic frame of mind, one is most likely to seize on those features which supposedly differentiate one from one's major international antagonist. For Japan this point of counter-reference, the thou than which one has to feel more holy, has been the West generally and in the twentieth century America more particularly. For Latin America, since the beginning of this century at least, it has been almost exclusively America.

---

[1] *Ibid.,* p. 353

[2] Willems, "Structure of the Brazilian Family," p. 343.

[3] John Friedmann, "Intellectuals in Developing Countries," *Kyklos,* 13 (1964), p. 524.

[4] William S. Stokes, "The Drag of the *Pensadores,*" *in* James W. Wiggins and Helmut Schoeck, eds., *Foreign Aid Reexamined* (Washington: Public Affairs Press, 1958), p. 63; see also Fred P. Ellison, "The Writer," *in* Johnson, ed., *Continuity and Change,* p. 97.

[5] Stokes, "The Drag of the *Pensadores,*" see the footnotes to these articles for reference to the large literature by Latin Americans and others emphasizing these points.

But in differentiating themselves from Americans, the Japanese could point to the beauties of their tight family system; their patriotic loyalty to the Emperor contrasting with American selfish individualism; the pacific subtleties of Buddhism contrasting with the turbulent stridency of Christianity; and so on. But it was not as easy for a Latin American to establish the Latin American differentiae in terms of family, political, or legal institutions. He had to fall back on "spirit" and attitudes; and since the most visible American was the businessman, he tended—*vide arielismo* as Ellison describes it—to make his dimension of difference the materialist-spiritual one. Thus by scorning American devotion to technology and profit, he made something of a virtue out of the stark fact of economic backwardness. For their part the Japanese had enough superior arguments with which to fortify their uncertain sense of their superior Japaneseness without resorting to this one, with its inhibiting effect on indigenous economic growth.[1]

While much of the anti-United States sentiment is presented in the context of left-wing critiques, *pensadores* of the right—those who uphold the virtues of tradition, Catholicism, and social hierarchy—also are aggressively opposed to North American culture, which they see as "lacking culture, grace, beauty, as well as widespread appreciation of aesthetic and spiritual values."[2] And a report on the writings of Chilean conservative intellectuals states that over 100 works have been published which "are as hostile to basic United States social, economic and political patterns as to Russian communism."[3]

The values fostered by the *pensadores* continue to be found as well in much of Latin American education. Most analysts of Latin American education agree that, at both university and secondary school levels, the content of education still reflects the values of a landed upper class. Even in the second most developed Latin American country, Argentina, a study of national values points out that the traditional landed aristocratic disdain for manual work, industry, and trading continues to affect the educational orientations of many students. When an Argentine seeks to move up, "he will usually try to do so, not by developing his manual skills or by accomplishing business or industrial feats, but by developing his *intellectual* skills. He will follow an academic career typically in a field which is not 'directly productive' from an economic point of view—medicine, law, social sciences, etc."[4]

As Jacques Lambert has put it, "A ruling class deriving its resources from landed property looks to education for a means not of increasing its income but rather of cultivating the mind. The whole public education system has been organized as a preparation for higher education, and more particularly for the type of education provided in the faculties of law, which gave

---

[1] Dore, "Latin America and Japan Compared," p. 245.
[2] Pike, *Chile and the United States,* p. 251.
[3] *Ibid.,* p. 254.
[4] Fillol, *Social Factors in Economic Development,* pp. 17–18.

instruction not only in law but also in political and social science, for a class of political leaders."[1] There is considerable resistance at both secondary and university levels to changing the curriculum to adapt to the needs of mass education in an urban industrial society. President Lleras of Colombia, for example, has complained that students in the secondary schools "are studying the same courses as in the 19th century."[2] The Brazilian sociologist Florestán Fernandes suggests that the "democratization" of education in his country has meant "spreading throughout Brazilian society the aristocratic school of the past."[3] The school here reinforces the disdain for practical work, and diffuses these values among the upwardly mobile. As he puts it:

> Education has remained impermeable to economic, social and political revivalist influences. Misunderstanding and contempt of popular education has subsisted, and the excessive prestige enjoyed by the humanistic culture of the old upper class, as patrons of a corresponding type of anti-experimental book-learning has been perpetuated. The school continues to be an isolated institution divorced from man's conditions of existence and specializing in the transmission of bookish techniques, potted knowledge and routine intellectual concepts. Formal education, in a word, is guarded from any impact that would adjust it to the constructive social functions which it should properly carry out in a society aiming at homogeneity and expansion.[4]

In Chile, one prominent educator, Julio Vega, wrote in 1950 "that education must begin to emancipate itself from the social prejudices which lead 99 per cent of those entering the *liceo*—somewhat the equivalent of the United States high school, but organized around an entirely different curriculum and dedicated to a different social purpose—to want to be professionals, so as to gain access to the world of the aristocracy." And many have argued that the educational system has taught middle-class Chileans "to think like an aristocrat of the past century and to hold in disdain manual labor and those who perform it."[5]

These generalizations about the strength of the traditional humanist bias in Latin America may be bolstered by reference to comparative educational

---

[1] Jacques Lambert, "Requirements for Rapid Economic and Social Development: The View of the Historian and Sociologist," *in* de Vries and Echavarría, eds., *Social Aspects of Economic Development*, p. 64.

[2] Robert W. Burns, "Social Class and Education in Latin America," *Comparative Education Review*, 6 (1963), p. 232.

[3] Florestán Fernandes, "Pattern and Rate of Development in Latin America," *in* de Vries and Echavarría, eds., *Social Aspects of Economic Development*, pp. 196-197; see also Oscar Vera, "The Educational Situation and Requirements in Latin America," *in* de Vries and Echavarría, eds., *Social Aspects of Economic Development*, pp. 294-295; and Wagley, *An Introduction to Brazil*, pp. 103-104.

[4] Fernandes, "Pattern and Rate of Development," p. 196.

[5] Pike, *Chile and the United States*, pp. 288-289. "There is a lengthy list of works suggesting that the educational structure in Chile foments class prejudice, leading the middle class to shun labor and the laboring classes, while striving to emulate the aristocracy," p. 442, footnote. This work contains a detailed bibliography.

statistics. Latin America as an area lags behind every other part of the world in the proportion of its students taking courses in engineering or the sciences. As of 1958–1959, 34 per cent of all West European undergraduates were studying science or engineering, in contrast to 23 per cent in Asia (excluding Communist China and India), 19 per cent in Africa, and 16 per cent in Latin America.[1] The comparable figure for the major Communist countries including the Soviet Union and China is 46 per cent.[2] China now trains more engineers per year than any country except the Soviet Union and the United States. And 90 per cent of all China's scientists and engineers have been trained since 1949.[3] In Uruguay, on the other hand, slightly over half the students in higher education have been enrolled in faculties of humanities, fine arts, and law, about 10 times as many as in the scientific and technical faculties. In Chile, in 1957, less than one sixth of the students were studying science or engineering, and the increase in the numbers in these faculties between 1940 and 1959 was less than the growth in total university enrollment. "In Communist countries, of course, the proportions are almost exactly reversed; Czechoslovakia had 46 per cent in scientific and technical faculties and only 6.4 per cent in humanities, arts, and law."[4] Among Third World nations, only Israel with 42 per cent of its students in science and engineering, and Nigeria with 40 per cent, approached the Communist nations in degree of dedication of higher education to development training objectives.[5]

The situation is now changing in some Latin American countries; but it is significant that a recent comparative analysis of trends in higher education completed for UNESCO notes particularly that, as compared to other regions, in Latin America there have "been no concerted efforts . . . to strengthen interest and achievement in science and the related fields."[6] In the largest Latin American country, Brazil, enrollment in universities has increased 10 times, from 10,000 to 101,600, between 1912 and 1961. However, the percentage of the total studying engineering was 12.8 in 1912 and 12 in 1961.[7] A study of students in 17 middle schools *(ginásios)* in São

[1] J. Tinbergen and H. C. Bos, "The Global Demand for Higher and Secondary Education in the Underdeveloped Countries in the Next Decade," O.E.C.D., *Policy Conference on Economic Growth and Investment in Education, III, The Challenge of Aid to Newly Developing Countries* (Paris: O.E.C.D., 1962), p. 73.

[2] Frederick Harbison and Charles A. Myers, *Education, Manpower and Economic Growth* (New York: McGraw-Hill, 1964), p. 179.

[3] *Ibid.,* p. 88.

[4] *Ibid.,* pp. 115–119.

[5] James S. Coleman, "Introduction to Part IV," *in* J. S. Coleman, ed., *Education and Political Development* (Princeton: Princeton University Press, 1965), p. 530.

[6] Frank Bowles, *Access to Higher Education,* Vol. I (Paris: UNESCO, 1963), p. 148.

[7] Robert J. Havighurst and J. Roberto Moreira, *Society and Education in Brazil* (Pittsburgh: University of Pittsburgh Press, 1965), p. 200. And engineering in Brazil and other parts of Latin America often means the traditionally socially prestigious field of civil engineering, not mechanical, chemical, or industrial.

Paulo indicates that the large majority hoped to enter one of the traditional prestige occupations. And Brandão Lopes comments that his findings indicate "the permanence of traditional Brazilian values relating to work in an environment in which economic development demands new specialties."[1] The absence of French Canadians in leading roles in industry has been explained as a consequence of Canada's educational system, which resembles that of Latin America. Until the 1960's secondary education in Quebec was largely "based on private fee-paying schools," whose curriculum reflected "the refined traditions of the classical college. In the main, French Canadian education was never geared to the provision of industrial skills at the managerial or technical level. The educational system was inappropriate for the kind of society that by 1950 Quebec was becoming. It was an outstanding example of institutional failure."[2]

Another reflection of the strength of "aristocratic" values in the Latin American educational system is the phenomenon of the part-time professor. It has been estimated that less than 10 per cent of the professors at Latin American universities receive salaries intended to pay for full-time work. As one Uruguayan professor once said to me, "To be a professor in this country is a hobby, a hobby one engages in for prestige." Obviously when men spend most of their time earning their livings away from the university, often in an occupation such as the law which is unrelated to their academic work, they cannot be expected to make major contributions to scholarship, or to devote much time to guiding students.[3]

To describe this system as "aristocratic" may seem ironic, but comparative research on other subjects indicates that the "conception that social service is performed best when [one] . . . is not paid, or is paid an honorarium, is basically an aristocratic value linked to the concept of *noblesse oblige.*" Conversely, inherent in equalitarian ideology "has been the principle that a man should be paid for his work."[4] In a comparative analysis of the position of leaders of voluntary organizations in the United States and various European nations, I presented data which indicated that there are many more full-time paid leaders of such groups in the United States than in much of Europe. And I concluded:

> The inhibitions against employing a large number of officials permeate most voluntary associations in the European nations and reflect the historic assumption that such activities should be the "charities" of the privileged classes. The absence of a model of *noblesse-oblige* in an equalitarian society fostered the American

---

[1] Brandão Lopes, "Escôlha ocupacional e origem social de ginasianos em São Paulo," *Educação e Ciencias Sociais,* I (1956), pp. 61, 43–62. This study is reported in Wagley, *An Introduction to Brazil,* pp. 125–126.

[2] Porter, *The Vertical Mosaic,* pp. 92–93.

[3] Benjamin, *Higher Education,* pp. 60–66, 94–96, 120–123.

[4] S. M. Lipset, *The First New Nation,* p. 195.

belief that such voluntary associations, whether they be the "March of Dimes," social work agencies, or trade unions, should be staffed by men who are paid to do the job. In a sense, therefore, it may be argued that the very emphasis on equalitarianism in America has given rise to the large salaried bureaucracies which permeate voluntary organizations.[1]

In the early days of the Latin American and European universities, they were staffed either by members of well-to-do families or the clergy. Such academics required no financial support from the university.[2] The high prestige of the university in Latin America is to some extent linked to its identification with the elite, with the assumption that professors and graduates, "doctors," are gentlemen.[3] However, such an identity is not dependent on the universities' contribution to society, and is clearly dysfunctional in any society which seeks to develop economically, or to make contributions to the world of science and scholarship. And it may be suggested that the resistance to "modernizing" the curriculum and to "professionalizing" the professoriate stems from the desire to maintain the diffuse elitist character of the role of the intellectual.[4] In contemporary times, when relatively few professors in fact can support themselves from family income, the diffuse elite status of the professor encourages him to use the status to secure wealth or power outside the university. Thus the professoriate as a status, as the equivalent of an aristocratic title, may be converted into high position in other dimensions of stratification. As one recent study of the Latin American university concludes about the behavior of the *catedrático,* the chairholder:

> With his name, title, connections, civil service status and life-long position ensured, he is often tempted to use his chair as a mere rung on the long social climb to power. Once made "catedrático," he no longer has to worry much about teaching and even less about research. Aided and sustained by his university post, he is at last free to launch up on [sic] a successful professional or even political career.
>
> It is expected that a full professor will amass a modest personal fortune in the exercise of his profession as a lawyer, doctor or engineer. . . . [Sometimes] these professional activities are also used as further stepping stones on the road to administrative, political or diplomatic positions. . . .[5]

[1] *Ibid.*

[2] Stokes, "The Drag of the *Pensadores,"* p. 70.

[3] Lambert, "Requirements for Development," p. 64.

[4] Ironically, the powerful leftist student groups in the various Latin American countries constitute a major force resisting university modernization. See John P. Harrison, "The Role of the Intellectual in Fomenting Change: The University," *in* Tepaske and Fisher, eds., *Explosive Forces in Latin America,* pp. 27–42. In Venezuela, they have opposed tightening up examination standards. See Orlando Albornoz, "Academic Freedom and Higher Education in Latin America," *Comparative Education Review,* 10 (June, 1966), pp. 250–256. For a collection of articles dealing with various aspects see David Spencer, ed., *The Latin American Student Movement* (The National Student Association, 1965).

[5] Rudolph P. Atcon, "The Latin American University," *Die Deutsche Universitätszeitung,* 17 (February, 1962), p. 27.

Economic Growth and the Role of the "Deviant"
in Anti-entrepreneurial Cultures

The argument that Latin American values are antithetical to economic development can, of course, be pitted against the fact that a considerable amount of economic growth has occurred in many of these countries. Clearly, in the presence of opportunity, an entrepreneurial elite has emerged. The logic of value analysis would imply that the creation or expansion of roles which are not socially approved in terms of the traditional values should be introduced by social deviants. This hypothesis is basic to much of the literature dealing with the rise of the businessman in different traditional societies.

In his classic analysis of economic development, Joseph Schumpeter pointed out that the key aspect of entrepreneurship, as distinct from being a manager, is the capacity for leadership in innovation, for breaking through the routine and the traditional.[1] From this perspective the analysis of the factors which resulted in the rise of an entrepreneurial group leading to economic growth under capitalism is comparable to the study of the conditions which brought about anticapitalist revolutionary modernizing elites of various countries in recent decades. The approach which emphasizes the theory of deviance assumes that those who introduce change must be deviants, since they reject the traditional elite's ways of doing things.[2] As Hoselitz puts it, "a deviant always engages in behavior which constitutes in a certain sense a breach of the existing order and is contrary to, or at least not positively weighted in the hierarchy of existing social values."[3] In societies in which the values of the dominant culture are "not supportive of entrepreneurial activity, someone who is relatively outside of the social system may have a particular advantage in entering an entrepreneurial activity. The restraints upon entrepreneurial activity imposed by the network [of social relations] would be less effective against such a person. Thus, an immigrant may be outside of many of the networks of the nation and freer to engage in entrepreneurial activity," in other words, freer socially to deviate.[4]

If we assume, in following up such generalizations, that within the Americas the value system of Latin America has discouraged entrepreneurial activity, while that of the English-speaking Protestant world of the United States and Canada has fostered it, then a comparative study of the backgrounds of entrepreneurs in these countries should reveal that those of Latin America are recruited disproportionately from sociological deviants, while those of

---

[1] Joseph Schumpeter, *The Theory of Economic Development* (New York: Oxford University Press, 1961), pp. 74–94.

[2] Bert Hoselitz, "Main Concepts in the Analysis of the Social Implications of Technical Change," in Hoselitz and Moore, eds., *Industrialization and Society,* pp. 22–28.

[3] Hoselitz, *Sociological Aspects,* p. 62; Peter T. Bauer and Basil S. Yamey, *The Economics of Underdeveloped Countries* (Chicago: University of Chicago Press, 1957), pp. 106–112.

[4] Louis Kriesberg, "Entrepreneurs in Latin America and the Role of Cultural and Situational Processes," *International Social Science Journal,* 15 (1963), p. 591.

North America should come largely from groups which possess traits placing them inside the central structures of the society. An examination of the research data bearing on this hypothesis indicates that it is valid.

In many countries of Latin America, members of minority groups, often recent immigrants, have formed a considerable section of the emerging business elite. "In general it appears that immigrants took the lead in establishing modern manufacturing before World War I [in Latin America]."[1] Recent studies in various countries reveal comparable patterns. Frequently, these new entrepreneurs come from groups not known for their entrepreneurial prowess at home, such as the Arabs and the Italians, although Germans and Jews are also among those who are to be found in disproportionate numbers in business leadership. A study of Mexican business leaders found that of 109 major executives, 26 had foreign paternal grandfathers; among the "32 outstanding business leaders in Mexico, 14 reported a foreign paternal grandfather."[2] Analysis of the backgrounds of 286 prestigious entrepreneurs, taken from the Argentine *Who's Who*, indicates that 45.5 per cent were foreign born.[3] However, many of those born in Argentina are "among the first generation born in the country."[4] Classifying the sample by origins, Imaz reports that only 10 per cent came from the traditional upper class, and they, as in many other Latin American countries, are concentrated in industries which processed agricultural products, so that their roles in industry are an extension of their position as a landed class. Among the rest, almost all are of relatively recent foreign origin.[5] Data from a survey of the heads of 46 out of the 113 industrial establishments in Santiago, Chile, which employ more than 100 workers indicate that 76 per cent of them are immigrants or the children of immigrants.[6] An earlier study of the Chilean middle class reports that as of 1940 the overwhelming majority of the 107,273 foreign born in the country were in middle-class, largely self-employed occupations.[7] In Brazil also "the majority of industrial entrepreneurs are immigrants or descendants of relatively recent immigrants."[8] Thus

---

[1] Strassmann, "The Industrialist," p. 164.

[2] Raymond Vernon, *The Dilemma of Mexico's Development* (Cambridge: Harvard University Press, 1963), p. 156.

[3] Imaz, *Los que mandan*, p. 136.

[4] *Ibid.;* see also Germani, "Strategy of Fostering Social Mobility," pp. 223–226; and Zalduendo, *El empresario industrial*, p. 10. The census of 1895 reported that 84 per cent of the 18,000 business establishments were owned by foreign-born individuals. Cochran and Reina, *Entrepreneurship in Argentine Culture*, p. 8.

[5] Imaz, *Los que mandan*, pp. 138–139.

[6] Briones, *El empresario industrial*, p. 10.

[7] Julio Vega, "La clase media en Chile," in *Materiales para el estudio de la clase media en la América Latina* (Washington, D.C.: Pan American Union, 1950), pp. 81–82, as cited in Pike, *Chile and the United States*, p. 279.

[8] Benjamin Higgins, "Requirements for Rapid Economic Development in Latin America: The View of an Economist," *in* de Vries and Echavarría, eds., *Social Aspects of Economic Development*, p. 169.

in São Paulo, 521 enterprises out of 714 were owned by men in these categories.[1] In the other economically developed states, Rio Grande do Sul and Santa Catarina, "almost 80 per cent of the industrial activities . . . were developed by people of European immigrant extraction."[2]

Similar patterns may be found in the less-developed and more traditional countries. Thus, in a recent study of Peru, François Bourricaud traces in detail the continued control of members of the ancient oligarchy over much of the economic life of the country, their maintenance in much of agriculture and traditional business and banking of the *patrón* system, and family and clan control. However, in the new and risky enterprises, those which have produced the new rich of the country, one finds many recent immigrants.[3] In Colombia, a country like Peru with relatively little immigration, a study of the members of the National Association of Industrialists reports "that in 1962, 41 per cent of a sample of business leaders in Bogotá were immigrants from other countries."[4] In Panama, in 1940 before the decree "nationalizing" commerce, "nearly 45 per cent of the men actively engaged in commerce or manufacturing were foreigners."[5]

The various studies of the backgrounds of the Latin American entrepreneurial elite indicate that on the whole they are a well-educated group; the majority of them in most countries are university graduates. And a study of the origins of students at the University of São Paulo suggests that much of the separation in career orientations between those of native background and others takes place while in school. Thus, the proportion of students of non-Brazilian background is higher among the students than in the population of the city; only 22 per cent are of purely Brazilian descent. Even more significant is the fact that students with a higher proportion of foreign-born ancestors tend to enroll in the "modern" faculties, such as economics, engineering, pharmacy, and the like. Those with preponderantly Brazilian family backgrounds are more likely to be found in the more traditional high-prestige schools such as law and medicine. And the author of this study comments:

> The children of foreign-born parents . . . are more inclined to take advantage

---

[1] Emilio Willems, "Immigrants and Their Assimilation in Brazil," *in* T. Lynn Smith and Alexander Marchant, eds., *Brazil, Portrait of Half a Continent* (New York: Dryden Press, 1951), p. 217. These apparently are largely from Italian, German, Jewish, and Lebanese backgrounds. See also Pereira, "Middle Class and Middle Management," p. 316; Richard Morse, "São Paulo in the Twentieth Century: Social and Economic Aspects," *Inter-American Economic Affairs,* 8 (Summer, 1954), pp. 21–23, 44; George White, "Brazil: Trends in Industrial Development," *in* Kuznets, Moore, and Spengler, eds., *Economic Growth,* pp. 57, 60–62.

[2] Wagley, *An Introduction to Brazil,* p. 87.

[3] François Bourricaud, *Le Pérou: Une oligarchie face aux problèmes de la mobilisation* (unpublished manuscript, 1965), chap. I, pp. 29–31.

[4] Aarón Lipman, "Social Backgrounds of the Bogotá Entrepreneur," *Journal of Inter-American Studies,* 7 (1965), p. 231.

[5] Biesanz, "The Economy of Panama," p. 9.

of the new opportunities in occupations which have emerged from the economic development of the city of São Paulo. One should consider the fact that in Brazil, the schools of Law and Medicine convey special social prestige to their students. It is easier for a not completely assimilated adolescent of foreign descent to ignore that prestige than for a "pure" Brazilian.[1]

Similarly, at the University of Chile, the School of Physics suffers from low prestige, "which diminishes the attractiveness of the field. . . ." A recent study of Chilean university students reports:

> Who, then are the students in this school? Why have they rejected the natural and well-formed paths of career choice? The most obvious are those who are immigrants or sons of immigrants—primarily German refugees and Italian emigrés. . . . A second and frequently overlapping group is composed of students who are critical of the traditional alternatives.[2]

Immigrant and minority groups have shown comparable abilities to take advantage of, or to create, opportunities in other parts of the underdeveloped world. Thus in sub-Saharan Africa, Arabs, Indians, and to a lesser extent Chinese form a large part of the commercial world. In southeast Asian countries, Chinese constitute almost the entire business community; Indians were important in Burmese economic life before they were expelled. It should be noted that it is not only immigrants who have been disproportionately successful. Minority religious groups such as Christians have entered the universities in relatively large numbers in various Asian states, even where they are a tiny minority in the entire population. In Indonesia, for example, over 15 per cent of the new students entering Gadjah Mada University in 1959–1960 were Christians, although few people adhere to Christianity. In general in southeast Asia, there is "a relatively high proportion of youth[s] from minorities enrolled in universities and [they have a] . . . reputation as better academic achievers than youth[s] from majority elites. Such minorities . . . include the Karens and the Indians in Burma, the Chinese in Thailand, the 'burghers' in Ceylon, the Bataks and Chinese in Indonesia, and other Christians in all these countries."[3]

The creative role of the deviant, or the outsider, has in part been conceptualized by the term "marginal men," those who for various reasons are partially outside the culture in which they are living, are less socially integrated in the structures which maintain conformity, and are therefore not as committed to the established values of the larger order. Hence they are

---

[1] Bertram Hutchinson, "A origem sócio-econômica dos estudantes universitários," in Hutchinson, ed., *Mobilidade e Trabalho* (Rio de Janeiro: Centro Brasileiro de Pesquisas Educacionais, Ministério de Educação e Cultura, 1960), p. 145.

[2] Myron Glazer, *The Professional and Political Attitudes of Chilean University Students* (Ph.D. thesis, Princeton University, 1965), pp. 78–79.

[3] Joseph Fischer, "The Student Population of a Southeast Asian University: An Indonesian Example," *International Journal of Comparative Sociology*, 2 (1961), pp. 225, 230.

more likely to be receptive to possibilities for change.[1] An analysis of those who successfully took advantage of the opportunity to shift the use of land in the vicinity of São Paulo from subsistence agriculture to lucrative commercial crops (mainly the growth of eucalyptus for firewood) points up this process. Over 90 per cent of those who became small-scale, relatively well-to-do entrepreneurs were recent settlers in the area, "immigrants or children of immigrants . . . or members of a small but flourishing Protestant sect (the *Evangelistas*) . . ."

> Almost all of the recent settlers were as poor as the *caboclos* [the native, lowest-status rural dwellers] when they arrived. They managed to see new alternatives when they arose, to buy up small plots of land and gradually increase their holdings, mostly at the expense of the *caboclos*. . . . It is worth testing . . . the proposition that *participation in newly valued activities among members of low economic and prestige classes varies inversely with length of residence in a locality.* Old settlers at depressed levels have inherited habits of belief, a morality and expectation of role rights and obligations associated with their statuses . . . that they are only slowly adaptable in the presences [sic] of altered opportunities. One of the most striking occurrences in the changing situation within the *municipio* under consideration is the fact that several *caboclos* sold or were seeking to sell their properties of [sic] prospective entrepreneurs, and then turned around and hired their labor out for wages.[2]

The traits which are often associated with economic innovation lead their bearers to be frowned upon or even hated by those who adhere to the conventional traditions of the society, or who resent the success of others. Thus in Brazil, Gilberto Freyre reports that many of non-Portuguese descent have:

> . . . shown a lack of finer moral scruples which has given many of them the reputation of being morally or ethically inferior. . . . [Their actions which lead to success in politics and business] are given as an example of the fact that the sons of "immigrants" are morally inferior to the sons of old Brazilian families as political leaders, businessmen, and industrial pioneers. Of course, sons of immigrants who follow such careers are freer than the members of old and well-known families from certain moral controls that act upon men deeply rooted in their towns or countries or regions.[3]

It is indicative of the extent to which Latin Americans identify entrepreneurial or commercial abilities as alien to their tradition and values that ethnic myths are invented to explain the success of those of native background who do succeed. Thus both in Colombia, where the citizens of

---

[1] See Robert Park, *Race and Culture* (Glencoe: Free Press, 1950), pp. 345–392; Everett Stonequist, *The Marginal Man* (New York: Russell and Russell, 1961).

[2] Siegel, "Social Structure and Economic Change in Brazil," pp. 399–400 (emphases in the original).

[3] Freyre, *New World in the Tropics,* p. 161.

Antioquia have evidenced entrepreneurial abilities far exceeding those of other sections of the country, and in Mexico, where residents of Monterrey have shown comparable skills, the story is widely believed that both groups are descended from *maranos*, secretly practicing Jews who publically changed their religion after 1492.[1] These stories have been disproven by historical research, but the fact that many accept them as gospel tells much about attitudes toward entrepreneurship. The same factors may be involved in Gilberto Freyre's report, citing various writers, that the major center of business enterprise in Brazil, São Paulo, is "probably the nucleus of the Brazilian population with the largest strain of Semitic blood."[2]

The logic of the analysis suggested here, however, does not agree with the thesis that innovating entrepreneurs in developing societies must be recruited disproportionately from the ranks of social deviants, as some have interpreted data such as these. Rather it points with Weber to the fact that many minority groups have not shown such propensities. Clearly the Catholic minorities in England, or other Protestant countries, were much less likely than the general population to engage in entrepreneurial activity. In his analysis of the divergent consequences for economic behavior of Protestantism and Catholicism, Max Weber pointed to the greater business accomplishments of the Protestant *majority* as compared to the Catholic *minority* in Germany.[3] The key issue, as Weber has indicated, is the value system of the various groups involved. Latin America and some other less-developed, traditional societies are so vulnerable to economic cultural deviants because the predominant values of the host culture are in large measure antithetical to rational entrepreneurial orientations. Where national values support economic development, the Weberian emphasis on value would suggest that the innovating business elite would be drawn not from deviants but rather from the in group, from persons with socially privileged backgrounds.

An examination of the social characteristics of North American business leaders in both Canada and the United States bears out these assumptions. Compared to most other nations in the world, the United States and English-speaking Canada have been among the most hospitable cultures to economic development. The Protestant ethic as fostered by denominations spawned by Calvinist and Arminian origins strongly influenced all classes in these societies, the United States somewhat more than Canada. And a study of

---

[1] Strassmann, "The Industrialist," p. 166.

[2] Gilberto Freyre, *The Masters and the Slaves. A Study in the Development of Brazilian Civilization* (New York: Alfred A. Knopf, 1963), p. 36. Freyre does not evaluate this thesis; rather as with many other tales concerning Jewish traits and abilities, he seems to be gullibly accepting. "The farmers with a deep love for the land and a thorough knowledge of agriculture were sometimes abused or exploited in Brazil by those of their fellow countrymen whose passion was for commercial adventure and urban life—most of them probably Jews." *New World in the Tropics*, p. 50.

[3] Max Weber, *Protestant Ethic and Spirit of Capitalism*, pp. 38–46.

the business leaders of the United States in 1870, the period of its takeoff
into industrial development, indicates that 86 per cent of them came from
colonial families settled in the country before 1777. Only 10 per cent
were foreign born or the children of foreign born.[1] Over 98 per cent of the
post-Civil War business elite were Protestants. Although the proportions of
those of non-Anglo-Saxon, non-Protestant, and foreign-born parentage have
increased over the years, they have always remained considerably lower
than their proportions in the population as a whole.[2] Canadian data are
available only for the post-World War II period, but it should be noted that
Canada's emergence as a major industrial society largely dates from the war.
Previously its economy somewhat resembled that of Argentina, being largely dependent on agricultural exports. The Canadian case is extremely interesting since the country is composed of two separate cultures—English
Protestant and Latin Catholic. And a comprehensive report on the Canadian elite shows a clear-cut picture: where cultural values congruent with
entrepreneurship are ascendant, the business elite will be recruited largely
from the dominant culture group, not from minorities. Thus those of Anglo-
Saxon Protestant background are overrepresented, while those of Latin
Catholic, and minority origins are underrepresented.

> An examination of the social origins of the economic elite shows that econom-
> ic power belongs almost exclusively to those of British origin, even though this
> ethnic group made up less than half of the population in 1951. The fact that eco-
> nomic development in Canada has been in the hands of British Canadians has long
> been recognized by historians. Of the 760 people in the economic elite, only 51
> (6.7 per cent) could be classified as French Canadians although the French made
> up about one-third of the population in 1951. . . . There were no more than a
> handful who . . . could be classified as top-ranking industrialists in their own
> province.
> Ethnic groups of neither British nor French origin, which made up about one-
> fifth of the general population, were hardly represented at all. There were six
> Jews (.78 per cent of the sample as opposed to 1.4 per cent of the general popu-
> lation). . . . [O]nly 78 (about 10 per cent) were Catholic . . . [while] 43 per cent
> of the population in 1951 was Catholic.[3]

In seeking to account for the low representation of French Canadians in
the economic elite, even within Quebec, John Porter points out that the
evidence does not fit the assumption that it is largely a result of the greater
power of the British Canadians. For French Canadians do quite well in
other power structures, e.g., politics, the intellectual world, and religion.

---

[1] Suzanne Keller, *The Social Origins and Career Lines of Three Generations of American Business Leaders* (Ph.D. Dissertation, Columbia University, 1953), pp. 37–41.
[2] See S. M. Lipset and Reinhard Bendix, *Social Mobility in Industrial Society* (Berkeley: University of California Press, 1959), pp. 137–138.
[3] Porter, *The Vertical Mosaic,* pp. 286–289.

French weakness in industry seems related to elements in their culture comparable to those in much of Latin America.

The varying origins of the business elites of the American nations clearly indicate that "out" groups, such as ethnic-religious minorities, are given the opportunity to innovate economically when the values of the dominant culture are antithetical to such activities. Thus, the comparative evidence from the various nations of the Americas sustains the generalization that cultural values are among the major factors which affect the potentiality for economic development.

Although I have focused on the direct effects of value orientations on the entrepreneurial behavior of certain groups, it should be clear that any given individual or group supports the values of their effective social environment. Although national values may discourage entrepreneurial activities, ethnic or religious subgroups, or links to foreign cultures may encourage them for those involved. One explanation of the comparative success of members of some minority groups in Latin America, such as the Anglo-Argentines, is that they continue to respect their ancestral national culture more than that of their host society. The fact that many ethnic minorities in some Latin American nations continue to send their children to schools conducted in their ancestral language and to speak it at home attests to their lack of acceptance of national culture and values.

The key question basically is whether one is involved in a network of social relations which sustain or negate a particular activity. Viscount Mauá, Brazil's great nineteenth-century economic innovator, though a native Brazilian, was adopted while in his early teens by an English merchant in Rio de Janeiro; his biography clearly indicates that he became "alien" within his native culture, that English became his "native" language, the one in which he thought and wrote his private thoughts.[1] Conversely, as we have seen, many successful entrepreneurs are drawn away from total commitment to their business life by an involvement in social networks and reference groups which supply more prestige than their vocation. One of Argentina's most successful entrepreneurs, who was an immigrant, built up a complex network of industrial companies, took the time to study at the university, accepted an appointment as an associate professor of Economics and Industrial Organization at the University of Buenos Aires, when he was 50 years of age, sought to secure a regular chair three years later, and bought a 6,600-acre *estancia,* on which he spent much time.[2] To facilitate the emergence of a given new role in a society, it is necessary to help create

---

[1] Anyda Marchant, *Viscount Mauá and the Empire of Brazil* (Berkeley: University of California Press, 1965), pp. 81, 83, 208–209, 241.

[2] Cochran and Reina, *Entrepreneurship in Argentine Culture,* pp. 147–151. It is worth noting that his two sons studied for their Ph.D.'s abroad, and that both are professors, one in economics and the other in sociology.

social recognition for it within meaningful subgroups. The leaders of Meiji Japan have provided an example of the way in which one nation did this. To raise the prestige of the business class,

> . . . social distinctions [were] granted to the presidents and main shareholders of the new companies. The presidents were given the privilege of the sword and family name. They were appointed by the government, as officials were. A president could walk directly into the room of a government official while common people had to wait and squat outside the building. Many other minor privileges were granted.[1]

It is important to recognize that the introduction of new activities by those linked to foreign cultures or minority religions is not simply one of the various ways to modernize a society. Innovations which are associated with socially marginal groups are extremely vulnerable to political attack from those who would maintain traditional values. Consequently efforts at economic modernization, changes in the educational system, or social customs which are introduced by outsiders may have much less effect in modifying the central value system than when they are fostered by individuals who are members of the core group, as occurred in Meiji Japan.

Although much of the discussion thus far has involved the presentation of evidence concerning *the* Latin American value system, it is obvious that there is considerable variation *among* Latin American nations, as there is among the English-speaking countries. Thus, many of the distinctions which have been drawn between Argentina and Uruguay on the one hand and Brazil on the other refer to the greater equalitarianism and universalism in the former two. Or the earlier and greater degree of working-class consciousness in Chile (indicated by the strength of Marxist parties) as contrasted with Uruguay and Argentina may be a consequence of the greater elitism, ascription, and particularism of Chile, which was a major center of population concentration under colonial rule, while the values of the latter two were modified by their later formation as immigrant cultures.

Uruguay (and to a somewhat lesser extent Argentina) differs from the rest of Latin America in being relatively committed to a historically rooted equalitarian ideology. This value orientation stems from the effects of widespread immigration, which helped provide a mass urban base for reformist political movements. As Gino Germani indicates, immigration "played a great part in the destruction of the traditional pattern of social stratification."[2]

The emphasis on equalitarianism in both Argentina and Uruguay is perhaps best reflected in the extension of their educational systems, which

---

[1] Johannes Hirschmeier, *The Origins of Entrepreneurship in Meiji Japan* (Cambridge: Harvard University Press, 1964), p. 35.

[2] Germani, "Strategy of Fostering Social Mobility," p. 226. Argentinian cultural traits are discussed in Fillol.

have long led all other Latin American nations in the proportions attending school, from primary to university. This commitment to education may
have played a major role in facilitating economic growth during the late
nineteenth century and the first three decades of the twentieth. However,
when equalitarianism is associated with particularistic and ascriptive orientations, it seemingly serves to strengthen the concern with security mentioned
earlier, and early successful pressures (more in Uruguay than Argentina)
for welfare-state measures. Both countries, today, face a major economic
crisis, brought about in large measure because governments responsive to
popular pressures have dedicated a large share of national revenues to welfare.

Efforts to do more than present loose illustrations of this type must await
systematic comparative work on all the Latin American republics, as sociologists at the Di Tella Institute in Buenos Aires are now doing.[1] They are
attempting to codify systematically a large variety of qualitative and quantitative materials, covering over a century, to test out various hypotheses
concerning the sources of differentiation within Latin America.

Changes in Value Orientations

The evidence presented thus far would seem to indicate that, regardless of
the causal pattern one prefers to credit for Latin American values, they are,
as described, antithetic to the basic logic of a large-scale industrial system.[2]
However, as noted earlier, it should be recognized that these descriptions
are all made in a relative or comparative context, that Latin American economic behavior is evaluated either in comparison with that in the United
States, or other developed nations, or against some ideal model of entrepreneurship. The value system of much of Latin America, like Quebec, has,
in fact, been changing in the direction of a more achievement-oriented,
universalistic, and equalitarian value system, and its industrial development
both reflects and determines such changes. Many Latin American entrepreneurs are hiring nonfamily members as executives, and in various ways have
acted contrary to the supposed norms. To some extent this may reflect the

---

[1] See Torcuato S. Di Tella, Oscar Cornblit, and M. Ezequiel Gallo, "Outline of the Project: A
Model of Social Change in Latin America," *Documentos de Trabajo* (Buenos Aires: Instituto Torcuato Di Tella, Centro de Sociología Comparada, n.d.).

[2] Alexander Gerschenkron has shown how entrepreneurial activities in nineteenth-century Russia
"were at variance with the dominant system of values, which remained determined by the traditional
agrarian pattern. . . . The nobility and the gentry had nothing but contempt for any entrepreneurial
activity except its own. . . . Divorced from the peasantry, the entrepreneurs remained despised by
the intelligentsia." He argues, however, that such cultural values may "indeed delay the beginning of
rapid industrialization," but they cannot stop it. Their effect, rather, is to hold back the pressures
for industrialization so that they finally burst out in periods of rapid growth. However, he also concludes that in Russia, "The delayed industrial revolution was responsible for a political revolution,"
i.e., the Bolshevik seizure of power. *Economic Backwardness in Historical Perspective* (Cambridge:
Harvard University Press, 1962), pp. 28, 59–62.

fact that a large segment of the creative and successful entrepreneurs are members of minority ethnic groups. More important perhaps is the fact that bureaucratic corporate enterprise has an inherent logic of its own; those who build such organizations, or rise within them in once-traditional societies, are either deviants who have the necessary new orientations, or men who develop them. Paternalistic feudal attitudes toward workers are characteristically more common in the less-developed Latin American countries than in the more industrialized ones, a finding which parallels the situation within Spain.[1] There, the more developed an area, the more "modern" the attitudes of its entrepreneurs.

Such developments have been analyzed by Fernando Cardoso in his study of the industrial entrepreneur in Brazil. The shift from the values of the *patrón* to those of the modern professional entrepreneur occurred with the emergence of large-scale industries, such as automobile manufacturing or ship building. He points out that the rapidity of the adjustments to modern orientations depends on the attitudes of the entrepreneurs involved. And the same individuals and companies often react in what appear to be contradictory ways. These dual orientations, modern and traditional, reflect in part the mixed character of the Brazilian economy, which may still be characterized as incipient industrial capitalism.[2] The heterogeneity of entrepreneurial environments and orientations has, as yet, prevented the emergence of a consistent ideology to which most adhere.[3] Hence, Cardoso points to changes in values with growing industrialization, although he does not challenge the general description of Latin American economic behavior, as still applying to much of the Brazilian present.

Values clearly change as societies become economically more developed.[4] Many of the generalizations made about Latin American or other relatively underdeveloped societies, in contrast to the United States or northern Europe, were made, and are still being made, about such countries as Spain, France, or Italy, when they are compared with more economically developed countries.

Only a short time ago, economic "stagnation" in these European Latin countries was interpreted as the consequence of values incongruent with enterprising behavior. That breakthroughs in development occur for a variety of reasons in different countries is obvious. Values dysfunctional to

---

[1] Amando do Miguel and Juan J. Linz, "Movilidad social del empresario español," *Revista de Fomento Social,* 75–76 (July–December, 1964).

[2] Fernando H. Cardoso, *Empresário industrial e desenvolvimento econômico no Brasil,* p. 157 and *passim.*

[3] A very similar point is made about the heterogeneity of outlook among the Argentinian entrepreneurs by Imaz.

[4] For a statement of the ways in which economic development may change values, see Albert O. Hirschman, "Obstacles to Development: A Classification and a Quasi-Vanishing Act," *Economic Development and Cultural Change,* 13 (1965), pp. 385–393.

economic growth may inhibit but not prevent growth, if other factors are favorable. As the history of various nations has suggested, processes or conflicts about values may foster the emergence of groups motivated to achieve economically. But conclusions such as these do not offer any prospect for change, other than to suggest the need for detailed careful study of the relevant factors suggested by social science theory in each country, or to simply add to the amount of investment capital available in a given country. I would like, therefore, to turn to a discussion of the various ways which seem open to those who deliberately seek to change values so as to foster the emergence of entrepreneurial elites.

The experience of Japan, the one non-Western nation which has successfully industrialized, suggests that the key question may not be the creation of new values so much as the way in which cultural ideals supporting tradition can give rise to those supporting modernity, that the shift from tradition to modernity need not involve a total rejection of a nation's basic values.[1]

In discussing this problem, Reinhard Bendix notes that in Weber's *The Protestant Ethic and the Spirit of Capitalism,* a study of the resolution of the contradiction between the coexisting traditional and modern within a developing society, Western Europe, the author observes that reformers continued to be concerned with their salvation and accepted the traditional, Christian devaluation of wordly pursuits. The emergence of the "spirit of capitalism" represented a direct outgrowth of this early antimaterialistic tradition of Christianity, a growth which occurred without replacing this tradition. Linking Weber's approach to the various analyses of the preconditions for Japanese development, Bendix points out that the Samurai under the Tokugawa regime became a demilitarized aristocracy loyal to the traditional Samurai ethic of militancy, even though the Tokugawa regime pursued a public policy of disciplined pacification, of the avoidance of conflict or competitive struggles to change a status or power relationship among the feudal lords. After the Meiji Restoration of 1868, the virtues of achievement were socially accepted. The traditional Samurai ethic applied to a competitive world now meant that any self-respecting Samurai was obliged to show his ability and desire to win. Thus in nineteenth-century Japan, as in Reformation Europe, "modern" economic orientations emerged through the application of traditional values and sources of individual motivation to new structural conditions, rather than the supplanting of one set of values by another. Since Japan and Western Europe are the only two noncommunist cultural areas which have developed successfully on their own, the finding

---

[1] For example, see Robert Bellah, *Tokugawa Religion* (Glencoe: The Free Press, 1957); James C. Abegglen, *The Japanese Factory* (Glencoe: The Free Press, 1958); Marion J. Levy, Jr., "Contrasting Factors in the Modernization of China and Japan," *in* Kuznets, Moore, and Spengler, eds., *Economic Growth,* pp. 496–536; and Hirschmeier, *Origins of Entrepreneurship.*

that achievement values seemingly emerged out of redefinition of traditional values, rather than the adoption of new ones, has obvious implications for those contemporary underdeveloped cultures which seek to industrialize.[1]

In seeking for culturally accepted orientations which will lead a section of the elite to "split off" and endorse "modern" values, Talcott Parsons suggests that nationalism, concern for the international status of one's society, can motivate those who are most oriented to foreign opinion to press for new attitudes toward industrialization. And within the existing elites such people are most likely to be found among intellectuals, especially "those who have had direct contacts with the West, particularly through education abroad or under Western auspices at home."[2] In the name of fostering the national welfare, major changes may be introduced, which would be more strongly resisted if they were perceived as serving the interests of a subgroup within the society, such as the businessmen. In Uruguay, governmental actions which are justified by a nonrevolutionary national development ideology are seen by the workers as another rationalization of the ruling class to consolidate its power.[3]

If the source of new development concerns is to be nationalism rather than self-interest, then the means are more likely to be perceived in the political rather than in an autonomous economic arena.[4] And within the political arena, it is necessary to dissociate the policies advocated from any identification with possible foreign control. In Latin America today, support of "socialism" as opposed to "capitalism" becomes a way in which intellectuals may advocate industrialization without being accused of seeking to foster foreign "materialistic" values which are destructive of the spiritual values of the society.[5]

A "socialist" ideology of economic development may be conceived of as a functional alternative to the Meiji elite's use of loyalty to the Emperor, Shinto, and the nation, when seeking to industrialize Japan. "To an important degree, socialism and communism are strong because they are symbolically associated with the ideology of independence, rapid economic development, social modernization, and ultimate equality. Capitalism is perceived as being linked to foreign influences, traditionalism, and slow growth."[6]

---

[1] See Reinhard Bendix, "Cross-Cultural Mobility and Development," in Neil Smelser and S. M. Lipset, eds., Social Structure and Social Mobility in Economic Development (Chicago: Aldine Publishing Company, 1966), pp. 262–279. See also Bert Hoselitz, Sociological Aspects, pp. 8–82; and Hirschmeier, Origins of Entrepreneurship, pp. 44–68.

[2] Talcott Parsons, Structure and Process in Modern Society (New York: The Free Press, 1960), pp. 116–129.

[3] Solari, Estudios sobre la sociedad uruguaya, p. 172.

[4] See also Gustavo Lagos, International Stratification and Underdeveloped Countries (Chapel Hill: University of North Carolina Press, 1963), pp. 3–30, 138–160.

[5] Ellison, "The Writer," pp. 96–100.

[6] S. M. Lipset, "Political Cleavages in 'Developed' and 'Emerging' Polities," in Erik Allardt and

The problem which can best be met by a revolutionary nationalist ideology justifying the rejection of the past has been well put by Gerschenkron:

> In a backward country the great and sudden industrialization effort calls for a New Deal in emotions. Those carrying out the great transformation as well as those on whom it imposes burdens must feel, in the words of Matthew Arnold, that
>
> > . . . Clearing a stage
> > Scattering the past about
> > Comes the new age.
>
> Capitalist industrialization under the auspices of socialist ideologies may be, after all, less surprising a phenomenon than would appear at first sight.[1]

In formulating such ideologies, Latin America is at a disadvantage compared with the new nations of Asia and Africa. Most of the latter have recently attained independence under the leadership of mass parties whose revolutionary ideology subsumes the values of equalitarianism, achievement, universalism, and collectivity orientation. Traditional practices may be attacked as antithetical to the national interest and self-image. In much of Latin America, however, many traditional values and practices are regarded as proper parts of the national identity. Supporters of these traditional practices cannot be challenged as being antinationalist. Conversely the initial steps toward attaining a national economic system in the United States were facilitated by its being "in many senses an underdeveloped country when it was transformed into a new nation-state by a revolution led by a new elite." The new United States faced the need to break down the particularistic loyalties and values of the "indigenous" aristocracy of each little colony. And under the aegis of the ideology proclaimed in the Declaration of Independence, the revolutionary elite modified "the social institutions inherited from the British to the needs of a continental political economy."[2] Latin America, however, did not use its revolutionary struggle for independence to legitimate major social and economic changes; rather, independence often confirmed the control of the traditional landed class in power. Hence, as segments of the elite have awoken in recent decades to the need for such changes, they find it difficult to create the political institutions and national consensus needed to foster new values.

Perhaps Mexico is the best example of a systematic effort at value change in Latin America. The Mexican Revolution transformed the image and legitimate political emphases of the nation. It sought to destroy the sense of

---

Yrjo Littunen, eds., *Cleavages, Ideologies and Party Systems* (Helsinki: The Westermarck Society, 1964), p. 44.

[1] Gerschenkron, *Economic Backwardness,* p. 25.

[2] Robert Lamb, "Political Elites and the Process of Economic Development," *in* Bert Hoselitz, ed., *The Progress of Underdeveloped Areas* (Chicago: University of Chicago Press, 1952), pp. 30, 38.

superiority felt by those of pure Spanish descent by stressing the concept of *mexicanidad,* and by a glorification of its Indian past.[1] There are almost no monuments to Spaniards from Cortés to independence in 1814. Emphasis on white racial descent is socially illegitimate. The values of the Mexican Revolution are similar to those of the other Western revolutions—the American, French, and Russian. Though Mexico clearly retains major elements of the traditional Latin American system, it is the one country which has identified its national ethos with that of equality and an open society. And with the sense of a collective revolutionary commitment to growth and egalitarianism, one finds that business activities, which are sanctioned by government approval, are presented as ways of fulfilling national objectives. A detailed account of the way in which the revolution affected value change concludes:

> [T]he Revolution fostered a shift from ascription to achievement as the basis for distributing income, and from particularistic to universalistic standards as the basis for distributing political and economically-relevant tasks among performers. . . .
>
> Finally, it is evident that the nationalistic character of the Revolutionary movement together with the broad area of congruence between politically significant new class interests and social goals has assisted the shift from self-orientation to collectivity orientation in the performance by the new elite of its social role.[2]

Many of the conclusions about the impact of the revolution on Mexican society which have been drawn from institutional and anthropological research have recently been reiterated in an opinion survey focusing on the effect of the revolution on political attitudes and behavior. The authors compared Mexican responses on a number of items to those of Italians, choosing the latter nation as another Latin, Catholic, semideveloped state which does not have a commitment to revolutionary ideals. Among their findings are:

---

[1] As one student of Mexican politics comments: "[T]he distinctive feature of a revolution is that it establishes new goals for the society; it reorganizes society, but it must first reorganize the values which that society accepts; a successful revolution means the acceptance as 'good' of things which were not regarded as good before, the rejection as 'bad' of things previously acceptable or commendable. . . . Prior to the [Mexican] revolution, the Indian was semiofficially regarded as an inferior being, to be kept out of sight as much as possible, being prohibited by Porfirio Díaz's police from entering the Alameda, the public park in the center of Mexico City, for example. After the revolution, Mexico's Indian heritage became a matter of national pride, to be stressed in her art and her history, to be studied at length in her universities." From Martin Needler, "Putting Latin American Politics in Perspective," *in* John D. Martz, ed., *The Dynamics of Change in Latin American Politics* (Englewood Cliffs, N.J.: Prentice-Hall, 1965), p. 25.

[2] William P. Glade, Jr., "Revolution and Economic Development: A Mexican Reprise," *in* Glade and Charles W. Anderson, *The Political Economy of Mexico. Two Studies* (Madison: University of Wisconsin Press, 1963), pp. 50–52; for a detailed account of the way in which the revolution affected changes in values see pp. 33–36, 39–43, 44–45, and *passim.*

In Mexico, 30 per cent of the respondents express pride in some political aspect of their nation—ten times the proportion of respondents in Italy, where only 3 per cent expressed such pride. A large proportion in Mexico also express pride in its economic system—in particular, they talk of economic potential and growth. In contrast, few Italians express pride either in the political aspects of their nation or in the economic system. . . .

There is some evidence . . . that the continuing impact of the Revolution explains part of the attachment to their political system that Mexican respondents manifest. Respondents in Mexico were asked if they could name some of the ideals and goals of the Mexican Revolution. Thirty-five per cent could name none, while the remaining 65 per cent listed democracy, political liberty and equality, economic welfare, agrarian reform, social equality and national freedom. . . . Those respondents who mentioned goals of the Revolution were then asked if they thought those goals had been realized, had been forgotten, or were still actively being sought. Twenty-five per cent of the 614 respondents in this category think the goals have been realized, 61 per cent think that they are still being sought, and only 14 per cent think they have been forgotten.[1]

The Mexican Revolution, of course, did not involve simply a symbolic transfer of power, as has occurred in a number of other Latin American countries. Rather it is the one major Latin American revolution in which genuine land reform has occurred. The old dominant class of large landowners has been eliminated. "The large landholders disappeared at the pinnacle of the social order, together with their luxury consumption, no-work value system and the belief in the innate inequality of social segments."[2] The rapid economic growth rate of Mexico in recent decades has been credited by many to the consequences of this revolution in changing the value system, in making possible the rise of a middle class that is self-assured about its own role. It "is fairly abstemious and frugal; it is devoted to modernization and education and recognizes economic achievement as a worthwhile end." Conversely, its neighbor, Guatemala, provides a case for "good comparative control" with a nation of similar social structure and history, but which has not changed its basic agricultural system and consequent class structure and value system, and shows little economic progress; the term retrogression would be more apt.[3]

The positive example of Mexico and the negative one of Guatemala and

---

[1] Sidney Verba and Gabriel A. Almond, "National Revolutions and Political Commitment," *in* Harry Eckstein, ed., *Internal War* (New York: The Free Press, 1964), pp. 221–222, 229.

[2] Manning Nash, "Social Prerequisites to Economic Growth in Latin America and Southeast Asia," *Economic Development and Cultural Change,* 12 (1964), p. 230; Pablo González Casanova, *La democracia en México* (Mexico, D.F.: Ediciones ERA, 1965), p. 41; Clarence Senior, *Land Reform and Democracy* (Gainesville: University of Florida Press, 1958).

[3] Nash, "Social Prerequisites," pp. 231, 232–233. See also Frank Brandenburg, "A Contribution to the Theory of Entrepreneurship and Economic Development: The Case of Mexico," *Inter-American Economic Affairs,* 16 (Winter, 1962), pp. 3–23.

many other countries as well suggest that those concerned with Latin American economic development and social modernization might best devote themselves to an analysis of the conditions for revolutionary transformation of class relationships, particularly at the current stage of development in the rural areas. Presumably the quickest way to initiate major changes in values is through social revolutions which remove those dominant strata which seek to maintain their position and traditional values. A recent study of sociological changes in Mexico concludes that in the new middle class, "there is evidence that the Revolution, by reducing the level of affluence and power of *cacique* families and by redistributing hacienda lands, has had a considerable psychological impact on the population in the direction of strengthening attitudes of independence and initiative and, conversely, reducing those of submissiveness."[1]

Analyses of the ways in which revolutions have fostered value change have pointed to how new regimes have sought to encourage economic development by changing the content of their education systems, not only in terms of more vocational education, but also through introducing achievement themes. In Mexico, through "the ideological values in Mexican socialism, achievement motivation was accorded a key position. . . ."

> The process of inculcating achievement values in 1939 through textbooks took at least two forms. First, the texts gave universalistic and achievement values to the worker movement. All workers were equal; their individual progress and status within the movement depended on their own aggressiveness and accomplishment on the job. This value orientation served to break down the traditional emphasis placed on social immobility and status achievement by birth and blood, both as-criptive-based values. Secondly, a high value was placed on the very activity of hard effective work, where men got their trousers dirty and their hands callused. Work was a noble and honorable endeavor in life. These achievement values were to be absorbed by the children who read how the son idolized his hard-working father. Later, in 1959 . . . in the field of education, the central idea presented to the child was the need to study, to excel, and to improve one's intellectual self. Related to the progress of education and to achievement was the stress placed upon developing personal discipline and a sense of responsibility.[2]

The educational system of Communist China has similarly exerted strong pressure on very young children for individual competitive achievement.[3] The teaching materials used in Chinese kindergartens in stories, songs, and games "reveal a highly sophisticated program of training conducive to

[1] Glade, "Revolution and Economic Development," p. 43.

[2] Walter Raymond Duncan, *Education and Ideology: An Approach to Mexican Political Development with Special Emphasis on Urban Primary Education* (Unpublished Ph.D. thesis, Fletcher School of Law and Diplomacy, 1964), pp. 167, 204–205.

[3] John Wilson Lewis, "Party Cadres in Communist China," *in* James S. Coleman, ed., *Education and Political Development,* p. 425; see also Richard H. Solomon, "Educational Themes in China's Changing Culture," *The China Quarterly,* 22 (April–June, 1965), pp. 154–170.

individual achievement motivation."[1] These are apparently designed consciously to break down the "non-competitive, group-oriented environment based on compatible relationships" fostered by the traditional precommunist family.

David McClelland has analyzed the emphases on achievement in Chinese education as reflected in the content of children's readers for "three Chinas," the Republican era of 1920–1929, Taiwan during 1950–1959, and Communist China for the same period. The stories of the 1920's showed a very low concern for achievement. The achievement emphases are markedly higher in Taiwan and Communist China, with the latter showing China "for the first time . . . above the world average."

> The predominantly U.S. influence on Taiwan has increased the amount of achievement concern in stories used there, but not as decisively as among the Communists on the Mainland. The quantitative data are supported even more strongly by qualitative analysis of the stories themselves. For instance the achievement concern in the Taiwanese stories is largely concentrated in tales of Western heroes—e.g., Magellan, Alexander Graham Bell, George Washington—whereas on the Mainland it saturates stories dealing with local and indigenous Chinese heroes.[2]

Data from various other nations undergoing ideological revolutions suggest similar conclusions. Thus the analysis of the content of children's readers in 1950 as compared with 1925 indicates that a "wave of high n Achievement . . . is common in newly independent countries."[3] This finding points up the earlier generalization that the old underdeveloped states of Latin America are at a disadvantage compared to the new ones of Asia and Africa in seeking political consensus for antitraditional values. Analysis of Russian children's stories in 1925 and 1950 also reveals a considerable increase in achievement themes between the two periods. And case studies of post-World War II Russian defectors "strongly suggest that n Achievement may be higher in individuals brought up wholly under the Soviet system since the Revolution than in an earlier generation."[4] A comparison of the actual n Achievement test scores of a sample of factory managers and of professionals in the United States, Italy, Turkey, and Communist Poland also suggests the positive impact of communist ideology on such orientations. The achievement orientation scores of the Poles were close to those of the Americans, and both were much higher than the Italians or Turks.[5]

---

[1] Lewis, "Party Cadres in Communist China," p. 425.
[2] David McClelland, "Motivational Patterns in Southeast Asia with Special Reference to the Chinese Case," *Journal of Social Issues,* 19 (1963), pp. 12–13.
[3] *Ibid.,* p. 10.
[4] McClelland, *The Achieving Society,* pp. 412–413.
[5] *Ibid.,* pp. 262, 288.

Education and the Motivation for Innovating Entrepreneurial Elites

Although revolution may be the most dramatic and certainly the most drastic method to change values and institutions which appear to be inhibiting modernization, the available evidence would suggest that reforms in the educational system which can be initiated with a minimum of political resistance may have some positive consequences. Changes in the educational system may affect values directly through the incorporation of modern values to which students are exposed; indirectly they may help to modify the occupational structure by both increasing the numbers trained for various "modern" professions and helping to increase the status of positions needed in a developing economy. Clearly the way in which nations conceive of elite status may affect the supply of talent available for leadership in economic development. Thus, a high evaluation of occupations associated with traditional sources of status—the land, the military, humanistic intellectual occupations, and the free professions—tends to direct talent into occupations which do not contribute much to industrial development. And in cultures with such occupational values, the children of the successful entrepreneurs of lowly, often foreign, origin frequently go to universities to find means of entering the learned professions, politics, the arts, or similar occupations. Such behavior is likely to reduce both the talent and capital available for entrepreneurial expansion.

To analyze the value system inherent in university structures in detail would take us considerably beyond the limits of this paper. A detailed effort to do just this by Michio Nagai, Japan's leading educational sociologist, argues that the values of higher education are in fact achievement orientation, universalism, and functional specificity, among others. Nagai derives the need for these value orientations in the university from a consideration of the requirements for genuine scholarly creativity. Universities which do not stress these values cannot be oriented toward the attainment of scholarly goals, and cannot protect themselves from outside interference with academic freedom.[1] There have been, of course, many universities, particularly in Latin America, which have not adhered to these values. Links with politics or religion have involved diffuse role obligations in which faculty have not been free to teach or publish findings in violation of the ideologies of groups of which they are a part. Ascriptive appointive, admission, or grading policies have sometimes reduced the adequacy of educational institutions as trainers of innovative elites motivated to achieve within a competitive system. But one may suggest that the more the universities of Latin America or other parts of the underdeveloped world are absorbed into the international world of scholarship, the more likely they are to reflect

---

[1] Michio Nagai, *The Problem of Indoctrination: As Viewed from Sociological and Philosophical Bases* (Columbus: Ohio State University Press, Ph.D. thesis, 1952, multilith), pp. 36–39 and *passim.*

the values of this reference group in their internal systems and to teach these to their students.

There is, of course, no simple relationship between the values of modern science and the way universities or even industrial concerns and government agencies operate in different countries. The Japanese system illustrates a formula whereby a "modern" nation may maintain particularistic and ascriptive traits while also developing rigidly universalistic and competitive patterns which guarantee the recruitment of talent into elite positions.

Members of various Japanese organizations, business, academic, or governmental, are given particularistic protection once they are admitted to membership. There is little competition for promotion or salary increases; men move up largely by seniority. Similarly, within the school and university system, little competitive grading occurs; almost everyone is promoted and graduated. And the graduates of various elite institutions are accorded almost ascriptive rights by others, e.g., leading business firms and government bureaus tend to hire most of their executive trainees from a few select universities, much as they have done for decades.

Universalism enters into the Japanese educational and business systems at two stages, first at admission to university, and second at entrance into the lower rungs of business or government executive ladders. The entrance examinations for Japanese universities are completely competitive; admission is solely a function of how well the students do on them, and many children of university professors, politicians, and the wealthy do not qualify for admission to the prestigious universities. Before admission, no one has any special claim to be accepted. Once admitted, however, grades do not serve as an important basis for future selection. While a prospective employer may not learn much about a student from his grades, he can be fairly certain that almost any graduate of Tokyo, Kyoto, Waseda, and other high-quality universities will be among the very top group in the country in general intelligence, and in ability to benefit from higher education. And as a further guarantee of quality there is another impersonal level of competition; job applicants must often take examinations as a precondition for civil service or business employment.

The Japanese system, therefore, permits particularism to operate in every personal relationship, while recruiting in a manner designed to ensure that the elite will be both highly motivated in achievement terms and well qualified. A teacher will not fail a student—i.e., someone with whom he has a personal relationship—nor will an employer or supervisor subject a subordinate to a humiliating lack of confidence. But the competitive entrance examinations, in which the examiners judge people with whom they have no personal relationship or obligation, meet the requirements of both particularistic and universalistic values.

It is significant that other industrialized societies which have emphasized ascription and particularism have also worked out means to handle the dilemma. In Britian, entrance to universities has not been difficult until recently, but final grading has been handled on a completely universalistic basis. Examiners from other universities are always involved in awarding final examination grades to assure that local faculty do not give special preference to their own students. And the grade which a graduate receives—first- or second-class honors, or lower—remains with him as one of the major attributes which defines his place in government, business, and other institutions for the rest of his life. In France there is universalistic competition in receiving grades and in being admitted to elite schools at various levels.

Conversely, it may be pointed out that a society which strongly emphasizes universalism and achievement in its values may permit a great deal of particularism and ascription. Political patronage has continued in America to a greater degree than in many more particularistic European nations; nepotism may be found in industry; influence and family background may affect admission policies to universities, e.g., the children of alumni and faculty are often given preference over those with better records even in some of the best universities. It may be suggested that where a society has strong norms which fulfill certain basic requirements of the system, it does not need explicit rules. North Americans will yield to particularistic obligations, but within self-imposed limits, to avoid harming the institution by helping incompetents. Hence the very emphasis on achievement and universalism in the North American value system would seem to reduce the need for the kind of rigidly universalistic examination system which exists in Japan, where all the normative pressure is in the direction of particularism. And North American institutions are much less inhibited about dismissing students or employees for lack of ability.

Thus it would appear that modernizing societies require either strong values or rules sustaining achievement and universalism. *They need not reject their traditional value system if they can work out mechanisms to guarantee that a large section of the elite will be composed of men who are highly motivated and able to achieve.* However, much of Latin America and some other nations in the less-developed parts of the world have not succeeded in doing either. Men from privileged backgrounds may be admitted to universities, take courses in which it is easy to pass and get a degree, and then secure a high position on the basis of whom they know, or through family ties. These countries have not yet found mechanisms to associate talent with elite status. And those reformist student movements which resist making admission and examination standards more rigorous are, in effect, helping to maintain the traditional order.

There is, of course, considerable pressure on many Latin American state universities to change because of the increasing numbers of applicants. Today, in some countries, large numbers fail to qualify for university entrance.[1] However, the entrance examinations have been subject to severe criticism in many countries for being biased in favor of those educated traditionally in private schools.[2]

An admissions system which is biased against the children of the less well-to-do also discourages enrollment in courses leading to modern vocations as distinct from the traditional elite ones. Studies of occupational choices of university students indicate that the career aspirations of the less well-to-do resemble those of youths from minority ethnic backgrounds. They are both more likely to seek to achieve through studying subjects like business, engineering, or practical sciences. The source of the class bias in recruitment to Latin American universities is not solely, or even primarily, in the preference given to those whose preuniversity training is in traditional subjects. Rather it lies in the fact that the road to university graduation requires a relatively high family income. And in poor countries, where most families have no possible economic reserve, they will not be able to sustain their children through the higher levels of schooling. In Latin America, about two thirds of all secondary school students attend private schools which charge fees, a factor which undoubtedly operates to increase class discrimination. As compared even to other underdeveloped regions, Latin America has done little to "identify and encourage able students . . . to provide programs for part-time students, although it is known that a sizeable proportion of the students in higher education support themselves through employment, and there is no program for external or correspondence students. Perhaps most important of all, the number of students who receive financial assistance must be discounted as negligible."[3] This situation, of course, means that the overwhelming majority of students at Latin American universities are from quite privileged backgrounds.[4] The distribution of class backgrounds may become more rather than less discriminatory in the future, if higher education does not expand rapidly. For greater selectivity brought about by a more rapid increase in demand than in places available will increase the relative advantage of those from well-to-do, culturally privileged homes, who can prepare for admission examinations after having attended good private schools, or having private examination tutors.[5]

Evidence that a deliberate policy to encourage students to take modern rather than traditional subjects can work in Latin America has been presented by Risieri Frondizi, former rector of the University of Buenos Aires, who reports that the initiation of "a program of fellowships, offered only

---

[1] Benjamin, *Higher Education*, pp. 67–71, 97–99, 123–127, 148–153.

[2] Bowles, *Access to Higher Education*, pp. 147–152.

[3] *Ibid.*, p. 148.

[4] Burns, "Social Class and Education," pp. 230–238; Kalman H. Silvert, "The University Student," *in* Johnson, ed., *Continuity and Change*, pp. 207–210.

[5] Havighurst and Moreira, *Society and Education in Brazil*, pp. 104–105.

in fields like science and technology," cut the number studying law in half within three years, while the modern subjects gained greatly.[1]

The rulers of Meiji Japan have provided an excellent example of the way in which a development-oriented elite consciously used the educational system both to provide the needed cadre of trained and highly motivated people and to enhance the status of those occupations needed for modernization. Shortly after the restoration, technical "education was introduced at the university and middle-school levels, and it covered a broad range of theoretical science and practical instruction in agriculture, trade, banking, and, above all, industrial technology."[2] In addition to the various government schools in these fields, Japanese businessmen helped start private universities such as Keio and Hitotsubashi, designed to train for executive business positions students who could absorb the norms of modern business rationality as part of their education.[3]

Another major problem of Latin American universities is the curricula and status orientations of students which encourage vast numbers to work for degrees in subjects which are not needed in large quantity. Educational policy often encourages such maladjustments by making it much easier to secure a degree in subjects such as law or the humanities rather than the sciences or engineering. Clearly it is an implicit policy decision to pass students in the former fields for less and easier work than in the latter, a decision which says, in effect, "We will overtrain and overencourage a section of our youth to aspire to occupational roles which are overcrowded and which do not contribute to social and economic modernization." Malcolm Kerr's comment about such policies in Egypt applies to many underdeveloped countries:

> The passively accepted assumption is that in these fields, where tuition fees are very low and nothing tangible is sacrificed by increasing the attendance at lectures, freedom of opportunity should be the rule. In reality, of course, a great deal is sacrificed, for not only does the quality of education drop, but a serious social problem is made worse, and thousands of students beginning their secondary schooling continue to be encouraged to aim for the universities rather than for the secondary technical education which would be more useful to themselves and to the economic progress of the country.[4]

These comments are clearly relevant to judging how education, particularly higher education, supports the elite in contributing to political stability and economic growth. First, as Arthur Lewis has suggested, there is some

---

[1] Risieri Frondizi, "Presentation," in Council on Higher Education in the Americas, National Development and the University (New York: Institute of International Education, 1965), p. 30.

[2] Hirschmeier, Origins of Entrepreneurship, pp. 127, 128-131.

[3] Ibid., pp. 164-171.

[4] Malcolm H. Kerr, "Egypt," in Coleman, ed., Education and Political Development, pp. 190-191.

reason to suspect that the status concomitants linked to education per se should vary with the proportion and absolute size of the population that is educated. A relatively small higher educational establishment will encourage the retention, or even development, of diffuse elitist values among university graduates, while if a large proportion of the university-age population attends school, the pressures should be in the opposite direction.[1] In much of Latin America, university students almost automatically "become part of the elite. It matters little whether a student is the son of a minister or the son of a workman. His mere enrollment at the university makes him one of the two per 1,000 most privileged in the land."[2] Conversely in the United States, with its mass educational system, few university graduates may expect to attain high status; many of them will hold relatively low positions in nonmanual work; and a certain number will even be employed in manual occupations. Where comparatively few attend universities, as in Britain, graduates who fail to achieve a status comparable to most of their fellow graduates will feel discontented; their reference group will be a higher successful group. The same analysis may be made with regard to the different implications of education for status concerns in the Philippines as contrasted with Senegal. A Filipino who attends the massive University of the Far East must know that few of his fellow students can expect an elite position; Senegalese students, like many in Latin America, however, know that among their classmates are the future economic and political leaders of the country.

A related consequence of increase in the numbers who attain higher levels of education should be an increase in the amount of high achievement orientation in a nation. Studies of the occupational goals of college students in nations with tiny systems of higher education suggest that the large majority of them expect positions in government work.[3] Since some form of white-collar employment must be the goal of college and secondary students, a sharp increase in their numbers should make talent available for a variety of technical and entrepreneurial roles. As Tumin and Feldman have indicated: "From the point of view of a theory of stratification, education is the main dissolver of barriers to social mobility. Education opens up the class structure and keeps it fluid, permitting considerably more circulation through class positions than would otherwise be possible. Education, further, yields attitudes and skills relevant to economic development and such development, in turn, allows further opportunity for persons at lower

---

[1] For a discussion of the consequences of moving from a small elite system to mass higher education in Japan, see Herbert Passin, "Modernization and the Japanese Intellectual: Some Comparative Observations," *in* Jansen, ed., *Changing Japanese Attitudes,* pp. 478–481.

[2] Atcon, "The Latin American University," p. 16.

[3] See K. A. Busia, "Education and Social Mobility in Economically Underdeveloped Countries," *Transactions of the Third World Congress of Sociology,* Vol. V (London: International Sociological Association, 1956), pp. 81–89.

ranks."[1] The thesis that sees positive effects from the expansion of universities has been countered by these arguments: a transfer of educational techniques from developed to underdeveloped societies sometimes results in dysfunctional efforts at innovation; an "overexpansion" of educational resources may create a frustrated, and hence politically dangerous, stratum whose political activities undermine the conditions for growth; the "educated" often develop diffuse elitist status and cultural sustenance demands so they refuse to work in the rural or otherwise "backward" parts of their country; the educated often resist doing anything which resembles manual employment; and rapid educational expansion results in many being poorly educated, while reducing the opportunities available to the small minority of really bright students.[2]

There is no doubt, of course, that the rapid expansion of an educational system may result in an oversupply of persons with relatively high expectations of employment, salary, and status. The increase in the numbers of educated people in a developing economy necessarily means that as education becomes less scarce it should command less status and income. The process of adjusting expanded levels of higher education to reduced rewards is obviously a difficult one, and often results in political unrest. And as W. Arthur Lewis has pointed out, "upper classes based on land or capital have always favoured restricting the supply of education to absorptive capacity, because they know the political dangers of having a surplus of educated persons."[3] One must, however, separate the problem of the possible political consequences of educational expansion from the economic ones. As Lewis indicates, "as the premium for education falls, the market for the educated may widen enormously. . . . The educated lower their sights, and employers raise their requirements. . . . As a result of this process an economy can ultimately absorb any number of educated persons. . . . One ought to produce more educated people than can be absorbed at current prices, because the alteration in current prices which this forces is a necessary part of the process of economic development."[4] The argument against expansion is largely political rather than economic, and calls for a detailed examination of the sociological consequences. Mexico affords an example of the way in which economic growth and emphases on new values may reduce the tensions inherent in rapid educational expansion. William Glade contends that although the educated were often frustrated in prerevolutionary Mexico, "the more or less steady expansion of the private sector activity

---

[1] Melvin Tumin with Arnold S. Feldman, *Social Class and Social Change in Puerto Rico* (Princeton: Princeton University Press, 1961), p. 7.

[2] H. Myint, "Education and Economic Development," *Social and Economic Studies,* 14 (1965), pp. 8–20.

[3] W. Arthur Lewis, "Priorities for Educational Expansion," O.E.C.D., p. 37.

[4] *Ibid.,* pp. 37–38.

since the mid-1920's" has meant a continuing demand for trained persons. "Secondly, . . . with the over-all expansion of the social, economic, and political structure there came a widening range of socially approved channels for the realization of achievement."[1]

To sum up the discussion of universities, the expansion of the educational system is of unquestioned benefit in providing the requisite skills, aspirations, and values essential to modern occupational roles. Not only is expansion required but the content of education also should be broadened. Specifically, education should be directed toward inculcating innovative orientations and teaching problem-solving techniques in all fields of knowledge. This would mean emphasizing and rewarding creative and independent effort on the part of students. The problem suggested earlier of the potentially disruptive political consequences of overproduction of university graduates would presumably be reduced if expansion is accompanied by a modernizing of the educational system. Underemployed graduates with modern innovative orientations are perhaps less likely to seek traditional political solutions to their plight, and more prone to look for other possible avenues toward achievement.

Proposals such as expansion and curricula change are easy to make but difficult to put into practice. Proposals to transform radically and to expand the educational system would meet, first of all, the opposition of present elites who are identified to some extent with the present system and see such changes as a threat. Considerable innovative skill may have to be applied to overcome such opposition.

The conclusion to this section on education also brings us full circle to a recognition of the need to change class relationships in order to foster a change in values. Governments and parties which are deliberately concerned with the need to change values must also seek ways to foster the rise of new occupational strata to status and power, and the reduction of the privileged position of old power groups, such as the land-linked traditional oligarchies, which have little interest in economic growth, social modernization, expanded opportunities for talent, or democracy and equality.

---

[1] Glade, "Revolution and Economic Development," pp. 44–46; for a general discussion of the conditions which affect student participation in various forms of politics see S. M. Lipset, "University Students and Politics in Underdeveloped Countries," *Minerva,* 3 (1964), pp. 15–56; and S. M. Lipset, ed., "Students and Politics," special issue of *Comparative Education Review,* 10 (1966), pp. 129–376.

Education and Political Development: The Latin American Case

W. RAYMOND DUNCAN

Public education conditions political action in developing societies. Literacy tends to produce individuals who are apt to follow election campaigns, who have political information, and who may feel themselves capable of influencing governmental decisions. It thereby creates a wider range of participants in political life.[1] Literacy also propels people toward various skills which in turn lead them to interest groups, parties, civil service, and other institutions. This specialization of labor diversifies the structure of political action, moving it toward modern forms.

The way in which individuals participate within modern institutions is shaped by the culture of politics defined as attitudes toward authority and leadership. These attitudes are formed in the home and church, in the workplace and school. Teachers and textbooks operate in this dimension to build

Reproduced, by permission, from *The Journal of Developing Areas,* 2 (January, 1968), pp. 187–210.

W. Raymond Duncan: Assistant Professor of Government and Assistant to the Vice-President for Academic Affairs, Boston University; author of several articles on political development and social change in Latin America, with special emphasis on Chile and Mexico. This article represents findings from part of a larger project on public education and political development which was started in Mexico in 1964 and continued in Colombia and Venezuela during the summer of 1965. The author gratefully acknowledges a travel grant from the Graduate School of Boston University to facilitate the research for this work.

[1] See Gabriel A. Almond and Sidney Verba, *The Civic Culture—Political Attitudes and Democracy in Five Nations* (Princeton, N.J.: Princeton University Press, 1963); also Karl Deutsch, "Social Mobilization and Political Development," *Political Science Review,* IV (September, 1961), pp. 493–514, where literacy, an indicator of social mobilization, is isolated as a force that expands the politically relevant sector of the population; Daniel Lerner, *The Passing of Traditional Society* (London: Free Press, 1958), pp. 57–64; Edward Shils, *Political Development in the New States* (The Hague, The Netherlands: Mouton, 1962), pp. 17–19.

the sense of national unity and to legitimize specific decision-making patterns that may range from democratic to totalitarian. Examples abound. Under Meiji leadership after 1890, Japanese leaders devised a new blend of filial piety, the samurai ethic, and obedience to the emperor as the curriculum for political indoctrination in the schools. In postwar Germany, American leaders attempted to de-Nazify and reeducate Germans to "democracy." When the French departed Laos, Laotian leaders printed secondary textbooks for the first time in the Lao language—a major effort toward building attitudes of national consciousness. More vivid evidence is found in countries that have experienced recent social revolution. In the non-Western world, Russia and China have placed enormous emphasis on public education as a means to control the rate and direction of political development within the parameters of variant Marxist-Leninist ideologies. Among the revolutionary elites of postcolonial states, those in Guinea, Mali, Ghana, Algeria, Egypt, and Indonesia soon changed the school curriculum to "indigenize" its content along specific ideological lines.[1] However, there are limitations to education as a means to change radically the political culture.

In Latin America the traditional political culture is one of authoritarian decision making, centralized control by a limited political elite, and dominant-submissive interpersonal relationships between the leaders and the led. Available evidence suggests that this underlying attitude set is present at a time when more literate people have progressively entered the political arena through diversified modern institutions. As a tentative hypothesis, then, it can be argued that the structure of politics changes more rapidly than the culture of politics. If this assessment is correct, and it must be admitted that it is contrary to currently accepted theory based on investigations in regions other than Latin America, then traditional attitudes will for decades continue to shape the decision-making processes within developing political institutions.

The difficulty with contemporary theories that evaluate education and political development is a tendency to equate increasing literacy with early change in underlying attitudes toward authority. The implication is that educated individuals in developing areas replace their particularist, ascriptive, and diffuse attitudes with universalist, achievement, and pragmatic

---

[1] Selected studies of education and political development include Herbert Passin, "Japan" in James S. Coleman, ed., *Education and Political Development* (Princeton, N.J.: Princeton University Press, 1965), pp. 304–312; on Russian education, several English works are available: *Soviet Commitment to Education* (Washington: U.S. Department of Health, Education and Welfare, 1959); Jeremy R. Azrael, "Soviet Education," in *Education and Political Development,* pp. 233–271; George Z. F. Bereday et al., eds., *The Changing Soviet School* (Boston, Mass.: Houghton Mifflin, 1960). On Chinese education see Stewart Fraser, ed., *Chinese Communist Education: Records of the First Decade* (Nashville, Tenn.: Vanderbilt University Press, 1965); C. T. Hu, "Communist Education: Theory and Practice," *China Quarterly,* X (April–June, 1962), pp. 84–97; Theodore H. E. Chen, "Elementary Education in Communist China," *China Quarterly,* X (April–June, 1962), pp. 98–122.

attitudes, the sine qua non of modernism.[1] The thesis of this article is that while education brings with it certain kinds of structural change examined below, it does not necessarily produce corresponding changes in the traditional culture of politics.

Literacy and Structural Change

In Latin America increased literacy can be correlated with interest group and political party formations, with widened election participation, with fewer insurrections, and with expansion of middle sectors desiring modernization. These changes in the structure of politics opened new channels for wider participation and established in some cases an institutional framework to accommodate on a permanent basis peaceful transitions of political power.

POLITICAL PARTIES AND CIVIL-MILITARY RELATIONS

Of the 10 Latin American countries with over 65 per cent literacy, relatively wide participation in politics occurs through interest groups, elections, and political parties (Table 1). Argentina is well known for its large labor movement inaugurated by Juan Domingo Perón, and six republics have modern indigenous parties devoted to social reform, industrialization, and national development: the Colorado party of Uruguay, the party of the Institutionalized Revolution (PRI) of Mexico, the National Liberation party of Costa Rica, the Christian Democratic party of Chile, the Communist party of Cuba, and the Democratic Action party of Venezuela. These modernizing parties of the 1960's range within individual party systems from the dominant single-party type in Mexico to the two-party system of Uruguay and the multiparty variety in Chile.[2] They aggregate diversified interests and help to insure regular and frequent elections according to constitutional norms and procedures, another index of modernization.

In the six countries mentioned above, high literacy rates and modern party systems appear to be related to fewer coups d'état and less military intervention in civilian political affairs. Uruguay has not experienced a successful insurrection in the twentieth century, and Mexico, Chile, and Costa

---

[1] See Alfred Stephen, "Political Development Theory," *Journal of International Affairs,* XX, no. 2 (1966), pp. 224, 228. See also, Russell H. Fitzgibbon and Kenneth J. Johnson, "Measurement of Latin American Political Change," *American Political Science Review,* IV (September, 1961), pp. 515–526, in which the assumption that modern institutional development is paralleled by modern attitudes seems implicit.

[2] The Christian Democrats defeated in September 1964 the Popular Action Front (FRAP), a Communist and Socialist coalition, by a vote of 56.6 per cent to 38.5 per cent in an election that produced an 87.41 per cent turnout of the registered electorate. It must be said that while more than one party operates in Mexico, the PRI clearly dominates the political system. The PRI itself, however, is composed of three major groups (labor, farm, and popular) which compete for power within the party. Presidential candidates must be acceptable to these groups, one factor which helps produce a party no longer governed by the traditional strongman as in the past.

Table 1. Literacy, Political Parties, and Coups d'État, 1945-1964

Country	Year of Census	Literate Percentage of Population	Modern Institutionalized Party	No. of Coups between 1945-1964
Argentina	1960	91	None[b]	2
Uruguay	1963	90	Colorados	0
Costa Rica	1963	84	National Liberation Party (PLN)	1
Chile	1960	84	Christian Democrats (CD)	0
Cuba	1953[a]	78	Communist (PCC)[c]	2
Paraguay	1962	74	None	4
Panama	1960	73	None	2
Ecuador	1962	67	None	3
Venezuela	1961	66	Acción Democrática (AD)	3
Mexico	1960	65	Party of the Institutionalized Revolution (PRI)	0
Colombia	1951	62	None	2
Peru	1961	60	Popular Alliance for Revolutionary Action (APRA)	2
Dominican Republic	1956	60	None	1
Nicaragua	1963	50	None	0
Brazil	1950	49	None	4
El Salvador	1961	49	None	3
Honduras	1961	45	None	2
Bolivia	1950	32	National Revolutionary Movement	4
Guatemala	1950	29	None	2
Haiti	1950	10	None	3

Sources: Literacy rates (ages 15 years and over) for the years noted are from the *Statistical Bulletin for Latin America,* produced by the Economic Commission for Latin America (ECLA) (New York: United Nations, 1966), III, No. 2, p. 36. The number of coups are cited by Martin C. Needler, "Political Development and Military Intervention in Latin America," *American Political Science Review,* LX (September, 1966), pp. 616-626.

[a] The literate percentage of Cuba's population is undoubtedly higher since 1953, given Castro's emphasis on adult literacy campaigns after the January 1959 revolution. For instance, out of a total population of 6,933,253 in 1961, some 707,000 illiterates (presumably over 15 years of age) were taught to read and write in that same year. See Richard R. Fagen, *Cuba: The Political Content of Education* (Stanford, Calif.: Stanford University Press, Hoover Institution, 1964), p. 11.

[b] Several institutionalized parties are not included in this column because they are more traditional than modern, e.g., Conservatives and Liberals in Colombia. Others are too small to command widespread participation, e.g., the Socialists of Chile. "Modern" means dedicated to social reform, industrialization, and national development.

[c] After the January 1959 revolution.

Rica have civilian-dominated governments. The military in Venezuela appears at present content to allow the Democratic Action party to run the government, and its nonintervention during the tense days of the December 1963 presidential election are positive signs for civilian predominance. In

Cuba the new military is well under the control of Fidel Castro, who has defeated military counterrevolution from the old professional army through a rebuilt armed forces, tight party organization, and personal control since January 1959. These six countries experienced a total of only six coups between 1945 and 1964 in contrast to 11 that occurred in the four weak-party states (Argentina, Paraguay, Panama, and Ecuador) that have over 65 per cent literacy. In the 10 republics below 65 per cent literacy, 23 coups occurred (Table 1).

These statistics suggest that a high literacy level, although insufficient in itself, is a necessary condition for less military intervention in civil affairs. The second basic condition appears to be development of a countervailing institution (the political party) able to aggregate interests, provide competent political leadership, and channel funding for economic development. The decline of the military acting as a civilian political institution can be a central index of modernization when it means redirection of scarce money and manpower from nonproductive military to productive economic investments; Costa Rica, Chile, and Mexico are cases in point. In contrast, Brazil allocates twice as much money to military spending as to education—a reflection of the role the military plays in Brazilian politics (Table 2). The problem of building countervailing institutions vis-à-vis the military is endemic in Latin America, given its authoritarian and violent history in which the military played a central role in maintaining political stability in the absence of legitimate political institutions after the wars of independence. Moreover, the importance of the military in transitional politics as a symbol of international power and prestige makes it a potent competitor with other national institutions for allegiance and loyalty.

LITERACY AND MIDDLE-SECTOR EXPANSION

Literacy is a stimulant to expansion of the middle sectors in Latin America by providing an educational base for semiprofessional and professional status, higher income, and social and political mobility. The 10 countries with over 65 per cent literacy have a higher percentage of their labor forces in intermediate and senior grades of industrial employment than the 10 countries of lower literacy levels, and Argentina, with the highest literacy, has the largest industrial management group.[1] Not surprisingly, most countries with over 65 per cent literacy have a higher per capita income than those under 65 per cent and are also more urbanized (Table 3).

The political importance of the middle-sector groups lies in the goals and aspirations which they tend to express. According to J. J. Johnson, who has written extensively on middle-sector formation in Latin America, these individuals identify closely with the nation-state as opposed to local

---

[1]Colombia and Brazil are exceptions. See Table 2.

Table 2. Investments by Latin American Governments
in Education and Defense, 1961–1965

Country	Year	% of Federal Budget Invested in Education	% of Federal Budget Invested in Defense
Argentina	1962	10.7	16.5
Uruguay	1961	2.9^a	8.5
Costa Rica	1965	28.1	3.1
Chile	1964	14.4	8.8
Cuba	–	–	–
Paraguay	1964	19.0	23.1
Panama	1964	17.9	–
Ecuador	1964	14.5	13.1
Venezuela	1965	12.2	10.6
Mexico	1964	24.4	10.5
Colombia	1965	12.5	24.4
Peru	1963	24.7	20.9
Dominican Republic	1964	13.9	20.2
Nicaragua	1964	17.0	15.3
Brazil	1964	5.8^b	14.0
El Salvador	1965	24.2	11.0
Honduras	1964	22.1	11.9
Bolivia	1963	24.4^c	11.8
Guatemala	1964	–	11.0
Haiti	1965	11.2	26.0

Source: Figures from "Situación económica: Producto e ingreso nacionales y finanzas," in *América en cifras 1965* (Washington: Pan American Union, Interamerican Statistical Institute, Organization of American States, 1965), pp. 103–128. These statistics may be misleading insofar as they do not indicate the breakdown of federal expenditures into primary, secondary, university, technical, or teacher-training sectors of education. They are nevertheless useful as a guide to governmental commitment to education in the process of nation building.
^{a} Includes investments in other social projects. *Ibid.*, p. 125.
^{b} Includes investments in cultural sector. *Ibid.*, p. 105.
^{c} Includes investments in fine arts. *Ibid.*, p. 104.

enclaves, want more public education in their countries, desire industrialization through state planning and intervention in the economic process, and tend to substitute the political party for the family as the center for political thought and action.[1] From the middle sectors have come the twentieth century leaders of the military, intellectual, and political world who give direction to social change and national government. Gustavo Días Ordaz of Mexico, Eduardo Frei of Chile, José Figueres of Costa Rica, Fernando Belaúnde Terry of Peru, and Romulo Betancourt of Venezuela are

[1] John J. Johnson, *Political Change in Latin America* (Stanford, Calif.: Stanford University Press, 1966 edition), pp. 1–14.

Table 3. Literacy and Middle-Sector Formation in Latin America

Country	Literate % of Population	Per Capita Income (U.S. Dollars at Current Prices)	% of Labor Force in Intermediate and Senior Grades of Employment in Secondary Sectors	% of Labor Force in Agriculture	% of Urban Population
Argentina	91	799.0	35.9	25.2	68
Uruguay	90	560.9	33.0	21.7	81
Costa Rica	84	361.6	22.3	54.7	36
Chile	84	452.9	21.4	29.6	66
Cuba	78	516.0	21.7	41.5	55
Paraguay	74	193.2	14.2	53.8	35
Panama	73	371.0	15.2	49.8	47
Ecuador	67	222.7	10.5	53.2	39
Venezuela	66	644.5	18.2	41.3	61
Mexico	65	415.4	16.9	57.8	50
Colombia	62	373.4	21.0	53.9	48
Peru	60	268.5	–	62.5	41
Dominican Republic	60	313.2	–	69.6	28
Nicaragua	50	288.4	–	67.7	37
Brazil	49	374.6	15.2	50.5	37
El Salvador	49	267.5	10.5	63.2	35
Honduras	45	251.7	4.5	93.1	25
Bolivia	32	122.3	7.6	49.4	37
Guatemala	29	257.7	7.7	74.9	30
Haiti	10	149.2	3.0	83.2	17

Sources: The per capita income figures are for 1961, from *The Economic Development of Latin America in the Post-War Period* (New York: United Nations, 1964), p. 51. Income distribution in Latin America is very uneven. Vast numbers of people receive amounts far lower than the average per capita income, and a privileged few enjoy incomes far higher. The other columns are from Egbert de Vries and José Medina Echavarría, eds., *Social Aspects of Economic Development in Latin America*, Vol. I (Paris: UNESCO, 1963), pp. 90–91.

middle-sector representatives. If more middle-sector groups means more interest in and more dedication and leadership toward modernization, then literacy again is a central impetus for change.

Education and Tradition

The foregoing examples suggest a clear connection between literacy and structural change. With the exceptions of Argentina, Ecuador, Panama, and Paraguay, relatively high literacy appears to be correlated with modern indigenous political parties, less military intervention in civilian government, and regular and frequent elections to effect legitimate, peaceful transitions of political power. Uruguay, Chile, Mexico, and Costa Rica are cases in point;

the Venezuelan and Cuban examples are too new to make an affirmative judgment though events since 1958 in Venezuela and since 1959 in Cuba (at least as far as a modernizing party is concerned) suggest a similar correlation. Since low literacy in 10 of the republics is accompanied by the virtual absence of modernizing parties, a high frequency of military interventions, and a limited middle sector, the evidence tends to support this approach to structural modernization through literacy.[1]

The central issue is not that institutional development is stimulated by increased literacy, but that the attitudes which condition political behavior within developing institutions must be examined more critically. Too often the assumption is that where interest groups, political parties, and elections exist, they reflect modern attitudes such as pragmatism, equalitarianism, achievement, and high national identification. This assumption can mislead one into believing that increased literacy not only builds the base for modern institutional development but also tends to change traditional, underlying attitudes toward authority, with the implication that democratic attitudes are being formed. If we are to understand the functions performed by political institutions in Latin America, the nature of relationships between leaders and followers, and the direction of evolving political systems, it is imperative to probe beyond institutional change into the cultural world of attitudes, values, and beliefs that shape interpersonal political action.

Limited studies of Latin American political cultures show a persistence of traditional attitudes in spite of modern institutional evolution and increasing literacy. One source of evidence is the work of John Gillin, a social anthropologist, which focuses upon ethos components in modern Latin America.[2] Gillin argues that Latin American attitudes and values are essentially personalistic (focusing upon inner unique differences between people), paternalistic, transcendental, fatalistic, attach great weight to hierarchy, and stress emotion as fulfillment of self. These attitudes and values, which encourage social and political inequality in terms of opportunity and status, are operative in most sectors of society (from illiterate to literate) and help to explain traditional perceptions and expectations at work within institutions. The dynamics of interpersonal political action in Latin America

---

[1] One could debate these correlations on the basis of Argentina alone, which does not fit this model of development even though it has the highest literacy in Latin America. Continued military intervention, instability, mass labor discontent, and no effective party leadership make Argentina a unique contrast to the general pattern. Another unique case is Bolivia at the end of the literacy spectrum: low literacy but with a relatively strong party from 1952 until late 1964 when President Victor Paz Estenssoro was overthrown by the military, led by General René Barrientos, vice-president.

[2] John F. Gillin, "Some Signposts for Policy," *in* Richard N. Adams *et al.,* eds., *Social Change in Latin America Today* (New York: Harper, 1960), pp. 14–62; Gillin, "Ethos Components in Modern Latin American Culture," *in* Dwight B. Heath and Richard N. Adams, eds., *Contemporary Cultures and Societies of Latin America* (New York: Random House, 1965), pp. 503–517.

include dominant-submissive relationships between leaders and the led that often result in personalist autocratic leadership by *caudillos* (political bosses) and *caciques* (local leaders).[1] Other traditional values linked to authoritarian leadership include *machismo*, expressions of manliness and action orientation, and *paternalism*, the expectation of protection by individuals in higher stations of life over others in lower positions.[2] These feelings, emotions, and beliefs that stress *people* rather than offices and impersonal institutions help to explain the oligarchical as opposed to democratic leadership that often prevails in Latin America and partially accounts for continued executive predominance in political life despite constitutional provisions for separation of powers and checks and balances. That educated people interact within these cultural parameters suggests that education per se has not significantly changed traditional perceptions and expectations. This hypothesis is supported by a study by Frank Bonilla and Kalman Silvert on education and national identification in which the authors found surprisingly low identification with the nation-state among highly literate and participant individuals in Argentina, Mexico, Chile, and Brazil.[3]

OTHER SOURCES OF EVIDENCE

These sources suggest that traditional values continue to shape perceptions and expectations of individuals in Latin America both during and after their attainment of higher levels of education.[4] The following list is by no means complete.

First, conservative and tradition-bound groups fall at both ends of the class spectrum of Latin American societies. They are likely to be illiterate unpoliticized Indians or *campesinos* (peasants) of the lower classes, or well-educated landholding or commercial elites of the upper classes. That educated conservative groups cling to the status quo and oppose major social and economic reforms suggests little direct correlation between high educational attainment per se and modern Western values. In the political sphere the educated conservative elites long dominated the system of national decision making, sometimes opposing widened secular and public

---

[1] Gillin, "Ethos Components in Modern Latin American Culture," pp. 509–511.

[2] *Ibid.;* also, Gillin, "Some Signposts for Policy," pp. 36–38.

[3] Kalman Silvert and Frank Bonilla, *Education and the Social Meaning of Development: A Preliminary Statement* (New York: American Universities Field Staff, 1961), mimeo. In another article by Silvert, "Some Propositions on Chile," *American University Field Staff Report,* West Coast of South America Series, XI, no. 1 (1964), he states that "the coexistence of a strong national modern community and at the same time a resistant traditional one is not unique in Chile." The key point is that such a traditional community is often well educated and highly politicized, which is what Gillin stresses.

[4] For application of this thesis to other areas, see Donald E. Weatherbee, "Traditional Values in Modernizing Societies," *Journal of Developing Areas,* I (October, 1966), pp. 41–54. Also, Ann Ruth Willner, "The Underdeveloped Study of Political Development," *World Politics,* XVI (April, 1964), pp. 481–482, in which she stresses continuity of traditionalism in modern politics.

educational opportunities for the broad mass of society. Their influence is clearly visible today. They can virtually stop the process of change in some countries (Haiti, Honduras, Ecuador, El Salvador, and Nicaragua) and impede it in other republics. For example, reformist presidents were elected in Chile and Colombia in 1964 and 1966, but they face stiff opposition from conservatives who are politically powerful bankers or congressmen in the national legislature.

Second, the phenomenon of national *caudillos* supported by educated members of society in postwar Argentina, Brazil, Colombia, Venezuela, and Peru suggests that authoritarian values are operative in educated Latin Americans just as they were in educated Germans and Italians during the 1930's and 1940's. While the political styles of Juan Perón in Argentina (1946–1955), Rojas Pinilla in Colombia (1953–1957), Perez Jiménez in Venezuela (1948–1958), and Manuel Odría in Peru (1948–1956) were different, they were all dictators initially supported by a sizable portion of the literate population—urban workers in Argentina and educated large landholders and businessmen in Colombia, Venezuela, and Peru.[1] Lesser known subnational *caciques* are in turn supported by both literate and illiterate people in rural Argentina, Colombia, Venezuela, and Peru, which helps to account for the politically passive and inarticulate rural populations in these countries.

Third, in Argentina, Brazil, and Ecuador, the traditional intervention of the military in civilian affairs has not been perceptibly reduced by increased professionalization, institutionalization, and leveling of the socioeconomic status of the officer corps. During a period when the officer corps are receiving more technical education in military colleges and when expansion of public education has given the lower classes increased opportunity to qualify for military schools, military insurrections have increasingly taken the form of attempts by the possessing classes to maintain the status quo. Moreover, postwar insurrections have been increasingly directed against constitutionally elected presidents and have become more violent as popular resistance to military intervention develops.[2] Higher educational attainment among the officer corps and expanded educational opportunities in the public schools have not resulted in increased reform orientations or democratic attitudes within the military. J. J. Johnson, long a student of civil militarism in Latin America, sums up the position by stating that

---

[1] See Tad Szulc, "The Dictators," *in* Robert D. Tomasek, ed., *Latin American Politics* (New York: Doubleday, 1966), pp. 41–55. For an excellent study of the wide appeal of General Gustavo Rojas Pinilla in Colombia, see Vernon L. Fluharty, *Dance of the Millions: Military Rule and the Social Revolution in Colombia, 1930–1956* (Pittsburgh, Pa.: University of Pittsburgh Press, 1957), pp. 130–158. The political setting leading to the Odría administration is examined by James L. Payne, *Labor and Politics in Peru* (New Haven, Conn.: Yale University Press, 1965), pp. 48–56.

[2] Martin C. Needler makes these points in his recent article, "Political Development and Military Intervention in Latin America," *American Political Science Review,* LX (September, 1966), pp. 616–626.

the "role of the armed forces has not changed basically under the impact of the massive transformation [where education is a key link in the transformation] that has taken place since World War I."[1]

Fourth, since the conquest, the upper classes of Latin American societies have accorded prestige and status not to manual work, industry, and trading, but to artistic and intellectual efforts. This traditional tendency has led to the study of the social sciences and medicine in higher education rather than the physical sciences or engineering.[2] This contempt for manual labor, imitated by the middle sectors of society, suggests the absence of the Western Protestant ethic identified so closely with thrift, industry, and economic development in the United States.[3]

Traditional distaste for manual work, beyond its immediate significance for Latin American industrial development, led to serious political repercussions in both the Cuban and Mexican revolutions. Most of the revolutionary leaders in Mexico and Castro in Cuba devoted major effort toward the construction and inculcation by radio, television, and textbooks of revolutionary national ideologies which stress the importance of work, achievement, struggle, and austerity for all members of society. Cuban textbooks, magazines, and newspapers (e.g., *Granma, Rebel Youth, The World,* and *Sierra Maestra*) continually idealize the workers in education, agriculture, and industry.[4] During the Lázaro Cárdenas and López Mateos periods in Mexico, government-printed textbooks focused upon work themes for all Mexican citizens.[5] Frequently the best workers in Cuba have become national heroes and are rewarded with free trips to China and the Soviet Union. These Cuban and Mexican emphases upon work in the new revolutionary ethics are designed to establish new patterns of national thought and participation; the need for them accentuates the tenacity of traditional cultural attitudes.

Fifth, high educational attainment has not significantly modified the extreme individualism and the deep respect for authority between leaders

---

[1] John J. Johnson, *The Military and Society in Latin America* (Stanford, Calif.: Stanford University Press, 1964), p. 101. See also pp. 102–104, 106. He discusses particularly the military in Brazil, Chile, Argentina, Venezuela, Ecuador, El Salvador, and Honduras.

[2] Tomás Roberto Fillol develops this thesis and applies it to Argentina in his *Social Factors in Economic Development: The Argentina Case* (Cambridge, Mass.: M.I.T. Press, 1961), pp. 16–18.

[3] The impact of traditional values and attitudes in Latin America on entrepreneurship is well explored by Seymour Martin Lipset in "Values, Education, and Entrepreneurship," *in* Lipset and Aldo Solari, eds., *Elites in Latin America* (New York: Oxford University Press, 1967), pp. 3–60.

[4] Evidence to support this point can be gleaned from the translations on Cuba by the Joint Publications Research Service (JPRS), Washington. See also Richard R. Fagen, "Mass Mobilization in Cuba: The Symbolism of Struggle," *Journal of International Affairs*, XX, no. 2 (1966), pp. 254–271; and Fagen, *Cuba: The Political Content of Adult Education* (Stanford, Calif.: Hoover Institution, Stanford University, 1964).

[5] Textbooks during the Cárdenas period strongly emphasized socialism based upon Marxist ideology. See Secretaría de Educación Pública, Comisión Editora, "Serie S.E.P.," third-year text. Socialism began to disappear from primary textbooks after 1940 and democratic themes reappeared.

and subordinates within the upper echelons of organized political life. As in the past, respect and authority is conferred more upon the *person* occupying an office or position than upon the office or position itself. Since it is often well-educated individuals who reach the upper echelons of political and economic organizations, the implication of *personalist* relationships is great. As Tomás Roberto Fillol argues:

> . . . since it is not the job or office that is the object of respect and value but the person who occupies it, and since having reached a higher position, his value orientations lead him to assume that he *Is* superior to his subordinates, the individual in a position of authority will not be likely to have self-doubts regarding the justification of such authority. He will tend to be more or less autocratic. Furthermore, since subordinates *Are* inferior, and thus not to be trusted in the performance of their functions, and since any failure or inadequacy in the socially acceptable performance of his job will reflect *personally* upon himself and his family, he will naturally be reluctant to delegate his authority and responsibilities.[1]

The upshot of these interpersonal relationships is limited sharing of effective decision-making power, fewer alternative choices available to political leaders, limited cooperation and dialogue between members of different political parties, and stifled development of impersonal institutionalized problem solving based upon compromise, bargaining, and reason—even though the political actors may be well educated.[2]

Sixth, a kind of informal education occurs when individuals become urbanized. They experience new relationships, are exposed to the demonstration effect of modern urban living, are available for recruitment into organized labor groups and political parties, and can listen to candidates at election time. The remarkable findings of studies conducted on urban working classes in Latin America is that education acquired through exposure to modern urban life brings little apparent revolution of rising expectations or deep explosive social discontent.[3] Rather, traditional authoritarian and paternalist attitudes often persist. Recent election returns from the slum urban areas of Lima, Caracas, Santiago, and Valparaiso illustrate the point: the shantytown districts of Lima favored General Manuel Odría,

---

[1] Fillol, *Social Factors in Economic Development*, p. 19.

[2] *Ibid.* See also Fluharty, *Dance of the Millions*, pp. 165–167; Ernst Halperin, *Castro and Latin American Communism* (Cambridge, Mass.: M.I.T. Press, 1963), pp. 2–3, in which he discusses the absence of a *homo burocraticus* mentality in Latin America. Interpersonal relations within political parties, based upon traditional attitudes and values, are examined by Robert E. Scott, "Political Parties and Policy Making in Latin America," *in* Joseph LaPalombara and Myron Weiner, eds., *Political Parties and Political Development* (Princeton, N.J.: Princeton University Press, 1966), pp. 331–367; see particularly pp. 338–340. The development of increased participation in political structures without corresponding development of effective organizations and institutions is the subject of Samuel P. Huntington, "Political Development and Political Decay," *World Politics*, XVII (April, 1965), pp. 386–430. On a similar theme, see Robert E. Scott, "Political Elites and Political Modernization," *in Elites in Latin America*, pp. 117–145, especially p. 121.

[3] Daniel Goldrich, "Toward the Comparative Study of Politicization," in *Contemporary Cultures and Societies of Latin America*, pp. 363–366.

the most conservative of four presidential election candidates in 1963; the shantytown vote during the Venezuelan presidential elections of 1963 in Caracas went to Arturo Uslar Pietri, a conservative intellectual and representative of business interests; and the shantytowns of Santiago and Valparaiso supported Eduardo Frei over Salvador Allende, the Marxist candidate, in the 1964 Chilean presidential elections. These election returns suggest a continuity of traditional values in spite of new social cultural experiences.

The Mexican Case

In order to investigate these contemporary political attitudes in Mexico, a questionnaire was devised and administered in Mexico City in 1964. The purpose of the questionnaire was to assess the relative impact of levels of education (a) on the authoritarian orientation so evident in the structure and culture of the Mexican political system, (b) on the formation of modern political attitudes associated with democratic egalitarianism, and (c) on the role and function of education as understood by the respondents to the questionnaire. Conclusions reached from such a questionnaire, while certainly neither final nor conclusive evidence, do indicate the direction and force of education in shaping Mexico's political culture. Evidence from this independent research in Mexico City can be linked with recent information gathered by Verba and Almond in connection with their study on *The Civic Culture,* and by Silvert and Bonilla in their work on *Education and the Social Meaning of Development,* to form a growing picture of education and attitude change in Mexican politics.[1]

QUESTIONNAIRE RESULTS

The questions asked, methodology followed, and correlation coefficients obtained are included in the Appendix of this study. In summary, the findings suggest that increasing levels of education within the sample did not correlate significantly with decreasing authoritarian attitudes. Second, the correlation coefficient between increasing levels of education and the modern political attitude scale was not significant (.0351), indicating that more education did not make the subjects of this sample more modern in their political perceptions. In short, increased education did not appear to accentuate the subjects' attitude toward democratic egalitarianism as defined within the framework of the questions asked (Table 8 of Appendix).[2]

---

[1] For other relationships between education and attitude formation, see Gabriel A. Almond and Sidney Verba, *The Civic Culture* (Princeton, N.J.: Princeton University Press, 1963); and Kalman Silvert and Frank Bonilla, *Education and the Social Meaning of Development* (New York: American University Field Staff, 1961).

[2] Almond and Verba found that, compared to citizens of the United States, Britain, Germany, and Italy, Mexican citizens expected less equal treatment by their governmental bureaucracy and the police. *The Civic Culture,* p. 108.

Indeed, for the employees of the Bank of Mexico, who had the highest level of education as a working class, the correlation coefficient was negative, rather than positive (Table 8).

The low impact of education as a direct socializing experience affecting authoritarian values is related probably not only to attitude formation in the family but also to the process of education itself. The Almond and Verba project revealed that the Mexican subjects felt little freedom to discuss unfair treatment in the school and rarely discussed problems with their teachers in comparison with citizens of the United States.[1] This pattern of authority in the school is also indicated by this survey, for in response to question one, teachers were the only occupational group to show a positive correlation between higher levels of education and increased strength of authoritarian attitudes.[2] The pattern characterized by rare discussion of problems and feeling of restraint in school decreased in the Almond-Verba study as higher levels of education were achieved. But given the heavy dropout rate of students before they reach higher levels, the basic pattern of authority in the school is highly significant.

THE MEXICAN CASE SUMMARIZED

Limited quantitative evidence gathered in Mexico indicates that authoritarian perceptions of the self in relation to others operate in the political system and condition relations between leaders and followers at all levels of political activity. This conclusion is confirmed by Mexican writers and spokesmen. Francisco González Pineda, in his *El mexicano: Su dinámica psicosocial* (1959) and *El mexicano: Psicología de su destructividad* (1961), describes Mexican attitudes toward authority which result in a compulsive attraction to strong personalist rule *(caciquismo)* in the form of a national president who serves as a kind of temporary absolutist monarch through a dominant single party that provides for "hereditary power" changed each six years.[3] In a work by Dr. Vincente Suarez Soto, *Psicología abismal del mexicano,* the author describes, as did Samuel Ramos in the 1930's, the deep sense of inferiority that pervades the Mexican people, producing in part general indecision and uncertainty resolved by a dominant president.[4] The upshot of authoritarian values and attitudes, as one Mexican senator explained it on the Senate floor on September 6, 1961, is oligarchical rule. He said:

---

[1] *Ibid.,* pp. 332-333.

[2] Question one reads as follows: Every decent person should have a feeling of love, gratitude, and respect for his parents. See Appendix.

[3] Both works published in Mexico, D.F., by Editorial Pax-México, Asociación Psicoanalítica Mexicana, A.C. See p. 53 in former and pp. 202-203 in latter.

[4] Mexico, D.F.: Secretaría de Educación Pública, Instituto Federal de Capacitación del Magisterio, 1962, Vol. I, pp. 142-143, of a two-volume work.

I wish to affirm vigorously and courageously that an oligarchy supported by the people governs in Mexico, an oligarchy that has made possible the leading of the nation into development [;] the difference between the Mexican elite and others is that ours is a revolutionary minority, while others in Latin America are of a military, clerical, large agricultural, or of a simple industrial financial type, and (as) conservative minorities they hold back from becoming revolutionary minorities [; they] do not think about the problem of transforming their people, but merely about development of properties and of their own businesses.[1]

The perseverance of these traditional authoritarian attitudes is all the more meaningful to development theory insofar as the indices of development are present in Mexico: urbanization, increasing literacy, mass media expansion, widening middle sectors, and an operative indigenous political party to accommodate the increasing number of literate people after the 1910 revolution. Before the 1910 revolution, Mexican leaders could claim only limited participation in the tightly controlled dictatorship of Porfirio Días (1876–1910). During these years, when 85 per cent of the population was illiterate, the labor sector remained undiversified and failed to organize into functional interest groups or national parties. After 1920, when literacy began to spread in Mexico, labor became more and more diversified and the base of political participation was extended in the 1930's to include first rural and factory workers followed by white-collar workers, teachers, civil servants, professionals, and intellectuals in the 1940's.[2] Through large interest groups these people began to participate in national politics through the large dominant Mexican party with its labor, farm, and popular interest group sectors. The party of the revolution, today called the Party of Institutionalized Revolution (PRI), became more and more institutionalized and began to provide the political machinery for selection and election of a

---

[1] Quoted by Frank R. Brandenburg, *The Making of Modern Mexico* (Englewood Cliffs, N.J.: Prentice-Hall, 1964), p. 3. Brandenburg, long a student of Mexican political development, concludes that Mexico is ruled by an elite which he calls the "Revolutionary Family." It is composed of the men "who have run Mexico for over half a century, who have laid the policy-lines of the Revolution, and who today hold effective decision-making power" (p. 3). This group includes the incumbent president, the president-elect (one every sixth year), several very wealthy individuals (or labor union leaders), and a few powerful national and regional political leaders. Other influential individuals of the political elite represent vested interests in finance, commerce, private industry, and agriculture (p. 4). Also, the closed procedure of selecting new presidents further illustrates limited political decision making within the PRI hierarchy (pp. 145–150). For other views on centralized decision making in Mexico, see Robert E. Scott, *Mexican Government in Transition* (Urbana, Ill.: University of Illinois Press, 1959), pp. 197–293. On the same theme, see Raymond Veron, *The Dilemma of Mexico's Development* (Cambridge, Mass.: Harvard University Press, 1963), p. 131.

[2] This is not to suggest that education produces industry but that increased education, during a time of industrialization, stimulates labor diversification as skills become more sophisticated. Education is of course a vital base for sustained industrialization. The chief concerns of this paper are relationships between education and political development rather than the stimulants to increased education, of which industry can be one.

new and different president each six years, for attainment of broad social reforms, and for communicating new national symbols (heroes, slogans, songs, and poems) designed to build national identification and to stimulate national integration and development. The PRI became the mechanism for wider sharing in governmental life.

The time frame of increasing literacy, labor diversification, and interest-group formation with the PRI is illustrated in Tables 4 and 5. These statistics are not meant to suggest that increased literacy was the single determinant of later political and economic modernization. They do suggest that because increasing literacy and labor specialization occurred concurrently with interest-group formation and their incorporation in the party structure, literacy was a vital impetus for politicalization. They further suggest that middle-sector expansion directly affects Mexican political development, for it has produced expansion of the PRI's popular groups (CNOP, Table 5)— a distinctly middle-sector organization composed of teachers, civil servants, professional women, small industrialists, and intellectuals. As an outgrowth of increasing literacy, the CNOP grew from its inception in 1943 to 1,848,000 members by 1959 at a time when the percentage of the literate population increased from 37 per cent in 1940 to 70 per cent in 1960. By 1964 this federation reached a 3,122,000 membership, making it the largest grouping in PRI. In short, the rise in levels of literacy has brought a major structural change within the dominant single party, where the largest division of participants is found in the middle-sector organization, CNOP, rather than in the divisions of less-educated individuals, the labor groups (CROM, CGT, CTM, and CNC). While vastly increased participation and social mobilization

Table 4. Increasing Literacy and Labor Diversification, 1940–1960

Year	Population	Literate % of Population	Agriculture No. of Workers	%	Industry No. of Workers	%	Services[a] No. of Workers	%
1900	13,607,272	15	–	–	–	–	–	–
1910	15,160,369	22	–	–	–	–	–	–
1930	16,552,722	29	–	–	–	–	–	–
1940	19,653,552	37	3,831	63.3	836	13.8	1,117	18.4
1950	25,791,017	66	4,824	58.3	1,222	14.8	1,774	21.4
1960	34,923,129	70	6,342	52.8	1,868	15.5	3,065	25.5

Sources: Figures for population and literacy percentages are computed from Mexican *Anuarios Estadísticos* for the relevant years. If *Anuarios* were not available, José I. Iturriaga's *La estructura social y cultural de México* (Mexico, D.F.: Fondo de Cultura Económica, 1951) contains similar statistical data. Figures in the "Agriculture," "Industry," and "Services" columns are from Ramón Ramírez, *Tendencias de la economía mexicana* (Mexico, D.F.: Escuela Nacional de Economía, Universidad Nacional Autónoma de México, 1962), p. 19.

[a]"Services" include transportation, communications, commerce, finance, and civil service occupations.

Table 5. Formation of Interest Group Sectors
(Participate through PRI)

Year Formed	Interest Group	Membership (1958)
1918	Regional Confederation of Mexican Workers (CROM)	35,000
1922	General Confederation Workers (CGT)	25,000
1936	Mexican Confederation of Laborers (CTM)	1,500,000
1938	National Farmers' Federation (CNC)	2,500,000
1938	Federation of Government Employees' Unions (FSTSE)	300,000
1943	National Federation of Popular Organizations (CNOP)	1,848,000[a]

Source: From Robert E. Scott, *Mexican Government in Transition*, pp. 166–167.
[a]Figure includes FSTSE membership.

(Deutsch's term) occurred, persistent traditional authoritarian attitudes continued to shape political interaction.

Conclusion: Implications for Research

Traditional values and attitudes in Latin America are in part the product of the Iberian conquest, which brought with it paternalist-political and religious authoritarianism accompanied by a rigid social hierarchy.[1] These conditions were not conducive to self-government during the colonial period and did not prepare the Latin American elites for independence. Instead, traditionalism produced authoritarian political systems in which followers tended to transfer power completely rather than delegate it temporarily to their leaders, and in which the idea that man is responsible for his own world never really took root.[2] Independence brought no legitimate substitute political institutions. Thus, anarchy ensued after independence had been won. Traditionalism in Latin America, not a solid foundation for the growth of democratic institutions as we know them in the United States, continues to condition the entire process of political development in spite of increasing literacy and expanding education.

To conclude that literacy can be correlated with various forms of increased engagement in politics, but not always with fundamental change in underlying attitudes toward authority, has future research implications.

[1] For a fascinating approach to traditional attitudes formation in Latin America, see Richard M. Morse, "The Heritage of Latin America," *in* Louis Hartz, ed., *The Founding of New Societies* (New York: Harcourt, Brace and World, 1964), pp. 123–177. The Indian and Negro heritages are also important in forming the weaker complements to dominant Iberian values. The mixture of whites and Indians has produced the mixed-blood mestizo, the man perhaps most achievement-oriented in Latin America today.

[2] *Ibid.*, pp. 172–173. The implications of these attitudes for democratic government, which requires specific historical experiences, is examined by Zevedei Barbu, *Democracy and Dictatorship: Their Psychology and Patterns of Life* (New York: Grove Press, 1959), pp. 12–23.

First, political development theory (or theories) must be applied carefully to individual Latin American polities if flaws in the theory are to be ascertained, reworked, and modified to fit reality. This task is essential in the continuing search for a general theory of political development. To date, most development theory is based upon research in the new nations of Africa and Asia, not upon Latin American evidence dating back to the colonial period and conditioned by a substantially different cultural setting.

Second, as new and productive uses of quantitative statistical analysis are devised, qualitative intuitive assessments based upon accurate and reliable information must not be given short shrift. If central links between political structures and political cultures, between institutions and values are to be discussed intelligently, then study of unquantifiable information should be geared to human judgment about social and political interrelationships.

Third, the decision-making and conflict-resolution process *within* emerging modern institutions should be a major concern. These processes include leaders, subordinates, issues, alternatives, ideologies, procedures, unwritten rules, and custom. They also involve political socialization (i.e., learning of attitudes toward authority in the home, school, and church) which we know in the case of Mexico is authoritarian with obedience and respect for authority as key values. In-depth study of these forces would help to expand the understanding of decision making within modern institutions. In spite of the growth of modern parties and increased politicalization cited in the six countries with high literacy, the important elements of personalism, *machismo, caciquismo,* and paternalism continue to shape the pattern of developing decision-making processes. One impact of traditionalism occurs in the broad spectrum of Latin American labor movements which have been organized and injected into the political system not from below as social mobilization increased but from above by strong leaders building a base of political power, e.g., Cárdenas in Mexico, Perón in Argentina, and Vargas in Brazil. Another impact of traditionalism is on the heavy commitment to equitable redistribution of the national income through state direction of the economy. This ideological objective suggests a strong element of historic paternalism and raises serious questions about economic development paralleled with social welfare programs (Uruguay is the classic case) which divert scarce funds from capital formation. These examples indicate that the pattern of political development in Latin America will be markedly different from that in the United States or Britain even though the indices of development—urbanization, literacy, and mass media circulation—appear to be similar.

Appendix: Study of Mexican Attitudes toward Politics and Education

The questionnaire consists of 42 items. Twelve of these questions are divided into two groups: eight items on personal information such as sex, age, place of birth, and level of education achieved and four general questions on the role of the Mexican school. The 30 remaining questions are divided into three equal groups of 10 questions covering (a) authoritarianism, (b) modern political attitudes, and (c) education in Mexico. Each of these 10-question sets constitutes an opinion-attitude scale which is designed to reflect the respondent's opinion-attitude toward each item or statement within the scale.[1] Five of the 30 questions are turned around and were later scored in reverse to obviate the tendency of a respondent to fall into a set pattern of agreement or disagreement with all items. The questionnaire was pretested, and several items were deleted or changed to make them more discriminating. The questions are of course mixed on the questionnaire to prevent the relationships between questions from becoming too obvious.

The subjects were given a wide choice of responses, ranging from strong agreement, through moderate agreement, slight agreement, undecided, slight disagreement, moderate disagreement, to strong disagreement. The subjects were asked to circle one of the numbers under each statement which registered their attitudes: +3, +2, +1, 0, -1, -2, and -3. Unmarked items were given the intermediate score of 4. These responses were converted into scores as follows: +3 became 7, +2 became 6, +1 became 5, 0 and unmarked items became 4, -1 became 3, -2 became 2, and -3 became 1. All turned-around items were scored in reverse order, with -3 equal to 1, etc.

These raw scores were then transferred to IBM cards, as was all background information, such as levels of education achieved, etc. This method was used to facilitate IBM determination of the correlation coefficients between the various groups of items in the questionnaire. A correlation coefficient is the mathematical expression of the degree of covariation that exists for any two variable items. The key point is that when there is no similarity between variables, the correlation is zero; when there is perfect similarity, the correlation is +1; and when there is perfect dissimilarity, the correlation is -1.[2] Correlation coefficients allow the investigator to gain information on the relationship between two basic variables, as in this

---

[1] This method of integrating several opinion-attitude scales into a single questionnaire was originated by Rensis Likert. See "A Technique for the Measurement of Attitudes," *in* R. S. Woodworth, ed., *Archives of Psychology,* 140 (New York: Columbia University Press, 1932), and Rensis Likert and Gardner Murphy, *Public Opinion and the Individual* (New York: Harper, 1938). The opinions reflected in this questionnaire also reflect political attitudes; the two are intimately related. See Gordon W. Allport, "The Composition of Political Attitudes," *American Journal of Sociology,* XXXV (September, 1929), p. 225, and Bernard Fensterwald, Jr., "The Anatomy of American Isolationism and Expansionism," *Journal of Conflict Resolution,* II (September, 1958), pp. 280–310.

[2] Fensterwald, "The Anatomy of American Isolationism and Expansionism," p. 296.

questionnaire, the relationship between levels of education and political attitudes reflected in the opinion scales.

THE OPINION-ATTITUDE SCALES

The Authoritarian Attitude Scale, one of the three scales employed in this research, consisted of the following questions:

1. Every decent person should have a feeling of love, gratitude and respect for his parents.
4. Most people who fail to get ahead in life simply don't have enough will power.
7. What this country needs is fewer laws and agencies and more courageous, tireless, devoted leaders whom the people can put their faith in.
10. Too many people today are living a soft life; we should look for the fundamental principles that require force and work.
13. The most important virtues that children can learn in the home are obedience and respect for authority.
16. No insult to honor should ever go unpunished.
19. It is good to spend money to construct schools, but in reality Mexico is spending too much to educate campesinos who aren't going to get ahead in life.
22. People can be grouped into two categories: weak and strong.
25. No normal, reasonable and respectable person could ever think of hurting a friend or parent.
28. It is essential for effective work that our bosses outline in detail what is to be done and precisely how to do it.

These questions were so stated that persons with strong authoritarian attitudes would be expected to agree with them.[1]

The Modern Political Attitude Scale, the second of three attitude scales, was composed of the following questions:

2. If a person wants to get ahead in life, it is better to have money than ability.
5. If a man works hard, is resourceful and creative, he can be very successful.
8. The way to resolve conflict between the different interest groups is through compromise.
11. If one wants to be successful in his profession, it is more important to be clever and imaginative than to be from a "good family."
14. In spite of industrialization and progress in education, the basic

---

[1] The questions on the Authoritarian Attitude Scale were taken from T. W. Adorno *et al., The Authoritarian Personality* (New York: Harper, 1950), pp. 226–227, 231, 237.

relationships among Mexicans are static and do not require a constant adjustment.

17. Mexicans possess many rights, the principal of which is equality before the law.
20. Personalism *(personalismo)* ought to rule in politics.
23. Through science we can hope to discover many things now unknown to the human mind.
26. In spite of what people say, the best way of telling the importance of people is through their family background.
29. It is not necessary that the program for progress of the nation be made from alternative courses of action.

Negative answers to questions 2, 14, 20, 26, and 29, and positive answers to all other questions were scored as modern political attitudes.

Attitudes on education as a central force for Mexican national development were placed into the following Functions of Education Attitude Scale:

3. Mexico should have a definite kind of educational system in order to reach its political and social goals.
6. Of all the roads to national development, formal and controlled education is the best.
9. If all men knew how to read and write and were well educated, they would act reasonably and peaceably in their relationships with each other.
12. A good system of education in Mexico ought to be controlled by the government and not left to chance.
15. Justo Sierra was right when he said that Mexico would be democratic if the importance of democracy were taught through the schools.
18. We can predict the social development of a country if we examine its system of education.
21. It is important that Mexicans have a uniform education in the schools if they want to avoid internal political conflict.
24. One of the principal functions of the school is to teach its students patriotism and a sense of civil responsibility in order that they may fit into Mexican society.
27. It is through a good system of education that Mexico can increase the number of citizens that believe in the ideals of democracy.
30. A country that has various systems of different education will only produce people that will later disagree politically.

Positive answers to these questions indicate several kinds of attitudes relative to education. Strong agreement with all the questions suggests that the respondent believes that education should be controlled by the government (a part of the authoritarian syndrome), that through education democratic values can be transmitted from teachers and textbooks to students, and that education is the central force in Mexican national development.

COMPOSITION OF THE SAMPLE

The questionnaire was distributed to 149 white-collar workers in the Federal District of Mexico.[1] Seventy-eight subjects, or 52 per cent of the sample, worked for the Sears Roebuck Company. Thirty-two subjects, or 21.5 per cent of the sample, worked for the Bank of Mexico. Seventy-nine subjects (53 per cent) were male while 70 (47 per cent) were female. The range in age was from 18 to 62 years.

The educational background of the sample was rather disparate. Fifty-one subjects (34 per cent) had completed university training, while 21 subjects (14 per cent) had begun but had not finished university studies. Thirty-five (24.5 per cent) had completed normal school for teachers or preparatory school for the university. Seventeen subjects (11 per cent) had completed secondary training, while 16 (10.5 per cent) had begun secondary studies but had not finished. Another interesting statistical breakdown is related to the time period during which the subjects attended primary school. Thirty-eight subjects (26 per cent) were educated during the 1930's, when socialist primary education was promoted in the public schools. Nineteen subjects (13 per cent) received their primary instruction before the socialist era, and 48 (32 per cent) went to primary school after the socialist era. These subjects were publicly educated, while the remaining 44 (29 per cent) were educated in private schools.

QUESTIONNAIRE RESULTS

Results from the questionnaire indicate moderate agreement with the authoritarian questions, where the mean score for seven of the 10 authority questions was over five. In the authority scale, attitudes of disagreement were registered as a mean score on questions 7, 19, and 22. On the Modern Political Attitude Scale, mean scores for agreement and disagreement were split evenly, five and five. The breakdown of mean scores is given below, where the score can be compared to the specific question. The strongest agreement was registered by the total sample in the education scale where eight of 10 mean scores were over five and two mean scores were over four. This would have been a likely prediction of the education scores, if the authoritarian scores were moderately high, since the questions on education were closely related to strong governmental control and to the

---

[1] Admittedly, 149 respondents is a very small base on which to build a theory. This case study, therefore, is not designed to erect a general theory. It does offer quantitative data for reaching tentative estimates of the limitations of education as an input to political development (in the realm of attitudes toward authority) and suggests that the rate of change in political cultures may be far slower than originally judged by political scientists.

authoritarian syndrome of opinions.[1] The pattern of mean scores for the total sample was:

Table 6. Mean Scores of the Three Opinion-Attitude Scales

Authoritarian Attitudes		Modern Political Attitudes		Attitudes toward Education	
Question	Mean Score	Question	Mean Score	Question	Mean Score
1	6.892	2	2.832	3	5.986
4	5.637	5	6.483	6	5.859
7	3.510	8	6.107	9	5.744
10	5.711	11	6.241	12	5.348
13	5.872	14	3.315	15	5.959
16	5.342	17	5.610	18	6.355
19	1.691	20	1.617	21	4.503
22	3.422	23	6.765	24	6.395
25	6.543	26	2.389	27	5.912
28	5.348	29	3.617	30	4.718

Other data from this study suggest that higher levels of education reduced the authoritarian attitudes only slightly; that is, as educational levels increased, authoritarian attitudes decreased relatively little. A correlation coefficient of −.3139 between higher levels of education and the authoritarian attitude scale (totals of 10 authoritarian questions) illustrates the point. Secondly, the correlation coefficient between increasing levels of education and the modern political attitude scale was not significant (.0351), indicating that more education did not make the subjects of this sample more modern in their political perspectives. Furthermore, as levels of education increased, the authoritarian attitudes built into the education scale decreased only slightly, as they did in the authoritarian attitude scale itself. The correlation coefficient between increasing education and the education scale was a slightly significant −.2881. The authoritarian scale and education scale were related in terms of a correlation coefficient of .4758, suggesting that as people in the sample were more authoritarian they believed that education should be controlled, be oriented to a specific policy, and be designed to inculcate democratic values, through control of Mexico's younger generations. Of course, this is a broad generalization based upon analysis of limited information; certainly exceptions to the generalization would exist within the total sample.

In order to investigate other relationships emerging from this study, subgroups were extracted from the total sample and then correlated with

---

[1] Agreement most probably reflects the de facto educational policy of the Mexican government, which approximates the elements embodied in the questionnaire.

Table 7. Correlation Coefficients between Increasing Education and the Authoritarian Attitude Scale

A.

Question	Male	m	Female	m	Teacher	m
1	-.2055	6.950	ns	6.826	.3998	6.593
4	ns	5.462	ns	5.840	ns	5.937
7	-.2844	3.212	-.3075	3.855	ns	3.156
10	ns	5.387	ns	3.855	ns	5.500
13	ns	5.712	-.2905	6.057	ns	5.593
16	ns	5.262	ns	5.434	.2259	5.093
19	ns	1.512	ns	1.898	-.3729	1.843
22	ns	3.062	-.2801	3.840	ns	3.437
25	ns	6.437	ns	6.666	ns	6.156
28	ns	5.150	-.2776	5.579	ns	4.750

B.

Question	Bank of Mexico	m	Sears Roebuck	m
1	ns	6.923	ns	7.000
4	-.3154	5.461	ns	5.623
7	ns	3.205	-.3775	3.844
10	ns	5.666	-.2445	5.805
13	ns	5.717	-.2518	6.051
16	-.2529	5.358	ns	5.415
19	ns	1.820	ns	1.157
22	-.2423	3.025	-.2276	3.584
25	ns	6.538	ns	6.701
28	-.2013	4.974	ns	5.792

C.

Question	Educated before and after Cárdenas Period [a]	m	Educated during Cárdenas Period	m
1	ns	6.802	ns	6.975
4	ns	5.816	ns	5.550
7	-.4008	3.352	ns	3.800
10	-.2338	5.704	ns	5.800
13	-.2230	5.507	ns	6.425
16	ns	5.225	ns	5.200
19	-.2380	1.690	ns	1.600
22	-.2557	3.774	ns	2.750
25	ns	6.338	ns	6.725
28	ns	5.366	ns	4.925

[a]Those subjects educated before or after the Cárdenas period were placed together in a separate group and correlated with levels of education.

increasing education. These correlations are given in Table 7. In general, the table indicates a weak relationship between increased (or higher) levels of education and decreased authoritarian attitudes. A notation of "ns" signifies that the correlation coefficient was not significant (between .2000 and –.2000). Mean answers are denoted by the "m" columns.

The relationship between the three scales and increased educational levels is summarized in Table 8.

Table 8. Correlation Coefficients between Increasing Education
and the Three Scales

	Authoritarian Attitude	Modern Political Attitude	Role of Education
Males	-.2372	ns	-.2561
Females	-.2949	ns	-.2501
Bank of Mexico	ns	-.2380	ns
Sears Roebuck	-.3369	ns	ns
Teachers	ns	ns	ns
Education before or after			
Cárdenas period	-.4832	ns	-.4059
Education during			
Cárdenas period	ns	ns	ns

Forecasting Manpower
and Education Requirements
for Economic and Social Development
in Peru

JAMES V. CORNEHLS

The decade of the 1960's has witnessed an enormous increase in both the theoretical and practical treatment of the strategic role of human resources in economic development. Ever since the pioneering studies of the residual factor in economic growth—growth in output not explained by increases in labor and capital—undertaken by Robert Solow, Moses Abramovitz, and others[1] and Theodore Schultz's early generalization that the rate of return on capital invested in improving the human factor is probably much greater than that used to increase the stock of reproducible goods,[2] economists have been increasingly concerned with the explicit treatment of human resources development as an integral element in overall planning for economic and social development.

The very nature of the development problem, speeding the economic and social modernization of a large number of backward sectors, suggests that developing countries must undertake simultaneously a wide variety of complementary activities on a large number of fronts. Human resource development is unquestionably one of the most important of these but, like all the others, cannot accomplish everything which might be usefully

Reproduced, by permission, from *Comparative Education Review,* 12, no. 4 (February, 1968), pp. 1-27.

[1] Robert Solow, "Technical Change and the Aggregate Production Function," *Review of Economics and Statistics,* 34 (August, 1957), pp. 312-330; Moses Abramovitz, "Resources and Output Trends in the United States," *American Economic Review,* 46 (May, 1956), pp. 5-23.

[2] T. W. Schultz, "Latin American Economic Policy Lessons," *American Economic Review,* 46 (May, 1956), pp. 425-432 and "Capital Formation by Education," *Journal of Political Economy,* 67 (December, 1960), pp. 571-583.

undertaken. The allocation problem persists, and consequently some choices become necessary regarding manpower policy and the kinds and amounts of training to be provided first and for whom. Choices are being made, many of them on a very rough-and-ready, rule-of-thumb basis, so that the use of more specific guidelines represents a distinct improvement over current practice. And it is now generally accepted that one of the major determinants in the process should be some variant of a broad cost/benefit analysis.[1]

A variety of model approaches, some more or less useful and more or less complex have been devised which attempt to provide answers to the foregoing questions.[2] These methods all have one common element, however; they seek to determine the quantity and kind of training which will yield the greatest impact in accelerated economic growth. The underlying argument is of course that rapid growth will generate most quickly the additional resources for the subsequent expansion and improvement of training facilities on all fronts. Hence, these approaches generally attempt to relate forecasted manpower requirements growing out of planned or forecasted economic sector growth patterns to the expansion and improvement of the formal and informal education system.

In late 1964 a manpower and educational research and development program of more than a year's duration was begun in Peru under the auspices of the Peruvian National Planning Institute and the Organization for Economic Cooperation and Development in Paris.[3] The United States Agency for International Development (USAID), through its Teachers College Columbia University Mission, became associated with this program from the outset. Numerous other Peruvian governmental agencies and educational entities provided varying degrees of support,[4] while computer programming for the data analysis was arranged for with the IBM del Peru.[5]

---

[1] In principle the measurement of costs/benefits in educational investment is a reasonable concept. In practice no entirely satisfactory method has been devised which satisfies everyone's criteria. There is little to be gained by belaboring the point that if a widely recognized and useful purpose will be served by any specific project, it need not necessarily await the prior outcome of a detailed cost/benefit analysis. But it should be clear in everyone's mind that it is indeed a useful project.

[2] Some examples of model approaches which seek answers to these questions are: H. Correa and J. Tinbergen, "Quantitative Adaptation of Education to Accelerated Growth," *Kyklos,* 15 (1962); Herbert S. Parnes, *Forecasting Educational Needs for Economic and Social Development* (Paris: O.E.C.D., 1962); and John Laska, "The Stages of Educational Development," *Comparative Education Review,* 8 (December, 1964), pp. 251–263. The latter, strictly speaking, is not a model approach, but a stage classification of countries which intimates that developing countries should try to emulate what the already developed countries have done.

[3] The complete results of this work, including a very detailed analysis of the evolution of the education sector during the past decade, were published in the document INP/OECD, *Desarrollo económico y social, recursos humanos y educación* (Lima, INP, 1966).

[4] Principal among these were the National Bureau of Statistics, the Ministry of Public Education, and the Employment and Human Resources Service of the Ministry of Labor.

[5] A comprehensive program was devised to sample data for the economically active population drawn from the 1961 Population Census and transcribed on 10 magnetic tapes.

The methodological approach employed was similar to that used in the Mediterranean Regional Project.[1]

Because most model approaches have a way of skirting some of the more complicated practical difficulties, any methodological approach to be operationally useful must be infused with a large element of common sense and enough flexibility to abandon rigor in the interest of realism. The manpower planning approach developed and refined in the Mediterranean Regional Project reflects this combination of abstraction and realism remarkably well. [2] Briefly, its salient features may be outlined as follows:

(a) Educational planning is approached from the manpower point of view. Thus that part of the population directly engaged in productive activity is given priority. This is in agreement with the criterion that education should have the greatest impact in contributing a maximum amount of additional resources which can be devoted to subsequent, greater educational effort.

(b) Educational planning is linked directly to economic growth forecasts for all major sectors of the economy. Thus manpower requirements foreseen provide maximum assurance that programmed educational development will be synchronized with sectoral development programs.

(c) A long-range perspective of 15 years (essential for educational planning) is provided through the extension of economic growth forecasts. However, since it is not likely that specific growth targets will ever be precisely met, the methodological framework provides adequate elasticity to allow for changes in the chief variables—and the parameters—through constant checks and subsequent revisions at key stages.

(d) The methodological framework (manpower approach) is not restricted to the formal education system. Manpower planning should and does allow for the consideration of all types of educational formation—formal, including primary, secondary and higher; and informal, including special institutions and on-the-job training programs.

(e) Even if there were general agreement regarding the criteria for measuring the returns to various types and levels of education, the

---

[1] The Mediterranean Regional Project represents one of the more fascinating contemporary efforts at broad, multicountry manpower and education planning. Teams of local country technicians and OECD technicians prepared long-range manpower forecasts and devised strategies for human resource and educational development for Italy, Yugoslavia, Greece, Turkey, Spain, and Portugal.

[2] Harbison and Myers have criticized this approach, mainly because of its use of productivity estimates in deriving sectoral employment estimates outside the manufacturing, construction, mining, and transportation sectors. Although considerable use of productivity estimates is implied, this is not the complete case. One of the stronger aspects of the approach is the allowance for incorporation of other criteria in forecasting employment in these other sectors.

required data for their measurement are not generally available in either developing countries or developed countries. Thus the programming of educational development in unison with overall development goals says only that the immediate return is greater for those members of the population who are engaged in productive activity and counsels only that the educational effort be related to independently established developmental priorities.

(f)   The methodological framework specifically allows for the inclusion of socially desirable goals such as universal primary education and adult literacy programs. And these are not merely adjuncts to an economically oriented approach; the approach calls for education for economic and social development.

(g)   Finally, and most important, it provides qualitative estimates of the needs for training from all sources and at all levels if the educational requirements for economic and social development are to be attained. This allows for programming enrollments, building activities, and so forth in fairly well-defined terms.

Economic planning in the public sector has been a declared policy goal of the Peruvian government at least since the inception of the National Planning Institute in 1962. Peru is basically a free-enterprise economy, and while considerable attention has been given to the private sector, the role of public policy in this regard has been primarily of a permissive nature or, at most, has involved the use of limited tax incentives, import and export controls, and credit policy to encourage desired activities in the private sector.[1]

The basic work of the Planning Institute has been centered on the completion of depth studies of Peruvian economic and social conditions,[2] the preparation of limited aggregate development goals and short-range public investment programs[3] (for one- or two-year periods), and the elaboration of specific projects for future public-sector implementation. As is the case in most developing countries, advances have been limited by the shortage of adequate statistical materials[4] and other data essential for planning purposes as well as by the general confusion inherent in first efforts at planning. It is within the framework of this system of fairly limited, short-range planning objectives that manpower and education planning in Peru must be evaluated.

[1] One such example is the 1965 tax moratorium for certain underdeveloped eastern areas of the Republic which is designed to encourage the location of new industry and subsidiaries of existing industries in this area.

[2] This consisted of a multivolume series of basic studies first published in 1963 under the title *Diagnóstico de la situación económica y social del país.* Part of the work of the Planning Institute has consisted in the annual updating of the original studies.

[3] *Plan de Inversiones Públicas, 1964–65* and *Plan de Inversiones Públicas, 1966* (Peru: INP).

[4] The recent Population Census, completed in 1961, was the first since 1940 in Peru, while the Economic Census of 1963 is the first in Peru's history.

As previously noted, manpower and educational forecasts are essentially a long-range enterprise, usually involving a minimum period of some 10 to 15 years. The reasons are reasonably apparent: the requirements for engineers, medical personnel, and technicians over the next one and one-half decades represent required inputs in the manpower training complex at the present time. This implies a general forecast of components such as the size of total GNP, its sectoral distribution, and the growth of the labor force over a long-range time period. Since the degree of accuracy in such forecasts is uncertain, even over the range of only a few years, the results are subject to a multiple margin of error over such a lengthy time period. This margin can be minimized to some extent by keeping occupational categories fairly broad and by building flexibility, in the form of plans for future readjustments, into the model. At any rate, the existence of uncertainties is something which must be lived with and provides no particularly valid reason for not venturing the closest approximations possible. Accordingly, the following steps were taken by the research group in Peru:

(a) They estimated the gross domestic product (GDP), breaking it down into sectoral components, through 1980. Projections through 1970 previously made by the National Planning Institute in its short-range public investment programs were employed, but the manpower research team itself in consultation with the responsible planning authorities made the projections for the period 1970–1980. The provisional nature of these estimates is well recognized, but at least a cursory examination of their basis is in order.

In the first place, the Planning Institute tentatively worked with two sets of aggregate growth rates, 5.5 per cent and 7 per cent. There seemed to be very little to be gained by working with alternate hypotheses in setting up preliminary manpower targets, since the flexibility of the method employed already allows for subsequent adjustments in the light of actual performance. In addition, several factors supported the adoption of the higher global growth rate:

1. A 7 per cent growth rate would appear to be attainable on the basis of past experience of the Peruvian economy and especially in view of current, active government intervention and public policies aimed at achieving a higher growth rate.
2. Available evidence regarding domestic and foreign capital mobilization and the capital/output ratio lend support to the higher growth rate.
3. The incremental output/employment ratio concept implies that the mere maintenance of current levels of employment is dependent on the achievement of a higher aggregate growth rate. In underdeveloped countries, the maintenance of full employment

is just as significant a policy goal as it is in the more advanced countries.

4. The rapid growth of the population, more than 3 per cent in the early 1960's, is a compelling factor in the achievement of an overall higher growth rate in Peru if an acceptable increase in per capita output is to be attained. While rapid population growth does not of course guarantee corresponding increases in output, the effective utilization of labor resources through conscious manpower policies can be a significant factor in growth.

(b)   They made a long-range estimate of the economically active population and its distribution among the various economic sectors. Overall labor force estimates were based on population projections and labor force participation rates for age and sex groups of the total population. The distribution of the labor force by economic sectors was based on relative rates of growth of these sectors (and hence their future estimated contribution to GDP), productivity estimates, implied employment policy objectives, and estimates of the job-creation capacity of the nonagricultural sectors.

(c)   They undertook a detailed evaluation of the educational, occupational, and sectoral structure of the present labor force on the basis of data drawn from the 1961 Population Census. The principal objectives served by this step were to provide a clear assessment of the overall manpower picture in Peru and to determine major structural deficiencies and required adjustments in terms of occupational and educational categories.

(d)   They postulated an improved occupational-educational structure consistent with aggregate manpower requirements and its sectoral composition for the 1980 target date. By taking into account the evolution of the current labor force, they were able to derive net requirements for the planning period.

The sectoral components of the aggregate growth rate in (a) above and the corresponding employment and productivity projections are given in Table 1. Several features of this table merit special comment. Output per worker in the industrial manufacturing sector is rather low at the present time, only some 47 per cent greater than overall output per worker, and surpassed by five other economic sectors. This reflects a heavy concentration—almost 50 per cent—of manufacturing employment in an antiquated textile manufacturing subsector. Peru's industrial manufacture, with the possible exception of the chemical products sector and a food processing sector based on a vastly expanded fishing industry,[1] lacks diversification

---

[1] In 1961 Peru became the world leader in the fishing industry, displacing Japan.

Table 1. Gross Domestic Product, Employment and Productivity

Economic Sectors	Base Year 1961			Target Year 1980		
	Employment (1,000's)	Gross Domestic Product (millions of 1960 Peruvian soles (S/.))	Output per Worker (1,000's of 1960 S/.)	Output per Worker (1,000's of 1960 S/.)	Gross Domestic Product (millions of 1960 Peruvian soles (S/.))	Employment (1,000's)
Agriculture and livestock	1,534.1	12,313.2	8.0	13.4	31,032	2,311.5
Fishing	21.1	1,010.6	47.9	73.4	3,123	42.5
Mining	66.3	5,221.8	78.7	139.1	13,076	94.0
Manufacturing	410.9	11,513.5	28.0	54.2	49,476[d]	911.7
Food and beverages	52.2	4,006.6	76.7	127.7	14,892	116.6
Textiles and clothing	191.8	2,141.5	11.1	22.7	7,421	326.1
Chemical products	14.4	1,416.2	98.3	169.9	6,679	39.3
Metals	55.7	1,934.3	34.7	73.3	10,934	149.1
Other	96.8	2,014.9	20.8	34.0	9,548	280.6
Construction	104.7	2,086.2	19.9	24.7	12,686	513.1
Energy	8.6	235.3[a]	27.3	56.0	1,648	29.4
Commerce	263.0	10,449.2	39.7	56.2	33,179	590.3
Banking, insurance and real estate	18.8	2,214.5	117.7	226.3	17,037	35.5
Housing	–	4,626.5	–	–	10,645	–
Transport and communications	93.9	3,193.0	34.0	49.9	12,686	253.8
Services	304.9	3,275.1	10.7	12.6	6,239	495.0
Government	171.8	4,642.8	27.0	40.4	16,199	400.8
Education	(65.9)[b]	–	–	–	–	(190.0)
Not specified	123.0[c]	–	–	–	–	147.1
Total	3,120.8[d]	60,781.7	18.7	32.8	197,026	5,824.7

Key to Table: [a]Estimated. [b]In government, 56.1; in services, 9.8. [c]Unemployed, 40.1; the remainder either seeking first job or not specifying economic sector. [d]Figures may not total due to rounding off.
Source: INP/OECD, *Desarrollo económico y social, recursos humanos y educación* (Lima: INP, 1966), pp. 3–28.

and employs rudimentary technology. At present, it is capable of providing only limited employment opportunities and will require modernization and rather heavy investments for some time to come.

Agricultural productivity follows the traditional pattern of an underdeveloped country, with commercially oriented export farms in the coastal zone differing markedly from highlands peasant plot farming. Nonetheless, given present and expected industrial employment opportunities over the next decade, agriculture will no doubt continue to absorb nearly 30 per cent of the expected increase in total employment. Manpower and labor training policies and programs must be geared to this reality.[1] Moreover, the movement from rural to industrial employment depends on improvements in agricultural investments and on better irrigation techniques; therefore, better-trained farmers in general are an item of first priority.

The fivefold expansion of employment in the construction industry, together with only modest productivity gains, reflects the conscious advocacy of a public employment policy in public works construction of all types and the use of unskilled labor resources to stimulate much needed housing, school, and other construction projects. The construction industry, for various reasons, is ideally suited for use as a transitional employment stage between agricultural and industrial employment.[2]

Table 2, deriving from (c) above, provides details of the projected occupational changes forecast for major occupational categories in the Peruvian economy.

The assumptions underlying the forecasted (target) changes in occupational composition are complex and diverse. They are basically derived from the treatment of economic sectors individually and the individual treatment of a number of occupational groups within categories on the basis of variables uniquely a function of the particular group. Thus in some instances the assumptions underlying structural occupational changes may be at variance as between sectors, while the overall changes depicted in Table 2 represent the reaggregation of individual sector and specific group components. As indicated in the previous section, changes in employment in the skilled-workers category reflect simultaneously the assumption of a higher unskilled/skilled ratio in the case of the manufacturing industry and a lower ratio in the case of the construction sector.

---

[1] One of the Peruvian government's major policy goals is the modernization of agriculture, and large sums are currently being invested in colonization schemes, agrarian reform, and irrigation projects. The success or failure of these programs depends, in great part, on the ability of the education system to provide the agricultural technicians needed to implement these programs and its adaptability to the needs of rural peasants.

[2] Specifically, a good deal of the labor input in construction can be of the manual, unskilled variety, especially if the choice of technology is deliberately geared to labor intensity. At the same time, involvement in elementary industrial operations requiring continuity, regularity, and cooperation is an excellent breeding ground for familiarity with industrial processes.

While it would be unnecessarily tedious to examine each of these individually, it may be useful to briefly discuss several sectors and occupational groups which are illustrative of the process.

Table 2. Labor Force: Current and Projected (Thousands of Persons)

Occupational Categories	1961		1980	
	Total	Survivors in 1980	Total	New Entrants
Scientific and technical professionals	15.5	9.7	55.9	46.1
	(0.50)[a]	(0.47)	(.96)	(1.23)
Nonscientific and nontechnical professionals	72.2	46.1	193.8	147.7
	(2.32)	(2.23)	(3.33)	(3.93)
Teachers	53.1	32.1	142.5	110.4
Others	19.1	14.0	51.3	37.3
Technicians	24.3	15.4	146.9	131.4
	(0.78)	(0.74)	(2.52)	(3.50)
Managers and directors	836.9	466.6	1,496.4	1,029.7
	(26.82)	(22.54)	(25.69)	(27.42)
In agriculture	794.0	441.5	1,391.9	950.3
Nonagriculture	42.9	25.0	104.5	79.4
Clerical	116.3	75.4	371.3	295.8
	(3.73)	(3.64)	(6.37)	(7.88)
Sales personnel	231.5	154.9	411.2	256.3
	(7.42)	(7.48)	(7.05)	(6.82)
Skilled workers	91.4	62.0	351.6	289.5
	(2.93)	(2.99)	(6.03)	(7.71)
Agricultural	1.5	1.0	—	—
Nonagricultural	89.9	61.0	—	—
Semiskilled, unskilled and family workers	1,603.8	1,136.9	2,615.7	1,478.7
	(51.38)	(54.97)	(44.91)	(39.41)
Agricultural	733.1	522.1	875.9	353.7
Nonagricultural	870.6	614.8	1,739.8	1,124.9
Others	26.1	17.0	34.8	17.7
	(0.84)	(.82)	(.59)	(.47)
Not specified	102.5	85.3	147.1	61.7
	(3.28)	(4.12)	(2.52)	(1.64)
Totals	3,120.8	2,069.6	5,824.7	3,755.0
	(100.00)			

[a]Figures in parentheses are percentages.
Source: Derived from INP/OECD, *Desarrollo económico y social*, pp. 3–47, 3–63, 3–76, 3–79.

Within the agricultural sector two significant government objectives may be mentioned: (a) a large-scale irrigation and technical improvements program and (b) an extensive agrarian reform and colonization scheme.

The first of these is reflected in a large expansion of the number of technicians and scientific and technical professionals, the combined total of which only amounted to 1,400 in 1961, compared with a total agricultural employment of 1.5 million. In addition, the ratio of professionals to technicians was 1.5 to 1.

It was assumed that the vast extension of technical services connected with agricultural extension work, survey and mapping and maintenance of facilities would be reflected primarily in an enormous increase in the technicians group—from 550 in 1961 to 25,000 in 1980. At the same time, independent estimates of the number by agricultural officials postulated a workable technical relationship of about one professional per 10 technicians in agriculture.

The projected increase in agricultural proprietors was a function of several factors: (a) normal population increase in agriculture less (b) an assumed industrial employment absorption rate of one third the natural rate of increase and (c) an estimated rate of creation of new farm units based on Agrarian Reform Commission projections. While the latter is heavily dependent on unforeseeable political factors, the residual categories of skilled and semiskilled agricultural labor do little violence to the training implications.

The manufacturing sector allows for considerably more precision in quantitative specifications than do other economic sectors. Partly this is a result of the relatively close relationship between occupational structure and levels of productivity for some of the more significant technical categories such as scientific professionals, technicians, and skilled labor; partly it stems from the availability of much more precise data drawn from the 1963 manufacturing census.

The assumption made about these groups is that the future structure of labor force will closely approximate the equivalent structure of current higher productivity firms in manufacturing subsectors. But it was also assumed that structural deficiencies like those between sectors, identified from the census data, would be corrected to provide for a more uniform distribution of skilled technical personnel among the five subsectors analyzed.

In the case of other occupational groups, additional variables were employed. For forecasting sales and clerical personnel, these included factors such as projected sales volume and the general expansion of markets; for forecasting needs for managers and directors, number of firms was used.

At another level, specific occupational groups within an occupational category were projected independently of any economic sector on the basis of specified variables. Two such examples are medical doctors and their corresponding auxiliary medical personnel and teachers.

The number of medical doctors was projected on the basis of health officials' estimates of minimally acceptable health standards expressed as ratios of doctors to population. Auxiliary medical personnel were projected as a function of the former, again employing health officials' estimates of technically derived ratios designed to meet certain medical standards.

The expansion of the teaching staff is, in effect, a residual factor deriving from all other categories. It is circular in that teachers are both an input and an output, and their number is arrived at through successive approximations. Functionally, the figures derive from assumed teacher/student ratios, an assumed attrition rate, and the progressive upgrading of the educational levels of the current teaching force.

Perhaps the most important single conclusion to be drawn from Table 2 is the massive training effort needed. Because of the high rate of growth of the population—assuming only a fairly constant labor force participation rate—nearly two thirds (64 per cent) of the 1980 labor force will be new entrants. In countries with more modest rates of population growth, approximately the inverse would be true, with 33 per cent of the economically active being new entrants. In one sense this places an enormous strain on the education system over the next two decades, but in another sense allows for the rapid overall upgrading of the economically active population.

From an occupational viewpoint, Peru's most urgent requirement is for scientific and technically trained personnel at all levels. Implicit in this is some redistribution of the present trained manpower, which is concentrated in particular sectors and geographical areas. The shortage of technical personnel reflects the well-known traditional emphasis on the humanities and law which prevailed for many years. Some change has already taken place in this regard—for example, the establishment of the Universidad Agraria, Universidad de Ingeniería, Cayetano Heredia (Medical School) and the rapid growth of secondary technical education facilities and SENATI (skilled-worker training financed by industry)—but there is still room for much improvement. In 1964, 73 per cent of enrollment in higher education was concentrated in the normal schools, faculties of education, and the humanities.

There is a great shortage of semiprofessional technical personnel in all fields of economic activity. Aside from several three-year faculties in the universities for the training of medical technicians and a few other semiprofessionals, no special facilities for training at this level exist at present, although there are plans.[1] Coupled with the shortage of skilled workers,

---

[1] The Peruvian government is currently negotiating a long-term loan with the International Bank for Reconstruction and Development which will include the construction and equipping of five junior colleges for the training of intermediate-level technicians.

there is a large gap between the most highly trained industrial workers and the next most highly trained, which makes communication and articulation between the various work activities difficult and limited.

Another occupational anomaly is the fact that many workers with specialized training are not employed in their field of greatest competence. Although some wastage of this sort is always to be expected, the degree to which it occurs in Peru may reflect two factors: failure of the education system to provide the real training needed to qualify for a particular job[1] and a poorly organized and poorly integrated labor market. An important illustration of these two phenomena can be observed among the graduates of secondary technical schools. The low quality of training imparted does not really prepare skilled workers without considerable additional on-the-job training, while industrial firms display a marked preference to hire low-wage, untrained labor off the street and to train these workers themselves. Industry is not taking into account the tax investment already involved in training secondary technical school graduates, and perhaps the only effective way to deal with this problem is through the long-range upgrading of the entire labor force and the removal from the market of cheap labor.

Of special importance for the educational system then is the need to provide 325,000 new professional and semiprofessional workers. This forms a rational basis for university expansion and for the provision of intermediate-level education. It also provides the basis for a more rational and equitable division of labor among the many specialized institutions of higher learning.

Sales and clerical workers represent another half million new workers to be added to the labor force in the forecasting period. Female employment in the secretarial and bookkeeping fields will be in demand, and secondary-commercial and regular secondary schools for girls must take these needs into account. The net increase of skilled workers projected is 290,000. While many of these will be trained outside the formal education system (on-the-job programs, SENATI, the Army, etc.), a large number (44,000) will still have to come from the secondary technical schools. And almost 200,000 (including secondary technical graduates) should have completed primary school.

The foregoing are purely economic requirements in the sense that we have heretofore been dealing with only the economically active population. It is at this point that the specified social goals of the country must be incorporated. The economic requirements are generally derived from technical

---

[1] Ministry of Education estimates indicate that at present only somewhere in the neighborhood of 10 to 15 per cent of the secondary technical school graduates find employment in their field of specialization. Responsible observers attribute this primarily to the lack of adequate equipment in technical schools, low quality of the technical teachers, and noncooperation of private industry with the schools.

specifications. The social goals are, by definition, nontechnically specified, generally via the political process.

Peru is committed to the goal of 100 per cent enrollment of all relevant age-group persons at the elementary level. In addition, strong commitments to adult literacy programs and to secondary school enrollments exist apart from purely economic considerations. An additional factor is the goal of providing greater balance than has previously existed between the educational opportunities of males and females and between urban and rural areas.[1]

However, because participation rates in the labor force after graduation are less than 100 per cent, there is a sense in which purely social goals are also implicitly met in the process of providing for the economic requirements. Nearly two million projected graduates will simply not be engaged in directly productive economic activities but will nonetheless possess varying degrees of educational and skill levels.

The quantitative impact of these broad occupational changes and incorporated social goals on the formal education system is given in Tables 3 and 4. The translation of economic and social requirements into their educational equivalents involved three basic steps:

(a) Total manpower needs for economic and social goals were converted into numbers of graduates required at the various levels and for the various branches of the education system during the entire planning period. With respect to the economic requirements, allowances were made for wastage, since a certain proportion of new graduates will not be economically active.

(b) Enrollment levels and absolute new enrollment requirements were derived, using specified hypotheses regarding expected completion ratios for the various levels and branches of education.

(c) Teacher requirements and administrative and auxiliary personnel requirements were estimated in the light of these enrollment factors.

An important consideration in the translation of manpower requirements into their educational equivalents is the manner in which "appropriate" education is defined. For some groups, especially scientific and technical professionals, there are reasonably objective criteria. For many other groups the relationship is much less clear, while the numbers of graduates required are highly sensitive to the upgrading of the educational qualifications associated with an occupation. No attempt was made to rigorously define these equivalents for any occupational group other than professionals and some semiprofessionals—medical and agricultural technicians especially. But an overall upgrading was assumed in the following general terms for certain groups.

[1] These goals have been officially defined by the Commission on Education and Human Resources.

Table 3. Graduates Needed by Level and Branch (Thousands of Persons)

Educational Levels and Branches	1961-80	1961-66	1967-70	1971-75	1976-80
Primary	5,582.5	768.0	832.1	1,711.4	2,271.0
Secondary	1,325.5	171.6	209.6	398.3	546.0
Regular	1,111.1	145.6	176.4	333.6	455.5
Technical[a]	214.4	26.0	33.2	64.7	90.5
Agricultural	42.5	3.9	6.8	13.6	18.2
Industrial	107.1	12.3	15.2	31.3	48.3
Male	64.4	6.8	8.2	18.4	31.0
Female	42.7	5.5	7.0	12.9	17.3
Commercial	64.8	9.8	11.2	19.8	24.0
Day	57.7	8.9	10.1	17.5	21.2
Evening	7.1	0.9	1.1	2.3	2.8
Intermediate (junior college)	15.0	0.1	2.0	5.7	7.2
Higher	262.6	48.6	53.5	73.4	87.1
Normal school	90.0	15.0	16.4	27.1	31.5
University	172.6	33.6	37.1	46.3	55.6
Education	36.7	10.6	9.9	9.0	7.2
Humanities	59.6	11.3	15.3	16.3	16.7
Medicine	13.7	2.5	2.1	3.6	5.5
Science	26.1	2.9	3.1	6.9	13.2
Engineering	36.5	6.3	6.7	10.5	13.0

Note: Intervals are not the same due to the fact that 1967 represents the earliest year in which the programming of enrollments to accomplish these goals can be undertaken.
[a]Day school only.
Source: INP/OECD, *Desarrollo económico y social,* p. 4-07.

In 1961, only 53 per cent of teachers had completed secondary school, while 13 per cent had only an elementary school education. It was postulated that by 1980, 63 per cent of these should have completed normal school and another 34 per cent university work in faculties of education. The satisfaction of these requirements is fundamental, since the success or failure of much else depends on the quality of the teaching force. Among the remaining nonscientific and technical professionals, it was postulated that two thirds should have completed university work, while the remaining one third would require a minimum of general secondary education, complemented in some cases by additional, nonuniversity special training.

In the semiprofessional/technician category, an analysis of the 1961 Population Census revealed a notable structural deficiency in the composition of the labor force. This group, which in many more-developed countries

Table 4. Enrollment Requirements (Thousands of Persons)

Educational Levels and Branches	1964	1967	1970	1975	1980
Preschool and primary	1,836.3	2,279.2	2,651.6	3,278.8	3,839.5
Secondary	319.9	451.0	571.2	751.2	949.1
Regular	260.3	362.8	462.8	618.3	770.8
Day	229.7	313.6	399.8	544.7	681.9
Evening	30.6	49.2	63.0	73.6	88.9
Technical	59.6	88.2	108.4	132.9	178.3
Agricultural	7.0	12.4	16.2	20.7	27.5
Industrial	24.8	36.6	45.4	60.3	90.2
Male	13.7	20.2	26.3	38.1	61.8
Female	11.1	16.4	19.1	22.2	28.4
Commercial	27.8	39.2	46.8	51.9	60.6
Day	15.1	21.3	25.0	28.1	32.1
Evening	12.7	17.9	21.8	23.8	28.5
Intermediate (junior college)	0.4	1.6	3.5	4.7	5.6
Higher	63.5	82.3	86.5	98.4	123.9
Normal school	12.1[a]	18.6	23.3	25.7	29.2
University	51.4	63.7	63.2	72.7	94.7
Education	11.8[a]	14.6	12.1	8.7	8.7
Humanities	22.7	28.0	24.8	24.2	24.2
Medicine	3.8	5.2	6.6	10.2	15.7
Science	4.3	5.7	8.0	15.4	28.2
Engineering	8.8	10.2	11.7	14.1	17.9
Total	2,220.1	2,814.1	3,312.8	4,133.3	4,918.1

[a] Normal school enrollments refer only to primary school teachers. Secondary, secondary technical and physical education teachers are included in education.

Source: INP/OECD, *Desarrollo económico y social,* p. 4–19.

constitutes an important middle-level operations group, represented .0075 of the labor force, totaling only 24,000 persons. Further analysis revealed that the latent demand for this category was strong, since of the 24,000 persons occupying such positions only 9 per cent had received any training above the secondary level. Indeed, 34 per cent of those occupying such positions had only completed elementary school.

Of the 132,000 new entrants to the labor force by 1980, it was postulated that at least one third should be graduates of technical secondary schools and 11 per cent graduates of the projected regional technical two-year colleges. Another 40 per cent should receive scholastic and extrascholastic training beyond the secondary level from a wide variety of specialized training programs, while the remainder will receive training on an ad hoc basis.

Small-farm operators compose the bulk of new entrants (92 per cent) into the managers and directors category. These two very distinct groups were analytically separated in determining educational requirements.

By and large, elementary school education and the use of agricultural extension services for informal training were assumed for most of the small-farm operators. The remainder of the nonagricultural managers and directors were assumed to be divided between some 40 per cent with university-level training, another 40 per cent with some form of secondary training, and a residual—principally managing small commercial establishments, shops, etc.—not rigorously defined.

The only other group to be mentioned specifically here is the very strategic category of skilled workers. While 75 per cent of these had received only elementary education or less in 1961, of the annual average of 285,000 new entrants to the labor force envisioned in the period considered, some 44,000 should be secondary technical graduates and another 90,000 with special training beyond the elementary level such as the National Apprenticeship Program (SENATI). The remaining half emphasize the importance of expanding and encouraging on-the-job programs and training programs in the armed services for skilled workers already in existence.

Wastage, defined as graduates who do not enter the labor force upon completion of their studies, implies that the actual quantity of graduates at all levels and for all branches must be considerably greater than real requirements. The actual participation rates of graduates of the various levels and branches are somewhat different, since they are principally influenced by the proportion of women graduates (lower activity rates), the level of education attained (higher activity rates for professionals), and the type of education completed (lower activity rates for general studies than for technical training).

Wastage, defined as dropouts at all levels and in a more limited sense repeaters, requires that new enrollments be much greater than expected graduates. There is also the additional requisite that all graduates beyond the primary school level must first have completed the previous educational levels leading up to advanced training.

Thus the total number of new graduates required over the entire programming period comes out to be approximately 5.6 million primary school graduates, 2.1 million of whom will enter the labor force and 1.8 million of whom will go on to the completion of secondary studies. Of the 1.8 million, approximately 630,000 may be expected to enter the labor force while 280,000 continue in higher education. Of the graduates of this latter group, some 224,000 may be expected to enter the labor force.

The breakdown into periods given in Table 3 also depicts the growth and changing distribution of graduates that is envisaged. Thus the 1961–1966 interval illustrates approximately what the education system is doing now, while the more or less steady increase at all levels and in all branches implicitly takes into account the time factor needed for the expansion forecast. Thus graduates of intermediate-level training, of which there were almost none in the 1961–1966 period, should rise to something over 7,000 during the five-year interval, 1976–1980.

An ancillary problem in the determination of numbers of required graduates deserves mention, albeit only brief. This is the question of dropouts and the role they play in satisfying graduate goals. Graduates, for the purposes of the program, include all students enrolled in the final year of an educational cycle. In the majority of cases this assumption has only limited effects. Students enrolled in the last year actually graduate in high proportions, either immediately or within the span of a few years. In addition, with few exceptions a person enrolled in the final year of an educational level has attained a degree of qualification that very strongly influences his occupational status. In practice, especially in a country such as Peru, he will have roughly similar options to those of an actual graduate. Dropouts before the final grade of an educational level are treated as graduates of the next-lowest educational level.

Estimates of total enrollment for specified years were derived by interpolating on the basis of first-year and last-year enrollment. Thus it may be seen in Tables 3 and 4 that for the total of 7.2 million new graduates in the entire period, total enrollment must be something over the four million level in 1975 and about 4.9 million in 1980. In contrast, due to the much higher labor force participation rates, total enrollment in higher education institutions in 1980 will represent less than one half of the total number of higher education graduates for the entire period.

In addition to the quantitative and qualitative (structure of enrollment by level and branch) factors implicit in the foregoing, something must be said about the qualitative educational standards of the school system. It is imperative that educators formulate ambitious programs of qualitative improvement designed to make the education system as productive as possible. This is of course already being done and will undoubtedly be continued. These activities will bring about changes in school completion ratios. Higher retention rates and improved completion ratios mean less enrollment to achieve stated graduate goals. While it is extremely difficult to forecast accurately the proportion of enrolled students who will go on to complete the educational cycle in which they are enrolled, some general hypotheses were needed, primarily in the form of goals. The completion ratio hypotheses employed are given in Table 5. The importance of achieving these goals cannot be overemphasized, since the continued loss of large numbers of the school population through dropouts is an enormous economic and

Table 5. Estimated School Completion Ratios (Graduates per 100 Enrollees)

	1964	1970	1975	1980
Primary	30.1	41	61	70
Secondary				
Regular				
Day	56	58	61	65
Evening and night	43.4	54	60	65
Technical				
Agricultural	56	60	66	70
Industrial				
Men	31	38	48	60
Women	31	38	48	60
Commercial				
Day	37	44	49	58
Evening and night	26	36	42	50
Intermediate (junior college)	–	66	70	75
Higher				
Normal school	90.1	81	84	85
University				
Education	80	80	80	80
Humanities				
(4-year sequence)	71.2	68	73	75
(5-year sequence)	33.2	55	64	70
Medicine				
(4-year sequence)	100	66	70	70
(6-year sequence)	76.7	71	75	75
Sciences	48.6	66	68	70
Engineering	76	70	74	78

Source: INP/OECD, *Desarrollo económico y social*, p. 4–12.

social waste and will ultimately require a significant increase in forecasted enrollments, buildings, and teachers if manpower needs are to be met.

In light of the foregoing, several specific proposals for improving the productivity of the education system may be briefly indicated. The most obvious of these are the implied improvement brought about by the training of highly qualified teachers and providing for the extended use of teaching materials, textbooks, and school equipment. Others are a more rational education budget (more attention to capital expenditures), economic assistance programs for needy students, and improved orientation of training in the light of special studies of student needs and plans. These are the significant problems to which the professional educators must turn their attention. Upon their rapid resolution hinges the success or failure of all the foregoing.

Perhaps the most important single consideration involved is the economic feasibility of the forecasted requirements. While there is very little to be gained by first setting up financial constraints and then gearing proposals to these limits (this represents antiquated economic thinking and almost inevitably leads to an inadequate and underfinanced program), the costs of undertaking such a program must be realistically assessed and allocation priorities defined. A more positive approach involves the assessment of manpower needs, the development of the most technically efficient means for meeting these needs and a look at what can be done to implement them. There is real room for some imaginative new ideas concerning educational finance, both in the developing and the developed economies. One which Peru might well consider very seriously is the use of local taxation, labor, and raw materials together with the encouragement of local groups to get into the education field themselves. The local and regional financing of some of the more straightforward educational costs, such as buildings and equipment, would not only make it possible to do a great deal more, but also free central government educators to concentrate on the issues of curriculum, school dropout, textbooks, and teacher training.

Other areas for imaginative finance involve the tapping of labor union and industrial funds for skilled-worker training, the more extensive use of the armed services for training purposes, and the encouragement of domestic production of expensive school equipment.

But most of all, every effort must be taken to improve the efficiency of all training systems. This is by far the most effective device for acquiring new financial resources without any corresponding absolute increase in the budget. In Peru, it is not at all improbable that as much as a one-third gain might be realized by a concerted attack on waste, inefficiency, and duplication of functions.

While it was not possible to accurately estimate the overall costs of implementing the foregoing, because of the lack of appropriate cost data, an attempt was made to forecast an operating budget for the year 1975 (Table 6). At present, many deficits must be made up because of past failures to provide adequate educational finance, especially regarding capital expenditures. Unequipped or only partially equipped buildings have already been constructed and unqualified teachers have been incorporated into the education system in an effort to put bodies in front of packed classrooms. These existing imbalances will require a considerable initial financial outlay in order to bring the system up to qualitative standards, though much can be accomplished through relatively inexpensive reorganization and the elimination of waste.

Table 6. Estimated Education Budget: 1975 (Millions of 1960 Soles)

		Current Expenditures				Capital Expenditures	
	Total	Wages and Salaries	Goods	Services	Indirect[a]	Construction	Equipment
Total	10,239.3	8,393.8	570.5	416.9	409.5	288.2	160.4
Administration	512.0[b]	460.8	20.5	30.7	–	–	–
School operation	9,113.0	7,748.7	537.7	378.0	–	288.2	160.4
Preschool and primary	4,617.6	4,173.9	131.8	87.9		168.0	56.0
Secondary	2,966.2	2,452.6	212.9	143.6		93.8	63.3
Regular	2,150.6	1,822.8	145.0	103.5		54.9	24.4
Day	1,904.0	1,605.8	127.7	91.2		54.9	24.4
Evening and night	246.6	217.0	17.3	12.3		–	–
Technical	815.6	629.8	67.9	40.1		38.9	38.9
Agricultural	149.0	119.3	12.5	6.9		5.5	4.8
Industrial	489.0	355.9	43.2	26.2		31.4	32.3
Men	361.4	251.2	33.7	21.4		26.6	28.5
Women	127.6	104.7	9.5	4.8		4.8	3.8
Commercial	177.6	154.6	12.2	7.0		2.0	1.8
Day	97.9	83.7	6.6	3.8		2.0	1.8
Evening and night	79.7	70.9	5.6	3.2		–	–
Intermediate (junior college)	40.2	30.3	4.5	3.0		1.5	0.9
Higher	1,489.0	1,091.9	188.5	143.5		24.9	40.2
Normal schools	210.2	144.6	41.3	20.7		2.4	1.2
Universities	1,278.8	947.3	147.2	122.8		22.5	39.0
Education	93.2	76.5	9.3	7.5		–	–
Humanities	259.4	192.0	36.3	31.1		–	–
Medicine	292.5	193.2	44.2	38.6		5.5	11.0
Science	291.8	201.2	31.0	25.8		13.0	20.8
Engineering	341.8	284.4	26.4	19.8		4.0	7.2
All other	614.3[c]	184.3	12.3	8.2	409.5[d]	–	–

Key to Table: [a]Transfer payments, social security reserves, etc. [b]Five per cent of 10,239.3. [c]Six per cent of 10,239.3. [d]Four per cent of 10,239.3.
Source: Derived from INP/OECD, Desarrollo económico y social, p. 4–44.

The operating and capital budget given in Table 6 represents expenditures equivalent to approximately 7.0 per cent of the estimated 1975 GDP and may be compared with Peru's 1965 percentage outlay of 5.7 per cent. This increase is certainly not unrealistic, as many lucrative areas of potential finance have yet to be tapped, while a considerable portion of the current deficit could be met through international borrowing. More than anything else, it represents a more rational structure than the present budget, which is heavily weighed down by salaries and administrative costs.

Detailed analytic cost studies of the various categories of Peruvian public education expenditure have been rendered virtually impossible up to now by the use of a traditional administrative budget employing vague categories of expenditure. In addition, the large degree of autonomy exercised by the various branches of the educational service in shifting moneys from proposed budget outlays into educational demands of a more immediate nature which arise during the course of the fiscal year has further complicated such analysis. Finally, virtually nothing is known about the cost structure of educational expenditures in the private sector, which accounted for almost a tenth of elementary school enrollments, more than one fourth of secondary enrollments, and nearly one third of normal school enrollments in 1964. All this has hindered an historical analysis of changing cost structure during the period of most rapid educational expansion, 1961–1965. Thus the budget proposals formulated here are of a normative character with a view to rationalizing public outlays on education and providing the basis for the future analytic treatment of expenditures.

The gradual adoption (since 1963) of functional budgeting in the public sector is beginning to have an effect in drawing attention to the need for cost/benefit analysis of various types of educational expenditures. It is also serving to promote the concept of long-range budgeting independent of the vicissitudes of year-to-year legislative budget slashing.

The growth of public and private outlays on education has proceeded at an average annual rate of almost 30 per cent during the period 1960–1965. This has meant that educational expenditures have grown from 3.1 per cent of the gross domestic product in 1960 to 5.7 per cent in 1965. Most of this increase is of course attributable to the expansion in public outlays. Nonetheless, the rate of increase in private expenditures on education has proceeded at an annual average of approximately 26 per cent, primarily as a result of the high profitability of providing private education, which is in turn a function of the inability of the public system to keep pace with the growth in demand.

It is extremely unlikely that such a pace will be maintained. Indeed, if it were, and given even optimistic projections of growth in total output by 1975, education expenditures would then constitute close to 12 per cent of the estimated gross domestic product.

The 1975 working budget postulated here would call for an average annual increase in expenditures of about 13.5 per cent for the next decade. However, as previously indicated, it presupposes the acquisition of external long-term financing for heavier capital outlays in the earlier years, during which existing deficiencies must be made up. What are its prospects?

Some of the factors portending favorable results have already been mentioned in other parts of this paper. The likely prospect of World Bank financing for secondary technical schools, comprehensive high schools, and regional technical colleges is one. The gradual adoption of a system of functional budgeting and its corresponding impact on cost rationalization and improved efficiency, along with the growing recognition of the need for other than year-to-year allocation of public moneys for educational projects of long-term duration, are others. The completion of overall public-sector investment programs and the integration of manpower requirements with general development objectives should afford additional impetus. Finally, the trend towards modernization of fiscal practices and tax reforms should lead to an expanded base of public revenues, while the achievement of cost efficiencies in an ever-growing number of public enterprises will provide more services out of existing revenues.

An important factor militating against the realization of the foregoing in budgetary terms as well as in real terms is the very significant issue of teachers' salaries. As already indicated, one of the principal problems in the education system to date has been the disproportionately high share of expenditures represented by salaries and wages, 93.5 per cent in 1965. Beginning in 1965, this component was radically affected by the application of a new law calling for the progressive application of an estimated 25 per cent across-the-board increase in all teacher salary scales and the provision for automatic cost-of-living adjustments in future years. The cost implications of this law have been difficult to assess because of the extremely complex nature of teacher salaries. Teachers may receive supplementary remuneration in addition to the basic salary scale for up to nine or 10 different factors: altitude, distance from national boundaries, rural-urban location, length of service, and so on.

The other major factor is of course an unknown, the rate of growth of the economy as a whole. This is highly sensitive to international price movements for raw material exports and the degree of internal political stability. While planning can only seek to minimize these exogenous effects, it is important always to recognize that a 1 or 2 per cent variation in the overall rate of growth would have serious repercussions not only on the education system but on the entire public sector.

Educational planning is characterized by a good deal of circularity, in the sense that many of the outputs of the system are also inputs. The most obvious of these is the case of teachers. Once initial output targets have been formulated, the teachers required to train these graduates must also be trained by the system of which they are to become a part. Teachers are also a critical variable in the entire program because their presence (or absence) in the appropriate quantities, qualities, and specialties spells the ultimate success or failure of the plan. Finally, teachers' pay represents about two thirds of the cost of education. Small variations in their rate of remuneration can have very serious budgetary implications.

The availability of adequate supplies of well-trained teachers is a function of several factors. The most important of these are: (a) the rates of remuneration for teachers as compared with the rates of remuneration elsewhere in the economy for persons of equivalent training; (b) the availability of adequate facilities to train the numbers of teachers in the categories where they are needed; (c) the criteria used for judging teacher qualifications; (d) nonmonetary benefits associated with the teaching profession; (e) the existence of alternative employment opportunities; and (f) the present stock of partially employed teachers and trained teachers who are not currently working as teachers, but who may be drawn back into the system.

The average annual rate of increase in the number of teachers required to meet Peru's manpower requirements during the period of this program is considerable, nearly 6,000 new entrants annually.[1] A more serious obstacle is the need to meet the proportionately much greater demand for teachers in the areas of science and technology, especially in higher education.

Comparability in rates of remuneration between academic and nonacademic persons varies among the different levels and specialties. At the primary and general secondary levels teachers' salaries are highly competitive and, in addition, alternate employment opportunities are not so extensive. The previously noted teachers' salary law which went into effect in 1965, along with an already existing virtual oversupply of primary school teachers, should insure adequate staffing at these levels.

The supply of teachers for the secondary technical schools has been deficient in both quantity and quality. This reflects several factors. Individuals with scientific and technical training are in strong demand throughout the economy. Salaries of secondary technical teachers have not been comparable to salaries of general secondary teachers. Facilities for training secondary technical teachers have been in short supply and have been poorly equipped and poorly staffed. Two parallel lines of action are suggested: (a) the use of differential salary scales to hold qualified teachers and (b) the rapid expansion of present teacher-training facilities and/or the conversion of some existing teacher-training facilities for use in this area.

The most severe shortage of teachers occurs in higher education and most particularly in the scientific and technical fields. Individuals with these

[1] See Table 7.

Table 7. Net Teacher Requirements by Educational Level
of the Teachers, 1961–1980

Educational Level of the Teacher	Total: 1980	Net Requirements 1961–1980
With primary	3,680	–
With general secondary	15,060	2,000
With technical secondary	1,910	1,000
With normal school	79,080	69,570
With university		
Education	24,925	22,405
Humanities	6,800	6,060
Medicine	2,671	2,501
Science	4,222	3,922
Engineering	3,352	2,892
Other training	330	–
Totals	142,460	110,350

Source: Derived from INP/OECD, *Desarrollo económico y social,* p. 4–34.

qualifications are at a premium throughout the economy. Salaries in the academic profession are at a strong competitive disadvantage and most teachers at this level hold other positions simultaneously. This situation, in and of itself, is not conducive to a healthy academic atmosphere nor to the encouragement of scientific research. The uncoordinated expansion of Peruvian universities in recent years has further aggravated the condition by spreading the existing supply of university professors ever more thinly and by encouraging the expansion of courses in general studies which are cheaper to provide.

The normal growth of the economy will occasion an ever greater demand for professionals in the scientific and technical fields as manufacturing, building, and research industries expand. The already short supply of qualified persons will push salary scales even higher and could result in an absolute drain on the present staff of universities unless bold measures are taken to insure an increase in their supply and to establish competitive salaries and other fringe benefits. This is the area of highest priority if future manpower requirements for teachers are to be met.

As is the case in general development planning, the most formidable barrier to educational planning is the gap between plan formulation and effective implementation. Ideally, planners and executors should work hand in hand so that plans are formulated with a clear view to their practicality and early incorporation.[1] In actual practice such an ideal is difficult to attain.

[1] Alvin Mayne provides one of the best single expositions of the problems of effective planning in his little volume, *Designing and Administering a Regional Development Plan* (Paris: OECD, 1961).

The general guidelines laid out in this program make no pretensions to being an education plan. They are intended only to provide a broad framework of general priorities within which the actual task of detailed educational planning can proceed in a more orderly fashion, consistent with national development goals. The major task has been to identify specific problem areas where policy decisions must be made.

Every effort has been made to involve Peruvian educators in the actual planning process, and representatives from the Ministry of Education, the Ministry of Labor and the universities' planning office have been directly involved. The principal limitation in this regard is that the persons directly involved are not higher-echelon decision makers in the educational system. Directors of educational branches, who would never be available to actually participate in such planning, are often not fully aware of the ways in which they might fruitfully apply the results in their own areas. There is a strong tendency in Peruvian educational circles to regard the plan as an end product itself.

The Peruvian educational system is, on paper, highly centralized. What this means is that the central ministry holds the purse strings and dispenses favors. But in actual practice, centralization does not mean a highly coordinated set of policies and decisions, the very thing which is essential for implementing new educational programs on a broad scale. Directors of educational divisions and regional officers enjoy a remarkable degree of autonomy regarding the content, direction, and day-to-day operations of their particular sphere of operations.

Educators, to be effective planners, must be in a position to program long-range activities, some of which will not bear fruit for several years. This is dependent on guaranteed financial commitments, or at least a reasonable degree of certainty regarding next year's budget. The annual education budget in Peru is at present subject to legislative whims. The primary effect has been to trim almost all capital expenditures in the current education budget to a bare minimum. And the prospects for further increases in educational expenditures are circumscribed by the fact that education already accounts for nearly one fifth of the federal budget.

Although pockets of firmly entrenched resistance to educational innovation can be found, these are not as widespread as is sometimes believed. In addition, they are probably outnumbered by pockets promoting change, though it must be admitted that the influence of the former may still be greater. But such resistances can always be worked around.

There is room for a considerable amount of continuing research regarding the content of education (especially higher and secondary-level technical education). The extension of manpower analysis on a regional basis is one very fruitful area for further research and the universities may be in a stronger position to implement this research than anyone else. For one thing, the regional planning of university programs and university staffing is dependent on regional assessments of the universities' role in regional manpower needs, so that the two are complementary.

Within the framework of overall manpower and employment possibilities, too little attention has been given to the role of deliberate public policies and infrastructure investments of a labor-intensive character. While the lure of technologically improved methods of construction and public works involving intensive use of capital is superficially appealing, allocative efficiency and the provision of employment opportunities must be the political rationale in most developing countries. A potentially invaluable area of research is concerned with the social costs and benefits of trade-offs between productivity gains and employment in a few strategic sectors.

While the obstacles to effective educational programming (only a few of which have been mentioned here) are formidable enough, there are encouraging signs that a large part of these requirements will be at least partially fulfilled. There seems to be something of a ground swell of popular support for implementing educational reforms which will meet the nation's development needs. The steps already being taken in response represent a considerable forward thrust in the eventual explicit inclusion of considerations of manpower and education forecasts in all areas of economic development planning and analysis.

The Political Economy of Education

MARTIN CARNOY

Research done in the economics of education over the last decade generally takes the structure and goals of the education system as given. Empirical studies have related schooling to increased incomes, participation in the labor force, and planning for economic growth maximization. More recently, economists have begun delving more explicitly into the school structure by means of production functions which treat the school as a multiproduct firm. They relate various inputs such as teacher preparation and student's home background to student achievement and attitudes (Levin, 1970a). But none of these studies proposes a theory of schooling; they merely test the relative effectiveness of measurable school inputs in producing some measurable school outputs.

The empirical results of these economic studies, plus those in the sociology and politics of education, suggest a distinct pattern: education systems in most countries are geared to *select* a "fortunate few" (Clignet and Foster, 1967) who are trained as elites and subelites in the social structure of the country. To understand this educational process and its implications for current research in the economics of education, this study turns to elite analysis.[1] The fundamental assumption of this analysis is that elites are much more socially cohesive than nonelites. An elite is a relatively small group which

Copyright 1970 by Martin Carnoy. Not to be reprinted in any part without the expressed permission of the author.

Stanford University. The author would like to thank Samuel Bowles, Henry Levin, and Soren Holm for helpful comments. Walter Reynolds contributed to earlier drafts. The Stanford Center for International Studies assisted in the final preparation of the paper.

[1] See Lipset and Solari, 1967, pp. vii–viii.

comprehends its policy-making power (Mills, 1959). It is held together by this responsibility, by its small size, and by oligopoly (collusive) arrangements in its use of resources (Baran and Sweezy, 1966). The analysis assumes that the elite is organized and exercises monopoly control over many facets of economic, political, and social life. A society may have competing elites with different interests. Each elite group is organized and attempts to structure institutions to favor its interests. On the other hand, the nonelite generally does not exhibit social cohesiveness (or is prevented from doing so by the elite), so members of the nonelite behave largely as individuals, competing with each other for rewards (Marx, 1935). Even when different elites compete with each other, their differences rarely include any elimination of the elite/nonelite hierarchy.

Sociologists tell us that a primary function of modern elites in less-developed countries has been to try to make societies and their education systems development-oriented—to change traditional, predominantly ascriptive societies, where father's occupation determines son's occupation, into meritocracies, where education taken by the son determines his occupation (Halsey et al., 1965). These sociologists have generally assumed that the heart of the development problem lies in the transition from traditional to modern. However, they also tend to characterize the traditional-modern problem as if it were a dichotomy rather than a continuum. This characterization is misleading. It leaves us with the simplistic notion that a society is hierarchical and not development-oriented if traditional, and not hierarchical and development-oriented if modern (Lipset in Lipset and Solari, 1967). In reality, the modernizing elite replaces the traditional, but in turn imposes its own value hierarchy (Raskin, 1971; Illich, 1968).

These values, according to sociologists, include those which characterize a modern society: people are judged by their achievements, by a general standard (universalism), and in terms of the specific positions they happen to occupy in this set of values; schooling largely replaces role ascription based on mother's and father's roles in the society. But the meritocratic schooling system, theoretically giving everybody an equal chance to enter the elite, in fact functions on the basis of merit norms which favor the ruling group, whether the group be traditional or modern (Bowles, 1970a, 1971). In all but a few revolutionary societies in which the elite places itself in the role of specifically destroying the usual relationship between elites and nonelites, the characteristics of the ruling elite are urbanism and Westernism. Children of those already in the elites and subelites—not surprisingly—tend to advance farther in the meritocracy than do the children of those unfamiliar with elite values (Lauter and Howe, 1970).

Even so, modern values tend to diffuse the elite, and modern societies have a much broader, less well-defined elite than do traditional societies. It is more difficult to work with the concept of a policy-making elite in a highly modernized, diffuse society such as the United States (Mills, 1959) than in a country like Nicaragua, which is run by a few families. In the latter, the connection between policy making and the elite is very direct; in the former, it is the pervasiveness of elite values which indirectly guides the educational system. Elite control of the educational system in a more socially mobile society is carried out through socializing people who rise through the system, whether they are from the elite or not. They are taught that the system as it exists maximizes social welfare (Illich, 1970). It is not difficult to convince those who succeed in such a system that it is indeed basically just and sound. They become its advocates, and once in the elite, tend to maintain the system in its present form, even if the system is biased against nonelite groups and even if they come from such a group. Maintenance is often expressed in terms of safeguarding the quality of education, implying that any changes in education which would favor nonelites would also lower the value of education to others. While working through such elite values widely held in the society, the maintenance of the current education system is in the individual interest of those who succeed in it. The system tends to protect their status and income position vis-à-vis nonelite groups. Since in both modern and traditional societies, the consistency of individual interest with elite values is an important condition of elite control, the pervasiveness of elite values passed down through the hierarchy plays an important role in maintaining the status quo even if it is not in the interest of a high proportion of the members of that society.

This paper is concerned primarily with the role of education systems in economies which are development-oriented—those already influenced by modern elites. Schooling is touted as an important allocator of socioeconomic roles in such economies, and the ruling group becomes subjected to great pressures from nonelites to provide education for everyone (social demand). Since education is held up by the elite as the legitimator of their rule and as the means to gain economic advantage and social status, access to education becomes a crucial political issue.[1] A dilemma for the elite is how to satisfy the social demand for more and more schooling *without* giving away economic and policy-making power. The current structure of the schools solves this dilemma by restricting the high return (in terms of higher income) component of formal education to schooling levels accessible almost exclusively to the elite. Within levels of schooling, the curriculum, teachers, and other inputs are more efficient producers of achievement and modernization for those who enter school with an already higher level of these outputs. The high return component of education is distributed to those with elite characteristics rather than to nonelites. This

---

[1] The more modern (sociologically) the society, the more members of the nonelite pass through the educational system to attain elite or near-elite status. If the educational system does not permit at least some individuals from the nonelite to pass through, education would no longer be accepted by nonelites as a means of attaining status.

leaves most of those who believe in education as a road to economic success with more education but little absolute increase in income or political power. Potential disillusionment creates a second dilemma: if the elite provides education without economic (or at least other intangible) benefits, they may be promoting their own overthrow. The elite can deal with this problem by becoming more hierarchical (dictatorial), by attempting to expand the opportunities for employment, or by both means. Again, however, the first line of defense is the education system itself. Schooling socializes the individual to believe that if he fails, it is his fault, not the system's (Kozol, 1967). The system is fair, he is taught; he, the failure, has not met its needs or requirements. If the individual is convinced of this, even lack of employment will not seem unreasonable to him (Illich, 1968).[1]

Social scientists have long recognized this elite bias in the education system, but they have chosen to ignore that a system with this bias forms its strategy of skill production primarily on political grounds—on income and status distribution considerations—and only secondarily on considerations of maximizing economic growth or the potential social contribution of all members of the society (Smyth, 1970). Economists assume, tacitly, that all students (parents) can choose the amount and nature of skill production desired. They do not recognize that the institutions themselves determine students' future roles through tracking, property tax base financing, and the nature of school social relationships (on this last point, see Friedenberg, 1965).

Ignoring the structure of the system has influenced the type of questions asked by economists and often caused misinterpretation of their results. Rates of return to investment in schooling have been estimated for a number of countries (*Journal of Human Resources,* 1967; Psacharopoulos and Hinchliffe, 1970*)* and for the United States over time (Becker, 1964). These rates do not exhibit a pattern explainable by neoclassical capital theory alone. Countries at different stages of development, with significant differences in the rate of expansion and average level of schooling, have similar patterns of return rates. Other studies of rates of return and income (Hanoch, 1967; Michelson, 1969; Welch, 1967; Blair, 1970) show that different identifiable groups in the economy have significantly different rates of return to investment at the same level of schooling

Production function estimates for the school as a firm assume that schools that produce education for children of elites and nonelites are maximizing the achievement output of schools for both groups (Hanushek, 1968; Kiesling, 1967). Yet the combination of resources used seems to be more nearly efficient for the former than for the latter (Levin, 1970a). The normal

---

[1] The advent of technology has provided another possibility for the elite to avoid political problems. The tendency to provide education in "neutral" or "objective" fields such as engineering or other technical professions allows the nonelite to participate—if they participate at all—in economic gains but makes them very apolitical.

reaction is that the schools are blatantly discriminatory, but the functions estimated by these economists may be misspecified. Schools may be efficiently producing a set of outputs for elites different from that for nonelites.

The need for a theory of education is most apparent in the planning of educational investment. Why are some planning models clearly more acceptable to policy makers than others? Why are plans for some parts of the education system left to politicians, while other parts are considered to be in the realm of educational planners? (Harbison and Myers, 1964). What is the context in which planners determine the educational needs of an economy? If plans are to accurately reflect the forces influencing educational output, they will have to take account of these forces much more specifically.

In this paper, I hypothesize a dynamic model of rates of return to different levels of schooling based on the elite-formation school system described above. The model explains how a monopoly rent to investment in schooling shifts over time to higher and higher levels of schooling and is eliminated when nonelites dominate the enrollment of any schooling level. The three parts of the paper which follow the model discuss its relationship to current work on rates of return to schooling, school production functions, and educational planning.

Part One

Figure 1 describes the effect that a typical educational expenditure pattern has on the social rate of return to schooling over time. The social rate of return is the rate to total expenditures on schooling, both private and public.[1] The pattern is divided into four periods. In period I, all the rates of return rise, but the rate to primary expenditures rises more rapidly than to secondary or university expenditures. In period II, the rate to primary falls rapidly, and that to secondary rises. The rate to university stays fairly constant and probably below the secondary rate. In period III, the social rate to primary reaches equilibrium.[2]

Also in period III, the rate to secondary schooling falls and the rate to university rises. By period IV, the university rate begins to fall and the secondary rate has reached its equilibrium level. Finally, the university rate also falls.

---

[1] The rate of return to schooling is estimated from the equation $0 = \Sigma y_i/(i + r)^i$, where y_i represents the costs (negative y_i) and benefits (positive y_i) associated with taking more schooling. Private cost is largely income foregone. Social benefits are usually assumed to equal private benefits—the increased income associated with increased schooling.

[2] The level of the equilibrium rate to primary depends, to some extent, on the rate of return to corresponding risk physical capital. There are two reasons why the rate to primary may be lower than the rate to physical capital. 1. Imperfections in the market for physical capital make it difficult for those investing in primary school to get investment funds, thus raising the rate of return to physical capital above the mean for the economy. 2. Primary schooling is heavily subsidized. Cash requirements for investment in primary schooling are low, leaving such an investment as one of the few available to small investors—this would tend to drive the rate to schooling below that of physical capital. See Psacharopoulos, 1970 for some comparison of returns to schooling with returns to physical capital.

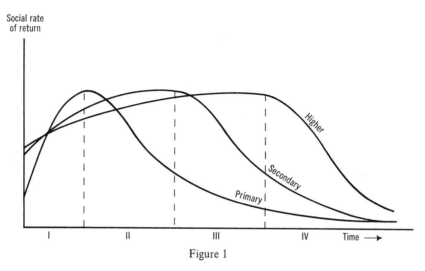

Figure 1

While Figure 1 depicts a hypothetical pattern of the economic return to schooling over time in a developing country, it can be argued that the paths of both economic growth (industrialization) and the growth of the educational system are fairly universal and that these universal paths generate universal patterns of skill production and concomitant effects of such patterns.[1] The rise in the rate of return to investment in each level is generally caused by an increase in demand for labor with that level of skills in the economy. The supply of primary school graduates lags behind demand in period I, the supply of secondary lags behind demand in period II, and the supply of university graduates lags behind demand in period III.

The rise in wages of primary-school-trained labor in period I raises the income foregone during school of those who attend secondary school and therefore tends to hold down the rise in rates of return to secondary expenditures. As the supply of primary schooling graduates increases relative to demand, it becomes increasingly difficult for those with no schooling to find jobs. Labor force participation to employment rates of unschooled labor tends to fall, especially among young people, during the end of period I and the beginning of period II. This causes income foregone of attending primary school to fall, and *private* rates of return to primary schooling to rise.[2] However, the increase in primary school graduates also reduces the unemployment adjusted wages of these graduates. Private rates of return

[1] This should not be taken to mean that the paths are necessarily "natural" paths. Rather, a conscious choice has been made by modern elites to develop (with subsidies) the industrial sector rather than the agricultural.

[2] The private rate of return can be approximated by $r = y/c$, where $y =$ net benefits of additional schooling and $c =$ income foregone, or the absolute income level of those of school age with the next-lower level of schooling. As income foregone (c) decreases, r increases.

rise, but because there is an important public expenditures component of primary schooling cost unaffected by labor force participation, social rates rise less than private rates and eventually fall with increased unemployment.

As labor force participation employment rates (and unemployment corrected wages) of primary school graduates fall, the effect is particularly important among young graduates. The income foregone of secondary school students falls correspondingly, and the private rate of return to secondary school rises rapidly. The social rate may also rise, but less than the private rate. As the output of secondary schools increases relative to demand, the labor force participation rate of those with secondary schooling falls, and their mean adjusted income also falls, driving the social rate down. The private rate, however, continues to rise, since income foregone falls even further (young primary school graduates find it even more difficult to get work) and its weight in the private rate is much greater than in the social rate. Ultimately, the same sequence of events occurs at the university level. The private rate of return to a given level of schooling can be rising while the social rate is falling. Families are induced by the high private rate to take more schooling for their children even though the social rate may be falling. This action drives the social rate even lower. If the total of schooling costs were borne by the family, there would be no divergence between the private and social rate, and families would undoubtedly take less schooling than under subsidized conditions. They might also be less willing to accept the school system as it is and its failure to produce social mobility except for a few.[1]

The length of all periods depends on a number of variables: (a) the stock of physical capital per capita,[2] (b) the rate of investment in physical capital, and (c) the rate of increase of output of each schooling level. The increase in output of schools is, in turn, a function of the rate of return to taking that level of schooling (the higher the private rate, the greater the political pressure for schooling services) and the political strength of those who already have schooling to keep others from getting it.

Because of the effort of the elite (or subelite) to maintain its income and status in the economy, the decreasing side of the rate-of-return curve for each level of schooling is different in nature from the increasing side. The decline in the rates is in every case due to the increase in supply relative to the demand for skills associated with that level of schooling. However,

---

[1] Both Blaug (1969) and myself (1970b) find that many aspects of human capital investment behavior can be explained in India and Puerto Rico, respectively, by the divergence of the private and social rate of return to schooling.

[2] The stock of physical capital per worker may be high because of high minimum wages (and high unemployment). The per capita measure is more useful, since it reflects the *potential* of the economy to employ skills.

in the period of increasing rates, the socioeconomic background of the student body is much more homogeneous than in the period of decreasing rates. As the primary schooling expands, for example, that level ceases to educate students largely from higher socioeconomic backgrounds. With expansion, the system differentiates between those students with elite characteristics and those without. As I shall show in the discussion of school production functions, the increase in performance, job expectations, and self-esteem added by the school to students with nonelite characteristics is never large enough for the nonelites to offset their lower cognitive and noncognitive knowledge at school entry. Even in an absolute sense, elites increase their school performance more than nonelites (Guthrie et al., 1969). Therefore, the rate of return to taking additional schooling could be lower for nonelites than for elites. The model (Figure 1) refers to the rate of return to investment in schooling alone, not to the rate of return to investment in schooling and home education together. If home background differences are not netted out of the measured rate of return (see below), the apparent difference between the rates of return to elite and nonelite groups is even greater.

On the up side of the rate-of-return curve, the economic value of additional schooling is increasing and the variance of the rate of increase among the students in school tends to be low. On the down side, the economic value of schooling falls, despite possible increases in the quality of teachers (replacement of primary-school-educated teachers teaching primary school by secondary-school-educated teachers, for example). In addition, the variance of the rate of decrease increases as the mean declines, in part because the system of education discriminates between elite and nonelite groups.[1]

As large numbers of students begin to enter primary school, the purpose and nature of primary school changes. In the period I phase, primary school prepares students to assume roles as skilled or white-collar, versus unskilled workers (see occupational distributions in Carnoy, 1964; Thias and Carnoy, 1969). The students have a sense of elitism: if they learn to read and write, if they graduate from primary school, they are virtually assured of a job in what is, in period I, a status position. They are being trained as a subelite. The move to universal primary schooling, at least in part a public response to the rising rates to investment in primary schooling, turns the primary school into a firm which socializes individuals to become good citizens, and to select particularly successful students for professional training in secondary school. In period II, elite formation, which had taken place at all

---

[1] These statements assume that the return side of the rate-of-return equation varies while cost remains essentially constant. However, as discussed above, the cost of schooling may also vary, especially the private cost. In general, the private cost (income foregone) will be falling or constant on the up side of the rate-of-return curve (see above), falling somewhat at the beginning of period II, and constant (essentially nonexistent) thereafter.

three levels in period I, shifts out of primary school. There are not enough industrial or high-status service jobs to go around for the rapidly increasing numbers of primary school graduates, and this interacts with the educational process to change the function of primary schooling (Abernethy, 1969). Neither teachers nor students see primary schooling as an end in itself.

At the same time, however, there is an increased demand for secondary-school-trained teachers due to the expansion of primary schooling. The demand for secondary-school-trained people generated by the replacement of foreign technicians, the growth of service industries and the growth of the government sector also increases. Secondary schools usually expand slowly at first relative to demand, and the rate of return to investment in secondary schooling increases.[1] In period III, secondary school enrollment expands rapidly. The purpose of secondary schooling changes from elite formation to socialization and selection for elite formation in the university. In most countries this is a gradual process, first moving into the lower years of the secondary cycle and ultimately to the entire cycle. The secondary level ceases to become an exclusive club for already highly socialized students and the screening process for elite status moves upward from the primary level (Thias and Carnoy, 1969). Secondary teachers, accustomed to teaching rather articulate elite-to-be, become custodians for many who are simply out of the labor force for a year or two, or who are to be channeled into vocational training (Lauter and Howe, 1970). At the same time, secondary schooling clearly differentiates between those who are to go on to universities and those who are not. The former group receives elite education which permits access to a university. As in primary schooling during an earlier period (II), the variance in returns to secondary school expenditures is much higher in period III than in period II.

The expansion of secondary schooling (period III) requires more university-trained teachers. Government in most countries expands, becomes more bureaucratically complex, and demands more university graduates. As in the primary-secondary relationship, the relative decrease in secondary wages tends to slow the increase in salaries for university types, but other factors, such as government job requirements, tend to offset this trend in period III.

---

[1] In Latin America, the large proportion of students in private secondary schools, and possibly the sensitivity of the private schooling sector to expansion and contraction of the economy, may be the cause of surprisingly stable rates of return to investment in secondary schooling in Latin America (Carnoy, 1967). Similarly, private Harambee schools in Kenya have attempted to expand secondary education outside federally accredited schooling, but they have not, for the most part, been recognized by the government. Many Latin American private schools and the Kenyan Harambee schools represent an effort by nonelites to break elite efforts to restrict secondary schooling. A different set of private schools in Latin America allow the elite to avoid the decrease in educational quality imposed by an expansion of public secondary schools. The elite is convinced that the lower average quality of output of the secondary schools affects their children's schooling adversely.

In period IV, the supply of university-trained labor increases much more rapidly than demand. University training gradually changes from a form of elite professional training to a means of further socializing students to accept subelite roles in society and to try to keep them out of the labor force for an additional four or more years. Even when university training ceases to be a path to elite roles for the average student, there will always be some institutions—either certain universities in the country or certain foreign universities—which take on (or continue) the function of elite formation. The secondary schools then screen in several ways: those who will not continue beyond secondary education, those who will go to the run-of-the-mill university, and those who will be in the elite. However, the students who go to the run-of-the-mill university can get a second chance to enter the elite by attending graduate or professional school in one of the elite-formation institutions.

At both secondary and university levels, the transformation of the level as a whole from an elite to a socialization-selection orientation still leaves a number of institutions in an elite-formation position. In Mexico, a number of private high schools retain their elite-formation status; in Kenya, the seven national secondary schools; in the United States, the academic track of a number of suburban high schools, the private preparatory schools, and the New York City entrance exam public schools (Bronx Science, Music and Art, etc.); and in Great Britain, the public schools. At the university level, the same division occurs in those countries which have a number of universities.

The model outlined here describes changes in the function of schooling as the percentage of the age cohort attending school increases relative to the growth of the economy. Different levels of schooling assume different roles as the expansion of enrollment occurs. The corollary of the relationship between rates of return and the period of educational-economic development shown in Figure 1 is the possibility of predicting the pattern of rates of return to investment in various levels of schooling and of predicting the function of each level by observing a country's gross national product per capita, the rate of economic growth, enrollment rates at the different levels and socioeconomic background differences between students at different levels of schooling. Two or three of these variables may be sufficiently good predictors. In terms of studying schooling as a distributor of skills, the model distinguishes between the primary outputs of schooling (achievement versus socialization) in the different periods of development. The model also indicates that the contribution of schooling to different groups in the society varies according to their political power or their ability to gain control of resources associated with elite-oriented education. The following sections describe what the model implies for the main lines of research in the economics of education.

Part Two

THE RATE OF RETURN TO SCHOOLING

Economists first became interested in education because of its role as an input into economic growth. Expenditures on schooling came to be recognized as being at least in part an investment by an individual in his future earning capability. Despite its possible limitations as a planning tool, the treatment of education as an investment in human capital and the rate-of-return analysis associated with it is seen by many economists as the basis of understanding the relationship between education and the economic system.

The results of several studies dealing with education and income and the relative value of investing in different levels of schooling have shown that average pecuniary earnings of individuals with more schooling are higher than earnings of those with less schooling. If the increase in earnings is attributed entirely to increased schooling, as most of these studies assume, the rate of return which equates the discounted value of cost and returns over lifetime is considered the yield of investment in schooling. This rate in usually compared to yields on other investments.

Table 1 presents rates of return to formal schooling in 27 countries (Psacharopoulos and Hinchliffe, 1970). The countries cover a wide range of product per capita, and school enrollment levels. It would seem that the rates could be used to test the model of Figure 1. However, they do not represent overall conditions in the country to which they apply: the rates are usually measured only for urban, employed males. In some countries, this group is representative of a large fraction of the labor force; in others, such as the African and Asian countries covered, it is a small minority. Furthermore, as is discussed in more detail below, the rates do not represent the return to schooling alone. Since the socioeconomic background of those with various levels of schooling differs from country to country, the correction for nonschooling effects would also vary. The unadjusted rates are therefore not comparable among countries even if they accurately reflect unemployment in the urban labor force and the rate of investment in education for rural employment.[1]

Nevertheless, one can relate the unadjusted rates to enrollment rates to check if the results are at all consistent with the hypothesized model. Since the stock of physical capital (as approximated here by gross domestic product per capita) affects the level of rate of return to schooling somewhat independently of enrollment rate, the relationship between rate of return and enrollment rate is estimated with the variation in GDP per capita held constant. The growth of GDP per capita is also included as a variable. As a check

---

[1] Besides these methodological points, it should also be noted that the rates have in many cases been crudely calculated. Since they are highly sensitive to errors in estimation, especially on the cost side, large over- or underestimates of rates are common. Wherever possible, I have tried to describe such errors in the footnotes to Table 1.

Table 1. Social Rates of Return to Schooling, Enrollment Rates, Gross Domestic Product per Capita, and Economic Growth Rates, by Country for Various Years, Primary, Secondary and University Levels of Schooling

Country	(1) Year	(2) Primary Rate of Return	(3) Primary Enrollment Rate	(4) Secondary Rate of Return	(5) Secondary Enrollment Rate	(6) University Rate of Return	(7) University Enrollment Rate	(8) GDP/Capita	(9) Economic Growth Rate
United States	1959	–	–	14[a]	82	10[a]	1,576	2,361	0.4
Canada	1961	–	–	14[a]	56	15[a]	725	1,774	0.6
Puerto Rico	1960	21	70	22	46	16	1,186	661	4.6
Mexico	1963	25	50	17	12	23	337	374	1.6
Venezuela	1957	82[b]	42	17	10	23	230	730	3.8
Colombia	1965	40	56	24	19	8	307	320	1.4
Chile	1959	12	68	12	23	9[c]	364	365	0.8
Brazil	1962	11	46	17	12	14	182	261	4.0
South Korea	1967	12	66	9	33	5	760	146	6.6
Israel	1958	16	63	7	36	7	625	704	4.4
India	1960	20	20	13	31	13	281	73	1.8
Malaysia[d]	1967	9	56	12	28	11	142	280	2.8
Philippines	1966	8	56	21	34	11	1,931	250	1.4
Japan	1961	–	–	7	79	6	510	464	5.8
Ghana	1967	18	35	11	34	16	70	233	-0.8
Kenya	1968	22	48	20	6	9	59	118	4.4
Uganda[e]	1965	66	32	50	7	12	19	84	1.4
Zambia	1960	12	28	–	–	–	–	144	4.8
Great Britain	1966	–	–	5	96	8	382	1,660	2.4
Germany	1964	–	–	–	–	5	396	1,420	3.5
Denmark	1964	–	–	–	–	8	545	1,651	4.2
Norway	1966	–	–	7	69	5	375	1,831	4.2
Sweden	1967	–	–	10	44	9	647	2,500	4.0
Belgium	1967	–	–	–	–	9	384	1,777	3.4
Netherlands	1965	–	–	6	91	6	902	1,490	3.2
Greece	1964	–	–	3	38	8	374	478	3.8
New Zealand[f]	1966	–	–	20	71	13	1,005	1,931	3.0

Table 1: Sources

Columns (1), (2), (4) and (6):

General source: George Psacharopoulos and K. Hinchliffe, "Rates of Return to Investment in Education and the Impact on Growth and Development: An International Comparison," London School of Economics, Higher Education Research Unit, 1970 (mimeo.).

United States: Giora Hanoch, "An Economic Analysis of Earnings and Schooling," *Journal of Human Resources,* II, no. 3 (Summer, 1967), pp. 310–329.

Canada: J. R. Podoluk, *Earnings and Education,* Canada Dominion Bureau of Statistics, 1965.

Puerto Rico: Martin Carnoy, "The Rate of Return to Schooling and the Increase in Human Resources in Puerto Rico," Stanford University, 1970 (mimeo.).

Mexico, Venezuela, and Chile: Martin Carnoy, "Rates of Return to Schooling in Latin America, *Journal of Human Resources,* II, no. 3 (Summer, 1967). For Chilean rates shown here, see footnote 11 adjusting rates shown in Table 7 of that article.

Colombia: M. Selowsky, "The Effect of Unemployment and Growth on the Rate of Return to Education: The Case of Colombia," Harvard University, *Economic Development Report,* 116 (November, 1968).

Brazil: S. A. Hewlett, "Rate of Return Analysis: Role in Determining the Significance of Education in the Development of Brazil," 1970 (mimeo.).

South Korea: Kim Kwang Suk, "Rates of Return on Education in Korea," USAID, 1968 (mimeo.).

Israel: Ruth Klinov-Malul, "The Profitability of Investment in Education in Israel," The Maurice Falk Institute for Economic Research in Israel, Jerusalem (April, 1966).

India: M. Blaug, R. Layard and M. Woodhall, *The Causes of Graduate Unemployment in India* (London: The Penguin Press, 1969).

Malaysia: O. D. Hoerr, Development Advisory Service, Harvard University (unpublished), reported in Psacharopoulos and Hinchliffe, "Rates of Return to Investment."

Philippines: D. Devoretz, "Alternative Planning Models for Philippine Educational Investment," *The Philippine Economic Journal,* 16 (1969).

Japan: M. J. Brown, "Mass Elites at the Threshold of the Seventies," *Comparative Education* (London), forthcoming.

Ghana: K. Hinchliffe, "Educational Planning Techniques for Developing Countries with Special Reference to Ghana and Nigeria." (M. Phil. dissertation, University of Leicester, 1969.)

Kenya: Hans Heinrich Thias and Martin Carnoy, *Cost-Benefit Analysis in Education: A Case Study on Kenya.* Economic Department, IBRD, November, 1969 (EC–173).

Uganda: John Smyth and Nicholas Bennett, "Rates of Return on Investment in Education: A Tool for Short-Term Educational Planning Illustrated with Ugandan Data," *The World Yearbook of Education* (London: Evans Brothers, 1967).

Zambia (Northern Rhodesia): R. E. Baldwin, *Economic Development and Export Growth* (Berkeley: University of California Press, 1966).

The following European and New Zealand rates are all reported in Psacharopoulos and Hinchliffe, "Rates of Return to Investment":

Great Britain: L. Magler and R. Layard, "How Profitable Is Engineering Education?" *Higher Education Review,* 2, no. 2 (Spring, 1970).

Germany: Klaus-Dieter Schmidt and Peter Baumgarten, "Berufliche Ausbildung und Einkommen," *in* A. E. Ott, ed., *Theoretische und Empirische Beiträge zur Wirtschaftsforschung* (Tübingen: Motz, 1967).

Denmark: N. B. Hansen, "Uddannelsesinvesteringernes Rentabilitet," *Nationaløkonomisk Tidsskrift,* nos. 5–6 (Copenhagen, 1969).

Norway: J. Aarrestad, *On Urbyttet av å Investere i Utdanning i Norge,* Norges Handelshøyskole Samfunnsøkonomisk Institutt, Bergen, 1967.

Sweden: Leif Magnuson, Department of Economics, University of Stockholm (unpublished).

Belgium: W. Desaeyere, "Een Onderwijsmodel voor Belgie, Deel 2," Katholieke Universiteit te Leuven, Centrum voor Economische Studien, 1969 (mimeo.).

Netherlands: P. de Wolff and R. Ruiter, *De Economie van het Onderwijs* (The Hague: Montinus Nijhoff, 1968).

Greece: H. Leibenstein, "Rates of Return to Education in Greece," Harvard University, *Economic Development Report,* 94 (September, 1967).

New Zealand: B. J. Ogilvy, "Investment in New Zealand Education and Its Economic Value, 1951–1966." (M. Com. dissertation, University of Auckland, 1968.)

Column (3):

UNESCO, *Statistical Yearbook, 1966* and *1967.* Enrollment rates taken from Table 2.5 for year five years previous to column (1) year. The rationale for this is that the average person with primary school training is assumed not to enter the labor force for five years after he leaves primary school. So the effect of enrollment rates on rate of return would be lagged by at least five years. The enrollment rate for the column (1) minus five years is corrected to a six-year length primary school program, so that all ratios represent a six-year equivalent primary enrollment as a percentage of five- to 14-year olds in the country. Length of primary school in each country is taken from Table 2.1.

Column (5):

Ibid. General secondary education only. The enrollment rate is taken for year three years previous to column (1) year. Enrollment rate is corrected to a four-year length secondary school program, so that all ratios represent a four-year equivalent secondary enrollment as a percentage of 15- to 19-year olds in the country.

Column (7):

Ibid. University enrollment is estimated as the number of university students per population 15 years old and older. The enrollment rates are taken from Table 2.10. The correction for population 15 years old and older is based on population data from United Nations, *Demographic Yearbook, 1960–1969.*

Column (8):

George Psacharopoulos, "The Economic Returns to Higher Education in Twenty-Five Countries," London School of Economics, Higher Education Unit, 1970, Table 1.

Column (9):

United Nations, *Statistical Yearbook, 1968.* Economic growth rate is taken as the average percentage change in gross domestic product per capita in the period t-5 to t, where t is the year shown in Column (1).

Notes

    a. The rates for the U.S. and Canada as reported are private rates. The rates as shown here have been lowered in accordance with the difference between private and social rates as estimated in W. L. Hansen, "Total and Private Returns to Investment in Schooling," *Journal of Political Economy,* 71, no. 2 (April, 1963), pp. 128–140.

    b. The 82 per cent rate represents the return between illiterates and six years of schooling. Income foregone is assumed to be zero. Both facts imply that the rate is seriously overestimated. It has been omitted from the regression estimates below.

    c. The rate as reported in Homberger and Selowsky is 12 per cent, but as shown in Carnoy, "Rates of Return to Schooling," 1967, this is an overestimate. The 9 per cent rate is approximate.

    d. Rates shown here are underestimates of unadjusted rates, since they have been corrected for nonschooling factors.

on the interaction effect between GDP per capita and enrollment rate at the secondary and higher education levels, countries are divided into those which were developed and those which were less developed in the year rates were measured. The former include all those with more than $750 GDP per capita plus Israel and Japan. Since there are no primary rates available for the higher enrollment rate countries, it is not possible to relate the rates over the entire range of development levels.

The regression estimates of rates of return as a function of enrollment rate, GDP per capita, and the rate of growth of GDP per capita are the following:

I. *Primary schooling* (all countries included)

$$(1) \quad r_p = 18.32 - 0.0183 \, N_p \qquad\qquad R^2 = 0.001$$
$$ (8.22) \quad (0.1550)$$

$$(2) \quad r_p = 15.69 + 0.0056 \, y \qquad\qquad R^2 = 0.016$$
$$ (4.38) \quad (0.0124)$$

$$(3) \quad r_p = 19.39 - 0.104 \, N_p + 0.0109 \, y \qquad R^2 = 0.036$$
$$ (8.23) \quad (0.196) \quad\;\; (0.0158)$$

II. *Secondary schooling* (all countries included)

$$(4) \quad r_s = 17.65 - 0.106 \, N_s \qquad\qquad R^2 = 0.228$$
$$ (2.10) \quad (0.0415)$$

$$(5) \quad r_s = 14.53 - 0.0017 \, y \qquad\qquad R^2 = 0.050$$
$$ (1.84) \quad (0.0016)$$

$$(6) \quad r_s = 17.65 - 0.137 \, N_s + 0.0016 \, y \qquad R^2 = 0.250$$
$$ (2.07) \quad (0.0563) \quad\;\; (0.0019)$$

IIa. *Secondary schooling* (less-developed countries)

$$(7) \quad r_s = 19.11 - 0.155 \, N_s \qquad\qquad R^2 = 0.105$$
$$ (3.48) \quad (0.125)$$

$$(8) \quad r_s = 14.01 + 0.0037 \, y \qquad\qquad R^2 = 0.015$$
$$ (3.15) \quad (0.0083)$$

$$(9) \quad r_s = 17.76 - 0.161 \, N_s + 0.0046 \, y \qquad R^2 = 0.128$$
$$ (4.14) \quad (0.124) \quad\;\; (0.0078)$$

---

e. Rates for Uganda are seriously overestimated, since they are based on differences between average incomes of employees with different amounts of schooling. This assumes that income differences are constant over lifetime. The Ugandan rates are therefore omitted from the regression estimates.

f. Ogilvy uses an alpha-coefficient of 0.5, but he probably overestimates unadjusted rates, since he also uses starting salaries of government employees as his base for estimates.

IIb. *Secondary schooling* (developed countries)

$$(10) \quad r_s = 12.76 \; - \; 0.040 \, N_s \qquad\qquad\qquad R^2 = 0.030$$
$$\; (5.77) \quad (0.080)$$

$$(11) \quad r_s = \;\; 4.40 \; + \; 0.0034 \, y \qquad\qquad\quad R^2 = 0.220$$
$$\; (3.82) \quad (0.0022)$$

$$(12) \quad r_s = \;\; 7.32 \; - \; 0.043 \, N_s \; + \; 0.0034 \, y \qquad R^2 = 0.025$$
$$\; (6.08) \quad (0.070) \qquad (0.0021)$$

III. *University* (all countries included)

$$r_u = 11.18 \; - \; 0.0009 \, N_u \qquad\qquad\qquad R^2 = 0.006$$
$$\; (1.58) \quad (0.0022)$$

$$r_u = 11.97 \; - \; 0.0013 \, y \qquad\qquad\qquad R^2 = 0.045$$
$$\; (1.52) \quad (0.0012)$$

$$r_u = 15.52 \; - \; 0.0005 \, N_u - 0.0013 \, y \; - \; 1.075 \, g$$
$$\; (2.32) \quad (0.0021) \qquad (0.0012) \qquad (0.511)$$
$$R^2 = 0.189$$

IIIa. *University* (less-developed countries)

$$r_u = 13.37 \; - \; 0.0012 \, N_u \qquad\qquad\qquad R^2 = 0.014$$
$$\; (2.02) \quad (0.0029)$$

$$r_u = \;\; 7.90 \; + \; 0.0148 \, y \qquad\qquad\qquad R^2 = 0.270$$
$$\; (2.55) \quad (0.0067)$$

$$r_u = \;\; 8.62 \; - \; 0.0020 \, N_u \; + \; 0.0150 \, y \qquad R^2 = 0.300$$
$$\; (2.65) \quad (0.0024) \qquad (0.0070)$$

IIIb. *University* (developed countries)

$$r_u = \;\; 5.87 \; + \; 0.0038 \, N_u \qquad\qquad\qquad R^2 = 0.190$$
$$\; (1.72) \quad (0.0023)$$

$$r_u = \;\; 4.69 \; + \; 0.0023 \, y \qquad\qquad\qquad R^2 = 0.190$$
$$\; (2.38) \quad (0.0014)$$

$$r_u = 11.25 \; + \; 0.0005 \, N_u \; + \; 0.0004 \, y \; - \; 1.16 \, g$$
$$\; (4.38) \quad (0.0024) \qquad (0.0014) \qquad (0.61)$$
$$R^2 = 0.44$$

Where r = rate of return to schooling (per cent) in year t;
N = enrollment rate in year t–5 (primary), year t–3 (secondary), or year t–1 (university);
y = gross domestic product per capita in year t;
and g = average growth rate of GDP in years t–5 to t.

Numbers in parentheses beneath coefficients represent standard errors of estimate.

The lack of any significant relationship between rate of return to primary school and enrollment rate with or without product per capita held constant indicates that these countries—only three of which have lower than a 40 per cent enrollment rate—may be already in the phase II or III stage of educational expansion. We would expect that with adjustment for socioeconomic background and unemployment, the level of the curve would shift downward. The adjustment would probably also shift the rates of the higher enrollment rate countries down more than it would those of the lower enrollment rate countries, since both the socioeconomic class difference between those who take primary and those who do not and the unemployment rate of those who take primary schooling is greater in the higher enrollment rate countries (see below).

With all countries taken together, the rate of return to secondary schooling is negatively related to enrollment rate, more so when GDP per capita is held constant. The coefficient of enrollment rate is more steeply negative in the less-developed than in the developed group. We would expect that the correction for socioeconomic class and employment would affect those countries with higher enrollments more than those with lower, so the coefficients of both enrollment and GDP per capita for adjusted rates would be smaller if the coefficient is positive and greater in absolute value if negative.

At the university level, the less-developed group of countries is characterized by a positive and significant relationship between GDP per capita and rate of return and a negative, but insignificant, relationship between rate of return and enrollment rate. In the developed group, rate of return is positively related to both enrollment and GDP per capita, but neither coefficient is significant. Again, as is discussed below, adjustments of the rate would decrease the higher enrollment country rates of return relative to less-developed countries. At the university level, adjustments would probably affect the less-developed group rates little because both secondary and university students in most LDC's are a very elite group.

Taken together, the observed unadjusted rates of Table 1 do not contradict the dynamic model shown in Figure 1 (see also Bowles, 1971). Primary rates are estimated to be rather insensitive to changes in enrollment rates and GDP per capita, which is consistent with the late period II and period III stages of Figure 1. For all countries together, there is a significant and negative coefficient of enrollment rate with respect to secondary school rate of return, holding constant GDP per capita. When the countries are divided into two groups, the coefficient of enrollment rate at the secondary level is even more negative for the LDC's than it is for all countries together, and is much less negative for the developed group. This pattern is consistent with the period III for the LDC's and a late period III or period IV for the developed group. The coefficient of enrollment rate for university rates of return is not significantly different from zero for either group of countries, which would be consistent with period III and early period IV pattern of rates. If the signs of the university-level enrollment rate coefficients were reversed for the two groups of countries, there would be more consistency with the model. However, adjusting the rates for socioeconomic background could well make the coefficient in the developed countries negative and greater in absolute value than for the LDC's.[1]

Until now, the issue of the comparative size of the rates at the different levels of schooling has not been discussed. The average primary rate (Venezuela and Uganda excluded) is 17.4 per cent; the average secondary rate (Uganda excluded) is 13.1 per cent; the average university rate (Uganda excluded) is 10.7 per cent. Although the shapes of the rate-of-return curves as shown in Figure 1 are not inconsistent with the observed data, the average rate at the different levels is. According to the model, rates of return to primary investment in late period II and period III should be below secondary and university rates, and secondary rates in periods III and IV should be below university rates. The rest of this section of the study argues that unadjusted rates do not correctly rank the rate of return to investment in schooling. The evidence offered suggests that despite the average unadjusted rates observed in Table 1, corrected rates of return would be consistent with the model presented above in level as well as shape of curves.[2]

There is evidence that such rates of return to investment in schooling, unadjusted for other factors—especially family background or environment—are overestimated for all schooling levels together and greatly overestimated for schooling levels in which *selection* is an important aim of the education process. In addition, the rates of return in Table 1 all refer to urban males (except the Chilean estimate, which is for employed urban males and females), so they may not accurately represent the rate of return to total investment in schooling—the investment that goes into rural males, urban and rural females and those who are unemployed. Since the investment in non-employed urban males and rural males and females takes place almost entirely at the primary level in developing countries, it is the primary rates that are most affected by including those groups in the estimates. In more-developed countries, analogously, it is the secondary rates that are most affected.

The adjustment of the rates for these other factors tends to lower the rates to each level of schooling more in countries with higher enrollment

---

[1] It should be noted that the rate of return is positively related to GDP/capita at all levels; but only at the university level, and then only for the LDC's, does the coefficient of GDP/capita become significant (at a 10 per cent level of significance).

[2] From a policy standpoint, the Table 1 patterns of social rates have led Blaug, Bowles, Bowman, Carnoy, T. W. Schultz, and others to conclude that investment in primary education should have high priority in total public expenditure allocation to schooling. Without correcting for differential effect of socioeconomic background at different levels of schooling, however, it is not possible to compare primary rates to secondary and higher rates.

rates in that level. Adjusting the rates would tend to steepen the negative slope of the primary, secondary, and university curves. It is possible that the corrected rates for the developed set of countries in the university case could even be negatively sloped.

A number of studies make some adjustments in the estimates of rates (these studies are summarized in Blaug, 1965). They recognize that differences in schooling are not the only reason for two individuals' earnings to differ, and that therefore earning differentials may not be a good measure of the advantage of better education. Edward Denison, in his well-known study of the sources of U.S. growth, attributes 60 per cent of earning differences to additional schooling at the secondary level, and 66 per cent at the university level (Denison, 1962). He then applies these same figures to his European estimates (Denison, 1967). Of the estimates shown in Table 1, only Blaug et al., Hoerr, Ogilvy, and Thias and Carnoy correct the rates for nonschooling factors. Blaug uses alternative 60 and 50 per cent of income differentials attributed to additional schooling (the rates for India shown in Table 1, however, are unadjusted). The 60 per cent adjustment seems to have become a norm, and in the Denison and Blaug cases it is applied uniformly across countries and schooling levels.

Nevertheless, Blaug does try to rationalize the 60 per cent adjustment (alpha, as he calls it) on his British estimates (Blaug, 1965) and extends his rationalization to the Indian data. This represents a beginning effort (by an economist) to describe the effect of educational structure on rate-of-return estimates (Blaug, 1965, p. 216).

Estimates of the rate of return to schooling in Kenya attempt to take into account both socioeconomic background and other nonschooling determined ability variables which could influence earnings of urban males (Thias and Carnoy, 1969).[1] The results of adjusting earnings for these variables show that the social rate to investing in the last three years of primary school (10.8 per cent) is only 28 per cent of the unadjusted rate (38.4 per cent). When this adjusted rate is corrected for a possible primary school certificate effect, its share of the unadjusted rate rises to 36 per cent.[2] The adjusted social rate to investment in the first two years of secondary schooling (6.3 per cent) is 39 per cent of the unadjusted rate (16.3 per cent). The adjusted and unadjusted rates are almost the same, however, for the last two years of the secondary cycle, which implies that the selection process as of the middle 1960's ended with the first two years of the secondary cycle.

---

[1] If the value of all nonschooling inputs that contribute to a child's cognitive and noncognitive knowledge could be determined (Gintis, 1969), then one could add the cost of nonschooling inputs to schooling inputs and calculate the adjusted rate of return (Dugan, 1968). It is somewhat easier from a data standpoint to correct from the earnings side.

[2] The rate to investment in the second, third, and fourth years of primary school is not adjusted for examination score, only for socioeconomic background.

The Kenya study also adjusts urban primary rates of return for unemployment and weights in the rate of return for rural males. When all these adjustments are combined, the rate of return to investment in primary schooling for African males falls to about 12 per cent, using the unadjusted rates for employed urban males. The rate is about 9 per cent if the adjusted rates are used. This compares to a 22 per cent unadjusted rate of return to investment in the primary cycle.[1]

The unadjusted rate of return to investment in urban women's schooling in Kenya is considerably lower than rates to investment in males' schooling at the primary level (7 per cent for women versus 22 per cent for men for all primary schooling and 7 per cent versus 38 per cent for the last three years of primary school—the adjustment for socioeconomic class and ability may, of course, be greater for men than for women), but is about the same at the lower secondary level (19 per cent for women as compared with 24 per cent for men to investment in eight to 11 years of schooling). Since almost half of the students in primary school are women and only a small percentage of urban women are employed, the total social rate of return to investment in primary schooling may be closer to 5 per cent rather than to the 9 per cent estimated for males.[2]

These adjustments show that the unadjusted rates of Table 1 are not suitable for determining the social yield of educational investment. The reliability of unadjusted rates depends on the structure of the schooling system at the time the measurement is made. If schooling even at the primary level is fulfilling largely elite-formation functions (period I), then the adjustment of the rate for factors other than schooling will be relatively small. In period II the composition of primary school students changes, and the adjustment for nonschooling factors increases.

Two effects occur as schooling expands:

(a) A higher fraction of students who attend school voluntarily or involuntarily do not enter the urban labor force (the rates in Table 1

---

[1] Selowsky's estimates of rates of return for Colombia (see Table 1) are not adjusted for nonschooling inputs, but are corrected for unemployment and labor-force participation rates (the rates shown are not adjusted, however). The rates are estimated only for Bogotá, and perhaps because of this the unemployment correction does not produce great changes in the rates. At levels of schooling where income foregone enters as a cost, the unemployment correction also lowers the cost of going to school, so rates tend to fall little or may even rise.

[2] The issue of female education, however, goes beyond the differential earnings of females themselves. Perhaps much more than father's education, the role of the mother's education seems to be an important factor in determining a child's preparation outside the school and his motivation in school. For Kenya, we find that the average percentage of wage earners with literate mothers increases significantly as the average level of education of wage earners increases. The increase is more rapid than for father's literacy as a background variable. The "intergenerational" effect—despite heavy discounting because it occurs only in the next generation—may be important in absolute terms and may provide the *raison d'être* of educating females in the present economic structure. Education of females may be a key to raising human capabilities even though they themselves are usually permitted to contribute very little to present measured national income.

are measured for the urban labor force). Those who do not enter the urban labor force either are involuntarily unemployed, become housewives, enter the rural labor force, or are at leisure. The adjustment for employment probability in either the urban or rural sector (assuming that rates of return are estimated for both sectors) as schooling expands depends largely on the stock and change of the stock (investment) of physical capital.

(b) Unadjusted rates to investment in primary schooling or even rates adjusted for employment probability may fall slowly in period II if the relative stock of physical capital is large enough to absorb the larger number of graduates. But rates to investment in primary schooling adjusted for background and ability differences fall much more rapidly: observed income differences in the primary school expansion phase represent the return to schooling differences and the return to increasing (rather than constant) socioeconomic and ability differences between those who finish and those who drop out or never enter primary school. At some point in period III, when completion of primary school is attained by a high fraction of the age cohort, the differences in socioeconomic background and ability between those who never enter primary school and those who drop out may get very small. Differences in background and ability of those who finish and those who drop out tend to get very large. The rate to taking some years of primary school adjusted for background differences approaches the unadjusted rate. The rate to finishing primary school requires a large adjustment. At the same time, however, the rate of return to investing in primary schooling ceases to become a useful concept. Going to primary school usually becomes enforceably mandatory. Almost everybody attends in any case. Investing or not investing in primary school is no longer a real alternative.

The same pattern evolves in secondary schooling and, finally, in higher education. As each level of schooling—because of social demand—expands beyond its elite-producing capabilities, the observed return to investment in that level of schooling increasingly represents a return uncorrected for the probability of unemployment and a return to education received outside of school in the home. This phenomenon occurs because of the increase of human relative to physical capital in the economy and because differences in background and ability of students increases as the level of schooling changes from an elite producer to a selection stage for higher levels of schooling.

As mentioned above, two good indicators of the period of development of a level of schooling are: (a) the difference of parents' socioeconomic background between that level and the one below it, and (b) the student survival rate in that level of schooling. Table 2 shows that in Kenya the percentage of literate fathers rises from 9 per cent for those with zero to two years of schooling to 24 per cent for those with three to five years to 42 per cent for those with completed primary school.[1] The percentage then rises to 57 per cent for those with nine years and to 60 per cent for those with 11 years. Similarly, the percentage of literate mothers at each level rises from 3 to 7 to 17 to 30 to 31 per cent. Up to nine years (lower secondary cycle) there are great differences in parents' literacy for students who have finished each level of schooling over those who have not.[2]

Table 2. Parents' Literacy by Years of Schooling of Son,
Kenya, Urban Africans, 1968

	Years of Schooling of Son				
	0-2	3-5	7	9	11
Literate father (%)	9	24	42	57	60
Literate mother (%)	3	7	17	30	31

Source: Hans Heinrich Thias and Martin Carnoy, *Cost Benefit Analysis in Education: A Case Study of Kenya,* Economic Department, IBRD (Washington: November, 1969), Annex Table 5.4.

In the last two years of the secondary cycle, the differences are very small. The percentage of the age cohort that enters the last two years of secondary school and the percentage that drops out are also very small. This indicates that the primary and lower secondary cycle are selection stages and are already on the down side of their curve. Unless the whole structure of education changes in Kenya or unless the Kenyans discover a large source of new physical wealth, rates to investing in those stages will

---

[1] These figures are derived from labor force data. No distinction is made between those who attended primary school in rural areas and those who attended urban schools since those data are not available.

[2] I estimated a linear relationship between earnings, age, socioeconomic class, and education for all years of schooling in Kenya up to 11 years (for urban African males). The results are heavily weighted by primary school because of the high percentage of observations at that level. If one takes mother's and father's literacy as the single measure of socioeconomic background of urban African males, the parameters estimated for Kenya show that the average gain for the individual of having literate versus illiterate parents—education, age, tribe, and father's occupation held constant—is 125 Kenya shillings annually. Each year of schooling—the same variables held constant—raises earnings 32 Kenya shillings annually. It takes about four years of schooling (around the mean of five years of primary schooling) to make up for having illiterate parents in Kenya, not accounting for the interaction between schooling and parents' literacy. If a lot of other variables are held constant in the equation—occupation of individual, city in which employed, size of firm in which employed, sector of occupation, type of primary school attended (public or private), and whether currently taking additional training—the estimated value of both the literacy and schooling parameters falls, but the trade-off between schooling and parents' literacy remains the same: four years of schooling.

continue to fall. The political decision to allow the populace free access to primary and lower secondary schooling has been made. Subelites already in the labor force with that amount of schooling have lost any holding action they may have made against that political decision.

Similarly in Puerto Rico, the average socioeconomic class of parents (on a scale of 4 low to 0 high)[1] of rural male students changes little for students in the first and third grades, then drops from 2.88 to 2.73 between the third and sixth grades (Table 3), but only from 2.69 to 2.61 between the seventh and ninth grades. More than 40 per cent of those who enter rural primary school drop out before finishing the sixth grade, mostly between the third and sixth grades. About 30 per cent of those who enter the first grade enter the seventh grade and about two thirds of that 30 per cent finish the ninth grade. It is difficult to say how many rural students go to senior high school, since senior high schools are all in urban areas. It appears from these data, nevertheless, that rural primary school is still in the period II selection process and that rural junior high is still in a somewhat elite-formation stage (Carnoy, 1970a).

Table 3. Parents' Socioeconomic Class, Rural and Urban Male Students
by Grade of Student, Puerto Rico, 1967

Grade of Student	Rural Students	Urban students
1	2.93	2.17
2	2.91	2.21
3	2.89	2.25
4	2.80	2.12
5	2.78	2.21
6	2.73	2.04
7	2.70	2.16
8	2.62	2.06
9	2.61	2.04
10	–	2.08
11	–	2.07
12	–	2.06

Source: Martin Carnoy, "The Quality of Education, Examination Performance, and Urban Rural Income Differentials in Puerto Rico," *Comparative Education Review,* XIV, no. 3 (October, 1970), Table 2, p. 341.

On the other hand, almost all urban students who enter primary school in Puerto Rico complete junior high school (80 per cent), and 80 per cent of those complete senior high school. There is a gradual drop of male urban

[1] Socioeconomic class is defined by a Hollingshead two-factor index (father's education and occupation) ranging from a low socioeconomic value of 77 to a high of 11. The five classes are defined so that an equal number of urban Puerto Rican students falls into each category.

students' parents' socioeconomic class from 2.17 in the first grade to 2.06 in the twelfth grade. Most of this drop occurs in the first years of primary school. It seems that urban primary and secondary schooling in Puerto Rico are near the end of the period III stage, in which the upper secondary school selects those who will go to universities and those who will not. As the school system moves into the period IV stage, the selection takes place almost entirely *between* the secondary school and the university. However, the ability differences between those who finish secondary school and those who do not is probably great. At this stage, the important drop in percentage enrolled and socioeconomic class of parents occurs between the last year of secondary schooling and the first year at the university. In Puerto Rico, however, less than 30 per cent of the high-school-age Puerto Ricans attend urban senior high school. The average socioeconomic class of the urban ninth grader is much higher than that of the rural ninth grader, despite the selection process in rural schools up to that grade. The large difference in socioeconomic background appears between those who are not in high school and those who are. In effect, the school system in Puerto Rico screens by having two separate systems—urban and rural—with very different properties. This type of screening occurs in most countries, including highly developed ones such as the United States. In the U.S., the duality of the school system is more along color and class lines than along urban-rural lines. Thus, by separating the labor force by the type of schooling received, the rate of return can be somewhat "purified," since the major socioeconomic differences among students can be picked up. Each type of school system can then be categorized according to the model in Figure 1.

Based on these observations, we would expect that the correction for background and ability is much more important in Puerto Rico for rates to investment in rural primary and perhaps somewhat more important for rural junior high than for urban investment at these levels. The ability correction for urban students in senior high school may be more important than for rural students in (urban) senior high. The latter are clearly a highly screened group who, if they return to agriculture or rural areas, represent an elite. We would also expect that adjusted rural social rates of return to junior and senior high schools will fall in the future relative to primary school rates, while adjusted urban rates to these three levels should remain relatively equal.

In summary, the correction of unadjusted rates of return for socioeconomic class lowers the return to schooling alone. The correction is not constant across countries or across levels of schooling in the same country, but depends on differences in the socioeconomic background of students who attend different levels of school. It appears that the level of school in which the most strenuous selection takes place (i.e., the ratio of those who graduate to those who enter is the lowest) is the level at which the largest correction takes place. Large adjustments for socioeconomic background probably occur below the selection point as well, but probably not in levels above the selection point. Once strenuous selection takes place, socioeconomic background differences between students at higher levels are greatly reduced. Continuation of schooling beyond the selection point is much more a matter of individual choice rather than system choice, so social class differences between those who continue and those who do not are not as clear cut.

Just as an exercise, the average rates of Table 1 can be adjusted by a set of correction factors which depend on the level of enrollment and gross domestic product per capita. These correction factors are based roughly on those used by Denison and Blaug, and the results of the Kenya and Puerto Rico work discussed above. Table 4 shows that the adjusted rates do correspond to the ranking shown in Figure 1 in period III (less-developed countries) and period IV (developed countries). Of course, the results of Table 4 do not prove anything; they simply show that, using some reasonable correction factors, one can arrive at a set of adjusted rates whose pattern is consistent with the theoretical model.

Table 4. Average Rates of Return, Adjusted and Unadjusted,
by Level of Schooling

Level of Schooling	(1) Average Unadjusted Rate of Return (%)	(2) Correction Factor	(3) Average Adjusted Rate of Return (%)
I. Less-developed countries			
Primary	17.4	.4	7.0
Secondary	15.2	.8	12.2
University	12.7	.9	11.4
II. Developed countries			
Secondary	10.0	.6	6.0
University	8.4	.8	6.7

Source: Column (1): Table 1.
    Column (2): Factors are approximate and hypothetical, based on work by Blaug, Carnoy
        and Thias, and Denison.
    Column (3): Column (1) times Column (2).

Part Three
SCHOOL PRODUCTION FUNCTION

One of the ways to describe the school system and determine the way it distributes skills is to estimate how various school and nonschool inputs affect the academic performance of pupils, their self-esteem, and any other relevant measure of pupil output that is chosen. There has been a consider-able amount of this work done for the United States (Bowles, 1970b; Cole-man, 1966; Gintis, 1969; Hanushek, 1968; Kiesling, 1967; Levin, 1970a, b; Ribich, 1968) and some now beginning in developing areas.[1] The U.S. stud-ies corroborate that socioeconomic background is an important factor in determining students' performance in school.[2] More sophisticated studies which attempt to measure the effect of in-school variables on pupils' per-formance within socioeconomic groups or race find that the contribution of in-school factors changes from one group to another. Kiesling estimates that the expenditures per pupil variable has a much lower coefficient for children of professional persons when related to examination score than it does for children of lower socioeconomic groups (Kiesling, 1967; Table 1). Hanushek shows that both the verbal ability and experience of teachers have higher coefficients for urban blacks in the U.S. than for urban whites, so that increasing expenditures per pupil has a greater effect for blacks than for whites. At the same time, however, the coefficients are both rela-tively low (Hanushek, 1968).[3] Henry Levin and Stephen Michelson show that in one eastern city (using the Coleman data base) teachers' experience is an important variable in explaining test score variance for whites, but is not important for blacks; yet, verbal ability of teachers is a very important variable in explaining test score variance of blacks and only somewhat im-portant in explaining the test score variance of whites (Michelson, 1970).

Although only one of these studies uses anything but race as a social-class parameter, that one study (Kiesling's) shows the difficulty of increas-ing expenditures per pupil as a means to equalize test scores of pupils from different family backgrounds. For example, Kiesling shows that the mean score at grades four, five, and six of children of professional persons is 29.0 and the mean score of children of skilled and semiskilled workers is 19.6. Since the coefficient of the logarithm of expenditure per pupil for the chil-dren of skilled and semiskilled workers is 5.3, expenditures per pupil would have to be increased by 300 per cent (tripled) in order to overcome the 9.5 point difference in mean test score between these two groups. Although differences in test scores between races may measure more than social class differences, Levin and Michelson show that the verbal ability of teachers teaching blacks would have to be raised from the present mean of 21.8 to

---

[1] We make crude estimates of school production functions in the Kenya study. Furthermore, the World Bank is attempting to assess its investment in secondary schools in Tunisia through produc-tion function techniques, and John Ryan and Carlos Munoz, graduate students at Stanford, are in Iran and Mexico, respectively, estimating production functions for primary schools.

[2] Socioeconomic background in most of these studies refers to father's education or occupation, number of people in the household, and types of objects in the household. Race may also be con-sidered a socioeconomic factor. The studies are almost all concerned only with urban schools.

[3] The elasticity of verbal score is 0.164 for blacks and 0.125 for whites; the elasticity of experi-ence is 0.045 for blacks and 0.019 for whites.

a mean of about 34 in order to overcome the 11-point spread between the achievement score of white students (35) and the mean score of black students (24).

The Kenya study (Thias and Carnoy, 1969) estimates average examination score of pupils in each school as a function of in-school inputs for primary schools in two Kenyan counties and as a function of in-school inputs and a crude student socioeconomic level proxy for all federally maintained secondary schools. The proxy for socioeconomic background is the average education of males and females over 30 years old in the county in which the school is located. These are very unsophisticated functions compared to U.S. studies, but they give us some insight into the effect of in-school inputs in raising the average examination score in a school. As Kiesling has found for the United States, the effect of expenditures per pupil on variation in examination score when other variables are held constant is rather small in Kenya. For primary schools, one finds that performance on the Kenya primary examination is negatively and significantly (at a 5 per cent level of significance) related to the size of the school and positively related to the school's expenditures and teachers' salaries per pupil. However, the coefficient of per pupil expenditures on teachers is only 0.09, which means that it would require an additional 160 Kenya shillings ($22.40) per class (an increase of about 3.5 per cent in the cost of primary schooling) to increase the average class examination score by 3.4 points out of a mean score of 150 points. For a class with an average score below 150 points, the rate of return (in terms of increased future earnings) to such increased expenditures is 4.6 per cent. The rate to spending on a class with an average score above 150 points is much less.

All these studies show that it is possible to alter the allocation of resources in schools to increase the performance of nonelite students. It is also possible to allocate additional resources in ways which would favor some groups. If, for example, Levin's and Michelson's results are correct, then paying higher salaries to teachers with higher verbal scores rather than more experience favors black students. The results of relationships estimated for secondary schools in Kenya indicate that if new funds for secondary schools were spent on school boarding facilities in poorer areas rather than on more teachers per pupil in wealthier urban areas, examination performance would be raised in poorer regions relative to the urban centers.

What the U.S. data make clear, however, is that simply equalizing resources spent on schooling for children of different socioeconomic groups will not equalize academic performance. Given the present production functions for schools, a very large increase in funds would be necessary to overcome the difference in examination scores between lower-level and middle-level socioeconomic groups. But the production functions can only tell us how to allocate resources more efficiently within a level (or grade) of school, given the values and goals of the school system as they now stand. We can discuss increasing the percentage of poor children who do not drop out of primary (secondary) school or who get into secondary school (university), but in the context of the present schools I am discussing poor children who must become more middle class (or urban) and must function in a middle-class child's society. The production function estimates show that under such conditions it is highly likely that even if the poor child finishes a certain grade, he will not be at the same level of competence as the middle-class child. Gearing the school to maximize output in terms of elite group values guarantees that children of elite or subelite groups will come out ahead of nonelite children even if the resources devoted to instructing the latter are the same (or somewhat greater) than for children of the elite. In practice of course, resources per pupil are less for the poor, the rural, and the black, so the production function *and* the quantity of resources minimize the probability of equal outcomes.

A number of authors have noted the limitations in estimating production functions for schools as firms (Bowles, 1970b; Levin, 1970a, b). The production function assumes that an output is being produced in a technically efficient way. Firms (schools) are assumed to be on the production frontier. It is unclear, however, that schools as firms even know what their production functions look like. Economists are having difficulty determining the outputs of the schools. Our model points out the following about school production functions.

(a) The functions should be specified differently for different groups in the society. Schools produce primarily achievement and self-esteem for children of the elite but concentrate on teaching discipline and hierarchical passivity to nonelite groups. Higher achievement is a by-product of schooling for nonelite groups (Hess, 1968).

(b) If groups are not analyzed separately and functions for all groups estimated together, the average function has to be specified differently for different stages of development of the education system. In period I, the primary output of all levels of schooling is achievement and self-esteem; in period II, the average output mix changes in primary school to a stress on socialization.

If the functions are not correctly specified to represent what the schools are producing for a given group or at a given point in time, they will be correctly representing the production frontier only for the process of schooling the elite.

Part Four
EDUCATIONAL PLANNING

Almost all nations have attempted some degree of educational planning. The ostensible goal of such planning is to allocate resources to education more rationally—to meet the outputs of the educational system within the social, political, and economic goals of the society.

As a technician, the planner takes these goals as given. Since the goals are an integral part of the educational system, curriculum, classroom structure, and distribution of educational expenditures among various groups are political decisions which transcend the planner's role. Educational planning has therefore usually been limited to altering the number of students produced at each level of schooling.

It is almost universally true that the elite controls the educational system and its functions. The educational planner is thus an agent of the elite. He translates elite needs into operational models. In many cases, the needs of the elite include satisfying political pressure from nonelites, but, as pointed out above, this does not constitute a sharing of political and economic *control* of educational structure and functions with nonelites. Nonelites may gain increased access to schools as a result of political pressure, but they must learn and work under ground rules set by the elite. This has an important effect on the relative academic and economic performance of nonelites.

The literature is not at all explicit on the limited role of the planner. We are led to believe that planners are the guides rather than the guided. But, as Smyth has shown for post World War II Uganda, whenever technically rational educational plans conflict with the government's political needs, the plans are altered or ignored (Smyth, 1970). Planners either are not aware of their limited role or, more likely, identify with elite goals and needs. So their planning models assume that the current educational system is structured to maximize social welfare, and needs only more efficiency or more resources to do so. The models also ignore the socialization function of schooling and the change in this function as the school system expands: since the planner takes elite goals as given, he assumes correctly that any such change in socialization function is rational in terms of fulfilling elite needs.

Logically, the most popular planning techniques are those that least question the goals of the educational system. These constitute the social-demand approach, which projects the future need for schools, teachers, and other schooling inputs based on population growth and a desired (as stated in government or international agency documents) enrollment rate. This approach assumes that everyone wants more schooling (what is the source of this want?), that increased schooling increases welfare, and that the role of government is to meet, as rapidly as financially possible, the demand for different kinds and levels of free schooling. More sophisticated planning (manpower planning) follows the Soviet input-output technique, treating education and skills as an engineering problem. Skills are taken as inputs into the production process using fixed coefficients between output of goods and inputs of skills. Another set of fixed coefficients is used to describe the relationship between skills and number of years of formal schooling. Manpower planning primarily oils the gears of a country's economy with an abundant supply of skilled labor. The structure and needs of the economy are taken as given. The approach does, however, implicitly recognize political constraints on the actual planning of education. Manpower plans traditionally deal only with shortages of middle- and higher-level skills, assuming that the expansion of primary school is a political decision (Harbison and Myers, 1964).

Besides the social-demand and manpower approaches to planning, a number of other techniques have been developed for assessing the demand and supply of skills and the corresponding demand for schooling services. They can be divided into: (a) the econometric model approach, which describes the education-labor market system by a series of estimable equations; (b) the rate of return approach, which focuses on the relative yield of investment in education at different levels of schooling and the change in relative yields over time; and (c) the linear programming approach, which maximizes the economic value of investment in different schooling levels subject to a number of constraints and derives the amount of schooling inputs required by the optimum solution.[1] These three approaches are more analytical than the social demand and manpower approaches, since the former apply some sort of efficiency criteria to educational expenditure decisions. However, all approaches are servants of a given economic structure, not testing the efficiency of that structure in meeting the needs of nonelites, nor the efficiency of schooling in terms of alternative structures. This may appear to be merely a contentious point. Yet, no educational planning literature explains that optimum school output derived from elite objectives is not necessarily the same as optimum school output for nonelite-oriented development.

EDUCATIONAL PLANNING AND THE RETURN TO PHYSICAL CAPITAL

The aim of most educational planning is to reduce bottlenecks in production. If physical and human capital are complementary goods in production (it is assumed here that they are), as school output rises, lowering the relative price of human capital, the rate of return to physical capital rises. In the long run, *caeteris paribus,* firms would like to respond to increased rates by increasing the stock of physical capital. This would raise

---

[1] For detailed comparisons of these approaches, see Blaug, 1967; Davis, 1966; and Bowles, 1969.

employment possibilities, increase output, and lower prices of goods. In theory, then, the mean rate of return to human capital would increase in the long run. Meanwhile, however, the school system expands further as nonelites compete with each other for the limited increase in jobs (see Blaug, 1969). Wages for skills continue to fall, outracing the increase in physical capital, which is constrained by imperfections in the world capital market and by shortage of domestic savings for investment in physical capital suitable for industrialization. If wages for job categories are inflexible downward, employers substitute higher skills for lower skills in these jobs.

Average unemployment among less-skilled workers increases. In the short run, and even in the long run, the expansion of school output increases the rate of return to physical capital and distributes national income from owners of human capital to owners of physical capital. In the case of state enterprise, the human capital elite are the "owners" of physical capital. With an increase in the rate of return to physical capital, managers may expand the firm's physical capital, or the increase in rent may be used to expand the government bureaucracy since that serves the human capital elite, or the increase may be consumed by the elite. If foreign enterprise gets an increase in return to capital, it may choose to amortize the investment more rapidly, shifting the increase in return to the parent company.

In a private enterprise economy in which the owners of physical capital are a different group from the human capital elite, planned expansion of the educational system conflicts with the aims of human capital elites who are trying to limit the number of those with primary schooling and, later, of those with secondary and higher education. Manpower planners are probably most acceptable to human capital elites because they base their projections of middle and higher educational needs on *current* real wages of secondary and higher graduates. Since the educational systems of most developing countries are apparently in the period II or III (Figure 1) stage of expansion, these current real wages include sizable monopoly rents. Pressure from nonelites usually causes secondary and sometimes higher schools to expand their output more than the plan calls for, depressing wages of the educated elite and shifting their monopoly rent to the owners of monopoly physical capital.[1]

There are ways of sweetening this pill, however. One of the facets of educational planning in Kenya which amazes foreigners is that those attending primary school must pay about 40 per cent of the total cost of their schooling, while those in higher secondary school (twelfth and thirteenth years of schooling) and in the university pay nothing. This is rationalized by the

---

[1] Arthur Lewis argues for the overproduction of educated manpower to reduce the monopoly rent associated with current wages. He does not recognize explicitly, however, the gain to owners of physical capital from such a policy (Lewis, 1961).

plan as an effort to expand the quantity of middle-level and higher-level manpower. If the effort succeeds, it will decrease the growth of real wages of those skill levels. Yet, the private rate of return to taking higher schooling remains relatively high. Resources are simply transferred from the populace as a whole to children of elites in order to satisfy both the human and physical capital-oriented elites. There is another shift of resources that takes place if the enterprises hiring highly educated labor are willing to expand output: the lower cost of such skills lowers the price of goods produced. Goods produced for domestic consumption which have an important component of highly skilled labor (automobiles, television sets, and various services such as telephone, banking, insurance, etc.) are consumed largely by those with higher education. The downward pressure on incomes of more highly educated labor induced by expanding that level of schooling may also be partially offset by lower prices for those goods which that level of skilled labor consumes.

The conflict between human and physical capital owners is usually resolved by developing a vocational training track at the secondary level. Owners of physical capital desire cheaper skilled labor and would like to avoid bearing the cost of on-the-job training. Owners of secondary school and university human capital wish to keep the wages of academically trained labor high. There is pressure from nonelites to gain access to the high wages associated with secondary training. The compromise among the elites with competing goals—one wanting a rapid expansion of secondary school output, the other a much slower increase—is to increase secondary-school-trained labor but to keep it from being competitive with academic secondary output. Vocational training shifts the burden of skill development out of the factory into the public sector, subsidizing industry (owners of physical capital). Although vocational schools attract those primary students unable to enter the academic track, owners of physical capital are clearly better off with vocationally trained labor than if they had to train the labor themselves. The human capital elite is better off because they have reduced the rate of increase of the competing labor force.

The nonelites who get vocational training would appear also to be better off relative to a condition in which there were no secondary schooling available for them at all. However, they also appear to be aware that they have been assigned a low-status role in the economic hierarchy. Foster analyzes the difficulty of getting students for vocational schools in West Africa (Foster, 1965). The private rate of return to taking vocational schooling was apparently much lower there than to the academic track. In the United States, the vocational track of the general high school was conceived as a means of permanently assigning nonelites to certain roles in the economy (Lauter and Howe, 1970). Junior colleges, which in many ways serve the same vocational purpose today, have been described by Clark as also a means of "cooling out" students who may have otherwise demanded university training (Clark, 1965).

All these studies discuss the negative aspects of vocational training from the point of view of nonelites. As taxpayers, they subsidize specific industries (in California, the state junior college system has an industrial advisory board which suggests training courses to be given in the system); as students, they are assigned to roles as factory workers, low on the status ladder (the reader should not infer that factory work is inherently low-status work, only that societies that place great value on the white collar generally consider factory work as low status). Vocational schools often cannot guarantee that a graduate with specialized training can get a job which matches his training. The vocational school or track is, however, the logical outcome of the conflict between two elite groups. It is derived from their needs, not from those of nonelites.

PARTICULAR ASPECTS OF THE SOCIAL-DEMAND APPROACH

The large expansion of education promoted by the social-demand approach tends to be rhetorically acceptable to everyone, especially when applied to the primary level. State capitalist elites are willing to increase the average level of education continuously as long as the education system guarantees their children a better chance of attaining the high-level bureaucracy or technocracy than the children of nonfunctionaries. In a private enterprise economy, the real friends of the social-demand approach are "progressive" industrialists who benefit from their ownership of physical capital when there is a large increase in the educated labor force. The approach rationalizes the expansion of schooling even with low rates of return to investment in schooling on the grounds of significant external economies accruing to a greater stock of education in the labor force. It is implied that the externalities accrue to those taking education through better networks of communication or the teaching capabilities of more efficient co-workers. In most countries, however, these possible externalities are overshadowed by the direct nonpecuniary costs of disillusionment of the unemployed educated. The "externalities" referred to by the social-demand approach probably mean the direct increase in the return to owners of physical capital from a more educated labor force.

The social-demand approach is also supported by the ministry of education. This ministry has a bureaucratic interest in the expansion of education in any form, as long as it is federally controlled. The larger the education system, the larger the number of teachers and the more important the ministry. This bureaucratic interest is an important ally of the nonelites in the sense that it wants to expand schooling. It is not interested in sacrificing its power base, however, by trying to change the educational system in ways which would conflict with industrial or other elite interests in the country.

FOREIGN INVESTMENT AND FOREIGN AID

The role of foreign investment and foreign aid in this process is particularly important for many countries. In order to attract foreign investment in manufacturing, developing countries must provide a pool of skilled labor. Foreign firms pay more than domestic, attracting the more qualified middle-level and higher-level manpower to work for them. This brings pressure on the government from domestic owners of physical capital in addition to the pressure brought by foreign firms to produce this level of manpower. In many countries, however, foreign firms are almost the only users of higher-level manpower in the private sector. In either case, foreign firms exert a tremendous influence on the kind of higher-level manpower produced (business school graduates and engineers versus social and physical scientists), which influences the technology and growth pattern of the country outside the foreign sector.

Foreign aid has complemented the owners of physical capital in the kind of education it supports. The World Bank, Ford Foundation, and the Agency for International Development have all been actively supporting university and secondary education to eliminate bottlenecks in skilled inputs. Capital-intensive foreign firms and firms producing for export capture much of this transferred monopoly rent. The apparent losers are those in the human capital-intensive public bureaucracy, which employs a large fraction of the middle-level and higher-level manpower elite in developing countries. The transfer is also borne by the less-skilled and even the uneducated because of the downward substitutability of skills. As more highly skilled people are produced by the education system, the lowering of wages is passed through all levels of labor. Hence, labor as a whole, at all levels of skills, transfers income to the owners of physical capital.[1]

CONFLICTS AMONG ELITES

The conflict between owners of human and physical capital about whether the middle and higher education system should expand is compounded by subconflicts over who is to get and control the additional education once it is expanded. This is usually a struggle between elites of different subgroups, not between elites and nonelites (that struggle is concentrated over

---

[1] It is worth noting that the transfer of economic surplus to owners of physical capital is entirely consistent with Rostow's and others' theory of economic development, which calls for the promotion and reinforcement of modern development-oriented elites, especially those who are likely to reinvest accumulated physical capital. These elites are characterized as the driving force behind the transformation of the society from a backward, low-level equilibrium condition to a rapidly growing, innovating national state (Rostow, 1960). There is now considerable evidence, however, that so-called traditional elements in the economy are highly efficient allocators of resources and highly sensitive to economic stimuli (Schultz, 1964; Yotopoulos, 1968). Usually, elites are drawn from the already more affluent members of the society, even though traditional elements may be just as efficient.

whether the system should expand, not over control of the system once it does expand). In Africa, various tribal groupings fight over access to the university and the better secondary schools. In Latin America, traditional elites struggle with the new industrial elites over university control. In those places where there is a struggle among different groups, the expansion of higher education is difficult, since no group will allow expansion until control is established. In Mexico and Venezuela, for example, university expansion in recent years has occurred more smoothly than in Brazil, Colombia, or Peru, where the industrial elite is not fully in control of government policy making, and a higher fraction of owners of human capital are employed by the government itself.

The planning models discussed above take little of these considerations into account. More important, they yield results which are only acceptable if the results conform to the decision of the elite in power regarding education. Excesses of labor should be just as unacceptable to planners as shortages, but, in fact, both the social demand and manpower models accept excesses because of the welfare function implicit in the models. I have tried to show what the important income distribution elements in that implicit welfare function may be. In addition to the distribution of economic surplus between physical and human capital owners implied by some approaches to planning, all the models unquestioningly accept the elite nature of schools themselves. Planners are either unconcerned with the income distribution effects of the educational system or are unwilling to face the distributional consequences of their planning models.

Conclusion

I have tried to introduce a number of ideas in a few pages. Education is not necessarily development-oriented even if it produces a modern, Western elite. Any meaningful concept of development must include a specific theory of distribution of economic and social gains. If education has served to increase per capita income, it has done so in a very skewed manner, consistent with the elite's narrow view of economic and social development. Schooling has not been geared to the needs of nonelites. It has channeled the mass of people into becoming more useful to elite needs and wants. Even if schooling teaches skills to the nonelites and increases their income, there is serious doubt about whether education serving some different, less-elitist, economic, social, and political structure would not do all the things education is doing now much more efficiently for the great majority of the world's children.

Many of the characteristics of present education systems are derived from their centralization away from the local community to the state. More centrally controlled industrialization, political power, and education would serve the elites already in power. Centralization is a means to destroy traditional hierarchies and derive economic advantage from economies of scale. However, centralization has obtained these "necessities" for development at the price of destroying people's sense of control over their environment. It has forced them directly into an environment which is hostile to them without providing the means for their adjustment to and understanding of that new environment. Schools have been assigned this task, but because they are centralized they are also hopelessly inflexible to the needs of nonelites. I have described the economic effects of such a school system on various groups which pass through it. The model and my remarks are applicable to developed as well as less-developed countries.

What may be needed at all levels of development is a movement toward community control over the lives of community members. A communalization of development—accompanied by a drastic reduction of centralized power—would probably reduce the rate of advanced technology-oriented industrialization. But development of local communities would proceed at a much more rapid rate than under a centralized bureaucracy, especially if the specific function of the central government would be to shift public resources to even out development among different communities. Education and technology would have to be oriented toward the community level of development. Schooling would serve community needs. At higher levels of schooling, communities could come together to provide a single secondary school. Harambee schools, if oriented toward community needs instead of toward competing with the central power elite on its own grounds, would be a model of community secondary schools in an African setting. Regional universities, such as one or two now operating in Venezuela, seem to be much more useful for developing a community-oriented technology than are large, central universities.

One must ask whether the institutions which now control the educational system would allow any serious decentralization of this form. If community schools imply in any way a transfer of political and economic control of a country from elite to nonelite groups, or even from the ruling elite to another, nonruling elite, decentralization will not evolve. Indeed, no solution to educational problems may be possible without profound changes in a country's overall institutional structures.

References

Abernethy, David. *The Political Dilemma of Popular Education.* Stanford, Calif.: Stanford University Press, 1969.

Baran, Paul, and Paul Sweezy. *Monopoly Capital.* New York: Monthly Review Press, 1966.

Becker, Gary S. *Human Capital.* Princeton, N. J.: Princeton University Press, 1964.

Blair, Phillip. "Rates of Return to Schooling of Majority and Minority Groups in Santa Clara County." (Ph.D. dissertation, Stanford University, 1970.)

Blaug, Mark. "The Rate of Return on Investment in Education in Great Britain," *The Manchester School* (September, 1965), pp. 252-261.

Blaug, Mark. "Approaches to Educational Planning," *Economic Journal,* 77, no. 306 (June, 1967), pp. 262-287.

Blaug, M., R. Layard, and M. Woodhall. *The Causes of Graduate Unemployment in India.* London: The Penguin Press, 1969.

Bowles, Samuel. *Planning Educational Systems for Economic Growth.* Cambridge, Mass.: Harvard University Press, 1969.

Bowles, Samuel. "Schooling and Inequality from Generation to Generation." Paper presented at the Far Eastern Meeting of the Econometric Society, June, 1970a (mimeo.).

Bowles, Samuel. "Towards an Educational Production Function," *in* W. Lee Hansen, ed., *Education, Income, and Human Capital.* New York: NBER, 1970b.

Bowles, Samuel. "Class Power and Mass Education." Harvard University, 1971 (mimeo.).

Carnoy, Martin. "The Cost and Return to Schooling in Mexico: A Case Study." (Ph.D. dissertation, University of Chicago, 1964.)

Carnoy, Martin. "Rates of Return to Schooling in Latin America," *Journal of Human Resources,* II, no. 3 (Summer, 1967), pp. 359-374.

Carnoy, Martin. "The Quality of Education, Examination Performance, and Urban-Rural Income Differentials in Puerto Rico," *CER,* XIV, no. 3 (October, 1970a), pp. 335-349.

Carnoy, Martin. "The Rate of Return to Schooling and the Increase in Human Resources in Puerto Rico." Stanford University, 1970b (mimeo.).

Clark, Burton R. "The 'Cooling Out' Function in Higher Education," *in* A. H. Halsey *et al., Education, Economy, and Society.* Glencoe, Ill.: The Free Press, 1965, Chapter 36.

Clignet, Remi, and Philip Foster. *Fortunate Few.* Evanston, Ill.: Northwestern University Press, 1967.

Coleman, James S., *et al. Equality of Educational Opportunity.* Washington: U.S. Government Printing Office, 1966.

Davis, Russell G. *Planning Human Resource Development.* Chicago, Ill.: Rand McNally, 1966.

Denison, Edward F. *The Sources of Economic Growth in the U.S. and the Alternatives before Us.* Supplementary Paper No. 13. New York: Committee for Economic Development, 1962.

Denison, Edward F. *Why Growth Rates Differ.* Washington: The Brookings Institution, 1967.

Dugan, Dennis. "The Impact of Parental and Educational Investments upon Student Achievement." Paper presented at the 129th Annual Meeting of the American Statistical Association. New York City, August 21, 1969 (mimeo.).

Foster, Philip. "The Vocational School Fallacy in Development Planning," *in* C. A. Anderson and M. J. Bowman, eds., *Education and Economic Development.* Chicago, Ill.: Aldine Publishing Co., 1965.

Friedenberg, Edgar Z. *Coming of Age in America.* New York: Random House, 1965.

Gintis, Herbert. "Alienation and Power: Toward a Radical Welfare Economics." (Ph.D. dissertation, Harvard University, 1969.)

Guthrie, James, George Kleindorfer, Henry Levin, and Robert Stout. "Schools and Inequality: A Study of the Relationships between Social Status, School Services, and Post-School Opportunity in the State of Michigan." Report prepared for the National Urban Coalition, Washington, D.C., September, 1969 (mimeo.).

Halsey, A. H., Leon Floud, and C. A. Anderson. *Education, Economy, and Society.* Glencoe, Ill.: The Free Press, 1965.

Hanoch, Giora. "An Economic Analysis of Earnings and Schooling," *Journal of Human Resources,* II, no. 3 (Summer, 1967), pp. 310–329.

Hanushek, Eric A. "The Education of Negroes and Whites." (Ph.D. dissertation, Massachusetts Institute of Technology, 1968.)

Harbison, F., and C. A. Myers. *Education, Manpower, and Economic Growth.* New York: McGraw-Hill, 1964.

Hess, Robert, and Judith V. Torney. *The Development of Political Attitudes in Children.* Chicago, Ill.: Aldine Publishing Co., 1967.

Illich, Ivan. "The Futility of Schooling in Latin America," *Saturday Review* (April 10, 1968).

Illich, Ivan. "Why We Must Abolish Schooling," *New York Review of Books* (July 2, 1970).

Journal of Human Resources, II, no. 3 (Summer, 1970).

Kiesling, Herbert. "Measuring a Local Government Service: A Study of School Districts in New York State," *Review of Economics and Statistics* (August, 1967), pp. 356–367.

Kozol, Jonathan. *Death at an Early Age.* Boston, Mass.: Houghton Mifflin, 1967.

Lauter, Paul, and Florence Howe. "How the School System Is Rigged for Failure," *New York Review of Books* (June 18, 1970).

Levin, Henry. "A New Model of School Effectiveness," *in* Alexander Mood, ed., *Do Teachers Make a Difference?* Washington: U.S. Office of Education, OE-58042, 1970a.

Levin, Henry M. "A Cost-Effectiveness Analysis of Teacher Selection," *The Journal of Human Resources,* V, no. 1 (Winter, 1970b), pp. 24–33.

Lewis, Arthur. "Education and Economic Development," *Social and Economic Studies* (Jamaica), 10 (June, 1961), pp. 113–127.

Lipset, Seymour Martin, and Aldo Solari. *Elites in Latin America.* London: Oxford University Press, 1967.

Marx, Karl. *Value, Price and Profit.* New York: International Publishers, 1935.

Michelson, Stephan. "Resource Allocation: Reflections on the Law and the Data," *Inequality in Education.* Cambridge, Mass.: Harvard Center for Law and Education, 1969.

Michelson, Stephan. "The Association of Teacher Resourceness with Children's Characteristics," *in* Alexander Mood, ed., *Do Teachers Make a Difference?* Washington: U.S. Office of Education, OE-58042, 1970.

Mills, C. Wright. *The Power Elite.* New York: Oxford University Press, 1959.

Psacharopoulos, George. "The Economic Returns to Higher Education in Twenty-Five Countries." London School of Economics, Higher Education Unit, 1970 (mimeo.).

Psacharopoulos, George, and K. Hinchliffe. "The Rate of Return to Investment in Education and the Impact on Growth and Development: An International Comparison." London School of Economics, Higher Education Research Unit, 1970 (mimeo.).

Raskin, Marcus. *Being and Doing*. New York: Random House, 1971.

Ribich, Thomas. *Education and Poverty*. Washington: The Brookings Institution, 1968.

Rostow, Walt Whitman. *The Stages of Economic Growth, A non-Communist Manifesto*. New York: Cambridge University Press, 1960.

Schultz, Theodore W. *Transforming Traditional Agriculture*. New Haven, Conn.: Yale University Press, 1964.

Smyth, John. "The Political Economy of Educational Planning in Uganda," *Comparative Education Review*, XIV, no. 3 (October, 1970), pp. 350–362.

Tenenbaum, Samuel. "The Teacher, the Middle Class, the Lower Class," *in* Donald Adams, ed., *Introduction to Education: A Comparative Analysis*. Belmont, Calif.: Wadsworth Publishing Co., 1966, pp. 294–301.

Thias, Hans H., and Martin Carnoy. *Cost-Benefit Analysis in Education: A Case Study of Kenya*. Washington: Economics Dept., IBRD (EC-173), November, 1970.

UNESCO, *Statistical Yearbook, 1966* and *1967*. Tables 2.1, 2.5, and 2.10. Paris: 1968.

Welch, Finis. "Labor-Market Discrimination: An Interpretation of Income Differences in the Rural South," *Journal of Political Economy*, 75, no. 3 (June, 1967), pp. 225–240.

Yotopoulos, Pan A. *Allocative Efficiency in Economic Development*. Athens: Center of Planning and Economic Research, 1967.

Section 3:
Structure and Function of Educational Systems

Introduction to Section 3

The first contribution, by Joseph Farrell, although concerned with education and development, provides a radical departure from the readings in the previous section. The primary focus of the paper associates "educational structural differentiation," or the process and state of multiplication and specification of distinct elements within an educational system, with specific development criteria. Development, as explained by Farrell, refers to two distinct indicators. One is called "urbanization" and includes, among other criteria, per capita income, media distribution, consumption of energy, and percentage of the population living in urban areas; the other development indicator is called "information-processing capacity" and refers to the degree of structural differentiation existing in the political and economic subsystems which permits both increasing adaptation to the environment and more diverse information to flow among and between subsystems. Farrell remarks: "It is suggested, then, that there are two (at least) quite different dimensions of national development, information-processing capacity and urbanization. Each is hypothesized to be strongly associated with a different educational system dimension: information-processing capacity with educational structural differentiation, and urbanization with enrollment ratios."

Using data from 1950 and 1969 on Latin America, the author summarizes his findings as follows: "Information-processing capacity, in both the political and economic sectors, is highly associated with educational structural differentiation, and is very weakly associated with educational enrollment ratios. Urbanization, which captures much of the traditional view of development, is moderately well associated with both educational enrollment ratios and educational structural differentiation."

Farrell reports that GNP per capita showed a weak relationship to both enrollment ratios and educational structural differentiation, thus calling into question many previous studies which have relied upon this variable as a sole indicator of development. In addition, secondary-level enrollment ratios showed very weak associations with both development criteria. Thus Farrell comments: *"It appears that increasing secondary-level enrollments rapidly enough to raise the enrollment ratio at that level is a particularly ineffecitve path to development."* In his concluding remarks, the author suggests that for at least two aspects of development it is more important to analyze the structure of education and the diversity of information transmitted by school systems than to concern oneself with increasing the proportions enrolled in schools.

The next article, by Mark Hanson, approaches the development problem through an investigation of current reforms in the organizational structures and administrative procedures of the Venezuelan and Colombian educational systems. The author describes the decentralization under way in Venezuela designed to retain policy and procedural decisions at the ministerial level while providing for increased decision-making powers at the regional level. In Colombia, the author indicates that the national reforms are designed to reduce decision-making power at the state level and thus ensure greater adherence to official ministerial policy. Hanson suggests that the reforms are dissimilar: Venezuela is attempting to increase functional autonomy while decreasing the interdependence between the parent system and subsystems; Colombia is instituting lesser functional autonomy and increasing the interdependence between the national, state, and private systems. The author suggests that political pressures may constrain current reforms.

The third selection, by James Stimson and myself, investigates teacher perception of the organizational climate of 30 rural and urban Paraguayan primary schools. Continuing with the theme of educational decision making advanced by Hanson, the administration of a 69-item questionnaire to 258 primary teachers found the sample of schools to be ". . . characterized as static institutions with apathetic teachers who receive little in the way of social-need or task-accomplishment satisfaction." While supporting the contention that the schools in Paraguay reflect the relatively closed sociocultural environment of which they are a part, Stimson and I suggest that the nature of the centralized administrative framework has parallels in urban, lower socioeconomic areas in the United States and conclude that ". . . a more decentralized system in which there is access to and participation in policy making by schoolteachers and administrators might alleviate the lack of satisfaction gained from institutional participation."

The fourth contribution leaves the area of administration of educational programs yet continues to supply insight into the structure and function of educational systems. Phyllis Goldblatt utilizes multiple regression and factor analysis to explain spatial patterns in primary school enrollment differentials in Mexico. Employing a conceptual framework borrowed from human geography, the author views enrollment rates as an innovation being diffused through communicative patterns from urban to rural areas and from region to region within the country. Differential outcomes of the analysis are then examined by pinpointing influences which alter parental decisions to enroll children in school. Maps of the nation show enrollment rates as well as paradigmatic representations of the two analytic aspects of the study. The author surveys the results of the factors thought to be associated with the underlying enrollment patterns. She suggests that high enrollment rates in urban areas are associated with low levels of immigration, adoption of urban life styles, high manufacturing incomes, low proportion of males in white-collar occupations, and awareness by parents of potential returns of schooling to the individual. In the rural areas, the proportion of males engaged in agriculture, the level of technology employed in farming, and the proportion of agricultural laborers evidenced little relationship to primary enrollments. Instead, the existence of opportunities for child employment, adult literacy, and the adherence to traditional cultural traits exhibited considerable influence on rural enrollments.

Aparecida Gouveia concludes this section with a series of hypotheses linking socioeconomic changes in Brazil to the composition of teaching staffs in secondary schools. Choosing São Paulo and Pará as representative areas of relative development and underdevelopment, the author uses government statistics and a sample survey to investigate the proportions of males and females by social origin who are teaching in different types of secondary schools. In terms of the social origins of teachers, Gouveia asserts that over one half of the secondary teachers in academic schools come from the middle-middle and lower-middle classes. The São Paulo females, however, represent higher social-class backgrounds than do their Pará female counterparts and both São Paulo and Pará males. Dividing the teachers into subgroups according to the number of years each has been teaching, the author compares sex and social-class origins. Males, for example, who teach in academic schools were found to be characterized by social-class origins lower than those recorded some 20 years earlier. Gouveia discusses the more than threefold increase in female teachers over the last 20 years and the impact this increase has had on the total male-female social composition in schools.

Original Sources for Selections

Farrell, Joseph P. "Educational Differentiation and National Development: A Statistical Study," *Interchange,* 1, no. 2 (1970), pp. 62–72.

Hanson, Mark. *Educational Reform in Colombia and Venezuela: An Organizational Analysis,* No. 4 of Occasional Papers in Education and Development. Foreword by Russell G. Davis. Cambridge: Harvard University Graduate School of Education, Center for Studies in Education and Development, August 1970, 33 pp.

Stimson, James, and Thomas J. La Belle. "The Organizational Climate of Paraguayan Elementary Schools: Rural-Urban Differentiations," *Education and Urban Society,* 3, no. 3 (May, 1971), pp. 333–349.

Goldblatt, Phyllis. "The Geography of Youth Employment and School Enrollment Rates in Mexico," *in* Andreas M. Kazamias and Erwin H. Epstein, eds., *Schools in Transition.* Boston, Mass.: Allyn and Bacon, 1968, pp. 280–294.

Gouveia, Aparecida J. "Economic Development and Changes in the Composition of the Teaching Staff of Secondary Schools in Brazil," *Social and Economic Studies,* 14 (March, 1965), pp. 118–130.

Educational Differentiation and National Development: A Statistical Study

JOSEPH P. FARRELL

The purpose of this paper is to examine empirically, using cross-national data, some relationships between educational systems and national development. Although there is a vast and expanding literature on the role education may play in national development, there have been relatively few attempts to use the increasingly abundant cross-national data to test propositions that relate to some specified body of theory. Partly this lack of use relates to the fact that most of the data that are available regarding developing nations have been assembled by national or international agencies for social accounting purposes and are not particularly appropriate for testing or development of theory. Partly it relates to the fact that many of the concepts current in development theory are loosely defined and difficult to operationalize. (Indeed it is hard to find theories sufficiently developed to permit the deduction of testable propositions.) For whatever reason, one finds few studies that follow the logical progression of, first, isolating and clearly defining theoretically important dimensions or variables, second, developing measures of the variables and then using the measures to assess the relationship between the variables—in order either to test hypotheses or to suggest hypotheses for future testing. This paper represents an attempt to follow precisely this progression.

The concept of central concern here is *educational structural differentiation*. A thorough explication of this concept can be found in Adams and Farrell (1969). Briefly, it can be defined as both a process and a state. As a process it refers to the multiplication of one structural element into two or more structurally distinct elements, to the establishment of more-specialized

Reproduced, by permission, from *Interchange,* 1, no. 2 (1970), pp. 62–76.

and more-autonomous social units. As a state it refers to the number of structurally distinct specialized elements that exist in a system at a particular point in time.

The theoretical framework that suggests that this differentiation is a particularly important dimension of educational systems may be termed information-theoretic systems analysis. One starts with a notion of culture as a system of shared meanings attached to social objects—that is, shared information.[1] Any social system can be viewed as a mechanism or structure for the orderly processing or handling of such information. Environmental changes impinge as new information upon strategic factors within a system. A society can then be thought of as a complexly interacting set of subsystems (educational system, economic system, political system, etc.) joined together by communicative links or channels, along which information relative to changes in one part of the system is transmitted to other parts. In this view, development itself may be defined, to quote Young (1968), "as a nation's overall ability to process information" (p. 364). Black (1966) has recently expressed much the same view: "When one considers modernization as a process . . . one thinks of a continuous series of changes accompanying the growth of knowledge and its effects on man's way of getting things done" (p. 5).

But what kinds of effects are referred to? The thoughts of a number of scholars working primarily, but not exclusively, within the rubric of systems analysis converge on the position that the typical way in which a social system maps into itself information concerning environmental change is, in the words of Buckley (1967, p. 50), through elaboration or change of its structure "to a higher or more complex level," that is, through *structural differentiation.* As communicative links become more differentiated they are able to transmit or process a greater diversity of information, and various subsystems are increasingly able to respond to one another. To use the metaphor proposed by Easton (1965, p. 123), such differentiation amounts to opening new channels in the system through which information can flow.

---

[1] It should be noted that information is here construed more broadly than is typical in studies of communication and national development. Information is here taken to include not only gestures and words, whether communicated face-to-face or via the mass media, but types of organization, social institutions, social roles, technology, material, and so forth. As Cherry (1961) has noted: "Speech and writing are by no means our only systems of communication. . . . [In addition to gestures, expressions, position, etc., which make up the silent language,] we have economic systems for trafficking [sic] not in ideas but in material goods and services; the tokens of communication are coins, bonds, letters of credit, and so on. We have conventions of dress, rules of the road, social formalities, and good manners; we have rules of membership and function in business institutions, and families. . . . A 'code' of ethics . . . is a set of guiding rules governing 'ought' situations, generally accepted, whereby people in a society associate together and have social coherence" (pp. 4, 8). For a further explication of this view of information, which is central to the systems analytic perspective adopted here, see Buckley (1967, particularly pp. 48–50).

It is being suggested, in short, that there is an extremely important dimension of national development that has not generally been considered in empirical studies, which might be called "information-processing capacity" (Young, 1968, p. 364). One would expect to find highly differentiated educational systems in societies that rank high on this dimension. Most of the elements of highly differentiated educational systems are either (1) specialized information-producing entities (e.g., research institutes), or (2) specialized schools, which can be thought of as entities for the transmission of specialized information. One would expect to find such educational systems in societies that have a high capacity to handle such specialized information. Indeed, it is suggested that to establish a highly differentiated educational system is to establish a quite effective set of communicative links, between the educational system and other systems, and between the other systems themselves. It is, therefore, a major hypothesis of this study that *there is a strong association between educational structural differentiation and measures of information-processing capacity in other systems.*[1]

It is suggested further that the information-processing capacity of a national system is a dimension of development quite different from that to which the generally used indicators of development refer. The traditional data series used to measure development, such as per capita income, urbanization, radio, telephone and newspaper distribution, commercial energy consumption, etc., all have been found repeatedly to be highly interrelated. Several studies have found that under factor analysis these indicators yield one or a very few factor(s) (Berry, 1961; Caplow and Finsterbusch, 1964; Sawyer, 1967; Schnore, 1961). The difficulty is that no one knows for sure just what to call the factor(s). Following the policy adopted by Young (1968), the term "urbanization" is used here to refer to whatever it is that is indexed by the traditional development indicators. Any number of other terms might be used, of course, such as "wealth," "economic development," and so forth. However, it is commonplace to note that most of the phenomena to which traditional indicators refer are, in most developing societies, essentially urban phenomena. Indeed, much of the vast literature relating to national integration or nation building has to do with the difficulties of spreading such phenomena out from the urban area to the hinterland.

This dimension (or at least some of the indicators of it) has long been considered to be the most important aspect of national development, if not coterminous with such development. It cannot be ignored in a study such

---

[1] It is of particular note that differentiation has been given this key role in system adaptiveness in a variety of theoretical perspectives other than the one adopted here (see, for example, Coleman, 1965; Eisenstadt, 1966; Marsh, 1967; and Parsons, 1966). Consequently propositions regarding differentiation in educational systems may prove relevant to the work of scholars who prefer to study development from any of several theoretical or disciplinary perspectives.

as the present one if the findings reported are to be related meaningfully to previous work. However, it is not completely clear to what concept in the systems analytic framework urbanization maps. Perhaps it can best be thought of as referring to the volume of material outputs of the national system (particularly the economic system) as opposed to the system's capacity to process information, and hence to adapt.

If educational structural differentiation has any effect upon urbanization, it is probably indirect with information-processing capacity as an intervening variable. It is, however, likely that a high degree of differentiation in the educational system requires some minimal level of wealth, population concentration, and communications facilities in the wider society. Previous empirical work has found urbanization to be only moderately well associated with information-processing capacity (Young, 1968, p. 373). Thus, although there is probably some association between urbanization and educational structural differentiation, there is no compelling reason to suggest that the association is strong. Consequently, another hypothesis is that *there is a positive but moderate association between urbanization and educational structural differentiation.*

One final bit of empirical evidence cannot be ignored. Study after study has found educational enrollment ratios to be highly associated with indicators of urbanization.[1] For present purposes, enrollment ratios can best be thought of, as they typically are in cross-national studies, as rough surrogate measures of the volume of educational system output. Urbanization appears to create demands for raising educational enrollment ratios, as well as to generate and mobilize the resources required to begin to meet those demands. There is, however, neither theoretical argument nor evidence that suggests a very strong association between information-processing capacity and enrollment ratios. Consequently, a further hypothesis is that *there is a strong association between enrollment ratios and urbanization, but a weak association (if any) between enrollment ratios and information-processing capacity.*

It is suggested, then, that there are two (at least) quite different dimensions of national development, information-processing capacity and urbanization. Each is hypothesized to be strongly associated with a different educational system dimension: information-processing capacity with educational structural differentiation, and urbanization with enrollment ratios.

---

[1] For example, Harbison and Myers (1964, p. 39) report that enrollment ratios correlate as follows with GNP per capita: first-level enrollment ratio—.668; combined first- and second-level ratio —.732; second-level ratio—.817; third-level ratio—.735. Russet, Alker, Deutsch, and Lasswell (1964, p. 283) report that combined primary and secondary ratios correlate highly with such variables as newspaper circulation ($r = .88$), number of radios per 1,000 inhabitants ($r = .83$), number of persons per physician ($r = .86$), and so on. There is no need to cite further evidence on this point as the relationship of enrollment ratios with such variables as are here called urbanization measures has become almost folklore in the study of national development.

Methodology

The general approach to the testing of these hypotheses has been correlational. The nature of the analysis has of course been constrained by the nature of the available data. Since several of the variables of central interest are ordinally measured, all of the data have been ranked and a rank association statistic has been used. Ranking all of the data has the advantage of minimizing the effect of inaccuracies in the original information. The range of most series used is sufficiently wide that a very large absolute error is required to change a nation's rank to any appreciable extent. Considering the dubious quality of many cross-national data series, this factor is of some importance.

The particular statistic used is Kendall's Tau_c. This statistic provides a direct measure of the extent to which two rankings tend to be similar and is not analogous to the more commonly used product-moment correlation statistics. For example, if there are no ties on either ranking, the *absolute* value of Tau, not its square, indicates the proportional reduction in error of estimation made possible by a relationship. Values of Tau are thus typically smaller than product-moment correlation coefficients obtained for the same data. Personal interest and data availability have led to a concentration upon the Latin American nations.[1]

Abundant data on all the variables of interest here are available for around 1960 for Latin America. Synchronic associations tell nothing, of course, about direction of effect or causation. To get at these questions one needs, at least, measures of the same variables at different points in time. Data have been found for at least some indicators of each of the major variables of concern for 1950 as well as 1960.[2] It is possible therefore to examine the hypothesized associations both synchronically and diachronically.

Measurement of the two educational dimensions of interest here has presented little problem. Educational structural differentiation is measured for 1950 and 1960 by Guttman scales, which have been published elsewhere[3]

---

[1] The universe of nations used for this study includes all Latin American nations that were autonomous as of 1960. One nation, Cuba, was excluded because of data acquisition problems. The list of nations, then, includes the following: Argentina, Bolivia, Brazil, Chile, Colombia, Costa Rica, Dominican Republic, Ecuador, El Salvador, Guatemala, Haiti, Honduras, Mexico, Nicaragua, Panama, Paraguay, Peru, Uruguay, and Venezuela.

[2] The temptation to use the overtime data to construct indices of rates of change has been resisted. There are several methods for calculating such rates, each of which produces a different ranking of nations. It becomes impossible to interpret correlations using such change indices, for one cannot tell if the observed coefficients reflect the actual relationship between the variables or if they are a function of the particular calculating method used. (For an example of the difficulties in intepretation presented by change indices, see Baster, 1965, pp. 17–19.)

[3] The following items are included on this scale for 1960. They are listed by scale step, in order of decreasing popularity, the 12 items in step 1 being universally present in Latin America: (1) ministry of education, university, teacher-training institution, inspectorate, curriculum agency, preprimary school, primary school, secondary school, secondary vocational education, secondary

(Farrell, 1968, pp. 112–113; 1969). Enrollment ratios are measured at the primary, secondary, and higher levels for 1950 and 1960.

Two Dimensions of Development: An Empirical Preliminary

It is commonplace to assert that most of the frequently used measures of development are of questionable reliability and validity. Therefore, no attempt has been made to peg the analysis to one or a very few indicators of the two dimensions of development considered here. Rather, an attempt has been made to assemble data on a number of alternate indicators of the dimensions and to search for general patterns of association. However, before selecting measures of urbanization and information-processing capacity, two questions had to be faced: 1. Are these really separate dimensions of development? 2. If so, which among the large number of available data series best measure them? (Considering the results of previous studies, which have been noted, the first question can best be thought of as an hypothesis to the effect that there *are* these two separate dimensions.) Finding answers to questions of this sort would ordinarily be thought to be a job for factor analysis. Traditional factor analysis, however, is inappropriate for the data used in this study. Factor analysis requires metric data, whereas, as noted above, the data series used here are either ordinal scales or metric scales that have been converted to rankings. Therefore, a recently developed nonmetric analogue of factor analysis, Guttman-Lingoes smallest-space analysis, was used.[1] For information-processing capacity, 11 candidate measures, all suggested by the work of Young (1968, 1970), who first used the concept in cross-national studies, were tried. All but one of the time-specific measures in this set relate to 1960. Data were found that permitted replication

---

vocational school, secondary commercial school, secondary industrial or crafts-trades school; (2) special pedagogical training for secondary teachers, special education class, special education school; (3) ministerial advisory body, secondary agricultural school; (4) university-level teacher-training institution; (5) military school, university research institute in physical-biological sciences; (6) university research institute in social sciences; (7) university-level school of librarianship; (8) national educational planning agency; (9) national apprenticeship commission, ministerial research division; (10) university research institute in agriculture, university research institute in economics; (11) specialized military school; (12) university faculties of biology, chemistry, and physics; (13) ministerial audiovisual division, university faculties of sociology or anthropology, university faculty of graduate studies, specialized secondary industrial school; and (14) university research institute in education.

[1] The object of the smallest-space analysis in this example is to provide, in the smallest possible space (a two-dimensional space being smaller than a three-dimensional space, and so on), a graphic portrayal of a data matrix. The computer attempts to locate points, representing the variables in the matrix, such that the monotonicity in the order relationships among them is faithfully represented. If variable 1 is more closely associated with variable 2 than with variable 3, then point 1 should be closer to point 2 than to point 3. By examining the maps and coordinates produced by the analysis, one can quickly determine if there is regionalization in the space, that is, one can quickly determine if there are clusters of variables. The variables in a cluster will all be highly associated with one another, and less well associated with other variables or clusters. For a brief description of the technique see Laumann and Guttman (1966) and Laumann (1969). For a more technical discussion see Guttman (1968).

of two of these, a scale of industrial diversity and a scale of economic institutional development, for the date 1950.[1]

Data were collected on 29 candidate measures of urbanization for 1960, all of which have been suggested by one or more previous cross-national studies. Ten of these series could be replicated for 1950.

The 52 variables fit quite adequately within a three-dimensional space (coefficient of alienation = .171).[2] Table 1 presents the variables classified according to their clusterings within the three-dimensional space, and indicates the coordinates on the three principal axes that locate each variable within the space. Forty-six of the candidate variables can be classified into six groups, with six variables fitting no group. Three of the groups are not considered further in the analysis. Group IV contains only two variables, both mortality rates, measured at two points in time. Group V contains only one variable measured at two points in time. Group VI contains only two variables. What these three groups suggest for present purposes is that the eight variables they include, which it was thought could be used to measure urbanization, should not be so used.

Examination of the variables included within Groups I, II, and III suggests that there are indeed separate dimensions to the development process, as hypothesized. Group I contains most of the variables that were thought a priori to be measures of urbanization. Indeed, those included are precisely those variables most commonly used in statistical studies of development, such as GNP per capita, proportion of the population in cities, literacy rates,

---

[1] The items on the 1950 replication of the industrial diversity scale, in order of decreasing popularity, are as follows: (1) nation manufactures cement, (2) nation has petroleum refinery, (3) nation manufactures cotton yarn or fabric, (4) nation manufactures boots and shoes, (5) nation manufactures man-made yarn or fabric, (6) nation manufactures any nonferrous metal, (7) nation manufactures steel, and (8) nation manufactures wool yarn. The Latin American nations are ranked as follows on this scale, by scale step: (1) Haiti, Panama, Paraguay, Nicaragua, Honduras, Costa Rica, El Salvador; (2) Dominican Republic, Guatemala; (3) Uruguay; (4) Bolivia; (5) Ecuador; (6) Peru, Venezuela, Colombia; (7) Mexico, Brazil, Argentina; and (8) Chile.

The items on the 1950 replication of the economic institutional development scale, in order of decreasing popularity, are as follows: (1) no legal discrimination against foreign patent applicants; (2) member of Pan American Union of Technical Experts in the Field of Economic Sciences; (3) bureau of any world news agency; (4) member of South American Petroleum Institute; (5) exports any manufactured goods, bureaus of both United States and European news agencies; (6) member of International Council of Scientific Unions, exports manufactured metal and some other export, national unit of International Chamber of Commerce, member of International Office for Weights and Measures; (7) member of International Organization for Standardization; (8) national news agency; and (9) member of International Society of Soil Sciences. The Latin American nations are ranked as follows on this scale, according to scale step: (1) El Salvador; (2) Haiti, Dominican Republic, Nicaragua, Honduras, Costa Rica; (3) Panama, Guatemala; (4) Paraguay, Colombia; (5) Bolivia, Ecuador; (6) Venezuela; (7) Peru; (8) Mexico; (9) Chile, Uruguay, Brazil; and (10) Argentina.

[2] The coefficient of alienation attempts to index the extent to which the map produced by the computer in n dimensions fits the order relations in the input matrix. The smaller the coefficient, the better the fit. In this case, using only two dimensions produced a substantially higher coefficient, and therefore a much poorer fit, than when three dimensions are used. Going to four dimensions did not substantially lower the coefficient.

Table 1. Guttman-Lingoes Smallest-Space Coordinates for a Three-Dimensional Space: Development Indicators, 1950 and 1960, for Latin America

Group/Year	Variable	Dimension 1	Dimension 2	Dimension 3
I-1950	GNP per capita	-31.039	78.544	-11.789
	% of population in communities 20,000+	-61.146	40.153	-31.606
	% of population literate	-44.072	61.615	18.077
	Radio receivers per 1,000 population	-13.315	32.584	-2.661
	% of population white, 1940	-58.658	38.420	3.235
I-1960	Telephones per capita	-35.373	46.075	-18.433
	Per capita consumption of commercial energy	-37.725	38.409	-29.955
	Average rate urbanization, 1945-1955	-51.086	47.052	-32.542
	GNP per capita	-4.185	83.260	-1.952
	% of population in communities 2,500+	-32.695	33.430	-13.740
	% of population in cities 100,000+	-30.104	59.661	1.588
	Electricity generation, kwh per capita	-41.196	49.623	-2.620
	% of population literate	-18.636	57.692	18.565
	Newspaper circulation per 1,000 population	-35.680	74.706	-24.522
	Newsprint consumption	-38.405	44.983	-7.474
	Radio receivers per 1,000 population	-6.914	76.759	-26.623
	Motor vehicles per 1,000 population	-35.085	55.536	-22.480
	Calories consumed per day per capita	-27.502	40.502	13.500
	Proteins consumed per day per capita	-17.625	39.812	37.961
	Hospital beds per capita	-35.847	72.574	16.817
	% of urban population served by piped water	-67.645	69.614	8.332
	Persons per physician	-3.621	10.938	-29.846

II–1950	Scale of economic flexibility	−40.840	−3.118	−26.877
	Scale of industrial diversity	−58.049	−11.859	−33.784
	% of GDP due to manufacturing	−46.581	−33.087	−23.622
	Number of radio transmitters	−68.783	5.808	−32.765
II–1960	Young scale of economic flexibility	−62.356	.319	−16.336
	Young scale of industrial diversity	−50.574	.810	−36.964
	Number of patents filed with U.S. Patent Office	−49.864	11.769	−29.783
	Number of revolutions	−67.691	−18.232	−26.131
	Number of wars	−39.009	−31.616	−32.377
	% of GDP due to manufacturing	−47.371	−34.622	−35.561
	Number of radio transmitters	−100.000	−12.414	−37.945
III–1960	Young scale of communicability	−36.523	−9.543	11.216
	Lieuwen typology of armed forces in politics	−83.153	13.804	−9.098
	Shapiro classification of types of Latin American governments	−58.005	36.145	−63.526
	Cutright index of political development	−72.832	42.845	41.177
	Coleman index of political competitiveness	−42.185	17.141	8.725
IV–1950	Infant mortality rate	73.565	79.780	−33.499
	Gross mortality rate	43.918	87.887	−10.619
IV–1960	Infant mortality rate	52.610	93.394	−35.502
	Gross mortality rate	41.475	82.820	−34.066
V–1950	% of population economically active	100.000	−28.635	−6.252
V–1960	% of population economically active	75.478	−43.419	−23.195
VI–1960	Road density: km per 1,000 square miles	23.030	−8.016	90.000
	Rail density: km per 1,000 square miles	41.332	9.370	70.882
Random–1950	Annual average rate of urbanization pre-1950 intercensal period	70.229	60.303	−100.000
Random–1960	Industrial employment as a percentage of urban population	−16.013	−11.096	26.037
	Rate growth imports	4.678	−39.654	−55.175
	Social security coverage scale	−51.891	11.448	43.857
	Population	−47.628	−42.276	−52.258
	International mail flow	−18.839	73.751	−58.826

Sources of data for these tables are available from the author upon request.

mass communications indicators, indicators of electricity generation and energy consumption, and measures of diet quality and the availability of health services. The one surprise here is that the variable "percentage of population white," which has been suggested by Young (1970) as a measure of the lack of rigidity and hence of information-processing capacity in the political system, is in the same region as the standard measures of urbanization. Why this should be so is unclear.

The measures suggested by Young as indicators of information-processing capacity actually fall into two adjacent regions. Group II contains measures relating principally to the economic sector and Group III contains measures relating principally to the political sector. Two of the measures included in Group II were thought to be urbanization measures: percentage of GDP due to manufacturing and number of radio transmitters. The inclusion of the former within this region probably indicates that it is difficult to achieve a relatively high manufacturing output without a highly diversified industrial system. The inclusion of the variable "number of radio transmitters" suggests that this measure can best be thought of as indexing the availability, in one of the most important mass media of communication, of a number of competing sources of information.

Based upon this smallest-space analysis the variables in Group I have been used as measures of urbanization, and the variables in Groups II and III as measures of information-processing capacity in the economic sector and the political sector, respectively. With this information in hand it is possible to turn to an examination of evidence related to the hypotheses noted above regarding the relationships between educational dimensions and these dimensions of development.

Tests of the Hypotheses

The rank associations between the two educational dimensions and the two dimensions of development are reported in Table 2.[1] The first hypothesis suggests a close association between educational structural differentiation and measures of information-processing capacity in other social systems. This hypothesis is substantially supported by these data. All 11 of the measures of information-processing capacity in the economic system are very highly associated with educational structural differentiation. The mean association is .63, which is very high for Tau_c.

---

[1] In this type of study tests of statistical significance are irrelevant, and hence are not used. Significance tests are part of the mechanics of statistical inference, reasoning from the characteristics of an observable sample to the characteristics of an unobservable population. Here one is dealing with a patently nonrandom sample, the Latin American nations. Indeed, it is assumed that many of the relationships explored may well differ from one to another geographic area, and from any area to the total set. Moreover, such differences or similarities between areas and the total set are matters for empirical investigation rather than statistical estimation. The total population is not unobservable. (See Bakan, 1966, p. 428; Selvin, 1957.)

The five measures of political information-processing capacity, while less strongly associated with educational structural differentiation than are the economic measures, are nonetheless fairly highly associated with it. The mean association in this case is .44. Among these five measures, the Coleman index is most highly associated with educational structural differentiation, the Cutright index least well associated, with the other three measures falling in between. The relative strengths of these associations with differentiation in the educational system can perhaps be best accounted for as follows. As noted above, a highly differentiated educational system is very likely to be found in a society with a high capacity to use information in the economic sector—with a highly differentiated economic system. The demands for highly specialized information and personnel generated by such a system can best be communicated to the educational system in a society with a highly competitive political system. The Coleman index is based upon judgmental ratings of the overall competitiveness of the political systems involved. The general ability of a society to exchange information between varying power centers, which is tapped by Young's communicability scale (and less directly by the Lieuwen and Shapiro indices), is apparently of less direct relevance to an educational system—although these three indices have a moderately high association with educational differentiation—than is the competitiveness of the political system itself. Simply having long experience with competitively elected legislatures and executives (which is what the Cutright measure indexes) is clearly not very relevant to the ability of a society to transmit information from one sector to another. What is of importance is the extent to which various segments of the society may participate in the competition for legislative and executive offices. This distinction is particularly relevant in Latin America, as noted in a comment by Blanksten (1960, p. 481):

> Most of the major parties in the competitive systems of Latin America are what might be called "traditional" political parties. . . . The traditional parties draw their membership, in terms of the class system of Latin America, primarily from the upper class, with mestizos and Indians virtually excluded from direct participation in these parties.

The qualitative judgmental ratings used for constructing the Coleman index may much more nearly approximate the actual competitiveness of Latin American political systems. For example, Uruguay, in which one party has won every national election since 1868, is nonetheless rated as competitive on the Coleman index. Similarly, Mexico, where one party has long held a virtual monopoly of political power, is rated as semicompetitive. Conversely, Nicaragua, with an elective legislature and functioning political parties (and a consequent high score on the Cutright index), is classified as authoritarian on the Coleman index.

Table 2. Rank Associations between Information-Processing Capacity and Urbanization, and Educational Structural Differentiation and Enrollment Ratios, 1950 and 1960, for Latin America

Dimension of Development	Ed. Structural Differentiation		Enrollment Ratios					
			1950			1960		
	1950	1960	Primary	Secondary	Higher	Primary	Secondary	Higher
Information-Processing Capacity								
Economic—1950								
Scale of economic institutional development	.74	.64	.38	.36	.47	.38	.41	.53
Scale of industrial diversity	.66	.68	.21	.29	.38	.23	.35	.34
% of GDP due to manufacturing	.72	.78	.23	.33	.29	.12	.17	.31
Number of radio transmitters	.66	.73	.22	.28	.32	.26	.35	.32
Economic—1960								
Young scale of economic institutional development	.49	.61	.24	-.04	.38	.22	.26	.25
Young scale of industrial diversity	.73	.71	.27	.26	.26	.29	.37	.35
% of GDP due to manufacturing	.69	.69	.11	.13	.17	-.02	.08	.19
Number of radio transmitters	.47	.43	.06	.18	.02	.07	.20	.15
Number of patents filed with U.S. Patent Office	.69	.54	.23	-.05	.38	.22	.34	.36
Number of revolutions	.54	.65	.20	.19	.37	.22	.29	.29
Number of wars	.49	.51	.23	.28	.30	.23	.17	.33
Political								
Young scale of communicability	.45	.43	.34	.21	.30	.29	.30	.40
Lieuwen typology of armed forces in politics	.42	.41	.16	.02	.48	.22	.35	.45
Shapiro classification of types of Latin American governments	.42	.47	.06	-.30	.28	.13	.35	.31
Cutright index of political development	.34	.35	.38	.48	.34	.27	.35	.38
Coleman index of political competitiveness	.57	.58	.52	.46	.49	.54	.61	.56

Urbanization

1950

GNP per capita	.45	.34	.41	.00	.38	.33	.51	.36
% of population in communities of 20,000 or more	.59	.69	.48	.23	.51	.49	.54	.52
% of population literate	.35	.43	.73	.23	.60	.73	.61	.56
Radio receivers per 1,000 population	.53	.47	.57	.32	.52	.60	.56	.65
% of population white 1940	.27	.44	.29	.13	.43	.33	.55	.50

1960

GNP per capita	.28	.26	.40	.00	.38	.44	.43	.32
% of population in cities of 100,000 or more	.43	.42	.59	.17	.60	.63	.55	.63
% of population literate	.42	.43	.73	.20	.68	.78	.64	.63
Radio receivers per 1,000 population	.38	.41	.37	.08	.32	.46	.52	.42
Annual average rate of urbanization 1945–1955	.55	.58	.48	.02	.52	.50	.50	.41
Telephones per 1,000 population	.66	.55	.56	.22	.55	.61	.74	.58
Per capita consumption of commercial energy	.59	.55	.40	.10	.46	.42	.51	.44
% of population in communities of 2,500 or more	.61	.57	.55	.17	.57	.57	.60	.54
Electricity generation, kwh per capita	.46	.51	.47	.13	.51	.46	.63	.49
Newspaper circulation per 1,000 population	.41	.40	.46	.19	.54	.48	.62	.48
Newsprint consumption	.64	.57	.51	.30	.48	.54	.64	.57
Motor vehicles per 1,000 population	.58	.46	.39	.00	.47	.39	.58	.55
Calories consumed per day per capita	.54	.45	.47	.07	.38	.44	.47	.40
Proteins consumed per day per capita	.41	.34	.45	.07	.24	.44	.38	.38
Hospital beds per capita	.46	.32	.41	.30	.37	.46	.70	.49
% of urban population served by piped water 1958–61	.36	.35	.51	.10	.51	.47	.59	.52
Persons per physician	-.44	-.38	-.43	-.17	-.44	-.42	-.36	-.44

It is also hypothesized that enrollment ratios are highly associated with urbanization. What is striking in examining these associations is the fact that they are generally only moderately high. The mean rank association between urbanization measures and enrollment ratios is .44, far below the mean association between economic information-processing capacity and educational structural differentiation (.63) and at the same level as the association between structural differentiation and political information-processing capacity. Moreover, only 14 of the 132 associations calculated to test this hypothesis are above the mean association between economic information-processing capacity and educational structural differentiation. This generally moderate association between urbanization and enrollment ratios is surprising in light of previous studies that have, as noted above, consistently found this relationship to be very strong. The explanation arrived at in attempting to rationalize these conflicting results is as follows. Previous studies of this relationship have thrown almost all of the nations of the world, from the most developed to the least developed, into their statistical pots. Moreover, these studies have used the Pearson product-moment correlation statistic, or one of its derivatives. Unfortunately, product-moment correlation coefficients can be spuriously high if there are a few extreme values on either or both of the variables tested. Yet, for most urbanization measures, using all, or almost all, extant nations virtually assures the presence of a few extreme values at both the high and low ends of the distribution. Consequently previous studies, because of the joint effect of the samples and statistics used, have consistently overestimated the strength of this relationship. The present study, using a smaller more homogeneous sample of nations and a statistic not influenced by the presence of extreme values, presents a more accurate picture of the relationship between enrollment ratios and urbanization.

Enrollment ratios are also hypothesized to be weakly associated with information-processing capacity. The mean association of enrollment ratios with economic information-processing capacity indicators is .25; with political information-processing capacity indicators, .32. The only exception to the pattern of low associations is the Coleman index of political competitiveness, which is relatively strongly associated with both enrollment ratios and educational structural differentiation.

Finally, structural differentiation is hypothesized to be weakly associated with urbanization. The data do not support this hypothesis. Indeed, the mean association between educational structural differentiation and urbanization (.46) is slightly higher than the mean association between urbanization and enrollment ratios (.44). Of the 22 urbanization measures used, only nine are clearly more strongly associated with enrollment ratios than with structural differentiation. Seven are about as well associated with one of the educational dimensions as with the other, and six are more strongly associated with structural differentiation. It can be concluded, then, that both educational dimensions are moderately well associated with urbanization.

The following statements can summarize the findings presented thus far. Urbanization and information-processing capacity are separate dimensions of development. Information-processing capacity, in both the political and economic sectors, is highly associated with educational structural differentiation, and is very weakly associated with educational enrollment ratios. Urbanization, which captures much of the traditional view of development, is moderately well associated with both educational enrollment ratios and educational structural differentiation.

Relationships over Time

Having determined the general pattern of associations between the two educational dimensions and the dimensions of development considered here, one can turn to an examination of the pattern of these associations over time. This analysis uses only those variables for which data are available for both 1950 and 1960. This set of variables includes the scale of educational structural differentiation; primary, secondary, and higher-level enrollment ratios; two measures of economic information-processing capacity; and four measures of urbanization. Tables 3 and 4 are extracts from Table 2, presented for convenience of reference. Table 3 indicates the associations over time between urbanization and the two educational dimensions. Table 4 indicates the associations over time between information-processing capacity and the two educational dimensions. Tables 5 and 6 complete the picture, indicating, respectively, the associations over time between the two dimensions of development and the two educational dimensions.

Table 3. Rank Associations between Urbanization and Two Educational Dimensions, 1950 to 1960, for Latin America

Urbanization		Ed. Structural Differentiation		Enrollment Ratios					
				Primary		Secondary		Higher	
		1950	1960	1950	1960	1950	1960	1950	1960
GNP per capita	1950		.34		.33		.51		.36
	1960	.28		.40		.00		.38	
% of population urban*	1950		.69		.49		.54		.52
	1960	.43		.59		.17		.60	
% of population literate	1950		.43		.73		.61		.56
	1960	.42		.73		.20		.68	
Radio receivers per 1,000 population	1950		.47		.60		.56		.65
	1960	.38		.37		.08		.32	

*1960 data refer to percentage of population in cities of 100,000+ population.

The first thing that can be noted regarding these tables is that the general patterns of association hold up over time. Urbanization is about as well associated, at a moderately high level, with enrollment ratios as with educational structural differentiation. Information-processing capacity is much better associated with educational structural differentiation than with enrollment ratios, its association with differentiation being very strong.

Several observations seem useful regarding the data in Table 3. It is hardly surprising to note that of the four urbanization measures, literacy is most strongly associated with enrollment ratios. However, it is interesting to note that GNP per capita is least well associated with both educational dimensions. *This fact suggests that the many previous studies of education and development that have used GNP per capita as the only, or primary, measure of development, may have produced results that are misleading* (see, for example, Anderson, 1964, particularly pp. 3–5; Harbison and Myers, 1969, pp. 34–44; and Peaslee, 1967). It also suggests the importance of a point made earlier, that it is generally unwise to peg one's analysis to a single measure of a complex concept.

Urbanization in 1950 predicts both enrollment ratios and educational structural differentiation in 1960 better than either of the educational dimensions in 1950 predict urbanization in 1960. Urbanization is a slightly better predictor of enrollment ratios than it is of educational structural differentiation, but urbanization in 1960 is equally well predicted by both educational dimensions. In relation to this last point, it should be noted that the relatively low predictive power of enrollment ratios vis-à-vis urbanization is the result of the very low predictive power of the *secondary* level enrollment ratios. The mean rank association between this ratio in 1950 and the urbanization measures in 1960 is only .11, with a range from .00 to .20. If one considers only primary and higher-level enrollments in 1950, their mean rank association with urbanization is .51.

Turning to Table 4, it can first be noted that the variation among the four measures of information-processing capacity, in their relationships with education, is relatively small. None of these variables is as anomalous as is GNP per capita among the urbanization measures. As with urbanization, information-processing capacity in 1950 is a better predictor of both educational dimensions in 1960 than are the educational dimensions in 1950 predictors of information-processing capacity. Here too, the secondary enrollment ratio is the least powerful predictor of information-processing capacity. However, the differences are less dramatic. The mean association of secondary enrollment ratio in 1950 with information-processing capacity measures in 1960 is .15, whereas the mean associations of primary enrollment ratio and higher-level enrollment ratio in 1950 with information-processing capacity in 1960 are, respectively, .17 and .21. *It appears that increasing secondary-level enrollments rapidly enough to raise the*

Table 4. Rank Associations between Information-Processing Capacity and Two Educational Dimensions, 1950 to 1960, for Latin America

Information-Processing Capacity		Ed. Structural Differentiation		Enrollment Ratios — Primary		Secondary		Higher	
		1950	1960	1950	1960	1950	1960	1950	1960
Economic institutional development	1950		.64		.38		.41		.53
	1960	.49		.24		.04		.38	
Industrial diversity	1950		.68		.23		.35		.34
	1960	.73		.27		.26		.26	
% of GDP due to manufacturing	1950		.78		.12		.17		.31
	1960	.69		.11		.13		.17	
Number of radio transmitters	1950		.73		.26		.35		.32
	1960	.47		.06		.18		.02	

Table 5. Rank Associations between Urbanization and Information-Processing Capacity, 1950 to 1960, for Latin America

Urbanization		Information-Processing Capacity — Economic Flexibility		Industrial Diversity		% of GDP due to Manufacturing		Number of Radio Transmitters	
		1950	1960	1950	1960	1950	1960	1950	1960
GNP per capita	1950		.40		.39		.04		.18
	1960	.08		.18		.04		.27	
% of population urban	1950		.46		.63		.41		.25
	1960	.43		.34		.19		.39	
% of population literate	1950		.42		.68		.15		.11
	1960	.38		.34		.19		.28	
Radio receivers per 1,000 population	1950		.40		.47		.30		.13
	1960	.28		.20		.00		.20	

Table 6. Rank Associations between Educational Structural Differentiation and Enrollment Ratios, 1950 to 1960, for Latin America

Educational Structural Differentiation	Enrollment Ratios — Primary		Secondary		Higher	
	1950	1960	1950	1960	1950	1960
1950		.38		.50		.49
1960	.34		.36		.32	

enrollment ratio at that level is a particularly ineffective path to development.[1]

The data in Table 5 indicate that urbanization in 1950 is a considerably better predictor of information-processing capacity in 1960 than vice versa (mean rank associations are .34 versus .23), although neither relationship is consistently very high. Once again, GNP per capita is the least strong of the urbanization 1950 predictors. It is shown in Table 6 that educational structural differentiation in 1950 is a much better predictor of enrollment ratios in 1960 than vice versa (mean rank associations are .46 versus .34).

A Tentative Model

In order to pull together the major threads in the evidence thus far assembled, a simple model can be constructed depicting the interrelationships between the four dimensions. This model is presented in Figure 1.

The data used for this study, from which the model has been drawn, cannot of course be used further to test the model. However, through the use of the multiple association coefficient for Tau the adequacy of this model as a summary of the interrelationships evidenced in this body of data can be further demonstrated. For example, if the model is accurate, the simple

---

[1] Some interesting evidence presented by McClelland (1966), using a different sample of countries and a longer time period, tends to support this conclusion. McClelland's evidence suggests that while higher education expansion "seems to be part of the wave of high *n* achievement and economic growth, . . . secondary education has tended to expand rapidly *after* a wave of high *n* achievement and rapid economic growth, not before it or at the same time" (p. 273). Focusing on the individual rather than the nation, data collected in Rio de Janeiro and Buenos Aires suggest that secondary education is much less of an upward mobility guarantor, or status ratifier, for its recipients, than are primary or higher education (Adams and Farrell, 1966, chap. 2). Peaslee (1969, pp. 299, 302) has recently suggested what might be considered an explanation of the observed low predictive power of national-level secondary enrollment ratios—that secondary education expansion will have a significant impact on economic development only *after* a relatively high level of primary enrollment (close to half of the eligible age group) has been attained. To consider this possibility, the relationships between secondary enrollment ratios in 1950 and measures of information-processing capacity and urbanization in 1960 were recalculated, using only those nations that had attained by 1950 a primary enrollment ratio of .40 or greater. The mean association of secondary enrollment ratios 1950 with information-processing capacity 1960 changes from .15 to –.08 when only the high primary nations are used. The mean association with urbanization 1960 changes from .11 to .17. Peaslee's contention does not appear to hold for this set of nations. Even among Latin American nations that have already achieved high levels of primary enrollment, secondary enrollment ratios are very weak predictors of both of the dimensions of development considered here.

This finding should not be read as a blanket condemnation of *all* efforts at the secondary level. It has been possible to construct separate scales of the *differentiation* of Latin American educational systems at the secondary and higher levels for 1960 (Farrell, 1969). Secondary differentiation is more strongly associated with the four urbanization measures in 1960 used here than is higher-level differentiation, with a mean rank association of .41 versus .27. Although higher-level differentiation is more strongly associated with information-processing capacity than is secondary-level differentiation, both mean rank association coefficients are rather high (.67 versus .47). These data, all referring to the same point in time, do not speak directly to the question of prediction, but do suggest that there may be some relative merit to building a differentiated secondary system, even though raising enrollment ratios at this level may be a relatively ineffective effort to make.

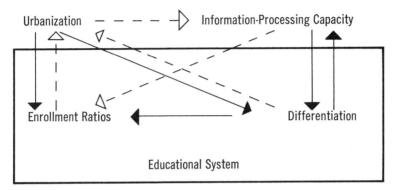

Figure 1. A model of some educational system dimensions of development relationships. Arrows indicate direction of effect over time. Solid lines indicate relatively strong associations. Broken lines indicate relatively weak associations. Absence of an arrow indicates a negligible association.

association between urbanization at one point in time and information-processing capacity at a later time ought to be much improved when the effect of differentiation at an intermediate time is added. However, one would not expect the relationship between urbanization at one point in time and information-processing capacity at a later time to be much affected by the addition of enrollment ratios at an intermediate time.

Data being available for only two dates, 1950 and 1960, it has not been possible to add in the effect of variables at an intermediate time. Rather, the additional variables for each simple association are considered at both the earlier and later dates. Thus for example, the simple association of urbanization 1950 with information-processing capacity 1960 is compared with the multiple association between the two when differentiation, at both 1950 and 1960, is multiplied in. That same simple association is then compared with the multiple association when enrollment ratios, at both 1950 and 1960, are multiplied in. The same procedure is followed all around the model. This somewhat roundabout technique is necessitated by the fact that the available multiple association statistic for Tau permits one to add in the effect of only one variable at a time (Moran, 1951). Thus one cannot determine the relative effect of a large number of variables simultaneously, as one can with more standard multiple-regression techniques using product-moment correlations.

The generalizations that summarize the results of these calculations are found in Table 7. To give some idea of the extent of improvement in the simple associations when different variables are added, the table shows the mean simple associations between each pair of dimensions and the mean improvement when measures of each of the other dimensions are added. For example, the mean difference between the simple association of urbanization 1950 with information-processing capacity 1960, and multiple

Table 7. Mean Improvement over Simple Rank Associations
between Educational Dimensions and Dimensions of Development
When Specified Multiple Associations Are Calculated, 1950 to 1960,
for Latin America

Association	Simple Association	Mean Improvement
Urbanization 1950 with information-processing capacity 1960	.34	
1. Much improved when differentiation added		.31
2. Not improved when enrollment ratios added		.03
Urbanization 1950 with differentiation 1960	.48	
1. Much improved when information-processing capacity added		.24
2. Not improved when enrollment ratios added		.04
Urbanization 1950 with enrollment ratios 1960	.54	
1. Not improved when information-processing capacity added		.02
2. Not improved when differentiation added		.04
Information-processing capacity 1950 with urbanization 1960	.23	
1. Improved when differentiation added		.18
2. Much improved when enrollment ratios added		.25
Information-processing capacity 1950 with differentiation 1960	.71	
1. Not improved when urbanization added		.04
2. Not improved when enrollment ratios added		.02
Information-processing capacity 1950 with enrollment ratios 1960	.31	
1. Much improved when urbanization added		.26
2. Improved when differentiation added		.13
Differentiation 1950 with urbanization 1960	.38	
1. Not improved when information-processing capacity added		.04
2. Improved when enrollment ratios added		.15
Differentiation 1950 with information-processing capacity 1960	.60	
1. Not improved when urbanization added		.02
2. Not improved when enrollment ratios added		.01
Differentiation 1950 with enrollment ratios 1960	.46	
1. Improved when urbanization added		.15
2. Not improved when information-processing capacity added		.02
Enrollment ratios 1950 with urbanization 1960	.38	
1. Not improved when information-processing capacity added		.06
2. Improved when differentiation added		.12
Enrollment ratios 1950 with information-processing capacity 1960	.18	
1. Improved when urbanization added		.12
2. Much improved when differentiation added		.44
Enrollment ratios 1950 with differentiation 1960	.34	
1. Improved when urbanization added		.14
2. Much improved when information-processing capacity added		.35

association of urbanization 1950 plus differentiation 1950 and 1960 with information-processing capacity 1960 is .31.

These results generally provide support for the model as a representation of the interrelationships between the four dimensions. There is only one surprise. The model would lead one to expect that differentiation would have a much greater effect than urbanization upon the simple association between information-processing capacity 1950 and enrollment ratios 1960. The reverse is the case. The fact that the results fit the model in all the other cases may indicate that variables not included in this analysis are particularly important in this one case. Most importantly, it should serve as a reminder that the model is a very crude representation of what are extremely complex relationships.

These multiple associations give added weight to the notion that educational structural differentiation is a dimension of considerable importance to the relationships between educational systems and their environments. To get some idea of the relative importance of each of the dimensions considered (the sort of information one gets easily from standard multiple-regression analyses), the mean improvements over all relationships in which each of the dimensions has been multiplied have been calculated. When all of the simple associations to which educational structural differentiation has been added are considered, the mean improvement is .2052. This is higher than the average improvement produced among all the simple associations when either of the extraeducational dimensions are added (.1220 for urbanization and .1237 for information-processing capacity) and is almost three times as high as the mean improvement when enrollment ratios are added (.0833). Moreover, the effect of differentiation on relationships between the two extraeducational dimensions is as great as its effect upon relationships that cross the boundaries of the educational system.[1]

---

[1] Data that have recently become available regarding 1967 GDP per capita in Latin America permit an exploration of one of these sets of relationships over a longer time span. The question that can be considered, if one wishes to use education as an instrument to contribute to development, is which should come first, development of the structure of the system through differentiation, or expansion of enrollment ratios? The data presented in this paper suggest that an initial concentration on differentiation may be more useful. Having measures of the two educational variables for 1950 and 1960 and one measure of urbanization for 1967 permits at least an approach to answering the question. Multiple associations with GDP per capita 1967 of (1) differentiation 1950 and enrollment ratios 1960 and (2) enrollment ratios 1950 and differentiation 1960 have been calculated. The mean multiple rank association with GDP per capita of enrollment ratios in 1950 and differentiation in 1960 is .39. When differentiation is taken at the earlier date, and enrollment ratios later, the mean multiple association is exactly twice as high (.78). It would appear that the best strategy is to concentrate first on differentiation. Alternatively, one can suggest that to raise enrollment ratios without first having a relatively differentiated system is not a particularly fruitful path to follow. Given that there is only one urbanization measure available for 1967, and that that measure is far from the most useful, these findings must be viewed with caution. They do however conform to what one would predict from the argument made in this paper.

Conclusion

The evidence just presented supports the original contention that to establish a highly differentiated educational system is to establish a quite effective set of communicative links, not only between the educational system and other systems, but between other systems themselves. If it is true that an increase in the ability of a system to process information represents an increase in the ability of the system to adapt to changes in its environment, and if such ability to adapt is one (at least) of the fundamental aspects of national development, then educational structural differentiation can indeed be said to be an exceedingly important dimension of educational systems in developing nations.

Some of the next steps to take in pursuing this line of inquiry are obvious. The data presented here refer only to Latin America. One must determine the extent to which these findings are generalizable to other geocultural areas. Additionally, there are several system structure concepts that have not yet been plugged into the analysis. One such concept is *segmentation*, the ramification or proliferation of a given type of element (e.g., an increase in the number of secondary commercial schools). Another concept of interest is system *population*. One assumes a close relationship between population and segmentation, in that the typical response to enrollment increases (actual or projected) is to build more schools of the existing types. It is important to discover how such measures of system scale are related to differentiation, and how all of these concepts are related to the *organization* or *integration* of systems. Presumably, if new elements are to contribute to the operation of a system, they must be integrated with the existing elements through some set of organizational linkages. And one also assumes that different patterns of system integration will have different consequences for the *output* of the system.

A full understanding of the interplay between educational systems and other national systems in the process of national development depends, among other things, upon the joint consideration of all these system concepts. However, even at this early stage in the work, one thing is clear. It is simply not enough—indeed for at least two important aspects of national development it may not be particularly important—to ask what proportion of the eligible population are receiving schooling, and to ask how the system may be expanded to raise that proportion. One must be concerned with the structure of the system; with the diversity of kinds of information being transmitted by the schools.

References

Adams, D., and J. P. Farrell. "Societal Differentiation and Educational Differentiation." *Comparative Education,* 5 (1969), pp. 249-262.

Adams, D., and J. P. Farrell, eds. *Education and Social Development.* Syracuse, N.Y.: Syracuse University Center for Development Education, 1966.

Anderson, C. A. "Economic Development and Post-Primary Education," *in* D. C. Piper and T. Cole, eds., *Post-Primary Education and Political and Economic Development.* Durham, N. C.: Duke University Press, 1964. Pp. 3-26.

Bakan, D. "The Test of Significance in Psychological Research," *Psychological Bulletin,* 66 (1966), pp. 423-437.

Baster, N. *Aspects of Social and Economic Growth: A Pilot Statistical Study.* Geneva: United Nations Research Institute for Social Development, 1965.

Berry, B. "Basic Patterns of Economic Development," *in* N. Ginsburg, *Atlas of Economic Development.* Chicago, Ill.: University of Chicago Press, 1961. Pp. 110-119.

Black, C. E. *The Dynamics of Modernization.* New York: Harper and Row, 1966.

Blanksten, G. I. "The Politics of Latin America," *in* G. A. Almond and J. C. Coleman, eds., *The Politics of the Developing Areas.* Princeton, N.J.: Princeton University Press, 1960. Pp. 455-531.

Buckley, W. *Sociology and Modern Systems Theory.* Englewood Cliffs, N.J.: Prentice-Hall, 1967.

Caplow, T., and K. Finsterbusch. *A Matrix of Modernization.* New York: Columbia University Bureau of Applied Social Research, 1964.

Cherry, C. *On Human Communication.* New York: Wiley, 1961.

Coleman, J. "Introduction," *in* J. Coleman, ed., *Education and Political Development.* Princeton, N.J.: Princeton University Press, 1965. Pp. 3-32.

Easton, D. *A Framework for Political Analysis.* Englewood Cliffs, N.J.: Prentice-Hall, 1965.

Eisenstadt, S. N. *Modernization: Protest and Change.* Englewood Cliffs, N.J.: Prentice-Hall, 1966.

Farrell, J. *A Cross-National Study of Education and Development Using Scalogram Analysis.* Washington: U.S. Office of Education Bureau of Research, 1968. (ERIC Accession No. ED 029353.)

Farrell, J. "The Structural Differentiation of Developing Educational Systems," *Comparative Education Review,* 13 (1969), pp. 294-311.

Guttman, L. "A General Non-metric Technique for Finding the Smallest Euclidean Space for a Configuration of Points," *Psychometrika,* 33 (1968), pp. 469-506.

Harbison, F., and C. A. Myers. *Education, Manpower and Economic Growth.* New York: McGraw-Hill, 1964.

Laumann, E. O. "The Social Structure of Religious and Ethnoreligious Groups in a Metropolitan Community," *American Sociological Review,* 34 (1969), pp. 182-197.

Laumann, E. O., and L. Guttman. "The Relative Associational Contiguity of Occupations in an Urban Setting," *American Sociological Review,* 31 (1966), pp. 169-178.

Marsh, R. *Comparative Sociology.* New York: Harcourt, Brace and World, 1967.

McClelland, D. C. "Does Education Accelerate Economic Growth?" *Economic Development and Cultural Change,* 14 (1966), pp. 257-278.

Moran, P. A. P. "Partial and Multiple Rank Correlation," *Biometrika,* 38 (1951), pp. 26-32.

Parsons, T. *Societies: Evolutionary and Comparative Perspectives.* Englewood Cliffs, N.J.: Prentice-Hall, 1966.

Peaslee, A. T. "Primary School Enrollments and Economic Growth," *Comparative Education Review,* 12 (1967), pp. 57-67.

Peaslee, A. T. "Education's Role in Development," *Economic Development and Cultural Change,* 17 (1969), pp. 293-318.

Russett, B. M., H. R. Alker, Jr., K. W. Deutsch, and H. D. Lasswell. *World Handbook of Political and Social Indicators.* New Haven, Conn.: Yale Univerity Press, 1964.

Sawyer, J. "Dimensions of Nations: Size, Wealth, and Politics," *American Journal of Sociology,* 63 (1967), pp. 145-172.

Schnore, L. "The Statistical Measurement of Urbanization and Economic Development," *Land Economics,* 37 (1961), pp. 229-245.

Selvin, H. C. "A Critique of Tests of Significance in Survey Research," *American Sociological Review,* 22 (1957), pp. 519-527.

Young, R. C. "A Structural Approach to Development," *The Journal of Developing Areas,* 2 (1968), pp. 363-375.

Young, R. C. "The Plantation Economy and Industrial Development in Latin America," *Economic Development and Cultural Change,* 18 (1970), pp. 342-361.

Educational Reform in Colombia and Venezuela: An Organizational Analysis

MARK HANSON

Foreword

Two words that are widely current in discussions of Latin American education are *reform* and *decentralization;* and the ills of overly centralized and unwieldy educational bureaucracies have been so pervasive and obvious that reform often begins with attempts at decentralization. The justification for the anguish and the activity is clear enough; in the face of rapid population growth, the schools are failing to deliver services that are adequate qualitatively or quantitatively. Substantial proportions of the school-age population are denied access to the system or provided an incomplete or ritualistic travesty of a basic education; and in some countries, despite heroic efforts at expansion, the absolute number of illiterates still continues

Reproduced from Occasional Papers in Education and Development, Number 4, 33 pp., August 1970, with the permission of the Center for Studies in Education of the Harvard University Graduate School of Education (Cambridge).

This study was conducted under the sponsorship of the Center for Studies in Education and Development (C.S.E.D.) of the Harvard Graduate School of Education. Financial support was provided, in part, by a Ford Foundation grant to Harvard University for research in education and Latin America. Also, financial support was received from the Corporación Venezolana de Guayana as part of the technical assistance and research activities of the C.S.E.D. in Ciudad Guayana, Venezuela.

Appreciation is expressed to the staff of the Centro de Servicios Educacionales who contributed to the author's understanding of educational matters in Venezuela. Also, a debt of gratitude is owed to Noel McGinn, Russell Davis, William Charleson and Steven Brumberg, who provided valuable advice and support. A special thanks to Julie Turkevich, who typed innumerable drafts.

The above-mentioned institutions and individuals are in no way responsible for the opinions expressed in this document. The author assumes full responsibility for any errors of fact or judgment that this document contains.

to grow. Still, the past two decades have brought a vast expansion of numbers accommodated in some fashion; and in the coming decade the emphasis is shifting to ways and means of making this coverage a more meaningful educational experience for the majority of children. Hence, educators, and politicians too, are seeking ways to reform and improve the schools. In the more traditional national systems the need for flexibility and adaptability to change leads inevitably to an examination of the possibility of decentralization.

This paper examines attempts at decentralization in Venezuela and Colombia; at least the word "decentralization" was used in both attempts to reform the respective systems although the writer shows that it had a very different meaning when applied in the two countries.

In Venezuela the national school system was in fact highly centralized: local school authorities had little autonomy and were "authorities" in name only; even the most routine decisions were made in the ministry at Caracas and passed down to the schools. The results, predictably, were: rigidity; lack of responsiveness, especially to pressures that were more than routine; and a considerable alienation or distance between local school men and ministry officials. The situation was almost a classic illustration of the ailment de Madariaga attributed to the Spanish government in its vain attempts to govern the New World before independence—the man on the distant scene understood but he carried out just enough of the directives to be comfortable.

The Colombian situation was quite different. Here the states had so much independence that the national government, empowered by law to establish policy and standards, was reduced to sending its money out and hoping for the best. State, municipal and private schools were the common pattern at both primary and secondary levels in Colombia, with the majority of primary schools state–run, and the majority of secondary schools under private auspices. The national government, which paid a substantial portion of teaching salaries, did not even have sufficient power to control the allocation of educational money so that it would be spent on education or to enforce standard qualifications for teachers.

Both countries and school systems were alike in that the schools were functioning poorly, wastage was high, and the quality of service was uniformly low.

In the Venezuelan decentralization the nation was divided into eight regions, and all ministries, including education, were directed to establish offices in the regions, to staff them, and to provide for regional planning, decision making and control. Paradoxically, there was centralized decentralization, directed and pushed and controlled from Caracas, as always. It is early to assess the effect of the Venezuelan decentralization attempt. The regional offices are established by law and the legislation and ordinances written, but much will depend on whether or not regional offices can be staffed by strong and competent people. At best, the decentralization has been taken only one step and it is not clear that there will be any increased authority or flexibility at the local district level. But the first move has been made, and instead of one lump of bureaucrats there will soon be eight.

Colombia with a different kind of problem adopted a different approach, but used the magic of the word "decentralization" to accomplish almost the opposite of what the word is generally taken to mean. In Colombia there were two major moves, and only the first might possibly merit the term decentralization, in that nine autonomous special purpose authorities were created to handle different levels and kinds of educational missions. The second component of the Colombian reform—the creation of regional educational funds I.E.F. (Fondos Educacionales Regionales)—actually lessened the authority of states in the control of schools. When the Colombian states signed the FER agreements they accepted the assignment of a *delegado* from the national government who had the power to approve and disapprove the allocation of funds for education. The nation now has a form of control that can be used to block misallocation of funds and enforce standards in teacher qualifications.

The paper also examines the possibilities of future reversals of the present policies and plans. One powerful influence that may block further progress is pressure for politically partisan patronage. In Venezuela the party in power makes good partisan use of teachers who have a strong position at the local level, and the power of selection of these teachers may not be lightly surrendered in the future. In Colombia teaching has been a popular form of local patronage for the state governors, and this may bring attempts to circumvent the assignment of teachers through merit and training.

The comparison of the Colombian and Venezuelan experience is particularly useful to illustrate that the same word can be used to describe phenomena that are almost completely different. Both countries did what they had to do, given the situation that confronted them before the respective reforms. Venezuelan schools were too dependent on the national ministry, whereas in Colombia the opposite was the case for state schools. Comparative analysis has the virtue of making both activities clearer in terms of each other. In both cases, it is fair to say that although procedures differed according to the differing situation, the aim was to improve education and to deliver a better service to more children. So reform goes on in the Latin American schools, and it is worthwhile to have it confirmed that there is no "typical Latin American" country or school. Each country is different; each school system is different; and each works out its educational destiny in its own way.

Russell G. Davis

Introduction

This paper offers a general perspective on policy making and policy execution within the context of pre- and posteducational reform in Venezuela and Colombia. The first stage of the paper identifies prereform decisional problems related to organizational structure and administrative processes. The second stage examines the modifications of these decisional problems implicit in the reform movements. The final stage is a comparison of the Colombian and Venezuelan reform movements with respect to the prereform decisional problems and the postreform systems modifications.[1]

Questions of organizational structure, policy, and administration are important at this time in Latin America because a number of countries have concluded that their traditional educational systems are not capable of meeting rapidly changing and increasing demands being placed upon them. Latin American educational systems can neither deliver adequate services to their populations nor insure that such services, when delivered, are appropriate in amount and kind to the requirements of the people. In short, nations forging the infrastructure of development are served poorly by educational systems designed historically to produce a social elite and serve agriculturally based economies.

In an attempt to provide greater support to the process of socioeconomic development, the Venezuelan and Colombian governments have incorporated a variety of goals into their educational reform movements, such as increased social and economic mobility of students, curricula more relevant to industrializing nations, reduced student dropout, upgraded teacher competence, and regionally differentiated education. A multifront assault is, therefore, being waged on educational problems in each country.

Rather than focus on any of the stated goals of the reforms, this paper examines the organizational and administrative changes necessary to make the desired outcomes possible. Because the reforms are in an embryonic stage of development, the reforms as "plans and strategies" will be analyzed as they reflect changes from the prereform systems. The specific variables of analysis will be *organizational structure and decision–making authority*. Policy making and policy execution are understood to be forms of decision making. Because Venezuela and Colombia are faced with very distinct organizational and administrative problems, a comparison of the two will be made to provide insight into the relationships between organizational structure and decision making in large–scale systems.

The analysis is based on data obtained through observation, documentary analysis, and interviews conducted over a period of several months with

---

[1] Unfortunately, at this writing the reforms in both countries are so recent that, as yet, it is not possible to obtain postreform measures of change.

educational officials at every level of the organizational hierarchies in both countries.

Conceptual Framework

The organizations analyzed in this paper are the educational systems of Colombia and Venezuela. Stinchcombe defines an organization as "a stable set of social relations deliberately created with the explicit intention of continually accomplishing some specific purpose."[1] An organization, then, is no more than a social mechanism designed to bring human and material resources to bear on an ongoing problem. Because the social mechanism consists of goal-oriented, interacting human beings, it is conceived of as a *social system*.[2]

Within the framework of a social system, human behavior must be so ordered that the actions of each member systematically contribute to a sequence of activity designed to accomplish a goal. The basic organizational unit which systematizes the ordering of human behavior is the *role*.

The role is elaborated here in terms of, among other things, task-responsibility and decision-making authority. A *hierarchy* is established in the system when roles receive varying degrees of task-responsibility and decision-making authority. The relationship between roles is referred to as *organizational structure*. An organizational structure, therefore, is a hierarchical network of roles ordered in such a way as to systematize human behavior toward achieving a goal.

Systematized human behavior, in its dynamic form, is conceptualized as a *process*. A chief function of organizational structure is the ordering of a series of processes essential for goal achievement. Most organizational theorists agree that the decision-making process is the center around which almost all other organizational variables are organized.[3]

There are, of course, various types of decisions, and each type is usually made at a specified level in the hierarchy. Policy and procedural decisions, for example, are usually made at the top of the hierarchy. These decisions establish objectives and select the procedures for achieving the objectives. Executive decisions are usually made at middle levels and routine administrative decisions at lower levels of the hierarchy.[4]

Social systems theory emphasizes that organizations are made up of systems which are subdivided into subsystems. The dependence of the

---

[1] Arthur L. Stinchcombe, "Social Structure and Organizations," *in* James G. March, ed., *Handbook of Organizations* (Chicago: Rand McNally and Company, 1965), p. 142.

[2] Talcott Parsons and Edward A. Shils, *Toward a General Theory of Action* (New York: Harper and Row, 1965).

[3] Herbert Simon, *Administrative Behavior* (New York: Macmillan, 1957).

[4] Max Weber, *The Theory of Social and Economic Organizations* (London: Collier-Macmillan Limited, The Free Press of Glencoe, 1964), p. 337.

relationship between subsystems and systems varies, of course, with each case. Students, for example, are more dependent on teachers than on janitors for learning experiences. Thus, there are degrees of independence between social systems. Gouldner states, "Systems in which parts have a 'high' functional autonomy may be regarded as having a 'low' degree of system interdependence; conversely, systems in which parts have 'low' functional autonomy have a 'high' degree of system interdependence."[1]

Prereform Organization of Education in Venezuela

The national Constitution contains provisions which fix the pattern of educational organization in Venezuela. In terms of structure, the nation must permit the existence of three educational systems: (a) national, (b) state, and (c) municipal. Private schools are permitted. A breakdown of the 1,877,212 students registered in primary and secondary schools in the 1968–1969 academic year is given in Table 1.[2]

Table 1. Venezuelan Student Enrollment

	Primary (%)	Secondary (%)
National schools	53.83	69.35
State schools	24.60	1.56
Municipal schools	7.20	2.14
Private schools	13.97	26.23
Autonomous schools	.38	–
Military schools	–	.69
	99.98	99.97

Because of the uneven distribution of students in the systems, education in Venezuela tends to be national education. A reform that is to have a far-reaching impact, therefore, must come through the national school system. The Ministry of Education is directly responsible for the national school system.

Prior to the reform, the ministry established the academic program to which all educational systems were required to adhere, although each system made its own administrative decisions, i.e., hiring, promotion, budget construction, etc. These administrative decisions, however, were made within a policy framework established by the ministry. (From this point forward, only the national school system will be discussed.)

ORGANIZATIONAL HIERARCHY AND AUTHORITY STRUCTURE

In terms of organizational structure, the Ministry of Education is the parent system (ultimate responsibility and authority) which has distributed

[1] Alvin W. Gouldner, "Organizational Analysis," in Robert Merton, Leonard Broom, and Leonard Cottrell, Jr., eds., Sociology Today (New York: Basic Books, Inc., 1959), p. 419.
[2] Ministerio de Educación, Más y mejor educación, División Técnica (1969), pp. 15, 38.

dependent subsystems throughout the country as a means of carrying out educational policy. As illustrated by Figure 1, the primary school system was divided into 21 regional zones, each of which maintained a regional supervisor as the chief educational officer. The regional zones were subdivided into districts, each of which maintained a district supervisor. There were over 100 districts in Venezuela. The educational officers immediately under the district supervisor were the local school directors.[1]

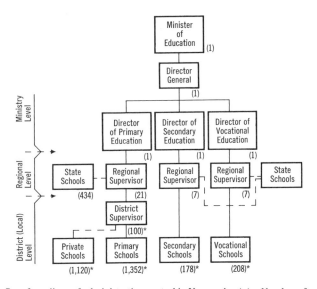

Figure 1. Prereform lines of administrative control in Venezuela. ( ) = Number of units; ——— = line of control; - - - - - = line of coordination; and * = approximate.

The secondary school branches (academic and vocational) maintained seven regional zones which were not subdivided into districts. Each local school director was responsible to a regional supervisor. A direct, unbroken chain of command, therefore, existed from the minister of education to the local school director.[2] An important question at this point becomes: where in the chain of command were the various types of pedagogical and administrative decisions made, and what were the consequences for the local school unit?

DECISIONAL POINTS

The Constitution assigns the president of Venezuela the task of creating and maintaining the system of national education.[3] Through the *Ley de*

[1]*Ibid.*

[2]At this writing, the educational reform had been implemented partially. In order to avoid confusion, the past tense is used to describe the prereform system.

[3]Venezuela, *Constitución.* Art. 136.

Educación (Educational Law), the president delegated the following responsibility and authority to the Ministry of Education: "The Ministry of Education will centralize the pedagogical activities of all official school plants in the country and provide the necessary coordination relative to the location, construction, equipment, teacher selection, and all that relates to the current organization of educational services. . . ."

This mandate includes, among other things: (a) planning and research functions for all national education, (b) determining the exact nature of the curriculum (content and teaching technique), (c) selecting textbooks, (d) defining the examination and evaluation process, (e) training teachers, (f) establishing in-service training programs, (g) constructing the educational budget, (h) managing the budget (control over all financial transactions), and (i) storing records.[1] These were some of the major decisional areas with which the ministry had to deal. How then was this decisional load distributed throughout the hierarchy?

After studying the *Educational Law,* reading the documents that flowed up and down the organizational hierarchy, and interviewing supervisors from the bottom to the top of the hierarchy, the writer found it was impossible to identify any decisions made below the ministry level which had any significant impact on the content or direction of administrative or pedagogical processes. The Center for Administrative and Social Research of the Venezuelan School of Public Administration reached a similar conclusion. The center reports:

> With respect to the teaching process, the organizational hierarchy leaves no room for anyone (at lower levels) to select alternatives of action designed to reach a specific goal, nor can they establish any goals. The directives come from the Ministry of Education to the Regional Supervisor and from him to the District and Rural Supervisors who in turn transmit them to the School Directors and teachers. The lines of authority are completely defined; all the plans, programs, evaluation methods, etc., are elaborated at the top of the organization and transmitted from one level to another until all members of the school community adopt the same conduct.
>
> With respect to administrative aspects, there are these few decisions made by the Supervisors: the transfer of teachers within the same school region, and the selection of teachers to attend in-service training programs. . . .[2]

The task of the supervisors, in other words, is "to provide and transmit according to the rules established by the Ministry of Education."[3] Before

---

[1] Venezuela, *Ley de Educación,* Arts. 7, 79, 90 y 93 *Reglamento General de la Ley de Educación* (20 de octubre de 1956), Arts. 1, 2, 61 y 66.

[2] Centro de Investigaciones Administrativas y Sociales, *Descentralización y desconcentración administrativa en el sector de la educación primaria,* Escuela de Administración Pública (Caracas, diciembre, 1967), pp. 56–57.

[3] *La Gaceta Oficial,* No. 899.

the reform, therefore, the ministry made the policy, procedural, executive and, in many cases, routine administrative decisions for the entire national school system.

CONSEQUENCES RELATED TO DECISIONAL POINTS

Concentrating decision-making authority at the top of the hierarchy had a variety of consequences for the local school unit, but the three most notable were decisional time lag, system rigidity, and psychological distance. Decisional time lag is the amount of time usually required for the Ministry of Education to respond to a decisional request initiated by a local school. Various types of decisional requests submitted by local school directors were monitored. Examples of such requests were calls for additional teachers for unexpectedly high enrollments, replacements for worn out or damaged equipment, and repairs for damaged school buildings. The school directors usually waited from six to 12 months for decisions to be made on their requests.

The six- to 12-month time lag, it should be noted, included only those requests which came up unexpectedly during the academic year. All requests initiated before the academic year began were programmed in advance and competently handled. The system had no rapid response capability for unanticipated developments because the locally based supervisors had no authority to intervene even in the more routine situations.

A second consequence of concentrating decision-making authority at the top of the hierarchy was system rigidity. Because a few men at the top were required to decide upon such diverse matters as academic program content, school construction, personnel, teaching technique, equipment, and budget management, there was a tendency to develop one standardized way of accomplishing each task. The standardized approach simplified the administrative problem at the top but was not adjusted to the socioeconomic variance between regions nor to individual student variance (i.e., attitude, aptitude, occupational expectations, etc.).

The rigidity derived from standardized practices also slowed the adoption of new developments in technique and content. The same primary school curriculum, for example, was used from 1944 to 1969. For 25 years, every student in Venezuela was subjected to the same unchanging body of knowledge which was developed before 1945![1]

A third consequence is referred to as psychological distance and is demonstrated in a study conducted by Gross et al. In a questionnaire issued to teachers and school directors of a large industrial city in Venezuela, Gross found the following:

---

[1] Ministerio de Educación, *Programas de educación primaria* (7 de diciembre, 1944).

(1) that approximately 75 percent of both the teachers and directors believe that "lack of any real understanding of a teacher's problems by the Ministry of Education" constitutes a serious or very serious obstacle that blocks a more effective performance of teachers; (2) that 63 percent of the teachers and 78 percent of the directors view the Ministry's lack of concern about the problems of their school as a serious or very serious obstacle; (3) that 48 percent of the teachers and 50 percent of the directors feel the Ministry constitutes an obstacle to improvement in the teachers' performance because it makes too many important educational decisions; and (4) that 45 percent of the teachers and 61 percent of the directors view the bureaucratic inefficiency of the Ministry as a serious handicap to the teachers' conduct. These findings show that the majority of the directors and approximately one-half of the teachers do not hold a positive image of the Ministry of Education and that they have strong reservations about its understanding or concern with the educational problems of their schools.[1]

In short, the elaborate mechanism designed to control decisions from the capital city often tended to overlook the fact that real human beings with individual needs and anxieties were trying to induce decisions which related to specific situations. Where the ministry saw the problems in terms of national statistics, the national school directors saw the problems in terms of angry parents, frustrated teachers, and a distorted learning process for students. Because of the extensive psychological distance between the teachers and the decision makers, the local school officials frequently exercised their option to do nothing which would require a great amount of time or create personal anxiety. The consequences of this practice were often dysfunctional for the educational process as a whole.

CONCLUSIONS

The Venezuelan national educational system was made up of subsystems (regions and districts) which reported to a parent system (Ministry of Education). Decision making was concentrated at the ministry level for all but the most routine decisions. Because the subsystems were so dependent on the ministry, their relationships can be characterized as having exhibited low functional autonomy and high system interdependence.

Consequently, at least three major dysfunctions can be attributed to this intersystem relationship: (a) a decisional time lag on unanticipated requests, (b) an organizational rigidity that could not be adjusted to regional as well as individual differences, and (c) a psychological distance between ministry officials and local school officials which had negative implications for motivation and morale.

---

[1] Neal Gross, Noel McGinn, David Napior and Walter Jewell III, "Planning for Educational Change: An Application of Sociological and Psychological Perspectives" (unpublished manuscript, Center for Studies in Education and Development. Harvard University, Cambridge, Mass., August 5, 1968), chap. 5, p. 6.

Prereform Organization of Education in Colombia

As in Venezuela, the Colombian Constitution established a federal system of government, and the educational organization parallels this form with national, state, and municipal school systems. Unlike Venezuela, the large majority of schools in Colombia are state and private schools. There are few national schools, and this characteristic makes the organizational and administrative problems very different from those of Venezuela.

ORGANIZATIONAL HIERARCHY AND AUTHORITY STRUCTURE

As in Venezuela, the president of Colombia is popularly elected and he, in turn, appoints the minister of education. As indicated in Figure 2, the minister of education sets educational policy for *all* the school systems in the country; however, *the ministry executes policy only for the few national schools it controls directly.* State governments and individual, private school directors are responsible for implementing most of the educational decisions made in the country.

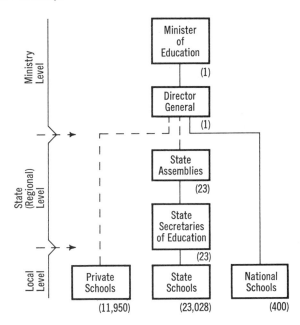

Figure 2. Prereform lines of administrative control in Colombia. ( ) = Number of units; ——— = line of control; and - - - - = line of coordination.

As a governing body, each state has a popularly elected assembly; the governor, however, is appointed by the president of the country. The governor of each state appoints a secretary of education who is the state's

Table 2. Colombian Student Enrollment

		Primary (%)	Secondary (%)
National schools	less than	1.0	6.5*
State and municiapl schools		80.1	40.0
Private schools		19.9	53.5

Source: Octavio Arizmendi Posada, *La transformación educativa nacional* (Bogotá, Colombia, 1969).
*Estimate.

chief educational officer. The secretary of education is responsible to the governor and the state assembly, and *not* to the Ministry of Education. This structural feature was at the crux of the prereform decisional problems in Colombia.

DECISIONAL POINTS AND RELATED CONSEQUENCES

Because of a national and state separation of powers, the prereform educational system in Colombia maintained a relatively decentralized, formal authority structure. The Ministry of Education dictated policy, and the individual state and private schools executed policy. Action-oriented decisions (as distinguished from policy decisions) were made at the state level, and the ministry had limited legal authority (and little available manpower) to intervene.

Every year, each state government appropriated money for state public expenditures—including education. Decisions concerning budget construction and management of public expenditures were, therefore, made at the state level.

However, over the years the national government played an increasing role in the financing of state education by augmenting state public expenditure budgets.[1] The national government earmarked money for public construction, housing, sanitation, education, and transportation. *The nation, however, lost control of the money once it entered into the accounts of a state.* Most of the national money was allocated for teachers' salaries.

According to informants highly placed in the Ministry of Education, state government officials regularly followed the practice of shifting funds from one budget item to another. Consequently, money earmarked for education was often used for building highways or purchasing health equipment rather than paying teachers' salaries.

Accordingly, the state educational systems have traditionally had difficulty meeting monthly payrolls. Often, teachers were not paid for as many as five or six months. Teacher strikes in primary and secondary schools

[1] Ley 97, Art. 9 de 1945.

were commonplace. At the end of each school year, only two or three of the 23 states were able to meet their salary obligations completely and close their financial books. *In short, the state governments regularly abused their decision-making authority by not adhering to official administrative policy as established by the Ministry of Education.*

Personnel decisions were also largely in the hands of the state secretaries of education and the private school directors. Even though the Ministry of Education had established a policy governing personnel matters, the states and private schools decided on all significant matters, for example: hiring, firing, promotions, transfer, and salary schedules. Consequently, individual state governments frequently made decisions which were not consistent with the official personnel policy established by the ministry.

The Ministry of Education, for example, officially established minimum requirements for hiring primary and secondary school teachers. Primary school teachers must be normal or secondary school graduates. When hired, they must be placed in a level of a four-level pay scale commensurate with their education and experience. The states, however, maintained an extra-legal fifth pay level for new teachers who did not meet the ministry's minimum hiring requirements.[1] In 1966, approximately 40 per cent of the primary school teachers employed in the schools did not meet the ministry's minimum hiring standards.[2] The hiring of unqualified teachers cannot be attributed to the fact that trained teachers were not available. In 1965, for example, 5,000 students graduated from normal schools. Of this number, only 1,600 entered the teaching profession.[3] In addition, teachers often were hired when no money was budgeted for their salaries.

In interviews, the writer received four explanations as to why states frequently hired teachers who did not meet the ministry's minimum standards. The first response offered economic reasons: the state budgets did not provide enough money to hire the quantity of teachers required at the higher salary levels approved by the ministry, and the states were therefore forced to hire unqualified teachers at an unofficial salary scale far below the approved scale. The second response gave political reasons: the state educational system was used as part of the local political patronage mechanism, and teaching posts were frequently given to the party faithful. The third response concerned personal comfort: qualified teachers did not want to teach in rural areas. The fourth response was a variation of the first two: unqualified individuals could be hired to teach at a below-scale rate (category 5), and the states did not allocate enough money in their educational

[1] Ley 111 de 1960.

[2] Jorge Octavio Díaz Velásquez, "Programa de capacitación del magisterio," Ministerio de Educación Nacional, Colombia, 1969, p. 14.

[3] Daniel Arango, *Informe del Ministerio de Educación al Congreso Nacional,* Ministerio de Educación Nacional, Bogotá, julio de 1966, p. 39.

budgets to hire teachers who met the minimum qualifications established by the ministry. The Ministry of Education concluded that the fourth response was closest to the truth.

CONCLUSIONS

By national law, educational policy was to be established by the Ministry of Education, and the state and private schools were to execute decisions in accordance with that policy. Because the individual state secretaries of education were not legally responsible to the Ministry of Education, the states were able to exercise their wills over their own school systems. The ministry had little authority to intervene even in cases where the states abused decision-making authority by acting outside ministry policy.

The state and private school subsystem, therefore, can be characterized as exhibiting high functional autonomy and low system interdependence. In Venezuela, it will be remembered, the relationship was exactly the opposite.

Venezuelan Reform Movement

The crux of the decision problems in Venezuela centered around the concentration of authority at the highest levels of the organizational hierarchy. Ministry officials tended to make policy, procedural, and executive, as well as many routine, administrative decisions for every subsystem in the national educational organization. Low-level supervisors did little more than serve as a communication link between the schools and the ministry. As a result, the system was characterized by rigidity, a significant decisional time lag, and a dysfunctional psychological distance between schoolteachers and directors, and the decision makers.

NATIONAL ADMINISTRATIVE REFORM

The national government in Venezuela is divided into ministries such as health, public works, transportation, treasury, and education. Each of these ministries has historically concentrated decision-making authority at the top of its own organizational hierarchy. Interdependence existed among these ministries because a major decision taken by any one of them usually required the collaboration of other ministries. For example, a decision to construct new highways made by the Ministry of Public Works necessarily required the approval and cooperation of the Ministry of the Treasury. Because of the mutual interdependence among ministries, there was little opportunity for any one ministry to delegate a significant amount of decision-making authority to regional levels. If any one ministry did delegate authority to a regional level, that regional office would encounter overwhelming problems in trying to solicit the cooperation of other ministries which maintained authority at the national level. Therefore, the president of Venezuela issued a decree designed to initiate a process of decentralization that encompassed the entire governmental administrative structure. The objective of the decree was to provide necessary administrative support to programs of regional development.[1]

The nation was divided into eight regions, each of which exhibited common socioeconomic characteristics. Under the reform, all of the ministries have been directed to establish offices in the eight regions, and regional activities are to be coordinated by a Regional Planning and Coordinating Office. The Regional Planning and Coordinating Office is responsible to the National Planning and Coordinating Office, which reports to the president. In short, a coordinated infrastructure has been created at the regional level which has been delegated the authority to plan and execute specific programs of development. Thus, any one regional office can draw support from the regional offices of other ministries of the government without having to depend on decisions from the capital city. A regional budgeting system has been created which enables the planning, coordination, and execution of programs from the regional level.

National Educational Reform

Consistent with the president's plan for general administrative decentralization (delegation of decision-making authority), the minister of education issued a decree progressively establishing offices in the eight administrative regions.[2] Among other things, the decree states that the regional offices will: (a) work in conjunction with the Regional Office of Planning and Coordination, (b) act as a mechanism of decision making (execution), advising, and coordinating in all aspects of pedagogy and administration surrounding programs of educational supervision, (c) coordinate plans of action with high levels of the Ministry of Education, and (d) exercise functions of control and evaluation of student, teacher, and administrator performance within the region. In short, the above-mentioned points have redefined the structure, roles (authority and responsibility), and processes of the educational subsystems.

STRUCTURAL CHANGES IN THE HIERARCHY

As indicated in Figure 1, the prereform system maintained three separate branches (primary, secondary academic, and secondary vocational) at the national, regional, and, in the case of primary education, district levels. Little contact and almost no coordinated decision making existed between the branches at the subministry level.

---

[1] Decreto No. 72, 11 de junio de 1969.
[2] Ministerio de Educación, Dirección Técnica, Número 10, 279, Caracas, Venezuela, 1 de septiembre de 1969.

Under the reform, each of the eight regions has been subdivided into zones and districts (Figure 3).[1] One supervisor is located at each level, and he has been given authority over all three educational branches. This structural change should have the effect of coordinating decision-making behavior within and between levels of the organizational hierarchy.

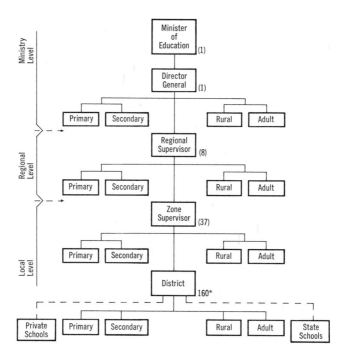

Figure 3. Postreform lines of administrative control in Venezuela. ( ) = Number of units; ——— = line of control; - - - - line of coordination; and * = approximate.

DECENTRALIZATION OF AUTHORITY

Through the delegation of authority, the decisional points have changed within the organizational structure. In the area of administration, the eight regional supervisors have the decision-making authority to construct and administer their budget (to be approved and coordinated by the ministry), hire and fire teachers, sanction personnel (faculty and students), maintain faculty and student records, and purchase equipment.

---

[1] EDUPLAN, *Plan General de Reorganización del Actual Sistema de Supervisión,* Comisión de Supervisión, Documento no. 15, Caracas, julio de 1968.

In academic areas, the regional supervisors have the authority to regionalize the curriculum, execute audiovisual aid and guidance programs, and evaluate student progress. Also, they have general supervisory control over the execution of academic programs in primary, rural, adult, and middle school education.[1]

Apparently, the zone and district levels have not been delegated any significant decision-making authority. Zone and district supervisors will continue to function as communication links between the schools and the regional offices.

CONCLUSIONS

By way of the reform movement, the Ministry of Education is divesting itself of the authority to make program execution and routine administrative decisions while retaining the authority to make policy and procedural decisions. A situation has been created which will permit increased functional autonomy and decreased interdependence between the parent system and its subsystems. If the reform movement is effective over time, it will, among other things, reduce the decisional time lag, increase the flexibility of the academic and administrative processes, and reduce the psychological distance between teachers, school directors, and supervising decision makers.

Colombian Reform Movement

The crux of the decisional problem in the Colombian educational organization was the peculiar structural-functional relationship between the Ministry of Education and the individual state governments. The ministry was charged with setting education policy for all educational systems; however, the state government and the private schools were expected to execute that policy. State governments often exercised wide latitude in their educational decisions, and significant differences developed between ministry policy and state practice. The ministry, in the meantime, was relatively powerless to do anything about abuses of authority at the state level.

NATIONAL REFORM IN EDUCATION

In December of 1968, the president of Colombia signed a decree which initiated an educational reform movement designed to solve many of the nation's major educational problems.[2] Programs were passed into legislation involving, for example, school construction, curriculum development, athletics, social and natural sciences, cultural development, language

---

[1] EDUPLAN, "Anteproyecto de Reglamento del Sistema Integrado de Supervisión Educativa," Comisión de Supervisión, Documento no. 18, Caracas, abril de 1969.

[2] Carlos Lleras Restrepo, Decreto no. 3157, 26 de diciembre de 1968.

development, university-level research, and the creation of 19 comprehensive high schools.

In order to implement these new programs, the Colombian government created nine semiautonomous educational institutes charged with achieving distinct program goals.[1] All of these institutes have been delegated well-defined policy-making and policy-execution authority to carry out their missions. These institutes, however, will not be analyzed in this paper because they are being undertaken *outside* the traditional framework of the Ministry of Education. In other words, new structures have been created for the new missions, and the leaders are not responsible directly to the minister of education.

One major program was created within the traditional framework of the Ministry of Education, and this program attempts to improve the decisional problems identified in the prereform organization. It is called the *Fondos Educacionales Regional* (FER) or Regional Educational Funds.

FER PROGRAM

The problem facing the minister of education was to create a plan which would lead the states to execute decisions along the policy lines defined by the ministry. This task had to be done in such a way as to neither violate constitutional states rights nor create a political fight. In short, states would have to agree to give up, or at least restrain, their authority voluntarily. The Regional Educational Funds (FER) program was created to resolve this problem.

A reorganization of the ministry again brought forth a clear definition of its formal decisional role: "The Ministry will have the role of formulating educational policy, coordinating its execution at the national level, supervising the operation of other organizations in the educational sector (state, municipal and private), and serving as financing coordinator."[2] The preceding quotation represents simply a restating of the historic mission of the ministry. In the writer's opinion, the FER program is a mechanism which puts enforcement "teeth" into this historic role.

CONTEXT OF THE FER PROGRAM

The key to the FER program is the national money which year after year has been sent to the individual states to help finance state education. The ministry's annual report says, "At the end of 1968 the Ministry sent a package of ordinances to the state governors which was to be submitted to the state assemblies for their consideration. The ordinances would authorize

---

[1] A description of objectives, responsibilities, and authority of the new institutes can be found in Octavio Arizmendi Posada, *La transformación educativa nacional.*

[2] Ministerio de Educación, "La reforma de la organización educativa," Serie: Transformación Educativa, no. 3, 1969, p. 7.

the state governors to sign a contract with the national government establishing the characteristics of the national (financial) assistance and authorizing the secretaries of education to initiate the reform."[1]

In order to make the FER contract as attractive as possible to the states, it was presented in a seductive form, for example: (a) the states would not be required to subscribe to the program, (b) it was billed as a decentralization project, giving the states greater control over their systems, (c) the nation would invest more money in state education, (d) advisors would be provided by the nation to assist state secretaries of education in their duties, (e) audiovisual equipment would be donated to the state educational systems, and (f) the national schools in each state would be placed under the administrative control of the corresponding state government. Underlying the offer, however, was the implication that if any state did not sign the contract, it would not receive any more national money to support state education. All 23 states (and the federal district) eventually signed contracts.

FER CONTRACTS

In signing the contracts with the ministry, the states agreed to adhere to many constraining clauses. Because the content of these clauses greatly limited the decision-making latitude previously enjoyed by the states, the states had, in fact, voluntarily surrendered much of their authority.

Among other things, the contracts require each state to:

(a) increase annually state appropriations for education consistent with the growth of the total state budget,

(b) hire only teachers who meet the qualification standards established by the ministry,

(c) replace all unqualified teachers (primary and secondary) within a period of two years (eliminate the illegal category 5),

(d) create positions for supervisors at the ratio of one for every 200 teachers,

(e) reorganize the state offices of education to agree with recommendations of the ministry,

(f) manage the wage-scale and personnel promotions consistent with ministry policy and national law,

(g) permit the ministry to supervise the state budgetary expenditures in education,

(h) demonstrate the availability of funds before hiring additional teachers, and

(i) accept the presence of a ministry official *(delegado)* authorized to supervise all matters mentioned in the contract and to investigate irregularities found in other parts of the state education system.

---

[1] Octavio Arizmendi Posada, *La transformación educativa nacional*, p. 19.

Each state (and the federal district) has its own FER fund. The national and state contributions to the fund must be placed in a bank account which is managed apart from the regular state budget. Expenditures for nonbudgeted items cannot be drawn from the account without the approval of the ministry's *delegado*. According to the contracts, if for any reason the state cannot meet its obligatory monthly contribution to the FER account or mismanages funds in that account, the national contribution to the fund must be returned immediately.[1]

CONCLUSION

Early it was pointed out that the Colombian government recently adopted a new set of national educational goals. In order to achieve these objectives, the Ministry of Education had to find a means of controlling and streaming state administrative processes. The FER program became the mechanism through which the ministry is striving for maximum state contributions to the national education goals.

By agreeing to the conditions of the FER contract, states have voluntarily accepted constraints on their decision-making authority. The Ministry of Education now has a tool to force the states to comply with official policy. At the end of the first year of the FER program, 20 of the 23 states had met their financial obligations on time. This was very different from previous years when only three or four of the 23 states annually had done so.

In short, under the FER program there exists a higher degree of interdependence and a lower degree of functional autonomy between the parent system and the subsystems.

A Comparison of the Venezuelan and Colombian Reforms

The educational organizations of both nations are similar in the sense that their respective constitutions provide for the existence of national, state, and municipal systems. The difference lies, however, in the percentage of students enrolled in the subsystems. As a consequence of unbalanced enrollment patterns, education in Venezuela tends to be national, whereas in Colombia it tends to be state and private school education. The decision-making processes in the two nations, therefore, are quite dissimilar.

In both countries, the ministries of education are charged with making policy decisions which govern the pedagogical and administrative components of the educational processes. In Venezuela, the ministry not only created the policy but executed it as well. In Colombia, however, the ministry created the policy, but individual states (and private schools) executed it. A major distinction between the two systems, then, was the hierarchical level at which major action decisions were made.

---

[1] Contrato No. 1, celebrado entre el Gobierno Nacional y el Departamento de. . . .

In Venezuela, the ministry tended to make policy, procedural, executive and, in many cases, routine administrative decisions. This concentration of decision-making authority had the dysfunctional effects of creating, among other things, a decisional time lag, a rigidity toward change, and a psychological distance between the ministry and the local schools. In an attempt to reduce these and other decisional problems the ministry has delegated decision-making authority to regional levels. An effort is being made to reduce the controls on the decision-making behavior of regional officials.

Colombia, on the other hand, is attempting to place narrower limits on the decision-making behavior of regional (state) officials. An effort is being made to force state officials to make decisions which are consistent with official ministry policy. The rationale is that a strict adherence to official pedagogical and administrative policy is the most effective means of systematizing behavior (teacher and administrator) according to patterns which are thought to be necessary if the nation is to achieve its educational goals.

Both nations are trying to arrive at organizational and administrative formulas which best support their educational goals. The hypotheses implicit in the two reforms are quite dissimilar. Starting from a prereform base, Venezuela is hypothesizing that a higher functional autonomy and a lower system interdependence between the parent system and subsystems will result in reduced uniformity and greater adaptability to local needs. Colombia, on the other hand, hypothesizes that lower functional autonomy and higher interdependence between the parent system and the subsystems will lead to greater uniformity in behavioral processes resulting in a more systematized approach to achieving established educational goals.

After the educational reforms of the two nations have been fully institutionalized, certain structural and functional similarities will be evident. The ministries of education will make pedagogical and administrative policies; however, these policies will be executed at lower hierarchical levels. In addition, the ministries will supervise the execution of policies and, if deemed necessary, veto lower-level decisions.

Constraints to Educational Reform

Change does not come easily. Behavioral patterns maintained and reinforced by traditional decision-making processes always present formidable barriers to reform. The Venezuelan and Colombian attempts will not be exceptions to the rule. To this point in the paper an attempt has been made to demonstrate how the reforms are *supposed* to resolve decision-making problems inherent in the prereform systems. The analysis will be more complete, however, if some thought is given to the constraints which might impede the smooth and efficient operation of the educational reforms.

The constraints to be discussed here represent, by and large, the writer's perceptions of certain traditional behavioral patterns in Colombia and

Venezuela. It should be recognized that the writer's personal value system colors these perceptions. The following potential constraints to the reforms will be dealt with: (a) political power, (b) career management, and (c) fiscal management.

POLITICAL POWER

In Venezuela (at the national level) and in Colombia (at the state level) educational organizations were often treated as extensions of political institutions. Specific *educational* decisions were often made for good *political* reasons.

In Colombia, for example, decisions were often made at the state level to use educational funds for public projects which had greater visibility (plus political returns) than educational projects. Also, ministry officials were suspicious (and at the same time powerless to act) when large numbers of teachers were hired by state governments immediately prior to elections. When this situation occurred, there was reasonable assurance that the new "teachers" would be on the streets organizing voters rather than in the classrooms organizing children.

In Venezuela, the hiring and promotion decisions favored individuals of the same political persuasion as the party in power. In every community, no matter how tiny, there is at least one teacher; and he might be the only public official in the area. In poor areas the teacher stands out as a learned individual who commands respect, and his presence at the grassroots level can contribute to the political party's power base.

As reported earlier, decision-making authority was centralized and concentrated at the ministry level in Venezuela and at the state level in Colombia. The reform movements will alter the traditional focus of decision-making authority in both countries. The change will affect the educational *as well as the political institutions,* thereby creating a potential danger to the reforms. If the political parties feel their power is threatened seriously by the loss of control of the educational organization as a power base, a sustained drive might be made to reestablish the prereform decision-making patterns.

CAREER MANAGEMENT

A second constraint which might impede the change process can be characterized as career management decision making. Skilled and knowledgeable educators are scarce in Venezuela and Colombia. Because authority and responsibility are being delegated to regional levels in Venezuela and the Colombian ministry policy requires the creation of new supervisory positions at the local level, individuals with a higher level of training and experience will be required to move to outlying geographical areas (away from Caracas in Venezuela and the state capital cities in Colombia).

However, living and working in the capital city have always been thought of as status rewards for public officials. Also, the personal and family comforts afforded by the capital city are rarely duplicated in outlying areas. In both countries qualified individuals may resist (if not reject) any career management decision to move them into regional or local positions outside the capital cities.

The reform movements will be seriously threatened if some form of reward system is not created to overcome the reluctance of competent educational officials to leave the capital cities. The writer is unaware of any such reward system being built into the reforms.

FISCAL MANAGEMENT

Under the Venezuelan reform, budget management will be practiced for the first time at the regional level. Controlling the allocation of human and material resources from the regional level will signal a dramatic downward shift of executive authority from the ministry level. The loss of control over expenditures by officials at the ministry level may be viewed by some as a loss of personal power. As a result, a tendency to support officially but resist unofficially (perhaps unconsciously) might foster a behavioral pattern which impedes the process of change.

A danger to the Colombian reform will exist if the ministry loses its resolve to enforce strictly the budgetary constraints placed on the states by the FER contracts. If the states violate the conditions of the contract and are not penalized, the FER program will be reduced quickly to a meaningless piece of paper. The act of penalizing the states for violation of the FER contract will probably be interpreted by the states as a political decision rather than an educational one. If this proves to be the case, the ministry will be hesitant to enforce the terms of the contract out of fear that the political repercussions will have a damaging effect on the ongoing activities of the ministry.

A second dimension of the budget management problem will be fiscal accountability. In Colombia, the state educational officials will be required to confine their financial decisions to conform with ministry policy. In Venezuela, financial decisions will be made at regional levels for the first time.

The problem of fiscal accountability is magnified when financial decision-making authority exists at the middle levels in the hierarchy. More individuals, for example, are participating in the decision-making process. Also, no one office maintains all the information necessary to clearly identify: (a) how priorities have been established, (b) whether or not the priorities maximize pedagogical returns, and (c) whether or not fiscal decisions are made to adhere to the established priorities.

As middle-level officials go through the learning process required for these new responsibilities, a certain degree of inefficiency and waste will be generated. If this inefficiency and waste is brought to the public eye, pressures will be brought to bear which call for a return to the prereform decision-making patterns.

In short, the planning of a reform and the execution of that reform are two distinct problems. As the architects of change design their strategies, they cannot possibly comprehend all of the converging forces which will seek to retard, if not eliminate, their meticulously constructed programs.

At this writing the educational reforms are still in the balance. Only time will tell whether or not the commitments to success are strong enough to counteract the constraints that surround the new programs.

The Organizational Climate
of Paraguayan Elementary Schools:
Rural-Urban Differentiations

JAMES STIMSON
THOMAS J. LA BELLE

Social scientists concerned with the role of societal institutions have espoused numerous theoretical constructs regarding the nature of an institution in terms of its obverse relationship to society and culture. As James S.
Coleman (1965, 6) has stated: "Since Plato and Aristotle, political philosophers have affirmed principles embodied in the phrase(s), 'As is the state,
so is the school.'" Although no empirical studies are able to grasp both the
cultural and institutional components of such a relationship, it is felt that
some preliminary investigations have provided a sufficient rationale to pursue the collection of data to test generally the bonds between culture and
a specific institution, in this case, education (Crozier, 1964). As an added
dimension, the urban institutional and cultural pattern, as distinct from a
rural configuration, presents a contrasting environment from which to view
such a relationship. Although this investigation was conducted outside the
United States, it is hoped that its import will not be lost to educators in
this country. It is felt that such studies are needed to crystallize common-
alities in problem orientations across cultural boundaries and thus enable
scholars to better cope with their indigenous institutions and environments.

The Setting

The investigation was undertaken in Paraguay, a land-locked country in the
heart of South America—one of the least-developed independent countries

"The Organizational Climate of Paraguayan Elementary Schools: Rural-Urban Differentiations"
by James Stimson and Thomas J. La Belle is reprinted from *Education and Urban Society,* Volume
3, Number 3 (May, 1971), pp. 333–349, by permission of the publisher, Sage Publications, Inc.

Authors' note: Items from the OCDQ questionnaire are reprinted from *Theory and Research in
Administration* © 1966 with the permission of the publisher, the Macmillan Company.

in the world. Its economy is based principally on agriculture, livestock, and forest industries, which until recent times have been poorly utilized. It is a predominantly rural nation divided into two distinct regions by the Rio Paraguay: eastern Paraguay, the area of most concentrated population; and the Chaco. All major cities are located in the eastern part; they include Asunción, the capital, with 350,000 inhabitants. The nation itself is composed of a predominantly mestizo population (a mixture of Spanish and Guarani Indians) engaged in subsistence farming on small plots of land, which the peasants cultivate with wooden plows, but do not own. It is the only nation in Latin America in which one indigenous language, Guarani, is widely spoken by both descendants of Europeans and Indians; this serves to strengthen the Paraguayan sense of nationalism. Although divided by political feuds, the Paraguayan population is essentially a homogeneous one racially, socially, and historically.

Although it is considered an underdeveloped nation, Paraguay is not lacking in rich natural resources. At present, considerable energy is being directed toward establishing an industrial economy, constructing a road network, expanding air transportation, exploiting the natural resources of the land, and amplifying education and health services. These are key goals. Much of the national development effort depends on bilateral and multilateral funds which, although sporadic, are proving beneficial to social and economic progress. The World Bank and the Agency for International Development have aided Paraguay's modernization process by supporting projects to improve transportation, communication, and sanitation facilities.

Although Paraguay purports to be a democracy, it has had the same president since 1954. In 1963 and again in 1967, President General Alfredo Stroessner was challenged for the presidency, but his opposition was weak, and there was little doubt that the general would emerge victorious in either election.[1] This is not unusual; Paraguay has always been led by strong personalities. "Autocracy" and "dictator" are common terms that specify the realities of political life. Given the high level of functional illiterates, the cautious press, the low standard of living, the institutionalized contraband, the strength of the military, and the historically oriented Paraguayan political tradition, any attempt to establish a democratic form of government in this nation of two million people would be difficult.

The development of human resources through formal education has progressed slowly. Paraguay's expenditure for education is the lowest in the hemisphere, with only 1.6 per cent of the national income going to support the formal schooling process (Rockefeller, 1969, 101). The educational

---

[1] Prior to the most recent election, a constitutional convention was called to update the constitution. To the local political pundits this meant changing the constitution to let Don Alfredo Stroessner run for another term. The former constitution specified two five-year terms.

sector reflects the centralized political authority, where local education officials are left only a small margin of administrative responsibility. On paper, the curriculum followed in all primary and secondary schools is uniform and controlled by the Ministry of Education.[1] At all levels of the educational hierarchy, nepotism and favoritism form the foundation for the selection of educational personnel. It is apparent that political alignment and familial connections outweigh knowledge and skill as criteria for the appointment of teachers and administrators.[2]

Purpose of the Study

The general purpose of this study is to investigate Michel Crozier's (1964, 238) hypothesis that a given educational institution mirrors the cultural values and traditions characteristic of the social system of that society. Crozier views the institution from two perspectives. One derives from the internal organizational system and the patterns of behavior characteristic of that system. The other views the institution in terms of its relations with the society of which it is part. Crozier's attention is directed toward an exposition of the French educational system, which he characterizes as having "omnipotent central powers" and few ties with local authorities, parents, or the general populace (Crozier, 1964, 240). Such a characterization might easily be applied to the educational system of Paraguay. Here education is weighted in favor of the elite, and the system tends to reinforce the existing social structure by limiting access to those who exhibit an appropriate familial background and can afford the investment of time and money. It is hypothesized that the centralized system manifests impersonal relations, with pedagogy and curricula proving dysfunctional to those who do not command the symbols of elite status. The school, as Crozier suggests for France, acts as a sorting mechanism in selecting people to enter definite social strata.

If Crozier's contention that the education system of any culture reflects that society's social system, and if Paraguay is a closed, autocratic society, as suggested above, then the Paraguayan schools should mirror these external influences. In addition, such external demands might be expected to vary

---

[1] One common breach of the ministry's regulations concerns the teaching of all subjects in Spanish. In the countryside, where most children speak Guarani well and Spanish poorly, the teachers are forced to teach in Guarani; therefore, they frequently break the "Spanish only" rule.

[2] A good example of how tenuous and important these relationships can be is illustrated by the following story circulated in Asunción during the course of this study. One of President Stroessner's nieces was recently appointed head of one of the regional centers of education. Upon hearing of this, most of the teachers in the school were surprised. They weren't surprised because a relative was awarded the position, but they had anticipated that an older sister of the niece who was honored would get the position because she was more qualified and, in terms of familialism, was next in line. Locally, this decision was explained by a claim that the president knew the older sister was more qualified, but he was angry because she married a member of the opposition party and had had her first child in Argentina.

in terms of the urban-rural environment and thereby promote a differentiation in terms of institutional characterization through what here is referred to as organizational climate. In other words, by studying the education institution in both a rural and urban context, it is hypothesized that the institution will be characterized differentially. Given the variations in rural and urban life styles and the demographic indicators which tend to separate these populations throughout the world, one might expect, even in a centralized bureaucracy, institutions in the urban and rural areas to vary according to certain criteria. Because of the myriad of problems relative to formal education created by urbanization throughout Latin America and the hemisphere, and because of our limited knowledge of institutional variability in the urban and rural areas, a study of this type seemed important and appropriate. It was with these facts in mind that in 1968 we undertook an investigation of the organizational climate of Paraguay's elementary schools. The sample included 258 elementary school teachers working in 30 randomly sampled public and private schools located in rural and urban areas of the country.

The Instrument

The organizational climate of the schools was identified through the use of the Organizational Climate Descriptive Questionnaire (OCDQ) developed by Halpin and Croft (Halpin, 1966b; Halpin and Croft, 1962). This questionnaire permits one to describe the organizational climate of an elementary school through an analysis of social interaction within the school. The 69-item instrument describes typical situations and behaviors that occur in elementary schools, with a focus on three areas—the individual teacher, the group, and the principal. The OCDQ can be given in a group situation and requires no more than 30 minutes for administration. The questionnaire consists of Likert-type items; the respondent is asked to what extent a particular statement characterizes his school (Halpin and Croft, 1962). The five examples below are illustrative of the types used in the questionnaire.

(1) There is considerable laughter when teachers gather informally.
(2) Teachers ramble when they talk in faculty meetings.
(3) The principal sets an example by working hard himself.
(4) Faculty meetings are organized according to a tight agenda.
(5) The teachers accomplish their work with great vim, vigor, and pleasure.

The items of the OCDQ are divided into eight subtests, which were delineated by factor analytic methods. The four dimensions of disengagement, hindrance, esprit, and intimacy measure the teacher's perception of interaction as related to the faculty; the dimensions of aloofness, production emphasis, thrust, and consideration are measures of teacher perception of leader behavior. The eight dimensions form a profile of six types of organizational climate. Profiles of different schools can be compared with the Halpin and Croft prototypic profiles for the six organizational climates which were conceptualized.

The eight dimensions of organizational behavior were defined by Halpin and Croft as follows.

(1) Disengagement indicates that the teachers do not work well together. They pull in different directions with respect to the task; they gripe and bicker among themselves.

(2) Hindrance refers to the teachers' feelings that the principal burdens them with routine duties, committee demands, and other requirements which the teachers construe as unnecessary busywork.

(3) Esprit refers to "morale." The teachers feel that their social needs are being satisfied, and that they are, at the same time, enjoying a sense of accomplishment in their job.

(4) Intimacy refers to the teachers' enjoyment of friendly social relations with each other.

(5) Aloofness refers to behavior by the principal which is characterized as formal and impersonal. He "goes by the book" and prefers to be guided by rules and policies rather than to deal with the teachers in an informal, face-to-face situation.

(6) Production emphasis refers to behavior by the principal which is characterized by close supervision of the staff. He is highly directive and task-oriented.

(7) Thrust refers to behavior marked not by close supervision of the teachers, but by the principal's attempt to motivate the teachers through the example which he personally sets. He does not ask the teachers to give of themselves any more than he willingly gives of himself; his behavior, though starkly task-oriented, is nonetheless viewed favorably by the teachers.

(8) Consideration refers to behavior by the principal which is characterized by an inclination to treat the teachers "humanly," to try to do a little something extra for them in human terms.

The six types of organizational climate, placed on a continuum, are defined as follows.

(1) The open climate describes an energetic, lively organization which is moving toward its goals, and which provides satisfaction for the group members' social needs. Leadership acts emerge easily and appropriately from both the group and the leader. The members are preoccupied disproportionately with neither task achievement *nor* social-needs satisfaction; satisfaction on both counts seems to be obtained easily and almost effortlessly. The main characteristic of this climate is the "authenticity" of the behavior that occurs among all the members.

(2) The autonomous climate is described best as one in which leadership acts emerge primarily from the group. The leader exerts little control over the group members; high esprit results primarily from social-needs satisfaction. Satisfaction from task achievement is also present, but to a lesser degree.

(3) The controlled climate is characterized best as impersonal and highly task-oriented. The group's behavior is directed primarily toward task accomplishment, while relatively little attention is given to social-needs satisfaction. Esprit is fairly high, but it reflects achievement at some expense to social-needs satisfaction. This climate lacks openness, or "authenticity" of behavior, because the group is disproportionately preoccupied with task achievement.

(4) The familiar climate is highly personal, but undercontrolled. The members of this organization satisfy their social needs, but pay relatively little attention to social control in respect to task accomplishment. Accordingly, esprit is not extremely high simply because the group members secure little satisfaction from task achievement. Hence, much of the behavior within this climate can be construed as "inauthentic."

(5) The paternal climate is characterized best as one in which the principal constrains the emergence of leadership acts from the group and attempts to initiate most of these acts himself. The leadership skills within the group are not used to supplement the principal's own ability to initiate leadership acts. Accordingly, some leadership acts are not even attempted.

(6) The closed climate is characterized by a high degree of apathy on the part of all members of the organization. The organization is not "moving"; esprit is low because the group members secure neither social-needs satisfaction nor the satisfaction that comes from task achievement. On the whole, the members' behavior can be construed as "inauthentic"; indeed, the organization seems to be stagnant.

Method

The Organizational Climate Description Questionnaire was translated into Spanish by 30 Paraguayan teachers interning at the University of New Mexico in 1966.[1] In Paraguay, the OCDQ was administered to all teaching faculty at the 30 elementary schools chosen by means of a table of random numbers from a list of schools provided by the Ministry of Education and located in and near the city of Asunción.

All the schools in the study were classified as either rural or urban and as either private or public by the Ministry of Education. Because of the lack of private rural schools in metropolitan Asunción, they were not included in the study. Most of the urban private schools were under the control of the Catholic church, but subject to the same governmental control over curricula as those of the public sector.

In order to ensure anonymity, schools were not identified by name and participants were instructed to omit their names from the questionnaires. To determine which of the six climate profiles was most similar to a given school's profile, individual school profiles were constructed on the basis of

---

[1] Professor Frank Angel, who has been involved in educational development programs throughout Latin America, supervised this translation.

standardized subtest scores. We then compared the statistically treated data from the OCDQ for each school with each of the six prototypic profiles, and in each instance emerged with a profile similarity score. After the profile similarity score had been computed for each prototypic profile, we selected the prototype with the smallest sum. This prototype indicated which climate best characterized the school.

Cross-Cultural Validity

Inasmuch as the instrument used to measure social climate has not been widely used in cross-cultural comparisons, validity data across cultures are sparse; it is anticipated that the results of this exploratory study will add to the accumulating evidence in this direction. It was assumed that the English-Spanish translation of the instrument by Paraguayan normal school teachers was an adequate method of translation for use in Paraguay. It was also assumed that the 69-item questionnaire was appropriate for use in a foreign school system which reflects, in part, United States models.

Results

Table 1 shows the numerical breakdown of the sample of schools by number, location, and control, as well as the total and average number of individual faculty members for each of the categories. Eleven schools were classified as rural-public, with a total faculty of 88 and an average of 8.0 faculty members per school. In the urban category, six schools were classified as private, with a total of 45 teachers and an average 7.5 teachers per school; 13 schools were classified as public with a total of 125 teachers and an average of 9.6 teachers per school. A total of 258 teachers in 30 schools were administered the questionnaire with an average of 8.6 teachers per school.

Table 1. Schools by Location, Control, and Size of Faculty

| | Rural Schools | Urban Schools | |
	Public	Private	Public
Schools n	11	6	13
Faculty n	88	45	125
Faculty average n	8.0	7.5	9.6

Table 2 presents the number of teachers in each school and the climate prototypes for each public, urban school. The lowest sum represents the climate categorization of that particular school. Following this pattern, it will be noted that the lowest sum for each elementary school indicates that 10 out of the 13 schools are characterized as closed and three are characterized as paternal.

Table 2. Number of Teachers and Prototypes for Urban Public Schools

Schools	Teachers n	Climate Prototypes					
		Open	Autonomous	Controlled	Familiar	Paternal	Closed
1	9	100	105	91	75	50	36
2	8	119	100	63	107	74	38
3	8	114	104	61	98	89	46
4	11	104	86	78	86	68	46
5	12	116	115	76	94	55	27
6	8	95	96	103	66	62	42
7	7	97	75	94	80	72	53
8	13	90	78	73	89	69	71
9	8	86	89	80	76	69	66
10	7	88	81	91	64	62	70
11	10	99	98	82	81	62	40
12	13	101	97	70	98	75	46
13	11	82	73	72	80	70	76

Table 3 presents the number of teachers in each school and the climate prototypes for each rural, public school. Of the 11 schools included in this category, nine are characterized as having closed climates, one as having a paternal climate, and one as having a controlled-paternal climate.

Table 3. Number of Teachers and Prototypes for Rural Public Schools

Schools	Teachers n	Climate Prototypes					
		Open	Autonomous	Controlled	Familiar	Paternal	Closed
1	5	82	83	69	82	73	75
2	7	94	84	85	84	71	66
3	12	115	96	80	95	66	31
4	11	90	75	63	90	70	62
5	5	95	84	64	101	74	62
6	7	113	120	73	95	62	42
7	10	95	83	66	91	66	69
8	6	81	73	80	70	71	69
9	11	111	98	84	77	67	27
10	9	112	107	70	92	62	32
11	5	103	95	63	99	73	49

Table 4 presents the number of teachers in each school and the climate prototypes for each private, church school located in an urban area. Five of the six schools are characterized as having a closed climate and one is characterized as having an autonomous climate.

Table 4. Number of Teachers and Prototypes for Urban Private Schools

Schools	Teachers n	Climate Prototypes					
		Open	Autonomous	Controlled	Familiar	Paternal	Closed
1	7	97	79	86	79	63	53
2	11	119	104	79	89	70	15
3	8	99	73	83	86	76	56
4	6	117	93	81	83	82	30
5	7	78	54	66	76	73	82
6	6	111	117	73	85	60	51

Discussion

A clear climate pattern can be discerned for the sample of 30 Paraguayan elementary schools included in this study. Twenty-four schools exhibited a closed climate, four schools exhibited a paternal climate, one school had a controlled-paternal climate, and one school demonstrated an autonomous climate. In accord with the Halpin and Croft climate continuum this seems to indicate that the sample of Paraguayan schools is characterized as static institutions with apathetic teachers who receive little in the way of social-need or task-accomplishment satisfaction. Furthermore, the institutions, with the exception of one private, church-operated, urban school, are characterized by principals who jealously guard the power and control over both the suggestion and implementation of leadership acts.

On the basis of these empirical data, it seems that the schools do reflect the wider social constraints characteristic of the political and social institutions of Paraguay. This supports the idea that the schools in a closed society mirror that society's social system and, as the most important institution for formal socialization, perpetuate that system.

Other studies using the Halpin and Croft OCDQ (Novotney, 1965; Gentry and Kenney, 1967) have found significant variations in regard to school climate in the United States. These studies indicate that in a random sample of schools in the United States, both urban and rural, some schools emerge as being characterized by open climates while others demonstrate closed climates. This fact indicates the variations which exist from school to school and from community to community in a decentralized educational system which is dependent upon local funding and control.

Halpin (1966a), however, after checking data on the OCDQ for various areas in the United States, found that schools located in urban-core areas were characterized by closed climates. He feels that this phenomenon is in some way related to such variables as the usually large size of such schools, the high population density, and the lower socioeconomic status population representing the integration or lack of integration of several racial or ethnic groups. He also attributes the preponderance of closed climates in urban-core areas to the usually large size of the school system and the normally pyramidal structure existing in the administrative hierarchy of such systems.

The results of the present study, when viewed in relation to the Halpin survey, would indicate that the existence of a school in a highly structured and centralized administrative framework, when combined with lower socioeconomic populations who have little access to the benefits of the external society, will most likely be characterized by the teachers as being closed. It is the teachers who feel the impact of such a climate, and it is they who will most likely reflect the despair and lack of esprit in their schools.

Paraguay's elementary school institutions, reflecting as they must the wider societal values, preoccupations and fears found in the culture as a whole, have no choice but to mirror those covert cultural manifestations and educate within the established constraints. Yet the teachers, when queried on their perceptions of the organizational climate of the schools, present their dissatisfactions with the system and indicate their apathy with a stagnant organization. Perhaps the only way to change the climate of the Paraguayan elementary schools is to await changes in the wider social and cultural environment. Perhaps schools will then mirror the new norms and values and, as Jules Henry (1963, 287) has pointed out, have no choice but to "train children to fit the culture as it is."

The same conception might be brought to bear on the closed inner-city schools in the United States. Because education must reflect the wider sociocultural patterns, the institution itself can only respond to external influences and demands. Those who place great confidence in the institution to act as innovator or even catalyst in terms of sociocultural change should be aware of the underlying patterns upon which the institution is built. Those who expect the school to somehow lead the society as a model of egalitarian behavior, for example, must keep in mind the society's very slow progress in promoting equality in access to resources, housing, and political representation for minority populations. To isolate the school from these external realities and view it as a panacea to overcome societal ills is not in concert with its integral place in the society and culture to which it belongs.

Apparently the nature of the Paraguayan society permeates both urban and rural institutional configurations, whereas the evidence indicates only urban, inner-city schools in the United States are so perceived. As has been suggested, perhaps the best explanation of this phenomenon rests with the sociocultural milieu; yet it is also apparent that the centralized administrative bureaucracy is common to both Paraguayan urban and rural schools, as well as to U.S. inner-city schools. It is possible that a more decentralized system in which there is access to and participation in policy making by schoolteachers and administrators might alleviate the lack of satisfaction gained from institutional participation. This line of inquiry in regard to cultural factors and to the comparisons of urban-rural, centralized-decentralized school systems deserves further thought and investigation. Such studies might prove supportive of experimental programs to increase local community involvement in school operation and to improve teacher perception of the role and function of the educational institution.

References

Coleman, J. S. "Introduction: Education and Political Development," *in* J. S. Coleman, ed., *Education and Political Development*. Princeton, N.J.: Princeton University Press, 1965.

Crozier, M. *The Bureaucratic Phenomenon*. Chicago, Ill.: University of Chicago Press, 1964.

Gentry, H. W., and J. B. Kenney. "The Relationship between the Organizational Climate of Elementary Schools and School Location, School Size, and the Economic Level of the School Community," *Urban Education*, 3 (1967), pp. 19-31.

Halpin, A. W. "Change and Organizational Climate," *Ontario Journal of Educational Research*, 8 (Spring, 1966a).

Halpin, A. W. "Organizational Climate Description Questionnaire," *in Theory and Research in Administration*. New York: Macmillan, 1966b.

Halpin, A. W., and D. B. Croft. "The Organizational Climate of Schools," *Research Report SAE 543 (8639)*. Washington: U.S. Office of Education, 1962.

Henry, J. *Culture against Man*. New York: Vintage, 1963.

Novotney, J. M. "The Organizational Climate of Parochial Schools." Ed.D. dissertation, University of California, Los Angeles, Calif., 1965.

Rockefeller, N. A. "Quality of Life in the Americas," Report of a U.S. Presidential Mission for the Western Hemisphere, August 30, 1969 (mimeo.).

The Geography of Youth Employment
and School Enrollment Rates in Mexico

PHYLLIS GOLDBLATT

If the people of a country are caught up with the rising expectations for development, they must be ready to adopt changes. The ways in which new ideas spread across a country and the readiness with which people utilize them will determine how successful a nation will be in the total process of modernization.

Primary schooling is often viewed as an agent of change. It is presumed to promote new skills, to allow people to consider alternatives to old ways, to offer incentives to greater efforts, and to encourage national unity through a common language and familiarity with other parts of the population. But primary schooling in developing countries may also be viewed as the dependent variable, the new trait or innovation that diffuses through the society in various patterns. This paper is concerned with an analysis of factors that explain spatial patterns in the diffusion and distribution of primary school enrollment rates in Mexico. The principal methods used are factor and multiple-regression analyses.

The theoretical framework takes as its starting point the diffusion theories of certain human geographers, derived in part from the "gravity models" of central-place theories but as modified by work at Lund, Sweden.[1]

Scholars working with central-place theory have developed a technique

Reproduced from *Schools in Transition*, pp. 280–294, 1968, by author permission.

The author is indebted to Mary Jean Bowman for her helpful comments on the manuscript. The author, however, is solely responsible for any deficiencies in the text.

[1] Torsten Hägerstrand, "Quantitative Techniques for Analysis of the Spread of Information and Technology," *in* C. Arnold Anderson and Mary Jean Bowman, eds., *Education and Economic Development* (Chicago: Aldine Publishing Company, 1965), pp. 244–280.

for measuring the influence of one population aggregate upon another as a function of size and distance. It has been assumed that the larger a population of place B the more influence it will have on a population in place A. The greater the distance from A to B the less is B's effect on A. To obtain the population potential of A we would divide the population of each other place, B_1, B_2, B_3 by its distance from A, distance $_1$, $_2$, $_3$, etc. and sum the results. Fattahipour[1] tested out this concept of population potential in a study of the diffusion of education in Iran but found it inadequate: both the central and intermediate cities remained self-contained with little spill-over of educational stimulation to the hinterlands.

The Lund geographer Hägerstrand has applied a rather different model, embracing information fields and resistances to the study of diffusion in space. He found a remarkable stability in the geographic pattern for the diffusion of many innovations (including schooling) over a 200-year period. He identified established centers from which innovations spread, and these centers appeared to form a status order. Ideas from the innovation centers were more likely to be accepted. What he calls information fields are communication channels; the most effective flow of information followed the tellings[2] between people. As indexes of these interpersonal linkages he used telephone usage and migration routes. Mass media appeared to promote new ideas only when supported by person-to-person communication.

But people do not always accept new ideas when they first hear of them. Reactions depend upon the economic and cultural setting and how a particular innovation fits into that setting—hence the concept of resistance, the degree of ease with which particular new ideas are accepted for any given intensity of tellings. Some new ideas may be adopted almost immediately, some only after repeated tellings, some not even then.

Education fits into this model in several ways: First, using Hägerstrand's general model as a guide, this paper discusses the enrollment of six- to 14-year olds in the states of Mexico as the innovation being diffused. Spatial variation in enrollment will be treated first as a function of information fields, approximated by patterns of communication from urban to rural areas and across regions of the country. These variations will then be examined from the resistance side of the model, examining traits of populations in one area versus another that affect parental decisions to enroll their children in school. In many instances, direct measures of information fields and decision factors cannot be obtained and indirect indexes must be used.

The spatial distribution of educational attainments of adults can fit into the Hägerstrand model in other ways. Thus, rather than the enrollment rates of children (treated as the innovation or dependent variables) the

---

[1] Ahmad Fattahipour-Fard, "Educational Diffusion and the Modernization of an Ancient Civilization: Iran" (Ph.D. dissertation, Department of Education, University of Chicago, 1963).

[2] "Tellings" refers to the exchange of information between people who meet and talk informally.

education levels of adults may be viewed as a proxy variable for intensity of tellings. That is, it is assumed that educated adults have more contacts with new ideas, and a locality with a large proportion of educated adults would have a more rapid rate of interchange of information relevant to decisions about schooling.

The level of adult education can be considered from the resistance side also, making people more eager or more opposed to keeping their children in school for both economic and noneconomic reasons: the more educated the adults the greater the presumption that aspirations for children's education will be high, simply viewing education as a value in itself, any economic returns aside.[1]

Mexico provides a good case for this kind of analysis, apart from the unusual amount of information available. In the early 1900's Mexico was characterized by a population 80 to 90 per cent rural. Rural Mexico was backward and underdeveloped, inhabited largely by poor, illiterate peasants, under the domination of *hacendados,* or owners of manorial estates. About 85 per cent of the population was illiterate, and only one quarter of the school-age children were in school. During the past third of a century or more there has been rapid development on all fronts. The leaders of the 1910 revolution attempted to break down the restrictions of class and region surrounding education and to use the schools as instruments of change.

The Geographic Patterns of Primary School Enrollment Rates

Although access to schools has broadened over the past generation or more, wide variation in their use and effectiveness persists. Some states remain almost wholly traditional while others have most of the earmarks of modernity, and the Federal District is one of the most modernized urban areas in the world. It is in the North generally and in particular parts of the central plateau (mainly in the capital district) that progress has been most marked. The three states facing south on the Pacific are most retarded: Guerrero, Oaxaca, and Chiapas. The northern states are better off than most of the central plateau, the latter displaying extremely diverse levels of development within a densely populated region.[2]

The three illustrative maps showing proportionate enrollments of six- to 14-year-old children in urban (Map 1) and rural (Map 2) areas highlight the diversities of development among the parts of Mexico. The overall enrollment

[1] Of course there are also correlations between education attainments of adults and other variables, like occupations, that affect demands for educated people and enter into the content of the tellings. However, the pertinent variables in this connection are those providing more direct indications of demands for educated people.

[2] In most of my analyses the Federal District has been omitted, for it would distort most of the distributions and often lead to overstated correlations. It would have been preferable to use *municipios* (counties) as units rather than states, but the labor entailed in handling thousands of *municipios* would have been prohibitive—and fewer items of information are available for *municipios* than for states.

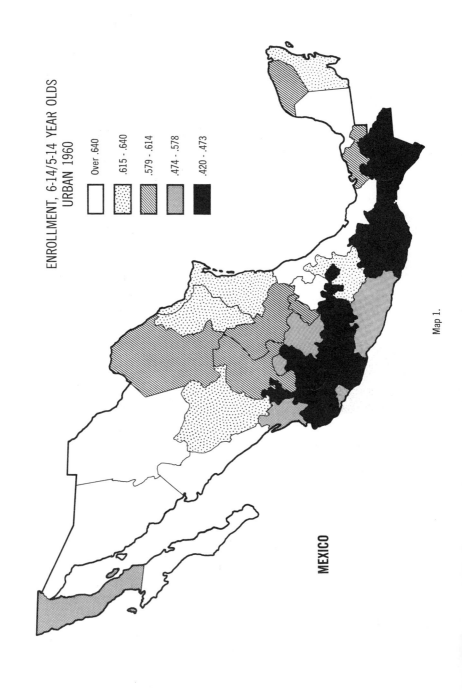

ENROLLMENT, 6-14/5-14 YEAR OLDS
URBAN 1960

Over .640

.615 - .640

.579 - .614

.474 - .578

.420 - .473

MEXICO

Map 1.

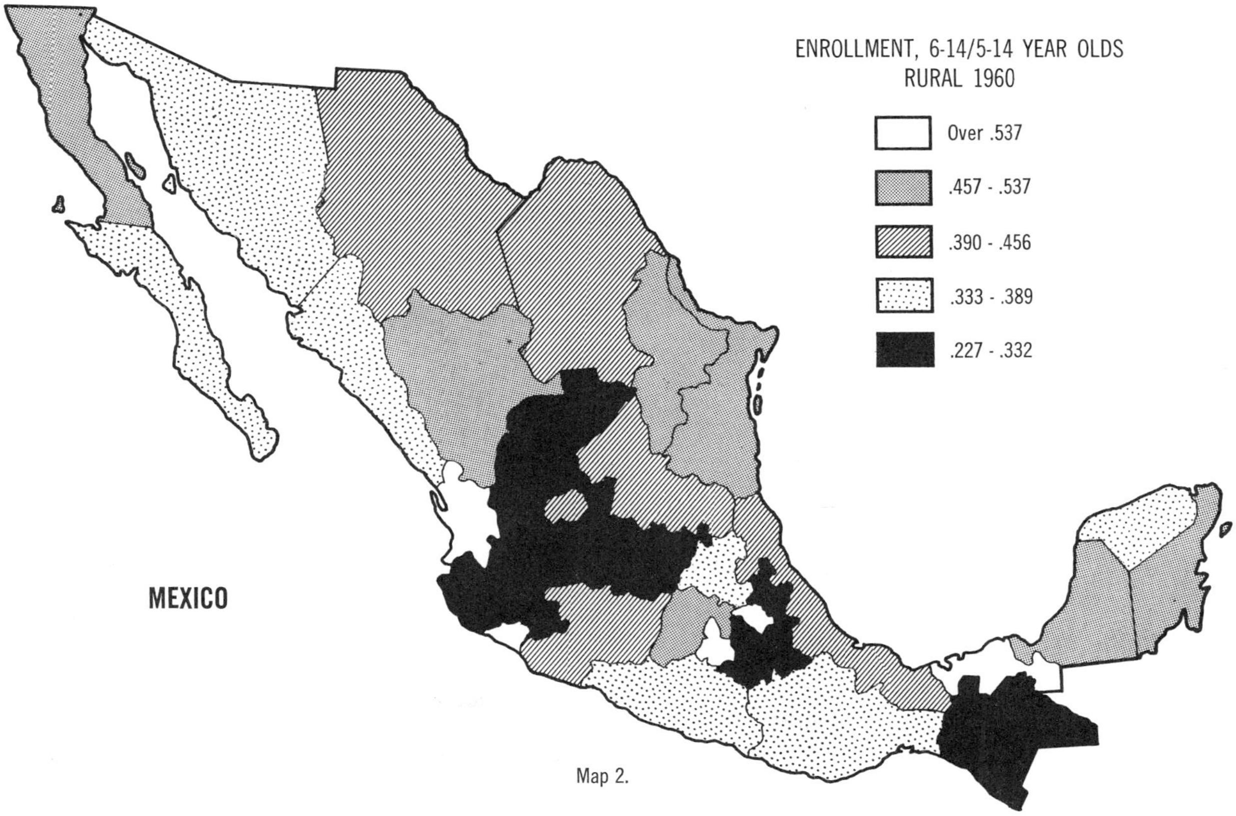

ENROLLMENT, 6-14/5-14 YEAR OLDS
RURAL 1960

Over .537

.457 - .537

.390 - .456

.333 - .389

.227 - .332

MEXICO

Map 2.

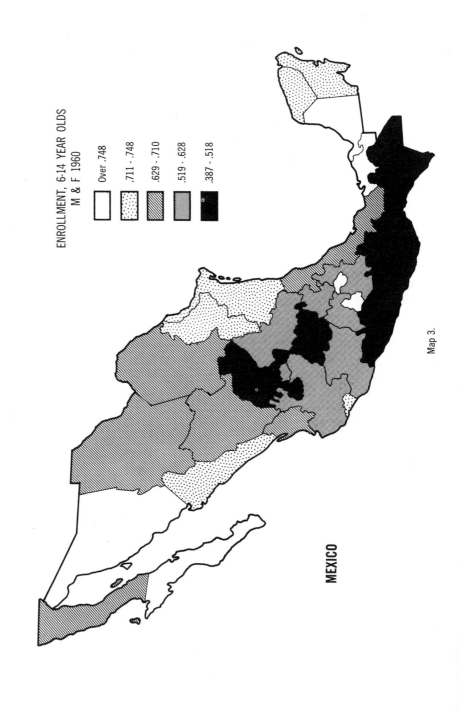

ENROLLMENT, 6-14 YEAR OLDS
M & F 1960

Over .748

.711 - .748

.629 - .710

.519 - .628

.387 - .518

MEXICO

Map 3.

rate (Map 3) provides a good general image of regional development, both cultural and economic. In the South there is also a clustering of states, but this time at low levels of school enrollment. The extreme diversity between North and South and the complex variations in the central group of states suggest that the gradient patterns implied in conventional population-potential models would not provide an adequate explanation for the observed pattern.

A first survey of some of the factors that can be presumed to underlie the geographic pattern portrayed in the maps is provided by the correlation matrix (Table 1). The literacy of urban males 40–49 years old has a positive association with enrollment of six- to 14-year olds in urban areas (.385). The proportion of urban males literate in the 40- to 49-year-old age group has a negative relationship to the employment of eight- to 11-year olds (–.512). With rural males the pattern is the same, a low (but positive) association between the literacy of older males and enrollment of youths in school (.105). At the same time there is a negative relationship between literacy of older men and the employment of children (–.777). Adult literacy clearly enhances enrollment of children in school and is associated with low enrollments (–.315) in urban areas and even more strongly in rural areas (–.571).

In the zero-order correlation matrix (Table 1) traditionalism, as indicated by going barefoot,[1] has little connection with either urban or rural enrollment rates (.004 and .112 respectively).

Yet there are negative correlations between going barefoot and adult literacy, which is correlated with enrollments. (The proportion of males barefoot is related to the literacy of older urban males –.656 and to the literacy of older rural males –.492.) This prepares one for the reordering of some of these relationships that will emerge when some multiple regressions and partial correlations are explored below.

Table 1. Illustrative Correlations between Educational and Other Variables Mexico (Units = 32 States)

	1	2	3	4	5	6	7
1. Enrollment, 6–14's–urban	—						
2. Enrollment, 6–14's–rural	–.085	—					
3. 8–11 year-old males employed	–.315	–.571	—				
4. Urban males age 40–49 % literate	.385	–.055	–.512	—			
5. Rural males age 40–49 % literate	.105	.490	–.777	.463	—		
6. % males employed, agriculture	–.129	–.338	.679	–.580	–.663	—	
7. % males barefoot	.004	.112	.480	–.656	–.492	.606	—
8. Not immigration	–.016	.417	–.542	.501	.458	–.568	–.504

[1] The proportion of males going barefoot as opposed to those wearing *huaraches* or shoes is used as a proxy variable for adherence to the traditional culture.

Variations in Enrollments as an Aspect
of Rural-Urban Communication Fields

Two diagrams were drawn to represent the information and the resistance sets of factors respectively. The actual variables available for analysis are put in the rounded boxes and the concepts or hypothetical variables in the square boxes. The goal is to explain enrollment of children in school, and the network of relationships displayed reflects the causal hypotheses derived from the Hägerstrand model and other sources. Although one may start with overall enrollment rates by states, there are distinctive characteristics of the rural as against the urban patterning of influences and behavior that are especially interesting.

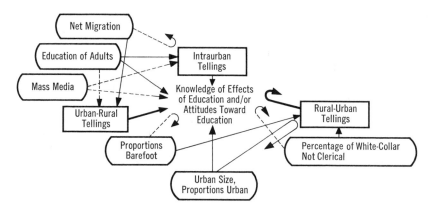

Figure 1. Information and Communication.

I begin with Figure 1 on information and communication fields. Information can flow within either urban or rural areas and between them—through intraurban and intrarural tellings. The intrarural tellings were not put in the diagram, however. The straight arrows indicate positive influence on diffusion of knowledge about the effects of education and tellings that convey attitudes favorable toward education. The arrows that turn back on themselves indicate negative effects. When an element in the chart has a traditionalist influence, arrows from it to Knowledge of Effects of Education and/or Attitudes toward Education turn back or reverse themselves. Here one has factors that impede or delay the spread of information and the orientations to education upon which the decisions to enroll and continue in school are based. Hereafter I shall refer to such arrows as "reversing arrows."

One would expect innovations to diffuse mostly within and among urban places with weaker influence to the surrounding hinterlands. Also, areas with high rates of immigration presumably have greater opportunities and higher levels of economic modernization; a priori one would expect higher enrollment rates. These assumptions were generally upheld in zero-order correlations. However, more-refined analysis points to distinctive urban types. Controlling for other key variables, the simple relationships may not hold. Thus in Table 2, regression in urban enrollment rates of children six to 14 were depressed by large immigration rates in cities of any given level with respect to manufacturing incomes and percentage of men in white-collar jobs. Given these controls, the less the immigration rate in the state the higher the enrollment (partial correlation –.506). Figure 1 shows a reversing arrow from net migration to intraurban tellings. Evidently, newly arrived migrants bring their traditional rural culture, tend to live in self-contained neighborhoods, and only belatedly accept the emphasis on schooling. Where there are many of them they pull down enrollment rates.

In pursuing the time dimension further, contrasting 1960 with 1940 enrollments as dependent variables, enrollments at the later date were not as well explained as were the 1940 enrollments. There were heavy migrations over that 20-year period, but while residences may change families may retain contact with their former localities. Thus with movements of people subareas become less homogeneous and the spatial web of tellings loses some of its previous distinctiveness and clarity.

When I consider rural-urban tellings I am thinking of towns that are strongly influenced by their surrounding rural areas. There is both persistence of indigenous traits and low levels of income. Thus a high proportion of males going barefoot suggests the presence of towns functioning as trading places for rural people. Examination of the occupation mixes within the white-collar category reveals distinctive urban types.

One might expect a high proportion of white-collar workers to be related to areas of high literacy of adults and high enrollment rates of children, i.e., areas that are progressing. Instead (Table 2, regression 1) high enrollments appeared with high manufacturing incomes (.486) but a low proportion of males in white-collar occupations (–.318). The anticipated facilitating effect of white-collar employment was not revealed. A reexamination of the underlying data showed clearly that the regressions were confounded where many traders outweighed the other nonmanual categories in the white-collar occupational group; proportions of clerical workers give quite different results.

A high proportion of the state population residing in urban places presumably diffuses knowledge about education, and the proportion living in cities has been growing rapidly. That proportion is higher in the northern states, which also display a closer connection between urban and rural development. However, development in rural areas may reflect special irrigation projects, for example, rather than the spread of modernizing influences from the urban center. In other parts of Mexico, and especially in the South,

Table 2. Partial Correlation Coefficients (Selected from Best Regressions) between Enrollment Rates for Six- to 14-Year Olds and Other Factors

	Urban	Rural
(1) % of males in manufacturing with incomes over 500 pesos	.486*	
% of males in white-collar occupations	-.318†	
R^2 = .248		
(2) % of males in manufacturing with incomes over 500 pesos	.651*	
% of males in white-collar occupations	-.311†	
Immigration rate of state	-.506*	
R^2 = .441		
(3) % of males barefoot	-.586*	
Literacy %, urban females age 40–49	.688*	
R^2 = .473		
(4) % of males barefoot		-.465*
Literacy %, rural males age 40–49		.629*
R^2 = .404		
(5) % of 8- to 11-year olds employed (outside family)		
(with employment of children included, the literacy		
rate of 40- to 49-year-old rural males dropped out)		-.571*
(6) Literacy %, rural females age 40–49		-.270
% of 8- to 11-year olds employed		-.581*
R^2 = .372		
(7) % of 8- to 11-year olds employed		-.561*
% of dwellings with radio		-.223
R^2 = .360		
(8) % of males in agriculture with incomes over 500 pesos		-.305†
% 8- to 11-year olds employed		-.608*
R^2 = .389		
(9) % of males barefoot		-.536*
% of 8- to 11-year olds employed		-.717*
R^2 = .520		

* Significant at .01. † Significant at .05.

Note: Regressions were programmed to drop out variables the partial correlation of which had an F value less than 1. In selecting variables for regressions, no two variables with loadings of over .8 on the same factor were used.

urban places as yet seem to exert comparatively weak modernizing effects upon the surrounding rural people.[1]

Determinants of Resistance to Diffusion of Education and Variations in Enrollment Rates

Some clues to the factors that influence people when they decide whether or not to send their children to school have emerged from these data. The data for the most part referred to spatial aspects of communications and the direction and intensity of tellings, i.e., the information field. Within any such field, how readily an innovation is adopted depends upon the factors that determine resistances; these latter are explored as a decision model in Figure 2. Again the rectangles are concepts and the rounded boxes are independent variables that proved to be important. Two of the rectangles refer to costs and availability of schooling. One is ability to afford schooling, one is the visibility of economic returns to schooling, and one is value attitudes or cultural traits and noneconomic preferences.

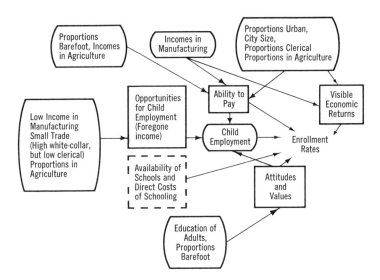

Figure 2. Resistance (plus and minus). Rectangles: concepts, not measured directly. Entries in boxes with rounded ends: each entry indicates a variable or set of variables used in the empirical analysis.

---

[1] The mass media—as exemplified by movie attendance and possession of radios—did not stimulate enrollments; this is consistent with Hägerstrand's emphasis upon person-to-person communication.

The direct costs of schooling (in the rectangle with dashed lines) were not represented by any variable. At the level of elementary school such costs are small and differ little from one area to another. For availability of schools we had one variable: proportions of elementary schools that did not contain the full range of six grades. However, that variable is ambiguous in that it may be as often an index of pace of expansion as of availability. Furthermore, local availability is itself a function of local pressures for schooling. More important on the cost side are opportunities for child employment and the costs in foregone income that such opportunities entail. Though children legally are not to be employed, child employment is widespread enough for the census to tabulate the eight- to 11-year olds separately among the economically active population.

Levels of income in agriculture and in manufacturing were used as indicators of ability to pay for schooling. In this context the proportions of males going barefoot can be interpreted as a level of living index though it is also a cultural index.

I will first discuss the urban patterns. In the urban setting a high level of income for employees in manufacturing was a powerful stimulant to enrollment of children. In the multiple-regression analysis for urban enrollments this index of ability to pay for education was more important among urban populations than the level of employment of children (which was dropped by the F test). The influence of parental education came in with a strong positive value in regressions that included proportions of males barefoot. The latter was a strong depressant on enrollment rates when controlling for parental education (see regression 3). Whether children in towns go to school is a function predominantly of parental economic ability, the visibility of education payoff in future earning power, in the immediate environment, and a positive attitude toward education on the part of adults (as inferred from adult literacy and urban style of dress).

In the factor analysis a strong modernization factor emerged; it had high loadings for urban population, high manufacturing income, clerical employment, few males in farming—and high enrollments of children. Juxtaposing regressions 1 and 2 leads to identifying a type of city with high manufacturing incomes, a small newly arrived or transient population, and a large proportion of other than tradesmen among the white-collar men.

In parallel fashion, an effort was made to isolate elements of the rural social structure that could explain variability in rural enrollments. The proportion of males in agriculture, the level of farm mechanization, and the proportion of agricultural laborers showed little influence upon enrollments (these variables were eliminated by the F tests at 1.00).

Level of incomes from agriculture had virtually no effect upon enrollment except when I controlled for the proportion of males in agriculture and employment of children, and then income worked in reverse; thus low farm incomes actually raised enrollment rates at any given child-employment level (Table 2, regression 8). Although I could speculate concerning the complex of factors that lie back of this result, the data do not permit any firm explanatory inference.[1]

Child employment is placed centrally in the diagram on resistance because of its logically key place in the schooling decision matrix. Yet this variable washed out in the urban regression even as it dominated the rural ones. Does this mean that foregone opportunities for child employment are unimportant in cities? That clearly is not the case. Martin Carnoy[2] found that employed children earned substantially more in the cities he studied than in his rural localities. Among urban populations foregone earnings are a relatively large cost in the last years of elementary school. Nevertheless, he found that despite high urban foregone incomes, urban rates of return to investment in the fourth to sixth years of primary school run to 30 or even 40 per cent. This finding is consistent with our regressions. Despite high opportunity costs, relatively fewer children are employed in Mexico's cities than in rural areas, and rates of child employment fail to explain differences in urban enrollment rates precisely because other factors dominate: visibility of returns to schooling, high parental incomes, parental education and participation in modern culture versus many unassimilated immigrants living (barefoot) in the poorer residential areas of cities.

In rural areas, where returns to schooling are less visible, ability to pay is generally lower, and there is less variation in these traits. Here the extent of opportunity for child employment comes to play a pervasive part in determining school enrollments. While the opportunities themselves cannot be measured directly from the available data, the uses people make of those opportunities and the correlates of such use can be studied. The data indicate that such use and the extent of such opportunities in rural areas are greatest where there are moderate proportions of males in agriculture, low incomes in manufacturing, and many small traders (indicated by high white-collar but low clerical proportions). Among rural populations, once factors inducing child employment are allowed for, male literacy disappears and female literacy becomes an insignificant factor (regressions 5 and 6). When child employment is not taken into account, the degree of cultural traditionalism and adult literacy are important (regression 4). Indeed, cultural

---

[1] In equations (6), (7), and (8), the negative partial correlation coefficients for females literate, dwellings with radios, and males in agriculture with incomes over 500 pesos seem surprising. While no one is significant (with the partial exception of agricultural income over 500 pesos), the fact that all three have negative associations is something of a puzzle. Other correlations suggest that each of the independent variables is a reasonably firm one, but rural enrollment rates have a wide range of error. What equations (6), (7), and (8) do demonstrate is that, once account has been taken of eight- to 11-year olds employed, the other variables add little to the explanation of rural enrollment.

[2] Martin Carnoy, "The Return to Education in Mexico: A Case Study" (unpublished manuscript, The Brookings Institution, March, 1966).

traditionalism retains an influence even after the factors producing high employment of children are allowed for (regression 9).

In summary, the Mexican data support Hägerstrand's emphasis on face-to-face tellings as the crux of the functioning of an information field. Evidence on this includes low correlations of urban with rural enrollment rates and low adult literacy correlates in the central area. Even more strongly, this thesis is supported by the negative immigration effect. In contrast to Sweden, however, Mexico is a bicultural land and has recently been experiencing a shaking loose of old geocultural patterns as subcultures move into new locations. Thus I find that 1960 trait clusters are geographically looser than those for 1937. Mexico displays strong culture change.

The urban settings range from the so-called "urban" that is essentially the gathering place and community crossroads of traditional rural society (which still lag in enrollments) to modern cities where incomes are high and returns to education are clearly visible.

Variations in school diffusion among rural populations suggest that opportunities for child employment play a key role, with ability to pay and visible returns generally too low to neutralize deterrent effects of foregone income opportunities.

Throughout, in both rural and urban life, the importance of cultural variabilities is clearly evidenced. The adoption of urban ways and the literacy of the older generation act as supportive factors in receptivity to the education of youth. Urban enrollments had the best R^2 with the culture variables, adult female literacy and proportion of males barefoot; and the barefoot variable came through in almost every rural regression in which it was included.

The implementation of centrally designed plans for education may meet countless hidden constraints among groups of illiterate people bound to a traditional culture. In designing programs, central planners must be aware of the subtleties in the diffusion of education and its relationship to the socioeconomic structure, both in deciding goals and in determining the most effective areas on which to focus their efforts.

Economic Development and Changes in the Composition of the Teaching Staff of Secondary Schools in Brazil

APARECIDA J.GOUVEIA

Introduction

THE DATA

Two kinds of data are used in this paper: school statistics put out by the Brazilian Ministry of Education, and information collected in 1963 in a sample survey study carried out under the joint sponsorship of the University of Chicago and the Instituto Nacional de Estudos Pedagógicos. The survey includes samples of teachers from five states in different regions but at this stage IBM processed data are available only for two units, namely São Paulo, which is the most industrialized and one of the most urbanized states of Brazil, and Pará, in the Amazon Valley, the least-developed region of the country.

Secondary education in Brazil encompasses a seven-year period after five years of elementary school. Five alternative courses or "branches" are offered to students at this level: the academic, the normal or teaching preparatory, the industrial, the commercial and the agricultural. The sample includes teachers from the various alternative courses in schools located in the state capital as well as in smaller urban centers. In the state capital a certain number of schools was randomly chosen out of a list of all the schools which had students in all grades in 1962. Outside the capital, where such a list would not be feasible, a certain number of towns was selected according to the following design:

1.   The towns were stratified according to the size of the 1960 urban population. Three strata were delimited:

Reproduced, by permission, from *Social and Economic Studies,* 14 (March, 1965), pp. 118–130.

    a. less than 15,000 inhabitants,
    b. 15,000 to 50,000 inhabitants, and
    c. more than 50,000 inhabitants.
  2. A certain number of towns was randomly selected in each stratum and in each town all secondary schools were included.

      In each school selected, in the state capital as well as in the chosen towns, one third of randomly selected teachers was asked to complete a questionnaire.

Following this procedure, 748 questionnaires were obtained in São Paulo and 214 in Pará. As to the official statistics used in this paper, they refer to the total teaching staff of secondary schools in the two states.[1]

HYPOTHESIS

The analysis presented in this paper started from the hypothesis that the composition of the staff of secondary schools reflects the changes in the general labor market which accompany urbanization and industrialization. More precisely, as society becomes more urbanized and industrialized, that is, as a result of competing opportunities found in the expanding secondary and especially tertiary sectors of employment, secondary school teachers tend to include: (a) a smaller proportion of males; and (b) a smaller proportion of individuals from the upper-middle class and larger proportions coming from lower origins, including families of manual workers.

    A first attempt to investigate this hypothesis was to be made by examining groups of teachers from different types of communities at a given point in time—1963. Two unequally developed states are included in our analysis, and information is available for teachers from very small towns (1,000 inhabitants) as well as from large cities, including the city of São Paulo, which has four million people.

    At the same time, as the 1963 teaching personnel included individuals who entered the occupation along a period of approximately 30–35 years, comparisons will be made between groups of teachers who started more recently and teachers who started less recently. However, in order to accept this type of test one has to accept at least one of the following assumptions: (a) the dropout rate is very small and thus might be ignored or (b) dropouts are not too few but they occur at random so that the individuals who remain in the occupation do not constitute a special group. At this point in our analysis no preference is expressed and both assumptions are tentatively accepted. Intercohort comparisons will thus be used to infer about changes in teacher social origins, and chiefly because no more direct means are available.

---

[1] Ministério da Educação e Cultura, Serviço de Estatística da Educação e Cultura, Rio de Janeiro: *O Ensino no Brasil em 1943* and *Sinopse Estatística do Ensino Médio, 1962*.

On the other hand, it will be possible to use a more direct longitudinal approach to focus on changes in sex composition, since sex distributions are found in published statistics for a period of 20 years.

Sex Composition

PROPORTIONS IN 1962

Since official records will be used to compute sex proportions in different points in time, the same source will be employed to examine the composition of contemporary groups. As 1963 statistics were not available when this paper was planned, the analysis will be based mostly on data referring to 1962. In some points, however, 1961 statistics have to be used.

The proposed theory says that the proportion of males among secondary school teachers decreases as society becomes more urbanized and industrialized. Accordingly, the proportion of male teachers is expected to be much smaller in the state of São Paulo than in Pará. As can be seen in Table 1, men represent a little over half of the total teaching staff of secondary schools, and the difference between the two states is very small. However, when attention is focused on the various types of schools, it can be seen that in general the male ratio is slightly higher in Pará than in São Paulo. The only exception is found in commercial schools, which show a difference in the wrong direction, i.e., a higher proportion of men in the more- rather than in the less-developed states.

Table 1. Male Secondary School Teachers
in Two Unequally Developed States, 1962

	Type of School					
State	Academic	Commercial	Industrial	Normal	Agricultural	Total
	%	%	%	%	%	%
Pará	55.4	67.9	80.0	36.1	88.9	56.1
São Paulo	51.2	77.9	64.9	34.4	80.6	55.8

Source: Ministério da Educação e Cultura, Serviço de Estatística da Educação e Cultura, Rio de Janeiro: *Sinopse Estatística do Ensino Médio, 1962.*

At the same time, in São Paulo as well as in Pará, as shown in Table 2, the differences between the state capital and the smaller towns do not follow a consistent direction: certain types of schools present more male teachers in schools outside the state capital, in others the percentage difference is in the opposite direction. As a matter of fact, if the total sample of secondary school teachers is considered, in both states, the difference between the capital and the smaller towns, although slight, runs contrary to what was to be expected on the basis of our theory.

From what could be seen, the comparisons among different groups of teachers at a given point in time cannot be said to support the part of our hypothesis referring to changes in sex composition.

Table 2. Male Teachers in Different Types of Communities, 1961

São Paulo

Type of Community	*Type of School*					
	Academic	*Normal*	*Commercial*	*Industrial*	*Agricultural*	*Total*
	%	%	%	%	%	%
State capital	53.4	28.2	83.4	73.9	–	59.5
Smaller towns	51.7	38.7	76.1	59.1	83.1	55.2
Total	52.0	36.5	78.3	65.5	83.1	56.6

Pará

State capital	53.3	49.6	70.9	61.1	88.9	59.4
Smaller towns	73.6	23.6	91.7	–	–	56.4
Total	59.4	36.9	69.5	61.1	88.9	58.7

Source: Ministério da Educação e Cultura, Serviço de Estatística da Educação e Cultura, Rio de Janeiro: *Ensino Médio por Município, 1961.*

SERIAL DATA STARTING IN 1943

The yearly statistics published by the Ministry of Education make it possible to trace the evolution of the teaching staff of secondary schools starting in 1943. It would not be safe to go farther back in the past because secondary schools were classified in a different way and the statistics referring to previous years would not be strictly comparable to the data for the last two decades.

As can be seen in Table 3, in 1962 the number of teachers was three

Table 3. Growth of Secondary School Teaching Personnel, 1943–1962

Year	Academic		Commercial		Industrial		Normal		General Total	
	Total	*Females*	*Total*	*Females*	*Total*	*Females*	*Total*	*Females*	*Total*	*Females*
	São Paulo									
1943	100	100	100	100	100	100	100	100	100	100
1950	159	203								
1962	322	519	284	375	203	193	611	738	319	481
	Pará									
1943	100	100	100	100	100	100	100	100	100	100
1950	199	240								
1962	383	564	285	396	59	24	285	396	297	372

Note: There were no agricultural courses of the secondary level in 1943.

Sources: Ministério da Educação e Cultura, Serviço de Estatística da Educação e Cultura, Rio de Janeiro: *O Ensino no Brasil em 1943* and *Sinopse Estatística do Ensino Médio, 1962.*

times as large as in 1943. And, incidentally, it can be seen that in this period the rate of growth was slightly greater in São Paulo than in Pará. However, the most important fact shown in the table is the part contributed by women. The observed numerical growth has resulted chiefly from the increase in the number of female teachers. At the end of two decades the number of females was almost five times as large as it was in the beginning of the period in São Paulo, and almost five times as large in Pará.

The academic schools have shown to be most vulnerable to female ambitions. In 1943 women represented less than one third of the total teaching body of schools of this type. The percentage has grown to 50 per cent in a period of two decades. The normal school rate of female expansion comes second, but the base line is here larger than in academic schools, since in 1943 more than half of normal school teachers was female. The encroachment has been much slower in commercial schools, chiefly in the state of São Paulo. As to industrial schools, the female ratio has, in fact, decreased from 1943 to 1962, as can be seen in Table 4. An explanation for such an exception might be found in the nature of the industrial courses that have grown in the last years—mechanics, land surveying, electronics, etc. The subjects taught are more appealing to male than to female students, and teachers are mostly men.

It is worth emphasizing that the differences observed in sex composition of the teaching staff of the various types of schools in São Paulo and in Pará are the same.

Table 4. Expansion of Female Participation in Secondary School Teaching, 1943-1962

	% of Female Teachers					
Year	Academic	Commercial	Industrial	Normal	Agricultural	Total
			São Paulo			
1943	30.4	16.8	36.9	54.3	–	29.3
1962	48.9	22.1	35.1	65.5	19.4	44.2
			Pará			
1943	30.3	23.1	47.5	51.7	–	35.0
1962	44.6	32.1	20.0	63.5	11.1	43.9

Sources: Ministério da Educação e Cultura, Serviço de Estatística da Educação e Cultura, Rio de Janeiro: *O Ensino no Brasil em 1943* and *Sinopse Estatística do Ensino Médio, 1962.*

It can thus be said that the examination of serial data referring to a period of 20 years clearly supports the anticipated sex composition trend, as shown both by São Paulo and Pará data. On the other hand, it should be kept in mind that the cross- or horizontal comparisons of contemporary groups of teachers have failed to show the expected results.

Social Origin
PROFILE IN 1963
Teachers in Academic Schools

The analysis will start by focusing on the sample of teachers from academic schools. Teachers in this type of school constitute by far the largest group among secondary schools in Brazil.[1]

In São Paulo, as well as in Pará, a little over half of the individuals who were teaching in academic schools in 1963 can be said to have come from the middle-middle and lower-middle classes. Using the father's occupation as a criterion to determine social origin, the occupations included under these two labels were mostly medium and small shopowners, government employees with first-level or no supervisory functions, secondary and elementary teachers, sales clerks and routine nonmanual workers in general. The remaining part of the 1963 teaching personnel was roughly equally divided between the individuals from families of manual workers on one side, and the individuals from the upper-middle class on the other. The occupations represented in this upper stratum were mostly the professionals, public administrators, managerial personnel in large companies, and owners of substantial concerns in business, agriculture and manufacturing. It thus can be seen that the occupation includes a sizable proportion of lower-mobile individuals, namely, the teachers whose fathers were ranked as upper-middle class. In my scale, which represents a modified version of the prestige scale used by Hutchinson in his studies of social mobility in Brazil,[2] secondary school teachers are ranked as middle-middle, i.e., above elementary school teachers but below the traditional professions and other occupations which require college education. This position was confirmed by the results obtained by asking the teachers in the sample their opinions about the prestige of different occupations. Secondary school teaching turned out to be ranked eleventh on a list of 18 occupations, i.e., it was ranked not only below the professions but also below the grade of laboratory technicians which, in Brazil, does not require a college education.

The extent of intergenerational mobility is seen in Table 5. Four levels are shown for fathers' occupations—one manual and three nonmanual. The suggestion is that the teachers who have ascended constitute the largest group among the mobile individuals. But the proportion of the ones who have come down is not negligible.

On the basis of the proposed theory, the proportion of teachers coming from the upper-middle class should be larger, and the proportion from the two lower classes should be smaller, in Pará than in São Paulo. However,

---

[1] As of 1962, teachers in academic schools represented 54.2 per cent of the total teaching staff of secondary schools in Pará, and 61.3 per cent in São Paulo.

[2] Bertram Hutchinson, *Trabalho e mobilidade* (Rio de Janeiro, Centro Brasileiro de Pesquisas Educacionais, 1960).

Table 5. Social Origin: Academic Teachers

Social Origin	Mobility Status	State of São Paulo		State of Pará	
		%		%	
Upper-middle	Down mobile	24.2		15.9	
Middle-middle	Stationary	31.7		26.1	
Lower-middle	Upper mobile	26.3		40.2	
Manual	Upper mobile	17.8		17.8	
Total		100.0	(281)	100.0	(107)

Source: Sample survey data.

when the percentages in the total state samples are considered no significant differences are found between the two states.

On the other hand, if instead of looking at the total state samples one focuses on the male and female subgroups, the conclusion has to be reached that Pará teachers are different from São Paulo teachers, but not exactly in the way that I had anticipated. The origins of male teachers are about the same in the two states (the percentage differences in Tables 6 and 7 would be in the expected direction were they large enough to be significant). But, surprisingly, São Paulo female teachers come from higher origins than Pará female teachers.

Table 6. Sex and Social Origin: Teachers in Academic Schools in São Paulo

Social Origin	Males		Females	
	%		%	
Upper-middle	16.2		31.7	
Middle-middle	28.7		34.5	
Lower-middle	27.2		25.5	
Manual	27.9		8.3	
Total	100.0	(136)	100.0	(145)

Source: Sample survey data.

Table 7. Sex and Social Origin: Teachers in Academic Schools in Pará

Social Origin	Males		Females	
	%		%	
Upper-middle	19.0		11.4	
Middle-middle	23.9		29.5	
Lower-middle	38.2		43.1	
Manual	19.0		15.9	
Total	100.0	(63)	100.0	(44)

Source: Sample survey data.

When one looks at the two sex groups in each state, one can see that in São Paulo female teachers come from higher origins, or more precisely, include more individuals from the upper-middle class and fewer from manual origins as compared to the male group. In Pará, there is no significant difference between the two groups.

To sum up, the three groups—Pará male, Pará female and São Paulo male—show the same social composition. São Paulo female teachers are the ones who depart from the others in that they come from higher origins.

The conclusion to be reached is that secondary school teaching is not very attractive to men from the upper-middle class in either state. Less than one fifth of male teachers in academic schools can be said to have come from that level. However, in São Paulo, for some reason, the occupation happens to be quite attractive to upper-middle class women, who represent one third of the female group.

Why should not secondary school teaching be equally attractive to Pará upper-middle class women? A first explanation would be in terms of the salary levels in the two states. Teacher salaries are lower in Pará than in São Paulo and, conceivably, low salaries could discourage Pará upper-middle class women from entering the occupation. However, were such an explanation valid, the proportion of men from that level should be lower in Pará than in São Paulo. But this is not found to be true; the suggested difference between the two states is small and not statistically significant.

In São Paulo, where the samples are large enough to allow partitions within each type of school, the data show that in all types of schools most women come from the two upper strata, namely, the upper-middle and the middle-middle, whereas most men come from the two lower strata. In all types of schools, manual origins represent one fourth of the male group whereas among female teachers manual origins reach that proportion only in commercial courses. Although in the normal and commercial courses the difference between the sexes is slight and not statistically significant, the suggestion is that the tendency prevails all over.

Teachers in Other Types of Schools

If sex composition is left aside for a moment and comparisons are made among the total samples, certain differences in social composition can be observed among teachers who represent the different types or branches of schools. The commercial type shows the larger, and the academic shows the smaller proportions of individuals from working- or manual-class families.

As can be seen in Table 8, the normal and the industrial courses are somewhere in between the two extremes, in the following order: the normal courses seem to be closer to the academic, and the industrial closer to the commercial. However, a more interesting fact is revealed by Tables 9

Table 8. Social Origin of Teachers in Different Types of Schools: São Paulo

Social Origin	Type of Schools				
	Academic	Normal	Industrial	Commercial	Agricultural
	%	%	%	%	%
Upper-middle	24.2	23.0	15.1	15.9	22.6
Middle-middle	31.7	32.4	31.4	20.6	22.6
Lower-middle	26.3	24.3	26.1	30.2	32.3
Manual	17.8	20.3	27.3	33.3	22.6
Total	100.0 (281)	100.0 (74)	100.0 (172)	100.0 (126)	100.0 (31)

Source: Sample survey data.

Table 9. Social Origin of Male Teachers in Different Types of Schools: São Paulo

Social Origin	Type of Schools				
	Academic	Normal	Industrial	Commercial	Agricultural
	%	%	%	%	%
Upper-middle	16.2	16.7	13.4	14.7	25.0
Middle-middle	28.7	20.8	26.1	18.6	16.6
Lower-middle	27.2	25.0	29.8	32.3	29.2
Manual	27.9	37.5	30.6	34.3	29.2
Total	100.0 (136)	100.0 (24)	100.0 (134)	100.0 (102)	100.0 (24)

Source: Sample survey data.

Table 10. Social Origin of Female Teachers in Different Types of Schools: São Paulo

Social Origin	Type of Schools				
	Academic	Normal	Industrial	Commercial	Agricultural
	%	%	%	%	%
Upper-middle	31.7	26.0	21.0	20.9	−(1)
Middle-middle	34.5	38.0	50.0	29.2	−(3)
Lower-middle	25.5	24.0	13.2	20.9	−(3)
Manual	8.3	12.0	15.8	29.2	−(−)
Total	100.0 (145)	100.0 (50)	100.0 (38)	100.0 (24)	100.0 (7)

Source: Sample survey data.

and 10. It refers to the part played by women in regard to the observed interbranch differences. As previously shown, male teachers come in general from lower origins as compared to female teachers. Now it can be seen that the social origin of males is about the same in all branches or types of schools and that the female teachers are the ones responsible for the observed differences.

The variation among the female groups is clearly shown by the percentages representing working-class origins in the several branches. That percentage is very small in academic courses, slightly larger in industrial and normal schools, and reaches more than one fourth in commercial schools. Teachers in agricultural courses seem to be closer to the academic and normal rather than to other vocational courses, but the sample for agricultural courses is too small to allow separate comparisons of males and females.

In Pará, from what can be seen in the total samples, the conclusion is that there are no significant interbranch differences, and the social composition of the teaching personnel as a whole is about the same presented by the total group of academic teachers in São Paulo. Thus, there is the same phenomenon seen in São Paulo but with a different manifestation; in São Paulo, where there are sex-related differences in social origin, significant differences are observed among the various types or branches of schools. In Pará, where there is no difference between the male and the female groups, there are no interbranch differences.

Teachers in Different Types of Communities

In São Paulo, where the samples are large enough to allow subpartitions, the comparisons show that in general there is no relationship between teachers' social origins and type of community in which the schools are located. The only exception is shown by the teachers of the first four grades in academic courses. This category includes smaller proportions of working-class individuals in schools located in the state capital as compared to schools located in other towns. However, in the upper grades of academic courses, as well as in all the other types of courses, there are no significant differences between teachers in the large state capital and teachers in other communities.

INTERCOHORT COMPARISONS

In São Paulo, where there is a certain number of older teachers in each branch or type of school, the samples can be divided into three categories, namely: (a) individuals who entered the occupation less than 10 years ago, (b) individuals who started 10 to 19 years ago, and (c) individuals who have been in the occupation for 20 or more years.

According to my theory, the younger as compared to the older cohorts are expected to present the following characteristics:
a. smaller percentages of individuals from the upper-middle class, and
b. larger percentages of individuals from the lower-middle and working classes.

As interbranch variations in social origin are observed, the analysis will be made by keeping the groups representing the various types of schools separate.

Table 11 presents the data on teachers in academic schools. In fact, as expected, the percentage of individuals from the upper-middle class is smaller among the teachers who have been in the occupation for less than 10 years than in the oldest group. On the other hand, although the precentages corresponding to the lower-middle and working classes seem to indicate a larger proportion of these strata in the more recent groups as compared to the oldest group, the suggested difference is small and not statistically significant. This being so, my hypothesis would be only partially confirmed.

Table 11. Changes in the Social Composition of the Teaching Staff
of Academic Schools: São Paulo

Time in Occupation	Social Origin				
	Upper-middle	Middle-middle	Lower-middle	Manual	Total
	%	%	%	%	%
Less than 10 years	20.6	31.5	29.7	18.2	100.0 (165)
10 to 19 years	25.0	32.5	22.5	20.0	100.0 (80)
20 or more years	38.9	30.6	19.4	11.1	100.0 (36)

Source: Sample survey data.

However, if the male and the female groups are examined separately, as is done in Tables 12 and 13, the anticipated trend is clearly seen in the data referring to male teachers. The two expected phenomena, namely, a significant reduction in the proportion of upper-middle class individuals and a significant expansion of the two lower strata, are seen to have taken place in a period of approximately two decades (Table 12). And it is worth noticing that the gain shown by the two lower strata has resulted chiefly from the increase in the number of teachers from families of manual workers.

Table 12. Changes in the Social Composition of Male Groups:
São Paulo, Teachers in Academic Schools

Time in Occupation	Social Origin				
	Upper-middle	Middle-middle	Lower-middle	Manual	Total
	%	%	%	%	%
Less than 10 years	11.6	24.6	30.4	33.3	100.0 (69)
10 to 19 years	12.2	36.6	24.4	26.8	100.0 (41)
20 or more years	34.6	26.9	23.1	15.4	100.0 (26)

Source: Sample survey data.

Those facts can hardly be seen in the total sample because they are disguised by the greater expansion of the female groups in which the changes,

Table 13. Changes in the Social Composition of Female Groups:
São Paulo, Teachers in Academic Schools

	Social Origin				
Time in Occupation	Upper-middle	Middle-middle	Lower-middle	Manual	Total
	%	%	%	%	%
Less than 10 years	27.1	36.4	29.2	7.3	100.0 (96)
10 to 19 years	38.5	28.2	20.5	12.8	100.0 (39)
20 or more years	50.0	40.0	10.0	–	100.0 (10)

Source: Sample survey data.

although apparently in the same direction, are far from clear (in fact, among females the intercohort differences are not statistically significant).

As to teachers in normal schools, the sample is small and the proportion of men much smaller than in academic schools. The conjunction of these two facts makes intercohort comparisons meaningless. At the same time, on the basis of intercohort comparisons no changes can be said to have occurred among teachers of commercial and industrial schools in the last decades. Those two groups, which are mostly male, included already approximately 50 per cent of teachers from working-class families 20 years ago.

From a certain point of view, the very fact that the anticipated changes are not observed in all groups of teachers represents an asset. Were the phenomenon observed both among male and female teachers and in all types of schools, the argument could be raised that it could merely reflect changes which have occurred in the structure of the total population. And no conclusion about changes in the level of recruitment sources could be reached without first discarding that hypothesis. On the contrary, if the changes are not general, but they do occur in certain groups, some conclusion can be derived without much concern about conceivable changes in the total society.

In the state of Pará, the samples are small and most teachers (65–75 per cent) entered the occupation less than 10 years ago. Consequently intercohort comparisons within branch and sex subgroups are not feasible. However, no suggestion regarding changes in social composition comes from the examination of the total sample of secondary school teachers. And apparently there is no serious objection against treating the Pará teachers as a nondiversified group since in this state, as previously shown, no significant social origin differences are found either between male and female teachers or among teachers in the various types of schools.

RESULTS FROM THE TWO APPROACHES

The attempted comparisons among contemporary groups failed to show the expected results. However, certain unanticipated facts emerged which are of some interest. For instance, besides showing the hierarchy of the different groups of teachers, from the "high" academic to the "low" commercial, and besides documenting the extent of the differences among the various groups, the analysis has served the purpose of revealing the part played by women who were shown to be entirely responsible for the observed interbranch variations. At the same time, there was no reason to expect that the difference between the male and the female teachers, observed in all types of schools in São Paulo but more markedly so in academic courses, would not be found also among Pará teachers.

Consequently, the whole picture turns out to be rather more complex than the one that I had first imagined. São Paulo teachers are in fact different from Pará teachers but not exactly in the anticipated way. They are different because they constitute a more diversified group. To start with, the male and the female subgroups show different social profiles, whereas in Pará the two profiles are about the same. Secondly, in Pará there are no interbranch variations, whereas in São Paulo significant differences among the various types of schools are observed. And this not only because the various branches have different proportions of female teachers but also because women's social origins vary from branch to branch.

As to the comparisons among groups of teachers who have entered the occupation at different points in time, they have served the purpose of unfolding the sequence of facts that have resulted in the present features of the teaching personnel in the various types of schools. In the same way, they have shown how the two subgroups—the male and the female—have departed from each other in a period of two decades. By pinpointing the differential evolution of the two subgroups, clearly seen in the largest São Paulo group—the academic—the analysis has shown how the anticipated trend, namely, the debasement in the level of recruitment sources, finds support in the data referring to the social origins of male teachers.

In Pará no change in social composition has been suggested by the comparison between older and more recent teachers. However, there is a point which is worth considering. Pará teachers are newer in the occupation as compared to São Paulo teachers. Three fourths of the individuals who were teaching in academic schools in 1963 had been in the occupation for a period of less than 10 years, whereas in São Paulo a little over half of the teachers were classified in that category. To explain this difference, the idea occurred that the teaching personnel growth might have started more recently in Pará than in São Paulo. But this hypothesis cannot be maintained, as shown by the statistics put out by the Ministry of Education. As Table 3 indicates, the growth rate was not smaller in Pará than in São Paulo in the first part of the period considered: 1943–1950; on the contrary it was even larger. It is true that the growth rates in those years are different in part because of the size difference in the numerical bases from which the two states started in 1943; the basis is smaller in Pará than in São Paulo. Nonetheless, as the growth in the more recent period was larger in that state, the proportion of the total teaching personnel which has been in the occupation for 10 years or longer in Pará should be at least as large as the proportion found in São Paulo.

If that hypothesis is thus discarded, the conclusion follows that teacher turnover is greater in Pará than in São Paulo. If one accepts this conclusion, the hypothesis might be raised that dropouts would be greater among teachers from the upper-middle class than among teachers from the lower strata. In this way, selective dropout could explain the percentages corresponding to the male teachers in Pará, or more precisely, the nonexistence of social origin differences between the more recent teachers and the older teachers *who have remained in the occupation* in this state.

At the same time the hypothesis of selective dropout would also explain the difference shown by the profiles of the female groups in the two states, namely, the smaller percentage of women from the upper-middle class in Pará as compared to São Paulo. To put it in another way: given the fact that dropouts are much more frequent in Pará than in São Paulo, the idea is that in the first state the dropouts would occur as much among men as among women, but mostly among individuals from the upper-middle class. In São Paulo, where the occupation shows higher retention indices, the male as well as the female teachers (including the ones from the upper-middle class) who started 20 or 30 years ago have remained, but the occupation has no longer been able to attract, or at least to attract in the same proportions, men from upper-middle-class families.

As plausible as it might be, the suggested interpretation is merely an ex post facto hypothesis. But it is attractive because of its heuristic value. If valid, it takes account of more than one finding, and interestingly enough, of findings which have emerged from different approaches.

Conclusions

This paper has shown the growth of female participation in secondary school teaching in the last 20 years. It has also documented the extent of the differences in social origins of individuals who teach in different types of schools. Moreover, it served the originally unintended purpose of showing how the social profiles differ from the male to the female groups. And by thus revealing sex-related differences in social origin the analysis has to a certain extent been able to indicate how the level of recruitment sources for male teachers has lowered markedly in São Paulo academic schools.

On the other hand, as interested as one might be in the substantive results, a comment should be made about a methodological point which has some theoretical implications.

The results obtained by comparing different groups of individuals who were teaching at a given point in time could be examined against longitudinal data on sex composition found in serial publications encompassing a period of 20 years. At the same time, intercohort comparisons were used as a counterpart for results derived from comparisons focusing on the social origins of contemporary groups of teachers in different communities. It happens that the findings resulting from the direct and the indirect longitudinal approaches differ from the inferences suggested by the horizontal comparisons among contemporary groups. The discrepancy between the two types of results suggests that the superimposition of the pictures presented by societies which are in different stages of development in a given historical moment does not give a fair idea of the changes that occur through time.

It seems that more and more the degree of similarity in certain aspects of social life tends to be greater than would be expected on the basis of the demographic and economic indices shown by the various national or even cross-national units. Chiefly when there are no language or political barriers to communication, ideas and practices in education (and perhaps in other areas as well) travel faster than economic development. It would not be risky to say that many of the problems which afflict Latin America today result from the fact that the changes in the structural bases of society lag behind the changes in ideas and aspirations.

Under such circumstances, the concept of *reverse* cultural lag might have some heuristic value.

Section 4:
Social and Educational Change

Introduction to Section 4

In the first selection, Leila Sussmann chronologically traces the development of the Puerto Rican educational system, showing how United States economic and political influence benefited the island by enabling early expansion of the educational system as well as national development in general. The author reveals the social and academic changes which have occurred in Puerto Rican secondary and, to some extent, university enrollment rates, resulting in both socioeconomic status parity and segregation. In her historical survey, the author suggests that educational quality at the secondary level was not sacrificed to rapid expansion of enrollment in the early decades of this century. In the 1920's public high schools were characterized as college-preparatory institutions and carried considerably more prestige than the private high schools. But following rapid expansion in the 1940's and 1950's and the advent of the comprehensive high school, this trend was reversed with the private high schools fulfilling the academic, college-preparatory function. Sussmann remarks that the quality of the public secondary schools and the universities dropped as double sessions, static per pupil expenditures, cuts in instructional time, lowered teacher quality, and general expansion transformed them into popular rather than middle and higher socioeconomic status institutions. She shows how, between 1944 and 1960, the middle classes began to withdraw to the private schools, whose quality and prestige were subsequently improved. She suggests that as a result of educational expansion, an "egalitarian ethos," and the absence of a preindustrial class structure, Puerto Rico remains an exception to the general pattern characteristic of the United States and Western Europe, where parity of enrollment at the secondary level did not occur until after the demands of the middle classes had been satisfied. At the same time, however, Sussmann remarks: ". . . the Puerto Rican case also suggests that rapid democratization of access is accompanied by segregation of the social classes into separate schools of disparate quality."

Viewing education and social change in five Caribbean societies, Joseph Farrell examines the effect education has as a broker institution in the shift from social pluralism to heterogeneity. A plural society is identified as one in which there are more than two subcultural groups which do not share basic institutions and in which there is a superordinate minority ". . . preoccupied with problems of maintenance and control and discouraging acculturation of the subordinate majority." Heterogeneous societies, on the other hand, ". . . are subject to ethnic group, class, residential, or some other form of segmentation. . . ." Viewing these two polar societal types, Farrell suggests that when institutions act in concert with one another, behavior change may result in movement in either direction.

The author asserts that under given circumstances in moving from a plural to a heterogeneous state the school is able to change values by the following means: student association with different reference groups, students acting as if they had internalized values of the superordinate group, alignment with particular status levels, association with values characteristic of specific professions, and role playing. The author also suggests that schools can be characterized as universalistic rather than particularistic and as achievement-oriented rather than ascriptive, and that they are potentially able to act as catalysts to activism rather than determinism. Schools are also seen as capable of raising student aspiration levels and promoting more favorable attitudes toward education. Farrell cautions the reader, however, not to interpret these potential outcomes as automatic simply because schools are located in subordinate areas of a plural society.

The author indicates that Haiti, because of the historical divisions between mulatto and black and the cultural differences between urban and rural areas, can be considered plural, with schools which have not served as broker institutions. Jamaica is presented as a society moving from pluralism to heterogeneity, with the schools acting in concert with other institutions in fostering integration. Because of the existence of a relatively small superordinate group of white and a small middle class of colored on the one hand and the rural Negro and East Indian on the other, Trinidad is classified as plural. Densely populated Barbados, although manifesting class and color differences, is classified as heterogeneous because all sectors, including the rural areas, share the same institutions. Puerto Rico, although colonized and therefore more likely to emerge as plural, is called heterogeneous due to the predominanlty European background of the populace throughout the island and the role of several institutions serving in concert as brokers. Farrell concludes that although schools can act as broker institutions, they alone cannot effect the requisite changes which would result in a movement from plural to heterogeneous.

The final two articles look at education in Bolivia and Cuba, societies which have experienced social, political, and economic revolutions. The article by Lambros Comitas seeks to analyze the Bolivian Revolution of 1952 and the effect the educational system has had on sustaining the revolutionary posture. Comitas remarks: ". . . every revolutionary society, to be in fact revolutionary, needs to initiate and support a revolutionary education, even if only for a relatively limited period of time." The author analyzes the traditional division between blancos and Indios in the Bolivian context, suggesting that education until the 1920's and 1930's was an urban phenomenon serving only the needs of the former while sustaining a plural society which effectively restricted social mobility.

Comitas discusses the revolution of 1952, which saw the nationalization of tin mines, the advent of universal suffrage, and considerable agrarian reform, thus weakening the power of the elite over the masses. The new Code of Education was in evidence by 1955. The urban areas, however, continued with a traditional academic curriculum which was organizationally separate from the rural system designed to educate the campesino child to adequately function in his own environment. The author reports that there were no secondary or higher education facilities built in the rural areas; thus the new code continued to foster and support the traditional social stratification.

Since 1952, evidence has indicated that enrollment rates have expanded and that the number of schools built has increased, even though the same, prerevolution problems exist, i.e., Spanish is the language of instruction and tends to divide rather than integrate the population, rote learning is indicative of the teaching-learning process, teachers are poorly trained and paid, student absenteeism and desertion rates remain high, and illiteracy rates are relatively stable. Comitas concludes: "This cursory review suggests that, in education, the revolution of 1952 and the 14 years of MNR dominance did little to modify the hierarchical order of the socially significant segments of Bolivian society and did little, if anything, to provide new, institutional forms of social articulation."

The article by Gerald H. Read views the educational system in Cuba since Castro. Read discusses the four main educational goals of the communist state, including universal, free schooling through the university; the development of a Marxist orientation; the fostering of polytechnic education; and the incorporation of the working masses into the educational system. Although the author suggests that little attention was paid to the ideological component in education until 1965, since that time an aggressive effort to express ". . . the thesis that the essence of socialist humanism is man, a free creative being, possessing the productive powers that enable him to produce for the sheer pleasure of doing so" has been evident, and drawn largely from Karl Marx. The area of polytechnic education has been in evidence since 1964, attempting in part to manifest the ideological component by combining manual and intellectual work, and the author suggests it is a central principle in all educational deliberations in Cuba. The rural populace is included in the educational effort through classes held at the place of work or in farm centers designed to both advance individuals to higher education levels as well as to provide special technical and vocational skills. There are also special programs designed for girls and women from the outlying areas who attend boarding schools and then return to their community to expand the party's influence and to teach. Rural development and increased education for the rural populace are apparent priorities. Read suggests that present projections for educational demand will most likely exceed national production. In addition, it is expected that the teaching profession will absorb more than half of the graduates from secondary and higher institutions in the future in order to meet the demand for increased schooling.

Original Sources for Selections

Sussmann, Leila. "Democratization and Class Segregation in Puerto Rican Schooling: The U.S. Model Transplanted," *Sociology of Education,* 41 (Fall, 1968), pp. 321-341.

Farrell, Joseph P. "Education and Pluralism in Selected Caribbean Socieites," *Comparative Education Review,* 11 (June, 1967), pp. 160-181.

Comitas, Lambros. "Education and Social Stratification in Contemporary Bolivia," *New York Academy of Sciences, Transactions,* Series II, 29, no. 7 (May, 1967), pp. 935-948.

Read, Gerald H. "The Cuban Revolutionary Offensive in Education," *Comparative Education Review,* 14 (June, 1970), pp. 131-143.

Democratization and Class Segregation in Puerto Rican Schooling: The U.S. Model Transplanted

LEILA SUSSMANN

The genius of American schooling is its "commitment to popular education."[1] This commitment is the essence of the U.S. model in Puerto Rico. The goal is to provide schooling for as many youths to as high a level as the economy will permit. If selection is necessary due to scarce resources, the criterion should be ability, but ability tempered by consideration for the socially caused disadvantages of lower-class homes and schools. So runs the egalitarian ethos of Puerto Rico education.

Along with the populist bent of her ideology, Puerto Rico's educational system has been shaped by rapid economic growth since World War II. The island gained semiautonomy in 1940. With the impetus provided by the war, the new government launched a successful campaign of industrialization. The rising gross Commonwealth product made greater resources available for education, and the growing literacy of the labor force was a lure for investors. It is well known that the success of the famed Operation Bootstrap owed much to Puerto Rico's unique political and economic ties to the United States. As U.S. citizens, Puerto Ricans have the right to migrate to the continent free of quota restrictions. Large numbers of young adults exercised this right in the 1940's and 1950's, thereby helping to keep population growth within manageable bounds.[2] Since the island is part of the U.S.

Reproduced, by permission, from *Sociology of Education,* 41 (Fall, 1968), pp. 321–341.

The research on which this article is based was supported by the Social Science Research Center, University of Puerto Rico, and by the U.S. Office of Education, Cooperative Research Project 1018.
[1] Lawrence A. Cremin, *The Genius of American Education* (New York: Vintage Books, 1965), chap. 1.

[2] Stanley L. Friedlander, *Labor Migration and Economic Growth: A Case Study of Puerto Rico,*

defense system, none of her budget need be spent for defense. Her integration into the U.S. tariff and monetary systems is attractive to continental investors. Because Puerto Rico has no representative in Congress, she pays no federal taxes. At the same time she received direct and indirect federal aid during the postwar period estimated by one scholar at more than $175 million a year.[1]

These economic advantages have few parallels in other developing countries and for that reason Puerto Rico's educational development is an atypical case. Nevertheless, rapid achievement of mass schooling is becoming a more influential pattern throughout the world, and its outcomes, even under special conditions, are worth study. Three of the important outcomes in Puerto Rico will be mentioned briefly here and discussed more fully below.

First, Puerto Rico has emulated the U.S. both in striving after numbers and leaving quality to take care of itself. For a country of her wealth, she has a school system characterized by high enrollment ratios and low quality. Her enrollment ratios rival those of the most industrialized nations of Europe; but indexes of school quality resemble those of less-developed countries.

Second, "equal educational opportunity," in one meaning of that phrase, is well realized in Puerto Rico. In 1960 there was an unusually close approach to equal rates of attendance at senior high school and university for youths of diverse social origins, this, despite the fact that only a third of the eligible age group was in senior high school and fewer than 8 per cent in B.A. programs at the university. The upper and upper-middle classes had nothing like the disproportionate share of selective education that their counterparts long maintained in the older industrial nations.

Third, accompanying the postwar enrollment expansion and the democratization of access to higher schooling, there appeared a sharp social-class segregation of secondary schools. The private sector of secondary education was increasingly preferred by middle-class families. By 1960, public and private high schools were different worlds, socially and academically. The private schools recruited mainly from the top-ability quintile and the higher social classes, while the public high schools had a heterogeneous social and academic composition. Social-class and ability segregation were creeping into university education as well.

As I have shown in detail elsewhere, Puerto Rico constitutes an exception to the rule that the demand of the working classes for selective education

---

The MIT Press, 1965, estimated that but for this emigration, consisting heavily of adults of child-bearing ages, Puerto Rico would have had 52 per cent more people in 1962 than she actually had, p. 49.

[1] Gordon Lewis, *Puerto Rico, Freedom and Power in the Caribbean* (New York: MR Press, 1963), p. 183.

does not begin to be met until the middle-class demand has been filled.[1] (This is the rule for the countries for which there are data, at any rate.) In Puerto Rico equality of access to senior high school for children of different social classes was closely approached while the enrollment of the upper and upper-middle classes was still under 50 per cent. My main point here is that this radical democratization of access was accompanied by social-class segregation of the high schools, in this case a cleavage between the public and private sectors. This is a new form of educational inequality since the private schools, attended exclusively by high-status youths from educationally strong families are, by virtue of that fact if no other, qualitatively superior to the heterogeneous public high schools. The academic achievement of the private school graduates is strikingly superior to that of the graduates of the public high schools.

Democratization of access has had similar consequences in the United States. Not only our neighborhood elementary schools, but also our high schools and colleges are social-class segregated and correlatively ability segregated to no small degree.

The phenomenon is old, but I suspect that segregation has sharpened as mass access to higher education has progressed. Inequality of access may be waning, only to be replaced by differential chances to get a high-quality education, which in its way is just as significant. While the educational level of the whole population has risen, the educational gap between the social classes, especially if measured by amount learned rather than years of schooling, may be as wide as ever. To prove such an assertion for the U.S. is a huge undertaking, although important fragments of documentation are at hand.[2] In the small Commonwealth of Puerto Rico, some parts of the process—democratization of access accompanied by social-class segregation of the high schools—stand out clearly.

Numbers and Quality in Puerto Rican Schooling

The economic and educational history of Puerto Rico from the American occupation to 1960 falls into three periods: 1899–1927; 1928–1940; and 1940–1960. During the first period, American investment flowed into corporate sugar plantations. Gross product and social-overhead capital

---

[1] Leila Sussmann, "Summary Review by the Rapporteur," *Social Objectives in Educational Planning* (Paris: OECD, 1968), pp. 15–27.

[2] On social-class segregation of elementary schools, cf. Robert Herriott, and Nancy St. John, *Social Class and the Urban School,* New York: Wiley, 1966; on the high schools, cf. Natalie Rogoff Ramsy, "The Clientele of Comprehensive Secondary Schools in the United States," *Social Objectives in Educational Planning* (Paris: OECD, 1968), pp. 67–83; on the colleges and universities, cf. Martin Trow, "The Democratization of Higher Education in America," *The European Journal of Sociology,* III, no. 2, 1962, pp. 249–257; and Peter Rose, "The Myth of Unanimity," *Sociology of Education,* 37, no. 2, pp. 129–149.

increased, but population grew even faster. Most of the sugar profits returned to the continent and the Puerto Rican people remained very poor.

At the time of the U.S. occupation, the population was 77 per cent illiterate. Ninety-two per cent of the children aged five to 17 were not in school. In accord with its declared intention that the people of its territories should gain full citizenship, the U.S. government began establishing a system of compulsory schooling. The goal of universal education enjoyed wide support in the island, and the growth of schooling in Puerto Rico during the first 25 years of U.S. rule was substantial. It is difficult to find a yardstick to measure just how substantial. U.S. and Puerto Rican authorities habitually made the comparison with the continental United States, and of course found Puerto Rico's school system lagging. Comparison with countries at the same level of economic development in 1925 would be more appropriate except for the fact that Puerto Rico, as a colony, was exempt from many expenses independent nations must bear. She spent 45 per cent of insular and municipal receipts on education in 1925 as compared with an average for the continental states of 28 per cent of state and local receipts. Thus, although she had a larger proportion of her population in the school-going ages than North Carolina, the state which came nearest in this respect, and she was also poorer, Puerto Rico spent as much per pupil on education in 1925 as did North Carolina.[1]

Another possible but imperfect comparison could be made with nations which had reached Puerto Rico's 1925 economic development level around 1958. This comparison is convenient because the data are readily available. It puts Puerto Rico at an advantage in the sense mentioned above. She is being compared with independent nations which could afford to spend less on education; but it puts her at a disadvantage in the sense that the emphasis on education as the route to development was worldwide in 1958, as it had not been in 1925. For example, few European nations had more than 10 per cent of the age group enrolled in secondary education in 1925; the U.S. had 25 per cent and Puerto Rico had 8 per cent.

If the comparison with nations equally developed in 1958 is made, using Harbison and Myers' tabulations of UNESCO data, Puerto Rico in 1925 falls into the range of the partially developed or Level-II countries. As compared with those countries, her elementary school enrollment was above the mean and her secondary enrollments were just at the mean.[2] Enrollments in higher education cannot be compared because there are no data on how many Puerto Ricans were receiving higher education abroad. Harbison and Myers include those students in their reports on Level-II countries.

---

[1] *A Survey of the Public Educational System of Porto Rico* (New York: Bureau of Publications, Teachers College, Columbia University, 1926), chap. VIII, "Financing Public Education in Porto Rico."

[2] Frederick Harbison and Charles A. Myers, *Education, Manpower and Economic Growth* (New York: McGraw-Hill, 1964).

Puerto Rico was a little below the Level-II mean in teacher/pupil ratios. This stood not so much for very large classes as for double sessions: a three-hour school day which allowed one teacher and classroom to serve two groups of pupils, morning and afternoon. Half-time schooling at the elementary level has been Puerto Rico's characteristic means for raising school enrollments within the limits of her resources. In 1925 the short school day was partly compensated for by a long school year: 180 days as compared with North Carolina's 139 days and an average for the continent of 164 days.[1] Puerto Rico's per pupil expenditure in elementary education in 1925 was more than three times that of the Latin American partially developed countries in 1958.[2] As a result the teachers were, on this comparison, well paid, well trained, and of high caliber. An investigation by a team of educators from Teachers College found that students going into elementary teaching were above the academic average of high school graduates and equal in academic quality to freshmen entering the liberal arts courses at the University of Puerto Rico at the time.[3] The holding power of the Puerto Rican schools was well above the Level-II average: fourth-grade pupils on the island were 45 per cent as many as first-grade pupils while the Level-II mean was 18 per cent as many.

The most striking indication that the quality of Puerto Rico's schools in 1925 was high for a country with so little wealth comes from the results of Stanford Achievement Tests administered by the investigators from Teachers College. The tests, translated as literally as possible from the English, were given to over 10,000 children in grades two through 12, chosen to represent all geographical areas of the island. There were examinations in Spanish, English and arithmetic, and also in science, history and literature. Since the latter three subjects were not taught at all in the Puerto Rican elementary schools—the time was devoted instead to teaching English—the children did very poorly in them. However, in the language and arithmetic tests they were close to, and sometimes above, the U.S. continental norms. In arithmetic computation and reasoning the children in the first four grades surpassed the continental children even on some tests administered in English. They also did better in the early grades on the Pinter nonlanguage mental-ability tests. U.S. children overtook and slightly surpassed the Puerto Rican pupils at grades seven, eight, and nine.[4]

Rough though these comparisons are, they support the view that mass

---

[1] Teachers College, *Survey of the Public Educational System*, p. 406.

[2] Puerto Rico spent $50 (in 1958 U.S. dollars) as compared with Bolivia: $6; Brazil: $10; Ecuador: $12; Guatemala: $17; Paraguay: $5; Peru: $14; for the Latin American data, cf. *Conference on the Financing of Education for Economic Growth*, Paris: OECD, 1960, "Financial Aspects of the Educational Expansion in Developing Regions," p. 13.

[3] Teachers College, *Survey of the Public Educational System*, pp. 296–298.

[4] *Ibid.*, chap. III, "Measurement of Results of Instruction."

expansion of schooling at whatever cost to quality was *not* the educational policy of Puerto Rico in 1925. There was great pressure from the urban areas for faster growth of secondary education, but the Teachers College consultants recommended giving first priority to universal elementary education of high quality.

Any debate which might have arisen concerning priorities was stilled by the world depression which reached Puerto Rico in 1928. The island went into an economic decline lasting until 1940 which brought the growth of elementary school enrollment ratios to a halt. The same was true of changes in holding power and double sessions. Pupil/teacher ratios became even less favorable than they had been. The urban-rural gap in school facilities, always large, grew larger. According to Education Commissioner José Gallardo in 1943, ". . . the existing differences in available facilities in the urban and rural zones of each municipality . . . are almost incredible." Only the senior high schools gained ground; their enrollment ratio went from 8 per cent of the age group in 1925 to 23 per cent in 1947 while their pupil/teacher ratio remained at 30. Thus the urban demand for higher secondary schooling remained strong and effective, despite U.S. expert opinion.

The next distinct phase of educational growth dates from World War II to 1960. Wartime investment stimulated a spurt of economic development. Puerto Rico drew immense vitality from her newly won autonomy and from the brilliance of her first elected governor, Luis Muñoz Marín. He and his lieutenants initiated Operation Bootstrap which raised the Puerto Rican Commonwealth's gross product from $391,105,000 in 1940 to $1,878,000,000 in 1962 and per capita income from $213 to $680.

With increased financial resources at their disposal and the growth rate of the school-age population declining, the Puerto Rican government in 1950 set new school enrollment goals to be reached by 1960. The goals were reached before the target date. A few statistics will convey just how great an expansion of school attendance was compressed into a decade. In 1950, 72.5 per cent of the six- to 12-year olds were enrolled in elementary school, and in 1960, 82.6 per cent.[1] In 1950, 32.4 per cent of the 13- to 15-year olds were enrolled in junior high school and in 1960, 52.9 per cent. In 1950, 17.6 per cent of the 16- to 18-year olds were enrolled in senior high school and in 1960, 32.1 per cent. The proportion of high school seniors going on to a bachelor of arts college program did not rise during the decade. On the contrary, it fell slightly, but the proportion of the college-age group entering a four-year college course did increase. Eighteen years was the modal age of University of Puerto Rico freshmen. Enrollment in the freshman year of a B.A. program as a proportion of 18-year olds was

---

[1] The statistics come from the annual reports of the Commissioner of Education, published in Hato Rey, Puerto Rico.

2.7 per cent in 1945, 5.6 per cent in 1952, and 8.6 per cent in 1960. If the college-age group is defined as 18- to 21-year olds inclusive (as Puerto Rican official statistics define it), the number attending a college or university in 1960, including two-year curricula, was 16 per cent of the age group. Using 20- to 24-year olds as the college-age group, the proportion, including two-year curricula, was about 12 per cent.

Contemplating these school enrollments in 1960, Puerto Rican officials found them too low, but the United Nations Yearbook called them unusually high for a country of Puerto Rico's income. A comparison with Harbison and Myers' cross-national data for the same period bear out the UN interpretation. By 1960 Puerto Rico belonged economically either at the top of their Level-III range, the semiadvanced countries, or at the bottom of their Level-IV range, the advanced countries. Her GNP per capita was midway between the Level-III and Level-IV means. Her percentage of population engaged in agriculture was at the mean of Level IV. But her proportion of population in the school-going age cohorts was still as high as that of *any* semiadvanced country. Puerto Rico had not attained the low birth rate of the most industrialized nations. Nevertheless, her school enrollment ratios equaled the mean of Level IV, the advanced countries.

Data collected by the OECD from its member nations (all of them Level IV by Harbison and Myers' yardsticks) calculate school enrollment ratios in a different way from UNESCO, which favors Puerto Rico even more.[1] By this method of calculation her school enrollment ratios were equal to those of the most-advanced industrial countries in the world excepting only Canada and the U.S.

On indexes of quality, however, Puerto Rico did not match the Level-IV countries. Both her recurrent per pupil expenditures and her pupil/teacher ratios were inferior to theirs, despite the fact that she was still spending a higher proportion of GNP on education—5 per cent—than any of the advanced countries. These resources were spread wide and thin. For five of the years between 1947 and 1957 the proportion of all elementary pupils on double session rose to an unprecedented 75 per cent. The pupil/teacher ratio went up to 60. There were no substitute teachers in the elementary

[1] The OECD data come from *Targets for Education in Europe in 1970: Policy Conference on Economic Growth and Investment in Education,* Paris: OECD, 1962. The UN data used by Harbison and Myers calculate school enrollment ratios by dividing the number enrolled in school *at a given level* by the total number in the age groups considered broadly eligible for that level. The OECD enrollment ratios divide the total number of children of an age group enrolled in school *at any level* by the total number in the age group. Since the UN includes ages five and six in its elementary (unadjusted) age group, Puerto Rico, where children tend not to enter school before age seven, is at a disadvantage in those comparisons. On the other hand, the general tendency toward overageness in the Puerto Rican school system gives it an advantage in the OECD 15- to 19- and 20- to 24-year comparisons, since in the island many 15- to 19-year olds are in school at lower than the appropriate level and many more 20- to 24-year olds than in the more advanced countries are still in the process of obtaining their first degree in higher education.

schools. That fact, plus the high rate of teacher absences (due to low morale) left classes uncovered to an extent of 5 per cent loss in the children's instructional time. Holidays were frequent. According to a report of the Superior Council of Education, the school year, subtracting teacher absences and holidays, lasted seven months. This is more than a month shorter than the school year of 1925.

The low morale among teaching staff contributed to an acute teacher shortage. A government planning report said that from 1955 to 1958 teachers had been leaving their jobs twice as fast as they were being trained.[1] It was difficult for the school system to compete with the private sector for educated personnel. In contrast to 1925 the teaching profession was not recruiting outstanding people. Students at the College of Education of the University of Puerto Rico had the lowest entrance examination scores of any freshmen in the University.[2]

> In order to staff classrooms the standards for *normalista* training are distressingly low. For example one professor found that his *normalista* class had a third-grade-level reading proficiency in Spanish and a second-grade-level reading proficiency in English. Math and science teachers in the public schools frequently have never taken these subjects in college, and many English teachers cannot speak English.[3]

The high schools, too, underwent great changes between 1950 and 1960. In the 1920's the public high schools of Puerto Rico had been college-preparatory institutions. Their curriculum was academic, offering English, Spanish, history, mathematics, French, Latin, science, and some home economics and manual training. They were located in the large cities and had room for only 8 per cent of the age group. They recruited meritocratically, on the basis of elementary school grades. After a probationary first year, adjustments were made. The competitive places in these public high schools were highly prized. They were the training ground for those who would go abroad to universities and return to the best positions in government, the professions, and commerce. The private high schools were patronized by students who had failed to gain acceptance in the public.

By the 1950's the public high schools were enrolling nearly a third of the age group. Commercial and vocational schools had been built to meet a growing demand. Graduates of these nonacademic curricula increased by 78 per cent in the 1940's as compared with a 121 per cent increase in

---

[1] Beresford Hayward, "The Future of Education in Puerto Rico, Its Planning," Department of Education (October 6, 1961), mimeo.

[2] Leila Sussmann, *High School to University in Puerto Rico*, final report of Cooperative Research Project No. 1018 (Washington: U.S. Office of Education), pp. 64–73.

[3] William H. Knowles, "Manpower and Education in Puerto Rico," *in* Harbison and Myers, eds., *Manpower and Education: Country Studies in Economic Development* (New York: McGraw-Hill, 1965), p. 116. "*Normalista* training" refers to a two-year college course leading to a diploma in elementary school teaching.

graduates of the college-preparatory course. In the 1950's the tables were turned; commercial and vocational graduates increased by 196 per cent as compared with an 85 per cent growth in college-preparatory graduates.[1] At this point Puerto Rico implemented a long-standing U.S. recommendation for comprehensive high schools. The college-preparatory course was dropped, leaving the general curriculum as the sole academic course of study. A few metropolitan high schools offered all three curricula: general, commercial, and vocational, and many offered the general and commercial courses. Rural high schools offered *only* the general curriculum. The academic requirements of the general curricula were actually a bit lower than those of the commercial and vocational; however, the general course left room for many electives, while the other two curricula were filled up with special, nonacademic requirements. In effect the college-preparatory curriculum became informal. Able, college-oriented students in the general curriculum were encouraged to take many academic electives while the others were encouraged to select easier courses. My 1960 sample survey of Puerto Rican high school seniors showed that the general curriculum attracted the most-able and least-able students while the other two curricula drew from the middle of the ability range.[2]

This transformation of the Puerto Rican public high school differed in several ways from the shift to the mass terminal high school which had occurred in the U.S. a generation before. Although most Puerto Rican high school graduates of the 50's did not go to college, a majority were *oriented* to going there. Fifty-eight per cent of all high school seniors in my 1960 survey said they planned to go to college. This was slightly higher than the proportion of high school seniors who had said they had college plans in the U.S. ETS survey of 1955. However, the proportion of Puerto Rican students actually entering college the following autumn was lower than in the U.S.[3] Furthermore, in Puerto Rico the difference in college plans among students in the different curricula was very slight. Commercial and vocational students had college plans almost as frequently as general curriculum students, but the rates of actual college *entry* differed sharply among planners from the different curricula. In short, the high school became a mass institution which was de facto terminal for most of its graduates, but it

---

[1] Sussmann, *High School to University*, p. 9.

[2] *Ibid.*, p. 97. The survey was based on a random sample of Puerto Rican high schools stratified by public or private control and by size. In the case of each of the 14 high schools in the sample, the entire senior class (with the exception of a few who could not be reached) filled out a paper-and-pencil questionnaire. The sample included 10 per cent of Puerto Rico's 139 high schools and high school seniors. For a detailed description of its selection, cf. *High School to University*, Appendix B.

[3] The U.S. college plans data come from *Background Factors Relating to College Plans and College Enrollment among Public High School Students,* Princeton, N.J.: Educational Testing Service, 1957. The Puerto Rican data come from Sussmann, "Summary Review," p. 97.

continued to be defined by its clientele as a college-preparatory institution. There was constant public pressure to make reality match this definition. Recalling Martin Trow's description of the two transformations of the U.S. high school, first from a select, college-preparatory academy to a mass terminal institution; and then to a mass college-preparatory institution,[1] it looks as though Puerto Rico telescoped these two transformations into one.

In all the public high schools in 1957–1958 there were only five qualified physics teachers. Five hundred mathematics teachers were needed but only 39 were qualified. The social studies, best supplied of the academic subjects, had 384 qualified teachers for 564 positions.[2] It is not surprising that under these conditions, student achievement declined:

> A large company that hires only high school graduates reported that it rejects 70 percent of job applicants due to failure to pass a simple test in mathematics and mechanics designed for ninth graders. The Vocational Rehabilitation and Education Division's new technical school, selecting high school graduates with at least a B average, requires three years for a two year training course in order to overcome deficiencies in mathematics, Spanish, and English.[3]

The University of Puerto Rico was also in trouble qualitatively. One of its most sympathetic consultants, Rexford Guy Tugwell, called it "little more than a junior college." Not much upper college work was offered since, due to the students' poor preparation, it took the better part of four years to cover the work of freshman and sophomore level. In a report on the University of Puerto Rico written in 1959, Frank Bowles estimated that many freshmen arrived at the U.P.R. with a deficiency of a whole grade level in terms of preparation.[4] One could never discover this fact from looking at admissions records. My analysis of these showed that freshmen entering the U.P.R. in 1960 had many *more academic credits* in their high school records than entrants of 1952 or 1944;[5] yet their professors found these groups of freshmen successively less prepared.

Except that it deluged the students with a plethora of introductory courses, the university made no institutional effort to overcome their

---

[1] Martin Trow, "The Second Transformation of American Secondary Education," *The International Journal of Comparative Sociology*, II, no. 2 (September, 1961).

[2] Hayward, "Future of Education in Puerto Rico."

[3] Knowles, "Manpower and Education," p. 118.

[4] Frank Bowles, "Preliminary Report on Certain Aspects of the Study of Institutions of Higher Learning," Superior Council on Education (University of Puerto Rico, 1959), mimeo. Another reason there was virtually no upper college work was the serious lack of articulation within the university program. The first two years were spent in the College of General Studies, where all students were presumably introduced to world culture. During the second year, students entered one of the five colleges in which they would major and there, because the work in General Studies was not trusted as a foundation, they were put through another battery of courses introductory to their major fields.

[5] Sussmann, *High School to University*, pp. 22–24.

academic deficiencies.[1] Many students handled the problem by registering for an overload of courses and then withdrawing just before final examinations from those they thought they would fail. The U.P.R. permitted such overloads and withdrawals without penalty. The courses dropped could then be repeated and passed another year, or the student could keep taking new courses until he had, by trial and error, passed a sufficient number to graduate. This was often a long, discouraging process. A majority of entrants never obtained a degree. My data, compiled from individual records of all students who entered as freshmen at the Rio Piedras campus in 1952, show that 33 per cent obtained a B.A. within four years; 13 per cent obtained one within eight years; and 54 per cent had not obtained a degree by 1960.[2]

Toward the end of the 1950's, talk of a "crisis of quality" in the schools led to a round of evaluations by Puerto Rican educators and outside consultants. The Superior Council on Education administered tests in arithmetic, Spanish and English to 32,942 pupils in grades four, six, nine, and 12. Unfortunately, the published results contained no bench mark comparisons with any outside group or previous period, so that the overall scores are very difficult to interpret. Important internal comparisons were made, however. Urban students did consistently better than rural, and students on single session did consistently better than those on double session in every subject. The report furnished a few illustrations of what is described as the "very unsatisfactory situation." In the fourth grade 57 per cent of the pupils answered the problem of "16 minus 7" incorrectly; 59 per cent could not multiply 9 by 8. Nineteen per cent in the sixth grade and 13 per cent in the ninth grade could not subtract 31 from 60; 81 per cent in the sixth grade and 77 per cent in the ninth grade could not divide 3/4 by 6/12.[3] A team of European consultants reported that in many fourth grades they visited 20 per cent to 50 per cent of the pupils could not read.[4]

Nearly all observers agreed that achievement levels were down since 1940.

---

[1]With the possible exception of the College of Engineering at Mayagüez, a campus on the west coast of Puerto Rico, separate from the main campus at Rio Piedras. Although engineering students have the highest entrance examination scores on the average of any students at the university, this college requires five years for its B.S. degree.

[2]As Frank Bowles has pointed out, the university has no statistics on this and other important topics. It was necessary to go back to individual records to tabulate these data; cf. Bowles, "The High Cost of Low Cost Education," in Seymour Harris, ed., Higher Education in the United States: The Economic Problems (Cambridge, Mass.: Harvard University Press, 1960), p. 200.

[3]Ismael Rodriguez-Bou, "Evaluation: Results of the Examinations Administered in Several Areas to Several Grade Levels in the School System," Superior Council on Education (University of Puerto Rico, 1958), mimeo.

[4]"The Educational System in Puerto Rico: Recommendations and Suggestions" by Christian Casselmann, Professor of Education, University of Heidelberg, Alberto Borghi, Professor of Education, University of Florence, Italy and Morten Bredsdorff, President, Teachers' College, Vordinborg, Denmark (May, 1959), mimeo.

The increase in double sessions, the lowered quality of teaching personnel, the cuts in instructional time all contributed to the decline. However, part of it was due to the fact that the expanded school system had finally reached the most disadvantaged sector of the child population, those "first generations" to attend school who need a *higher* investment of instructional resources to attain the achievement levels of children whose parents have been schooled. But Puerto Rico's investment per elementary school pupil was virtually unchanged in 1960 from what it had been in 1925: $56 per year as compared with the earlier $50.[1]

The huge effort of the 1950's attained its goals. Nearly every Puerto Rican child had his "chance at school." The high schools were transformed from elite to popular institutions, and the same was true of the university. The price was a decline in quality throughout the system. Half-time schooling plagued the elementary schools. The high school students who were university bound took more academic courses than their predecessors and apparently learned less. The university had a huge dropout problem and lacked a true upper college. Many Puerto Rican educators said that the 1950's having been the decade of expansion, the 1960's must become the decade of quality improvement. But popular pressure for still further expansion of high school and university places was very strong. Slowing down the growth in favor of raising the academic standards could prove politically difficult for a popularly elected government.

Egalitarian Policy

Behind the expansion of the Puerto Rican school system in the 1950's was a passionate concern for equal educational opportunity. Frank Bowles' 1959 report on higher education claimed ". . . Puerto Rico has accepted and tried to meet the need for expansion without recognizing that standards have been lowered in the process. Thereby the lowered standards have become embedded in and have affected all tax supported education in the Island."

If the educators gave too little thought to quality, it was because of their overriding devotion to equity. They wanted as nearly as possible to "equalize" educational chances. The spirit in which they made policy is well expressed in the following quotation:

> At the present time there are 7 towns with first grades organized in single sessions (a six-hour school day) and 10 with second grades organized (in single sessions). The total number of children in these grades on single sessions reached 8209 last year. There were also 12,106 in these three grades on interlocking sessions (a five-hour school day) which makes a total of 20,315. That is to say that by organizing all the first, second, and third grades on double sessions (a three-hour day) it would be possible to make room for 20,315 new pupils next year. In this way,

[1] In 1958 U.S. dollars.

the opportunities of those now in the first three grades would be equalized and at the same time opportunity would be increased for 20,000 of those who are not in school. Why should 664 first grade students have a double opportunity, that is to say a complete day of classes when all the rest who are 74,499 have to make do with a half day? Why should one-fourth of those in third grade receive a full day while three-quarters receive only a half day? [1]

One can point to many educational policies of the 1950's which sacrificed quality to equity, at times with awareness of the price. An instance was the continued practice of giving preference to children past the normal school-entry age over those who had just reached it, in admissions to first grade. The Teachers' College report criticized this practice in 1925, pointing out that overage children had a high dropout rate, whereas younger children tended to remain in school longer, and thus to be a better investment risk. The Puerto Rican educators knew the facts, but they felt it unjust to children who were originally excluded from school for lack of space to deprive them altogether of their chance to get an education. Hopefully, with further expansion, the younger children could be accommodated a year or two later. However, expansion never quite caught up with the need. Overage entrants continued to receive preference, and as a consequence the Puerto Rican school system has unusually large numbers of students who are older than the proper age for their grade level.

The rejection of any form of ability grouping in the elementary schools also had an egalitarian rationale. In particular, separating more-able pupils from the others so that they could have an enriched curriculum or go through the regular one faster was considered a kind of an unacceptable elitism.

The college-preparatory curriculum was dropped in the 1950's and the general, commercial, and vocational curricula incorporated into comprehensive high schools in order to guarantee what the British call "parity of esteem" for all three courses of study. To the same end, the Superior Council on Education dropped *all specific subject requirements* for entry to the University of Puerto Rico. In theory, this opened the way to the university for graduates of any of the three high school curricula. They were all made eligible, that is, to take the university entrance examination. No doubt this formal equality of chances to enter the university supported the heavy college orientation which I described above. But, as I pointed out, the facts were at variance with the doctrine. Competition for university entry was becoming more intense because the proportion of high school graduates who applied for admission grew, while the proportion of graduates admitted remained the same. As a result, the number of high school academic credits

---

[1] Pablo Roca quoted in I. Rodriguez-Bou, *La doble matrícula en las escuelas de Puerto Rico* (December 17, 1950), pp. 11-12, mimeo. The translation from the Spanish is mine.

on the records of entering freshmen at the U.P.R. rose steadily, *after* the formal requirements for academic courses were dropped. Graduates of the commercial and vocational curricula lost out on the entrance examination for lack of this academic preparation. My data show that in 1960 their entrance examination performance was poorer than that of graduates of the general curriculum even with ability test scores held constant.[1]

In the 1950's too, an island-wide competitive entrance examination became for the first time part of the University of Puerto Rico admissions procedure. Prior to that, entrance had been based on high school grades. However a study by the Superior Council on Education in 1948 demonstrated that a graduation index of "B" from a small (usually rural or small town) public high school was predictive of about the same univeristy performance as a grade of "C" from a large (usually metropolitan) high school. The entrance examination was intended to correct for these differences in high school standards. However the policy adopted was actually a compromise. The high school graduation index and the entrance examination score were given equal weight and averaged to form the admissions index. Using the entrance examination alone would have been more purely meritocratic, but it would have penalized the rural as compared with the urban applicants and the public school as compared with the private school applicants. For instance, the entrants to the College of Education in 1960 had scored second in their entering class on the basis of high school graduation indexes, but last on the basis of their entrance examination scores. They consisted disproportionately of girls from rural and small town high schools. Had admission to the university been based on the entrance examination alone, some of them would not have been admitted. Thus the meritocratic principle was tempered with the populist one, keeping the road to the university open for a good many youths whose homes and earlier schooling had left them academically disadvantaged.[2]

Equality of Access

The extent to which youths of different social origins gain access to senior high school and university education is only partly a matter of social policy. Aspirations to higher education have diffused far more rapidly to every social stratum in U.S. and Puerto Rican society[3] than in European. In the

---

[1] Sussmann, *High School to University*, pp. 138–141.

[2] Another possible reason for using high school grades as part of the basis for admission was that the College of Education would have had difficulty recruiting students if rural and working-class girls had been excluded from the University of Puerto Rico. In the cities the most able *public* high school girls took the commercial curriculum and thus were siphoned off early from the pool of potential teachers. Girls who attended private high schools entered the College of Humanities at the university rather than the College of Education.

[3] For detailed data on the diffusion of education aspirations in Puerto Rico, cf. Melvin Tumin

U.S., high enrollment ratios have been cause and consequence of the diffusion. However, the relationship between the enrollment ratio in secondary or higher education and parity of attendance rates as between the social strata is not a simple one. Expansion of the enrollment ratio is not necessarily associated with increased parity. Within limits total enrollment and parity of access for the different social stata can vary independently. For instance, a doubling of places in British grammar schools from 12 per cent to 23 per cent of the age group resulted in only a small reduction of social-class differentials in rates of attendance. Of course when enrollment approaches 100 per cent, as in the U.S. high school, it is self-evident that social-class differentials decline. In fact when the enrollment from the upper social strata approaches saturation, further expansion can only come from below and *must* result in some equalization of social-class attendance rates.

The evidence is that the expansion of selective education in Europe has not so far been associated with a decline of social-class differentials in access. The upper and upper-middle classes have continued to receive a disproportionate share of the new places. In the U.S., access to high school education for children of the manual strata seems to have leveled up only after the attendance rate of the nonmanual strata was close to its ceiling. Something similar appears to be true in higher education. Expansion since 1947 has been associated with some equalization of attendance rates between the manual and nonmanual classes. However, the equalization set in at a point when 78 per cent of nonmanual sons and 66 per cent of nonmanual daughters who graduated from high school were attending college; for the professional and technical classes the percentages were 83 and 78. Thus the U.S. is no exception to what has been the rule: substantial room in selective schools is made only after the demand of the nonmanual strata has been filled.

It is striking, therefore, that Puerto Rico *is* an exception to the rule. On the island only 32 per cent of the age group was attending high school in 1960, as compared with 87 per cent in the U.S. Yet, if the parity ratio of the two sets of high school seniors are put side by side, it is clear that parity of access was as far advanced in Puerto Rico as in the U.S. with the exception of children of farm laborers. It was much farther advanced than in Bridgeport, Connecticut, or Seattle, Washington, at the time (1930) when only 30 per cent of *their* youths were in high school. And this parity of access was achieved despite the fact that the nonmanual classes in Puerto Rico still had an attendance rate in the twelfth grade of less than 50 per cent. Recruitment to the prestigeful status of high school senior in Puerto Rico was radically democratic.[1]

and Arnold Feldman, *Social Class and Social Change in Puerto Rico* (Princeton, N.J.: Princeton University Press, 1961), especially chaps. 3, 4 and 7.

[1] Sussmann, "Summary Review," p. 21.

Recruitment to the status of college freshman was less so. Still, a comparison of parity ratios for freshmen at the University of Puerto Rico in 1960, when 8.6 per cent of the age cohort were entering B.A. programs, with freshmen in the U.S. which had 20 per cent of the age cohort entering them, suggests that Puerto Rico will also achieve parity of access to higher education at an earlier stage of growth of universities than the United States. Recruitment to higher education there is already more democratic than it is in European countries with similar enrollment ratios.[1] Puerto Rico's mass education system clearly follows the U.S. pattern and, in some ways, is outrunning its model. In particular, the Commonwealth has admitted large numbers of urban working-class youths to the privilege of higher schooling at a time when more than half the offspring of the middle classes are still denied it.

Social-Class Segregation

Equal access is not the whole of equal educational opportunity. If high schools and colleges were alike in quality and prestige, it would be. But that situation is most nearly approached in countries where access is severely exclusive. In the U.S. the secondary schools and the colleges and universities are extremely diverse in curricula, in the social and ability composition of their clientele, and in the prestige of their diplomas. Mass extension of higher schooling has been accompanied by internal differentiation. A nonselected mass student population with a wide range of preparation, capacity, and occupational aspirations can only be served by a diversity of educational offerings. The diversity is not random, however. In high schools and colleges, as well as elementary schools, the social and academic composition of the student body varies sharply from institution to institution and quality is positively correlated with the presence of a high proportion of high SES students. Thus: "Educational inequalities linked to social class differences are not wiped out by the growth of mass higher education, but find their expression in the internal differentiation of the system."[2] Unequal access to high school and university is replaced by unequal access to schooling of high quality.

In the U.S. social-class segregation in education is masked by the size and heterogeneity of our school systems. Although it exists to a considerable degree, it has not been the socially visible irritant that racial segregation has become. The more socially visible fact has been the overall expansion. In Puerto Rico, the expansion and democratization of high school education and the withdrawal of the middle classes to private high schools were pretty much compressed into a space of 15 years. Between 1944 and 1960 the public and private sectors expanded with equal speed but their relative

---

[1] *Ibid.,* pp. 17 and 19.
[2] Martin Trow, "Democratization of Higher Education," p. 239.

prestige was abruptly reversed. The private high schools, largely Catholic, became the prestige institutions where formerly they had been receivers for the public high school rejects. Whereas in 1944, U.P.R. freshmen were 84 per cent public school graduates and 16 per cent private school graduates, in 1960 they were 69 per cent from the public and 31 per cent from the private high schools.[1] The two groups of high school students were becoming mutually hostile and the existence of private schools was a potential political issue.[2]

In 1960 the private and public high schools catered to very distinct clienteles. The social composition of public and private high school seniors in my 1960 sample is shown in Table 1. The socioeducational index used to classify students in the table is a combination of father's occupation and education.[3] More than half of the private high school seniors and less than a fifth of the public came from the top two SES strata. Data which indicate the trend toward increasing difference in the social composition of public and private high schools between 1944 and 1960 are shown in Table 2, which gives the social composition of University of Puerto Rico entrants from the public and private sectors.

Table 1. Socioeducational Status of Public and Private High School Seniors in Puerto Rico, 1960

SES Stratum		Public	Private	Total
		%	%	%
I	(High)	8	28	11
II		10	25	12
III		16	23	17
IV		29	12	26
V		25	12	23
VI	(Low)	12	—	11
N (100%)*		(1,279)	(251)	(1,530)

*A few cases where socioeducational status could not be determined are omitted from the table.

High school seniors in my 1960 sample were given a group ability test. The results for the public and private sectors are shown in Table 3. Fifty-nine per cent of the private high school seniors scored in the top quintile. Private high school students scored higher in every subject than the public school seniors in the achievement tests administered by the Superior Council on Education in 1959. The graduates of private high schools showed

---

[1] Sussmann, *High School to University*, p. 39.

[2] Lewis, *Puerto Rico*, p. 464.

[3] For a detailed discussion of how the index was constructed, see Sussmann, *High School to University*, Appendix C.

Table 2. Occupations of Fathers of Public and Private High School Graduates Admitted to the U.P.R. at Rio Piedras

Occupation of Student's Father	Public			Private Catholic			Other Private		
	1944 %	1952 %	1960 %	1944 %	1952 %	1960 %	1944 %	1952 %	1960 %
Professionals, semiprofessionals and higher white-collar	30	20	18	33	34	50	37	48	69
Lower white-collar	6	11	15	6	10	13	7	13	10
Retail proprietors	22	20	16	31	30	17	30	19	10
Manual workers	23	23	32	18	9	10	11	2	5
Farm owners and managers	12	11	8	10	7	5	9	2	1
Farm laborers and farm foremen	1	1	2	–	–	–	–	–	1
Other	6	14	9	2	10	5	6	16	4
Total	100%	100%	100%	100%	100%	100%	100%	100%	100%
	(N = 542)*	(N = 907)	(N = 1,148)	(N = 51)	(N = 143)	(N = 390)	(N = 54)	(N = 95)	(N = 138)

*This table is not based on a sample, but includes all entrants at Rio Piedras, U.P.R.

Table 3. Ability Distribution of Public and Private High Schools Seniors,
in Puerto Rico, 1960

Ability Quintile	Public	Private
	%	%
Top	19	59
Second	21	13
Third	20	13
Fourth	19	7
Bottom	21	8
(N = 100%)	(1,312)	(253)

increasing superiority between 1944 and 1960 on the University of Puerto Rico entrance examination and in grade indexes at the end of the freshman year. In 1960, private school entrants to the U.P.R. scored higher on the entrance examination than the public school entrants, even with ability held constant, a fact which suggests that they were not only a more-able group but had received superior high school training.

The pattern of academic and social segregation of high school students obtained in 1960 had the effect of canceling out the correlation between social class and ability *within* the private schools on the one hand and *within* the general curriculum of the public high schools on the other, although there was such a correlation for high school seniors as a whole. However, the correlation between students' SES and ability reappeared at the university, where public and private school graduates were merged into one student body. As late as 1944, there was no correlation between father's occupation and entrance examination scores among freshmen entering the U.P.R. However, by 1952, a correlation had appeared and in 1960, it had become stronger (Table 4). The same was true of grades at the end of the freshman year (Table 5).

Using these data to hypothesize about the past, I would surmise that prior to the 1950's the correlation between social class and measured ability was screened out at the public senior high school level by a selective and meritocratic admissions policy. The expansion of secondary education allowed the correlation to appear in the high school population as a whole; but the segregation of public and private sectors eliminated it within each sector. However, the state university, which kept itself accessible to the graduates of all high schools, was then faced with the problem of handling the gap between its socially and academically superior and inferior students. Already in 1960 there were distinct patterns of recruitment to the several colleges on the main campus of the U.P.R. at Rio Piedras. The colleges of natural science and humanities recruited, respectively, the boys and girls

Table 4. Occupational Status of Students' Fathers and Mean Examination Score
by Year, University of Puerto Rico at Rio Piedras

Occupational Status of Students' Fathers	Mean Entrance Examination Scores		
	1944–1945	1952–1953	1960–1961
Professional, proprietary and executive	238	137	170
Semiprofessional and higher white-collar	236	129	161
Lower white-collar	248	128	157
Small business	228	122	151
Skilled labor	239	121	146
Semi- and unskilled labor	230	117	143
Farmer	213	111	145
Farm laborer	—*	—*	138

*Fewer than 10 cases.

of highest social status and academic ability. The College of Education
recruited the lowest-status, least-able girls. The colleges of business, pharmacy and social sciences recruited the least-able boys and also the mid-
dling-ability groups of both sexes. Despite these differences, these colleges
remained united as one huge urban campus. However, the movement for
community colleges, already strong in 1960, will relieve the Rio Piedras
campus of some of its financially and academically poorest students. It will

Table 5. Occupational Status of Students' Fathers and Mean Freshman Index
by Year, University of Puerto Rico at Rio Piedras

Occupational Status of Students' Fathers	Mean Freshman Index		
	1944–1945	1952–1953	1960–1961
Professional, proprietary and executive	2.13	2.46	2.49
Semiprofessional and higher white-collar	2.35	2.34	2.34
Lower white-collar	2.46	2.33	2.14
Small business	2.15	2.24	2.06
Skilled labor	2.13	2.20	2.10
Semi- and unskilled labor	2.30	2.33	2.04
Farmer	2.00	2.20	2.06
Farm laborer	—*	—*	1.89

*Fewer than 10 cases.

also add a new stratum of still-poorer students (academically and financially) to the bottom of the pyramid. It is predictable that a further expansion of higher education will bring with it more internal differentiation still, although whether there will be much growth of private higher education is not clear. In 1960, the private denominational universities of Puerto Rico were somewhat easier to enter than the state University of Puerto Rico. Their academic standards differed little from the U.P.R.'s. A private university of high quality did not seem a likely possibility. However, there were pressures for decentralization of the U.P.R., which had three campuses and over 20,000 students. The most probable development is a further differentiation of social recruitment and quality within the state system of higher education.

Conclusion

The case of Puerto Rico demonstrates that access to selective schooling for the children of different social strata can be roughly equalized at a point where the enrollment ratio of the upper strata is not near saturation. Since this did not occur in either Europe or the U.S., the Puerto Rican exception is important. It suggests that the same might occur in other industrializing countries although the factors conducive to such a development are not clear. Speed of educational expansion together with a strong egalitarian ethos seem to be two favorable conditions. A third, perhaps, is the absence of a strongly developed preindustrial class structure.[1]

However, the Puerto Rican case also suggests that rapid democratization of access is accompanied by segregation of the social classes into separate schools of disparate quality. By the time education reaches the stage of mass expansion (which democratization implies), there are always some strata with several generations of experience in higher schooling, while the newest strata to be recruited are sending their first generation into secondary and higher education. The educationally privileged are both able and motivated to maintain their privilege by self-segregation into elite schools. Thus a new source of educational inequality is generated, illustrating John Vaizey's thesis that ". . . even if a wholly egalitarian ethic prevailed in the public sector . . . , the provision of private facilities would always tend to restore the inequality prevailing in the economy as a whole."[2]

Whether the inequality is fully restored in Vaizey's meaning—that the distribution of education can be no more egalitarian than the distribution of income—is an unanswered question. A slightly different question, also unanswered, is whether mass-education societies like the United States and

---

[1] This factor was suggested by Philip Foster, "Secondary Schooling and Social Mobility in a West African Nation," *Sociology of Education,* 37, no. 2, pp. 150–171.

[2] John Vaizey, "Some Dynamic Aspects of Inequality," in *Social Objectives in Educational Planning* (Paris: OECD, 1968), p. 51.

Puerto Rico actually show smaller differences in educational achievement between social strata than industrial societies with selective secondary and higher schooling. Martin Trow suggests that they do: ". . . this is a very different kind of link between social class and educational opportunity than that provided by an elite university system which simply excludes the bulk of the lower classes from exposure to any kind of higher education."[1] Trow may be correct. Yet, it also seems possible that mass higher education reflects the society's high standard of living without obliterating the differentials which persist within the general affluence.

---

[1] Trow, "Democratization of Higher Education," p. 239.

Education and Pluralism
in Selected Caribbean Societies

JOSEPH P. FARRELL

An understanding of the role of education in effecting social change is seen today to be critically important for the planning of education in developing societies. This paper examines the effect that education has had on one type of social change, the shift from pluralism to heterogeneity, in several Caribbean societies.

"Education," as used here, means only formal, purposeful learning experiences—schooling. In order to define "pluralism" it is first necessary to clarify two concepts central to such definition: society and cultural institutions. "Society" will here refer only to "territorially distinct units having their own governmental institutions."[1] "Cultural institutions" are "standardized modes of co-activity."[2] Examples include marriage, blood revenge, family, property, etc. These tend to form systematic clusters, or subsystems (such as the kinship subsystem, including institutions like marriage, levirate, and family) or the government subsystem, including law, parliament and police, and other such regulative institutions. Not all institutional forms will be found in all societies. I will be concerned primarily with the "basic institutional system,"[3] which includes kinship, education, religion, property

Reproduced, by permission, from *Comparative Education Review,* 11 (June, 1967), pp. 160–181.

The author wishes to thank Professors Don Adams, John Laska and Helen Safa for their comments and suggestions.

[1] M. G. Smith, "Social and Cultural Pluralism," *Annals of the New York Academy of Sciences,* 83, Art. 5 (1960), p. 760.

[2] *Ibid.,* p. 766.

[3] M. G. Smith, *The Plural Society in the British West Indies* (Berkeley, Calif.: University of California Press, 1965), p. 82. The basic institutional system is analogous to Nadel's "compulsory institutions," S. F. Nadel, *The Foundations of Social Anthropology* (Glencoe, Ill.: Free Press, 1951), p. 120, and Linton's "culture core," R. Linton, *The Study of Man* (New York: D. Appleton-Century Co., 1936), chap. 16.

and economy, recreation, and certain sodalities. Participation in the forms of these peculiar to a given group is a requisite of membership in that group.

A "plural society" is a society wherein (a) there are two or more distinct subcultural groups sharing no basic institutions and (b) the superordinate group is a distinct minority preoccupied with problems of maintenance and control and discouraging acculturation of the subordinate majority.[1] It is important to note that this is a special use of a term which has been given, in both popular and professional literature, a confusing variety of meanings. Most commonly the term plural society is applied to societies which exhibit some form of ethnic or class segmentation (e.g., the U.S. is often called plural because of the diversity of ethnic backgrounds within the population). Used in this way the term lacks analytic power and is therefore almost meaningless for a scientific investigation. Pluralism is here used to refer to a particular and extreme form of segmentation. Some distinctions may clarify the matter.

(a)   It is quite possible to have a society with ethnic minorities which is not plural. If a number of basic institutions are shared, there is no pluralism but rather what Leonard Broom has called "congeries of minorities."[2]

(b)   Pluralism is not identical with class stratification. A plural group may occupy only one national stratum or may spread over several. The distinction is clearly marked by Smith:

> Class patterns represent differing styles of life, but the conceptual difference between such life styles and culture as a way of life is profound. Life styles can and do change without involving any change in the institutional system. Within class-stratified societies, such as those of the Hausa or in Britain, the various strata or classes hold common economic, religious, familial, political, and educational institutions, but the condition of cultural and social pluralism consists precisely in the systematic differentiation of these basic institutions themselves.[3]

(c)   Pluralism is not necessarily consonant with urban-rural differentiation. As with social classes, urban and rural populations tend to differ in life styles rather than in basic institutions. Often, however, in plural societies, it is an urban minority, with separate institutions, which controls a rural majority.

Societies which, while not plural, are subject to ethnic group, class,

---

[1] Smith, "Social and Cultural Pluralism," pp. 767 and 772. Government is the only institution which must be shared, for without it there would be no society. Control of the political institutions rests, however, in the hands of the superordinate minority; it is the instrument of maintenance and control.

[2] Leonard Broom, "Urbanization and the Plural Society," *Annals of the New York Academy of Sciences*, 83, Art. 5 (1960), p. 884.

[3] Smith, "Social and Cultural Pluralism," p. 769.

residential, or some other form of segmentation, are "heterogeneous." The determination of whether a society is plural or heterogeneous, then, is a matter for empirical research, focusing on institutional forms and their underlying value systems.

A final useful point is made by Charles Wagley, who views plural societies as occupying one end of a temporal continuum.[1] As societies move away, both in structure and in time, from pluralism, they become not homogeneous (it is difficult to conceive of a truly homogeneous society) but heterogeneous.

It will be noted that this view of society differs importantly from that of the system theorists, from Weber and Durkheim to Parsons, whose conception of a viable society posits the existence of a commonly shared set of basic institutions and values, a normative consensus, the necessity of which is dictated by the integrative function they perform. Plural societies, as here defined, are of interest precisely because they lack such an integrative mechanism; the constituent groups do not share values and institutions. Plural societies depend for their order on regulation by explicit or implicit force. Thus, if a society moves from pluralism to heterogeneity, it moves from dependence on regulation by force for order to dependence on normative consensus for integration.

This shift involves, at the manifest level, changes in behavior; the members of the subordinate group(s) begin to practice new institutional forms, those of the superordinate group. Since institutions "involve patterned activities, social relations, and idea-systems"[2] there will be, at the latent level, substantial changes in value orientations accompanying the institutional changes. This does not imply a one-to-one correspondence between changes in behavior and changes in values, as a certain amount of asymmetry in this regard is to be found in even the most well-integrated society, but indicates rather that there will be a rough correspondence between the two levels of change. This shift from pluralism to heterogeneity, then, is a special case of acculturation.

The types of institutional changes which must occur have been specified above. The question of value changes is both more subtle and more complex. Since we are examining a shift to a social order with a normative consensual base, the pattern variables devised by Talcott Parsons to describe such a society can be used. According to Lloyd Braithwaite, "This process of acculturation implies the introduction and partial acceptance of universal and achievement values in spheres in which particularistic and ascriptive values were previously dominant."[3] This does not necessarily mean that

[1] *Ibid.*, p. 779.

[2] Smith, *The Plural Society*, p. 14.

[3] Lloyd Braithwaite, "Social Stratification and Cultural Pluralism," *Annals of the New York Academy of Sciences*, 83, Art. 5 (1960), p. 819.

the old value patterns suddenly disappear but rather that there is a shift toward the new.

These descriptive category names—"ascription," "achievement," "particularistic," and "universal"—can be regarded as opposite ends of two separate continua, the first having at its poles particularistic and universal values, the second ascription and achievement. As their names imply, particularistic values represent a concern only with one's particular group, while universal values represent a concern with all groups, or at least with a more universal group. Since the meaning of ascription is less obvious, we can best turn to Parsons:

> Ascription: the normative pattern which prescribes that an actor in a given type of situation should, in his selections for differential treatment of social objects, give priority to certain attributes that they possess (including collectivity memberships and possessions) over any specific performances (past, present, or prospective) of the objects . . . the role expectation that the role incumbent in orienting himself to social objects in the relevant choice situation, will accord priority to the objects' given attributes (whether universally or particularistically defined) over their actual or potential performances.[1]

Performance, then, has nothing to do with one's ascribed place in society. One is more or less "born into" a position, with no chance for change. Achievement would represent a value set which atrributes position on the basis of actual or potential performance.

Related to the move toward achievement is a switch from a deterministic to an activistic value set. The former views all of life as determined by forces outside direct human control, which can only be propitiated in one manner or another. This is the orientation which views all events as the results of fate or luck. If such an attitude is prevalent there is not likely to be much attention given to achievement, since success would be regarded as indicative not of individual worth, but of individual good fortune. The opposite end of this particular continuum, activism, views men's fate as essentially controllable through their own efforts.

Another facet of this change, or perhaps another way of viewing it, is concerned with levels of aspiration, expectation and opportunity. Briefly, level of aspiration has to do with the values and institutions considered by a group or individual as ideal. Level of expectation concerns the values and way of life the group or individual actually expects to hold or attain. Level of opportunity is the realistically available possibility. What normally happens as a society moves from pluralism is an identification by the subordinate group(s) with the institutions and values of the superordinate; their level of aspiration is raised.

---

[1] Talcott Parsons and Edward Shils, "Values, Motives and Systems of Action," *in* Parsons and Shils, eds., *Toward a General Theory of Action* (Cambridge, Mass.: Harvard University Press, 1951), pp. 82–83.

It is of course possible for the change to move in the other direction, that is, for a heterogeneous society to become plural. This has normally occurred in societies which have been conquered or colonized, or where large numbers of laborers of a different ethnic group have been imported.

When I explore the relationships between education and changes both in values and behavior I am asking, in a sense, a question which has challenged philosophers for millennia and social scientists for decades: Why do men think and behave as they do? This is a question not amenable to easy answers, and the evidence available permits only tentative generalizations. Some of the ways in which education seems most likely to affect values and behavior are discussed below.

In considering the role of the schools in this process of institutional (behavioral) and value change, one point must be kept in mind. Schools are not, by themselves, effective instruments of such change. Education must be part of a set of superordinate economic, political and social institutions which together (or more correctly in sequence) penetrate the subordinate community. There is a great deal of evidence that schools placed in rural villages, with no supporting institutions, either do not "take" or, occasionally, become part of the traditional socialization process.[1] Frank and Ruth Young, in a series of comparative studies, have shown that the institutional development of small communities is both systematic and sequential and that schools are not the first urban institution to penetrate into the hinterland.[2] The same phenomenon has been observed in recent studies of Philippine communities.[3] But given the existence of a school in a rural area, the question of how it influences behavior and values remains.

A common way to view the role of the school in this connection is as an agent of occupational socialization. This is certainly one of the traditional roles assigned to schools. The school either provides skills which are salable in the labor market (how to be a carpenter, how to be an accountant, etc.) or, more commonly, provides the necessary tool skills (reading, writing, etc.), general knowledge, and, perhaps most essential, the certification which open up a whole new class of occupations to the student. Obviously, this will be of little importance if those jobs which provide access to situs of social, economic or political power are open only to members of the superordinate group, and if only the most menial jobs, or none at all in the money economy, are permitted to members of the subordinate group(s).

[1] Cf. the discussion about two Burmese villages in Manning Nash, "The Role of Village Schools in the Process of Cultural and Economic Modernization," Social and Economic Studies, 14 (March, 1965), pp. 131–143. [See pages 483–497, this volume. 1972. Ed.]

[2] Frank W. and Ruth C. Young, "Social Integration and Change in Twenty Four Mexican Villages," Economic Development and Cultural Change, 8 (July, 1960); and "The Sequence and Direction of Community Growth: A Cross-Cultural Generalization," Rural Sociology, 27 (December, 1962), pp. 374–386.

[3] Linda Nelson, University of Hawaii, personal communication.

This again emphasizes the point that the schools are not likely to be able to initiate the process of change from pluralism to heterogeneity but rather play a part in the process once begun.

Occupational socialization is, of course, a special case of the general socialization process in which schools have always been designed to play a part. The school is always the carrier of a culture, in this case, the superordinate culture. A particularly useful way to view the socializing role of the school in this special case is to use the "broker" concept developed by Eric Wolf.[1] Brokers are members of subcultural groups who have links to both the superordinate and subordinate cultures and thus mediate between the one and the other. Generally they are representatives of, or participants in, national-level (superordinate) institutions. The schoolteacher serves in subordinate areas as an important broker. He is an agent of a national institution and is usually an outsider, embodying an alien culture. At the same time, if the school is a functioning institution within the local community, he is, by virtue of his position and education, almost automatically a member of the local elite, and as such his behavior and attitudes may be taken by members of the community as models. Students themselves often come to form part of the broker class in that their school experience forges new links for them with the outside world. In addition young people who have been to school are quite likely to migrate to urban (superordinate) areas, and it has often been noted that such migrants form a most important link between urban and rural cultures. Also, the school is a unique national-level broker institution in that it is the only such institution in which everyone (at least among the younger people) is theoretically eligible to participate. Not all members of the community will serve in the military, not all will join labor unions, not all (particularly not women in many cases) will participate in the national occupational system, but all will enter the schoolhouse.[2]

Thus, the school, as a broker, is a carrier of superordinate behavior and values. It is this last point which leads us into a consideration of the role of the school specifically in effecting the value changes suggested earlier as essential to the shift from pluralism to heterogeneity. A few initial points about the role of the school in attitude and value formation are in order. Careful examination of the research in this area leads to few easy generalizations, but the following would seem to be possible ways in which schools can and do change values. (a) Schools provide children with new reference

---

[1] Eric Wolf, "Aspects of Group Relations in a Complex Society: Mexico," *American Anthropologist*, 58 (December, 1956), pp. 1065–1078.

[2] For a more complete discussion of the broker concept, as it applies to education, see "Education and National Integration," *in* Don Adams and Joseph P. Farrell, eds., *Education and Social Development*, Draft Report (Syracuse, N.Y.: Center for Development Education, Syracuse University, 1960), chap. 3.

groups. Older students can serve as brokers for younger students. (b) Children can be taught perhaps to act as if they had internalized superordinate values, since changed behavior need not require immediate value change, and psychologists suggest that behaving or expressing opinions contrary to one's private values often results in modification of the latter. (c) Success in school, particularly among those few who are selected for higher levels of education not available to all, may enhance students' self-perceptions and stimulate them to adopt values seen as appropriate to their roles as "leaders." (d) It has been observed that students preparing, particularly at the higher levels of education, for particular professions have a tendency to adopt the values prevalent among the current members of the profession. If they are preparing for a profession in the superordinate sphere students are likely to adopt superordinate values. This is the value change aspect of occupational socialization, which was discussed above in connection with behavior change. (e) Role playing has been found to be effective in changing values. Schools, by providing several years of rehearsal for superordinate roles, may in this fashion serve to stimulate value change—(d) above may be a specific case of this.[1]

Concerning the specific value changes associated with a shift away from pluralism, I have suggested a move from particularistic to universal values. Lloyd Braithwaite, writing about Trinidad, has come to the following conclusion: "In any case, formal education even on the lowest levels, seems to be almost intrinsically linked with a universalistic scale of values."[2] The school, in its broker role, exposes children to an entirely new culture. Kathleen Wolf, in her study of Puerto Rico, discovered in the rural peasant community that the mere presence of the teacher from the outside "suggests alternatives to the existing way of life which were unknown to the older generation."[3] Similarly, one could say that success in school, with its paraphernalia of grading, competitive examinations, and so forth, inherently demands a certain modicum of achievement motivation and competitiveness.

A shift from determinism to activism was suggested as a necessary concomitant of the above. Schools, by demanding mastery of a given body of

---

[1] Cf. Don Adams, "The Study of Education and Social Development," *Comparative Education Review,* 9 (October, 1965), pp. 261–262; Don Adams and Joseph P. Farrell, "The Measurement of Education and Social Development," *Malaysian Journal of Education,* 3 (June, 1966); Geraldine Holmes, "Implications of Attitude Change Theory for Formal Education in Developing Nations" (Center for Development of Education, Syracuse University, 1965), mimeo.; and for an example of (d) see discussion of Argentina *in* Kalman Silvert and Frank Bonilla, *Education and the Social Meaning of Development* (New York: American Universities Field Staff, Inc., 1961).

[2] Lloyd Braithwaite, "Social Stratification in Trinidad: A Preliminary Analysis," *Social and Economic Studies,* 2 (October, 1953), p. 54.

[3] Kathleen Wolf, "Growing Up and Its Price in Three Puerto Rican Sub-Cultures," *Psychiatry,* 15 (November, 1952), p. 411.

knowledge which is a selected portion of the total environment, may encourage an activist attitude toward the whole environment. Brameld has found that Puerto Ricans are definitely activistic and that the efforts of the Division of Community Education, dealing operationally with human problems and vocational education, seem particularly to encourage this value orientation. The Division of Community Education has discovered that the success of its programs for encouraging activism is highly correlated with educational level in the community.[1] Similarly, a study by Icken in Puerto Rico noted that urban respondents, with more education, emphasized personal responsibility when explaining failure in life and that in rural areas determinism decreased as education assumed greater importance.[2]

If the school is performing its role of occupational socialization, it can also be expected to raise the level of aspiration of its patrons (or to ratify and encourage an already raised level). That such is the case is indicated by Smith's study of rural schoolboys in Jamaica and Edithe Clarke's study of three Jamaican communities.[3]

The general thrust of the preceding analysis is well summarized, and the interrelatedness of the analytically separated value changes is well described by Kimball and McClellan:

> Formal schooling does mold children, especially when it supplements other influences on the child. It does this less by virtue of what is taught than by the ways schools select and motivate. A curriculum consisting of memorizing nonsense syllables would not be as effective as the usual one, but it would not be entirely ineffective. It would serve as hurdles for pupils, and those coming out at the other end would be of proved intelligence. . . . In all school systems the classroom activities create aspirations in children by the very operations of learning and by the experience of succeeding or failing. Enterprise and drive are learned by the successful pupils through achievement and by the element of universality or objectivity involved in formalized learning.[4]

Thus each of the suggested value changes necessary to a shift from pluralism to heterogeneity can theoretically be, and in some cases has actually been, influenced by attendance at school. There is one final effect of schooling which Tumin and Feldman discovered which is extremely important: a shift in attitude toward schooling. They found in Puerto Rico that an

---

[1] Theodore Brameld, *The Remaking of a Culture: Life and Education in Puerto Rico* (New York: Harper Co., 1959), pp. 125 and 384.

[2] Helen M. Icken, "From Slum to Housing Project: A Study in Social Transition" (New York: Columbia University, 1962), pp. 33–34. Unpublished study.

[3] M. G. Smith, "Education and Occupational Choice in Rural Jamaica," *Social and Economic Studies*, 9 (September, 1960), p. 343; and Edithe Clarke, *My Mother Who Fathered Me: A Study of the Family in Three Selected Communities in Jamaica* (London: George Allen and Unwin, Ltd., 1957), p. 166.

[4] Solon T. Kimball and James E. McClellan, *Education and the New America* (New York: Random House, 1962), p. 16.

increase in education resulted in an increased respect for education, a sharpened perception of its importance, an increased feeling of its accessibility, and an increased desire for education for one's own children.[1] This seems particularly important in effecting the development of an educational growth spiral.

In no way is the discussion above meant to imply that placing schools within the subordinate culture of a plural society will automatically result in behavior and value changes requisite to participation in superordinate institutional forms. Even if the schools "take" in the subordinate areas there is no guarantee that they will be effective instruments for such change. The literature concerning education in both the "West and the rest" abounds with examples of failure in this regard.[2] But anyone with experience in schools also knows that children who have been to school are different from those who have not attended or have attended for a shorter period of time; and there are examples, some few of which have been cited above, of success in value and behavior change. What this analysis attempts to do is to indicate, where such change occurs as a result of schooling, the mechanisms which appear to be operating.

The relevance and utility of this analytic approach can be illustrated further by turning to an examination of the social, and particularly educational, situation, past and present, in several Caribbean societies. Although having much in common they have had varied colonial experiences, and the consequent synthesis of European and non-European elements has created in each a different culture pattern. Two, Haiti and Jamaica, will be considered in some detail, and selected relevant aspects from the experience of three other societies, Trinidad, Barbados and Puerto Rico, will be briefly discussed.

Haiti

During the seventeenth century the western third of the island of Hispaniola, under Spanish control, was a center for buccaneers. France gradually took over and in 1697 her claim to the territory was recognized by Spain. Under French domination the area became one of the world's richest colonies, exporting vast quantities of sugar cane. The population was overwhelmingly black and enslaved, with a small group of mulattoes occupying the limbo between their white fathers and black mothers.

There was during this period no public education. Wealthy planters sent

---

[1] Melvin M. Tumin and Arnold S. Feldman, "Status, Perspective, and Achievement: Education and Class Structure in Puerto Rico," *American Sociological Review,* 21 (August, 1956), p. 471.

[2] As Eisenstadt has said, "There are certain inherent potentialities built into the very process of education and its relation with other parts of the society that make the outcome uncertain." Shmuel N. Eisenstadt *in* Don C. Piper and Taylor Cole, eds., *Post-Primary Education and Political and Economic Development* (Durham, N.C.: Duke University Press, 1964), p. 27.

their legitimate children to France. Occasionally, a mulatto, being "his father's son," would receive a mainland education. The attitude toward education for the Negro is perhaps best expressed in the words of one M. de Villaret, who wrote at the time:

> The French government has realized that the need for extending and generalizing instruction—appropriate no doubt for the education of a free people—is incompatible with the existence of our colonies, which depends upon slavery and color distinction. . . . It would therefore be dangerously imprudent to tolerate schools for the Negroes.[1]

There was no need to worry about tolerating such schools, for none existed.

During the dying years of the eighteenth century social ferment reached a fever pitch. The mass of black slaves greatly outnumbered the whites. The mulattoes, freed by an act of the French government, were frequently educated; accepted by neither white nor black, they served as a catalyst for black resentment. The result was a revolt which gained Haitian independence in 1803. The mulattoes, with their superior education, gained control of the society and reigned supreme for considerably more than a century. As time passed palace revolts became more frequent and more violent, until in 1915 the United States felt compelled to move troops in.

One of the main themes of Haitian educational development clearly appeared during this time: the neglect of the rural population, which has always comprised the vast majority of the citizenry. Until 1848 there were no rural schools. In that year a law was passed stipulating that rural communities were to establish schools "when the financial situation permitted." This provision allowed the law to remain virtually a dead letter.[2] Following the American troops came the usual brigade of educational advisors, concentrating upon the rural school problem. Their efforts resulted in the establishment, using American capital, of a rural teacher-training institution and 74 rural schools.[3]

Politically, the period of United States domination was peaceful. Orderly elections were held in 1930, and the troops were withdrawn in 1934. Tranquility, however, left with the troops. The mulattoes once more took over and economic chaos ensued. There have been several revolutions since. In 1946 Dumarsais Estime, a black, came into power, his avowed policy being to break mulatto power. In 1950 another revolt brought Paul Magloire in. During his reign racial tensions were somewhat reduced, the mulattoes being given a breathing spell. In 1957 François Duvalier gained control and has carried Estime's policies to unexpected extremes.

---

[1] Mercer Cook, "Recent Developments in Haitian Education," *Education,* 76 (June, 1956), p. 611.

[2] *World Survey of Education* (Paris: UNESCO, 1958), Vol. 2, p. 497.

[3] *Ibid.*

Curiously, during the regimes of Estime and Duvalier, in spite of their campaigns against the mulatto, education of the black masses in the rural areas has continued to be neglected. Urban teachers receive more pay and are more highly trained. They work under more favorable conditions, having at least some equipment and teaching in schools which are less primitive than those in the hinterland. Although Haiti has very few qualified teachers, 90 per cent of those who have had professional training are in urban areas.[1] This is a reflection of the fact that secondary teachers are more highly trained than elementary teachers, and all secondary schools are in urban areas, as are all vocational and commercial institutions, due to the traditional attitude that secondary education is appropriate only for the privileged few.[2] Typically the only substantial efforts in rural areas have been made under outside impetus—that of the United States during the 1920's and of the United Nations during the 1950's. This neglect of rural areas would seem to indicate that the division in Haitian society is as much rural-urban as black-mulatto (these being largely but not entirely coincident), with the revolutions determining simply which segment of the small elite gets the rewards of control.

Haiti is a plural society. As Bastien has stated, the urban 15 per cent of the population is French-oriented and generally despises the completely different culture of the masses in the rural areas and does everything possible to separate itself from the folk culture.[3] Smith, after surveying the literature, has concluded that "there is a marked consensus on the existence of two different cultures in that country."[4] Oscar Vera has concluded that the availability of education "corresponds to the characteristics of the social structure of this country."[5] The deliberate deprivation of education has been one of the tools used to maintain the separateness of the institutional systems. Manipulation by the superordinate urban group of access to education has been one of the tools used to effectively block the acculturation of the rural masses.[6] Under such conditions the few schools which have been established in the subordinate culture area, under outside

---

[1] George A. Dale, *Education in the Republic of Haiti,* Department of Health, Education and Welfare, Office of Education Bulletin 1959, No. 20 (Washington, D.C.: Government Printing Office, 1959), p. 23.

[2] *Ibid.,* p. 67.

[3] Remy Bastien, "The Role of the Intellectual in Haitian Plural Society," *Annals of the New York Academy of Sciences,* 83, Art. 5 (1960), p. 844.

[4] Smith, *The Plural Society,* p. 55.

[5] Oscar Vera, "The Educational Situation and Requirements in Latin America," *Social Aspects of Economic Development in Latin America* (Paris: UNESCO, 1963), Vol. 1, p. 286.

[6] It must be pointed out that education has aided in the acculturation of the urban blacks. It was mentioned that the urban elite culture is no longer exclusively mulatto. Bastien has testified *(The Caribbean Scholar's Conference, Caribbean Studies Special Report,* 1962, Rio Piedras, Puerto Rico, 1962, p. 11) that it was public education which allowed the urban blacks to break the mulatto monopoly.

impetus, can hardly function as broker institutions, in fact can hardly function at all.[1]

Jamaica

Originally Jamaica was a Spanish possession, but in the middle of the sixteenth century the British landed and the island was officially ceded to them in 1670. Jamaica has thus inherited its elite culture from Great Britain rather than from Spain. It became, along with Sainte Domingue (Haiti), a fabulously wealthy sugar supplier. Although there was much slave unrest and revolts were sporadically attempted, the island remained under British control. In 1838 the slaves were freed by an act of the British Parliament. The greater share of them, having had experience with subsistence farming on the plantations, left for the back country, becoming self-sufficient peasants. This loss of labor contributed to the decline of the sugar plantations, which were already beginning to feel the effects of an international market collapse.

Jamaica's educational development has been governed, of course, by colonial policy. Both in structure and curriculum the schools have been very British, consisting of a large primary system sharply separated from a much smaller secondary system, with a few university students at the apex of the pyramid. This system began to develop fully only late in the nineteenth century when the notion of state responsibility for mass education became firmly imbedded in the British mind. Previously, almost all education was provided by religious or private groups.

A closer look at education reveals more clearly the effect it had upon the original pluralism of the slave society. In the preemancipation society there were few schools of any note for the planters' white children. Each parish had a barely adequate primary school. In addition there were three higher-level schools, one in Kingston, one in St. Anne, and one in Port Antonio, which gave "a moderately bad education, including some study of languages."[2] The entire system suffered from the fact that anyone with the means sent his children to England to be educated. These children, however, frequently failed to return to Jamaica, or, if they returned, came back poorly educated for plantation life.

This effect of white education contributed to a general lack of qualified (or unqualified) whites to fill positions above the laborer rank. Into this gap moved the free colored. Some of them had an English education, most had some education, and they were generally more highly skilled and better trained than the English clerks and indentured servants at the bottom

---

[1] Ronald Hilton, "Education in the Caribbean: Government Policies" in Curtis A. Wilgus, ed., *The Caribbean: Contemporary Education* (Gainesville, Fla.: University of Florida Press, 1960), p. 38.

[2] Philip D. Curtin, *Two Jamaicas: The Role of Ideas in a Tropical Colony* (Cambridge, Mass.: Harvard University Press, 1955), p. 56.

of the white heap. These free colored, aspiring to the institutions and values of the whites, and rejecting those of the blacks (those who controlled slaves were generally harsher than their white counterparts), and wishing to avoid field labor, the mark of slavery, concentrated in the towns, where there were more educational and economic opportunities, and thus more possibilities for fulfilling their aspirations. Leonard Broom has pointed out that although the white elite was land-based, and thus acquisition of land was eventually necessary to ratify elite membership, among the aspiring colored "for the first few steps up the ladder some training was more important than some land."[1] Of particular importance was the possibility of moving into journalism, trade or law, which were avenues into politics. The colored had gained such strength politically that they were declared by the Assembly in 1830 equal to whites in civil and political rights. There were several colored members of the Assembly at this time and the colored population outnumbered the white substantially. The enrollments of Wolmer's Free School, one of the "big three" on the island, are indicative of both the numerical increase of the colored and their rise in status (Table 1).[2]

Table 1. Enrollments at Wolmer's Free School

Year	White	Colored
1815	111	3
1820	116	78
1825	89	185
1830	88	194

This brief history of the rise of the colored again illustrates the point that schools cannot function as brokers independently of other forces for change. For example, they could hardly have served the colored as agents of occupational socialization for elite positions had the paucity of the white population not necessitated opening such positions to nonwhites.[3] Although there were isolated cases of educated Negroes, the great mass of the black population was completely illiterate at emancipation. Slaves, as in Haiti, were not seen as needing any schooling, and such an exposure to ideas was viewed as potentially dangerous.

Thus, at emancipation Jamaican society consisted of three groups: a small white population which was in control but which had neither the numbers nor the education to occupy all key positions in the power structure; a slightly larger colored group which had used education to move into

---

[1] Leonard Broom, "The Social Differentiation of Jamaica," *American Sociological Review,* 19 (April, 1954), p. 118.

[2] Curtin, *Two Jamaicas,* p. 240.

[3] Cf. Broom, "Social Differentiation of Jamaica," on this point.

the gaps in the structure, gaining for themselves a measure of power; and the great mass of uneducated black slaves. After emancipation the colored and whites remained in power, the colored gaining power as a result of the economic failure of the white-dominated plantations and the consequent decline in the white population.

The problem of educating the newly freed slaves was left almost entirely to the missionaries. The British government did grant £30,000 per year to charitable foundations and missionary societies for Negro education in all the colonies, but this grant was withdrawn in 1845 and the island Assembly, for a variety of reasons, failed to replace it. The Jamaican government, finding itself unable to cope with the social problems created by the post-emancipation rise in the aspirations of the black masses, which was viewed as a threat to the status of the ruling class, abolished the constitution in 1865 and placed control of the island entirely in the hands of the Crown. In this social turmoil the colored identified their interests completely with the whites and were perfectly willing, with the whites, to exchange political responsibility for status protection.[1]

The new colonial government began to take a more active interest in education and in the latter half of the nineteenth century both its quantity and quality increased. The gains were particularly noticeable in the rural areas, although they remained behind the urban areas, as they are today.[2]

Although there is general agreement that present-day Jamaican society exhibits substantial cleavages, there is disagreement as to the nature of the divisions. Some, such as Kerr and Broom,[3] maintain that the discontinuities mark a class-stratification pattern, while Smith maintains that the society is still plural.[4] There is, however, general agreement that three main societal groups continue to exist: the dominant (superordinate if plural) almost entirely urban whites; the subordinated primarily rural blacks; and the colored who occupy an intermediate position. Smith indicates that the colored share with the whites a number of institutions and are using education as a means of occupational mobility, thus continuing the pattern established before emancipation.[5] For the colored, then, education has been and still is an important broker institution, contributing to their integration into the elite culture.

That there is still a distinct cultural split between the urban white-colored elite and the largely black rural masses is quite evident. Smith notes that the "inequality of educational opportunities . . . is an important condition

---

[1] Smith, The Plural Society, p. 153.

[2] George W. Roberts, The Population of Jamaica (Cambridge, England: Cambridge University Press, 1957), pp. 78 and 81.

[3] Smith, The Plural Society, p. 56 and Broom, "Social Differentiation in Jamaica."

[4] Smith, The Plural Society, chap. 7.

[5] Ibid., p. 175 and pp. 166–167; cf. also Broom, "Social Differentiation in Jamaica," p. 119.

of social and economic differentiation."[1] Data from 1960 indicate that rural education is still quantitatively and qualitatively inferior to urban education. At the primary level the enrollment ratio in Kingston was near 100 per cent while it was below 60 per cent in some rural parishes. At the secondary level rural St. Mary's Parish, with 6 per cent of the population, had less than .5 per cent of the total enrollment, while St. Andrew's and Kingston, with 25 per cent of the population, had 53 per cent of the total enrollment.[2] Roberts and Abdulah have quite recently noted that although there is a "convergence toward a common level, manifestly the urban areas still enjoy a substantial advantage over the rural."[3]

Several points may put this urban-rural difference into its proper perspective. First, Ruscoe has noted that at the secondary level the statistics tend to overemphasize the difference somewhat, since rural students competing for secondary places frequently give relatives' addresses in urban areas as their home addresses, since it is generally felt that urban secondary schools are superior to those in rural areas.[4] From this I can also suggest that some rural inhabitants do have access to urban education, with its superior occupational socialization potential. Secondly, as the earlier analysis suggests, the mere presence of a school in a rural area is not proof that it is acting as a broker—its ability to function depends upon other conditions. Smith's study of rural Jamaican schoolboys, previously cited, demonstrates that although schooling raised the students' aspirations, the economic situation they faced after leaving school did not allow them to fulfill these aspirations, and they gradually blended back into the traditional subordinate culture.[5] Seaga's study, on the other hand, of a rural village which is exposed to urban influences and in which there is some opportunity for occupational mobility indicates that students who are judged capable and who pass the third (advanced) Jamaica Local Examination "are expected to seek further training in the professions of teaching, nursing, or postal clerkship."[6] In short, rural education in Jamaica (and the figures cited above indicate that although quantitatively inferior to urban education it is still widely available), given the existence of other superordinate institutions, principally economic institutions, can act, and in some cases has acted, as a broker between the superordinate and subordinate cultures.

---

[1] Smith, *The Plural Society,* p. 167.

[2] Gordon C. Ruscoe, *Dysfunctionality in Jamaican Education,* Comparative Education Dissertation Series, No. 1 (Ann Arbor, Mich.: University of Michigan Press, 1963), pp. 14–15.

[3] G. W. Roberts and N. Abdulah, "Some Observations on the Educational Position of the British Caribbean," *Social and Economic Studies,* 14 (March, 1965), p. 149.

[4] Ruscoe, *Dysfunctionality in Jamaican Education.*

[5] Smith, "Education and Occupational Choice."

[6] Edward Seaga, "Parent-Teacher Relationships in a Jamaican Village," *Social and Economic Studies,* 4 (September, 1955), p. 200.

Thus one can conclude that education has long served as a broker institution for the colored section of Jamaican society and is now serving that same function for some of the black rural masses. The schools are thus contributing to the shift from pluralism to heterogeneity which appears to be occurring in Jamaican society.

Trinidad

During the seventeenth and eighteenth centuries, when slavery formed the base of the social structure of most Caribbean societies, Trinidad was relatively undeveloped. Thus, when emancipation occurred, in 1838 (the British having annexed the island in 1797), the freed slaves were able to retreat from sugar plantations to unoccupied Crown lands. The labor shortage thus created resulted in the importation of thousands of indentured laborers from British India. Most of these returned to India when their indenture was completed, but enough remained that their descendants make up a good share of the present population of Trinidad. In 1959, of a population of approximately 815,000, roughly 470,000 were Creoles (Negroes or colored) and more than 300,000 were East Indian, the small remainder of the population being made up of British, Chinese, French, Venezuelan, Portuguese, Syrian, and other groups.[1] These unusual historical circumstances (British Guiana is the only other Caribbean society with a substantial proportion of its population East Indian) have produced an extremely complex system of social segmentation on the island. Thus, any brief discussion risks considerable oversimplification.

Trinidadian society could now be described as plural, with a quite sharp ethnic differentiation between Creoles and East Indians overlying the plural segmentation. The superordinate group consists of the small, mostly white, elite and the somewhat larger, principally colored, middle class. These two segments, according to Braithwaite, share a number of values and institutions[2] and are sharply differentiated from the subordinated, mostly rural, group, which is itself sharply divided into Negro and East Indian sections.

The role played by education both in meliorating, and in some cases aggravating, the sharp divisions in Trinidadian society is instructive. During the nineteenth and early twentieth centuries the division between the colored and the white elite was quite sharp, and the colored could not have been properly included in the superordinate group. When the barriers began to break down, however, due to a set of economic and political changes in both Trinidad and in Great Britain which are much too complex to detail here, education served the same broker role for the colored as it had in

---

[1] John P. Augelli and Harry W. Taylor, "Race and Population Patterns in Trinidad," *Annals of the Association of American Geographers,* 50 (June, 1960), p. 123.

[2] Braithwaite, "Social Stratification in Trinidad," p. 153.

Jamaica starting more than a century earlier: it provided them with the qualifications for newly opened superordinate occupations and for ratifying their newly acquired status.[1]

The rural subordinate Creoles and East Indians have received little education and, indeed, appear little interested in it where schools have been provided, as the supporting institutions which allow education to perform as a broker are largely absent. In the towns, however, where such supporting institutions are present, the subordinate groups view education much as do the colored, and encourage the attendance at school of those of their children who appear to have a chance to obtain a free secondary education.[2]

The East Indians who have moved into urban areas have experienced much the same value and behavior changes as have the colored. Crowley argues that they are "culturally indistinguishable" from their white, colored or black neighbors of the same class.[3] This high degree of assimilation and loss of ancestral culture has alarmed some of the East Indian elite and has led to a greatly increased emphasis on separate Hindu and Moslem schools, where Hindustani is taught, the Indian anthem sung, and various other attempts made to stimulate Indian nationalism. Even though they have been largely unsuccessful in their efforts, as most urban East Indian children still attend school with their Creole age mates and the only available teachers for these separate schools are "among the most Europeanized of all Trinidadians,"[4] these schools have exacerbated the already suspicious relations between the Creoles and East Indians.[5] This once again demonstrates that conscious attempts to use the schools as cultural brokers (in this case attempting to acculturate children to an Indian culture) will fail in the absence of supporting institutions. It further indicates that providing or allowing separate schools for minority groups, while often politically necessary, can be a dangerous practice from the standpoint of societal integration.

Barbados

The island of Barbados presents a remarkable contrast to Trinidad. It is one of the most crowded areas in the world, and has been for centuries. As long ago as 1640 there were approximately 200 persons to the square mile,[6] and the current density is well above 1,400 persons per square mile.[7]

---

[1]*Ibid.,* pp. 56–62.

[2]*Ibid.,* p. 132.

[3]Daniel J. Crowley, "Cultural Assimilation in a Multiracial Society," *Annals of the New York Academy of Sciences,* 83, Art. 5 (1960), p. 852.

[4]*Ibid.,* p. 853.

[5]Inez Adams and J. Masuoka, "Emerging Elites and Culture Change," *Social and Economic Studies,* 10 (March, 1961), p. 89.

[6]J. H. Parry and P. M. Sherlock, *A Short History of the West Indies* (London: Macmillan Co., 1960), p. 56.

[7]Smith, *The Plural Society,* p. 311.

Culturally this dense population is, and has been almost since emancipation, heterogeneous rather than plural. There are substantial class differences, with class standing and color relating quite highly, but all classes share essentially the same cultural institutions. The whole cultural pattern, as Starkey noted some time ago, "is essentially English, and the outward material evidences to the contrary are largely a veneer overlaying the cultural core. . . . Every Barbadian, white, black, or colored, thinks of himself as a member of Anglo-Saxon society."[1] More recently Lowenthal has testified that urban influences permeate all but the most remote areas. "Most of Barbados' rural communities are remarkably urban. A characteristic description is that 'Barbados is a city, where sugar grows in the suburbs.' "[2]

The factors creating this distinct (for the Caribbean) cultural uniformity are quite numerous, including the inability of the freed slaves to remove themselves from sugar cultivation after emancipation, as they did in Jamaica and Trinidad, the nature of Barbados' white colonists,[3] and the high level of education which has long existed in the island. The role of the school as a broker institution and as an avenue for occupational, and hence class, mobility was early recognized in Barbados. For example, in 1875 the Mitchison Commission, a group of prominent Barbadians appointed by the House of Assembly to investigate educational practices on the island, expressed confidence that the primary schools (there were then over 160 in existence) were instilling in the lower-class (Negro and colored) pupils such upper- and middle-class virtues as "obedience, order, punctuality, honesty, and the like."[4] The commission also advocated the use of education as an avenue of social mobility and specifically rejected any color bar, stating that "an avenue of advancement for the very able of all classes must exist to recruit a stable middle class, as in England, and to stimulate primary education. . . . But it is not only desirable that the best stratum in each primary school should gravitate upwards . . . ; it will also conduce to the interests of the community and the stability of its institutions, if the very best units in that best stratum be placed, through means of access to our highest type of education, within reach of the best social and professional positions."[5] The question of universal primary education was not even considered worth debating, its value being considered self-evident.

---

[1] Otis P. Starkey, *The Economic Geography of Barbados* (New York: Columbia University Press, 1939), p. 6.

[2] David Lowenthal, "The Population of Barbados," *Social and Economic Studies,* 6 (December, 1957), p. 472.

[3] Starkey tells this story fairly well. He also notes that even shortly after emancipation the Negroes aspired to such "white" cultural goals as owning land, raising sugar for profit, and living near the urban areas. Starkey, *Economic Geography of Barbados,* p. 118.

[4] Shirley Gordon, "Documents Which Have Guided Educational Policy in the West Indies: The Mitchison Report, Barbados, 1875," *Caribbean Quarterly,* 9 (September, 1963), p. 38.

[5] *Ibid.,* pp. 35 and 38.

The result of this early and continuing emphasis on education can be seen in some recent educational statistics. In 1960 only 1.8 per cent of adult Barbadians had never attended school, 83 per cent had had at least four years of schooling, and 16 per cent had been to secondary school, the latter figure being the highest in the British West Indies and being approached in the Caribbean only by Puerto Rico.[1] Concerning the effect of this high level of education on social integration, Lowenthal, noting the overwhelming literacy of the island, has testified that almost everyone is "accessible to the dissemination of ideas as well as of goods and services."[2]

Thus education in Barbados, one of the least plural societies in the Caribbean area, has long been available to persons of all colors, has been extensively patronized, and continues to be used as a means of class mobility.[3] It has served Barbados well as a broker institution.

Puerto Rico

Due to a peculiar nexus of historical circumstances Puerto Rico never was a plural society. Most of its rural workers were pure European, except along the coasts where Negroes were used on the sugar plantations.[4] However, when the United States took control of the island in 1898, introducing a new superordinate culture, a plural society could easily have developed, conquest being one of the most common causes of pluralism. The conscious avoidance of such a development by the United States and the deliberate effort to acculturate the Puerto Ricans is a familiar story.

Following on the heels of the U.S. troops came the usual brigade of workers, bringing roads, health-improvement measures, and schools. During the military occupation an education survey was made, a bureau of education established and school laws enacted. These laws attempted to transplant the American system whole and entire into Puerto Rico. The commissioner of education, appointed by the president of the United States, had complete control over schooling. The first commissioner, Dr. I. M. Brumbaugh, described as "a man fanatically devoted to salutes to the flag and lusty renderings by the children of such patriotic songs as *America, Hail Columbia,* and *The Star Spangled Banner,* reported after only one year's efforts that the average Puerto Rican child already knew more about Washington, Lincoln, and Betsy Ross and the American Flag than did the average child in the United States."[5] This statement reflects the consciously acculturative tone of American educational policies at the time.

---

[1] Roberts and Abdulah, "Educational Position of the British Caribbean," pp. 145-147.

[2] Lowenthal, "The Population of Barbados," p. 495.

[3] George E. Cumper, "Household and Occupation in Barbados," *Social and Economic Studies,* 10 (December, 1961), p. 408.

[4] P. E. James, *Latin America,* third edition (New York: Odyssey Press, 1959), p. 782.

[5] Earl P. Hansen, *Puerto Rico, Ally for Progress* (Princeton, N. J.: D. Van Nostrand Co., Inc., 1962), p. 115.

During the first four decades of the century substantial progress was made (although perhaps not so spectacular as Brumbaugh's glowing report would have one believe), considering the dearth of facilities available in 1898. A normal school was established in Rio Piedras early in the century. Enough eight-year elementary schools were established that by 1920 one out of three school-age children was in class, compared with one of 15, 20 years earlier.[1] Secondary schools developed less rapidly, but generally they were built as needed. In 1903 the University of Puerto Rico was established. By 1925 more than half of the school-age children were in school, mostly in the lower four grades.[2] The primary enrollment ratio grew more slowly after reaching .50, as might be expected. Table 2 traces this growth after 1930.[3]

Table 2. Primary Enrollment Ratio after 1930

Years	Enrollment Ratio
1931–34	.54
1935–39	.55
1940–44	.57
1945–49	.61
1950–54	.66

The imposition of an essentially foreign educational system created certain very difficult problems. Many innovations were resented by the native teachers and administrators, although they knew better than to complain openly. Perhaps the grossest example of this conflict was the language problem. Official policy from the start of the occupation was that the language of instruction should be English. Children were thus expected to learn the three R's in a language utterly alien to them. Slowly it became apparent that this policy was "not only not teaching Puerto Rican grade school pupils English, but was preventing them from learning anything else."[4] The problem remained unresolved until the island was allowed to appoint its own secretary of education, since which time instruction has been in Spanish, with English required as a second language.

It is not being suggested here that all Puerto Ricans are, or should be, completely acculturated to mainland culture. Nor is it suggested that the schools alone have been responsible for the remarkably rapid acculturation

[1] Juan José Osuna, *A History of Education in Puerto Rico* (Rio Piedras, Puerto Rico: Editorial de la Universidad de Puerto Rico, 1949), p. 242.

[2] Lloyd Blauch and Charles Reid, *Public Education in the Territories and Outlying Possessions*, Staff Study No. 16 of the Advisory Committee on Education (Washington: U.S. Government Printing Office, 1939), p. 104.

[3] UNESCO, *World Survey of Education*, Vol. 2, p. 1283.

[4] Osuna, *Education in Puerto Rico*, p. 184.

which has taken place. What is of note is the fact that schools have been used as *one of a set* of broker institutions which have effected the transformation of Puerto Rican society.

Conclusion

The conceptual scheme presented in the first part of this paper represents a synthesis of ideas developed in a number of different contexts by several scholars over the past few years. The separate, brief studies of five differing but roughly comparable Caribbean societies have indicated that education can serve as a broker institution in plural societies, but that it cannot alone effect the shift from pluralism to heterogeneity. Two points suggest themselves as being particularly important.

(a) The school is a broker institution. Not only does the school itself serve as a broker, a carrier of superordinate culture in subordinate areas, a socializing agent of the superordinate culture, but it turns out into the community individuals who can form a broker class. In order to serve as a broker between two cultures an institution must be part of both, which leads to the second point.

(b) The school needs the support of other institutions. This point bears repeated emphasis because it seems so frequently to be overlooked in practice. The school must be linked with other institutions which give its "message" meaning and value. If the school is attempting to prepare students for superordinate roles there must be possibilities for participation in a number of superordinate institutions; there must be openings in the occupational system, for example, or the availability of both formal communications media and such informal media as political parties, labor organizations, cooperatives, etc. It is at best useless to prepare students for a way of life which they will have no opportunity of following. If this principle is often ignored by planners, it is certainly recognized by members of subordinate cultures, as witnessed by the massive apathy toward education found in areas where schools have been established with no supporting institutions.

Education and Social Stratification
in Contemporary Bolivia

LAMBROS COMITAS

The Bolivian Revolution of 1952 is regarded by many as the only significant social revolution in contemporary South America. Whether this revolution effected any radical change in the stratification system, however,
still remains open to question, since Bolivia has received a minimum of
scientific attention in comparison to most other Latin American countries.
This paper attempts a limited analysis of this critical question through the
examination of one key area of social activity, that of education. While the
dangers of a relatively narrow focus on a multifaceted problem are many, I
should stress, in defense of the procedure, that the core importance of
education makes it a productive point of entry for the study of complex
social systems. As anthropology shifts to research of complex sociocultural
units, the theoretical and methodological necessity for the systematic development of such vantage points becomes obvious.

To place the substantive argument which follows in clearer perspective,
I must first deal briefly with two linked issues—first, the functions of education in society, and, second, the social structure and stratification system
of traditional Bolivia.

In any social system, those institutions integrally involved with education
can have but one of two basic social functions. The first and most significant function is to maintain and to facilitate the existing social order. This

Transactions of The New York Academy of Sciences, Vol. 29, No. 7, pp. 935–948, L. Comitas.
© The New York Academy of Sciences; 1967; Reprinted by permission.

This paper was presented at a meeting of the Division on April 24, 1967. An abbreviated version
was presented at the 65th Annual Meeting of the American Anthropological Association, Pittsburgh, Pennsylvania, November 17-20, 1966.

The author was a professor at Teachers College, Columbia University, New York, when this article was written. [Ed.]

function appears to have been operative in the overwhelming majority of societies known. Education, in these cases, provides a fundamental mechanism for maintaining the sociocultural status quo through systematic and culturally acceptable training of the young for effective participation in the system. In general, the more stable and enduring the society and its culture are, the more congruous is the fit between education and the total system. Where stability is the operative function, any disjunction between education and the social system is predictably remedied through reform of the educational institutions and not through reform of the society. The objective of such institutional reform is to correct the balance and congruity, thereby readjusting the threatened social equilibrium.

In a number of relatively rare cases, the function of education is revolutionary in nature—to promote and secure the restructuring of a given society through the deliberate introduction of a type of education significantly different from that offered to the older generation. In these cases, educational change historically has followed drastic social, political, and economic upheaval and has been utilized by the new leadership to consolidate, to protect, and to refine the revolutionary gain. Education, in these instances, plays a more dynamic and creative social role, helping to reformulate the structure and reorient the values of society. This is a more positive and, I believe, a more defensible view than that taken by Talcott Parsons, who argues that the extreme concern of revolutionary regimes with education reflects their need to discipline, in terms of revolutionary values, the population over which they have gained control but which did not participate in the revolutionary movement (Parsons, 1951, p. 528).

Historic examples of the revolutionary function of education are relatively uncommon. Certainly for the twentieth century there are only limited examples even though this century has probably experienced more revolutionary activity than any comparable period in the past. Turkey under Kemal Ataturk in 1923, the Soviet Union in the 1920's, present-day China with its Red Guards and drastic educational upheaval, and undoubtedly Castro's Cuba, supply us with illustrations of thoroughgoing revolutionary systems of education. In these nations, as in a few others, education was or is being used to carry forward the social restructuring by preparing young citizens for life in a manner and with a content which radically breaks with the traditions of the past. In essence, a true revolution requires the development of a new education to help build the new society as well as to safeguard against social reaction and regression and the possible collapse of the new system. However, if over a period of time, the revolution is consolidated and protected, the function of education shifts from revolution back to one of social maintenance—to help assure the stability of the new order. Consequently, while the revolutionary function in education is of fundamental importance in any radical and permanent reformation of society, it is, almost by definition, transitional in nature. The social raison d'être for its existence diminishes once the social reorganization has been established. If this argument holds, every revolutionary society, to be in fact revolutionary, needs to initiate and support a revolutionary education, even if only for a relatively limited period of time. It follows then that an analysis of education in a society labeled revolutionary should be uniquely suited to assess the intensity and social impact of any centralized attempts to change the traditional patterns of stratification since such attempts are the keys to a successful and completed revolution and education an integral part of the process. In addition, through the examination of the organization, operation, objectives and content of education, a significant portion of the conscious and unconscious intent of a revolutionary regime can be gauged. It is with these particular ends in mind that I turn to an examination of pre- and postrevolutionary Bolivia.

Bolivia has an estimated population of only 3.5 million, one of the smallest in South America, despite the fact that it is the fifth largest country on the continent. In economic terms, it competes with Haiti as the poorest nation in the New World, with an estimated per capita income of approximately $150 a year.[1] Culturally, Bolivia is almost prototypical of the Indo-American culture area as defined by Elman Service (1955). Fully two thirds of the population are racially and culturally identifiable as Aymara or Quechua Indians, the impoverished descendants of the Incaic high civilizations of aboriginal America. The high density of this indigenous population at the time of conquest, the complexity of the pre-Hispanic Indian societies, the harsh nature of the highland environment and the specific forms of socio-economic exploitation were all significant variables in the formation of a social system which existed throughout much of the country's colonial and Republican history, and in some aspects persists to the present day.

Following the conquest, a sharply segmented society developed, consisting at first of two absolutely differentiated, hierarchically placed social sections, articulated only through the economic and regulative pressures of the socially superordinate segment, which was and remained numerically very small. Composed of the original Spanish settlers and their descendants and of a small but steady infusion of other Europeans, this superordinate group was the carrier of either Hispanic or Western European culture or the creolized variants of it. With its control of the latifundia and the other strategic resources of the territory, with its domination of a theoretically centralized

---

[1] Accurate economic statistics for Bolivia are difficult to obtain. However, the 1966 edition of the *Gallatin Annual of International Business* puts Bolivia's per capita income at about $154, the second lowest in Latin America, Haiti being the lowest. This positioning compares favorably with that established in Mikoto Usui and E. E. Hagen's reliable 1957 survey, *World Income*, which lists Bolivia's per capita income as $99, the lowest in Latin America, and Haiti's at $100, the second lowest.

but essentially loosely integrated political system, and with its preference for Castilian to the almost total exclusion of native languages as mediums of communication, this closed social segment developed aristocratic values and the behavior to match. Not unexpectedly, then, the sociocultural gulf between the groups and the requirements of the economic system gave rise to upper-segment convictions and rationalizations that Indians were sub-human, no more than beasts of burden, and carriers of a culture that could only be despised.

The subordinate segment was totally Indian, and it included the vast majority of the colonial population. Its adaptation to European cultural patterns was selective and incomplete. Only those European elements nec-essary for social and economic survival were assimilated or syncretized. Consequently, a considerable portion of the culture of this social segment remained indisputably either Aymara or Quechua and, over time, even European-derived patterns developed an identifiably Indian cast.

As in the rest of the Andean highlands, two organizational alternatives were possible for the rural indigenous population, depending to a large de-gree on local circumstance. For inhabitants of economically marginal lands, the modal reaction to the conquest was social retreat and coalescence into substantially closed, corporate communities with the concomitant develop-ment of defensive attitudes and behavior. For the indigenous inhabitants in fertile and accessible regions there was no choice; forced labor on the latifundia was the rule. In either situation, the Indian population was rele-gated to subordinate, sometimes almost slavelike, positions in the social hierarchy, positions which generated deferential cultural attitudes and styles toward members of the upper segment. Deference and servility were the reactions to force, and there is no evidence to indicate that this behavior and the accompanying values demonstrated even grudging acceptance of or consensus about the rightness of the social system. A peasant, speaking of the life of less than 20 years ago, said:

> Before we were slaves because we were stupid, we didn't understand what was going on. We didn't have anybody to defend us and we were afraid to do any-thing for fear that the patron would beat us. We didn't know why we were beaten. We didn't know about our rights. (Muratorio, 1966, p. 5.)

Throughout almost all of its postconquest history, Bolivia was socially and culturally segmented: the *blancos,* or masters and exploiters, were cul-turally European, and they occupied the highest-status points in the society; the *indios,* or exploited workers, were culturally Aymara or Quechua, and they filled the lowest-status position of the system. A structurally inter-mediate social segment developed later. Generally referred to in Bolivia as Cholos, the members of this stratum are analogous to the mestizos and La-dinos of other Latin American countries. Primarily town and city dwellers,

Cholos, of either Indian or mixed descent, have taken much of Hispano-Bolivian national culture, but they are not culturally homologous to the superordinate segment. Concentrating on small businesses, middlemen operations and transport, Cholos traditionally have been disliked by the elites, feared by the Indians, and avoided by both.

In political terms, early Bolivia and the viceroyalty of which it was a part can best be categorized as a conquest state with a stratification system based on the unilateral application of force. Later developments during the Republican period did little to effect fundamental changes in the bases of social inequality. Social accommodations to force did not lead to acceptance of the system. In this regard, Bolivia was never feudal, as was medieval Europe, where unequal distribution of opportunity could be part of the normal order of things and where social consensus could validate inequality (Smith, 1966, p. 166). In a recent article M. G. Smith has referred to a variety of basically nonconsensual societies as "unstable mixed systems." He notes for the Latin American variants in this category, among which I would include Bolivia, that:

> Systems of this sort may endure despite evident inequalities, dissent and apathy, partly through force, partly through inertia, partly because their organizational complexity and structural differentiation inhibits the emergence of effective large-scale movements with coherent programs. (Smith, 1966, p. 172.)

For present purposes, it is not necessary to find the precise sociological label for traditional Bolivia. It suffices to state that rigid stratification was at the root of the system, that aspects of cultural and social pluralism were evident, and that the structure successfully inhibited social mobility. Status in traditional Bolivia was characteristically ascriptive, based on birth into a particular social stratum and community. Differential rewards accrued to each social segment, and the system of distribution of such rewards was first protected by naked force and then by a juridical and political system dominated by the elites.

In such a social framework, it is not difficult to understand why systematic formal education for the Indian population was not considered a necessary governmental or social function for well over four centuries. The efforts made in education, particularly at the university level, were essentially reserved for the children of the social elite and were located in urban centers of population. Urban education in Bolivia has long continuity.[1] Aside from

---

[1] During the colonial period, educational institutions, located principally in the cities and large towns, were under the direction of the Roman Catholic church. With independence, public education became the responsibility of the government. At this time, Marshal Sucre promulgated legislation establishing primary, secondary and vocational institutions in all capitals of departments. During the first decade of the twentieth century, the structure and content of Bolivian education, still primarily located in areas of large population concentration, was strongly influenced by a Belgian

occasional lip service to the idea of Indian education and the occasional mission or parochial school in the countryside, almost no educational facilities were extended to the Indian until 1929. In that year, the state decreed that agricultural proprietors with more than 25 workers were obliged to establish primary schools on their estates for the Indians and that these schools were to be under the direction of the minister of public instruction and the rector of the university (Flores Moncayo, 1953, pp. 340–343). From the little evidence available and given the temper of the majority of landholders, the edict had little practical effect. From the early 1930's through 1951, there was growing agitation from the more socially conscious members of the elite for the development of educational facilities for the rural masses. In part, this agitation stemmed from the socially broadening experiences of the Chaco War (1932–1935), in which Indians were taken into the army and, for the first time, left the Altiplano and the high valleys (Quitón, 1963, p. 2). For some Bolivians with high status, the unique experience of fighting alongside the Indian against a national enemy allowed for the development of more benign attitudes toward the indigenous population. It is during this difficult period of Bolivian history that the problems of the Indian began to be considered seriously by the intelligentsia and that the first hesitant action was taken to provide the Indian with a modicum of education. Just prior to the war, in 1931, WARISATA, the forerunner of the *núcleos escolares campesinos,* or Indian nuclear schools, had been opened (Pérez, 1962, pp. 80–95). The nuclear model, a radical concept in rural training, provided for a central school which was located generally in a large pueblo and which supported a number of smaller and more limited sectional schools in surrounding villages and hamlets. In 1935, a supreme decree authorized 16 such nuclear clusters throughout Bolivia, a very limited step towards the solution of the problem of Indian education. Nevertheless, the rhetoric and stated intent of this decree is of significance in that the lack of social cohesion in Bolivia is clearly enunciated and the value of education in effecting a change is posited:

> It is the obligation of the State to integrate the native classes into the life of the country, invigorating their education in all the centers of the Republic and to assist equally the different ethnic groups that comprise the nation. (Flores Moncayo, 1953, p. 349.)

In the early years, from 1931 and up to 1944, the curriculum of the nuclear school was formal and academic, similar to that of the urban primary schools and the other rural schools maintained for non-Indians. It had little or no specific relationship to the need of the *campesinos* (Nelson, 1949, p.

---

educational mission led by Dr. George Rouma, a pupil and colleague of Dr. Ovide Decroly, the noted Belgian educator.

22). In 1945, however, on the advice of an American educational mission,[1] all rural education was reorganized. While retaining the nuclear school format, the basic objective became preparing Indians for rural life. In theory, these schools offered to the *campesino* child a four-year curriculum emphasizing agricultural and vocational subjects and personal hygiene and giving secondary importance to reading, writing, and arithmetic. The language of instruction in these schools tended to be Spanish. Justification for a markedly different system and content of education from that offered to the urban population was seen in the distinct needs of the *campesino,* "... a man who works the land, who holds the spade and plow and who has a different life from the urban man." (Quitón, 1963, p. 2.)

Despite these stirrings, the expansion of educational facilities in the countryside before 1952 was fundamentally limited. Until 1946, only 41 nuclear centers with 839 small sectional schools had been established (Nelson, 1949, p. 16). On the eve of the revolution, these numbers had not changed significantly. By 1951 (and here I must utilize unreliable government figures), only 12.9 per cent of the rural school-age population—ages five to 14—had ever been matriculated at any school (Plan Bienal, 1965 [?], p. 10). At that time, the official illiteracy rate for Bolivia was about 70 per cent, from which I estimate an illiteracy rate for the rural population of well over 90 per cent. Linguistically, the process of *castellanización,* or the attempt to make Spanish speakers of the Indians, had made little headway. Few rural Indian women knew Spanish, and a very large majority of men remained monolingual in either Aymara or Quechua. Semitrained teachers, an emasculated curriculum, lack of financial and political support from the government, and attacks from local landlords kept expansion and progress to a minimum. From all indications, it can safely be concluded that the impact of formal rural education in prerevolutionary Bolivia was weak, that it had little apparent effect in integrating the social segments, and that it had accomplished little, if anything, towards the amelioration and economic uplifting of *campesino* life. In the Bolivia of 1951, there remained an almost perfect congruence between the pattern of social stratification and the marked differences in the national allocation and use of educational resources.

In 1952, a combination of social and economic events forcibly propelled Bolivia into the twentieth century. After a series of coups and countercoups, the Nationalist Revolutionary Movement (MNR)[2] assumed power. The MNR,

---

[1] In September 1944, an agreement was signed between the Bolivian Ministry of Education and the United States government creating the Cooperative Educational Program to assist in the development of Bolivian education. In 1948, this organization was replaced by the Interamerican Educational Cooperative Service (SCIDE), which was sponsored, in conjunction with relevant Bolivian ministries, by the United States International Cooperation Administration. SCIDE gave technical assistance in rural education, industrial education, and agricultural vocational education.

[2] The Movimiento Nacionalista Revolucionario was founded in 1940 by Victor Paz Estenssoro

a party of urban intellectuals and politicians with widely differing ideologies, led, guided and occasionally diverted the several elements in Bolivia clamoring for change and recognition. With a sweeping platform of social reform, in total opposition to the ideas and wishes of the traditional elite, the MNR had to assure itself of the support of the Indians, that social segment which until this time had never been allowed participation in Bolivian national life. To ensure this support, a number of basic socioeconomic actions were taken which transformed the power shift of 1952 into a frontal attack on the traditional order of Bolivian society. First, universal suffrage was granted to all adults, with no requirements for literacy or understanding of Spanish. Secondly, pressured by the tin miners, the most highly politicized workers in the country, the MNR nationalized the vast holdings of the three most important tin barons. Finally, and most importantly, propelled more quickly by the extralegal seizures of latifundia lands by organized *campesinos,* the government legislated a national agrarian reform, returning to the Indians land that once belonged to their forefathers. Through this legislation and its execution, the government, supported by *campesino* strength, weakened the power of the superordinate segment. The partial redistribution of the country's national resources and the newly mobilized, but politically potent, force of the *campesinos* formed the scene for social change.

Although the social fabric of Bolivia was unquestionably altered during the 12 years of MNR control, the extent and form of this restructuring is as yet unclear. In addition, significant questions still remain as to how far the revolutionary leadership intended to carry its reform, to what extent it was willing to institutionalize and legitimatize change, and to what degree they were ready and able to incorporate the Indian into the new system so as to permit his free competition for position in society. In short, was the government the fulcrum for deliberate change of the traditional principles which regulated access to advantageous status positions?[1] Satisfactory answers to these questions are difficult to find; inadequate and sometimes misleading national statistics, lack of archival research, and the pervasive fog of official propaganda tend to obscure the issues, as important as they are to both scholar and administrator. However, as I have already indicated, an examination of education since the revolution of 1952 should suggest some answers. Theoretically, if the political transformation of 1952 was revolutionary in its essence, education should clearly reflect this fact.

---

and Hernán Siles Zuazo with a platform of social change and nationalism. In 1951, the MNR unexpectedly received the largest number of votes in the general election, but the takeover of the government by a military junta prevented the party from taking power at that time.

[1] Utilizing one issue, these are the same fundamental questions raised by Richard W. Patch (1960) and Dwight B. Heath (1963) in their debate over whether agrarian reform in Bolivia was a result of grassroot pressure or of central government action.

Despite the social and economic crises which beset the new government, by 1955 it had implemented a new Code of Education, laying out the structure of an educational system which exists to the present. The basic goal of the new education was to integrate the nation. In the words of President Paz Estenssoro in 1955, "The educational system which we are introducing corresponds to the interests of the classes which constitute the majority of the Bolivian people." (SORO, 1963, p. 206.)

Organizationally, the code provides for a multiple division of educational responsibility, allocating such responsibility to a number of governmental and quasi-governmental bodies. In this schema, the Ministry of Education, for example, has direct authority only for urban education—the formal schooling of children living in the cities, the capitals of departments and provinces, and other large population centers. In this urban system, legal provision is made for preschool, primary, secondary, technical-vocational and university cycles for the clientele which it serves. Furthermore, the ministry has the additional responsibility of training teachers for its own school system, of preparing the curriculum, of setting the length of the school year, and of almost all other academic and administrative matters. Philosophically, the objectives of urban education are little different from those of prerevolutionary days and fall well within the Western tradition from which they were derived. On the primary school level, for example, the school is seen as the catalyst for the cultural formation of the child, taking into consideration its idiosyncratic characteristics and its biological, physical and social needs. The social structural significance of this practically independent section of Bolivian education is that it coincides, to a very considerable degree, with the Spanish-speaking sectors of the population and with those geographical areas dominated by the descendants of the traditional elites, the small and amorphous middle class, and the Cholos. In this regard, the urban system continues, with minor modifications, the Bolivian tradition of a classic, academic education for the socially and economically privileged segments of the nation.

The Ministry of Peasant Affairs (Ministerio de Asuntos Campesinos) is responsible for the education of the rural population as well as for other activities directly relevant to rural life. Through fundamental education, the goal is to train the *campesino* child to function in his milieu and to aid in the uplifting of the rural community. Deliberately, all instruction is given in the Spanish language, continuing the policy of *castellanización,* so that eventually, in theory, a common language will unify the nation. Provisions are made for nuclear schools, sectional schools, vocational-technical schools, and rural normal schools, but none for secondary schools or for university-level work. The stated objectives of rural education are basically different from those of urban education: to develop good living habits in the *campesino* child; to teach literacy; to teach him to be an efficient agriculturalist; to develop his technical and vocational aptitudes; to prevent and to terminate the practices of alcoholism, the use of coca, the superstitions and prejudices in agronomy; and finally to develop in the *campesino* a civic conscience that would permit him to participate actively in the process of the cultural and economic emancipation of the nation (Ministerio de Educación y Bellas Artes, 1956, p. 136). This system of rural education, in essence, is a continuation and expansion of the experiments of the 1930's and 1940's. While it is a system designed for the cultural and economic uplifting of the *campesinos,* significantly it provides no mechanism for the movement of the rural student into the secondary and university cycles. Structurally, except for the possibility of limited training in the rural normal schools or through migration to the cities, the *campesino* terminates his education at the end of the primary cycle, if he is fortunate enough to reach that stage.

Several numerically less important systems of primary education also exist. For example, the *Corporación Minera de Bolivia* (Comibol), the national mining corporation, administers and supports schools in the mining areas, and *Yacimientos Petrolíferos Fiscales Bolivianos* (YPFB), the national oil corporation, is responsible for schooling in the oil and oil-refining territories. Although an educational coordinating council exists,[1] with representatives from all agencies concerned, in fact, each agency with educational responsibility has de facto control of the educational destinies of its clientele.

With well over a decade having elapsed since its inception, what have been the results of this educational structure for rural Bolivians? Most importantly, there has been a substantial physical expansion of the rural school system. By 1965, there were 5,250 government and private schools in the countryside, a fivefold increase over prerevolutionary days. Admittedly, many of these schools are little more than crude adobe shelters. Nevertheless, by 1964, 38.2 per cent of the rural school-age population was registered at school, an increase in enrollment of about 250 per cent since 1951 (Plan Bienal, 1965 [?], p. 10). In six Altiplano and Yungas communities with rural schools which were studied by anthropologists during the period

---

[1] The purpose of the Consejo de Coordinación Educacional is to ensure the basic unity of Bolivian national education. It is chaired by the minister of education and includes among others, the director general of education, the director general of rural education, the general inspector of education for the schools of the state mines and petroleum areas, the national director for the protection of minors and children, and the director of vocational education. Other interested ministries are also represented.

[2] This is a three-year project of the Research Institute for the Study of Man under Peace Corps Grant No. PC(W)-397. The basic objectives of this anthropological-epidemiological study are to assess the impact of Peace Corps public health programs in Bolivia and to provide social scientific guidelines for future public health programming in Bolivia and in structurally similar contexts. The research included intensive community studies of Sorata, Coroico, Reyes, San Miguel, Compi and Villa Abecia, as well as several shorter, selected studies of surrounding villages.

from 1964 to 1966,[2] the percentage of inhabitants who claimed any elementary schooling ranged from 31.3 per cent to 49.4 per cent, with a mean of 43.4 per cent. However, few *campesinos* in these communities progress further than the second year. For example, in one Yungas high valley community from this sample, composed of long-resident Negroes and transplanted Aymara, the mean number of years of education for ages 12 to 22 is 2.2 years for the Negroes and 2.0 years for the *campesinos*. The mean number of years of education for those over 22 years, and therefore less affected by the educational reform of the MNR, is 0.12 years for the Negroes and 0.71 years for the *campesinos*. (Newman, 1966, p. 78.)

One sign of the value placed on education by Indians is that the majority of rural schools have been constructed by *campesinos* with materials donated and gathered by the community and with only limited state aid. Schweng reports on Pillapi, an expropriated hacienda near Lake Titicaca:

> ... the interest in education the campesinos showed was moving. After the first school was built in 1955 at the expense of the project, the other schools were built by the campesinos themselves. They made the adobe bricks, leveled the ground, dug the foundations and provided all the unskilled labor. (Schweng, 1966, p. 54.)

However, a serious drawback is that over 90 per cent of these schools lack adequate furniture and sufficient teaching materials. The rural normal schools lack laboratories and libraries; the few industrial schools lack machinery for practical lessons and, as a result, students and student teachers learn only theory without practical experience.

Despite rudimentary facilities, however, the educational aspirations of the *campesinos* are very high. Many *campesinos* perceive education as the catalyst for social mobility, as the means by which they or their children will escape from the hard and unremitting toil on the land. Theoretically, by learning Spanish and attaining literacy they can more readily move to the urban centers and find better employment; if they choose, they can begin the process of becoming Cholos. Others see education as a general panacea for their life condition but have little idea as to what specifically can be gained from it. For some in this group, education is endowed with magical qualities. There are even a few *campesinos* who view education as necessary for the preservation of a traditional way of life. This particular point of view was lucidly presented by a *jillikata,* or leader of a traditional *ayllu* in an isolated community in the hills overlooking the Altiplano.[1] His

---

[1] This is a community in the Province of Carangas situated at approximately 14,000 feet above sea level. It is possible, from the pueblo site, to view almost the entire Antiplano region of the Andes. The community is part of an enclave of Aymara-speaking campesinos, partly surrounded by Quechua populations. Archeologically and anthropologically, this relatively inaccessible and little-studied section of Bolivia offers much to the serious scholar.

position, while simple, was structurally revealing: since the central government requires literacy as a prerequisite for holding local political office,
the paucity of eligible candidates makes it possible for traditionally unacceptable persons to be selected. This often has led to intracommunal clashes
between the official and the traditional systems of authority. Consequently,
in one old man's opinion, schools were necessary to provide a supply of
literate and traditionally acceptable leaders. In essence, he was choosing to
change just enough so as not to have to change. Formal education, where
it exists, may well have different meanings for the population. Nevertheless, as noted by Olen E. Leonard in a recent study of the Altiplano:

> The school is the source of greatest pride in each community. Almost all the
> heads of families seem to admit that the improvement of their educational system
> has been one of the better attainments of communities during the last decade.
> (Leonard, 1966, p. 26.)

However, for the less than a third of the rural school-age population attending school,[1] the possibilities for learning are limited. To begin with the
teacher is required to teach in Spanish even though he may be less fluent
in that language than in his native Aymara or Quechua. The non-Spanish-
speaking Indian children are instructed in the first grade, therefore, in a
language they cannot understand. To compound the problem, an extreme
form of rote instruction is utilized: As the teacher speaks, the child copies
the words into his course book, which is graded for accuracy, neatness and
artistic quality. Memorization and recitation are uniformly stressed almost
to the complete exclusion of the use of observation and experimentation.
Lack of equipment and lack of training on the part of the teachers effectively preclude any vocational or technical training, so that the student generally receives only rudimentary instruction in the fundamentals of reading,
writing, and arithmetic. With the language barrier, which is never completely surmounted, much of even this hard-learned literacy is eventually
lost. Schweng makes much the same point for his Altiplano community:

> In their educational effort, the schools were handicapped by the Govern-
> ment's insistence on using the schools as an instrument of "castellanización," for
> forcing the use of Spanish on non-Spanish speaking Indians to the exclusion of
> their native tongue. The mother tongue of the children of Pillapi was Aymara
> and no other language was spoken at home; the women spoke Aymara only and
> there were only a few fathers who spoke even a little Spanish. But in the schools,
> from the first grade, the language of instruction was Spanish and Aymara was not
> taught at all. The continuation of this policy after the Revolution was in strange

---

[1] Although in 1964, 38.2 per cent of the school-age population in the rural areas were officially
counted as being registered in schools, the number actually in full attendance was and continues to
be much lower. One estimate for 1961 (SORO, 1963, p. 199) is that only about one in 10 rural
children attended school.

contrast with the cult of the Indian encouraged by the Government and the freedom given for the use of Indian languages, Aymara and Quechua, in politics. Forcing Spanish made teaching very difficult and the educational effort wasteful. Without opportunity for using the language most children soon forgot the little Spanish they picked up at school in the two years they customarily attended. They learned less than would otherwise have been the case. (Schweng, 1966, pp. 54–55.)

The policy of *castellanización* has also compounded problems of cultural and ethnic identity. If one of the basic objectives of the rural school is to cultivate a sense of pride in being an Indian and a *campesino,* then instruction in Spanish, a language inextricably associated with the superordinate elements of Bolivia and of little direct value in an Aymara or Quechua community, widens rather than narrows the social gap. The language of instruction in this case tends more to divorce, rather than weld more closely, the student and his rural context. In any case, the goal of making Spanish the cornerstone of national cohesion is far from being realized. For example, of the four basically Aymara communities in the study sample, none had more than 1.2 per cent monolingual Spanish speakers, and these were almost always government officials assigned to the community. Aymara monolinguals ranged from a high of 84.4 per cent in one community to a low of 42.5 per cent in the most acculturated village. Self-professed bilinguals in Spanish and Aymara ranged from a low of 10.5 per cent to a high of 49.6 per cent.[1]

Aside from linguistic barriers and a truncated and unrelated curriculum, the low quality of rural education is also a function of the inadequacies of rural teachers. While urban teachers are required to have a secondary school and a normal school diploma, rural teachers need only a primary school certificate, plus six months in a rural normal school. In many cases, even these minimal requirements are not met, so that a large number of rural teachers have not completed the primary school. Teachers' salaries are low in all parts of the country, averaging about $40 a month. As a result, teachers' attendance in school is often sporadic, since other work is sought to augment the income. This is particularly true of male teachers. In addition, with a politically strong teachers' union which makes it almost impossible to fire a teacher, the educative process stagnates. A normally short school year is shortened further by student participation in scores of national and religious holidays which require days of special preparation before the event, by political crises which close the schools, by teachers' strikes, and by teacher absenteeism.

[1] Data on language were generated from a census collected at an early date in all communities studied by the Research Institute for the Study of Man. A comprehensive sociological survey, which included a long section on language and education, was undertaken at the close of the field study in 1966. These data are currently being computer processed and will be utilized as the basis for several forthcoming papers and reports.

As a consequence, the *campesino* child receives, from the rural school system, little formal preparation for modern life, and this is clearly reflected in the educational statistics. Student absenteeism rates are very high and usually attributed to the need for the child to assist in family work, but they are also related to the actual, as opposed to the stated, content of the programs, the lack of teacher preparation, and the scarcity of teaching aids and classrooms. The desertion or dropout rate is extraordinarily high. Of each 100 *campesino* children ages five to seven years, only 37 enter the first grade, and six complete the sixth terminal year (Plan Bienal, 1965 [?], p. 15). Finally, the problem of illiteracy has not been solved. While the official illiteracy rate has been modestly reduced from 68.9 per cent in 1950 to 63 per cent after 14 years (Plan Bienal, 1965 [?], p. 5), I would speculate that even this limited gain was made in the urban areas.

In providing expanded educational opportunities for the *campesinos,* the MNR corrected what it believed was a glaring injustice of the old order. As far as a limited economy permitted, the *campesino* was granted the right of formal schooling, which in the past had been essentially reserved for the privileged classes. In this regard, the government provided an institutional structure to help meet the rising aspirations and demands for education. In many of the remote areas of Bolivia, the school, for the first time, became a factor in the socialization of the *campesino* child. Abstractly then, the very extension of educational services to the rural masses can be considered revolutionary.

An analysis of the structure and content of rural education, however, leads to diametrically opposed conclusions. The Balkanization of the educational enterprise, the multiple allocation of responsibility, the differing educational goals for different socioeconomic groups, in my opinion, lead inevitably to further qualitative distinctions between these groups. In fact, the more efficient each section of the total educational system is in the training of its wards, the more distant becomes the ideal goal of integration through education. Furthermore, since the divisions of Bolivian education correspond closely with the old social divisions of Bolivian society and since the rural segment is virtually barred from participation at the secondary and university levels, the effect is to institutionalize, in education, the stratification patterns of the past. Given the structure of education, there is no opportunity, short of physical relocation and cultural transformation, for the *campesino* to receive that level of training which will allow him to compete successfully for the advantageous positions in society. It is of more than academic interest to note that most of the sharply stratified societies which have made resolute moves toward modernization and toward a consensual form of social structure select unitary systems of education to aid in the process.

Conservative rather than revolutionary thought is also seen in the content of rural education. Subject matter and mode of instruction reflect both patronizing and paternalistic features. A leitmotif of the educational philosophy is the suppression of all cultural elements in *campesino* life which are considered dysfunctional, but little is offered to replace that which is suppressed. When this is combined with the central decision to give highest priority to training for rural life, the *campesinos,* from an educational perspective, are sealed off from social movement in the society. A short-run gain for the national economy is a long-term investment in the continuance of a sharply stratified state. I do not argue here for absolute homogeneity for all sectors of Bolivian education, but for Bolivian youth to have institutionalized opportunities to move, if qualified, from one differentiated educational sector to the other. This would provide an important condition for an open society and would decrease the social dangers which will ensue when unrealistic aspirations hinged to education are not realized.

This cursory review suggests that, in education, the revolution of 1952 and the 14 years of MNR dominance did little to modify the hierarchical order of the socially significant segments of Bolivian society and did little, if anything, to provide new, institutionalized forms of social articulation. It is obvious that, whatever else the directives were that emanated from the center of the system, they were not revolutionary in effect. The considerable social change which Bolivia has experienced during the last 14 years seems to be more the result of a partial splintering of the traditional order than a thoroughgoing social reform. It is a change generated, in the main, by an uncoordinated but mass pressure from a discontented social base. One can then speculate that the post-1952 phase of Bolivian history represents a period of *campesino* coalescence and emergence which, if not diverted, will lead to serious upheaval before resulting in reform and social regrouping. In this present process of coalescence, any opportunity for formal education is of value. This is perhaps the true legacy of the present system.

Acknowledgments

I am grateful to the Research Institute for the Study of Man, New York City, to the Institute of International Studies, Teachers College, Columbia University, and to the Columbia-Cornell-Harvard-Illinois Summer Field Program for research support while I was in Bolivia for varying periods of time during 1964, 1965, and 1966.

References

Flores, Moncayo, José. *Legislación boliviana del indio: Recopilación 1825–1953.* La Paz, Bolivia, 1953.
Heath, Dwight, B. "Land Reform and Social Revolution in Bolivia." Paper read at 62nd Ann. Meeting, Am. Anthropological Assoc. 1963. Mimeo.

Leonard, Olen E. *El cambio económico y social en cuatro comunidades del Altiplano de Bolivia.* Instituto Indigenista Interamericano, Serie Antropología Social, No. 3. Mexico, 1966.

Ministerio de Educación y Bellas Artes. *Código de la educación boliviana.* La Paz, Bolivia, 1956.

Muratorio, Blanca. "Changing Bases of Social Stratification in a Bolivian Community." Paper presented at 65th Ann. Meeting Am. Anthropological Assoc., November 17-20, Pittsburgh, Pa. 1966. Mimeo.

Nelson, Raymond H. *Education in Bolivia.* Washington: Federal Security Agency, Office of Education, Bulletin No. 1, 1949.

Newman, Roger C. "Land Reform in Bolivia's Yungas." M.A. thesis, Columbia University, New York, 1966.

Parsons, Talcott. *The Social System.* New York: Free Press, 1951.

Patch, Richard W. "Bolivia: U.S. Assistance in a Revolutionary Setting," *in* Richard W. Adams, ed., *Social Change in Latin America Today.* New York: Random House, 1960. Pp. 108-176.

Pérez, Elizardo. *WARISATA: La escuela-Ayllu.* La Paz, Bolivia, 1962.

Plan Bienal. "Plan del sector de educación y formación profesional, 1965-66." La Paz (?), Bolivia, 1965 (?). Mimeo.

Quitón, Carlos. *Proceso de la educación rural y educación fundamental en Bolivia.* Boletín Indigenista No. 1, April 1963.

Schweng, Lorand D. "An Indian Community Development Project in Bolivia," *in* Arthur H. Niehoff, ed., *A Casebook of Social Change.* Chicago, Ill.: Aldine Publishing Co., 1966. Pp. 44-57.

Service, Elman. "Indian-European Relations in Colonial Latin America," *Am. Anthropologist,* 57, no. 3 (1955), pp. 411-425.

Smith, M. G. "Pre-Industrial Stratification Systems," *in* Neil J. Smelser and Seymour M. Lipset, eds., *Social Structure and Mobility in Economic Development.* Chicago, Ill.: Aldine Publishing Co., 1966. Pp. 141-176.

SORO (Special Operations Research Office). *U.S. Army Area Handbook for Bolivia.* Washington, D.C.: The American University, 1963.

The Cuban Revolutionary Offensive in Education

GERALD H. READ

With the Alliance for Progress in Latin America in complete disarray and the explosive reaction to Governor Rockefeller's forays south of the border dramatically recorded by the mass media for the world to study and analyze, it is important to report the degree of success Cubans have had in their revolutionary offensive in education. The reader must judge for himself the impact that the Cuban educational model may have upon the restless nations south of the United States border.

The revolution that came to Cuba 10 years ago brought with it many changes and a style of life quite in contrast to the one which had existed for centuries. Superficially the revolution has imposed a conceptual and institutional structure similar to that found in the socialist countries of Eastern Europe and China, but in operation the Cuban version is unique and radically different.

The government espouses a totalist ideology, maintains a single party with a one-man leadership committed to the practice of its ideals, and operates under extensive but relatively relaxed surveillance and control. The party asserts monopolistic direction of all mass media. All organizations and their activities are centrally controlled and ordered. The ultimate goal of the educational establishment is to remold and transform every individual under its control in the image of an ideal called socialist humanism, and of a political system labeled communism.

The "grand design" of Cuban revolutionary education can best be described in terms of four major goals which are being pursued simultaneously:

Reproduced, by permission, from *Comparative Education Review,* 14 (June, 1970), pp. 131–143.

(a) making education universal from nursery school through the university, so that knowledge, science, and technology will be made available to all, (b) developing a Marxist orientation in education, (c) combining education with technological principles, productive work, and research, and (d) incorporating the working masses into education.

Making Education Universal

The most significant achievement of the Castro regime in its first 10 years of existence has been the establishment of genuinely free co-education of all types of schools and on all levels, by eliminating registration fees and tuition, and by providing free text books, school supplies, scholarships, and economic aid for thousands of young people, peasants, and workers who otherwise would never have had the opportunity to secure an education. The principle of universality of education through state control and management has been put into effect for the first time in the history of Cuba in order to meet the social, economic, and cultural needs of its children and adults, as well as the needs of a technologically developing nation.

This indeed is a huge undertaking for a newly established revolutionary government and involves a great investment of human resources and money for a nation that is still industrially underdeveloped, but it is a necessary investment if a successful and widespread transformation to a socialist state is to be achieved.

The minister of education, José Llanusa, has repeatedly said "the proposed draft of the Law for Compulsory Secondary Education will soon be discussed," but no date has ever been set. In January 1969, however, he filled in a few more details of the proposed law relative to measures for enforcement. "The responsibility for compliance with the law will fall on the parents, and the law will also include measures to be taken in case of noncompliance. Discussions will be held with all the people concerning this law. Their opinions will be taken into consideration, block by block, work center by work center."[1]

The new program forecasts a huge demand for secondary school teachers. Many young people will have to be enrolled in the pedagogical institutes of the three universities or in a special center in Camagüey for a five-year course after having graduated from the new technological institutes. An organized effort is already being made to direct into the pedagogical institutes those who have served as monitors.

Developing a Marxist Orientation

Castro gave little personal attention to the ideological mission of the schools in the early years of the 1960's. Slow and laborious spadework to this end,

---

[1] José Llanusa, "Creando una nueva conciencia," *Bohemia* (January 24, 1969), pp. 58-60.

however, was undertaken by cadres from the Trade Union of Education and Scientific Workers (SNTEC). In advance of the thoroughgoing reformulation of objectives, revision of course content, reorientation of teaching procedures, and a reconstruction of teacher education, the trade union conducted a series of conferences for the purpose of ideological orientation. At one of these meetings, on December 13–15, 1961, Gaspar Jorge García Galló, the secretary-general, made very clear the source and inspiration of the new pedagogical theory and practice.

Those who are going to study in the primary school during these years will become adults in a society different from that of today; let there be no doubt about it. The society in which the children will live, for whom we are working in these programs, will be Communist when they are adults. Communist! I suppose that you have studied the program approved by the 22nd Congress of the Communist Party of the Soviet Union. [October 17–18, 1961.] If some have not studied it, note here that one ought to study it and he who has only read it, note that he ought to study it.[1]

Later in this same meeting, Secretary García made the point that the schools could not be refashioned in a short time but that a long-range plan was contemplated.

What is proposed is to train active and conscientious builders of the communist society. But this cannot be achieved immediately by means of simple decrees and administrative orders of the new revolutionary authority. It is not enough to meet here and agree to modify all the plans of study. This will require a longer time and it will be achieved to the degree that the old educators are reeducated and a new mentality is created, a new socialist mentality.[2]

The real revolution in education got under way after October 1965 when the July 26th movement was converted into an organized Communist party of Cuba. In June, 1965, the minister of education, Armando Hart Dávalos, proclaimed the start of a new phase in educational development which would be marked by an aggressive effort to secure an ideological transformation in the moral and social consciousness of every citizen. He resigned his post as minister shortly thereafter to become the organizing secretary of the Communist party of Cuba. A hundred-member central committee, a six-man secretaryship, and an eight-man political bureau assumed responsibility for coordinating the party's ideological pronouncements and programs, which for the most part emanated from the office of the first secretary, Fidel Castro.

Castro gradually succeeded in putting together what can be called a system of attitudes, beliefs, values, assumptions, ideals, and goals—in short, an

---

[1] Gaspar Jorge García Galló, *Conferencia sobre educación* (Havana: Imprenta Nacional Unidad, 1962), p. 5.

[2] *Ibid.*, p. 7.

ideology. He used this, in August 1968, as a whip for chastising Czecho-slovak socialists who, he claimed, were sacrificing glorious ideals for the illusory immediate material gains that would come from commercial ties with the imperialist powers of the West. What were the glorious ideals which the prime minister had come to hold so dear, even to the point of support-ing the invasion of a socialist country?

> ... those beautiful aspirations that constitute the communist ideal of a classless society, a society free from selfishness, a society in which man is no longer a mis-erable slave to money, in which society no longer works for personal gain, and all society begins to work for the satisfaction of all needs and for the establishment among men of the rule of justice, fraternity, and equality.[1]

These are the stated aspirations and ideals that now guide and direct Cas-tro's educational visions and revolutionary endeavors. They explain his role as a messianic leader who cannot tolerate opposition. They explain his identification with Marxism, because this ideology expresses what he has come to believe. They explain his acceptance of organizational Leninism because it provides the discipline and control which his previous political grouping had failed to achieve. They explain the overriding concern of all Cuban educators and teachers, for the formation of the "new man" in a rev-olutionary society is the principal subject of the revolution.

With the abolition of private property, capitalistic exploitation, and po-litical dependence, Castro believes that the first large goals of the revolution have been successfully reached. He has proclaimed that Cubans are now free and, under prevailing revolutionary conditions, can prepare themselves through education for their ultimate fulfillment, or state of "grace." This fulfillment should come with the humanization of labor, when all Cubans will be capable of discovering, assimilating, and mastering the content of their work. "The possibility of a man's being motivated by the content of his work is in direct relation to the individual's knowledge and his cultural level; the lower his cultural level, the less work motivates him."[2]

Addressing his audience at the University of Havana, the prime minister asserted that "the revolution cannot reconcile itself with the idea that in the future there should always be a minority in society with a monopoly on technical and scientific knowledge and a majority shut out from this knowledge." He has even promised that "in Cuba someday the university will become universal and the entire nation will study at the university level."

Labor in the future is to become a pleasure. "When work is completely

---

[1] Fidel Castro, "Discurso para analizar los acontecimientos de Checoslovaquia," *Ediciones C.O.R.,* August 23, 1968 (Havana: Instituto del Libro, 1968).

[2] Fidel Castro, "Discurso para honrar a los martires del 13 del marzo, 1969," *Ediciones C.O.R.* (Havana: Instituto del Libro, 1969).

ordered by man's intelligence, completely controlled by man's intelligence, it ceases to be hard, animal work." Hence Castro is saying that "it is impossible for us to conceive of the development of the people's education without including in our conception . . . the development of every potential capability, of all the potential intelligence of that people." On the other hand, awareness of the importance of manpower development in a technological and developed society is always evident in his plans. "The levels of development that this country will reach can be measured only by the percentage of young people carrying on advanced studies. It will be measured by the total number of citizens engaged in such studies."[1]

This entire conceptual framework is historically known as socialist humanism. It is a relevant and convenient concept to use in marking out the direction and shape of a truly revolutionary education, but it is neither new nor original. Almost never does Castro identify the historical or contemporary sources or sanctions for his beliefs, values, attitudes, and goals. They are always presented as the thoughts of Fidel Castro. But much of the theoretical orientation of his speeches over the past few years appears to come from an early work of Karl Marx, *The Economic and Philosophical Manuscripts of 1844,* which expounds the thesis that the essence of socialist humanism is man, a free creative being, possessing the productive powers that enable him to produce for the sheer pleasure of doing so. Castro agrees with Marx that once work is taken from the exploitative circumstances of the capitalistic society, it will become an artistic creation.[2] The ultimate reason for revolutionary effort, Castro asserts, is to secure the release of the spiritual energy of man and thereby bring into being a society in which man will be able to cultivate the life of the mind and exercise his creative abilities freely in work. In this utopia, after the day's labor is completed, the educated Cuban citizen will devote his leisure to the cultivation and enjoyment of the arts and sciences.

The theoretical framework of Cuban education, therefore, is a peculiar mix of Marxism and Castroism. Leninism is almost never mentioned. The nationalism and independence of Castro is so great that Marx is seldom directly quoted. It is best, perhaps, to identify the conceptual guidelines as Castroism while recognizing that the sources are to a large extent those of Marxism and socialist humanism. Educational structures and practices, on the other hand, are much less dependent upon imported sources, although even here borrowings from the socialist countries of Eastern Europe may be observed.

Although Castro is still committed to socialist humanism and has kept it in a rather fluid state with varying interpretations, all evidence points to

---

[1] *Ibid.*

[2] Karl Marx, "Economic and Philosophical Manuscripts," *in* Eric Fromm's *Marx's Concept of Man* (New York: Frederick Ungar Publishing Co., 1961).

the beginnings of a more systematic ideology, perhaps even a dogmatism. On September 28, 1968, he asserted with great confidence: "We can state that it has taken years for revolutionary conscientiousness to triumph in our masses . . . and I believe that it has actually been during this past year that the triumph of the Revolution has become most evident in the consciousness of the masses of our capital."[1]

The prime minister conceives of the party, the state, the society, and the individual collectively providing for the education of the present and future generations. At the closing session of the National Meeting of School Monitors, September 17, 1966, he spoke of the task that had fallen to the revolution. "The most sacred of all of our obligations has been that of how we are going to form our children and youth . . . our triumph in this great historic mission will depend upon the measure in which we are capable of solving correctly the problem of the formation of our new generations." Then he spoke of the parents' responsibility and that of society in general. "The greatest offense that can be committed against a human being and against society, the gravest offense that a father or mother can commit, is to permit his child not to attend school." And finally in a true humanistic spirit he declared: "It will not be the law, it will not be the coercive force of the state but, rather, social conscience that imposes on each citizen the idea that he cannot commit the crime of creating an ignoramus or of bringing an ignoramus into the world."[2]

In a speech to the trade unions of Cuban workers on August 30, 1966, in his role of first secretary of the party, Fidel described the dual responsibility which he had to shoulder: "Revolutionary processes have two facets. One is the theoretical facet and the other is the practical facet. One is revolutionary theory, which inspires and guides the struggle of the oppressed, and the other is what revolutionaries practice."[3]

Castro is at his best in projecting utopian tomorrows, but the professionalization of revolutionary schooling is quite a different and much more exacting task, which he has delegated to a specialist in physical education, José Llanusa, minister of education. Llanusa has been a close collaborator of the prime minister since the guerrilla days in the Sierra Maestra Mountains. No one in Cuba today is more devoted to the task of furthering the ideological orientation of the entire educational establishment. On August 18, 1968, he addressed the Makarenko Pedagogical Institute in Havana, where he directed this challenge to the graduating class: "You must help develop your students as Communists, representatives of generations that

[1] Fidel Castro, *Discurso en el acto conmemorativo del VIII Aniversario de los Comités de Defensa de la Revolución, 28 de septiembre de 1968* (Havana: Instituto del Libro, 1968).

[2] "National Meeting of School Monitors," *Granma* (September 25, 1966).

[3] Fidel Castro, *Speech to the Closing Session of Trade Unions of Cuban Workers, August 30, 1966* (Havana: Instituto del Libro, 1966).

will be better than yours—which, in turn, will doubtless be better than ours. That is the revolutionary pledge you are making today to the Revolution. You must be concerned about the conduct of students . . . the ideological formation of those students."[1]

On January 24, 1969, "creating a new conscience" was the theme for the minister of education's address to the activists who were responsible in the party for indoctrination in all educational, scientific, and cultural institutions. The aspiration of the new revolutionary pedagogy, he emphasized, was "the creation of a new scale of values in which man and his complete development are the fundamental considerations." What should be the relation of the individual to the collective? The minister took great care to say: "This means a complete development of his individuality for the benefit of collective interest, based on the revolutionary and international principles our leaders have taught us." The "New Cuban Man" which this pedagogy is to create must be one "for whom work is enjoyment and not obligation, and for whom study is a permanent process. A man of culture, science and technology."[2]

To achieve these ends, the minister of education has conceived a strategy called the "Mass Line." The leaders of the revolution patiently and repeatedly describe and explain in their major addresses the grand design of the new education and all the difficulties being encountered in putting it into operation. They elaborate upon the plans and strategies they have proposed, tried out, or hope to put into action to meet the operational problems. All of the mass organizations, government agencies, and party branches are then called upon to cooperate in getting the educational program moving forward. Llanusa has said that the "Mass Line" is not simply a theoretical postulate; it is a revolutionary reality, a style of work. To be more specific, he declared: "Revolutionary pedagogy must be everyone's concern, a consistent application of the anti-bureaucratic methods which Fidel teaches us. . . . Everyone teaching, everyone learning, everyone working, everyone devoted to national defense, everyone creating for the revolution."[3]

A similar line was taken at the Seventh National Assembly of the People's Organization in Education. "We need teachers whose motivation is to form new men. . . . True revolutionary teachers who will replace the turncoat teachers who deserted their country."[4]

There is no record of the reaction of the teachers to Llanusa's proposal that all vestiges of special material incentives would have to be eliminated

[1] José Llanusa, "There Are 1533 New Primary Teachers," *Granma* (August 19, 1968).

[2] José Llanusa, "Creando una nueva conciencia," *Bohemia,* 4 (January 24, 1969), pp. 58–60.

[3] *Ibid.*

[4] Manuel Castro, "VII National Assembly of the People's Organization in Education," *Granma* (September 11, 1966).

from the teaching profession. "Only those capable of making sacrifices should be admitted to the profession." He went on to say: "They will be the ones who find their incentives in the awareness that they are constructing the new society, forming the new men." This high ideal is already being achieved, he told the assembly: "even now our young people, inspired . . . by the example of Che, as well as by what our leaders are teaching them, no longer speak of vocation, but rather they speak of the greatest vocation, that of being a revolutionary." And in almost the same spirit as John Kennedy at his inauguration, Llanusa concluded: "The new generation does not ask which occupation is best paid or most secure but rather, what does the Revolution need? Where can I discharge my duty?" On the other hand, he conceded that "giving scholarships and making available reading materials, and similar measures were the best ways to stimulate workers in education to improve professionally."[1]

At the final session of the plenum of the Union of Pioneers of Cuba, in August of 1968, the first secretary of the Young Communist League (UJC), called upon the UPC to shoulder the responsibility for creating "the man of the 21st century, the man that Che dreamed of, the man who will be inspired by his example."[2] It was to that end that 270 graduating high school seniors from schools throughout Las Villas Province made a 26-kilometer trek to the site in the mountains where Che had his headquarters. Here they were granted their diplomas and one of the seniors read the class oath.

> We swear to direct our future activities as university students toward attainment of the Communist society, sparing no physical or intellectual effort, training to be technicians capable of contributing to the elimination of underdevelopment in our own country or in any place throughout the world in which such knowledge may be needed.
>
> To find the essential motivation for our work and future plans in love of mankind, the dream of developing the man of the 21st century, without designing ambitious or geographic frontiers, with a profound international spirit, depending on neither moral nor material incentives. To struggle against routine, dogma and schemata. . . . To maintain the ideological struggle, taking an active part in the revolutionary process, as regards both the methods of political roles and our own development as students and future technicians, and maintaining an intransigent spirit in the face of vice, weakness and ambition. . . .[3]

Polytechnical Education

Education throughout Latin America has been and still is highly verbal, intellectual, and formal, with a disdain for the technical and practical. A similar charge against Soviet education had been made by Premier Khrushchev

---

[1] Llanusa, *Bohemia,* 4 (January 24, 1969), pp. 58-60.
[2] Lino Oramus, "National Plenum of Union of Pioneers of Cuba," *Granma* (September 2, 1968).
[3] "Las Villas High School Students," *Granma* (August 30, 1968).

in 1956 when the party led a movement in the U.S.S.R. to introduce into the schools a closer connection between school and life, instruction and productive work, scientific theory and practice. The Soviet school reform of 1958 provided for general, polytechnical, labor education intimately linked, and all Eastern European socialist nations have applied this concept in their educational programs. The Cubans have studied these experiences and have developed their own interpretations and applications. Combining education with technological principles, productive work, and research is now a principle that guides all deliberations of educational committees, technical teams, study groups, conferences, and seminars at all levels. It is the rationale for the "Schools Go to the Countryside" program in which students voluntarily contribute their vacation periods to work assignments on farms or in industries or public works.

This polytechnical program started on May 25, 1964, under a law which proclaimed that the new concept of education would run the entire span of the educational system from the first grade through the university. The ideological aim is to develop a new attitude toward life, work and the working class, and to overcome the tendency of students to develop a bookish outlook on life.[1]

The then minister of education, Armando Hart, went to the U.S.S.R. in 1961 to study its educational system and methods. The Trade Union of Educational and Scientific Workers of Cuba, modeled after that of the U.S.S.R., conducted seminars throughout the island on the theoretical and operational meaning of polytechnical education. Ivan Grivkov of the U.S.S.R., Lu Ting-Yi of China, and Alfred Wilke of the German Democratic Republic contributed descriptions of the operation of polytechnic education in their countries to a trade union publication.[2] Later *Tres experiencias sobre la politecnización* illustrated how three Cuban schools had interpreted and applied polytechnical education.[3]

Secretary-General García had this to say at a national seminar of the teachers union: "When teaching is oriented in accordance with the socialist transformation of our economy, it will have to undergo profound changes in the context of the programs, the methods that are employed for its realization, the textbooks, and the teaching aids." He fully realized that the most serious problem would be faced in converting the teachers. "This transformation in the orientation of education will be gained only after a long and stubborn fight . . . the most intense battle will be freeing it from the old traditions which separate manual and intellectual work . . . the work

---

[1] Armando Hart, "Resolution 392 of the Revolutionary Government on the Polytechnization of Instruction, May 25, 1964" (Havana: Ministry of Education, 1964).

[2] El Sindicato Nacional de Trabajadores de Enseñanza y la Ciencia, *La politecnización* (Havana: SNTEC, 1964).

[3] García Galló, *Conferencia sobre educación*, p. 5.

of the National Union of Education and Scientific Workers will have to be in the vanguard."

Another step toward a more utilitarian education was taken in 1968 when the Plan for Technological Instruction converted all the agricultural cattle-raising technological institutes into military centers. There are now 23 institutions in this program under the direction of the Office of Military Centers for Intermediate Education in the Ministry of the Armed Forces. The technical and teaching portions of the programs are supervised by the Ministry of Education. Students live under strict military discipline at boarding institutions and complete their military draft obligations while they study.[1]

Major Belarmino Castilla Mas, deputy minister for technological military training, directs all intermediate-level technological training, sets priorities, and developed the strategy for the changeover to the new system. He has asserted: "It is our job to determine where and how this army of technicians is to be trained, where we are to employ these human resources and in which direction the efforts must be aimed." The major will also have full responsibility for determining "the rational use of the teaching personnel."[2]

Castro was candid in giving another reason for combining secondary education with military training:

> . . . nothing makes a military commander happier than to have a technological school assigned to one of his units. Indisputably, any youth with one or two years of senior high or technological education finds it easier to learn military techniques and is much more capable of learning the handling of complex military equipment in a short time. Military units have a hard time training personnel composed of young people with only a second-, third -, or fourth-grade education.[3]

The Plan for Technological Instruction will also include the transitional preuniversity secondary school which will be converted into institutes of science and humanities. The first hint of this came in a speech by Castro on November 16, 1968. "In the future we will no longer have what we term *bachillerato.* [Preuniversity secondary school.] Instead, there will be technological institutes for the study of sciences. . . . But they will all be technological institutes with different specialties according to the studies to be carried out in the future or the use to be made of this training."[4]

Will this military training be similar to the ROTC arrangement found in American universities? What will be the status of the regular armed forces? Some hint as to what he has in mind appeared in an article recognizing

[1] Vincente Cubillas, "Ernest Thaielman Tech Fulfills Goal of Training," *Granma* (March 10, 1968).

[2] E. Gonzalez Manet, "The Principal Task of Our Youth," *Granma* (June 9, 1969).

[3] Fidel Castro, "Discurso en resumen séptimo aniversario de la derrota del imperialismo yanki en Playa Girón, abril 19 de 1968," *Ediciones C.O.R.* (Havana: Instituto del Libro, 1969).

[4] *Ibid.*

the fifth anniversary of the promulgation of the Military Service Law: "At the present time tens of thousands of young students drawn from our technological and high schools make up our military units."[1] This article then went on to distinguish between the Revolutionary Armed Forces, as an organization of cadres-on-call, and the regular troops, which are the students on active duty at each of the institutes. Moreover, the schools of the future will not only be in the army but will also be in the country. This was made clear in an address by Castro on December 8, 1968. ". . . it will no longer be today's '45-Days School Goes to the Countryside'; by then it will be the 'School in the Countryside.' "[2] On March 13, 1969, he was even more certain that this would be the case. "In the future we will have the Schools in the Countryside. . . . The first of these will soon be under construction."[3]

Worker-Farmer Education

The National Office of Worker-Farmer Education in the Ministry of Education's elementary school division seeks to upgrade the meager knowledge of the peasants and workers which was acquired during the literacy campaign or after a few years of schooling. Improvement courses are given for adults (14 years of age and above) to advance them to the third-grade, sixth-grade, and through the basic secondary levels. Classes are held in work and farm centers, usually in the evenings or before the work shift begins. More than 15 million textbooks, technical pamphlets, workbooks, magazines, and newspapers have been printed by the Ministry of Education and distributed without charge to participants in these programs.

Completion of the basic secondary course opens the way to further education in the upper secondary classes, the worker-farmer preparatory faculties of the universities, or special technical and vocational courses for adults. The worker-farmer faculties, created in 1964 with branches in many cities and towns, undertake crash courses to prepare adults for entrance into various schools and the universities. In order to enroll in one of these faculties one must be a member of the trade union, armed forces, Ministry of Education, or mass organizations. The time schedule is coordinated with workshifts; classes are usually held at the place of work. Experience derived from these courses has led Castro to predict that: "In the future, practically every plant, agricultural zone, hospital, and school will become a university."[4]

---

[1] "Fifth Anniversary of Promulgation of Military Service Law," *Granma* (November 26, 1968).

[2] Fidel Castro, "Discurso a la Universidad de Oriente," *Bohemia,* Supplement (December 13, 1968).

[3] Fidel Castro, "Discurso para honrar a los martires del 13 de marzo, 1969," *Ediciones C.O.R.* (Havana: Instituto del Libro, 1969).

[4] Fidel Castro, "Construimos un país para todos con el trabajo de todos," *Bohemia,* 50, Supplement (December 13, 1968).

Adult education also includes the Women's Educational Advancement Program. This program brings thousands of farm girls and women from the Sierra Maestra Mountains and other remote places to boarding schools which prepare them politically and educationally to return to their own areas to expand the party's influence and to teach. The Ana Betancourt School for Farm Girls is one of these institutions. Founded in 1961 at the suggestion of Fidel Castro, it has an enrollment of more than 10,000 and is under the direction of the Federation of Cuban Women. It is housed in more than 300 mansions where the wealthy elite formerly lived.[1]

Study and work camps are maintained for delinquent youths between 14 and 17 years of age who for various reasons have not completed the sixth grade. This is a very active program designed to bring these youths back into the mainstream of society. The principle is: "Work should be the great teacher of youth."[2]

Over 460,000 adults were enrolled in courses in 1968; from 1962 to 1967, 365,720 persons completed the sixth grade and 578,444 the secondary courses.[3] This program of adult education is exceptionally important in view of the massive exodus of the educated classes from Cuba during the past 10 years. It is still common to find people with a sixth-grade education in charge of state farms, factories, and other important work centers. Some have served adequately, but the pressing need is for better-educated administrators and supervisors.

Since 1959, schools have increasingly reflected Castro's attempt at total control of everyday life and activities, thoughts and attitudes, although one wonders if regimentation can ever be achieved and maintained to the degree reached by the socialist countries of Eastern Europe. The island at the present time can be characterized as a vast reformatory, or, more charitably, a comprehensive school, with the party showing no sign of discouragement in its mission to inculcate revolutionary enthusiasm, commitment, and morale. The leadership has given top priority to rural development and a regeneration of the masses through education in the spirit of the July 26th movement and ideological evangelism. The revolutionary offensive has demonstrated above all else that the appetite for education is insatiable, is still growing, and will continue to grow faster than the national production. If present projections become a reality, the teaching profession will absorb more than half the graduates of higher and secondary institutions.

If Cuba is to resist the domination of the great powers, she must develop her agriculture and industry. Serious problems arise, however, when the

---

[1] *Granma,* August 1968.

[2] Justina Alvarez, "A School Where Country Girls Learn and Teach Simultaneously," *Granma,* December 4, 1966.

[3] "La educación en números," *Cuba,* p. 50.

educational system must be geared to meeting pressing societal needs and their required fulfillment outweighs all other ends, including even human freedom. The utopian and commendable dreams of Fidel Castro, which flow from his belief in the possibility of a better life for all Cubans, are in danger of being reduced to purely economic strategies.

Cuban education is increasingly becoming a victim of economic planning and systematization, in spite of everything Castro has done and said in efforts to prevent it. On the other hand, it may be that this is what the revolution is all about and to reverse the process is to deny the revolution. The supreme sacrifice that José Martí preached was to die for Cuba. He was strongly opposed to placing personal rights above the national welfare, for only *patria* mattered. Martí proclaimed: "He who loves the fatherland cannot think of himself."

Whatever the final judgment may be, Cuba in the past decade has witnessed a political, social, and pedagogical revolution. Cubans who have lived and are living through it will never be the same, and the future of Cuba will surely be different if Castro achieves his educational goals. "All soldiers, all students, all workers. An army of the people advancing along the three fundamental paths toward progress: educational development, defense of the country, and productive work."

Section 5:
Perspectives on Students and Schools

Introduction to Section 5

The article by Daniel Goldrich presents cross-national questionnaire results from agrarian laborers' sons who attend vocational schools in or near the capital cities of Panama and Costa Rica. He finds that these peasant families have provided a home environment which is relatively politicized and cohesive and which encourages the sons to take advantage of educational programs as one of the government services provided in the city. Goldrich suggests that family disintegration is not a characteristic of this new urban sector and that the existence of political extremism, when it is evident, is a result of the structure and performance of the political system existing in each of the respective nations. He further suggests that these potential leaders of the urban mass are not characterized by extremism but instead by an increasingly moderate political style.

Robert Havighurst and Aparecida Gouveia, in the second selection, report on their investigation of 16,156 middle school students representing five Brazilian states. The authors indicate a positive relationship exists between the socioeconomic level of the family and attendance at the secondary level. The relationship appears to become more positive as students enroll at higher levels; middle- and upper-status students emerge with a similar opportunity to attend middle schools whereas lower-status students, in terms of the proportion of lower-status families in the society, emerge with a relatively small opportunity. Lower-status students are more likely to enroll in commercial, industrial, and agricultural schools, whereas the middle-status and upper-status students are heavily enrolled in academic and normal schools.

The authors suggest that although few differences exist among socioeconomic status levels in student attitude responses, considerable difference is evident between states and between urban areas. They report: "It appears that young people attending middle schools in the more industrialized and urbanized areas have attitudes more conducive to the support of and participation in social change which is directed toward greater individual autonomy and greater social complexity." The study also found that, depending upon the state, between 25 per cent and 60 per cent of boys at the end of the first cycle and between 40 per cent and 75 per cent of boys at the end of the second cycle are employed. Of those employed, 85 per cent work 30 or more hours a week. The authors indicate that lower-status boys are more likely to be employed than higher-status boys.

Aparecida Gouveia, in the third selection, analyzes the unusually heavy middle and upper socioeconomic class student attendance at predominantly private industrial schools in São Paulo. Taking father's place of birth as the criterion for difference in nationality, while at the same time controlling for social class, the author found no difference among second-cycle enrollment rates for Brazilians, Japanese, Italians, Portuguese, and Spaniards. The classification "other" immigrants, however, indicates a heavy concentration of enrollment in industrial schools irrespective of social-class background. The very small proportion of the total enrollment accounted for by the "other" immigrants is explained as a structural rather than an ethnic difference. The Brazilian middle- and upper-class students, who account for the enrollment concentration, apparently attend industrial schools as a result of the level of industrialization evident in São Paulo and because of the large number of new job opportunities available after a middle-level specialization in such areas as chemistry or electronics.

T. David Williams, in an article on Guatemala, discusses both the restrictive nature of year-end examinations intended to ensure high quality and the relationship between the planned versus the actual function of specialized secondary schools. Using data from a survey of examination performance for male students, Williams suggests that the relatively high failure rate works against the lower classes since academic ability may be less important than the ability to financially support prolonged attendance at school. The author presents student questionnaire responses for two specialized secondary schools, one for middle-level technicians and the other for rural teachers, which indicate that few students in either institution intended to pursue the careers for which they were being trained. Williams asserts that such discrepancies result from increased material and nonmaterial rewards in alternative careers which prove more attractive than the intended goals of both the institution and the student.

Occupational choice of secondary students in Caracas, Venezuela is the subject of the paper by Gordon Ruscoe. Presenting data from questionnaire responses of nearly 3,000 third- and fifth-year students, the author analyzes the problems inherent in providing incentives to students who represent different socioeconomic backgrounds and who express different reasons for pursuing various educational and occupational goals. Ruscoe suggests that successful education and national development planning is contingent upon providing ideological and material incentives to students in order to ensure their pursuance of identified occupational needs. He suggests that long-term programmatic use of incentives must be accompanied by information on various occupations and should be directed toward students with lower socioeconomic status backgrounds who feel that income, working conditions, job satisfaction, and the needs of the nation are important considerations when choosing an occupation.

Original Sources for Selections

Goldrich, Daniel. "Peasants' Sons in City Schools: A Inquiry into the Politics of Urbanization in Panama and Costa Rica," *Human Organization,* 23 (Winter, 1964), pp. 328–333.

Havighurst, Robert J., and Aparecida J. Gouveia. "Socioeconomic Development and Secondary Education in Brazil," *International Review of Education,* 12, no. 4 (1966), pp. 397–413.

Gouveia, Aparecida J. "Preference for Different Types of Secondary School among Various Ethnic Groups in São Paulo, Brazil," *Sociology of Education,* 39 (Spring, 1966), pp. 155–166.

Williams, T. David. "Discrepancy between Goal and Function in Educational Planning: The Guatemalan Experience," *Comparative Education Review,* 13 (June, 1969), pp. 196–208.

Ruscoe, Gordon C. "Individual Decisions and Educational Planning: Occupational Choices of Venezuelan Secondary Students," *International Development Review,* 10 (June, 1968), pp. 20–25.

Peasants' Sons in City Schools:
A Inquiry into the Politics of Urbanization
in Panama and Costa Rica

DANIEL GOLDRICH

It is frequently assumed that the extremely rapid urbanization of Latin America will generate political extremism and instability, based on the bitter protests of the new urban mass, which aspires high but must live on the margin of survival. The flow of subsistence farmers and agrarian laborers to the cities has been intellectually accommodated by social scientists only in a very crude way. Although the folk-urban continuum has been challenged by a series of empirical studies, the newly urbanized are still uncritically expected by many observers to exhibit signs of social disorganization threatening a progressive susceptibility to demagogic political leaders.

Challenging this perspective on urbanization is a group of disparate studies of the urban poor, which, taken together, suggest a range of factors operating to impede the politicization of this sector and to promote acquiescence in existing sociopolitical conditions or even affirmation of them.[1] But equally important is the question of political leadership of the urban poor. On the whole the urban lower class has few resources permitting political

Reproduced by the permission of the Society for Applied Anthropology from *Human Organization,* Vol. 23, No. 4, Yr. 1964.

Daniel Goldrich is in the Department of Political Science, Institute for Community Studies, University of Oregon, Eugene, Oregon.

He wants to express appreciation for research support to the Carnegie Foundation, the Institute of International Studies and Overseas Administration and the Office of Scientific and Scholarly Research at the University of Oregon, and the Office of International Programs at Michigan State University. Robert Sandels and William Wroth assisted him in Costa Rica. Thanks are also expressed to the directors and students of the schools used in this study.

[1] These studies are analyzed in the author's "Toward the Comparative Study of Politicization; with Special Reference to Latin America" (forthcoming). [This note was written in 1964.–Ed.]

activity or the exercise of political influence. There has been a strong tendency on the part of academic observers to perceive the subsociety of poverty as a homogeneous one, and thus they have failed to isolate conceptually and then observe any limited stratum from which might be recruited people capable of giving leadership to the submerged of the cities and pressing their demands before the much higher status (whether traditional, oligarchical, or reformist) political elite.

This report focuses on a rarely studied stratum: peasants' sons who have moved to the city and are enrolled in vocational-mechanical arts secondary schools. These sons of agrarian laborers are among the most fortunate stratum of the new urban lower class. While limited on the whole to working-class occupations, they will have attained a secondary level of education and valuable skills, distinguishing them from the great bulk of those of similar background who are destined to the insecure, impoverished life of the urban Latin American petty-service worker or unskilled factory worker.

This stratum would not be expected to provide recruits for elite sociopolitical roles, but it would seem one of the likeliest sources of any representation of the new urban mass. This is because these students are limited in the main to manual laboring occupations, automatically relegating them to lower status, and probably deterring the development of the strong identification which students of middle-class origin or aspiration tend to develop with traditional oligarchies of wealth, status, and power.[1] This strong drive on the part of middle-class students to win privilege and prestige rather than to restructure society along egalitarian lines helps explain the weakness of reformist and revolutionary forces in urban Latin America today. (The high valuation of prestige and privilege by superficially reformist university students has apparently been widely sensed among those who often find themselves the object of university students' verbal political protection—the slum dwellers. Frank Bonilla has found that 90 per cent of *favelados* in his study believe that university students

do *not* give sincere help to people living in *favelas*.[2])

The following aspects of the students' socialization and political orientations will be examined: the extent to which their families were aware of and involved in politics during the students' childhoods; the extent and quality of their continuing relationship to their parents; and an assessment of the relative moderation or extremeness of their orientations concerning current sociopolitical problems, democratic constitutionalism, the political leadership, and the extent of their satisfaction or frustration arising from their quest for social and political mobility.

---

[1] See the analysis of the urban middle sectors in Claudio Veliz, "Obstacles to Reform in Latin America," *The World Today,* XIX (January, 1963), pp. 18-29.

[2] Frank Bonilla, "Rio's *Favelas:* The Rural Slum within the City," an American Universities Field Staff Report (August, 1961), p. 10.

Up to now, the few studies of the impact of urbanization on behavior and attitudes have been of the independent case-study type. Although the present study is comparative in nature, the generalizability of its findings and conclusions cannot really be estimated until there is a greater accumulation of related empirical research. And while the extent and problematic character of Latin American urbanization are not by any means represented in their most extreme form in Panama or Costa Rica, the problems of these two countries are substantial and their pattern of urbanization fits the general Latin American one.[1]

Methodology

The Panamanian students attend the only vocational-mechanical arts secondary school in the capital. There was only one school in the Costa Rican capital, San José, corresponding to the Panamanian, and because of its small number of students in the last years of training, I decided to add a counterpart school in the nearby *meseta central city* of Heredia (only 15 minutes removed from San José by bus). Questionnaires were distributed in the classroom to all of those in the last three years of the secondary cycle in Panama and the last two years in Costa Rica. Only the older grades were included because of the relative complexity of the questions and the length of the questionnaire. The respondents were not asked to give their name, and assurances of the confidential nature of the study were given. The number of purposefully distorted questionnaires was very small.

This report focuses only on those students who indicated their fathers' occupation as agrarian laborer. These undoubtedly include some independent peasants with small holdings as well as farm laborers, but no further

---

[1] A recent report on urbanization in Latin America has treated Panama as an exception to the general pattern.

. . . for each country, excluding Panama, and for each intercensal period, the rate of increase of the population living in cities of 20,000 plus has been higher than the corresponding rate for the total population of the country, and *a fortiori,* than the population living in localities of less than 20,000 inhabitants. In Panama, from 1940 to 1950 both the population in small localities and that in the rural areas grew more rapidly than that of Panama City and Colon— the two cities with more than 20,000 inhabitants. This represents a very significant deviation from the general pattern.

Population Branch, Bureau of Social Affairs, United Nations, "Demographic Aspects of Urbanization in Latin America," *in* P. Hauser, ed., *Urbanization in Latin America,* International Documents Service (New York, 1961), pp. 96–97.

However, data for the subsequent decade indicate that the annual growth rate for Panama City between 1950–1960 was 5.1 per cent, that of the remainder of the country, 2.7 per cent, and of the country as a whole, 3.3 per cent. Apparently, the 1940–1950 decade in Panama *was* a deviation from the general pattern in Latin America, but the more recent data indicate that it was a deviation for Panama as well. The country's experience for the past decade has been typical for Latin America. A confusing factor in computation has been the extension in 1950 of the city limits, but the statistics cited above on the city's growth from 1950–1960 are based on a comparison of the same, demographically urban, *corregimientos.* See *Panamá en cifras,* Dirección de Estadística y Censo, Panama, November 3, 1961, pp. 1 and 18.

distinction is possible with the present data. The number of such students was 48 in the Panamanian school and 51 in the two Costa Rican schools.

The Social and Political Background of the Students' Families

Both national samples come from agrarian families where the father has completed a substantial amount of education, by Latin American rural standards. Half the fathers have had some primary education, and half have completed primary school, representing by the same standard a substantial attainment. This image of a relatively advantaged stratum of the peasantry is reinforced by data on their political involvment. About 40 per cent of both national samples report having had a family member or relative who had participated in government or politics. On another item concerning the degree of parents' political participation during the respondents' childhoods, one third of each sample reported a substantial parental involvement, and only one third to one sixth reported no such activity at all (Table 1).

Table 1. Parental Education and Parental/Familial Political Activity

	Panamanians	Costa Ricans
	%	%
Father's education		
None	15	0
Some primary	35	51
Completed primary	37	45
Some secondary	11	4
Completed secondary	2	0
N	(48)	(51)
Participation of family member or relative in government or politics	40	37
N	(48)	(51)
Extent of parents' political participation during student's childhood		
Much	6	6
Some	26	30
Little	36	48
None	32	16
N	(47)	(50)

These students' backgrounds suggest a picture contrary to that of the new urbanite confronted abruptly by a modern society and a complex government for which he has no psychological preparation. The craftsmen and skilled workers produced by these urban vocational schools are recruited from peasant families the great bulk of which have provided a fairly politicized familial environment prior to urban migration. This indicates that the characterization of rural Latin America as "effectively outside the nation," or prepolitical, is too gross in the very important respect that the more advantaged and ambitious peasant families who seek high socioeconomic status within the urban working class for their sons are aware of and involved in the political system. This in turn suggests the hypothesis that urban migration in pursuit of education and social advancement may be to a significant degree a function of those peasant families who perceive the personal relevance of government, who realize that such governmental services as vocational education exist and who mobilize their resources to take advantage of them. Certainly what has been found here suggests the fruitfulness of a more refined model of the urbanization process, that would take into account the phenomenon of rural politicization.

Family Cohesion

In just these sorts of families one might expect to encounter a high degree of intergeneration tensions, for there is probably considerable pressure on the son to succeed, to take advantage of the opportunity made possible by family sacrifice, etc. The son will be exposed to a school environment probably differing to a substantial degree from that of his home. The occupation for which he is being prepared probably has a structure and ethos that differs greatly from the agrarian pursuits of the father. On the contrary, however, we find indicators of a high degree of family cohesion.[1] For example, the family apparently continues to be central in the son's political socialization after he (if not his family) moves to the city and enters the vocational educational institution. Asked to select two advisors from a list including "father, friend, mother, relative, teacher, student organization, and other," three fourths of both national samples indicated they would go to father, mother, or relatives for "the best political advice." One half would go only to a family member, while another one fourth would go both to a family member and to teacher, student organization, or friend. More significantly, these proportions do not change when we focus on the highly politicized among the students (Table 2). (I am considering the highly politicized to be those students who report either: frequent discussion of politics with family, friends, or officials; frequent discussion of the Cuban Revolution; attending political meetings; or participation in political demonstrations.) Even in Panama, where there is a very strong relationship between high politicization and high participation in school organizations and where the school seems to be a more important locus of politics than in Costa Rica, the highly politicized are just as strongly oriented to family members as political advisors.

Additional data on the importance of the family to these students

---

[1] The pattern found in this comparative study is quite similar to that reported by Oscar Lewis for a group of migrant families in Mexico City. See his "Urbanization without Breakdown," *Scientific Monthly*, LXXV (July, 1952), pp. 31–41. Similar findings are also reported by Douglas Butterworth, in "A Study of the Urbanization Process among Mixtec Migrants from Tilantongo in Mexico City," *América Indígena*, XXII (July, 1962), pp. 257–274.

Table 2. Family Cohesion

	Panamanians		Costa Ricans	
	Total	Highly Politicized	Total	Highly Politicized
	%	%	%	%
"Who could give you the best advice on politics?" (Select 2)				
Family (father, mother, relative)	52	52	48	50
School organization, teacher	13	7	12	8
Friend, other	2	4	0	0
Family + school organization, etc.	18	18	18	22
Family + friend, etc.	4	4	8	6
School organization + friend, etc.	11	15	14	14
N	(46)	(27)	(50)	(36)
"How important are the following matters concerning anyone you might want to marry?" Her acceptance by your family				
Much	85	81	80	80
Some	2	4	20	20
None	13	15	0	0
N	(45)	(26)	(50)	(35)
Her interest in getting ahead socially				
Much	42	46	44	43
Some	7	12	37	39
None	51	42	19	18
N	(45)	(26)	(48)	(33)
Her acceptance by your friends				
Much	27	23	34	30
Some	24	35	38	37
None	49	42	28	33
N	(45)	(26)	(47)	(33)

reinforce the foregoing conclusions. They were asked whether the following factors concerning any girl they might consider for marriage were of "much, some, or little importance": acceptance of the girl by his family, acceptance by his friends, and her interest in getting ahead socially. Eighty per cent of each sample indicated that acceptance by their family was of much importance. Only half that proportion thought that "her interest in getting ahead socially" was of similar importance, and fewer still found acceptance by friends to be of such importance. Thus the family is still highly important as a source of sanctions and values for the vast majority of these students.[1] Regardless of the influence of the school on so many aspects of their lives, the family appears to be a far more important group for the

[1] Pearse comes to the same conclusion about migrant families in Rio de Janeiro, in his "Some Characteristics of Urbanization in the City of Rio de Janeiro," *in* P. Hauser, ed., *Urbanization in Latin America,* p. 200. See the analysis of his and related studies by R. M. Morse, "Latin American Cities: Aspects of Structure and Function," *Comparative Studies in Society and History,* IV (July, 1962), pp. 473–493.

students than peers in major areas of decision (political advice and mate selection). And even with the obvious salience of social mobility in the lives of these students, in that (a) they are the extremely fortunate few among the vast stratum of rural migrants to the cities and (b) through secondary education they have already attained considerably higher social status than their fathers, family views on prospective spouses seem to be considered far more important in mate selection than the latter's own commitment to social elevation.

The conclusion must be that if this critical sector of the new urban working class turns toward political extremism, it will not be a function of the oft-hypothesized social disorganization attending rapid urbanization and with its roots in family disintegration, but of factors of a political nature. Furthermore, the pattern found among both our samples suggests the hypothesis that only the stable families among the agrarian lower class can mobilize the initiative and the resources to support the secondary education of their sons in the city.

Political Extremism

If social disorganization resulting from disintegration of the family may be ruled out as a particular characteristic of this critical sector of new urbanites in the two countries, then the existence of political extremism within this sector must be a function of other factors. The most obvious source of political extremism would seem to be political—protracted periods of ineffective government. In this regard the two countries sampled offer a clearcut test, inasmuch as the Panamanian government has but recently begun to act to ameliorate the conditions of working- and lower-class life, while the Costa Rican has been (although somewhat discontinuously) engaged in welfare state programs since the early 1940's. Whereas no reformist party has played a role of any significance in Panamanian politics to the present time, two of the three major Costa Rican parties share responsibility for reforms. The traditionally styled, personalist, diffuse Partido Republicano Nacional of Rafael Calderón Guardia was dominant during 1940–1948, and in alliance with the Communists enacted labor legislation and a social security program. The Partido Liberación Nacional, organized by José Figueres on a more professional programmatic, expressly welfare statist basis, controlled the national executive and legislature during 1953–1957, when public housing, other welfare, and industrial development programs were inaugurated.

Although the distribution of political orientations among the Costa Rican students by no means reflects a complete commitment to constitutional democracy, satisfaction with the political leadership, or acquiescence in the current allocation of socioeconomic status and political influence, these students differ substantially from the Panamanians in the expected direction.

While the vast majority of both groups agrees that there is

a need for agrarian reform [and for] the rich to pay much higher taxes than they now do,

these issues are much more salient for the Panamanians. Only one third of the Costa Ricans agree strongly with the former statement, compared to two thirds of the Panamanians. One fourth of the Costa Ricans agree strongly with the latter statement, compared to three fifths of the Panamanians. Discontent over these matters appears to be reflected in the evaluation of the political leadership: the Panamanians are evenly divided in response to the statement

The majority of the public officials work in behalf of the public interests,

while over two thirds of the Costa Ricans are in agreement. The Panamanians' dissatisfaction with public policy and public officialdom probably has contributed to their relative disinclination to accept gradualist constitutional democratic rules of the political game. Some 73 per cent of the Costa Ricans compared to 54 per cent of the Panamanians agree strongly or moderately with the proposition that

Violence should never be used to settle political questions.

Although two thirds of both groups endorse in some degree the statement that

Freedom of speech and assembly should be unlimited,

they diverge in sanctioning unconstitutional practices as a means to a desirable policy. Two fifths of the Panamanians and one fifth of the Costa Ricans agree strongly that

If a government is doing a good job it should remain in office, even though it means postponement of elections.

If we focus on the highly politicized portions of the samples, these international differences are in most cases even greater (Table 3).

The apparent dissatisfaction of the Panamanians is not simply a case of an abstract orientation, for a great deal of personal frustration seems to exist in relation to these matters. Both sets of students were asked to respond to the statements

Only if things change very much will I attain the success I want, [and] Only if things change very much will I attain the political influence I want.

In addition, they were asked

What is most important for success in this country: hard work, skill, family position, or money? [and] What is most important for political success in this country: hard work, political program, family position, or money?

On the latter pair of items, I am assuming that if the respondent selects

Table 3. Orientations toward Issues, Public Officials, and Constitutionalism

	Panamanians		Costa Ricans	
	Total	Highly Politicized	Total	Highly Politicized
	%	%	%	%
"This country needs a great agrarian reform."				
+3*	66	64	33	36
+1/+2	30	28	61	58
−1/−3	4	8	6	6
N	(44)	(25)	(49)	(36)
"The rich should pay much higher taxes than they now pay."				
+3	61	77	25	26
+1/+2	24	8	39	40
−1/−3	15	15	36	34
N	(46)	(26)	(49)	(35)
"The majority of the public officials work in behalf of the public welfare."				
+1/+3	48	44	68	69
−1/−3	52	56	32	31
N	(40)	(25)	(50)	(35)
"Violence should never be used to settle political questions."				
+2/+3	54	44	73	76
+1	23	28	15	15
−1/−3	23	28	12	9
N	(43)	(25)	(48)	(33)
"Freedom of speech and assembly should be unlimited."				
+1/+3	68	68	64	74
−1/−3	32	32	36	26
N	(44)	(25)	(45)	(31)
"If a government is doing a good job, it should be allowed to remain in office even if it would mean the postponement of elections."				
+3	39	50	18	22
+1/+2	34	25	35	42
−1/−3	27	25	47	36
N	(41)	(24)	(51)	(36)

*The six response categories range through strong agreement (+3), moderate agreement (+2), slight agreement (+1), slight disagreement (−1), moderate disagreement (−2), to strong disagreement (−3).

either of the first two factors, he tends to see the channels to social and political success as open, whereas a selection of either of the last two factors (family position, money) reflects a belief that the channels are closed, that opportunities for social and political mobility are limited. Both Costa

Ricans and Panamanians see the need for substantial change if they are to attain what they want in life, but the Costa Ricans express faith that the present system will accommodate them, in sharp contrast to the Panamanians. Sixty-one per cent of the Costa Ricans see the need for major changes if they are to attain the desired success in life, and almost as many, 53 per cent, see the social system as open. Almost all of the Panamanians, 91 per cent, see the need for major social changes, but only 44 per cent see the system as open. Seventy-three per cent of the Costa Ricans see the need for major changes if they are to attain the political success they want, and an equal preponderance, 72 per cent, see the political system as open. Among the Panamanians, 81 per cent see the need for major political changes for personal political success, but only 30 per cent see the system as open. The hard core of frustrated students would seem to be those who see the need for major changes in both society and polity for personal success, but who see both systems as closed. Only 2 per cent of the Costa Ricans exhibit this extreme degree of frustration, compared to 25 per cent of the Panamanians. Among the highly politicized, the difference is somewhat greater: 3 per cent of the Costa Ricans to 33 per cent of the Panamanians (Table 4).

Thus critical subgroups of the stream of rural migrants to Latin American cities differ very greatly in their orientations toward the polity. Sociopolitical extremism is not the invariant product of urbanization among the sons of *campesinos* and *peones,* but varies rather with the structure and performance of the political system. In fact, data from Costa Rica indicate that the urbanizing sons of agrarian parents are more moderate in political style than their parents. As indicated above, two strains of social reform exist in Costa Rica, one being the highly personalist, traditional-style *calderonista* movement, the organized aspect of which is the PRN and which has been allied in the past with the Communists; the other being the more "Western"-style, programmatic PLN. (The weakest of the three major parties is the conservative PUN.) The parents of these Costa Rican students are reported to be about equally divided between the PRN and the PLN, with a minority supporting the third party or holding no party affiliation at all. The students themselves are slightly more affiliated with the PLN than their parents and give substantially less support to the PRN. Furthermore, the students report an even higher ratio of PLN to PRN supporters among their friends (a more urban group in origin?). Thus there seems to be an attrition of support for the inherently more extremist styled reform movement among the students undergoing the transition from rural to urban life and a rise in support of a party that has exhibited more moderate political behavior. Again, this difference is even greater among the highly politicized (Table 5). And apparently, this generational change associated with the process of urbanization is not occurring as a function of general family

Table 4. Prospects for Personal Political Frustration

	Panamanians	Costa Ricans
	%	%
1. "Only if things change very much will I attain the success I want."		
Agree	91	61
Disagree	9	39
N	(44)	(49)
2. "What is most important for success in this country?"		
Hard work, skill (open)	44	53
Family position, money (closed)	56	47
N	(48)	(49)
3. "Only if things change very much will I attain the political influence I want."		
Agree	81	73
Disagree	19	27
N	(42)	(48)
4. "What is most important for political success in this country?"		
Hard work, program (open)	30	72
Family position, money (closed)	70	28
N	(47)	(50)
Proportion who agree on both items 1 and 3 and see the system as "closed" on both items 2 and 4:	25	2
N	(48)	(51)
Among the highly politicized:	33	3
N	(27)	(36)

Table 5. Partisanship: Father, Mother, Self, and Friends (Costa Ricans)

	None	PLN	PRN	PUN	Mixed	N
	%	%	%	%	%	%
(As reported by students)						
Father	12	39	33	16	0	(51)
Mother	4	43	39	14	0	(51)
Self	24	45	25	6	0	(51)
Friends	12	47	14	6	21	(51)
Among the highly politicized						
Father	14	42	30	14	0	(36)
Mother	6	44	39	11	0	(36)
Self	17	53	25	5	0	(36)
Friends	6	55	14	6	19	(36)

disintegration. The students may be deviating over time from their parents' partisanships, but there is no indication, as previously indicated, that disharmony within the family has attained substantial proportions.

Summary, Conclusions, and Suggestions

This article poses the suggestion that the mass of rural migrants to Latin American cities has relatively little capacity for political action, let alone sustained revolutionary action, and that its political influence will be a function of the extent to which potential leaders within this social stratum are politicized, and the direction in which they are politicized. Vocational secondary school students of rural lower-class origin appear to be among the few potential leaders of the stratum.

The literature on the behavioral and attitudinal consequences of urbanization is scanty, and even less attention has been paid potential political leaders of the rapidly expanding urban lower class. This study of Panamanian and Costa Rican peasants' sons in city schools finds (a) that a large proportion of these families were oriented toward urban, "national" life during the students' childhoods and helped probably to prepare them for migration and the opportunities available in the city, a case of anticipatory political socialization and (b) that strong ties continue to exist between the students and their parents, the former relying on the parents for political advice, as well as advice and direction in other areas of personal decision. The extent and degree of this relationship suggests the hypothesis that it is primarily the relatively stable agrarian lower-class family that can mobilize the psychological and material resources to support the secondary education of their sons in the city. Therefore, within this group of potential leaders of the urban mass, any political extremism would not seem to flow from social and familial disorganization. This study finds on the contrary that (c) urbanization is associated with an increasingly moderate style in politics.

Future inquiry must focus on the extent to which such groups as these students actually serve as links between the political elite (and counterelite) and the mass of lower-class urbanites, with its huge admixture of rural immigrants. When the elite (or counterelite) needs support and turns to "the popular masses," does it go through such people as the educated, skilled sector of the working class, or are there more direct relationships between high and low? In the rare case of uprisings by slum dwellers, how is this mass mobilized? What is the role in such events of these students and particularly the frustrated among them, or adults with equivalent educational and demographic backgrounds?

Socioeconomic Development
and Secondary Education in Brazil

ROBERT J. HAVIGHURST
APARECIDA J. GOUVEIA

Introduction

Under twentieth-century conditions, secondary education has two major societal functions.

(a) To contribute to the economic development of the society.

(b) To increase the degree of social integration of the society: the meaning of social integration is the tying together of various social, economic and racial groups into an interacting social system in which every person has the opportunity to achieve a social and economic status which he desires if he is willing to work for it and has the requisite abilities.

In a big country, such as Brazil, one sees both functions being served with different degrees of efficiency in different regions of the country, and even in different sections of the same state, as in the differences between the major city and the remainder of the state. Even in a more industrialized big country, such as the United States, the two functions are served with different degrees of effectiveness in different regions.

This study was made in Brazil, the largest and most variegated Latin American country.

Reproduced, by permission, from *International Review of Education,* 12, no. 4 (1966), pp. 397–413.

This is a shortened version of a paper presented at the Round Table on Educational Sociology of the International Sociological Association in Evian, France, in September 1966. The work reported is part of a research project on Secondary Education in Transitional Societies, supported by Carnegie Corporation of America.

MIDDLE SCHOOLING IN BRAZIL

The term "middle schooling" stands for the Portuguese phrase *ensino médio* and covers a wide variety of schools that follow after the unitary primary school in Brazil. Generally speaking middle schooling in Brazil may be a seven-year process, following a five-year period of elementary schooling that starts generally at age seven. Thus the period of middle schooling is from ages 12 to 18 inclusive. Graduates of most middle schools may enter a university, while other middle schools of a limited vocational type give a diploma that indicates the qualifications of the holder for a technical job. The phrase "secondary education" will not be used frequently because its Portuguese equivalent, *ensino secundário,* refers only to the academic or university-preparatory secondary school.

Admission to the middle school is by examination. Very few graduates of the five-year primary school can pass this examination, and many primary schools offer only a four-year course. Consequently, most Brazilian children who aspire to enter a middle school take an "admission course" given by a private school or by a group of teachers who combine to form a tutoring institution. Since these cost money, the middle school admission examination acts to limit the numbers of children from low-income families. On the other hand, the fifth-year course in the public schools of the larger cities is becoming more widespread and more efficient as a preparation for the admission examination. In 1963 the Federal Council on Education ruled that any pupil who successfully completes the fifth year of primary school may enter a middle school without an entrance examination unless the school is so crowded that it must apply an examination as a criterion of admission.

The system of middle schools is very complex in Brazil. There are several different types of schools, and the schools may be operated by the state, federal government, churches, and private individuals and groups. The middle school is divided into two cycles, the first of four years and the second of three years. The first cycle, called the *ginásio,* takes pupils normally from 12 through 15 years of age and gives them a basic general education. However, there are also commercial schools, industrial schools and a few normal schools which have first-cycle "basic courses" of two to four years.

The second cycle consists of the academic *colégio,* commercial, industrial, and agricultural schools, and normal schools which train teachers for primary schools.

To further complicate the picture, many middle-level schools operate day and night programs, and the night schools are sometimes more crowded than the day schools. Students attending night schools are likely to be employed, and above the "normal" age. The median age of the sample of students in our study in the fourth year of the first cycle was 17, and the median of the students in the third year of the second cycle was 20, both of these ages being two or three years above the age of a student who started primary school at the age of seven and progressed normally without repeating a grade and without dropping out for employment.

Growth of the Middle School

A striking phenomenon in Brazil is the growth of middle schooling since about 1930, when a modern system of schools was developed. Enrollment has more than doubled during every decade since 1930 and continues to grow currently at a rapid rate. Only about a quarter of the enrollment increase is due to increase in the absolute numbers of youths of middle school age. These numbers have increased about 30 per cent at each decade. Table 1 shows the enrollment gains by branch of school.

Table 1. Growth in Middle School Enrollments (1960 = 100)

Year		Academic Secondary	Commercial	Normal	Industrial	Agricultural	Total
1931		6	10	19	–	–	
1935		11	12	24	14	–	
1940		20	26	23	22	–	
1945		28	44	21	64	10	31
1950		45	39	36	75	33	44
1955		67	60	64	77	76	66
1956		72	67	70	76	62	71
1957		77	75	82	81	68	77
1958		84	83	87	85	85	84
1959		90	91	90	89	90	90
1960	Relative No.	100	100	100	100	100	100
	Absolute No.	904,000	194,000	93,600	26,081	6,428	1,224,000
1961		110	110	110	117	106	110
1962		123	124	125	140	109	124
1963		138	135	158	212	129	140
1964		151	139	187	263	162	155

Source: Instituto Brasileiro de Geografia e Estatística: *Statistical Bulletin,* 89 (Rio de Janeiro, January–March, 1965).

Private schools account for about 56 per cent of student enrollment. Private schools dominate the field of commercial education, while public schools have most of the industrial courses. In the academic secondary school and the normal school the public and private schools have about equal numbers of pupils, with the public schools gaining an increasing proportion in the last decade.

Description of the Study

A major part of the research centered around a questionnaire given to students in the last year of the first and second cycles respectively. The questionnaire contained items concerned with family background, student attitudes toward occupations, student values and attitudes with respect to various aspects of changing social and economic life, and student work experience.

In order to get the range of the country, students were studied in five states. The most modern and industrial state of São Paulo was one of them. Also the southernmost state, Rio Grande do Sul, was studied because it has a substantial central European immigrant influence, with a significant though small proportion of Lutherans. It is more rural than São Paulo, but more urbanized than the other three states. These two states are in the South. While only 9 per cent of Brazilian territory lies below the Tropic of Capricorn, this is a rolling, fruitful and well-watered area that contains 30 per cent of the 80 million Brazilians and produces much of the industrial goods and more than its proportionate share of the national income. From the North we chose the state of Pará, which is situated at the mouth of the Amazon. Though the state is heavily rural, 88 per cent of middle school pupils in Pará are in Belém, the capital city. Two of the northeast Atlantic-fronting states are included, Pernambuco and Ceará. Both of these states are rural, although Pernambuco has for its capital Recife, the major industrial city of the northern half of Brazil.

An attempt was made to study a representative sample of pupils in each state. This was done separately for the capital city and the remainder of the state. For the capital city a list was made of all the middle schools, grouped according to the categories mentioned above. For example, one group consisted of all the academic schools of the second cycle, public, day shift, and for both sexes. For each of these categories the enrollment was ascertained of pupils in the final grade of both cycles in the year 1962. It was then decided to study a certain percentage of the students which might vary from one category to another so as to avoid too-large numbers in the more numerous categories. The quotas range from 5 per cent in the most numerous categories to 100 per cent in the least numerous. Finally, in order to get the requisite number of students thus agreed upon, schools in a category were chosen by a method of random numbers until the quota was reached. All students in the final year of a school so chosen were asked to fill out the questionnaire. If this produced too many questionnaires, some were eliminated by a method of chance. The data from the different categories of schools could then be combined later through using a system of "multipliers" when it was necessary to get totals for a particular state or a particular cycle or for the capital to be compared with the interior of a state.

For the sample of a state outside of the capital city, a simplified method was necessary, at the expense of the representative quality of the sample. The cities within the state were grouped into three categories as follows: large cities with more than 50,000 inhabitants, medium cities with 15,000 to 50,000 inhabitants, and small cities with less than 15,000 inhabitants. Among the cities of a given size category, a certain number were chosen by chance, the ratios varying from one state to another. The total number of students whose questionnaires were used ranged from 5,835 in São Paulo down to 1,113 in Pará, and amounted to 16,156 in all.

Results
REGIONAL DIFFERENCES IN MIDDLE SCHOOL ATTENDANCE

Since Brazil is such a large and variegated country, the regional differences must be seen and understood in order to understand the social functions of middle schooling. The regional differences in socioeconomic factors are illustrated in Table 2. The states in the study are located in the northern, northeastern, and southern regions. The regional differences in attendance at middle schools are documented in Table 3, which shows the proportions of pupils in the middle schools in relation to the total populations of the five states that were studied in this research. These proportions vary from 1.66 per cent for the state of Ceará (northeast) to 3.66 per cent for the state of São Paulo. These are all substantially below the proportions to be found in the United States.

Table 2. Regional Comparisons on Indices of Human Resources Development in Brazil

	North	Northeast	East	South
Per capita income, 1958, US$ of 1957	136	95	274	321
Primary school enrollment % of age group 6–10, 1958	69	48	72	96
University students, 1958, % of age group 20–24	—	0.69	1.68	1.68
Professionals of university level per million population, 1950	—	936	—	3,701
% literate age 13–19	—	44	64	84

Source: Robert J. Havighurst and Roberto J. Moreira, *Society and Education in Brazil* (Pittsburgh, Pa.: University of Pittsburgh Press, 1965), chap. 1.

Similar to regional differences are those between the major city of a state and what the Brazilians call "the interior" of the same state. This is mainly an urban-rural differentiation since most of the Brazilian states are predominantly rural and they tend to have one major concentration of population in or around the state capital. Middle school attendance is relatively higher

Table 3. State and Regional Differences in Middle School Attendance

	Total Enrollment (thousands)	% of Total State or Regional Population
Brazil, 1964		
South		
São Paulo	541	3.66
Rio Grande do Sul	173	2.87
North		
Pará	31	1.77
Northeast		
Pernambuco	81	1.82
Ceará	60	1.66
All Brazil	1,893	2.42
U.S.A., 1960*		
South	5,675	10.3
North Central	5,085	9.8

Source: Instituto Brasileiro de Geografia e Estatística: *Anuário Estatístico do Brasil–1965*. United States Census–1960. Series PC(2)-5A.

*The figures for the United States are based on the numbers in the age group 12–18 inclusive who are enrolled in school.

in the state capital than in the remainder of the state in all five states in this study.

Sex Differences

There are some sex differences in attendance at middle schools which also vary by regions. In general, boys outnumber girls slightly in the middle schools of the southern states, while girls outnumber boys slightly in the northern and northeastern states.

SOCIOECONOMIC DIFFERENCES IN MIDDLE SCHOOL ATTENDANCE

The major factor in determining middle school attendance is socioeconomic status. The occupation of the father was taken as the index of socioeconomic status. The student was asked to state the occupation of his father in enough detail to indicate what kind of work he did, how much responsibility he had, how much land he owned, etc. The occupational scale was an adaptation of the one devised by Hutchinson for his study of social mobility in São Paulo (1960).

Hutchinson's seven levels were grouped into three, called high, middle, and low. The A or high level includes levels 1 and 2 of the seven-point scale and is equivalent to upper and upper-middle class in the usual North American social science terminology. The middle level includes levels 3 and 4 of the seven-point scale, and is equivalent to lower-middle class. The other three levels of the seven-point scale are included in the C or low level, which contains manual workers. However, in our particular study there were very few unskilled workers who were fathers of pupils in middle schools.

Differences between the First and Second Cycles

As can be seen in Table 4 (A and B), the second cycle tends to have higher proportions of high-status students than the first cycle. This is true for the states of São Paulo, Rio Grande do Sul, and Pernambuco. Also, in all five

Table 4. Socioeconomic Origin of Students: All Types of Middle Schools
Percentage in a Given Category

A. First-Cycle Students

Social Origin	São Paulo	Rio Grande do Sul	Pernambuco	Ceará	Pará
		CAPITAL			
High	21.3	21.4	11.5	17.4	15.3
Middle	49.9	50.6	55.0	61.7	52.3
Low	28.0	28.0	33.5	20.9	32.4
Total	100.0 (1,729)*	100.0 (741)	100.0 (668)	100.0 (658)	100.0 (450)
		INTERIOR			
High	15.4	14.1	15.2	10.7	10.5
Middle	49.6	55.1	54.6	69.7	51.4
Low	35.0	30.8	30.2	19.6	38.2
Total	100.0 (1,807)	100.0 (2,121)	100.0 (467)	100.0 (482)	100.0 (241)

B. Second-Cycle Students

		CAPITAL			
High	24.8	27.6	23.3	15.2	18.2
Middle	48.3	54.0	56.9	66.4	58.6
Low	26.9	18.4	19.8	18.4	23.1
Total	100.0 (1,129)	100.0 (697)	100.0 (841)	100.0 (591)	100.0 (358)
		INTERIOR			
High	16.2	20.1	23.9	9.3	8.7
Middle	57.1	58.2	54.6	75.8	60.9
Low	26.7	21.7	21.5	15.0	30.4
Total	100.0 (897)	100.0 (1,241)	100.0 (132)	100.0 (151)	100.0 (16)

*Absolute numbers in the table in parentheses.

states the second cycle has fewer low-status students than the first cycle. Still, the differences between the two cycles are not great ones. Perhaps the differences would be much greater if the first year of the first cycle were compared with the last year of the second cycle. Possibly, by the close of the first cycle, the effects of family social status on middle school attendance have largely become established. However, it may be true that even at the beginning of the first cycle these effects are fairly visible.

Socioeconomic Differences between Capital and Interior

Although the differences between capital and interior are seldom statistically significant, there is a strong and apparently reliable tendency for the capital to have more high-status students than the interior cities. The most likely explanation is that there are proportionately more high-status families in the capital than in the interior and proportionately more lower-status families in the cities of the interior.

INDICES OF OPPORTUNITY THROUGH MIDDLE SCHOOLING

In order to compare the states more carefully, an "index of opportunity through middle schooling" has been computed.

A crude index of this type may be calculated on the basis of the data available for the five states and is shown in Table 5. This index is the percentage of youths who attend middle school for some period of time, as little as a few months and as much as the full seven years. It is computed as follows: the percentage of middle school pupils coming from families of each of the three socioeconomic levels is based on the data in Table 4. This is done by weighting the enrollment figures for first and second cycle and for capital and interior of Table 4 according to the enrollment data supplied for these states by the reports of the Ministry of Education. Thus, on the assumption that our samples are reasonably representative of the five states, we have crude estimates of the socioeconomic distribution of middle school pupils in each state. Next, the middle school enrollment is estimated as a certain percentage of the number in the age group 12–18 inclusive. This is done by taking the figure for Brazil as a whole, 14 per cent as of 1964, and adapting it to each of the five states by using the data in Table 3 which give the middle school enrollment as a certain percentage of the total Brazilian population. Using the figure 2.42 per cent of the total Brazilian population enrolled in middle schools in 1964, the 14 per cent of the 12–18 population for all of Brazil may be corrected for each of the five states, and ranges from 9.5 for Ceará to 21 for São Paulo.

Finally, there is need of data on the distribution of the total age group, 12–18, according to socioeconomic status. The estimates in Table 5 are made as follows: Havighurst and Moreira (1965) estimated the percentage distribution of the employed population in Brazil by regions for 1950

Table 5. Indices of Opportunity through Middle Schooling

Socioeconomic Status	% of Total Number of Middle Sch. Pupils in the Various SE Groups	Middle Sch. Enrollment As % of Age Group 12-18	% of Total Age Group 12-18 in the Various SE Groups	% of Youth Who Attend Middle School for Some Period
São Paulo		21		
A High	18		6	63
B Middle	51		17	63
C Low	31		77	8.5
Rio Grande do Sul		17		
A	18		6	51
B	55		17	55
C	27		77	6.0
Pará		10.2		
A	15		4	38
B	54		12	46
C	31		84	3.8
Pernambuco		10.5		
A	15		3	53
B	56		12	49
C	29		85	3.6
Ceará		9.5		
A	14		3	44
B	66		12	52
C	20		85	2.2
U.S.A.		74*		
A	13*		10	100*
B	39		30	97
C	48		60	59

*These figures refer to grades 10-12 of the American secondary school and to the age group 16-18. Cf. Robert J. Havighurst and Bernice L. Neugarten, *Society and Education* (Boston: Allyn and Bacon, 1961).

according to socioeconomic status. These estimates have been corrected for a general increase in Brazil of the proportions of upper- and middle-status occupational positions since 1950, and also for the fact that upper-status people have fewer children in Brazil than lower-status people. The estimates are crude and may be in error for any given status group by as much as two or three percentage points.

The "index of opportunity through middle schooling" is given in the fourth column in Table 5. It is obtained by multiplying the first two columns together and dividing by the third column. It is the percentage of youths from a given socioeconomic level who attend middle school for some period.

Since the estimates are crude, especially in the third column, the results in the fourth column are correct only in order of magnitude. The results most subject to error are those for the upper-status group, which is so small a percentage of the total age group that an error of two or three percentage points can throw the opportunity index off by 25 or 50 per cent. However, the results for the lower-status group are quite stable and reliable and indicate clearly the level of opportunity through middle schooling and the variation in this level among the states.

In general, it seems likely that children of middle-status families have about as much opportunity through middle schooling as do children of upper-status families. This conclusion would be modified if we took completion of a second-cycle course as the criterion of opportunity. As Table 4 shows, the upper-status students have higher relative indices of second-cycle attendance than of first-cycle attendance in São Paulo, Rio Grande do Sul, and Pernambuco.

For comparison purposes, the figures for the United States of America are given in Table 5. The number, 74, in the second column is the percentage of the age group 16–18 who reached the highest three grades (10–12) of the American secondary school in 1964. Similarly, the numbers in the first column are the percentage distribution of students in the highest three grades of the secondary school according to socioeconomic status.

DISTRIBUTION OF THE SOCIOECONOMIC GROUPS AMONG THE DIFFERENT TYPES OF SCHOOLS

Youths of the various socioeconomic groups are not distributed evenly among the various types of schools. Table 6 shows how the students from lower-status families are distributed. As would be expected, youths from working-class families are more likely to attend commercial, industrial, and agricultural schools than they are to attend academic and normal schools. Especially in the second cycle, the academic and the normal schools are heavily high and middle status in composition.

An interesting exception to the general rule is seen in the composition of the second-cycle industrial schools of the city of São Paulo. Several of these schools specialize in training chemists for the prosperous chemical industry of Brazil. Large numbers of boys from middle- and high-status families attend these schools, partly as a way of getting a good business job and partly as a way of preparing for engineering and exact sciences in the university.

ATTITUDES TOWARD SOCIOECONOMIC DEVELOPMENT

There is a relationship between the values and attitudes of people and the

Table 6. Percentages of Students of Working-Class Origin
in Different Types of Schools in Capital Cities

Type of School	São Paulo	RGS	Pernambuco	Ceará	Pará
	FIRST CYCLE				
Academic	21	24	31	20	26
	(1,105)*	(421)	(402)	(514)	(294)
Commercial	49	36	53	32	51
	(337)	(95)	(124)	(57)	(78)
Industrial	69	66	64	55	76
	(287)	(165)	(142)	(87)	(41)
Agricultural	0	45	0	0	46
		(60)			(37)
	SECOND CYCLE				
Academic	15	14	17	17	14
	(263)	(346)	(419)	(355)	(197)
Commercial	47	25	26	34	34
	(226)	(245)	(217)	(47)	(112)
Industrial	20	46	50	0	0
	(449)	(26)	(12)		
Normal	20	16	22	16	18
	(226)	(80)	(186)	(189)	(49)

*Numbers in parentheses are the base numbers from which the percentages are calculated.

level and rate of economic development of their society. Thus the social attitudes of young people are one element in the complex of factors that make for development of the society. Consequently we have attempted to study some of the attitudes of Brazilian youth that are presumably relevant to socioeconomic development.

The two attitude scales which seem to be most useful for the purpose are called the modernism-traditionalism scale and the initiative-ambition scale. These are both designed to measure attitudes toward participation in a modern industrial democratic society such as those of persons who are autonomous and welcome social change and social complexity.

The modernism-traditionalism scale is adapted from one developed by Joseph Kahl for use with adults in Brazil (1962). It contains 16 items, such as the following, with the instruction to the student to indicate much or little agreement or much or little disagreement.

"It is better to work for a relative than for a stranger."

The initiative-ambition scale is adapted from a "risk-taking scale" developed by Williams for use with employees of business concerns in the United States (1962). This was designed to measure propensity to take risks as against the seeking of security. It consists of eight pairs of job descriptions, the respondent being asked to choose one of each pair as his preference. One example is:

(a) A job in which I succeed very well or fail completely.
(b) A job in which I will never be a great success, but in which I will never fail completely.

These two attitude scales were given to second-cycle students. The results are shown in Tables 7 and 8.

Table 7. Scores on Modernism-Traditionalism Scale by State, Sex, Socioeconomic Status, and Capital-Interior Residence: Second Cycle

State		Number	% in Each Category on Scale			
			1 (mod.)	2	3	4 (trad.)
São Paulo	Total	2,106	18.4	33.3	28.0	20.3
Entire state	Male	1,045	19.5	32.8	29.2	18.5
	Female	1,012	17.2	33.8	27.0	22.0
Status	A	437	19.5	36.3	24.5	19.7
	B	1,136	18.0	32.3	29.0	20.7
	C	533	18.6	32.4	28.9	20.1
	Capital	1,166	20.0	36.4	28.2	15.4
Interior	Large city	398	19.1	31.7	28.1	21.1
	M and S city	493	14.0	27.4	27.8	30.8
*Rio Grande do Sul**	Total	684	35.7	33.8	22.8	8.1
Capital	Male	488	33.0	30.2	23.9	12.8
	Female	196	38.5	37.5	20.8	3.3
*Pará**	Total	377	13.4	25.0	31.2	30.3
Capital only	Male	149	14.9	25.7	30.7	28.7
	Female	197	12.3	26.2	28.5	33.0
Pernambuco	Total	806	9.3	27.9	32.3	30.5
Capital	Male	394	10.4	27.4	33.3	28.9
	Female	412	8.3	28.4	31.3	32.0
*Ceará**	Total	584	6.5	20.4	24.8	48.1
Capital	Male	262	8.5	18.9	25.4	47.2
	Female	322	4.9	21.7	24.4	49.0
Status	A	91	6.8	24.5	26.1	41.3
	B	388	6.0	20.4	25.4	48.0
	C	105	7.7	16.5	21.8	54.0
Interior	Large city	71	5.6	11.3	22.5	60.6
	M and S city	77	5.2	13.0	26.0	55.8

*Multipliers used with data on capital city.

Modernism-Traditionalism

There is no reliable difference among students between socioeconomic groups on the modernism-traditionalism scale. Such differences as do exist are between states, between the capital and the interior, and between the sexes. The states rank in the following order from modern to traditional: Rio Grande do Sul, São Paulo, Pará, Pernambuco, Ceará. The students in the capital are more modern than the students in the cities and towns of the interior. Boys are slightly more modern than girls on this scale, but the differences are small, and in Rio Grande do Sul girls are slightly more modern than boys.

Initiative-Ambition Scale

On the scale of initiative-ambition, or risk taking, there is little or no difference between socioeconomic groups, but there are substantial differences between states and between sexes. The states follow the same order as they do on the modernism-traditionalism scale. The capital-dwelling students are higher on this scale than the interior dwellers. And boys are substantially higher than girls on this scale.

Inferences from the Attitudes Scales

The two attitude scales support each other, except for sex differences. It appears that young people attending middle schools in the more industrialized and urbanized areas have attitudes more conducive to support of and participation in social change which is directed toward greater individual autonomy and greater social complexity.

Table 8. Scores on Initiative-Ambition Scale by Socioeconomic Status: State, Capital-Interior Residence, and Sex

	Mean Score								
	Socioeconomic Status*				Mean for State	Capital	Interior	Male	Female
State	A	B	C	D					
	High			Low					
Rio Grande do Sul	4.94	4.58	4.52	4.72	4.62	5.06	4.39	5.03	4.16
São Paulo	4.91	4.47	4.45	4.53	4.52	4.94	4.01	5.02	3.99
Pará	4.48	3.95	3.91	3.41	3.92	3.99	3.42	4.61	3.50
Pernambuco	4.28	3.72	3.57	4.00	3.78	3.95	2.78	4.23	3.42
Ceará	3.41	3.13	3.10	3.73	3.19	3.35	2.60	3.92	2.71

*The four socioeconomic levels, A, B, C and D, are based upon the occupation and the educational level of the respondent's father. Levels A and B are similar to levels A and B of the other socioeconomic scale. Levels C and D, if combined, would be approximately equivalent to level C of the other scale.

It is also clear that there are almost no reliable differences in these attitudes among middle school students that are related to their socioeconomic origin. Tables 7 and 8 indicate that the high-status youths may be slightly above the others on the scale of initiative-ambition, but not of modernism-traditionalism. There is also a suggestion that the small low-status group in Table 8 are slightly above the middle groups on the scale of initiative-ambition. But none of these socioeconomic differences compares in magnitude to the differences between states and between capital and interior within a state.

Since the middle school students who come from low-status families are only a small fraction of low-status youths in Brazil, it is quite possible that a representative sample of youths would show large socioeconomic differences on these attitude scales. The study made by Kahl (1962) of Brazilian adults indicated that there was a considerable relationship between scores on Kahl's modernism-traditionalism scale and socioeconomic status among Brazilian adults.

The inference we draw is that youths from lower-status families who enter middle schools and stay four years or more are a selected group—selected for attitudes which are conducive to individual autonomy and social complexity. We do not know whether they had these attitudes when they entered middle school or learned these attitudes from the middle- and upper-status students and from the teachers with whom they associated in school.

Students in the Labor Force

One of the striking facts about middle school students is their tendency to be employed while they attend school. About 60 per cent of São Paulo boys at the end of the first cycle are employed, and about 75 per cent of males at the end of the second cycle. In Pará, which has the lowest employment rate of students, 25 per cent of boys in the first cycle and 40 per cent of males in the second cycle are employed. About half as many girls are employed. Table 9 shows the employment rates for males of the two cycles in the capital cities. Students of commercial schools have the highest rates of employment. This is probably due in part to the fact that most commercial schools are privately operated and charge a substantial tuition fee, which may be beyond the means of students' families to pay. However, it is also due to the fact that business is expanding rapidly in Brazil and needs employees, and must get them wherever they can be found. In this situation, the existing body of students may be drawn into the labor force in large numbers.

Furthermore, students tend to work nearly full time. The proportion among employed students who work 30 hours a week or more is well above 85 per cent in the more industrialized states and it is almost as high among first-cycle students as among those in the second cycle.

Table 9. Students Who Are Employed: Male Students in Capital Cities
Percentage Employed

Branch	São Paulo	RGS	Pernambuco	Ceará	Pará
		FIRST CYCLE			
Academic ginásio	45	22	34	37	18
Commercial	81	92	75	75	50
Industrial	65	32	16	6	9
		SECOND CYCLE			
Academic-scientific	30	34	34	38	28
Commercial	95	92	83	80	91
Industrial	61	65	17	–	–

If a system of middle schools serves an important societal function by providing workers who are still students, the structure of the school system should reflect this fact, as does the Brazilian system in several ways.

For one thing, there are many night courses, in both first and second cycles, and the students in night courses have a high employment rate. Also, the school day is relatively short, not requiring more than four or five hours of attendance per day at school in the day courses, and somewhat less in the evening courses.

Another characteristic of middle school students in Brazil is their relatively advanced age in comparison with the age they would have if they entered secondary school at 11 or 12 and finished seven years later. A considerable group of students are three or more years older than the "expected" age, and these students have a high employment rate, no matter what kind of school they attend.

The students from homes of lower status are much more likely to be employed than students from higher-status families. Thus the opportunity to earn a living makes it possible for children of families with modest incomes to continue their studies. The actual jobs held by middle school students are overwhelmingly office jobs. They work in business offices, banks, and stores.

Conclusions

From this analysis of middle schooling in Brazil it appears that the system is contributing to the economic productivity of the society by training young people for a wide range of "middle-level" jobs which do not require a high degree of specialized training, but can be learned by young people with the knowledge and skills that they acquire in middle schools. The commercial schools have an important part in preparing young people for clerical jobs. The industrial and agricultural middle schools serve relatively small numbers of students, though they have grown rapidly in the most recent years. Thus, for the skilled trades and the jobs as technicians the middle schools are not an important source of trained manpower.

While training these young people, the middle schools also provide a degree of social integration by bringing youths of various social-class backgrounds together in school, and by giving opportunity for upward mobility to a number of working-class youths. Nearly all middle schools have at least some students of working-class origin, although the academic schools which are not public-supported generally have a rather small minority of these students. The proportion of the total number of youths of working-class background who get into middle schools is quite small, although in absolute numbers it is substantial. This proportion varies from 8.5 per cent in the progressive state of São Paulo to 2.2 per cent in the rural and conservative state of Ceará. When this is compared with 59 per cent of working-class youths who get into senior high school in the United States, it can be seen that the Brazilian middle schools are far from contributing as much toward social integration as they do in an affluent and highly urban industrial country.

References

Hutchinson, Bertran. *Trabalho, Status e Educação*. Rio de Janeiro: Centro Brasileiro de Pesquisas Educacionais, Ministerio de Educação e Cultura, 1960.

Havighurst, Robert J., and Roberto J. Moreira. *Society and Education in Brazil*. Pittsburgh, Pa.: University of Pittsburgh Press, 1965. Chap. 1.

Kahl, Joseph A. "Urbanização e Mudanças Ocupacionais no Brasil," *América Latina,* 4 (October–December, 1962), pp. 21–30.

Williams, Lawrence K. "Development of a Risk-Taking Scale." Unpublished Working Paper. Cornell University School of Industrial Relations, Ithaca, N.Y., 1962.

Preference for Different Types
of Secondary School
among Various Ethnic Groups
in São Paulo, Brazil

APARECIDA J. GOUVEIA

Secondary schooling in Brazil is a seven-year process which follows a five-year period of elementary schooling that generally starts at age seven. The seven-year sequence is divided into two cycles: a basic course of four years and a more specialized three-year course. At either cycle, the system includes five types of courses: academic, commercial, industrial, agricultural and normal or teacher preparatory. At the first cycle, about four fifths of the total enrollment is concentrated in academic courses. A certain redistribution takes place at the end of the first cycle, when half of the girls enter normal schools and a substantial proportion of male students are diverted to other vocational courses, as shown in Table 1.

In 1960 the total enrollment in secondary schools represented 11.5 per cent of the population in the 13–19 age group. Since school enrollments, especially at the secondary level, are growing faster than the country's population, the ratio is expected to be a little higher as of 1965.

As might be expected on the basis of such limited attendance, the chances for secondary education are unevenly distributed. Apart from regional and urban-rural differences, there is marked selectivity along social-class lines, the working class being in general heavily underrepresented among secondary school graduates. However, the degree of social selectivity varies according to type of school. It is higher in academic than in vocational courses, except for normal schools, which are mostly attended by girls and in general do not rank lower than academic courses. Among vocational courses,

Reproduced, by permission, from *Sociology of Education,* 39 (Spring, 1966), pp. 155–166.
Aparecida Gouveia is a professor at the University of São Paulo.

Table 1. Enrollment in Secondary Schools, Brazil, 1962

Cycle	Type of School					Total Number (100.0%)
	Academic	Commercial	Industrial	Agricultural	Normal	
First	83.0%	11.6	2.2	0.4	2.8	1,128,510
Second	41.2%	30.0	3.6	0.5	24.7	335,761
Total	73.4%	15.8	2.5	7.8	0.5	1,464,361

Source: *Sinopse Estatística do Ensino Médio* (Rio de Janeiro: MEC, Serviço de Estatística da Educação e Cultura), 1962.

the industrial ranks the lowest, as 50 per cent or more of the student body comes from working-class homes. The pattern is about the same for both first- and second-cycle courses and, according to the best available evidence, prevails throughout the country.

The low prestige attached to industrial courses, which is paralleled by the small enrollments, has been of some concern to those in Brazil who are aware of manpower problems, especially the shortage of qualified middle-level technicians. It is believed that the avoidance of industrial courses is deeply rooted in feelings carried over from days in the not distant past when manual work, including crafts requiring the greatest skill, was left to Negro slaves. However, it seems that the phenomenon might better be seen as the result of competing alternatives in which the maximum premium is offered by academic courses that are the surest route to college, and secondly, by commercial courses, which do not appear too different in content from the academic. When only a small fraction of the total population gets to secondary school, most of those who reach this level aspire to occupations which require a college education.[1] Although the large majority in fact do not get that far, reality factors are not of the kind to discourage high aspirations when the student or his family makes a course choice at the end of elementary school, or even at the end of the first cycle, when a shift is theoretically possible.

Whatever the reasons for the low acceptance of industrial courses might be, they are certainly being counteracted in São Paulo, where in the second cycle they include substantial proportions of students from middle and upper-middle class families. As shown in Table 2, the large majority of the students enrolled in these courses in São Paulo come from nonmanual origins. As a matter of fact, in terms of social-class composition, second-cycle

---

[1] Among the second-cycle male students included in the sample that provided data for this paper, 50 per cent in vocational courses and more than 80 per cent in academic courses prefer occupations which require a college education. The sample will be described at a later point in this article.

Table 2. Percentage of Students of Nonmanual Origin in Different Types of Schools
(Male and Female)

Type of School	São Paulo	Rio G. do Sul	Pernambuco	Ceará	Pará
		Capital			
		FIRST CYCLE			
Academic	79.0 (1,105)	75.8 (421)	69.4 (402)	80.2 (514)	74.2 (294)
Commercial	51.0 (337)	64.2 (95)	46.8 (124)	68.4 (57)	48.7 (78)
Industrial	31.4 (287)	34.5 (165)	35.9 (142)	44.8 (87)	24.4 (41)
Agricultural	–	55.5 (60)	–	–	54.0 (37)
		SECOND CYCLE			
Academic	88.7 (248)	85.7 (346)	83.1 (419)	83.4 (355)	85.6 (197)
Commercial	53.3 (226)	74.7 (245)	74.2 (217)	64.0 (47)	66.1 (112)
Industrial	80.4 (449)	53.8 (26)	50.0 (12)	–	–
Normal	80.1 (226)	83.8 (80)	78.5 (186)	84.1 (189)	81.7 (49)

Source: Sample survey data.

industrial schools in São Paulo are much closer to the academic than to the vocational stream.

The situation found in São Paulo seems worth considering. As a "negative" case, it might throw some light on other aspects of the more general problem of social change. Since the topic seems to be of more than parochial interest, an attempt is made in this paper to account for the observed deviance.

As against similar courses in other states, which are maintained by the federal government, second-cycle industrial courses in São Paulo are mostly in private hands. As much as 92.1 per cent of the enrollment is concentrated in private schools.[1] But this is simply another indication of the acceptance enjoyed by this type of education in São Paulo. Private schools would not thrive if this type of education did not appeal to the kinds of students who can afford tuition fees which are as high as or even higher than the fees charged in academic courses.

Rather than looking for explanations on the basis of institutional or school characteristics, the focus of this paper is on the environment where these courses are thriving. The hypothesis is suggested that the main factor accounting for the acceptance of industrial schools in São Paulo is to be found in impulses originating from the economy. Except for the development of light industries in the southern state of Rio Grande do Sul and a few government-sponsored projects in the states of Minas Gerais and Rio

[1] *Sinopse Estatística do Ensino Médio* (Rio de Janeiro: MEC, Serviço de Estatística da Educação e Cultura), 1962.

de Janeiro, the great effort towards industrialization (which has been the leitmotif of policy makers in the last two or three decades) has resulted chiefly in a heavy concentration of industrial plants in the São Paulo metropolitan area. The modern factory buildings in the outskirts of the bustling city and the cars which are turned out in hundreds by Volkswagen, Simca, and Willys' plants are too conspicuous to go unheeded. Moreover, more earthly than the halo of technological accomplishments, the new jobs advertised in the bulky Sunday issue of *O Estado de São Paulo* pay good enough salaries to divert to industrial courses students who otherwise would choose the academic stream. This does not mean that occupations that require college education have lost their prestige. In fact, engineering is the most desirable occupation in the eyes of male secondary school students, the old respected medical profession ranking second. But to a good proportion of students, the well-paid jobs that can be obtained with a middle-level course in chemistry or electronics are much too close to be ignored.

The hypothesis is that a certain reassessment of the gains to be derived from the different types of schooling takes place as new opportunities are perceived in the labor market. Not only students, but parents as well, who in their school days would not have thought of following an industrial course, favor the practical training which is offered, sometimes, side by side with an academic course. The same would not be true of first-cycle courses. At this level, industrial courses would not enter the picture for students from middle- and upper-class families. It is not likely that the choice of a vocational course is even considered in those homes for children at the age of 12 or 13.

The assumption is that previous to the relatively recent developments in the economic sphere, people in São Paulo showed the same attitude that is found today in other parts of Brazil, and the discrepancy presently observed results from changes which have taken place in consequence of new opportunities in the job market. In fact, this hypothesis is already suggested by Haga in her analysis of São Paulo school enrollments.[1]

However, the picture becomes less clear when thought is given to the ethnic composition of the population in São Paulo. As of 1960, the population of São Paulo state represented 18.3 per cent of the total Brazilian population. It is estimated that more than half of the immigrants who entered the country since 1878 settled in this state.[2] A question is then bound to be raised. Is not the acceptance of industrial courses perhaps confined to immigrant groups who, from the very beginning, were more predisposed to industrial schools?

---

[1] Atsuko Haga, "Algunas Considerações Sôbre a Aceitação e a Procura dos Cursos Profissionais Industriais," *Pesquisa e Planejamento*, 6 (December, 1963).

[2] Fernando Bastos de Ávila, S.J., *L'Immigration au Brésil* (Rio de Janeiro: Êditora Agir, 1956), p. 114.

This question raises some difficulties. To begin with, clear-cut ethnic origins are not frequent in the present school population. The large immigration streams started towards the end of the nineteenth century, and intermarriage is relatively frequent in Brazil, not only among foreigners and local people, but also between individuals of certain immigrant groups.[1] However, even in the absence of intermarriage, one could not rule out *ab initio* the hypothesis of cultural diffusion through physical proximity, business contacts, and other kinds of secondary contacts.

This paper deals with the problem from a limited perspective. It focuses on the distribution of certain nationality groups among the various secondary school streams as shown in the present student population. The data come from a random stratified sample of senior students taking second-cycle courses in the city of São Paulo in 1963. Industrial and normal school students are overrepresented in the sample but, when necessary, weights are applied to correct for unequal proportions. The data are taken from questionnaires filled out for a larger research project on secondary students and teachers in five Brazilian states.[2] Unfortunately, in other states the number of immigrants' children is too small to allow meaningful comparisons.

Ethnic origin is defined by father's nationality, or, more precisely, by father's country of birth. Four groups are defined, as follows: Brazilians, Japanese, Latins, and others. The number of immigrants' children is not large enough to permit a more refined categorization. The sample includes 1,065 students, but more than two-thirds reported fathers born in Brazil. The Japanese are the only homogeneous group. Latins include fathers born in Italy, Portugal, and Spain. "Others" includes all other nationalities. This classification is very crude but it has some heuristic value, as will be seen.

As shown in Table 3, boys avoid normal schools, and girls are little-inclined to industrial courses. These tendencies are found in both Brazilian and immigrant groups. Given these sex-related propensities, the analysis will focus on male and female students separately.

Among males, the enrollment is parceled out among the academic, the commercial, and the industrial streams in equal proportions. However, examination of Table 3 reveals that this overall distribution results from different choice patterns. Brazilians tend to concentrate on academic courses, whereas immigrants tend to concentrate on vocational courses. However,

---

[1] As shown in G. Mortara, "Contribuição para o Estudo da Assimilação Matrimonial e Reprodutiva dos Principais Grupos Estrangeiros no Brasil," *Estudos Brasileiros de Demografia,* 1 (July, 1947), pp. 193–221.

[2] The larger project was carried out jointly by the National Institute of Pedagogical Studies of the Brazilian Government Ministry of Education and the Center for Comparative Education of the University of Chicago, represented by Professor Robert J. Havighurst. Financial support for a part of the study has been provided by Carnegie Foundation. The sample was taken from schools in the states of São Paulo, Rio Grande do Sul, Pernambuco, Ceará, and Pará. The data were collected in 1963.

Table 3. Enrollment in Various Types of Courses among Students
of Different Nationality Groups

Father's Country of Birth	Academic	Commercial	Industrial	Normal	Total Number (100.0%)
		São Paulo—Capital			
		SECOND CYCLE Males			
Brazil	42.0%	27.7	29.6	0.7	400
Japan	23.0%	41.4	35.6	—	45
Latin	21.3%	54.4	24.2	—	73
Other	29.8%	17.0	53.2	—	61
Total	36.7%	31.6	31.1	0.5	579
		Females			
Brazil	43.3%	25.5	6.5	24.7	349
Japan	50.5%	38.8	5.8	4.8	34
Latin	46.5%	27.9	5.4	20.2	57
Other	52.0%	20.0	17.0	11.0	46
Total	45.2%	26.5	7.3	20.9	486

Source: Sample survey data.

immigrants are not all alike. Latins prefer the commercial course. "Others" prefer the industrial course, and the Japanese stay somewhere in between these two streams.

Among female students, the academic stream contains almost half of the total enrollment. The remainder is divided between the commercial and the normal in roughly equal proportions, and a small fraction—less than 10 per cent—is found in the industrial. Differing from the pattern observed among male students, the preference of girls for academic courses is not confined to the Brazilian group, but prevails in all nationality groups. On the other hand, certain ethnic-related differences regarding the propensity to follow normal courses are evident. Among Brazilians and Latins, about one-fifth is enrolled in this stream, whereas among "others" and more so among the Japanese, normal school students represent much smaller proportions. At the same time, the proportion of industrial students, although still small, is shown to be larger among "others" than among Brazilians, Latins, or Japanese.

As observed, the choice of a course is related to ethnic origin, the propensity to follow an industrial course being more frequent among children of certain immigrants than among Brazilians, Japanese, and Latins. And this is true for both boys and girls.

However, the question might be raised whether these findings have something to do with the distribution of the various nationality groups along the social scale. In fact, as the data on social origins of students enrolled in the different streams suggest, the chance of attending a vocational course—industrial or commercial—is smaller for children from upper and upper-middle class families than for children from lower origins. Inversely, the working-class student who reaches the second cycle is much more likely to enroll in a commercial than in an academic course. At the same time, it is not absurd to think of certain inequalities in the social distribution of the different ethnic groups. For example, on the basis of what happens in the United States, where the phenomenon has received some attention, one could expect that more recent immigrants would more rarely be found at the top than at the bottom of the social scale. Thus it is conceivable that the observed ethnic-related differences in secondary school choice might simply reflect the socioeconomic position of the various groups.

As seen in Table 4, the social profiles of the various nationality groups are somewhat different. The upper category, which includes big landowners, big businessmen or industrialists, high political and administrative officials, university professors, physicians, lawyers, and other professionals, managers and personnel of equivalent prestige level, represents a smaller proportion among Japanese and Latins than among Brazilians and "others." However the proportion of "uppers" is somewhat larger in the group made up of "other" immigrants than among Brazilians.[1]

This finding runs contrary to the pattern to be expected on the basis of observed preferences for industrial courses. If the socioeconomic position of "others" is as comfortable as Table 4 indicates, they *should* be concentrated in the academic rather than in the industrial stream. Thus, from the distributions shown in the above table, one could still entertain the hypothesis that the concentration of Japanese and Latins in the commercial stream might have something to do with their position in the social hierarchy, but the distribution of "others" could not explain the concentration of these students in industrial courses.

In fact, as can be seen in Table 5, referring to male students, the preference for industrial courses observed in this group does not depend on social status. The subpartition results in small N's but the tendency is shown at

---

[1] Social status is defined on the basis of father's occupation. The three-level classification used in this paper results from a seven-point scale which was collapsed according to the following scheme:

Status Level	Original Categories
Upper	High and upper-middle (1, 2)
Middle	Middle-middle and lower-middle (3,4)
Lower	Manual work supervision, skilled and unskilled (5, 6, 7)

The original seven-point scale represents a modified version of the instrument used by Hutchinson in his studies of social mobility in São Paulo. B. Hutchinson, *Mobilidade e Trabalho* (Rio de Janeiro: Centro Brasileiro de Pesquisas Educacionais), p. 19.

Table 4. Socioeconomic Status and Father's Country of Birth
(Percentage in Given SES Category)

Father's Country of Birth	Socioeconomic Status			Total Number (100.0%)
	High	Middle	Low	
	Males and Females, São Paulo—Capital			
	SECOND CYCLE			
Brazil	27.8%	51.4	20.8	(749)
Japan	6.3%	69.6	24.1	(79)
Latin	14.6%	53.1	32.3	(130)
Other	39.3%	50.4	10.3	(107)

Source: Sample survey data.

all social-class levels. Among "uppers," "middles," and "lowers," the proportion attending industrial courses is larger among "others" than among students of other nationality groups. The data referring to female students show the same pattern although, as previously indicated, the inclination for industrial courses is far less frequent than among male students, and in the upper category Latins enter the picture, too (Table 6).

Thus, the greater propensity for industrial courses shown by "other" immigrants prevails all along the social scale. The same cannot be said of Latins' preference for commercial courses. As observed among Brazilians, the inclination for this type of schooling is related to social class. It decreases as one goes up the social scale; in other words, it decreases as the position of the student or his family improves. However, an examination of the two distributions suggests that, as compared to Latins, Brazilians turn their backs on commercial courses at a lower point on the social scale. Among Latins, the larger decline of enrollment in the commercial courses is observed between the middle and upper strata. Among Brazilians already in the middle category, commercial students represent only about one fourth of the total male enrollment in second-cycle courses. The remaining part is divided between the academic and the industrial streams in roughly equal proportions. Thus, for Brazilian boys from middle-class homes—sons of small businessmen, secondary or elementary schoolteachers, salesmen, bank clerks and the bulk of white-collar workers—the choice in São Paulo is chiefly between the academic and the industrial courses. As for Brazilians from other status levels, the chances are that the boy will most likely follow an academic course if he is an "upper," and a commercial course if he comes from a working-class family.

The picture first suggested by interstate comparisons is now somewhat clearer. The preference for industrial courses is, in fact, more frequent among certain immigrants than among Brazilians. However, the immigrants'

Table 5. Enrollment in Various Types of Courses among Male Students
of Different Nationality Groups and Different Social Levels

Father's Country of Birth	Secondary	Commercial	Industrial	Normal	Total Number (100.0%)
		São Paulo–Capital			
		SECOND CYCLE "Lows"			
Brazil	28.4%	45.5	25.1	1.0	(94)
Japan	–	74.1	25.9	–	(12)
Latin	12.1%	66.7	21.2	–	(27)
Other	40.0%	–	60.0	–	(7)
Total	22.9%	51.0	25.5	0.6	(140)
		"Middles"			
Brazil	36.7%	27.0	35.3	1.0	(194)
Japan	35.0%	28.1	36.8	–	(30)
Latin	19.5%	53.6	26.8	–	(37)
Other	27.9%	18.6	53.5	–	(28)
Total	33.3%	30.4	35.6	0.7	(289)
		"Highs"			
Brazil	60.9%	14.1	25.0	–	(112)
Japan	–	–	100.0	–	(3)
Latin	57.1%	19.0	23.8	–	(9)
Other	29.3%	19.5	51.2	–	(26)
Total	56.1%	15.0	29.0	–	(150)

Source: Sample survey data.

children make up only a small fraction of the student population, and this is not sufficient to explain what is shown by interstate comparisons. What really makes for the relatively high proportion of enrollments in industrial courses observed in São Paulo is the acceptance that these courses enjoy among middle-class Brazilians—not that the preference for this type of schooling is significantly higher than in other social strata, but chiefly because the Brazilians constitute the largest group in the student population.

From the viewpoint of the explanation originally suggested, it is also worth noticing that in none of the nationality groups is the choice of the industrial stream preponderantly a working-class phenomenon.

Yet, and especially considering the criterion used to define ethnic origin, the hypothesis could still be entertained that the acceptance of industrial courses among Brazilians in São Paulo would have something to do with

Table 6. Enrollment in Various Types of Courses among Female Students
of Different Nationality Groups and Different Social Levels

Father's Country of Birth	Secondary	Commercial	Industrial	Normal	Total Number (100.0%)
		São Paulo–Capital			
		SECOND CYCLE "Lows"			
Brazil	17.5%	55.5	3.6	23.4	(62)
Japan	32.0%	64.0	–	4.0	(7)
Latin	13.3%	53.3	3.3	30.0	(15)
Other	57.1%	–	28.5	16.4	(4)
Total	20.1%	54.3	4.0	21.6	(88)
		"Middles"			
Brazil	44.6%	17.8	7.8	29.8	(191)
Japan	51.4%	34.3	8.6	5.7	(25)
Latin	55.0%	25.0	2.5	17.5	(32)
Other	60.0%	7.5	15.0	17.0	(26)
Total	48.4%	19.9	7.8	23.8	(274)
		"Highs"			
Brazil	56.9%	19.6	6.2	17.3	(96)
Japan	100.0%	–	–	–	(2)
Latin	63.2%	–	21.1	15.8	(10)
Other	40.0%	40.0	17.5	21.5	(16)
Total	56.2%	20.5	8.6	14.7	(124)

Source: Sample survey data.

values brought by foreign immigrants. However, the available evidence does not point in such a direction, as Italians, Portuguese, and Spaniards, who are far more numerous than other immigrants, are no different from Brazilians as regards preference for industrial courses.[1] Moreover the group which shows the largest concentration of students in the industrial stream cannot

---

[1] The following data, referring to persons who entered the country in the 1874–1950 period, indicate the relative volume of the five major immigrant streams:

Italians	32%
Portuguese	28%
Spaniards	12%
Germans	5%
Japanese	4%

Source: *Anuário Estatístico do Brasil* (Rio de Janeiro: Instituto Brasileiro de Geografia e Estatística, 1951).

be said to represent a given culture or tradition, since it includes people as different as Russians, Syrians, Germans, Argentines, Egyptians, Hungarians, Greeks, Frenchmen, Lithuanians, Dutchmen, and Poles. These groups were lumped together because each is too small to be treated in a separate category.

The fact remains that relatively more industrial students are found in this residual category than in any other group. An explanation might be found in the very fact that these immigrants do not belong to any of the large groups. Being few, they cannot count on traditional anchorages; but for this same reason, they are more likely to discover new pathways. "They are prepared to see the range of objective opportunities in the new environment and are minimally restricted by prescribed commitments," as Siegel suggests in his analysis of successful migrants from northeastern Brazil who settled in a small community in the state of São Paulo.[1]

The ex post facto hypothesis proposed to explain the greater propensity to industrial courses shown by "other" immigrants would fit into Siegel's theoretical scheme. He deals with internal migrants and his key variable is recency of arrival. The problem discussed in this paper involves foreign immigrants, and the key variable would be the number of fellow countrymen. But the structural conditions are basically the same, as seen from the following quotation:

> . . . other things being equal, the perception of available choice behavior would be directly affected at the social-cultural level by what may be labelled status control. By status control is meant the total range of commitments and expectations which characterize the playing of social roles.

The proposition suggested in this paper is that the situation of the individuals who do not belong either to local groups or to the major migrant streams is propitious to the perception of new opportunities and reorganization of choice behavior.

Thus, the greater propensity for industrial courses shown by individuals who do not belong to the major immigrant streams would be explained on the basis of structural factors rather than on the basis of original differences in values.

A similar situation could perhaps account for some of the explained variance among Brazilians. Enrollment in industrial courses is expected to be more frequent among internal migrants who cannot count on a large network of kin or friends from their native towns than among people who have strong and numerous ties in São Paulo. Unfortunately, no data on geographical origins of Brazilians are available, and the hypothesis, which

---

[1] Bernard J. Siegel, "The Role of Perception in Urban-Rural Change: A Brazilian Case Study," *Economic Development and Cultural Change*, 5, no. 3 (1957), pp. 244–256.

might be applicable to choice behavior of any kind, remains to be investigated.

Summary and Conclusions

As opposed to what happens in other parts of Brazil, where industrial courses are attended mainly by lower-middle class and especially working-class students, in the city of São Paulo this type of secondary school attracts substantial proportions of students from more-favored origins. It is suggested that the new job opportunities resulting from the heavy concentration of industrial plants in the São Paulo metropolitan area make these courses more appealing to students from middle and upper-middle class families, who otherwise would enroll in academic courses. At the same time, the hypothesis is entertained that the discrepancy observed in São Paulo could be explained by the large influx of immigrants with different values.

This hypothesis is explored by examining the distribution of various ethnic groups in a sample of students from different types of secondary schools in São Paulo. Controlling for social class, no difference is found among Brazilians, Japanese, Italians, Portuguese, and Spaniards. But the group made up of immigrants from "other" countries, who are too few to be treated in separate categories, shows a greater concentration in industrial courses at all social-class levels. On the other hand, this would not be sufficient to explain the difference pointed out by interstate comparisons, for this group includes only a small fraction of the student population. In fact, the greater acceptance of industrial schools in São Paulo is shown to result mainly from choices made by middle-class "Brazilians" who are by far the largest group in the student population.

At the same time, there is no reason to believe that Brazilians have been influenced by values brought by immigrants, as the largest immigrant groups— Italian, Portuguese, and Spanish—are no different from local people as regards the inclination for industrial courses.

It is suggested that the greater propensity to industrial courses found among "other" immigrants could be explained on the basis of structural conditions resulting from the fact that being few in number, they lack traditional anchorages and thus are more likely to perceive new opportunities and follow new pathways.

Discrepancy between Goal and Function in Educational Planning: The Guatemalan Experience

T. DAVID WILLIAMS

History does not perhaps repeat itself, but an awareness of past experience does sometimes give the observer of the contemporary scene a melancholy impression of old tunes on new (but not always better) instruments. Educational reform is an old story in Guatemala, and few contemporary reformers can improve on the enthusiasm and imagination that prevailed during the two decades following the elevation to the presidency of General Justo Ruffino Barrios in 1873.[1] The country at that time had a relatively advanced educational structure,[2] and if articulate aspiration linked with enthusiasm were enough to create and sustain momentum, Guatemala would have become a showpiece for the virtues of educational planning.

The failure to achieve the promise of those years owes something to alternating periods of political instability and repression, which various governments have justified as the only alternative to instability. But these factors alone are not adequate to explain the inefficiency of the educational

Reproduced, by permission, from *Comparative Education Review,* 13 (June, 1969), pp. 196–208.

Research on this paper was carried out during the summer of 1965. Assistance was generously provided by members of the Oficina de Planeamiento Integral de Educación, especially Professors Elizardo Ureal and Carlo Morales. An even greater debt is owed to Professor Russell Davis of the Center for Studies in Education and Development, Harvard University. Any errors or deficiencies in the argument are due entirely to the author.

[1] The annual reports of the minister responsible for education are the best source. A useful secondary source is Carlos Gonzalez Orellana, *Historia de la educación en Guatemala,* Colección Científico-Pedagógica (Mexico: B. Costa Amic, 1960).

[2] See T. David Williams, "Educational Development in Ghana and Guatemala: Some Problems in Estimating 'Levels of educational growth'," *Comparative Education Review,* 10 (October, 1966), pp. 462–469.

system—its poor record in achieving the limited goals espoused by most political factions.

The attention of educational reformers appears to have been concentrated on either very long-range objectives or the minutiae of the internal organization of the schools—both proper matters of concern. Preoccupation with them, however, has led to neglect of an equally important matter, the process by which change within the educational system is effectively translated into change in the social or economic conditions of the nation.

If inattention to the topographical details of the "path to progress" meant merely that the chosen path was not as good as another, but that the goal could still be reached with some extra effort or time, the issue would perhaps be an academic one. It may, however, make progress negligible—the extra time and effort required exceeding the bounds of feasibility—or encourage movement in the wrong direction altogether.

This paper will examine two areas in which the Guatemalan educational system failed to achieve its goals. The system did not achieve "internal efficiency"—was not able to ensure high educational standards in the upper levels of the secondary system through apparently rigorous annual examinations from the first year of primary school onwards. Nor was it able to provide a highly specific link between the schools and the labor market through the establishment of secondary vocational schools, particularly those designed to provide technicians and rural schoolteachers.

Internal Efficiency: "Tough" Examinations and Academic Selectivity
THE STAGES OF EDUCATION

Primary education lasts six years[1] and is followed by three years of "basic" or prevocational (*ciclo básico*) junior secondary schooling designed to give the student sufficient exposure to postprimary work—in mathematics, science, and language—to enable him to choose a vocation. The various branches of senior secondary schooling (*ciclo diversificado*) may last from two to three more years, and are designed to prepare the student for either entry into the labor market (as teacher, technician, or bookkeeper, for example) or into the university.

Originally the two-year *bachillerato* course was regarded as the preuniversity course, but now almost all of the senior secondary graduates qualify for entry to one or another of the university faculties, so that the three-year teacher-training and technical tracks, while providing some degree of access to intermediate-level occupations, also provide access to higher education.

Finally, degree courses at the universities last from four to six years

---

[1] There is a preprimary program for children who do not speak Spanish and there are also some regular preprimary kindergarten schools for those who do. The primary program, however, does not depend on preprimary training, except that knowledge of Spanish is essential.

depending on the subject (but most taking five or six years). There are substantial provisions at this level for part-time students, and all courses are offered in the evening as well as during the day.

Schools are both private and public, with most students attending public school at the primary level. The average level of teacher qualification in the public schools is low by international standards but very much better than in the private schools. The private schools, on the other hand, have smaller classes and since many people are prepared to meet the costs of sending their children to them, it may be presumed that they have other, less easily identifiable, advantages. The private schools had an internal system of examining during the period covered by this paper, so examination results cannot be compared with those in the public schools. Reported examination results do show a much higher success rate than that obtained in the public schools, but it is not clear whether this was due to more lenient marking or to higher achievement levels.

There is a marked disparity between urban and rural educational performance. In several rural districts, few or no students were enrolled in the upper levels of primary school in 1964. No one knows how many rural students may have moved to urban schools after completing the first two grades, but it seems safe to say that the wastage rate in the rural areas is very high and comes early.

Failure in the examinations means that students must repeat the year, except in some cases when a secondary school student may be allowed to proceed to the next grade and to retake the examination he has failed.

THE FAILURE RATE IN EXAMINATIONS

Table 1 gives data on examination performances in public urban primary and *ciclo básico* schools by male students. Data from urban schools are used because they are the source of most secondary school students. This does mean, however, that the performance described below is, in fact, better than the average for the country as a whole since urban schools are, by most criteria, better than rural ones. Figures for male students are used for the sake of convenience—official data provide separate tables for male and female performances but no total. Male performances seem to have been slightly better than those of the females.

The examination toll in the *ciclo básico*—which is not intended to provide a terminal education—is much higher even than that in the primary schools. However, students who are only marginal failures are allowed to go into the next grade and may retake the examination without repeating the year.

It should be noted that Table 1 shows the proportion of *examinees* who pass the examination; about 20 per cent of those attending school do not take the examination, and there is a further difference between numbers enrolled and numbers attending.

Table 1. Examination Results in Public Urban Primary
and *Ciclo Básico* Schools, October 1963

Grade	Examinees	Passes	% Pass Rate
Primary			
1	24,597	15,311	62
2	16,072	12,121	75
3	13,440	9,708	72
4	10,977	8.165	74
5	8,804	6,820	77
6	6,604	5,855	89
Ciclo básico			
1	3,593	1,062	30
2	1,923	766	40
3	1,328	606	46

Source: *Informe de las labores realizadas por la Sección de Estadística Escolar, 1964* (Guatemala City: Ministerio de Educación Pública, 1965), pp. 22–23, 40.

Results in the upper secondary *ciclo diversificado* schools are close to those in the primary schools. In 1963, results for all public schools at this level showed an average pass rate of 70 per cent[1] although if successful candidates are related to enrollment, the figure would be closer to 50 per cent.

A student who qualified for entry to the university would thus have passed through 11 or 12 grades, each culminating in an examination which a substantial proportion of the candidates fail. Whatever the disadvantages to students of so severe an obstacle course throughout their school lives, the system should at least, one would suppose, produce graduates who are highly accomplished examinees: an intellectual precision squad poised for spectacular triumphs at the university. Instead, the proportion of students managing to graduate from the University of San Carlos—an institution which does not have an outstanding international reputation—is strikingly low. The university does not provide data on annual examinations, but it does give figures for the numbers entering each year and the numbers graduating, so that an estimate of the number of graduates can be given by looking at enrollment in one year and graduates five years later (this assumes a program lasts six years).

A large number of students attend on a part-time basis and these may have a higher wastage rate than the full-time students, but even if part-time students are assumed to account for three quarters of the university student

---

[1] The *Informe* (see source for Table 1) does not aggregate the results, but shows data for each type of school. This runs to several pages; the average given here is the average for each year in all types of school at this level.

Table 2. Freshmen and Graduating Classes at the University of San Carlos
1950 and 1955 Respectively

Faculty	Freshmen, 1950	Graduating, 1955	% Graduating
Agronomy	43	0	0
Economics	229	11	5
Law	537	16	3
Medicine	604	24	4
Chemistry	125	6	5
Humanities	329	16	5
Engineering	322	21	7
Total	2,189	78	4

Source: *Boletín Estadístico Universitario,* University of San Carlos, Office of the Registrar.

population and none of them graduate, according to the statistics, regular students still achieve a very low level of success; and certainly the part-time students, who take longer, account for some of the small number who graduate.

RIGOROUS SELECTION: SHADOW OR SUBSTANCE

It is possible that the examinations are so poorly constructed that they have no predictive value, or even that they test the wrong aptitudes (creative ability or even reasoning power may be handicaps if the answers to questions depend largely on the whim of the examiners). It was not possible to examine this hypothesis; however, it does not seem likely that this could account entirely for the failure of the selection process.

The system, which at first seems highly competitive, may in practice be highly restrictive: if even relatively good students are likely to fail and be forced to repeat the year, academic ability may become less important than the ability to bear the cost of an extended school career. The handicaps faced by students from low-income families are exacerbated. Because of home environment (including facilities for studying at home), students from low-income families are likely to do less well in examinations than students of similar ability from more-favored environments, and they are probably less likely to feel at ease in the predominantly middle-class atmosphere of the prestigious schools. If, in addition, relatively weak students from middle-class homes are able to carry on despite poor performance while relatively good students from lower-income homes have difficulty in lasting the course, selection is biased in a way quite different from that intended by the proponents of a severely selective examination system.

Table 3 shows the number of years taken by final-year primary students to reach the sixth grade, parental background, and the students' expectations

Table 3. Parental Background, Academic Success and Expectation of Further Study
among Final-Year Primary Students

Years Taken to Complete Primary Program and Parental Background	Expectations			% Expecting to Continue Full-Time Study
	Full-Time Study	Part-Time Study	No Further Study	
6 years				
White-collar	54	10	1	83
Blue-collar	34	29	3	52
7 years				
White-collar	28	6	1	80
Blue-collar	37	20	13	62
8 years				
White-collar	14	3	0	82
Blue-collar	13	22	6	28
9 years				
White-collar	4	1	0	
Blue-collar	1	6	2	

Notes to Table 3: N = 308. To test the negative hypothesis that parental background is not related to further study among students with similar academic records, contingency tables can be established for each group—six years, seven years, and eight years and over. The "no further study" category has to be combined with "part-time study" because there are insufficient observations in each cell to treat it as a separate unit. The chi-square values for each group exceed the values for .005, .01, and .005 respectively. The hypothesis that parental background and expectations of further study are unrelated can be rejected. It might be useful to show "the working" for the six-year group as an example:

Parental Background	Expectations		Total
	Full-Time Study	Other	
White-collar	0 = 54 (e = 43.6)	0 = 11 (e = 21.3)	65
Blue-collar	0 = 34 (e = 44.4)	0 = 32 (e = 21.7)	66
Total	88	43	131

The chi-square is 14.79. With one degree of freedom, 7.88 is the .005 value of chi-square.

of further study. Part-time study, a realistic expectation at the university level, is unlikely at the secondary school level and many students who say this is what they expect to do are likely to fall into the "no further study" group. Part-time study at this level probably means private tuition; it is most likely available to white-collar and affluent blue-collar students.

Table 3 is based upon the results of a survey carried out by the author in selected primary and secondary schools in Guatemala City. Four aspects of that survey should be stressed. First, students were divided into two groups: those whose fathers (or guardians) held white-collar jobs and those whose fathers held blue-collar jobs. Father's occupation was used in lieu of family income, although the match would not always be precise. It is unlikely that any from the white-collar group came from low-income families, but some from the blue-collar group may have been affluent. Unfortunately, it was not possible to get a more detailed breakdown, but it seems reasonable to suppose that the apparent nonacademic advantages that the "whites" had over the "blues" would also have been observed between more and less affluent subgroups of the "blues" if it had been possible to make this distinction.

Second, questionnaires were distributed only to students in the final year of primary and senior secondary schools. It is likely that a similar, though less pronounced, pattern would have emerged if data had been obtained on background, performance, and intention in other years.

Third, the responses of students to the question about how many years they had taken to reach the final grade may be inaccurate because of reluctance to admit failure. Almost one half of the students in the final primary year said they had gone straight through as did more than 60 per cent of those in the final year of senior secondary school. It was not possible to check these responses because there is, for a variety of reasons, much transferring from one school to another (even within the city) and few schools maintain records on individual students. If the figures are correct, there must be a high dropout rate after nine, 10 or 11 years of school. If there was bias due to concealment of failure, it would not affect the argument advanced below as long as the bias was shared equally by both groups. There may be a greater likelihood of this sort of bias among the white-collar group since academic failure is a greater offense to the cultural values of middle-class than to working-class communities, and the general environmental advantages of a middle-class home make it more difficult to rationalize failure. If a partial bias of this sort does exist it would strengthen the argument that nonacademic factors played a major role in the selection process.

Fourth, it was not possible to follow up with a study to investigate whether expectations were realized or not.

Only slightly over half of the most successful blue-collar students expected to continue, while in no group of white-collar students did less than 80 per cent expect to continue. The disparity is much greater among secondary school students (Table 4). Since some schools offer two-year senior secondary programs and some three-year programs, the categories have been changed to "completed in minimum time" and so on.

Most students who intend to go on to full-time study say that they completed their program without repeating. If this is accurate, it suggests that a substantial part of the subsequent failure is due to inadequacies in the examination system itself. But even as they stand, the figures do indicate a very high wastage rate associated with socioeconomic factors.

It is a commonplace that all societies "lose" a large number of able people from lower-income groups who, because of environmental handicaps, are

Table 4. Parental Background, Academic Success and Expectation of Further Study
among Secondary School Students

Time Taken to Complete Course and Parental Background	Expectations			% Expecting to Continue Full-Time Study
	Full-Time Study	Part-Time Study	No Further Study	
Minimum				
White-collar	44	39	9	48
Blue-collar	6	71	21	6
Minimum plus 1 year				
White-collar	4	11	7	18
Blue-collar	1	29	17	2
Minimum plus more than 1 year				
White-collar	5	5	2	42
Blue-collar	0	12	20	0

Notes to Table 4: $N = 303$. The data for the second and third groups cannot be translated into a contingency table because there would be some cells with too few observations. A chi-square test on the "minimum" group, to check the negative hypothesis that the variables are independent, gives a value larger than the chi-square for .005 and the hypothesis can be rejected.

either unable or unwilling to operate effectively in a school environment. It should perhaps be emphasized that the data given here refer to the small proportion of students of blue-collar origin who have overcome these obstacles and in some cases have achieved considerable success in spite of them. Moreover, because of the differences between the blue-collar and white-collar environments, equal performance will in general require greater natural ability from the "blues." But even among the most successful of these, only 6 per cent expected to continue with full-time education.

The Link between Formal Education and the Labor Market

The two secondary schools which train students for places in specific areas of the labor market are the Technical Institute and the Rural Teachers School at Chimaltenango (henceforth referred to as I.T.V. and Chimaltenango respectively). Their functions are well described by their names: the I.T.V. was established to provide middle-level technicians and thus to eliminate what is generally regarded as a bottleneck in the supply of skilled artisans and junior technical managers; Chimaltenango was designed to ease the critical shortage of trained teachers in rural areas—both by recruiting potential teachers for rural areas and by training them to deal with the special problems of rural students.

One of the problems with schools designed to meet a highly specific need is that their actual function may differ from their intended function. The additional training the students get increases the opportunities available to them; they become eligible for jobs (or further training) other than those for which they have been specifically prepared and, for various reasons, these other opportunities may be more attractive than the work they were intended to do.

The results of a questionnaire administered to final-year students at Chimaltenango and penultimate-year students at I.T.V.[1] indicate that few intended to follow the careers for which the schools were designed to prepare them. Many who would seek jobs for which they were being trained intended to do so temporarily or as a last resort; few looked with any favor upon the careers they were supposed to undertake. It will be argued later that their attitude is consistent with rational economic choice; the roots of failure lie neither in the educational institutions per se, nor in the students who attend them, but in the pattern of economic incentives prevailing in the society and, perhaps, in the administrators who believe that career patterns can be easily molded by changes in curricula.

SOCIAL BACKGROUND AND ACADEMIC PERFORMANCE OF STUDENTS AT I.T.V. AND CHIMALTENANGO

Both I.T.V. and Chimaltenango had a higher proportion of students from blue-collar families than the overall sample did. Overall, the "blues" comprised just under 60 per cent of the total; in both I.T.V. and Chimaltenango they accounted for almost 80 per cent.[2]

Overall the "whites" tended to have a considerably higher proportion of nonrepeaters than did the "blues," but in both I.T.V. and Chimaltenango the degree of success was similar for students from both groups. The data do not explain this difference. Perhaps these schools are a poor option for students from white-collar families and attract generally the weaker students from this group, whereas the vocational bias and scholarship provision make them relatively attractive to lower-income students; or it may be that the manual-rural content of the curricula reduces the cultural bias that favors middle-class students in orthodox academic schools.

Data from these schools do, however, support the idea that there is a striking difference between the expectations of "white" and "blue" students, regardless of academic performance. At I.T.V., 86 per cent of the best "whites" expected to continue full-time education compared with 17 per cent of the best "blues"; no "whites" expected to work full time, compared with 13 per cent of the "blues." The data from Chimaltenango were not quite as clear (the only student who actually wanted to work full time as a rural teacher was a white-collar student) but did correspond to the overall pattern.

---

[1] The final-year students were not available because they were doing practical work with various enterprises.

[2] The information about 10 per cent of the students at I.T.V. was insufficient. If this group were distributed in the same way as the others, 77 per cent of the students would be from blue-collar families.

THE CAREER INTENTIONS OF STUDENTS AT I.T.V.
AND CHIMALTENANGO

I.T.V.

Eighty per cent of the students in what was intended to be a terminal course expected to go on to the university on either a full-time or part-time basis. Insofar as they do what they expect to do, the purposes for which the I.T.V. was established will be frustrated. Established at considerable expense to provide intermediate technicians, it becomes instead another feeder institution for the university.

Of course, the students may not be able to do what they expect to do. In particular, those who planned part-time studies may not have appreciated the difficulties of the undertaking, and the very high wastage rate at the university has already been shown. But even if many I.T.V. graduates find that they eventually have to give up hopes of a degree, their expectations almost certainly affect the kind of job they would be willing to accept and, especially, its location. Until they have become resigned to the frustration of their hopes, they will not be prepared to accept jobs outside Guatemala City, and they will be unlikely to accept jobs in the city that do not give them enough spare time during the day for them to cover their home-study assignments in addition to guaranteeing them free time for evening lectures.

Most students wanted to study engineering at the university, with mathematics the second most popular choice. There are three possible explanations for this: first, the courses at I.T.V. qualify a student for further work in those areas; second, the I.T.V. attracts students interested in engineering and mathematics; and third, the type of education offered at I.T.V. stimulates enthusiasm for these subjects.

Other schools in the sample produced students who wished to study engineering but not in such large proportions as did I.T.V. and, although perhaps the numbers are too small to justify attaching much significance to apparent trends, students from other schools who are interested in engineering are overwhelmingly from white-collar homes: only two of the best "blue" students outside of I.T.V. intended to study engineering—and one of these was from the Rural Teachers College.

The I.T.V. serves perhaps a very useful function as a "bridge" to engineering courses at the university. It may be that learning a trade provides a very good foundation for engineering studies and, even more, for practical engineering work. This is not, however, what the I.T.V. was intended to do. Designed to meet the shortage of artisans, it is increasing the supply of an entirely different group—professional engineers; designed as a terminal course, it is seen by students as a bridge to higher studies.

Chimaltenango

Only one student replied to the question "what would you *like* to do" by saying he would like to teach in a rural school. There were 17 students (27 per cent) who *expected* to work full time. Even so, most of these said they would like to study if possible so it is likely that even this group would be reluctant to accept jobs in rural schools except perhaps those near the capital, which are already relatively well supplied. It is probable that less than 10 per cent of this final-year class intended to do the work for which the institution had been established to train them. Moreover, only two students among those expecting to continue schooling intended to take a degree in education. The most favored subject was social work (14 choices), followed by agriculture (seven), engineering (six), domestic science (five), law (four), and mathematics (three). Other choices were veterinary studies, anthropology, science, biology, accounting, and humanities.

The curriculum at Chimaltenango may provide a useful background for many of the subjects the students wish to study at a higher level and there may be long-term educational benefits derived from having students exposed to a wide range of only loosely related experiences. These benefits would, however, be quite different from those anticipated by the proponents of highly specific vocational education.

Insofar as student expectations are a reasonably reliable guide to what students will actually do and insofar as the results obtained in 1965 are representative, it would seem clear that neither the I.T.V. nor the Rural Teachers College are fulfilling anything like the function that was their rationale.

THE STRUCTURE OF INCENTIVES

The apparent failure of these vocational courses raises two important points for educational planning. The first is that educational institutions should be examined for what they actually do, rather than what they are supposed to do. If vocationally oriented secondary schools are, in fact, providing a bridge to university work, the usefulness of their curricula for this purpose along with any other purposes actually being met should be examined. It may be that present curricula would meet these criteria, but they are not, in fact, being analyzed in this way. The second point is that one should seek an explanation for the divergence between the intended function and the actual one.

Reliable data on the relationship between educational level and incomes are difficult to obtain. It appears, however, that a very large gap exists between the earnings and possibilities for promotion of people with professional qualifications and those of people with intermediate (i.e., high school) qualifications.

Only a small proportion of the school-age population complete the six-year primary school course. Those who have completed a senior secondary program are in statistical terms members of a very small elite and will have already incurred substantial costs in the form of forgone earnings. If, for example, the average educational level in the country is three years, a graduate of I.T.V. will already have spent nine years beyond the average in formal education. Moreover successful completion of the I.T.V. program will usually provide qualification for entrance to the university. To increase substantially the supply of subprofessional technical workers, either salaries at this level must be raised so that the discounted cost and income streams of professional and subprofessional technicians are more nearly equal, or else the time required to obtain subprofessional qualifications must be reduced so that these qualifications are a feasible target for a much broader range of the population.[1]

The salary structure for schoolteachers reflects a similar disregard for economic realities, this time in a different direction. A secondary school graduate and a university graduate are paid according to the same basic scale, with a few extra "points" given for higher academic qualifications but even more for seniority in the post. It is possible—perhaps even likely—that a man who does not attempt a degree will be better placed after four years than a man of equal ability who has gone through the degree program with distinction.

Therefore, for the careers where higher education should be a prerequisite, the rewards are slight or even negative, while for the careers where attracting able preuniversity graduates is vital, the incentives virtually compel them to seek professional status.

The difficulties of attracting qualified teachers to the rural areas and of persuading potential teachers to take a degree and then become teachers are also due in part to a failure to appreciate the importance of providing incomes commensurate with the costs of acquiring these qualifications. At present rural teachers tend to be paid at a lower rate than teachers in the urban areas. The reason given for this is that it is less expensive to live in the rural areas. This is true, however, only in the sense that the standard of living is lower in rural areas: to obtain a comparable standard of living would be more expensive. Moreover, teachers who have already spent 12 years in formal education often wish to continue their studies, which they can do on a part-time basis in the urban areas. Time spent in the rural areas thus involves a considerable sacrifice of opportunity, so that if one is serious

---

[1] The principal costs for full-time students are the opportunity costs, and these rise substantially as the students complete successive stages of their educations. Many university students—and probably all those in the relevant group—are evening students who hold full-time jobs, and for them the opportunity cost is much lower. Only a small proportion of those who start at the university will graduate and some of the others may do the sort of job for which they were trained. Their choice of work while they are at the university and especially its location will, however, have been largely determined by the degree of access it allows to the university; their subsequent careers might be as significantly affected by the type and location of the job or jobs they have during their university days as by their secondary school experience.

about staffing rural schools with qualified teachers, perhaps one should offer compensation to teachers who, at least temporarily, forgo this opportunity.

But even raising economic incentives in areas where a serious shortage of appropriately trained manpower exists may not prove sufficient to remedy the problem. Perhaps nonmonetary factors, such as enhancing the prestige of certain types of work, would prove more powerful. But until proper financial incentives are used, it is fruitless to speculate about this point. In any event, economic incentives are a necessary, even if not sufficient, part of any effective manpower policy. The creation of educational institutions in order to meet an alleged bottleneck in the supply of skilled labor without due regard to de facto opportunities is most likely to lead, as it appears to have done, to the effective transformation of these institutions into something quite different from the purpose for which, at considerable cost, they were established and are being maintained.

Conclusion

This paper has been concerned with the failure of the educational system in Guatemala to achieve goals which, whatever their educational validity, appear to have had the approval of all major political groups. They are, moreover, goals which have appeared to be on the threshold of achievement for several generations and which were discussed with as much eloquence and enthusiasm 80 years ago as they have been in the last decade. It may be that achieving these goals requires a fundamental change in social structure which many of their proponents have not appreciated and which some of them might not be willing to accept. Debate has not, however, focused on these aspects of the problem; clearly, there has been a failure at the planning stage, or what should have been the planning stage, to work out the steps required to achieve the goals.

There have been two principal elements in this failure. The first has been the belief that the educational system can be considered independently of the social and economic environment in which the schools are placed: the attempt to establish an academically selective system has been frustrated because of a very high wastage rate due to nonacademic factors. The attempt to meet assumed manpower shortages for middle-level technicians and rural teachers has been frustrated because the graduates find their training has provided them with options that are more attractive than the jobs for which they were trained.

The second element in the failure to transform aspiration into achievement has been the low priority attached to empirical research as an instrument for clarifying and evaluating policy proposals. Policy makers have acted on assumptions about what ought to happen rather than what was actually happening, and these assumptions were rarely challenged because so little information was available.

Individual Decisions and Educational Planning: Occupational Choices of Venezuelan Secondary Students

GORDON C. RUSCOE

The planning of education in the emerging nations has been advocated as a means to meet manpower needs, to facilitate social cohesion, and to promote political integration at the national level. These goals of educational planning, assumed to be valid components of national development, are largely advocated without reference to the desires and decisions of the individuals whose education is to be planned. The importance of individual decisions is at best only partially recognized through attempts to couple educational plans with incentive systems designed to get the right people into the right educational and occupational slots through self-allocation.

Self-allocation, however, depends on more than the identification of needed occupations and the establishment of presumably compelling incentives. It rests finally on how well the incentives will attract sufficient numbers of individuals with the right qualifications into the appropriate types of education and subsequently into the appropriate occupations.

Reproduced, by permission, from *International Development Review,* 10 (June, 1968), pp. 20–25. (Copyright © 1968, Society for International Development.)

Gordon C. Ruscoe has been an associate professor in the Center for Development Education, Syracuse University, since September 1967, after a previous appointment at the University of California at Los Angeles. He received his Ph.D. degree from the University of Michigan in June 1963 and has recently completed *Latin American Students in the United States,* a monograph for the National Association for Foreign Student Affairs.

The author wishes to thank the University of California at Los Angeles Latin American Center and the UCLA Chancellor's Committee on International and Comparative Studies for their financial and operational support for this study. The author is indebted to Audrey Schwartz and Robert Butler, UCLA; Juan Guevara, Director, Centro Latinoamericano de Venezuela; and Senta Essenfeld and Sixto Guaidó, Secondary Guidance Section, Venezuelan Ministry of Education, for their invaluable assistance in carrying out the research.

Thus, the success of self-allocative processes and, indirectly, the success of educational planning cannot be accurately predicted without at least some assessment of how the individuals involved make occupational choices. Are these choices based on knowledge and experience, factors which could be externally altered to persuade individuals to opt for occupations needed for national development? Are the reasons for these choices open to reconsideration, given changes in an individual's perception of relative advantages of different occupations? Indeed, are externally devised incentives likely to be compelling at all? A partial answer to these questions may be made on the basis of research which the author has recently carried out on the occupational and educational decisions of secondary students in Venezuela.[1]

The occupational decisions of secondary students and how they are made are major determinants of future educational developments in Venezuela in at least three respects. First, students' decisions about their future occupations and about the training necessary to enter these occupations will shape higher education and consequently national development for many years to come. If students make the wrong decisions for want of sound information about occupations or about the educational means to attain these occupations, this may lead both to student dissatisfaction and to possibly major dislocations in Venezuela's future occupational and educational structures.

Second, either to fail to establish educational and occupational incentive systems or to rely upon incentive systems which are insufficiently compelling to attract university students into educational and national plans may wreak havoc with such plans.

Finally, while Venezuela has experienced significant educational growth since 1958, particularly in enrollments and new plants at all educational levels, the country still faces serious educational problems. Two problems are especially relevant to our present concern. First, the number of places in higher education and the necessary financial bases for university expansion have not kept pace with demands for these places by secondary school graduates. Second, university education continues to be plagued by unresolved conflicts over control, autonomy, finance, and purpose. The current impossibility of establishing viable interuniversity cooperation—not only between public and private universities but also among the public universities themselves—means inter alia that little concerted effort can be made at the university level to improve or redirect students' self-allocative processes

---

[1] The major instrument of the study was a 12-page questionnaire administered in late 1966 and early 1967 to nearly 3,000 third- and fifth-year students in *liceos* and *colegios* in and about the Caracas metropolitan area. In addition to background information about the student, the questionnaire contained questions about the occupational choice of the student, his reasons for selecting this occupation, his sources of knowledge about the occupation, his educational plans and his vocational-educational orientation. A preliminary report of the findings may be found in Gordon C. Ruscoe, "Vocational Choices of Secondary Students in Venezuela." (Unpublished paper.)

or even to assure that the most-able students are enrolling in and graduating from the nation's universities.

Occupational Choice

Given the impact which the occupational decisions of secondary students will have on future educational developments in Venezuela and the present inability of the higher education system to play a decisive role in shaping and redirecting these decisions once students have reached the university level, it is of more than passing interest to learn that 97.5 per cent of secondary students sampled in the present study aspire to professional occupations. Students do differ in the specific careers which they choose, e.g., doctor, engineer, lawyer, chemist, and university professor. Nevertheless, all the careers chosen fall within the general classification of professional occupations.

Clearly, to say that nearly all students choose professional occupations is not to say that they are equally committed to these choices. Such differences in students' commitments are important in determining likely reactions to incentives and appeals which seek to promote students' re-examination of their educational and occupational decisions and, where necessary, reformulation of decisions to correspond more closely to national needs. Students' commitments to choices are of course difficult to measure before they take specific action to implement their choices. But, given our concern in determining the likelihood that commitments can be altered before action is taken, by means of incentive systems, it is possible to examine those factors which seem to be the ingredients of commitment.

In our Venezuelan study five factors about occupational choice were used to explore differences in commitment: (a) reasons for making occupational choices, (b) expectations about the occuaption chosen, (c) length of time during which the occupational choice has been held, (d) sources of information about the occupation and its requirements, and (e) the extent to which the student knows individuals in his chosen occupation. In addition, it is possible by examining the last three factors together to distinguish between those students who have held their choices for a long period of time and who have had close personal contact with individuals, usually relatives, in their chosen occupations; and those students who have held their choices for only a short period of time and have had no personal contact with individuals in their chosen occupations. The former group may be considered high in both length of, and familiarity with, their occupational choice, while the latter group may be considered low in both length and familiarity. This measure of length/familiarity offers another way of gauging the extent to which occupational choices are open to change.

The reasons which students give for making their occupational choices are perhaps the best initial indicators of the ways in which students are likely to react to external incentives and appeals. Nine alternative reasons were offered in the questionnaire: (a) family advice, influence or tradition; (b) possibility of obtaining a large income; (c) the need of the country for specialists in the occupation; (d) learning to know oneself better; (e) work conditions; (f) the influence of teachers whom the student has known; (g) the social prestige of the occupation; (h) the example or influence of acquaintances who have the same occupation; and (i) advice or influence of friends (Table 1).

Table 1. Freqeuncy Distribution of Responses
to Reason for Occupational Choice

(1) Family	8.5%	(4) Self-knowledge	15.5%	(7) Social prestige	3.8%
(2) Income	9.7%	(5) Work conditions	27.8%	(8) Influence of acquaintances	5.0%
(3) National needs	26.3%	(6) Teacher	1.6%	(9) Influence of friends	1.7%

Notes: Each respondent was instructed to indicate which one of the nine alternative reasons he felt was most important in determining his occupational choice. Clearly, the response to this single item does not preclude other, less-important reasons which also might affect the respondent's choice. As will be seen in Table 2, however, responses to this single item do serve very well to distinguish among respondents on other questionnaire items.

Of the nine alternatives, only the first five received sufficient responses to be included in the analysis—family, income, national need, self-knowledge, and work conditions. Even a brief examination of the characteristics of students who choose each of these five alternatives suggests that we are dealing with five quite distinct groups. The characteristics of each of these groups may be seen in the following tabular form (Table 2). Groups designated by reason for occupational choice differ not only in other factors reflecting occupational choice and expectation but also in factors reflecting educational and socioeconomic background and future orientation. Several implications for educational planning and incentive systems may be drawn from these differences.

Appeals to University Students

First, and most important, given differential rates of university enrollment and academic success in Venezuela based on sex and socioeconomic background,[1] it is questionable whether sufficient numbers of university students to whom planning and incentives are directed are likely to respond.

[1] A disproportional number of male students continue to reach the universities in Venezuela. Thus, in 1965, while males constituted only 55.5 per cent of secondary *colegio* and *liceo* enrollment, males constituted 68.0 per cent of university enrollment. By university the percentage of male students was: Central 66.4 per cent, los Andes 70.6 per cent, Zulia 69.1 per cent, Carabobo 72.9 per cent, Oriente 79.6 per cent, Católica 54.4 per cent, and Santa María 80.4 per cent. (Calculated from: República de Venezuela, Ministerio de Educación. *Memoria y cuenta 1965*. Tomo II, Anuario Estadístico, 1966, pp. 187, 477.)

The socioeconomic bias in Venezuelan university enrollment has yet to be rigorously studied.

Those most likely to become university students are males from high socio-economic backgrounds. But these students are in fact those who give family influence and, to a lesser extent, self-knowledge as their major reasons for choosing their occupation. These same students are among the least interested in national needs and in income rewards from their chosen occupations. For this group planned educational incentives such as scholarship programs have little appeal, especially if the acceptance of such incentives requires enrollment in educational programs not normally endorsed by the family.

In addition, students in this group view their future lives as centering around family and friends. They have only moderate interest in their future socioeconomic status; more accurately, they are in general satisfied with maintaining rather than improving their status, which is already high. Because these students have such expectations and aspirations, it is improbable that educational incentives will be effective in redirecting their educational and occupational choices.[1]

The students most likely to respond to conventional incentives and appeals are those who report that their reason for their occupational choice is income or national need. These students, from low socioeconomic backgrounds, aspire to socioeconomic status higher than that of their parents much more frequently than do other students. And they are much more likely than are other students to believe that studies are the most important avenue to occupational success. Studies, however, are rather narrowly defined: these students are especially concerned with obtaining the necessary credentials for their chosen occupations, but they are little concerned with vocational education as education. That is, they see the principal role of education to be certifying rather than educating or training.

It would appear that many educational programs in higher education, provided that they offer appropriate economic incentives and certificates,

Because Venezuelan education does not differ significantly from that of most other Latin American countries, however, it is a warranted assumption that biases documented for other Latin American countries operate in Venezuela as well. See, for example: Hobart W. Burns, "Social Class and Education in Latin America," *Comparative Education Review,* 7, no. 1 (February, 1963), pp. 230–237. Consejo Superior Universitario Centroamericano, "Algunos aspectos socioeconómicos de la población estudiantil universitaria centroamericana del año 1962," *Recursos Humanos en Centroamérica,* Cuaderno No. 2 (October, 1963). Robert J. Havighurst *et al., La sociedad y la educación en América Latina* (Buenos Aires: Editorial Universitaria de Buenos Aires, 1962). (Especially chap. 10.) David Nasitir, "University Experience and Political Unrest of Students in Buenos Aires," *Comparative Education Review,* 10, no. 2 (June, 1966), pp. 273–281. Kalman Silvert, *The Conflict Society* (New York: American Universities Field Staff, 1966). Rev. ed. (especially chap. 7). Some indirect evidence specifically about Venezuelan university bias may be found in Gordon C. Ruscoe, "Educational Strategy and Occupational Choice: The Case of Secondary Students in Venezuela." (Paper submitted for publication.)

[1] There is no intended implication here or in the following comments that every student in the group has the characteristics being described. That is, we do not mean that traditional appeals and incentives are *totally* effective or ineffective for all members of any group. Rather, we are attempting to describe the likely reactions of the majority of each group.

Table 2. Distribution of Characteristics of Secondary Students Classified by Reason for Occupational Choice

Occupational Choice Characteristics

Reason for Occupational Choice	Source of Occupational Information[1]			Relative in Chosen Occupation[2]		Length of Time Occup. Decision Held[2]		Expectation about Chosen Occupation[2]						Score on Measure of Length/Familiarity[2]	
	Reading, Lectures	Personal Contact	Other Sources	Yes	No	4 Years or More	Less Than 4 Years	Use Abilities	Aid Others	Meet Nat'l Needs	Earn Money	Secure Future	Other Expectations	High	Low
Family	38.9	41.7	19.4	47.7	51.3	40.9	59.1	24.7	15.3	8.2	2.3	24.7	24.8	51.7	48.3
Self-knowledge	49.2	25.8	25.0	31.7	68.3	24.9	75.1	19.3	23.3	13.3	2.0	18.7	23.4	28.3	71.7
Work conditions	47.2	22.2	30.6	32.7	67.3	37.3	62.7	32.7	14.8	7.6	1.9	21.7	21.3	26.0	74.0
National needs	51.7	23.9	24.4	23.2	76.8	42.1	57.9	17.9	18.7	31.1	2.0	19.5	10.8	28.8	71.2
Income	54.5	26.7	18.8	24.8	75.2	21.7	78.3	15.2	12.1	8.1	14.1	32.3	18.2	17.9	82.1

Current Characteristics

Reason for Occupational Choice	Sex[2]		Socioeconomic Status[3]			Secondary School in Which Enrolled[2]		Sec. Div. in Which Enrolled or Intend to Enroll[2]		Secondary School Grades[4]		
	Male	Female	High	Medium	Low	Public	Private or Parochial	Sciences	Humanities	High	Medium	Low
Family	55.4	44.6	82.4	17.6	0.0	26.3	73.7	79.8	20.2	27.2	49.4	23.4
Self-knowledge	32.3	67.7	68.7	24.4	6.9	42.2	57.8	63.4	36.6	26.0	52.0	22.0
Work conditions	49.6	50.4	66.2	28.2	5.6	49.4	50.6	76.5	23.5	24.4	49.3	26.3
National needs	62.0	38.0	63.4	30.7	5.9	53.7	46.3	85.0	15.0	16.3	52.9	30.8
Income	46.3	53.7	54.6	39.2	6.2	54.7	45.3	72.5	27.5	21.6	49.5	28.9

Future Orientation

Reason for Occupational Choice	Educational Orientation [2]					Socioeconomic Aspirations [3]			
	Vocational Education	General Education	Education for National Needs	Titles and Certificates	Other	Much Higher Than Parents'	Higher Than Parents'	Same As Parents'	Lower Than Parents'
Family	50.0	20.5	4.5	17.0	8.0	20.7	34.0	41.5	3.8
Self-knowledge	44.4	19.0	5.9	18.3	12.4	24.4	37.0	36.1	2.5
Work conditions	52.6	14.0	4.8	18.7	9.9	26.5	39.2	28.4	5.9
National needs	50.2	10.9	10.5	13.2	15.2	27.6	47.7	21.5	3.2
Income	34.4	15.6	4.2	32.3	13.5	40.8	45.7	12.3	1.2

Notes: Percentages rather than actual numbers are reported in this table in order to facilitate reading. Statistical tests reported are based on the actual numbers of responses, however. Because the following sections of the paper are devoted to consideration of the salient differences among groups for each of the items included in the table, no extended discussion of the data is included at this point.

Some comments about the types of data reported are appropriate, however. First, all items required single responses. For example, each student selected only one response to describe his expectations about his chosen occupation or to describe his educational orientation. Second, differences among groups of students for each item, while statistically significant, do not result in mutually exclusive categories. Thus, 82.4 per cent of those who indicate that family considerations were paramount in determining their occupational choices come from high socioeconomic backgrounds, but 17.6 per cent come from intermediate backgrounds.

Finally, two items require further explication. Socioeconomic status is a composite item which includes occupation of parent or guardian, sources of family income and sources of student school financing. Secondary school grades are presented as high, medium, or low. Venezuelan grading is based on a 20-point scale. Although 19 and 20 are officially described as high grades, in practice very few students have such high averages. In our study, high grades were considered 16 or above, medium grades 13–15, and low grades 12 or below. This classification corresponds closely to that proposed by the North American Association of Venezuela for credential evaluation. (See: Isabel M. Gouverneur, "A Guide to the Evaluation of Venezuelan Academic Credentials." Caracas: North American Association of Venezuela, 1965.)

[1] The chi-square computed for differences among groups for this item is barely significant, falling between the .10 and the .05 levels of confidence.

[2] The chi-square computed for differences among groups for each item is significant at greater than the .001 level of confidence.

[3] The chi-square computed for differences among groups for each item is significant, falling between the .01 and .001 levels of confidence.

[4] The chi-square computed for differences among groups for this item is significant, falling between the .05 and .02 levels of confidence.

would be attractive to these students. But because these are students from low socioeconomic backgrounds, they are unlikely to reach the university level in sufficient number.

It does not seem unreasonable to suggest that one curious potential result of current university planning would be the development of incentive systems which appeal to those effectively denied admission and which do not appeal to those who are admitted. To avoid this situation, two alternatives would seem to be available. On the one hand, attempts could be made to design incentives and appeals which would be meaningful to the predominantly upper and upper-middle class students currently enrolled in universities. The success of this alternative is, however, doubtful. These students, relatively unconcerned with personal economic gains and with national exigencies, would be enticed by only the most extravagant incentives and appeals. Particularly economic incentives would have to be so great that their costs would considerably outweigh the economic benefits to the nation by attracting a few students into needed occupations.

On the other hand, the likely positive reactions to conventional incentives by those students from low socioeconomic backgrounds who are currently not attaining university status in appreciable numbers suggest a second alternative—preuniversity intervention in educational and occupational selection.

Appeals to Secondary School Students

If the composition of university student bodies is to be altered in favor of those for whom conventional incentive programs are attractive, such alteration will require efforts at the secondary level to identify and assist students to reach a university.[1] One might argue that those students whom we have identified as concerned with income and national needs, given their rather low grades and their too-narrow views of education, cannot be expected, in sufficient numbers, to be successful university students. This may well be true. There is, however, a third group of students, those who give working conditions as their major reason for occupational choice, which might profit considerably from assistance and guidance at the secondary school level.

These students are fairly evenly divided between males and females, between public and parochial school enrollment, and between science and humanities specializations in secondary school. They would seem to be a potentially rich source of university students who could be persuaded to enter needed educational and occupational positions.

---

[1] This is in fact now being done in Venezuela on a small scale. IVIC (Instituto Venezolano de Investigaciones Científicas), concerned with the apparent lack of well-trained Venezuelan experimental scientists, has begun a program, under the direction of Dr. Luis Carbonell, associate director of IVIC, to identify last-year secondary school students who show aptitude for and interest in scientific investigation. These students are given financial assistance to attend a university and opportunities each summer to work at IVIC.

First, given their intermediate socioeconomic background, these students are not likely to be deaf to economic appeals. Second, these students are concerned with finding occupations which will allow them to make full use of their abilities and talents, concerns which can be linked with requirements in many needed occupations. Finally, this group is most oriented toward vocational education in the sense of education which will equip them to carry out their occupations successfully. The potentiality of this group, however, is not likely to be realized to a sufficient extent without intervention at the secondary level to ensure that these students are exposed to information about a variety of occupations rather than the traditional choices of law, medicine and engineering and that they are assisted in reaching and remaining in a university.

The contention that more must be done at the secondary level in order that educational planning and incentive systems can be effective at the university level raises two further issues which can be partially examined with the present data.

Programs at the secondary level to identify, assist and guide students to necessary university careers require something more than ad hoc, intermittent efforts of individual schools or teachers. Nationwide programs initiated by the national government and carried out by the Ministry of Education on a permanent basis, however, are, at least at this time, circumscribed. The private and parochial schools, although supervised by the government and required to follow minimal educational standards set down in national educational laws, would largely fall outside the program.

The exclusion of private and parochial schools would have two results. First, many of those students who are most likely to attend a university— i.e., those of high socioeconomic background—would be removed from the influences of such programs because they are enrolled in parochial and, to a lesser extent, private schools. Second, a good part of those who may require assistance to reach a university and who are more likely to respond favorably to conventional incentives are registered in public schools. Thus, while government programs limited to public schools will miss a good number of students likely to attend a university, such programs may well reach those very students who will most likely respond to and profit from the assistance offered.

In order to assess the effectiveness of programs initiated at the secondary level, it is necessary to consider the probable changes in occupational choice which might occur. Even assuming that a secondary-level program could be introduced into all secondary schools, public, private and parochial, it is likely to have quite different effects on different students. To a large extent differential effects are likely to result because students have been exposed to different kinds of information about their occupational choices and because these choices have been held for different lengths of time.

For example, those students who report family influence as the reason for their occupational choices have held their choices for some time and have depended for information on relatives engaged in the occupations rather than on other, more formal and remote sources. It seems improbable that such students will react to new information about other occupations by opting for these occupations.

In contrast, those students who have had to depend on more formal sources of information and who have held their occupational choices for only a short period are more likely to respond favorably to new information. Students who report income and work conditions as central reasons for occupational choice would fall into this classification.

Thus again those students who are for the most part enrolled in public secondary schools are the students most likely to respond to programs at the secondary level.

Conclusions

On the basis of data from secondary students in Venezuela, it is suggested that educational planning and incentive systems directed at university students are unlikely to cause these students, through self-allocation, to fill educational and subsequently vocational slots deemed necessary for national development. The lack of sufficient relationship between incentives and student self-allocation results primarily because most university students have already made certain educational and occupational decisions which are no longer open to extensive reconsideration, especially reconsideration postulated on incentives and appeals which have little meaning. External appeals to economic incentives, national needs, or increases in socioeconomic status largely fall on deaf ears.

This is not to say that increasing economic rewards for certain occupations and granting university scholarships to be applied only to certain courses of study are totally unproductive exercises. However, such exercises typically are too late with too little. They offer too little to students from high socioeconomic backgrounds, who have already in large numbers chosen occupations and educational means to these occupations endorsed by their families and known to them through their families and relatives. These exercises are too late because their appeals are appreciably more meaningful to those students who have failed to reach the university level in sufficiently large numbers.

Given these considerations, programs at the secondary level are needed which would identify students who are likely to allocate themselves among necessary occupations and which would assist these students to enter a university. Such programs would in the long run promote more efficacious educational planning by ensuring that incentive systems will be directed toward those students who are likely to respond favorably.

Section 6:
Rural Environments

Introduction to Section 6

J. Roberto Moreira describes the social and economic conditions as well as the problems of the educational system which existed prior to 1960 in rural Brazil. Through a discussion of special projects to alleviate rural problems, Moreira concludes that ". . . it is possible to create a local awareness of educational needs and to lead local people to care about education and help in realizing educational projects as well as making choices and decisions." He cautions, however, that, although such is a possibility, promoting education will also lead to urbanization; he suggests that education alone, without financial support to small landowners, improvement of farming techniques, agrarian reform, and increased social services, will be unable to fulfill either the needs of the rural dweller or the development goals of the nation.

Manning Nash analyzes four rural communities in his cross-cultural investigation of the role of schools in fostering modernization. Through a conceptual framework which he calls "multiple society with plural cultures," Nash describes the interrelationships among local value systems and the wider social, political, and economic structures of the nations of Mexico, Guatemala, and Burma. Through an analysis of the similarities and differences existing in educational orientations between the two major culture areas, the author suggests that the most common features underlying similarities are the poverty of the populations and the very high costs of providing primary education. Regarding the differences in the educational system, the author remarks that these ". . . are reflections of the larger social and cultural differences, and spell out at a micro-level the meaning of a recently sovereign nation in Southeast Asia with a Buddhist cultural tradition, oriented to reaching a form of democratic socialism, as against two Latin American societies with a Spanish-colonial heritage, being strongly involved in both Westernization and modernization." In the concluding section of the article, Nash suggests that social change must occur on the local and regional levels before the educational system will be able to change since community schools which are not affected by such external forces will likely remain as stabilizers or reinforcers of conservatism.

Education in rural Guatemala is the focus of the next two articles in this section. The first, by Robert Redfield, discusses education from both an institutional and a less formal, or noninstitutional, perspective. Redfield suggests that the school's role in preserving the local culture in highland Guatemala is minimal since little of the traditional heritage is dependent upon literacy and the instruction provided does little to support village life. However, education received outside school, primarily in the home, is characterized by Redfield as having a greater and a more meaningful impact since the tasks that are mastered and the knowledge acquired are reinforced through participation in daily activities which support the existing life style.

Differentiating between the Indians and Ladinos, Redfield finds that the nature of this out-of-school educational content, especially in terms of religious ceremonies and mythology, is different. He suggests that the contribution of ritual and myth to the Indian education process is greater since it is developed over generations and is relied upon in understanding, describing, and coping with the world as it exists.

In the second article on Guatemala, Oscar H. Horst and Avril McLelland describe the community of Ostuncalco, where the Mam Indians outnumber Ladinos but are economically subservient. In a discussion of the eight rural and two urban schools in the Ostuncalco educational system, the authors point to the problems of the limited facilities and supplies available to teachers and students and to how these and other limitations tend to be greater in rural schools attended primarily by Indians. The case study describes the administration of schools, the nature of the curriculum, the different types of certified teachers, and the reasons for nonattendance at school by students. The authors indicate that: "The situation in Ostuncalco clearly reveals that school facilities can be joint insofar as Indians and Ladinos are concerned and yet very unequal in opportunities for the children of these two culturally distinct groups of Guatemalans."

Horst and McLelland point out the school's role in reinforcing the existing structure, including the hostility which pervades Indian-Ladino relations, and its position as a relatively inaccessible institution for the economically poor.

The final selection in this section, by Gerardo and Alicia Reichel-Dolmatoff, is an excerpt from a larger anthropological study on Aritama, a village in northern Colombia. The village is characterized by two relatively distinct populations: the placeros, who live near the center of Aritama, represent the higher socioeconomic level and consider themselves forward looking and progressive; the lomeros, who are characterized by tradition and isolation, cling to accustomed ways of the Indian-oriented mountain peasant. The authors, through their description of the boys' and girls' schools in the community, suggest that the education received has a great impact on students. "In the first place, the child is systematically taught the high prestige value of good clothes and of ceremonial behavior and is made to abhor and to ridicule all manual labor and cooperative effort. . . . In the second place, 'knowledge' is reduced to a set of ready questions and answers, beyond which there is little or nothing added or learned."

The authors point to the different conceptions of what the school should consider its responsibility by drawing upon the perception of lomero and placero parents as well as those of the teachers and of the government. They also indicate that wastage rates are high in the schools, attendance is sporadic, and discipline is harsh; instruction centers on recitation, memorization, and copying. In conclusion, the authors suggest that "the composition of the student body" and "the cultural effects of the teaching methods" are the two problems inherent in the schools which tend to increase placero-lomero tensions in the village.

Original Sources for Selections

Moreira, J. Roberto. "Rural Education and Socioeconomic Development in Brazil," *Rural Sociology,* 25 (March, 1960), pp. 38-50.

Nash, Manning. "The Role of Village Schools in the Process of Cultural and Economic Modernization," *Social and Economic Studies,* 14 (March, 1965), pp. 131-143.

Redfield, Robert. "Culture and Education in the Midwestern Highlands of Guatemala," *American Journal of Sociology,* 48 (May, 1943), pp. 640-648.

Horst, Oscar H., and Avril McLelland. "The Development of an Educational System in a Rural Guatemalan Community," *Journal of Inter-American Studies,* 10 (July, 1968), pp. 474-497.

Reichel-Dolmatoff, Gerardo, and Alicia Reichel-Dolmatoff. "Formal Schooling," in *The People of Aritama: The Cultural Personality of a Colombian Mestizo Village.* Chicago, Ill.: The University of Chicago Press, 1961. Pp. 115-125.

Rural Education
and Socioeconomic Development
in Brazil

J. ROBERTO MOREIRA

From Semicolonial Rural Society to a Society in Transition

Since colonial times the Brazilian economy has been based mainly on the production of tropical goods and raw materials. The process of capitalization and industrialization, of which the first steps were taken at the end of the last century, was slow and met with many obstacles, especially the uncertainty of the international market for tropical products. As manufacturing did not develop until the beginning of this century, most foreign exchange credits had to be applied for the importation of consumer goods.

Because of this economic situation, the Brazilian way of life has been based predominantly upon rural activities, and this rural society could be neither rich nor bright. The manner in which Portugal settled the country during the sixteenth to the eighteenth centuries, the structure of the economy resulting from that settlement, and the related social organization precluded the development of an efficient rural technology in Brazil. The formula "latifundium + monoculture + slavery" characterized Brazilian social organization until almost 1900. Large estates, ruled by a kind of patriarchal family and worked by Negro slaves, divided the country into three classes—a small rustic aristocracy, slaves, and numerous poor landless peasants.

Agricultural technology was very primitive and, as the country was large, no care was taken to preserve the soil. No more than two generations of the same family would work the same land; they moved forward into new

Reproduced, by permission, from *Rural Sociology,* 25 (March, 1960), pp. 38–50.

The author is technical assistant to the Ministry of Education and Culture of Brazil and director of the National Campaign to Eradicate Illiteracy.

lands, neighboring or distant, as soon as the previous ones were exhausted. The *taperas* (country estates which have been completely abandoned and are in ruins) are today an important part of the Brazilian rural landscape. *Queimadas* (lands cleared by burning) were the first to be cultivated, and no fertilizers were used.

This primitive technology was so poor that when many American Southerners went to Brazil after the Civil War to continue their way of living there, they discovered that Brazilian slaves raised cotton in the same way as the American Indians planted and raised corn.[1]

The 1920 census reported a labor force of almost 10 million people, of whom about 80 per cent were concerned with primary production; yet only 1,706 tractors and no more than 142,000 plows were in use. The rate of productivity per rural worker was among the lowest in the world. About 80 per cent of the adult rural population was illiterate.

At that time coffee production and exportation constituted the foundation of the Brazilian economy, and only a few other extractive products could be considered as having some weight in the country's external trade. During the great world depression of the late 1920's and early 1930's, Brazil almost went bankrupt. From these economic difficulties arose a series of political troubles. The socioeconomic development from 1930 through 1946 was very well described by Spiegel[2] as chronic inflation and sporadic industrialization.

Industrialization was the result of the deficiency of exports. Lacking foreign exchange, Brazilians had to produce many of the needed consumer goods. However, when the international market demanded more tropical products, as it did just before the Second World War, the process of industrialization declined.

Nevertheless, industrial production increased at a mean annual rate of 3.2 per cent from 1930 through 1940. Output in agriculture decreased, however. New lands were no longer available, and agricultural technology was so deficient that no modern means of soil revitalizing could maintain the fertility of the lands in use.[3] The resulting economic imbalance was responsible for a general impoverishment of the common people. Landless peasants and owners of small despoiled rural properties emigrated to towns looking for jobs and better living conditions, but the urban labor market was unable to make jobs available to these unskilled migrants. The result

---

[1] Ballard S. Dunn, *Brazil, the Home for the Southerners* (New York: G. B. Richardson, 1866), p. 138.

[2] Henry William Spiegel, *The Brazilian Economy: Chronic Inflation and Sporadic Industrialization* (Philadelphia, Pa.: Blackiston, 1949).

[3] The cumulative rate of population increase was about 2.4 per cent; the industrial rate of increase was 3.2 per cent; the rate of agricultural production increase was about 1.6 per cent. Then the real increase of industrial production was 0.8 per cent and in agriculture it was -0.8 per cent (decrease); the Brazilian economy was almost stagnant from 1930 through 1940.

was the appearance of *favelas, malocas,* and *mocambos* (different kinds of small, unsanitary wooden cabins without water supply) on the borders of the towns and cities as homes of a marginal population.

After World War II many factors—among them, we must emphasize, the training of a large group of Brazilians in the United States in the fields of economics, political science, education, and the social sciences—contributed to set up short- and long-run programs for socioeconomic development, both with private and government participation. From 1948 through 1957 the gross national product increased at an annual rate of about 5.5 per cent. Special policies were adopted to attract foreign investments and to diversify exportable products in order to obtain more foreign credits. Foreign investments during these 10 years increased to about $5 billion, two thirds of which were made by American investors. This program is being retarded, however, by the world overproduction of coffee, for coffee represents almost half of Brazilian exports.[1] In 1957 the exports amounted to about $1.5 billion and imports to about $1.6 billion; the gross national product was $16 billion.

The Problems of Rural Brazil

Although Brazil is not yet a developed country, it is far ahead of its 1920 position. Per capita income has increased from less than $100 per year to about $260. A system of roads and railways has been developed, health conditions have been greatly improved, and educational opportunities have increased very rapidly. Nevertheless, the rural areas of Brazil, from which 60 per cent of a population of more than 60 million draw their means of living, are still far from prosperous.

To understand this situation we must consider the rural division of properties, the rural labor force, technology, and the social-status system. All of these show traces of the ancient latifundium + monoculture + slavery organization. Though there is no more slavery in Brazil, farm labor remuneration is low, and the social and job controls are such that in most of the interior areas the farms and plantations retain many features of the semifeudal and patriarchal colonial organization. But this is not as bad as it appears, because it is not too difficult to improve technology on large rural properties; as a matter of fact, rural economic improvement has begun. From 1950 on, the agricultural rate of real production exceeded the rate of population increase: 3.5 per cent against 2.4 per cent per year, which means a real increase of 1.1 per cent. But during the same period the real rate of industrial production increase was about 9.5 per cent per year,

---

[1] In 1957, 29.4 per cent of Brazilian exports were raw materials; 43.5 per cent, coffee; 25.5 per cent, foods and drinks; 0.7 per cent, chemical and pharmaceutical products; 0.1 per cent, machinery and vehicles; 0.4 per cent, manufactured goods; and 0.3 per cent, gold and money. Of the exports, 40.1 per cent were to the United States.

an indication of the unbalanced development of the Brazilian economy.[1]

The main problem of rural production in Brazil lies in the division of land. This division moves in two antagonistic directions: toward the large estate (latifundium), and toward the very small property (minifundium). Large estates are favored by many factors: capitalization and financial resources to increase holdings, nonlegal ways of obtaining land and court tricks to legalize the situation, misuse of temporary political power to get financial support for enlarged rural estates, and so forth. Small properties result from Brazilian legislation on patrimony; there being no birthright or primogeniture, at every new generation the estates are divided and redivided, if not sold, in order to permit a better partition and to pay the expenses of public inheritance transmission.

In 1920, rural estates smaller than 250 acres numbered 464,000; in 1940 there were 656,000 estates of less than 25 acres, and 975,000 with more than 25 acres and less than 250 acres. There was also an increase of large estates; the number of those ranging from 2,500 to more than 25,000 acres in 1940 was more than 27,000. In 1950 the number of small estates (less than 25 acres) increased to 711,000; those ranging from more than 25 to less than 250 acres numbered 1.1 million, and the largest estates (between 2,500 and 30,000 acres) increased to a total of 33,000. The total area of the rural estates increased from 430 million acres in 1920 to 495 million in 1940 and 580 million in 1950.

The owners of large estates find no great difficulty in improving production because they can obtain loans from official and private banks. Especially in the south and southeast parts of the country such improvement occurred after 1946. In 1940 the total number of tractors for agricultural activities in Brazil was less than 4,000; in 1950 they numbered 8,400, and in 1958 more than 30,000. The number of plows increased from about 500,000 in 1940 to about 1.9 million in 1958. Brazilian production of fertilizers was negligible in 1950, but rose to 14,000 tons in 1956; about 290,000 tons were imported in the same year.

Operators of the smaller properties, on the other hand, do not have the financial resources to buy the tools and other materials needed for better exploitation of their lands. They do not have the requisite knowledge to develop cooperative organizations. A national technological and ideological base for the progress of small farmers in Brazil is lacking.

In 1950 the labor force in agriculture comprised about 11 million workers (65 per cent of the total labor force of the country), of whom 55 per cent were owners and 45 per cent landless peasants. A landless peasant or a

---

[1] Source for these and other economic data: *Conjuntura Económica*, Nos. 9, 10, 11, 1958, and Nos. 1, 2, 3, 1959; a monthly digest of Brazilian finances and economy issued by the Getúlio Vargas Foundation, Rio de Janeiro. There is also an English-language edition of this magazine issued by the same foundation.

small holder in Brazil is often an illiterate, unskilled person who can obtain only a minimum income for survival. Landless peasants live in mud huts of one or two rooms, without piped water supply, water closets or any equipment other than rude beds, footstools, some vessels of earthenware, and such tools as a hoe, an ax, and a *facão* (a long, wide knife). They may have some furrows of black beans, corn, and cabbage near the hut, and also a few pigs, one or two cows, and a few chickens, which forage for themselves. The land on which the huts are constructed does not belong to the family. The owners permit the families to live on the land; in return the peasants work for the landlord during planting and harvest periods. Most of the peasants are sharecroppers, and about 40 per cent work for small wages.

In 1957 the mean annual salary for a rural worker or sharecropper in Brazil was no more than 6,640 cruzeiros, which in purchasing power is equivalent to no more than $250 in the rural areas of the United States. But the peasants have to buy only a few things because they may get most of their subsistence from the land on which they are permitted to live. No money is needed for the children's education or for health. When there is an elementary school nearby they send the children to attend the lessons, and all the pencils, notebooks and books must be furnished by the school. When possible, the school also gives the children some light lunch and some health care (mainly vermifuges and tonic medicines). For health treatment the Brazilian backwoodsmen use nonscientific medical personnel.

The family organization of these landless peasants is generally based on common-law marriage. Frequently, family organization is reinforced by legal marriage when a Catholic priest or missionary pays a visit to the area and persuades some peasants to accept the sacrament that since 1946 has been civilly recognized in Brazil. Marriage between relatives is very common because of the distance between settlements and the resulting isolation. The peasants organize themselves into large extended families with reciprocal aid and solidarity. It is very common also to reinforce the kinship linkage by means of godparenthood. But godparenthood is used also as a political device, being a means of linkage between rural political bosses and peasants. Through this linkage the bosses win a voting power, and the peasants believe that they have been assured protection and help from a powerful and influential leader.

Landless peasants in 1950 made up a labor force of five million workers (four million males and one million females), who provided support for at least 10 million more children, wives, godchildren, and relatives. These 15 million persons living in very low socioeconomic and cultural conditions represent the great challenge to Brazilian socioeconomic development because they comprise more than 29 per cent of the Brazilian population. Many of them, when it is possible to get some extra money, try to emigrate to cities and towns. There they will not attain even a proletarian status, but they can find unskilled and underpaid jobs, and the government has to give them some social and health assistance. As Andrew Pearse pointed out, they have in the *favelas, mocambos,* and *malocas* more social security and more possibilities for living than in the backward, underdeveloped areas, and this in spite of having a marginal position in the urban society.[1]

The second group of poor peasants is composed of the owners of very small properties (less than 25 acres). Supposing that each belonged to a different family, we would have no less than three million persons supported by that kind of rural property.[2] These peasants cannot produce any more than the landless ones; they can raise some crops, pigs, and chickens for their own consumption, but they have to work on some big farm for money to buy what they do not produce. Consequently, the only difference between them and the landless peasants is that they can sell out the small land they have in order to procure money with which to emigrate to urban areas.

The third group is more resistant to migration; they are owners of small and middle-sized rural estates ranging from 25 to 2,500 acres of land. They are able to make some money by selling part of their produce, and they strive to continue as rural landowners. The mean net income per family in this group ranges from about $300 per year to about $5,000. With their families, they make up a group of more than 3.9 million persons (in 1950 about 7.5 per cent of the Brazilian population). Together with the group of skilled rural workers (tractor drivers, managers, experts in agriculture or cattle raising, and so forth) who have jobs on the big farms, they form the upper-lower class and the middle class of rural Brazil. This group of small and middle landowners are the most responsive to adult education and community development programs.

The Problem of Education for Rural Areas

After 1930 many attempts were made to provide rural people with at least a part of the educational facilities allotted to urban areas. Because of the demographic condition of rural areas the kind of elementary school organized was the one-room and one-teacher school. In Brazil rural villages or hamlets are not common because of the nature of the rural technology and because of the economic fact that peasants need to have at hand some domestic animals, some vegetables, and some crops for immediate home consumption. Brazilian villages and towns are inhabited by people who live from commercial and handicraft activities. A village or a so-called rural town is generally a market place for agricultural products and a place where manufactured and other goods which rural people need are sold.

[1] Andrew Pearse, "Integração Social das Familias de Favelados," *Educação e Ciências Sociais* (Centro Brasileiro de Pesquisas Educacionais, Rio de Janeiro), II (November, 1957), pp. 245-278.
[2] This supposition is based on the fact that in 1950, out of a total population of 52 million, 17 million were economically active.

In principle, the one-room school presupposes a very good teacher because it assembles in the same class children of different ages, skills, and aptitudes. A good teacher is the result of culture and training; that is, he must be a highly educated person with capacity and social abilities for heterogeneous class management. Nobody with such qualifications in Brazil needs to apply for a teaching position in the uncomfortable and poor rural areas; such teachers can have good jobs in towns and cities. Consequently the rural teacher in Brazil is a person, generally a woman, who can scarcely read or write and who has had no pedagogic training.

In 1957 out of a total enrollment of about 5,900,000 pupils in elementary schools, only 2,109,000 were from rural families. As the estimated rural population of elementary school age was about 4,962,000 by that time, we can say that 2,853,000 rural children who should have been enrolled were not attending any school.

And this is not all. Because of the poor organization and teaching in rural schools, and because the school has no great meaning in the rural milieu, nonattendance and dropping out are quite frequent.[1] About 56.4 per cent of the rural pupils stay at school less than one and one-half school years; 12.6 per cent stay for two years, and 10.3 per cent for three years; only 18.7 per cent of them stay long enough to learn some basic writing, reading, and reckoning.

If the above is the situation as regards elementary schools, the condition of rural secondary schools is worse. The existing secondary schools are urban and academic. The federal government has been trying since 1940 to organize a system of technical secondary schools for agricultural teaching. In 1957 there were 35 such schools supported by federal funds and 14 supported by state funds. Their capacity was about 20,000 pupils, but no more than 4,370 were effectively enrolled. These schools appeal only to the interests of a few upper-lower class and lower-middle class people in the rural districts who look for employment as agricultural experts on the big modernized farms. Consequently these schools do not contribute to improving the technology of the middle and small tenants.

The educational, socioeconomic, and cultural situation in rural Brazil is not only a crucial challenge to the country's development; it also retards Brazilian industrialization, which depends upon an expanding purchasing power by the great majority of the active population—that is, the rural people.

The data on improvement of agricultural productivity in Brazil are mainly indicative of the situation on the large farms, as we have said. But this improvement, if translated in terms of productivity per capita or per worker, may lead to misinterpretation. For instance, the Economic Commission for

---

[1] See the author's report on Brazil in *World Survey of Education*, Vol. II, *Primary Education* (New York: UNESCO, 1958).

Latin America's Study of Agricultural Productivity found out that between 1945 and 1955 the Brazilian agricultural worker's productivity increased by about 39 per cent, but this is the result of improved production on big farms.[1]

According to Jacques Lambert, there are two different and contradictory Brazils. Both in the backlands and in the urban areas there is prosperity and also misery. Sometimes a rich, new, modern region contrasts with a neighboring poor, archaic, and decadent one. It is as if Brazil were living in two different ages of the same civilization: the medieval and the modern.[2]

The Attempts to Meet the Problems

In a new country, when the awareness of underdevelopment becomes critical and painful, and there is no previous experience to serve as a basis for meeting the situation, many possible solutions can be suggested and tried out. Since 1930 this has happened in Brazil. The national Ministry of Education and the state departments of education have shown unrest and anxiety. Numerous experiments have been tried, but the results have not been satisfactory.

We will report only the main projects of the federal government designed to help the states solve the problem of elementary education in rural areas.

In 1946, in accordance with a constitutional provision creating the National Fund for Elementary Education to supplement state and municipal funds for the enlargement and improvement of elementary schools, a plan was set up to apply the resources of the national fund according to regional needs.[3] From the total amount collected every year, 70 per cent would be applied to construct new school buildings, 5 per cent to improve teacher-training programs, and 25 per cent to create and maintain special schools for illiterate adolescents and for adult education.

From 1946 through 1958 more than 15,000 new school buildings were constructed and thousands of teachers were trained with federal help. About two million adolescents and adults learned to read and write in the night elementary schools that were created for this purpose. Nevertheless, most of the benefits of such a plan fell to the urban areas; urbanization is so rapid that all towns must educate innumerable migrants from rural areas. Even in Rio de Janeiro and in São Paulo, the two richest industrial cities of Brazil, the shortage of elementary schools remains a major problem.

In 1940 enrollments in elementary schools totaled about 7.3 per cent of the Brazilian population (2,900,000 pupils), and in 1957 that percentage

---

[1] *Survey of the Brazilian Economy* (Washington: Brazilian Embassy, 1958), p. 12.

[2] Jacques Lambert, *Le Brésil, structure sociale et institutions politiques* (Paris: Colin, 1953), pp. 64–65.

[3] The national fund resources are the result of a special documentary stamp tax of about 3 cents plus a percentage of the taxes on liquors.

rose to 10 (almost 6,000,000 pupils); clearly there has been a major effort to educate Brazilian children. Nevertheless, no less than 2,800,000 children of school age remain without schools, and the great majority of these children live in rural areas. In 1958 the proportion of illiterate persons aged 10 or over was estimated to be about 42 per cent. This failure to eradicate illiteracy promptly has given rise to sharp criticism of the government; Brazilians do not like to be considered a retarded nation.

After President Juscelino K. de Oliveira's inauguration in January, 1956, he asked the Ministry of Education to set up an intensive program to eradicate illiteracy. A committee was appointed and the present writer was made chairman and reporter of the studies and discussions. After a few months a project was prepared, but the committee expressed doubts as to its success on the grounds that the social and economic causes of illiteracy could not be removed by educational procedures.

In 1957, as co-director of the Brazilian Center for Educational Research, the author and a group of young educators and social scientists reached the conclusion that an experiment of extensive and complete education for a limited area could provide the basis for an exact evaluation of the possibility of eradicating illiteracy. Based on data already existent and on well-grounded assumptions, their proposal to the Ministry of Education and Culture was to set up demonstration areas in which complete fundamental education might be expected to bring about eradication of illiteracy. These pilot projects would provide estimates of costs and help to evaluate the methods and techniques for a nation-wide campaign.

The proposed project was inaugurated in January, 1958. At the beginning three limited areas were selected: Leopoldina in the State of Minas Gerais (eastern Brazil), Timbaúba in the State of Pernambuco (northeastern) and Catalão in the State of Goiás (western-central). Each area has a municipal town seat and a corresponding rural district. The three areas had about the same population, but differently distributed into rural, urban, and rurban populations. Leopoldina is more industrialized and its rural areas are more developed. Timbaúba has a very large poor urban area, a sizable marginal population, and the beginnings of industrialization; its rural area has many sugar-cane plantations. Catalão is more agricultural, being the town seat and mainly a small market place; but its outlook seems to be excellent because it is not far from Brasília, the future capital of Brazil, now being constructed.

The project is being carried on according to the following steps.

(a)   A rapid and complete survey of the area, with emphasis on economic activities, labor possibilities and trends, social structure and stratification, cultural patterns, and educational availabilities in order to evaluate the favorable and unfavorable conditions.

(b)   Social services to get the assent and support of the local people, to make them accept responsibilities, and to leave them some choices and decisions in regard to the proposed plans.

(c)   Establishment of the main lines of the project according to the opinions and choices of local people.

(d)   Continued objective checks on the experiment as a means to evaluate processes and results, correct mistakes, readjust methods, and forecast further consequences.

From the first reports we have reached the conclusion that in all three areas we have to provide the following.

(a)   Enlargement and expansion of the existent elementary school system in order to enroll all the population from seven to 12 years of age in an elementary school of five grades and to provide emergency classrooms and emergency education for people over 12 and younger than 16 who have had no opportunity to attend school.

(b)   To organize the elementary schools in such a way that all pupils, even the most retarded ones, will progress from grade to grade without the repeating that has been so common in Brazil.

(c)   To reconstruct the elementary school curriculum in terms of local conditions and possibilities, replacing abstract teaching methods with a more concrete set of activities incorporating local facts and local meanings.

(d)   To provide complementary prevocational schools both in rural and urban areas.

(e)   To change, as far as possible, the rural schools into small social centers, where not only children but all local people will have a place for meetings to study and discuss their problems.

(f)   To organize a system of basic education capable of leading the rural people to accept and practice more-productive agricultural and cattle-raising activities.

(g)   To provide places and means for training rural teachers selected from the rural population, and to equip them with knowledge and skills to lead rural people toward improved health and work conditions, and give them instruction in home economics.

(h)   To cooperate as far as possible with rural organizations and to seek technical assistance from the Ministry of Agriculture in the program of basic education.

(i)   Wherever possible to organize special classes for illiterate adults and to search for appropriate teaching methods.

(j)   To make full use of parent-teacher associations, clubs, recreational organizations, and citizenship education programs.

These 10 main recommendations of the project are being put into practical action, and each of them is stumbling upon specific local difficulties such as the socioeconomic conditions which we have described in the first two parts of this article. But one certainty we have already acquired: the rural common people can be easily awakened to the benefits of education, and they can do more for their own education than the socioeconomic conditions lead us to suppose. Reports from the experts in the field in the three areas emphasize the impatience of the local people for achievement of all the parts of the program.

Then we may say that it is possible to educate and improve the culture of rural people; it is possible to create a local awareness of educational needs and to lead local people to care about education and help in realizing educational projects as well as making choices and decisions. It is possible to train local young people for elementary teaching positions and to equip them with better techniques than teachers in many urban areas possess, because of their closer acquaintance with local needs and problems.

A major reservation concerns the results of such a program for improving rural life conditions. It is very probable that the people we are educating will not remain in their present areas: education will enable them to move to urban areas. The great number of landless underpaid peasants and poor owners of very small rural properties will not be able to improve their incomes by continuing to live in rural areas.

Hence we look toward a program that was set up by the Banco do Nordeste in cooperation with the United Nations Food and Agriculture Organization.[1] It is a kind of supervised loan and socioeconomic service to medium and small landowners in the rural areas of the northeastern region. This program is very well known today by the initials of the resulting operation: ANCAR, or Associação Nordestina de Crédito e Assistência Rural (Northeastern Association for Rural Loans and Social Services). The program is not entirely Brazilian; in many other countries somewhat similar projects are being carried on. The Brazilian novelty was the use of pilot projects before launching a full-scale program. In this way it was possible to adapt foreign experience to Brazilian conditions and potentialities. From the first efforts it was possible to elaborate techniques and socioeconomic methods for improving productivity on small farms. In a very general way we may outline the process in the following steps: (a) approach the landowner's family and get their own feelings and criticism of their living situation; (b) let them know the fundamental causes of that situation; (c) lead them to the conclusion that with some help they can improve the situation by themselves; (d) offer a reasonable bank loan which will be controlled according to the program to be set up for the particular farm; (e) study the soil and the economic possibilities of the farm and organize a specific program; (f) put the program into action and give all the needed technical assistance in order to make it successful; and (g) give to the peasant's family available social services in order to teach them to improve home conditions

---

[1] An official bank created by the federal government to finance the improvement of economic activities in the northeastern part of the country.

and follow better home economics practices. All the services are given completely free of charge, and the loan as well as the interest is to be paid back according to the net resulting productivity of the land. To meet the expenses for technical assistance and social services, the association relies partly on small contributions from the benefited landowners, but mainly on federal and state subsidies. The bank also contributes a subsidy that is a part of the interest payments.

After two years of successful experiments and program readjustments, ANCAR began to organize the benefited landowners into production cooperatives, thereby helping them to obtain more-substantial loans with which to buy modern agricultural machinery, fertilizers, selected seeds, and so forth.

This successful program is being enlarged and expanded all over the Northeast with due care to avoid any deterioration of methods, undesirable political implications, or attempts to misuse resources. A predominantly educational program of rural self-development—a long-term process of teaching, guiding, and counseling—cannot, in any event, be regarded in terms of rapid expansion.

Because of the good results already obtained, associations like ANCAR are being created in other Brazilian regions, with official support and subsidies. All of them are denominated by initials ending in "CAR" meaning literally "Rural Credit and Assistance," but also having the broader meaning "Rural Social Services, Technical Assistance, and Loans." In Rio de Janeiro the ABCAR, a national agency of the system, was organized.

In spite of their promising success, the "CAR" organizations are not the complete solution for low Brazilian rural productivity. They are merely a means of partial improvement that can be completed only if some reasonable and well-based agrarian reforms are brought about in the near future.

There is a great movement in Brazil in favor of agrarian reform and the matter is being subjected to discussion and debate in the federal congress. Brazilians are optimistic about such reforms because they realize that of the 600 million acres of private lands, only 200 million are under true cultivation or pasture. Only 70 million acres are regarded as not suitable for production. About 330 million acres are under private ownership but are not being utilized. The new west-central regions are now being reached by railroads and new improved roads which will make possible the exploitation of about 200 million acres of new land in this region. From eight to 12 million peasants could have sufficient land (330 million + 200 million acres) to cultivate if properly assisted financially, technically, and socially.

For this purpose ANCAR's experience could be a great help as an adequate program, having only to be adjusted to the different ecological areas of Brazil; but to expand such a program, the financial aspect cannot be forgotten. Has Brazil sufficient financial resources to do that at once?

The conclusion that we may draw from this report, insofar as we consider the actual Brazilian conditions, is that education alone is not capable of improving the rural conditions of life. Perhaps what is needed mainly is a means of better urbanization. Allied to an educational program must be improved organization of rural production, new sources of financial credit, better distribution of available lands, and programs for rural social services.

The basic experiments to eradicate illiteracy which we are carrying on can have major rural results if they have the support of these other plans.

The Role of Village Schools
in the Process of
Cultural and Economic Modernization

MANNING NASH

When a nation embarks on a deliberate course of modernization there is a clear and broad mandate for the educational system. Education serves as one of the principal means of social transformation. In a newly developing nation education is viewed by the elite and their planning agents as having two chief tasks: (a) to instill the skills required for the movement of the economy from a raw-producing, agricultural-export one toward an industrial, processing and diversified agricultural economy; and (b) to produce a modern nation of dedicated citizens from a population of peasants who have small experience and understanding of civic, consensual or mobilization politics. These tasks stem in part from the elite vision of the future and in part from their appraisal of the contemporary social structure.

The universities and secondary schools in nations like Mexico, Guatemala and Burma—the nations I shall use in this paper as empirical referents for the propositions advanced—are fairly amenable to planning, to elite control and to government pressure to get on with the tasks of modernization. Of course, I do not mean that the government can or does have its way easily with the universities and secondary schools. Indeed, the recent history of universities in Southeast Asia—especially Burma—and events in Guatemala during the 1950's indicate that universities have a built-in dynamic of independence, of resistance, and of political criticism. However,

Reproduced, by permission, from *Social and Economic Studies,* 14 (March, 1965), pp. 131-143.
Since the data were gathered in Amatenango, the schoolteacher has become much closer to the members of the indigenous community. An economic cooperative was formed and the teacher was, and is, instrumental in the moderate success of this enterprise. How and why the teacher accomplished this new integration merits further study.

the universities, their faculties and student bodies are visible, centralized, and, even if opposed to the government or the elite, are at least speaking and acting in the same idiom and in the same universe of expectations as those who seek to find the path and means toward modernity. Universities are, in fact, one of the spearheads of modernity in any developing nation, and, however ineffectual they may be at one or another moment, they are ineluctable sources or reservoirs of the culture of modernity and of the skills for economic transformation.

The village schools, on which I concentrate, are in a different relationship to the government and the elite, and play a more problematic role in the process of modernization. The village schools are numerous, decentralized, less open for inspection, less amenable to manipulation, and most importantly, they are set into local communities. Higher education, in most cases, forms its own community and relates to the world community of like institutions. But the village school is embedded in an organized local community and it has neither the resources nor the ability to set itself against or apart from the social system of which it is but an aspect. Not only is the village school part of a locally organized society, but the community itself is but an aspect of a complex nation, a larger social and cultural system.

In order to assess the possibilities and the probabilities of various local systems of education in the process of social change aimed at speeding modernization, the first tasks are the exploration of the relation of the school to the local community, and the stipulation of the place of the local community in the complex society that is the nation. Earlier, I have had recourse to the concept of a "multiple society with plural cultures" as one attempt to conceptualize the nature of social integration in Mexico and Guatemala,[1] and I have subsequently extended and modified this notion in trying to account for the peculiar articulation of Burma.[2] And I have found the concept to be heuristic in making a comparison between Latin America and Southeast Asia,[3] so I propose to use it now to see in what manner it helps to elucidate the role of village, local education in the process of modernization. The multiple society may be defined as:

> ... a segmented social order welding a territory and its population together by a single set of political and economic bonds. There is a class, or segment, which commands resources of national scope, carries in it the idea of nation, maintains relations with other nations, and is in some sort of touch with scientific, economic

---

[1] Manning Nash, "The Multiple Society in Economic Development: Mexico and Guatemala," *American Anthropologist,* 59 (1957), pp. 825–833.

[2] Manning Nash, "Southeast Asian Society: Dual or Multiple," *Journal of Asian Studies,* 23 (1964), pp. 417–423.

[3] Manning Nash, "Social Prerequisites to Economic Growth in Latin America and Southeast Asia," *Economic Development and Cultural Change,* XII (1964), pp. 225–242.

and political developments of the international community. It is this group, spread out through the national territory, in whom political control is vested and among whom political power is contested. The other segments of the multiple society are organized for regional or local purposes. They do not command political or economic power of national scope. They are, in contrast to the national elite, of small scale in social organization. Plural cultures are sometimes found in the multiple society. Not only is the political, economic, and ideological scope of the segments different, but their cultures may be also (e.g., in Burma the Kachins, Karens, and Shans are cases [and in Mexico and Guatemala the various Indian cultures are like this]).

The multiple society is different from our own in that the social and cultural variations are not class variations on a basically common culture in a single social structure, but rather the society exhibits poor articulation between segments, disparities in the principles of social structure from segment to segment, and allows only the national, elite elements to be organized for purposeful political action.[1]

In treating Mexico and Guatemala, the data come from the far end of the multiple-society continuum. The Guatemalan community is a mixed Indian and Ladino *municipio* in the Western Highlands, and details of its society and culture may be found in *Machine Age Maya.*[2] The Mexican Indian community of Amatenango del Valle is an extreme instance, even for Mexico. These Indian societies are in a tense bicultural situation and there is much antipathy and hostility between the Indians and the environing, superordinate Mexican nationals—here also called, as in Guatemala, Ladinos. The term Ladino is primarily cultural, not biological, and it means any person who speaks Spanish as his chief language, dresses like a member of the national society, and is culturally identified with a society beyond the local community. Indian-Ladino are polar opposites, and for the purposes of this paper the Ladinoized Indian, who does exist, will be ignored. In Amatenango, there is only one resident Ladino family, that of the schoolteacher.

Amatenango is a *municipio* with a town center of 1,469 persons and a rural periphery of 2,529. It is an all-Indian community, and more than 90 per cent of its population are born in the *municipio* and spend their lives there. It is, like other Mayan Indian communities in Meso-America, a distinct local society, united by blood and custom, living on its own territory and conscious of itself as an ethnic entity. The community makes its living by agriculture on a small-plot system combining the subsistence crops of maize, beans and squash with a cash wheat crop. It also is the pottery-producing center for a region between Tuxtla and Comitan. The community has many of the defensive features of the Indian peasantry of Meso-America, but it is nonetheless tied into the national society in at least three distinct and significant ways. First, the economic ties stemming from its

---

[1] Manning Nash, "The Multiple Society in Economic Development."

[2] Manning Nash, *Machine Age Maya* (Glencoe, Ill.: The Free Press, 1958).

position in the regional market economy give rise to the circulation of Mexican currency, the consumption of items produced in the national economy, the price levels being set by the forces of supply and demand on the larger stage of the region, and tenure of land being defined by the national legal code. Second, like other communities, Amatenango has been the object of special government attention. The Instituto Nacional Indigenista (INI) has for more than a decade carried out in this region a program of education, road building, sanitation, medical care, and agricultural and industrial innovation. Amatenango, for example, has a clinic sponsored by INI, a store and credit society, and a piped water system installed by the agency. Third, Amatenango is affected by the politics of Mexico, for the program of "incorporation" of Indians into the national society is implemented or ignored according to shifts in politics at the national level. Also, the *ejido* (government grant of communal land) is in the political arena, and some Amatenangeros have *ejido* land in the hot country about a day's distance from the *municipio*. And finally, just how the Indian will fare with the police, the courts, and in the myriad legal and contractual relationships Indians make with Ladinos is a function of the political climate of the nation as that is refracted in the backwoods of Chiapas.

Left on its own, that is, making a mental abstraction and eliminating from the scene all Ladinos, a community like Amatenango would not have any school at all. For the community itself continuity in culture and development of the skills needed for the maintenance of the society come through the informal means of ordinary socialization and enculturation. What is needed to be an Amatenangero is learned in the local social system, while what is needed to deal with outsiders may be learned in the local school. This puts the school and schooling in perspective: it is an extrinsic agency, part of the larger society, transmitter of a different cultural tradition, and by nature an agent of change and a source of new and wider mental horizons. That the school has not radically transformed the community or in fact made much of a dent in its illiteracy is a function of two facts: the major concerns of the people of Amatenango and the character of the incumbent schoolteacher.

The people of Amatenango are, because of their place in the multiple society and due to the long history of acrimonious ethnic relations in Chiapas, not concerned with becoming Ladinos, and the process of acculturation over nearly 400 years has not eroded the ethnic distinctiveness of the society, whatever cultural items and traits they have borrowed and accepted from Ladino society. The Amatenangeros have major interests in making a living, in the mundane business of getting along with neighbors, and in keeping the proper relationship between the society and the supernatural. For these ends, the school counts little. Nothing in the curriculum implements the ends of Amatenango Indians.

The school itself is set in the central square of the town center in an adobe building. The Ladino teacher and his family (his wife and daughters serve as assistant teachers) make their residence in the school compound. About 280 students (130 girls and 150 boys) are usually enrolled in the three grades that the school offers. (There is another school of about 50 students in the rural *barrio* of Madronal.) The major tasks of the school are the teaching of Spanish and the elementary skills of reading and writing. The normal language of the household and the streets of Amatenango is Tzeltal, and if anybody learns Spanish it is as a second language. Men in Amatenango have a much higher fluency in Spanish than do women. By rough percentages, for the town center, better than 85 per cent of the men are to some extent bilingual, while just the reverse is true for women, of whom more than 85 per cent are monolingual in Tzeltal. Among children from six to 12 years of age (in 1959, when all these data were collected in the field) the percentage of bilinguality of both boys and girls was about 75 per cent. What is clear from this figure is that the three or four years of school does instill some basic Spanish language skills in both boys and girls, but that men, because they travel, meet Ladinos, sometimes work for them and have other contacts with them, while women do not; hence men increase their Spanish over their lifetimes, while the Spanish of the women tends to erode and decay from lack of occasion for use.

The literacy rates, even in the most loosely defined notion of functional literacy, are about 15 per cent for the males, and under 5 per cent for the females, indicating the difficulty of transfer of the skills from school to everyday life, where they are not called for at all. The only reading matter I ever observed in Amatenango were comic books in simple basic Spanish, an occasional newspaper, and government decrees. Outside of the Indian officials in office, it is safe to estimate that the population of the town center collectively spends less than one hour a day in contact with the printed word.

The innovative potential of village education—for the school does follow the national curriculum and does try to instill some history, some geography, some patriotism, and some arithmetic as well as the national language and literature—is thus clearly circumscribed by the total operation of Amatenango as a society with its given value system and its place in a multiple social structure. It is further hampered by the character of the schoolteacher himself. The teacher and his family are socially isolated from the Indians. At night he locks up his school and his house, and, given the numerous guns he has, the place has something of the aspect of a fortress. The analogy is deliberate. The teacher is an alien in the midst of a people he does not understand and does not completely trust. On their side the Amatenangeros neither respect nor trust the schoolteacher. He leaves on any occasion, his life is tied to the nearby city, not the village, and even if he wanted to he could not get into the intimate daily life of the community. He is over-bearing, authoritarian, and not particularly gentle in his relations with the Indians. Furthermore he is a State of Chiapas employee, and hence not responsible to the local community, and they in no way influence the conduct or the content of teaching. The school scratches the surface of Amatenango life, because that life is oriented to its own concerns, and because the teacher is a social irritant in an alien community, not the representative, however humble, of respected *literati*.

What revolutionary or innovative potential schooling may in fact have when it is divorced from the constraints of local society is exemplified by a social experiment carried out in Indian communities about 20 years ago. There was a program of boarding schools *(internados)* instituted by the Mexican government to train some Indians in each community in Spanish speech and literature. Young boys and girls were taken from their families and put into boarding schools and kept from four to six years. Of the 10 taken from Amatenango into the program, all are now resident in Amatenango, all of them are still bilingual, and all of them are literate. Furthermore they have worked out to be something of an elite, in the sense that they relate the community to a Ladino world that they understand much better than their fellow villagers, and they have held the top offices in the village civil and religious hierarchy. They have, at least some of the men, moved over to a Ladino style of dress, and have comparatively expanded views of the world. Also some of them have taken on jobs (e.g., storekeeper) that no other Indian could handle, and furthermore they are the people who have married outside of the habitual rule of village endogamy. They have married Indian women from other communities who were Ladinoized enough to give up traditional Indian costume.

The boarding school experience does indicate that elementary schooling can result in important social change, even for people at the end of multiple society, but it must be withdrawn from the community constraints, when the community is organized as is Amatenango.

By way of contrast to Amatenango, but still of the same social type, is the Guatemalan Indian community of Cantel. In a double sense Cantel is a more sophisticated community of Maya Indians than is Amatenango. It apparently had a richer Mayan heritage (it is in the area where Quiché was and is spoken), and it has been in longer, more intimate contact with Guatemalan Ladino society than has Amatenango. If I can hazard a forecast, when the road net around Amatenango now in construction gets to the level that Cantel has enjoyed for 20 years, Amatenango will begin to approximate many of the structural and cultural features of Cantel. The *municipio* of Cantel is also more populous. Its town center (in 1954, when the field census was taken) had a population of 1,910 and its outlying areas had 6,585. In the town center *(pueblo),* on which I shall focus, the Indians accounted for 96.2 per cent of the population, and the remaining 3.8 per cent were Ladinos. In the *pueblo,* 17.7 per cent of the population were engaged in specialist occupations (not all of them full time) and more than a quarter of the work force was in the textile factory just across the river from the town center. In short, the town center was a bustling, cosmopolitan, and specialized place compared to the agricultural village of Amatenango. But still Cantelenos were a distinct social and cultural entity, both in objective fact and in their self-perception as Cantelenos whose customs were different not only from those of Ladinos but also from those of their Zunil, Almolonga, Totonicipan, or Quezaltenango neighbors.

There were in Cantel two schools. One was the national school, the other run by the factory for children of factory workers. The school attendance in Cantel was slightly better than that in Amatenango (my remarks and data are restricted to the town center and the canton of Pasac), but the difficulty of meeting the compulsory attendance of children from age seven to age 14 was about the same. Where school and work conflict in societies at this level of income, work always wins. Poverty coupled with familial agricultural production has the effect of drawing children out of school as soon as they are useful in the fields. Cantel's schools offered up to a sixth-grade education. But the enrollment figures are revealing: in the first three grades are 300 pupils; in the fifth and sixth grades combined there are only 20 pupils. Still, the fact that 20 students a year get up to the sixth-grade level gives Cantel a greater edge on the modernity and national-integration scales than Amatenango.

By the same loose definition of literacy, about 60 per cent of the Cantelenos are illiterate, and this is about the national average, while Amatenango was above the reported Mexican average. Bilingualism in the town center is much greater for women than it is in Amatenango, and most men can handle elementary Spanish.

The schools are, as they are in Mexico, agencies of the national government, transmitters of the national culture, and divorced from the community in regard to support or control. The schoolteacher is a Ladino, somewhat marginal to the community but not so nearly an alien as in Amatenango.

That the schools have not been more of a radical agent of social change than in fact they have been in Cantel is accounted for by two major facts. First, the poverty of the community and the nation keeps many children from more than three years of education, in which they barely learn the elementary skills; and second, the national government is, and has been, hesitant about how to incorporate Indians into the political society of Guatemala. Thus the schools are not seen nor used as catalysts in social change, but are confined to transmission of elementary skills, some patriotism, and some minor facts about history and geography. But these schools could, if an ideology activated them, if more resources were poured in, if more teachers were assigned, if more books . . . —but why catalogue the needs of any underdeveloped country?—act more forcefully as agents of change. This requires not only the necessary expenditures, but a clear and definite program among the national segment as to the role of the Indian in Guatemalan society. This program is but vaguely enunciated and defined, and this very hesitancy, plus the lack of scale in investment, keeps the schools in a marginal role in fostering modernity.

One strong index of the impact of both schools and factory on the children of Cantel is found in the occupational aspirations of school children. Interviewing (in 1953–1954 when all of the data were collected) 136 boys and girls between the ages of 10 and 15 in both the Pueblo and Pasac schools, for job preferences, revealed the predominance of a preference for artisan or specialist occupations. These occupational aspirations are at variance with the chief uses of manpower in the community and far exceed the foreseeable demand for the kinds of jobs and services selected by school children. What these aspirations seem to indicate is a continuance of the basic community values of self-employment and economic independence or self-sufficiency. Formerly these values were expressed in terms of landholding, but the pressure of a growing population on a fixed land base has moved the loci of the values to artisan or specialist occupations. This younger generation of school-educated are willing to try occupations which may cut them off from some of the roots of community life and possibly alienate them from the local society. It appears that schooling, even under the restricted conditions of Cantel, does have the potential for social change and mental expansion.

Part of the receptivity to change in the economic sphere among the school-educated of Cantel is intimately linked to the political events of the preceding decade, and points up again the fact that, in multiple societies structured like Guatemala, political events on the national scene are likely to be decisive in social and economic change in local communities. The school can and does act as an agency of the national society, and in the interaction between the school and the community lies an important source for receptivity or resistance to change.

In Cantel, the generational differences of the effect of both educational and political change are fairly clearly marked. The older generation lost much influence, power and respect to the younger, more literate and less traditional members of society,[1] and this is echoed even in the consequences of schooling. Of the adults attending a night school for literacy, only one thought of an occupation outside the traditional roster of Cantel (and, of course, those willing to come to night school on their own for the rewards or literacy represent the most progressive of the older generation). In short,

---

[1] Manning Nash, *Machine Age Maya.*

those who are "well built-in" members of the society and of middle age cannot afford the risks of mobility, of loss of social obligation and support and the adventures of new careers. This generational difference underlines yet another important generalization: in local communities the village school begins to instill different values from those of the local community, but adulthood, the claims of mundane life, the competition of the known with the unknown, and the absence of supporting institutions beyond the schools make these values, in most instances, atrophy and eventually disappear.

Through a contrast with another newly developing nation, Burma, the highlights of the place of village education in modernization may be, I believe, better approximated. The value of contrasting such culturally and historically disparate societies is akin to the role of litmus paper in bringing out the special ingredients of the differing social mixtures. And, of course, one reason for attempting the contrast is that I have field work experience in Burma, so that comparability comes as much from the general categories of social prehension as it does from the simple fact that the same mind and methods have gathered and interpreted the data of observation.

A review of the recent history of Burmese education is available in Tinker[1] (1962), and the current state of the university is well summarized in Fischer.[2] The description of the village schools I give is restricted to Upper Burma (above the 40-inch *ishopyet*) and stems from the period 1960–1961.

Burma, as a new nation, fits within the general category of a multiple society,[3] but its multiplicity is different from that of the Meso-American societies sketched earlier. Elsewhere, the multiplicity of Burma a decade after independence was characterized as:

A thin modern elite was the national segment of the new nation. There were administrators from the old civil service, the politicians schooled in agitational politics, the army officer corps, and a sprinkling of intellectuals, professional [sic], and businessmen. This group has been called the political class. It ruled over a peasantry, the "hill peoples," and the other non-national indigenous peoples. In lieu of the former colonial civil servants, nationals now filled all the ranks, and a single political party, driven by internal strife and jealousies, emerged as the legitimate political custodian of sovereignty. . . . The key to membership in the national segment is the command over some of the skills needed to run large and complex organizations of persons and resources. . . .[4]

Within this multiple, poorly articulated society, the peasants of Burma were to be turned into modern farmers, or industrial workers, and

---

[1] Hugh Tinker, *The Union of Burma,* third edition (London: Oxford University Press, 1961).

[2] Joseph Fischer, *Universities in Southeast Asia.* International Education Monograph No. 6 (Columbus, Ohio: Ohio State University Press, 1964).

[3] Manning Nash, "Southeast Asian Society: Dual or Multiple."

[4] Manning Nash, "Social Prerequisites to Economic Growth."

responsible dedicated citizens, enlisted in and implementing the elite's drive to the Burmese version of a welfare, socialist society. (All of this refers to a time before the second takeover of General Ne Win. His military coup does not much, so far, affect the structure of Burmese society. It has merely changed or eliminated some of the personnel in the elite segment, but it, too, seems to be groping for the keys to giving social vitality and meaning to slogans and programs of contemporary Burma.)

Burma is a relatively poor nation, and, given the wartime devastation, it has not the capacity to give all of its citizens a primary education. School attendance cannot be made compulsory. In 1960–1961, in Burma, of 30,000 village tracts, only about 10,000 had primary schools, and some had neither primary schools nor monastic schools (*kyaung* is Burmese for school, and a *pongyi kyaung* is a school run by monks in which literacy, some religious knowledge and some Pali are taught). There are not enough facilities to take all the children who are eligible for education, physical plant is likewise insufficient, and finally there is a shortage of qualified teachers.

I do not want to concentrate on the constraints in resources and personnel, but rather to characterize village schooling in Upper Burma to show the place of the school in the community, the relationship of the community to the larger society, and possibilities of the educational system as a means of implementing a transformation in the basic structure of Burmese values and social organization. The data come from two villages, one a mixed, dry-crop community south and west of Mandalay in the Sagaing region, the other a wet rice farming community in the Mandalay district about seven miles south of Mandalay. Between them, these two communities approximate the range of social and cultural variety among the peasantry of Upper Burma. Unlike Meso-America, the villages and communities of Upper Burma are not distinct cultural entities; rather they are variations on a common regional culture—local expressions of cultural organization of a tradition deep and widespread in the region. Further, villages do not have the restrictive, bounded social corporateness of Meso-American Indians. These villagers are inhabitants of a country known to them, the rural extension of Burmese society and culture. They are much more akin in their status to the Ladino in Guatemala than to the Indian, although even this analogy is somewhat misleading.

In the mixed-crop village there are two schools, one a government school, the other a *pongyi kyaung,* although both schools are housed in *pongyi kyaungs.* The physical plant of the schools is a modest wooden structure raised high on stilts. The government school contains both *koyin* (novices in the Burmese Buddhist order of monks, the *sangha*) and *kyaungtha* (secular students). In the village primary school there are 70 students (15 girls and 55 boys), while in the *kyaung,* taught only by monks, are 15 students.

The whole school population is then 106 students. With a population of 553, this is virtually everybody in the community who is eligible for school, even though attendance is not compulsory. This attendance reflects the greater wealth of a Burmese peasant village compared to a community like Amatenango, and it also indicates the high value placed on literacy and the role of the religious heritage of Buddhism, which for centuries has schooled the peasantry in the rudiments of reading and writing, and also it marks the great differences between being a multiple society with plural cultures when one of the cultures (as in Amatenango) is subordinate, and being the rural component of a continuous social organization (as in the Burmese peasantry).

Education for the village boy or girl virtually stops at the fourth standard and in the last two years only four students (two boys and two girls) have gone beyond the fourth standard.

The two schools are virtually identical in method and content of teaching, although the *pongyi kyuang* teaches some Pali and the Buddhist cosmology while the state primary school includes some history, arithmetic and general science. *Pongyis* occasionally strike recalcitrant students; state teachers have given up this practice. In a Burmese village the teacher's role is one of great respect and the social distance between teacher and pupil is correspondingly great. In traditional Buddhist belief the objects of great honor are: the Buddha, the Sangha, the Dhamma (the teaching of the Buddha), the parents and the teacher. At many public ceremonials children give honor to these five worthy objects. Teachers are considered the repositories of knowledge. The job of the teacher is to lead the student forth into the exploration of a fixed body of knowledge. The role definition of the superordinate, learned teacher vis-à-vis subordinated pupil, with the task structure of communicating fixed knowledge, makes teaching a rather rote business. Students have the goal of acquiring knowledge letter-perfect, not of innovating or of challenging or questioning either the teacher or the information he transmits. The teacher and his teaching are traditional authorities and the psychological stance of the pupil is that of "traditionality," a reverence for authority and for the pastness of things. Hence the method of teaching is oriented to train the memory, to stuff the mind, and to fix a respect for what is already known. Students are rewarded for feats of memory, for long, letter-perfect recitations, and for knowing answers to standard questions.

The method of teaching is much more suited to social continuity and stability than it is to social change and innovation. The village educational system is one of the agencies for cultural transmission; it is a means for the maintenance of the traditional culture. Other educational agencies in the village exhibit the features that the school does: learning by reverential junior from respected elder, stress on learning by rote, and reward for traditional knowledge. The village school is not detached from other educative agencies of the community, and hence does not have its own standards, ethics or momentum. It is only an extension of a local society teaching its young to be members.

In the abstract, education is one of the most highly valued things in Burmese life; in fact, support for schools and teachers at the local level is meager. Villagers do not support by contribution, by labor, or through organization in the local schools. That is the government's job and they have no social sense about government projects. The operative values of villagers are plain enough, both in their speech and in their activities when they are faced with real choices. They want to make a living, get along with relatives and neighbors, earn respect and honor, and lay up a store of *kutho* (merit), so that in the next life they may have a favorable rebirth. If education does not implement or bear on these concerns, it does not engage the interest of the villagers. As a consumption good, education is not in the village purview. Education should conduce to economic gain, and that is why village boys go beyond the fourth standard, to be clerks, teachers, or civil servants, to take on a middle-class style of life in an urbanized setting. Or education should lead to the enhancement of one's chances for favorable rebirths, and that is why monastic education is pursued. Finally education means a display of refined handling of common knowledge, for that is how an educated man gets respect. An education oriented to manipulating nature, changing the world, intellectual curiosity and exploration is not worth the villagers' time and resources. From this value stance it follows that girls get less education than boys, that attendance is spotty, and that every household or religious task has priority over education.

The teachers in this village are not native to it; they come from a nearby village. This may, in part, explain their inability to get local support for the school, but it does not account for their equally bad luck with national authorities. The village teacher is the lowest rung in the educational bureaucracy. Before making any demands his request must be processed through a bewildering hierarchy of officials. As the student before the teacher, so the teacher before superordinate officials has a feeling of powerlessness. His only means of coping is compliance in the official context. The teacher is aware that the basic educational decisions are political events. For him the educational system is at once too much and too little politicized; too much so because the political parties decide on the principles of education, and too little so because the teachers are an ineffective political organization.

A poor village in the Mandalay district, which makes its living by wet rice farming, amplifies and extends some of the contentions made above. This village has a primary school, and it exhibits the same teacher-pupil relationship and the same traditionality. It has that same element of *anade*— a complex value and attitude implicating reluctance or shame if a junior should question a senior or contradict his teacher. The school is also an embedded institution lacking autonomy or a dynamic of its own. The villagers do not control it, barely support it, and expect it to give their children only the minimal skills of functional literacy.

In the four standards of this school there are 110 children on the rolls: the first has 82, while the fourth has but 10. In the first are 36 boys and 46 girls, in the fourth, eight boys and two girls. The sex and numerical skewing manifests the economic facts of life in this community. It is poor. Many of the people do not have enough land to meet even the modest demands of the Burmese peasant. Rice growing is a labor-intensive activity for several months of the year. Education competes with child labor in the fields, and at age 10 or 11 (the fourth standard) children are useful field hands. Girls can help their mothers, as well as work in the fields, so they drop out more often than do boys. In the lower standards attendance is sporadic, and during the four months for which I have data, daily school attendance never exceeded 80 of the 110 on the rolls. Regular attendance is a problem unsolved.

The school is scheduled to have three teachers, but there is only one. There is a teacher shortage at the village level, and its causes are not obscure. The teacher who remained in this village is native to it; her family and friends live in it. Her job as teacher is a second income, for her husband also teaches in a nearby community. She does not have a modern, nor heavy investment in her teaching skills. She has only a seventh standard education, plus a year training course taken in the late 1930's. For her, village teaching is a reasonable, useful and not unexciting life. For the young graduate from a teacher training school life in a poor village is repellent. Being assigned to a strange village is almost a sentence to exile, boredom and frustration for a young graduate. The salaries and life style of beginning teachers do not compensate for these evils. It takes devotion and idealism for a rural schoolteacher to persevere with an assignment in a village.

This rice village indicates the pressure of poverty upon the Burmese village school. Poverty does not shape the Burmese village school, it is not the root of its difficulties; it merely exacerbates them. The point is here labored because there is a prevalent belief that money and means would solve all the ills of local education. What increased investment would do, in the absence of social and cultural change, is merely to shift schools like the one in the rice village toward the full achievement of the Burmese pattern as exemplified in the mixed-crop village and in the 36 villages I surveyed.

The comparisons in this paper may be summed up in two columns:

Burma	*Mexico-Guatemala*
Education tied to rest of institutions	School as extension of national society

Main task: enculturation	Oriented to change of values
Knowledge is not a novelty, does not touch major concern	Local support not relevant
	Authoritarian teacher-pupil rela-
Unoriented to change	tionships
Authoritarian teacher-pupil rela-	Knowledge not fixed
tionships	Motives for completion economic
Completion of primary school de-	Image of educated man partly tradi-
pends on economic opportunity	tional
Local support minimal	Teachers undertrained
Teachers barely trained	Major value: creation of citizens
Resources poor	Minor value: literacy
Image of educated person traditional	

What this profile shows (providing, in fact, it does fit more than the data from which it is derived and justifies the bold use of national society labels) is that the educational system in Burma differs from the systems in Mexico and Guatemala, the latter two belonging to a separate species. The similarities in the profiles stem from the relative poverty of the nations and the tremendous costs of implementing a primary education program at such a late stage in national history. The differences in the educational systems are reflections of the larger social and cultural differences, and spell out at a micro-level the meaning of a recently sovereign nation in Southeast Asia with a Buddhist cultural tradition, oriented to reaching a form of democratic socialism, as against two Latin American societies with a Spanish-colonial heritage, being strongly involved in both Westernization and modernization. These differences affect the method of teaching, the content of teaching, and the place of the village school in local communities and in national plans. The contrast also underlines the different potentials for a given local system of education to absorb and use creatively more investment. The mechanical formula of pouring resources into schooling is hence recast into a broader framework of viewing a set of social and cultural consequences and possible economic payoffs.

Three very general propositions about village schools in the process of social change may be hazarded on the basis of the foregoing:

(a) It is change in the economic, religious and interpersonal relations on the local and regional levels which is antecedent to change in the educational system.

(b) Local schools tend to be conservative agents, transmitting by means that reinforce local tendencies toward stability.

(c) Education becomes a force for social change only when the process of social change is well underway.

The practical and procedural consequences of these propositions are fairly self-evident. What is needed is to verify them with a wider sample than that given here. However, it is clear that the diagnostic tools of social science and its ability to distinguish between types of poverty and types of social systems are valuable ingredients in translating any plan into practice, and even in foreseeing, however opaquely, some of the consequences of a given course of action.

Culture and Education
in the Midwestern Highlands of Guatemala

ROBERT REDFIELD

When education is considered as it occurs in a modern society, we think
first of the school. In a primitive society there are neither schools nor peda-
gogues; yet we speak of the "education" of the primitive child. In so doing
we are, of course, recognizing a conception of education much wider than
the domain of the school; we are thinking of it as "the process of cultural
transmission and renewal"—a process present in all societies and, indeed,
indistinguishable from that process by which societies persist and change.

When we describe education in such schoolless and bookless societies,
we are likely to fix attention upon other institutions which obviously and
formally express and communicate the local tradition. Such are ceremony,
myth, tribal and familial symbols and stories, initiation ceremonies, and
men's houses. In these we recognize a certain fixity and emphasis of major
elements of culture, and we see that in their perpetuation and repetition
these elements receive restatement and are communicated to the young.
Indeed, we have come to think of primitive societies as providing a well-
organized and self-consistent system of institutions by which children are
brought up to think and act as did their fathers. In such societies we con-
nect education with traditional forms expressive of a rich content. In comparison with the educational effect of a katchina dance upon a Hopi child,
a chapter in a civics textbook seems pretty thin, educationally speaking.

To the invitation to give an account of the educational process, I respond
from a point of view of certain rural communities in the midwestern highlands of Guatemala which are neither modern nor primitive but in many

Reproduced, by permission, from *American Journal of Sociology,* 48 (May, 1943), pp. 640–648.

respects intermediate between a simple tribe and a modern city. Educational institutions among these rural mountain dwellers do not quite conform to either the primitive or civilized type. These people have schools, but the schools are of small importance. They have ceremonies and legends, but these forms do not have so much content as one might suppose. In these Guatemalan societies schooling is far from accomplishing what our educational experts claim generally for schools. On the other hand, ceremony and myth do not come up to the standard set by many primitive societies. In this part of the world there are no central and powerful educational institutions around which an essay can conveniently be written.

The situation is not without value, however, for students of the cultural process. In recognizing in this part of Guatemala the limited educational influence of schools, on the one hand, and of traditional forms, on the other, one is brought to see aspects of education which underlie all formal institutions. People in Guatemala do get educated (in the sense that the heritage is transmitted) with adjustments to meet changing circumstances, even though many of them never go to school and even though there are no great puberty ceremonies, with revelations of the sacred *alcheringa* and narrations of totemic myths, such as occur among Australian aborigines. In this paper I shall make some observations on certain features of these highland societies insofar as the educational process is concerned; and I shall, in particular, call attention to aspects of that process which are probably to be encountered in every society. I call attention to them because education is ordinarily studied without much reference to them.

As I look at the school in the little village where I once was resident, it appears to me to play a greater part in changing the culture of the people than in handing it on from one generation to the next, although its influence in the direction of change is indirect. Nearly all the time in the school is given to learning to read, to write, and to calculate. Some children acquire a fair command of these arts; others do not. The arts of literacy have many practical uses, and their possession carries some prestige. They improve the opportunities for gainful employment, and their possession disposes the individual to seek his fortune in the town or in the city. In some cases success in school leads to higher education in the city and so to participation in urban civilization.

The majority of people of this community are Indians; a minority are a Spanish-speaking people of mixed ancestry known as Ladinos. The cultures of the two groups are identical in many areas of experience; in others they are still notably different. Where both kinds of people live in the same settlement, both attend the same school. The school makes more change for the Indian than for the Ladino, because through association with the Ladinos in the school he learns Spanish and in not a few cases is disposed to put off Indian dress, to live in the manner of the Ladinos, and so to become a Ladino. There is here no obstacle of prejudice or law to prevent this not infrequent occurence. The school is one important institution, therefore, through which the Indian societies tend to lose members to the Ladino society and so ultimately to disappear.

As such an instrument of acculturation and culture change, the school is only one among a number of effective institutions. The penitentiary deserves mention, for, although its liberalizing influence is less widely distributed than in the case of the school, not a few individuals profit by this form of widened experience and return to the village with a new song, a new trade, and a less parochial view of life. The common custom of bringing up other people's children is also effective, as when the child is an Indian brought up in a Ladino household. Of such individuals it may later be said that "that Ladino is really an Indian," but the ethnic origin of the individual carries little or no social disadvantage and is quickly forgotten.

Considered as an institution helping to preserve the local culture, the role of the school is small. I venture the assertion that the abolition of schools in these highlands would leave the culture much as it is. Except for the texts of prayers recited on many occasions, little of the rural Ladino heritage depends on literacy. And, furthermore, is is only necessary that a few individuals in each society be literate so as to preserve access to written or printed sources. Indeed, for generations the Indian cultures in the more isolated societies have got along with a semiprofessionalization of literacy. A few individuals in each village or group of villages were trained to read the Mass; the central government sent from the city a literate person to deal with the written communications of formal government. The more pagan religious ritual was, and still is, stored, unwritten, in the memories of a small number of professionals. Their knowledge is highly specialized and is little understood by the layman.

The village school in this area devotes little time to instruction other than the purely technical; and the little "cultural" instruction which it gives has small support in other branches of the village life. Some instruction is given in Guatemalan history and geography. What is taught is not reinforced by books in the homes, because there are almost no books in the homes. Nor is the instruction closely related to the content of oral tradition. The knowledge that Columbus discovered America is perpetuated in the school and is possessed by most Ladinos as an item of information, but few people whom I interrogated were able to tell me that that discovery was the event commemorated by the little celebration which the government orders to occur each year in the village municipal building on October 12. (Of course the more sophisticated townsman understands the meaning of the occasion.) At any rate, Columbus is no tribal or village legendary hero.

As not a great deal is accomplished by formal instruction in the school, one might suppose the lack to be made up by a great deal of deliberate

inculcation and discipline in the home. At least with regard to the rural Ladino society, I am sure that this is not the case. Children are taught to do
what they are expected to do chiefly as an aspect of coming to perform
the tasks of adults. Moments of instruction are not segregated from moments of action. Boys are taught to farm and girls to cook as they help
their elders do these things. Along with instruction in the practical arts,
parents comment on conduct, saying what is "good" and what is "bad."
The word *pecado* is applied to innumerable interdicted acts, from those
which are regarded as mildly unlucky to those to which some real moral
opprobium attaches. Some parents will select a serious and special moment
in which to convey sex instruction, and sometimes other subjects will be
somewhat formally inculcated; but on the whole I should say that instruction in the home is casual and unsystematized.

Certainly it is not characteristic of this Ladino culture that the young
gather around the knees of the old to listen reverently to a solemn exposition of the holy traditions and sacred memories of the people. Indeed, in
this society, as in our own, it is hard to find the holy traditions, let alone
to get anyone to listen while they are expounded. Most instruction that
occurs in the home or outside it is connected with the practical arts of life.

It seems to me interesting that, while few of these Ladinos are today
teaching their children the prayers of their Catholic tradition, they do take
pains to teach them the traditional forms of address and salutation, which
in these cultures are complicated and elaborate. It is characteristic of this
people that requests and other communications are not abruptly and directly presented but are wrapped in highly conventional preliminary and
terminal utterances; also, in general, among them polite language is regarded
as seemly conduct.

It also seems to me that this formal language is a way in which people
preserve their personal lives from too easy invasion and that it is therefore
a useful art. It is, moreover, one which every man must practice for himself.
The case is different with the prayers. Apparently it is not thought sufficiently important that every child have formal language in which to talk
with God. It is, however, thought important that the prayers be recited by
someone on the occasions of novenas for the saints and following a death.
But all that is necessary is that one or a few persons be available to recite
the prayers. It would not greatly surprise me if in these villages the reciting
of Catholic prayers became a paid profession, as are now the reciting of a
Mass by priest or layman, the teaching of the spoken text of a dance-drama,
or the playing of the little flageolet which accompanies processions bearing
images of the saints.

This observation about the teaching of prayers and of mannerly speech
may be generalized into two wider characterizations of these Guatemalan
cultures. The point of view on life is practical and secular rather than

religious or mystical; and formal activity is more than usually large, it seems to me, in proportion to the content of symbolic meaning which underlies it. This statement I am disposed to make about both the Indian and the Ladino cultures, although there are differences of degree or kind in these respects between the two.

For the rural Ladinos it may be safely asserted that religious pageantry and mythology do not play a large part in the education of the individual. The Christian epic is known very incompletely; it exists in the form of many uncoordinated fragments of lore, and it is not vividly presented in any coherent or impressive way. These country people read very little sacred literature; they very rarely hear sermons; and there is no important traditional ceremony or drama in which it might be expressed. An exception in part must be made for the ninefold repetition at Christmas time of the journey of Mary and Joseph and for the little enactment of the birth of the child. The effigies of and stories about Christ, and in less degree and importance of and about the saints, do constitute a body of lore in which significant traditional conceptions are perpetuated. But these ceremonials occupy a very small part of the time and interests of the Ladinos, and the element of mere entertainment in them is very large.

For the Indian, more is to be said as to the contribution of ceremony and myth to the educational and cultural process. The cult of the saints is more elaborate, and ritual observances are more extensive. Justification for the statement that the culture of the Ladinos is more shallow or less integrated than that of the Indians is in part to be found, it seems to me, in the fact that most stories told among Ladinos—and they like to tell and to hear stories—deal chiefly with fairies, witches, talking animals, and the adventures of picaresque personages, and that these stories are not regarded as true and are not thought of as describing the world in which the individual lives. They are recognized as fanciful creations that serve to entertain. The Indian, on the other hand, is disposed to regard the stories which he tells as true. Taken as a whole, the Indian's stories deal with men and animals and supernatural beings that he believes to exist about him, and their telling helps to define and redefine the conventional world in which the Indian lives.

A story well known in the Indian village of San Antonio tells how St. Anthony was once a man who dwelt in that village as other men, and how, counseled by his friend, Christ, whom he sought to rescue when our Lord's enemies were after him, he took the form of a saint so as to help the village where he lived and worked. The story offers an explanation for the origin of every significant element of costume and accouterment in the effigy of St. Anthony as customarily fashioned and as it exists in the village church; and it explains and justifies by reference to the saint's divine will many of the elements in the cult now customary: the marimba, the masked dancers, the fireworks, incense, and candles. Indeed, except that the content of the story is of Old World origin, the story in feeling and form is quite like many origin or hero myths that are told among non-Europeanized Indians.

A study of the educational process among these Indians would certainly have to take into account the existence of these stories and the circumstances under which they are told. It is plain that their telling helps to communicate and perpetuate the tradition of the group. It is significant that in the Indian villages every man passes through a series of public services; that in the course of many of these employments he spends long hours sitting in the company of his age mates and his elders, and that the elders at such times tell stories and relate episodes. The Ladino society is almost entirely without such an institution.

The existence of such a story as the one about St. Anthony is another evidence of the power within a culture to make itself, if such an expression may be employed. We may be sure that no priest set out to teach just this story to the Indians of the village. The story has grown in the course of generations of speculation upon an effigy and a ritual already sanctified and mysterious. Indeed, we catch glimpses of this process today when we hear of Indians who have found new explanations for some element of decorative design in church, or when an cthnologist's informant begins to offer speculations of his own.

Yet I am struck with the fact that even in the case of the Indian cultures there is more form than content in their collective life. In this same village of San Antonio there is performed every year in Holy Week a series of ceremonies occupying several days. It is generally understood that these ceremonies are a representation of the Passion of our Lord, and a general air of gravity attends them. But in my notes is a list of elements of the ritual for which none of my informants has been able to offer any explanation at all. Structures are erected and taken down, and effigies are used to which no meaning is assigned other than mere custom. One could fill many hundreds of pages with a detailed account of the goings and comings, the processions, the handing over of effigies, the ritual drinking and bowing and the like, which custom provides must be carried on each year in one of the Indian villages among the groups of men in whose custody rest the images of the saints. On the other hand, even making liberal allowance for the relative difficulty of getting trustworthy information on the meanings of these acts, I feel sure that little could be said about the symbolic connections these acts have with the content of tradition. Yet, even insofar as these rituals have no symbolic meaning, they do maintain traditional ways within which behavior is regulated, and, therefore, they have their place in a broad investigation of the educational process in these communities.

The relatively formal or external aspect of much of the Guatemalan cultures is conspicuously illustrated in the dance-dramas. These are performed by Indians at most Indian festivals and very infrequently are performed by Ladinos at Ladino festivals. The observer sees a score or men dressed in brilliant and fantastic costumes, carrying highly specialized objects in their hands, and dancing, gesturing, and reciting long lines of set speech. The performance might be an enactment of some centrally important holy myth. It is, as a matter of fact, nothing of the sort. There are about a dozen dance-dramas known in Guatemala. Most of these have spoken text. Specialists possess these texts and at festival time are hired to teach groups of Indians to speak them and to perform the accompanying dances. The texts are in oratorical Spanish, and it is rare that an Indian understands well what he is saying. The general theme of the drama is known: if the dance called "The Conquest" is danced, the combat between Alvarado, the Spanish invader, and the pagan Indians is understood. But the tradition means little to the dancers; they will just as well enact Cortés' triumph over Montezuma, if that dance is cheaper to put on or provides a better show. The dance is performed, indeed, because a group of men is willing to put money and time into doing something lively for the festival. It may be compared to putting on a minstrel show in another culture, or hiring a merry-go-round. The comparison is not quite fair, but it suggests the truth.

In these societies of which I write, then, the educational process is not greatly dependent upon institutions organized for pedagogical purposes or upon organized and deliberate instruction within the family or other primary group. The ceremonial and other expressive customs which we find in every society are significant educationally here in Guatemala, too; but at least this one observer finds that, compared with some other societies, there is a great amount of formal machinery for the regulation of activities without corresponding symbolic content. To a marked extent the transmission of culture takes place within a complex of regulations: the traditional machinery of government and of ritual observances, the superimposed police control of the Guatemalan national government, and the general traditional emphasis upon forms of utterance and conduct.

Nevertheless, an investigation of the educational process in these communities would be far from complete if it were to consider only institutions, pedagogic or ceremonial, as elements in that process. Here, as elsewhere, the heritage of the group is communicated and modified in situations much less clearly defined than any of which mention has so far been made in this paper. I refer to that multitude of daily situations in which, by word and gesture, some part of the tradition is communicated from one individual to another without the presence of any formal institution and without any deliberate inculcation. This class of situations corresponds in a general way to what Spencer called the "primary forms of social control."

Let us imagine that we are standing unseen outside a house in the village where I am living. Within the house some Ladino women are praying a novena, and outside it six men and two boys stand around a little fire and talk. Someone compares the heaping up of pine cones made ready for this fire to the heaping up of twigs by Indians at certain places on hilltops where, by Indian custom, the traveler strokes away the fatigue from his legs with a twig and then adds the twig to a growing pile. As soon as the comparison has been made, one of the men beside the fire expresses derision at this Indian belief, which is well known to all present. Others briefly indicate similar disbelief in the custom. Another man then makes a remark to the effect that what does in fact serve to relieve tired legs is to rub rum on the ankle bones. A younger man—apparently unfamiliar with this remedy—asks how this can be effective, and the older man explains that the rum heats the nerves that run near the ankle bone and that the heat passes up the body along the nerves and so restores strength. The explanation is accepted; the apparent physiological mechanism provides a warrant for accepting the worth of rum as a remedy.

After a short period of silence, conversation begins about snakes, one man having recently killed a large snake. A young boy, apparently wishing to make an effective contribution to a conversation in which he has as yet played no part, remarks that the coral snake joins itself together when cut apart. The man who laughed at the Indian belief about tired legs scornfully denies the truth of the statement about coral snakes. Another older man in the group comes to the support of the boy and in a tentative way supports the truth of the belief as to coral snakes. A younger man says that it is not true, because he cut apart such a snake without unusual result. The skeptical man appeals to the company; another witness offers testimony unfavorable to the belief. The boy has not spoken again; the other man who ventured to support him withdraws from the argument. But this man wishes, it seems, to restore his damaged prestige. With more confidence he offers the statement that some animals *can* do unusual things: the monkey, when shot by a gun, takes a leaf from the tree in which he is sitting and with it plugs the wound. The smaller of the two boys, who has not yet spoken, adds that the jaguar can do this also. Discussion breaks out, several persons speaking at once; the trend of the remarks is to the effect that, although undoubtedly the monkey can do as described, the jaguar is unable to do so. The quick statements of opinion break out almost simultaneously, and very quickly thereafter the matter is dropped. The bystander recognizes that there is substantial consensus on the points raised; the boy is apparently convinced.

We may safely assume that in such a situation as this the states of mind of the participants in the conversation with reference to the points at issue differ from one another less at the conclusion of the conversation than they did at the beginning. The matter is not ended for any one of them, of course; subsequent experiences and conversations about fatigue, snakes, and monkeys will again modify their conceptions, or at least redeclare them. We may suppose also that the outcome of this particular conversation—an apparent consensus in favor of rum and against twigs, supporting the belief about monkeys and unfavorable to the beliefs about coral snakes and jaguars—will not be duplicated exactly in the next conversation that occurs among similar men on these subjects. We are not so simple as to suppose that by attending to this little talk we have discovered "the belief" of the Ladinos on these points. The personalities of the influential men, the accidents of recent experiences had with monkeys or snakes, and, indeed, probably also the general tone of the moment, which may or may not have been favorable to the serious reception of a marvelous story, are among the factors that have entered into the situation. They have brought about, not a conclusive conviction, but a sort of temporary resting place of more or less common understanding. We may think of the outcome of such little exchanges of viewpoint as the component of many forces. Because each man's state of mind at the time of the conversation is itself the component of many such forces, most of which have been exerted within the same community of long-intercommunicating men and women, it is likely to be not greatly different from that of his neighbors. Still, there are always individual differences; and it is largely in such little happenings as that which took place around the pine-cone fire that these differences are made influential and that they come to be adjusted one to another.

The episode may be recognized as one of that multitude by which the heritage is transmitted. It was a tiny event in the education of the people. Some part of the heritage with reference to the treatment of fatigue and with reference to the behavior of certain animals passed from older people to younger people—and, indeed, it passed also from younger people to older people, for oral education is a stream that flows through all contemporaries, whatever their ages.

At the same time it was a small event in which the culture of the group underwent a change. Some old people in the community tell me that when they were young they heard about the ability of the coral snake to join itself together and did not doubt its truth.

Perhaps the boy who advanced the belief received his first knowledge of it from such a grandfather. After this evening around the pine-cone fire he will treat grandfather's remarks with a new grain of skepticism. Some of the men who took part in this conversation have traveled and have lived in the city among men whose tradition disposed them more readily to laugh at the story of the coral snake, and the effects of such experiences were also registered in the outcome of the evening's conversation. The result of these various influences was to shift, though ever so slightly, the center of gravity of the community beliefs on these points.

Furthermore, the trifling occurrence was also an event in the transmission

of tradition from one group to another. No Indian took part in the conversation, but one man who was born an Indian but had lived long among Ladinos stood silent in the dark edges of the group. As an ethnologist who
has talked with Indians, I know that the belief about getting rid of fatigue
by brushing the legs with twigs is by them generally accepted, and great
credence is given to beliefs as to the ability of injured animals to treat
themselves. Now there has impinged upon that silent Indian a set of forces
tending to shift the center of his belief; and now, when he takes part in a
similar discussion among Indians, he is more likely to be on the skeptical
side of the center of consensus than if he had not been here this evening. It
is largely by the accumulating effect of innumerable such occurrences that
the culture of the Indians and that of the Ladinos are becoming more and
more alike.

We are not to suppose that it is always the Indian who is disposed to
change his mind so that it becomes more like that of the Ladino. For certain reasons the predominating trend tends to substitute Ladino tradition
for that of the Indians. But the Ladino has in 400 years taken on a great
deal from the Indians—the techniques of maize farming and the use of sweat
baths, to mention just two elements; and he still learns from the Indian.
The episode around the pine-cone fire could be matched by an episode in
which Indians, by showing Ladinos the nicked ears of wild animals as evidence, tended to persuade the Ladinos that these animals were indeed under
the domestication of a supernatural protector inhabiting the woods.

It is a fair guess that in any society the process of education depends
more on such events as represented in the conversation I have reported
than it does upon all the formal pedagogical devices which exist in the society. In the speech and gestures which take place in the home, in the play
and work groups, and wherever people talk naturally about matters that
are interesting to them, the tradition is reasserted and redefined. In these
situations the culture is not merely spoken about; it is acted out; it happens
before the eyes and even through the persons of children, who by this
means, in large degree, are educated. This basic part of the educational
process takes place in every society and probably to such an extent that
societies are greatly alike in this respect. Upon the flow of such experience
are erected those more clearly defined institutions of the folk traditions,
as well as the deliberate enterprises of pedagogy and propaganda. As to
these, societies will be found greatly to differ.

Comparing these particular Guatemalan societies with, let us say, that
of the French Canadian villages, I should say that here education is more
secular and more casual. These Guatemalan societies seem to me relatively
meager with respect to organized moral convictions and sacred traditions.
What the Indians tell me about the times of their grandfathers suggests
strongly that the Indian societies have lost in ceremonial richness, as I

suspect they have lost in the moral value and the integration of their local traditions. Because I have observed the influence of priests in other communities in maintaining a sacred tradition and in explaining symbolic significance of traditional rituals, I think it likely that, if, indeed, these societies have been becoming more casual and more secular, the lessened influence of the Catholic priests has been one factor in this change. The Guatemala of today is well regulated by secular government in the interests of public order and hygiene. My guess—which is to be tested by historical investigation—is that secular external regulation (important probably even in pre-Columbian times) has grown in later years, while that control dependent upon moral conviction and instruction and upon local tradition has declined. The school, for these rural people, is another form of external regulation rather than an expression of local tradition.

Whatever study of the history of this part of rural Guatemala may in fact show, the present situation in these societies suggests the question of whether a rich culture is compatible with a society in which the mechanisms for education consist chiefly of formal regulations and of casual conversation. The comparison between Indian and Ladino societies—alike though they are in their generally secular character—indicates a correspondence between certain characteristics of culture and certain characteristics of education. The Indian beliefs and tales have relation to current life, and more of them have moral content or depth than is the case with Ladino beliefs and tales. And, second, in the Indian societies there is a social-political-religious organization—a system of progressive public services through which all males pass—that is largely native to the community, that is a force in social control, and that involves relatively sacred things. This organization is largely lacking in the Ladino societies. These differences may be stated in terms of differences in the educational institutions of the two peoples: to a greater degree than is the case with the Ladinos, the Indians hear and tell stories that express and justify traditional beliefs; and by passing through the hierarchy of services the individual learns the ritual that is the inner and relatively sacred side of the formal civic organization. Emphasizing characteristics of these Guatemalan societies which are more evident in the case of the Ladinos than of the Indians, this paper concludes, then, with the suggestion that an education which is made up, on the one side, of practical regulation and instruction without reference to tradition and, on the other, has nothing much more compulsive and expressive in which to exert its influence than the casual contacts of everyday life is not likely to educate with reference to any greatly significant moral values.

The Development of an Educational System in a Rural Guatemalan Community

OSCAR H. HORST
AVRIL McLELLAND

Introduction

In the United States there is a constant preoccupation with the qualitative aspects of our educational system. This occurs in a nation where over 98 per cent of children between the ages of seven and 14 are attending school and where over 95 per cent of all inhabitants are considered literate. Thus, in terms of literacy and level of education, the United States is classified as highly advanced. Not so fortunate are the developing nations of the world.

Latin America, as a major world region, is classified as underdeveloped and shares many of the economic and social misfortunes which plague that sector of the world's populace. Within Latin America there is a wide diversity of educational attainment. Although seven nations may be classified as advanced or moderately advanced, these represent less than one quarter of the region's population.[1] The vast majority are less advantaged and among these are the inhabitants of Guatemala. Less than one quarter of its children between the ages of seven and 14 attend school; less than 30 per cent over 10 years of age are considered literate.[2] This Central American nation

Reproduced, by permission, from *Journal of Inter-American Studies*, 10 (July, 1968), pp. 474–497.

Oscar H. Horst is a member of the Department of Geography at Western Michigan University; Avril McLelland, a graduate student in the International and Area Studies Program at Western Michigan University at the time of this study, is now also a member of the Department of Geography [1972–Ed.]

The authors acknowledge the support of The National Science Foundation and a Faculty Research Grant provided by Western Michigan University for joint field research in Guatemala during the summers of 1966 and 1967.

[1] Inter-American Statistical Institute, *Characteristics of the Demographic Structure of the American Countries* (Washington: Pan American Union, 1964), p. 115.

[2] *Ibid.*, pp. 116, 128.

shares the distinction of being classified with five others as educationally "very backward," the lowest rung of educational achievement in the Western Hemisphere.

The educational system in Guatemala basically consists of preprimary, primary, secondary, and university levels. In Guatemala City and other main cities, one can find preprimary *párvulos* (similar to kindergarten classes) available to many of the five- and six-year olds. These, however, are found rather infrequently in smaller villages and are completely absent in rural areas. The primary level consists of grades one to six. In Guatemala there is a national law which makes it mandatory that all children between seven and 14 years of age attend school; however, it is obvious that this law is not strictly enforced. As Whetten states, "the law requiring compulsory attendance for children of school age is more of an expression of idealism than of expected compliance."[1] Completion of primary education is often difficult, for most rural primary schools terminate with the third or fourth grades.

Secondary education also consists of six years of study, the first three years being called *prevocacional* or *ciclo común,* in which all students follow the same courses. In the final three years, known as *vocacional,* the student may follow a program to become a teacher or one related to a number of other fields. If, after completing secondary education, a student wants to further his education, he may enter the university. Less than 0.3 per cent of all students beginning in primary education make it to the university.[2] A meaningful revelation of the manner in which the Guatemalan educational system functions at the primary level is disclosed by an examination of this topic as it relates to Ostuncalco, a highland community located in southwestern Guatemala.

Ostuncalco consists of a *cabecera* subdivided into four *barrios* and nine *aldeas,* which together comprise a *municipio,* one of 24 making up the department of Quezaltenango.[3] The term Ostuncalco is applicable to both the village and the *municipio* of which it is the *cabecera.* Within the 45 square miles of this *municipio* are crowded nearly 18,000 inhabitants, most of whom are impoverished quasi-subsistent agriculturalists. One fifth of this population is Spanish-speaking Ladino;[4] the remainder are Mam Indians, the great majority of whom are restricted to the use of their own Indian dialect.

---

[1] Nathan L. Whetten, *Guatemala: The Land and the People* (New Haven, Conn.: Yale University Press, 1961), p. 30.

[2] Consejo Superior Universitario Centroamérica, "El sistema educativo en Guatemala: situación actual y perspectivas," *Estudio de Recursos Humanos en Centroamérica,* 2 (Costa Rica: Ciudad Universitaria, 1964), p. 3.

[3] A department is comparable to one of our states and the *municipio* to a county. The *cabecera,* in this instance, would be equivalent to a county seat. The *aldea* is a political subdivision of the *municipio.*

[4] A Ladino is one who has culturally adapted himself to a Westernized way of life.

Most of the *municipio* of Ostuncalco lies above 8,000 feet in elevation. For six months (November to April) there is very little rain, and frost is a constant hazard. Although the eastern third of the *municipio* encompasses some flat terrain, the region is more nearly identified as a land of slopes. Increasingly, these are being encroached upon and subjected to erosion. A rapid decline in the mortality rates has produced increasing numbers of Ostuncalceños who are not well served by this environment. Consequently, many find it necessary to supplement their incomes by migrating seasonally to the adjoining low-lying Pacific coastal plain, to plant corn, to work on coffee or cotton estates, or to obtain other forms of employment. Both increased seasonal migration and improved local communication are serving to break down the walls of cultural intransigence that have for so long shielded this as well as other upland communities of Guatemala. Rising aspirations have contributed to social, political, and economic turmoil within Ostuncalco. The quest for education cannot be disassociated from this conflict of interests.

Stresses within the society of Ostuncalco are further complicated by the overtones of cultural strife between Ladino and *indígena* (Indian) elements of the populace, for the threads of social conflict are interwoven in the matrix of Indian-Ladino affairs. This poses an added dimension of concern in assessing the needs of an educational system in Ostuncalco, where Indians are numerically in ascendance but economically subservient to a minority Ladino element. The fact that Indians dominate numerically in Guatemala reveals the degree to which any remedial effort in education must be predicated upon an assessment of Indian affairs.

Until recently only primary school facilities have been available in Ostuncalco. In this respect the local citizens share a problem which is commonplace among their brethren in Guatemala, for less than 3 per cent of all Guatemalans over the age of 10 are able to avail themselves of secondary education.[1] A consideration of the status, the problems, the needs, and the prospects of the educational system of Ostuncalco is the subject of this paper. It is against this background that one may reflect upon the efficacy of an educational system in a developing land.

The Schools

The direction of the school system in Ostuncalco is primarily the responsibility of the district supervisor, a federal appointee with offices located in the departmental capital of Quezaltenango. He periodically inspects the schools in Ostuncalco and checks into such matters as program and student progress, the teacher's daily lesson plans, student and teacher absences, availability of materials, and in general tries to assess the operation of each

---

[1] Inter-American Statistical Institute, *Characteristics of the Demographic Structure of the American Countries*, p. 131.

school. The frequency of these visits varies from year to year and from school to school. Some teachers noted that their classes were inspected six or seven times a year, while others stated that the supervisor came much less frequently.

The district supervisor is not responsible for the maintenance of school buildings. This lies in the hands of a council in Ostuncalco, called the San Juan Junta Local de Educación, which provides that the buildings receive necessary care, such as painting, replacement of broken windows, and the like.

All but one school have an association known as the Comité de Padres de Familia. This is organized by the teacher, but the officers are parents. It is composed of both Indians and Ladinos, although teachers state that more Ladinos take part, particularly in the urban schools. Its purpose is to help schools fulfill some of their needs. The rural school in the *aldea* of Nueva Concepción recently required a kitchen in which to prepare milk for its students. Under the direction of a local committee, parents and members of the community joined together and built a structure in which the kitchen could be housed.

After years of stagnation there has been a slow but evident increase in the number of schools in the *municipio* of Ostuncalco. During the first four decades of this century there were only five schools—two urban and three rural. Since the Second World War period five rural units have been added. Ostuncalco presently has a total of eight rural and two urban schools.

Guatemalan rural schools leave much to be desired. The majority are one-room constructions within which all grades are housed as opposed to separate classrooms for each grade in the urban units. Only two of the eight country schools have more than one room. Five of the 10 schools in Ostuncalco are constructed of adobe. Of the remaining five, three are of crude wood construction and two are new buildings of stone and brick built under a community aid program.

Equipment and outside facilities are generally very limited in both rural and urban schools, although this is more evident in the former. Each classroom building is surrounded by a play yard, which frequently serves as a soccer field. An outdoor plot at each school also features a vegetable garden. The nature of the soil, the lack of fertilizer, the absence of tools, and other deficiencies make difficult the satisfactory maintenance of these projects. It is, however, incorporated as one of the duties of the teachers and is included as part of the school program. Toilet facilities, outdoor or otherwise, are nonexistent in most of the schools, particularly in the older rural units. Of the two new schools constructed under the Ydígoras Plan,[1] one has outdoor and the other indoor toilet facilities.

---

[1] Under the Ydígoras Plan the cost of school construction was divided in three ways: one-third

While most schools are not supplied with water, it is usually accessible at a nearby *pila* (fountain). Although the water supply is supposedly safe, contamination is always possible, and it is probably responsible for many of the intestinal afflictions which these people endure. The only attempt to minimize the harmful effect of the water is the boiling of it in preparing reconstituted milk for students.

All schools are supplied with desks and chairs. In some instances, students are provided with an individual desk and chair. On other occasions a six-foot bench-type chair and desk is shared by four or five students. Some of the materials for the latter type have in the past been donated to the schools by CARE. Out of the 10 schools, only two did not have a sufficient number of desks and here students shared space.

In only one school, the urban boys' school, is incandescent lighting provided for all classrooms. Lighting in the rest of the schools is very poor. Since most schools have only one or two doors and few windows, natural lighting is poor. Light, which is adequate on sunny days, is virtually eliminated when it becomes cloudy.

Interior walls in the urban and rural schools are anything but bare; however, in only one school were they decorated with examples of the students' work. Several teachers indicated that the Ministerio de Educación does not stress or encourage this practice. It is preferred that materials placed on the walls should have a purpose and be of some use. Most of the walls are painted a pastel color—blue, white, or pink. Items found on the walls are numerous and varied. Every school has pictures of the national flag and the national flower. Many also have attendance charts, maps of Guatemala and the department of Quezaltenango, calendars, and number and color charts. Other items such as illustrations of parts of the body and different kinds of animals and plants can also be found in the schools. These visual aids serve many useful purposes and are of benefit to the students.

One of the major problems confronting most Guatemalan schools is the lack of supplies and materials. Students are required to bring a notebook, pen, and pencil; however, the majority of students are limited in the number of items they can afford. This is due to the widespread poverty among these people, particularly the rural Indians. Since many families earn less than 80 cents per day, it is understandable why students lack adequate supplies. Furthermore, numerous families have three or four children of school age, thus multiplying financial requirements for schooling. Teachers in Ostuncalco purchase out-of-pocket many needed materials such as cardboard to make posters, some books, and crayons. It was somewhat surprising to note that teachers did not seem to be greatly disturbed by this.

was provided by the *municipio*, one-third by the Guatemalan government, and the remaining one-third by the government of the United States. A rural school in Monrovia and the village boys' school of Lorenzo Montúfar were constructed under this arrangement.

Urban and rural schools receive materials from various sources. The Ministerio de Educación, which is in charge of and directs the national education program, distributes a limited amount of supplies such as chalk, paper, ink, textbooks, and pencils. However, the items tend to be distributed in larger quantities to urban schools, particularly those located closer to the capital. Several rural teachers in Ostuncalco indicated that they had received only a few boxes of chalk during the course of a year.

The Alliance for Progress has also done much to help schools throughout Guatemala. It has distributed books covering such subjects as reading, language, and mathematics. In Ostuncalco these books were present, although a deficiency at many schools made it necessary for students to share them; when very few were available, teachers tended to use them as guides. Even within the *municipio* it was apparent that these materials were not equitably distributed, for they are more in evidence in the urban than in the rural schools.

As indicated previously, the lack of materials is a major problem confronting the Ostuncalco schools. A recent publication of the Oficina de Planeamiento Integral de Educación (OPIE) states:

> On all levels, in general terms, the scarcity of textbooks or consultation books is dreadful, and gravely influences the deficiency of the educational system: the misery in which the majority of Guatemalans live does not permit any hope that parents will be able to acquire the necessary books in sufficient quantity; the donation *(dotación)* of books will contribute to improving the quality of teaching in our country.[1]

Another organization providing aid to the local school system is CARE. It donates powdered milk and wheat. The wheat is made into rolls at a local bakery in the village and distributed to all 10 schools. The milk is prepared at each individual school daily by one of the students' mothers. Although the hot milk and bread are intended to be free for all students, several factors limit this. First, in order to have the bread made, it is necessary to pay the baker. In addition, other ingredients such as milk and sugar must be purchased. In an average month, it costs approximately $70 for this bread to be made. In order to defray this cost, each student is required to pay 15 cents every month. Although this does not appear to be a great sum of money, it is necessary to remember the limited earnings and the frequently large number of children per family. It would appear that more Ladino than Indian students can afford this food supplement. It is indeed unfortunate that the most needy are frequently least able to avail themselves of available sustenance. Each student receiving milk supplies his own tin cup, which is kept at school. One of the rural schools had just received from

---

[1] Oficina de Planeamiento Integral de Educación, *Diagnóstico de la educación guatemalteca* (Guatemala: Ministerio de Educación, 1964), p. 2.

the Alliance for Progress a new set of plastic cups, plates, and spoons.

It is obvious that there is a desperate need for more and better schools and school supplies, and that the lack of these is one of the major problems confronting teachers and their schools. The urban schools of Ostuncalco are providing minimally for the needs of those in attendance. The rural schools, which bear the responsibility of tending the needs of over four fifths of the school-age students in the *municipio* of Ostuncalco, are woefully understaffed, inadequately financed, and in every respect disadvantaged in terms of the two village schools in Ostuncalco. Although support by various independent agencies alleviates some of the local school problems, it by no means promises any basic remedy for the local educational system.

The Classrooms

As a guideline to teaching, the Ministry of Education publishes three books which the teachers follow. One is called *Programas de Estudio* (Study Programs) and is divided into three cycles. The first cycle is divided into grades one and two; the second, grades three and four; and the third cycle, grades five and six. An outline of material to be covered in eight subject areas is provided for each grade. The aims and purposes of each subject to be taught are described. The main points to be stressed are indicated and various activities are recommended as possible aids. Teachers in Ostuncalco, as well as those throughout the nation, follow these books. The subject matter tends to be directed toward the urban child and thus, unfortunately, does not always benefit rural children. A number of teachers noted that a separate school program oriented toward rural children would be most beneficial. Many topics currently taught, although significant, cannot be put to meaningful use by rural students due to differences in the urban and rural environments.

A second book published by the Ministry of Education and used by the teachers is the *Reglamento de evaluación educativa, exámenes y promoción* (Rules of Educative Evaluation, Examinations, and Promotion). This includes information concerning the grading system, when and how grade marks are to be given, and the way in which tests should be administered. It also includes examples of all forms which the teachers are required to fill out during the school year.

A final book, *Ley orgánica de educación nacional* (Organic Law of National Education), also written and published by the ministry, lists the objectives of the national educational system, stating the subjects that should be taught and the purposes and objectives of each one.

Between January and October all schools are in session five and one-half days a week. Urban schools meet in the morning between 8:00 a.m. and noon and in the afternoon from 2:00 to 4:00 p.m. Rural schools, however,

meet only from 8:00 a.m. until 12:30 or 1:00 p.m. On Saturdays, both rural and urban schools meet from 8:00 until 11:00 a.m. Saturday attendance, particularly in the rural schools, is so much reduced that one wonders
about the efficacy of holding classes. This feature in the scheduling of
classes again focuses attention upon a system which is geared for urban administration notwithstanding the needs of a dominantly rural society.

In classes, a variety of subjects are taught. The following are the general
areas taught by all primary teachers in Guatemala: Spanish language, mathematics, social studies, science, *educación estética* (art and music), health
and safety (includes physical education), *educación agropecuaria* (agriculture), and industrial arts and education for the home. Both the boys' and
the girls' urban schools have instruction by a music teacher who comes
twice a week from Quezaltenango. In rural schools this duty is undertaken
by the individual teacher.

All teachers in Ostuncalco make up daily lesson plans. These include subjects that will be taught and items they wish to stress with their students.
Teaching methods vary among instructors. For example, in the teaching of
reading, the majority of teachers use the phonetic method. Several mentioned that it was easier and quicker for the students to understand, particularly among the Indians.

In rural schools teachers must adjust their schedule so as to be able to
go from one grade to another. They also have to contend with the problem of trying to keep each group occupied while teaching other students.
The noise emanating from unoccupied students is an obvious distraction.
The daily schedule is more clear cut in the two urban than it is in the eight
rural schools, as each hour is specifically designated for a certain subject.

At about 10:00 a.m. on weekdays students are dismissed from class for
one-half hour of recreation. This may be organized under the teacher's direction but tends not to be. The boys participate in playing soccer, spin-
ning tops, or shooting marbles, while most of the girls stroll about, play
jacks, embroider, or observe the male students. Games such as tag or *los
animales* (similar to musical chairs) are played by all.

After the recreation period it is time for a *refacción* (snack). Hot milk
and rolls are passed out and generally are limited to those who pay the assessment for the preparation of this food. After the *refacción,* the students
return to their classwork until midday, when everyone departs for home.
As stated previously, students attending the two urban schools are obliged
to return from 2:00 to 4:00 p.m.

Tests are given throughout the school year; however, the most important
are at the middle and end of the year. The midyear tests are made up and
administered by the teachers and are called *parciales.* The final tests are
made by the Guatemalan Ministry of Education and are distributed to
schools throughout the nation. At this time, the teachers administer the

tests at schools other than their own. For example, a teacher from the *aldea* of Varsovia may go to Monrovia to give the tests, and the teacher in Monrovia may go to Pueblo Nuevo, and so on. A staff member of the Ministry of Education is also present. Besides these two major examinations, most teachers also give minor tests throughout the year. These are either made up by teachers or are taken from the students' workbooks.

Report cards (*certificados*) are given at the end of the school year. One copy is sent home with the child; another is sent to the Ministry of Education. In order to be promoted, a child in grades two, three, or four must receive a minimum of 51 points out of 100. A child in grades five or six needs a minimum of 55 points to pass. In addition to receiving a minimum number of total points, a child in grade two must pass at least four of the previously mentioned eight subjects, in grades three and four, five of the eight subjects, and in grades five and six, six of the eight subjects. In no instance, however, may a student be advanced without passing mathematics and Spanish language.

The year-end examination constitutes 50 per cent of the student's final evaluation; the examination given at the middle of the year is worth 25 per cent and the remaining 25 per cent is based upon quizzes or tests during the school year and the student's attendance record. If a student is absent for more than 20 per cent of all school days, he is not allowed to take the final examination and therefore fails. Beginning in 1966 prepared tests were not administered to first graders, for their promotions were henceforth based upon the teacher's evaluation of their ability to read and write.

During the school year there are holidays and numerous other occasions for which teachers organize special programs in which the students take part.[1] For example, on Mother's Day the students memorize poetry or songs and present them either individually or in groups to an audience of parents and relatives. From observations made, solo presentations, without exception, were given by Ladinos, with Indian students participating only in group activities. This may in part be due to the language barrier among the Indian children; however, there is a tendency for the Ladinos to stand out in class. They appear to be more extroverted than the Indian students, although this does not mean to say that all the Indians are passive in their actions.

All schools prepare a special program for Independence Day, September 15. Another important event is the program presented at the end of the school year. Parent participation varies, since it is difficult for many to come. It is understandable that a larger proportion of mothers than fathers comes to these programs. The fathers are generally out working in the fields or on the coast.

---

[1] There are a number of national holidays, such as "Promulgación de la Constitución de la República" (March 15), and "Aniversario de la Independencia Nacional" (September 15), as well as local holidays commemorating patron saints.

It is apparent that distinct differences exist between the Ladino-dominated urban schools and the rural schools, where the great majority of students are Indians. In urban schools the students are in class more hours per day, the student-teacher ratio is lower, they have a greater amount of equipment available, and there is a greater likelihood that an adequate educational program will be provided. If and when a rural child completes his primary schooling, he very rarely has the opportunity to pursue further education. Due to the importance of agriculture in their lives and to the need to work in fields many hours a day, the students are not able to put their acquired educational training to use.

At present the national educational program set up by the Ministry of Education is oriented towards the urban inhabitants who are, in most cases, Ladinos. This program does not fulfill the needs of the thousands of rural school-age children, mostly Indian, found throughout Guatemala.[1] Many subjects currently taught to rural students will not be utilized by them in their future life's work, and thus will be put out of their minds and forgotten. If this is the case, where does the value of their education lie? A change in the focus of activity in rural school programs is essential if the Indian is to place a higher value on education. Only when such training becomes meaningful in his everyday life will he make an attempt to acquire it for himself or his children.

The Teachers

The teachers in Ostuncalco are classified into three categories depending upon the amount of education they have had. The first of these is an *empírico,* one who has had only a primary education. A law, however, has recently been passed prohibiting people from teaching with only a primary education. Those who were teaching before this law was passed must now take up further studies. A second classification is that of a specialized teacher in rural education. These teachers have had at least two years of study beyond the primary level. The third category consists of teachers of primary education who are qualified to teach in urban or rural schools. This degree involves six years of education at the secondary level, the first three years being prevocational and the final three consisting of courses specifically intended for those persons planning on entering the teaching profession. Teachers in this final category are obviously best prepared as instructors.

---

[1] Joaquín Noval in "Tres problemas de la educación rural de Guatemala," *Cuadernos del Seminario de Integración Social Guatemalteca,* No. 1, 1959, explores this matter at some length. He notes that specific laws direct that the school year should be adjusted to distinct climatic and social conditions which characterize the various zones of the nation, and that timetables should be flexible in accordance with the needs, interests, and capacity of those being educated. He states that this is far from being the case in the instance of most rural schools, where little consideration is given to widely varying needs created by the diversity of physical, cultural, and economic conditions.

It is widely recognized that Guatemalan teachers are in need of more-thorough preparation. Whetten states that in 1955, "84 per cent of all the rural teachers in Guatemala were classified as *empíricos,*"[1] that is, possessing no more than a primary education. It is difficult for rural schools to employ teachers who have adequate training. Better-prepared teachers do not desire positions in small rural schools as long as openings are available in urban areas.

Another factor which discourages many people from entering the teaching profession is low salaries. An *empírico* teacher's beginning salary is about $70 per month; one holding a certificate in rural education starts at $80 per month; and a teacher in urban education starts at $100 per month. Salaries are not increased until after five years of service, at which time there is a 20 per cent raise. A similar increase is given every five years, over a maximum of 25 years. By this time, the teacher's beginning salary would be doubled. An *empírico* teacher's maximum salary then would be $140 per month and an urban teacher's would be $200.

In Ostuncalco, according to the 1965 records of OPIE, there were three *empírico* teachers, four specialized teachers in rural education and 17 teachers with a degree in urban education.[2] In 1965 salaries ranged from a low of $70 per month to a maximum of $180 per month. The average monthly salary for the Ostuncalco public school teachers was $142. There were two people earning $180, both of whom had earned a degree in urban education and had been teaching for over 20 years. The one teacher earning $70 per month was working towards her certificate in rural education, which she anticipated would bring an immediate increase in salary. She attended classes in the evenings and also during November and December, when public school is not in session.

Ostuncalco currently has a total of 25 teachers. Fourteen teach in the urban and 11 in the rural schools; 15 are women and 10 are men, ranging in age from 20 to 26. Seventeen of the teachers are married; four women and four men are single.

Ostuncalco teachers have taught various lengths of time, ranging from one to 39 years. It is obvious that once people enter the teaching profession, they tend to retain their job for a good number of years. However, during these years personnel may frequently be transferred within the local school system or to another system.

Half of Ostuncalco's teachers live in the city of Quezaltenango, which is approximately nine miles from the village of Ostuncalco. The remaining teachers live either in the village of Ostuncalco or in the *aldea* in which they teach. Of the 11 teaching in the rural *aldeas,* two live in Ostuncalco and

[1] Whetten, *Guatemala,* p. 199.
[2] Oficina de Planeamiento Integral de Educación (OPIE), *Questionnaires of 1965* (Guatemala: Ministerio de Educación), mimeo.

six reside in Quezaltenango. Only three reside in the *aldea* in which they teach. This supports the idea that most people having an education do not want to live in a rural area dominated by Indians. Several of the teachers interviewed expressed this feeling. Of the 14 teaching in the urban schools of Ostuncalco, six reside in Quezaltenango.

Living in Quezaltenango and teaching in Ostuncalco presents the teachers with a variety of problems. Perhaps one of the most important is the hour at which teachers must leave their homes in order to arrive at school on time. One teacher has to leave her house at 6 a.m. in order to catch a bus which passes through the *aldea* where she teaches. Disembarking from the bus, she then has to walk about two miles along a rough dirt road before arriving at school by 8 a.m. Twenty per cent of her salary is expended in transportation costs associated with her employment.

The primary mode of transportation for teachers living in Quezaltenango is the bus. Two teachers travel by motorcyle, and there is one teacher who rides a bicycle to school daily. Since they do not have a sufficient amount of time to return to Quezaltenango for lunch, they take their lunch and eat at the school or at a fellow teacher's home.[1] Keeping in mind the distance to the rural schools and added cost of transportation, it is understandable why one would seize the opportunity to teach in an urban school closer to his home if and when the opportunity should arise.

It is obvious that those having a higher degree teach in the village itself or relatively close by. Teachers having the least preparation tend to be located farther away from the center of town, which obviously places rural schools at a distinct disadvantage in relation to those located in urban centers. Deficiencies in providing the service of instruction to rural areas are further increased by the difficulty of obtaining substitutes to cover occasional absences of the teacher. It was reported that substitute teachers frequently are not provided in rural areas of Ostuncalco until the duration of the teacher's absence approaches one month.

When asked if they wished to continue teaching for the rest of their lives, most responded in the affirmative. There were several who hoped to enter another profession; several desired social work and another expressed interest in becoming a lawyer. A number of teachers replied that they wished to teach for only 20 years, or until they became tired, and then retire. A majority, however, stated they would like to change schools. This was especially evident among the 12 teachers whose homes were in Quezaltenango. At the same time, they noted the difficulty in obtaining a position in one of the Quezaltenango schools.

The previously cited problems associated with classroom situations are compounded by problems within the realms of the teaching profession.

---

[1] This applies only to the urban teachers, since the rural schools are not in session during the afternoon.

Finding adequately trained teachers to work in the numerous rural elementary schools is very often difficult, for qualified men and women shun the rural schools to work in the urban centers. Consequently, rural schools are frequently forced to hire persons who have had less than the minimum amount of education required to teach.

Only through efforts such as improving teacher training, increasing salaries, and improving schools and conditions in rural areas will Guatemala be able to attract the adequately prepared people needed to instruct her younger generation.

The Matrix of School and Human Affairs

Teachers in Ostuncalco are confronted with numerous problems, some of which have already been alluded to. One of the most vexing is related to student registration and attendance. The registration of students starts at the beginning of January and continues until about the middle of the month. Some teachers, particularly in the rural areas, go to homes and tell the parents when school will begin. At the same time a census is taken of the total number of school-age children living in each of the *municipio's* nine *aldeas* and four *barrios*. There is a very significant difference between the number of school-age children and those who register and attend school. For example, in one of these surveys conducted in the *aldea* of La Victoria in the beginning of January of 1966, out of a total of approximately 400 children between the ages of seven and 14, only 90, or 23 per cent, registered for school. In the *aldea* of Varsovia, only 120 of 212 school-age children were enrolled. For the *municipio* as a whole, approximately one third of the school-age children were registered although considerably fewer attend on a regular basis. In one of the rural schools there was a total of 49 children registered; however, on the day a visit was made at the school, only 26 students were present. At another rural school only 31 students out of the 46 enrolled were in attendance. Although less serious, attendance in the village schools is also a problem. A spot check indicates that attendance is better at the upper grade levels. Whereas absences in the boys' school may run 40 per cent in the first two primary grades, they appear to be on the order of 20 to 25 per cent in the upper two primary grades.

A number of reasons account for the lack of registration and attendance in the schools of Ostuncalco. In a survey conducted by OPIE in 1965, one of the questions concerned student attendance and the reasons for nonregistration and absences. Of the available choices, teachers cited the following in descending order of importance: (a) work, both agricultural and domestic, (b) illness, (c) poverty, (d) distance from school, and (e) little interest on the part of the parents. The teachers of Ostuncalco tended to give the same responses regarding this matter, thus indicating their awareness of the situation. The causes of absenteeism in urban and rural schools is also substantiated by an earlier survey of the Sección de Estadística Escolar of the Ministerio de Educación Pública, made available in 1962 and reported by Luis Arturo Lemus.[1]

The first and prime reason for absences is due to agricultural and domestic work performed at home. Children are looked upon as assets and are required to do a great deal of work in support of the family. Most *varones* (boys) are of great aid to their fathers in the *milpa*. When the father is away from home for any length of time his sons may be found at home taking on family responsibilities pertaining to household affairs. Many girls are absent from school because of the need to perform numerous domestic duties such as washing clothes or taking care of younger siblings. Boys or girls may also be sent on *mandados* (errands) by their parents. Rather than going to school for only part of the day, they remain at home working.

A further factor causing many absences occurs when entire families temporarily move down to the coast to work on the large estates. Although each *finca* and *hacienda* is responsible for maintaining a school for children of migrant workers, it is readily evident that most provide an inadequate educational program.

If a survey were to be taken, it would no doubt show that a disproportionate share of nonregistered students and those absent for agricultural or domestic reasons are Indian children, although some Ladinos would be included as well. Indians dominate in rural areas, where poverty is paramount. Thus it is not surprising that absenteeism on that account would be more prevalent among the Indians.

Listed second in importance as a cause of absence were student illnesses. Teachers interviewed stated that this is a prime problem. In Ostuncalco the mornings, especially in the winter, are cold. The children do not have adequate clothing to dress in accordance with the weather, and few wear shoes. Thus, poorly dressed, the children have lessened resistance to many common illnesses. This again is more predominant in the rural areas. Malnutrition is also to be reckoned with. Children and adults receive neither adequate nor proper foods such as green vegetables, eggs, and meats. Instead, items which could improve their diets are frequently taken to the market and sold.

Housing is inadequate and, with the exception of urban dwellings, many homes are one-room units. This room serves not only as a kitchen, but also as a living quarter. It is not uncommon to see livestock, chickens, and pigs running close by, if not in the house itself. Inadequate facilities for the disposal of human waste and an abundance of animal refuse about every household contribute to the lack of sanitation.

The third reason given for lack of attendance, poverty, is predominant

---

[1] Luis Arturo Lemus, "Situación de la educación nacional," *Humanidades,* IV, no. 11 (1965), p. 4.

in most areas and is interrelated with the aforementioned causes of absenteeism. Annual family income certainly does not exceed $200. Money which is earned must be spent on essentials. Thus, very little remains to be expended on school clothes, books, or supplies.

The number of absentees and nonregistrants is also directly related to the distance from home to school. In the rural areas many of the children live two, three, or even more miles from school. During bad weather, some students stay at home instead of going to school. This is of less importance in the *cabecera's* two urban schools, where most of the students live relatively close by.

Only one of the eight rural schools has a fifth grade, two include a fourth grade, and the remaining five end at the third grade. The lack of upper-level grades poses problems for rural youths desirous of continuing their education, for it necessitates going to the village schools, where the remaining primary grades are available. The number of students who come to the urban schools in order to complete their education is very small, for few families can undertake this financial burden.

A child living in the outlying *aldea* of La Esperanza and wanting to continue school beyond the third grade must either spend 30 cents for daily bus fare to Ostuncalco, or else live with a relative or friend in the village. In addition to transportation, textbooks and supplies must be purchased at an additional expenditure of $4 or $5 per year. For many Guatemalan families this would be equivalent to one-half month's income.

Finally, the attitude of parents toward education is listed as a significant factor in student registration and attendance. This attitude varies between Ladino and Indian and also within each of these cultural groups. Generally, most Ladinos and a few Indian families have an interest in and send their children to school. The remaining Ladinos and a minority of Indians are interested in education for their children (particularly their sons), but are financially unable to provide for it. A majority of the Indians apparently exhibit no interest in providing their offspring with an education. These attitudes are evidently born of the fact that when parents are themselves educated they place a higher value upon schooling, and that the Ladino rather than the Indian tends to be nominally educated.

In the *municipio* of Ostuncalco there are currently about 3,400 children of school age (ages seven–14) of whom 680, or one-fifth, are Ladino.[1] The remainder are Indian. Nearly all of the 280 Ladino school-age children in the village are registered in school, of whom approximately one half may be expected to complete a sixth-grade education. Opposed to this are 704 school-age Indians living in the four *barrios* of Ostuncalco, of whom about 30 per cent (202) are registered in school. On the basis of past experience,

---

[1] All figures cited in this paragraph have been approximated on the basis of limited census material and the personal accumulation of field data.

virtually none of these can be expected to complete six years of primary school. In the outlying *aldeas* of the *municipio* approximately one half of the 360 school-age Ladinos are registered. Of an estimated 2,050 school-age Indians only 12 per cent, or about 250, are registered in school, and it is doubtful if many progress beyond the first three years of primary school. Although no specific attempt has been made to assess the quality or functionality of literacy, it is readily evident that the problem of illiteracy in Ostuncalco is an Indian and a rural problem.

Ladinos tend to feel that the majority of Indians neither appreciate the value of nor even desire to have an education for their children. They state that Indians prefer to devote their time to working on their land and raising crops.

When Indian families were questioned, various opinions were stated, but for the most part it is evident that Indians express a disinterest that is probably based upon the realization that such an attainment is beyond the realm of their limited resources. This is, in some measure, reflected in an often-repeated phrase that education would be preferred, *"si Dios quiere"* (God willing).

For the reasons expressed above as well as others, disinterest in schooling and absenteeism are chronic problems, especially in the rural sector. To keep track of absentees each school has its *policía escolar* (truant officer). Failure of a child to enroll in or attend school is subject to disciplinary action by the truant officer. Men holding these positions are, for the most part, Indians. The question then arises as to why there is not an increase in school enrollment. One reason is that some people hide their children or send them away from the house when the truant officer heads their way. Another, perhaps more important reason, is the fact that one is not likely to tell on his friends. Since the officers and most of the rural people are Indians of the same locality who have known each other since adolescence, it is understandable that a matter of truancy would not be pressed.

Indians, limited in their use of Spanish and culturally removed from the "modern" ecoeducational system, have neither the desire nor incentive for an education as do their Ladino counterparts. Any aspirations for the education of their children are further frustrated not only by their financial inability to provide for it but also by the need for offspring to be gainfully occupied.

Indians surely are developing an increasing awareness of the value of an education, but due to a greatly accelerated growth in population over the past generation there is a rapid increase in the absolute number of Indians not attending school. On the basis of annual reports housed in the local archives in Ostuncalco it is estimated that 15 per cent of school-age children attended school at the turn of the century. This figure had increased to 20 per cent in 1935 and currently stands at 22 per cent; however, as a consequence of rapid population growth since the 1930's the number of school-age students not attending school has grown from 1,410 in 1935 to a current figure of 2,750.

It is readily evident that poverty and its attendant consequences are more inherent in the rural than the urban sector of Ostuncalco's populace. Nowhere is this more apparent than in the disproportionate investment of resources in education in rural as opposed to urban areas. The urban schools are better equipped, their teachers tend to be more adequately prepared and paid, and the schools are better staffed. Whereas there is a separate teacher for each grade in the two village schools, this is rarely found to be the case in the rural areas. Only two of the rural schools in Ostuncalco have more than one teacher, and even in these instances the teachers were responsible for more than one grade. There may be fewer students in each grade of the rural schools, but the student-teacher ratio is significantly higher. In the rural schools in 1966 there were 52 registered students for each teacher and 42 in the urban schools.

At the present time 11 teachers serve the rural schools of Ostuncalco. If the current high student-teacher ratio were to be maintained and all rural school-age children were in attendance, there would be a need for 46 teachers, or a fourfold increase in the number of teachers. If all children were in attendance, if a separate teacher were assigned for each grade, and if a reasonable student-teacher ratio of 30:1 were to be established, it would necessitate a staff of approximately 80 teachers, or a sevenfold increase over the current number of teachers employed. The urban schools are less poorly provided for, but the situation in the rural schools, multiplied many times over, indicates Guatemala's deficiency in the area of available teachers, to say nothing of the facilities required to service such an expansion in the nation's educational system.

Additionally disturbing is the rapid fall-off in students at the higher grade levels. In 1965 in the rural schools there were 184 first and 74 third graders. The two urban schools had enrolled 159 first, 96 third, and 54 sixth graders. A survey in 1966 reveals that for all schools in the *municipio,* 607 students were registered in the first two grades and only 141 for the last two grades of primary schooling. This rate of attrition does not, however, give a true overall picture, for the rate of dropouts among Indians is much higher than it is for Ladinos. For a variety of reasons, Indians are less pressed to pursue a formal education beyond the second year.

The efficiency of the school system of Ostuncalco is further taxed, particularly at the lower grade levels, by the dredge of students required to repeat a grade. A recent survey discloses that one fifth of the students enrolled in the first two grades of the two village schools are repeaters. The rate in rural schools is less only because children failing a grade are more likely to drop out than repeat a year of work. The foregoing indicates that a number of factors tend to discourage children from continuing in school. There is questionable efficiency in the utilization of resources for maintaining an enrollment in which such a large share of students is functionally equipped for little more than writing their names.

A number of quantitative aspects of school enrollment also need to be cited and reemphasized. With the exception of the rural school in the *aldea* of Sigüilá, the majority (ranging from approximately 70 to 100 per cent) of students are Indian. In the urban boys' school, Lorenzo Montúfar, 233 of a total of 381 students are Indian. In the girls' urban school, however, there is a larger proportion of Ladino students; of a total of 215 students only 65 were Indian. Of the combined enrollment in the two urban schools, slightly more than half are Indian; however, they are not equally distributed throughout all grades. They make up nearly two thirds of all students in the first two grades. In the third and fourth grades there are almost an equal number of Ladino and Indian students. In the final grade of elementary school nearly 95 per cent of all students are Ladino.

Another difference related to Indian-Ladino students has to do with their ages at the various grade levels. Theoretically, a child begins first grade at the age of seven and, progressing annually, he should finish his primary education at age 13. In most instances this is not the case. Though it is rare for a child younger than seven to be in the first grade, it is common to find a youth of 10 or 11 just beginning his education. Consequently, it is not at all uncommon to have children of diverse ages in the same grade. In the village in 1966 the ages of first graders ranged between seven and 13 and between seven and 12 respectively for the boys' and girls' schools. The range tends to be only slightly less in the rural schools. Generally speaking the Indian students in urban schools average one year older than their Ladino counterparts; in rural schools they tend to be two years older.

A significant difference also exists between the number of male and female students enrolled in and attending school. For example, in the rural schools of the *aldeas* of La Esperanza and Varsovia there are, respectively, a total of 48 and 106 students. There are 31 boys and 17 girls in the former and 71 boys and 45 girls in the latter. This is the trend in all rural schools, where male students outnumber females by about a two-to-one margin. In the urban schools 60 per cent of the registered students are males. In both instances, it is apparent that boys have a better chance for formal education.

The predominance of male students is not merely restricted to Ostuncalco but occurs in most, if not in all, areas of Guatemala. Many parents, particularly Indian, feel that an education is of greater value to the man, since it is he who is in charge of any business negotiations which must be made outside of the home. The woman, on the other hand, should be primarily concerned with duties confined to the house, and for these tasks it is not necessary to know how to read and write.

Variation in the availability of education to males as opposed to females, among rural as opposed to urban inhabitants, and among Indians as opposed to Ladinos has been indicated. The chance for a primary education for a rural Indian girl is exceedingly poor. Equally unlikely among the vast majority of all students in Ostuncalco is the acquisition of any form of education beyond the primary level.

Another instructional problem relates to the majority of Indians who, upon beginning school, do not know the Spanish language. Classes of *castellanización* are offered in eight of the 10 Ostuncalco schools. Students in these classes take part in a variety of activities; however, the main purpose of the class is to learn to speak Spanish prior to entry into the first grade. There are many who, upon entering first grade, still do not have a complete grasp of Spanish. This disadvantage creates an obvious gap between the Indian and Ladino students. The sometimes hostile Ladino environment and the requirement to speak a foreign langauge are not an altogether pleasing experience for many young Indian children.

The teachers of Ostuncalco are consequently confronted with language barriers between themselves and their Indian students. Teachers, for the most part, are not familiar with the Indian language; those who are know only a few words or common expressions. Older Indian students, better versed in Spanish, oftentimes act as interpreters for the younger students. Although most Indian students use Spanish when talking with the teacher, they use only the Indian dialect when asking a question of an Indian. During recreation periods, the Indian children revert to a boundless chatter in the Mam dialect.

Needless to say, this resistance to the use of Spanish probably accounts for a lack of association between Indian and Ladino students. One fourth-grade Ladino student at the girls' urban school stated that she had friends among the Indian students in her class since they spoke Spanish well. However, she said she did not speak to or pay attention to the smaller Indian children because their Spanish was very poor. There are assuredly many cultural barriers to the interaction between Indian and Ladino youths, but it is unlikely that any manifest themselves in a more tangible fashion than the inability to communicate because of the language barrier.

Although teachers are acquainted with a majority of their students' parents it is obvious that there is a considerable range of interaction between parents and teachers. In most of the *aldeas,* Ladinos tend to be more centrally located while the Indians are more widely dispersed and decentralized. Since most teachers are only school-hour residents of a community, their associations are restricted to Ladino or Indian parents who are in close proximity to the school. Many parents live several miles from school, and thus contact between teacher and parent is inconvenient and time consuming. Under such circumstances teachers are restricted to occasional visits to student homes, sometimes made in the case of an extended absence from class. Specially organized school programs presented by the students may attract parents from more distant sites.

The relationship between teachers and parents does not appear to be strained. Most parents described their child's teacher as being pleasant and friendly. One Indian father, however, expressed feelings of a different nature, and one cannot but wonder whether or not his negative attitude towards teachers was more representative of community thought. He felt that Ladino students received more attention from the teacher than the Indian students. In addition, he expressed the opinion that teachers separate the two groups of students, showing favoritism towards the Ladinos. His solution for this situation was that Indian parents should join together and replace the teacher. He felt that discrimination was definitely being practiced in the schools. He further mentioned that some *becas* (scholarships) are available, but they are given first to Ladinos and that the Indians do not have a chance.

Interviews with parents revealed that in general there are a number of things they would like to change about the school. It was apparent that there was a sentiment for separate schools, one for boys and another for girls. Another interesting suggestion was to have separate schools for Indians and Ladinos in the rural areas.

In the United States, the rule of separate but equal facilities has gone by way of the boards. The situation in Ostuncalco clearly reveals that school facilities can be joint insofar as Indians and Ladinos are concerned and yet very unequal in opportunities for the children of these two culturally distinct groups of Guatemalans.

Basic to an interpretation of the requirements of the educational system of Ostuncalco is an understanding of the relationship that exists between Indian and Ladino. Thus far, the character of interactions, and the cross-current of attitudes which seethe beyond the grasp of the casual observer have merely been alluded to. Opinions regarding this matter tend to be stated in muted terms, particularly by the Indians. In reality one senses that Indian-Ladino hostility is a pervading factor irrespective of what is being said by whom.

Questions were posed concerning the relationship between Indian and Ladino school-age youths. Several teachers (all are Ladino) indicated that both "races" are used to their own ways of living and that they do not bother one another; that there is no racial tension in the schools; that there is a natural pride in the Ladino, manifested in his dominating personality; and finally that no discrimination exists between the two groups. At variance to this were a larger number of teachers who felt that Indians are dominated and humiliated by Ladinos and subjected to running errands for them and that Ladinos are given preference for available jobs in the community. Ladino and Indian parents' attitudes concerning this question were also varied. Some expressed no awareness of the situation within the schools; however, there were others who agreed that the Ladino students had more influence. One Ladino mother stated that although they played together in school, the Indians and Ladinos *"no se quieren"* (do not like each other). An Indian mother said that her children could not take anything to school, such as a new toy, for the Ladino children would take it away. Observation of student participation in the Ostuncalco schools revealed that Ladino students do appear to be more active in class than do the Indians. This was observable not only in the classroom participation, but also during the recreational activities, where Ladino boys were more active and seemed to be in charge. During recreation periods the Indian and Ladino girls also appear to divide into separate groups. However, there were occasions when the two groups played and interacted together.

Among the dominant Ladino element of Ostuncalco, there are varying convictions as to the relative status of Indians in the community, but it is doubtful if many would support an effort to redress past wrongs immediately. The Indians are increasingly aware of their disadvantageous position in a community in which they are superior only in numbers. Again, however, they have little concept of the power which could be theirs through the organization of action to a common end. The educational system of Ostuncalco appears to reinforce the existing order. And even an improved educational system would be of little value for those to whom it was economically inaccessible.

Conclusion

The educational system of the *municipio* of Ostuncalco is totally inadequate to effect any meaningful solution for the 3,400 school-age children of today or the increasing numbers which it must come to bear. Added schools and teachers have been more than matched by increasing numbers of school-age children. The system is deficient in every conceivable realm of operation, even in its number of students; and deficiencies at all levels are merely more pronounced in rural than they are in urban Ostuncalco.

Supposing that facilities and teachers were available, even more overriding is the economic status of the populace of Ostuncalco. Increasing availability of educational facilities and larger teaching staffs would be poorly served if people, because they are poor or for other reasons, choose not to send their sons and daughters to school.

Funds for education are admittedly short, but a more disturbing factor involves the apparent inattention of properly placed officials to local needs as exemplified in the case of Ostuncalco. What is good for students in Guatemala City may or may not serve counterparts in a small Pacific Ladino or a highland Indian community. A high rate of repeaters or excessive dropouts before functional literacy is attained saps the limited resources of any administering unit. Should there be more primary schools through the third grade, or should there be fewer primary schools but all terminating in the sixth grade? Should more stress be placed on adult education so as to improve the environment of family aspiration? Would limited funds be better spent by educating the more educable—in other words, the Ladino? Can you afford to spread schools across a rural landscape, where teachers choose not to live, or should you concentrate them in towns and villages (to the detriment of rural youths), where the per student cost of producing a functionally literate individual would be significantly reduced? Since seasonal migration among Indian and Ladino has become an economic fact of life, is there a virtue in establishing a more flexible academic year, or in enforcing regulations which make the education of the young a responsibility of the *fincas* or *haciendas* to which youths have migrated with their families? These questions and many others are bound by a philosophical approach to education which does not readily lend itself to the flexibility required for either experimentation or the resolution of local community problems by the citizens of that community.

The limitation of resources does not enhance this situation. Under present conditions there may be, at worst, only a relative deterioration in the process of education in Ostuncalco. On the other hand, it is difficult to believe that there will be a rapid resolution of the problem.

Formal Schooling

GERARDO REICHEL-DOLMATOFF
ALICIA REICHEL-DOLMATOFF

About 45.2 per cent of all adults in Aritama have attended school (men 38.6 per cent, women 61.4 per cent). The illiteracy rate is 79.44 per cent for men, and 70.56 per cent for women.

Few people in Aritama are able to write more than their names, and fewer still can read a newspaper. Those who *can* read do so very slowly, moving their lips or reading aloud. Adults, when asked to write a few lines, will find all sorts of excuses for not doing so, saying that their eyes hurt, that they forgot their spectacles, or that their hands are trembling from some effort they have just made. However, many illiterates display pencils and fountain-pens clipped to their shirt fronts. One old man, who could be seen frequently sitting before his house with a book, admitted candidly that he had never learned to read but that he had acquired considerable prestige by pretending to do so, staring every day for a while at the open pages.

Some 20 villagers, all placeros, received part of their formal education in one of the lowland towns, and at least two went to high school and graduated from universities. However, of these people only a few have returned to their village; the majority have preferred to establish themselves in other towns.

Formal education as offered at the local government schools is a major factor in molding the young individual into the patterns of thought and action that are considered by the community to be desirable. Even one or two years of such education leaves a lasting impression upon him and inevitably influences his life in some important ways. Formal schooling in

Reproduced from *The People of Aritama: The Cultural Personality of a Colombian Mestizo Village,* pp. 115–125, 1961, with the permission of The University of Chicago Press (Chicago).

Aritama is at least a century old. The first schools, which were founded by Catholic missionaries, were taken over by the government in later years and are known at present as "rural schools" *(escuelas rurales)*. Administrative officers of these schools are appointed directly by the secretary of the municipality who, in turn, is an appointee of the director of public education in the capital of the department. All departmental directors are responsible to the Ministry of Public Education in Bogotá, a special section of which is dedicated to the organization and promotion of rural schools all over the country.

In the Corregimiento of Aritama there are seven rural schools. Aritama proper has two schools, one for boys and one for girls, both established in the last century. In the satellite hamlets there is no segregation, children of both sexes attending "mixed schools" *(escuelas mixtas)*. The boys' school in Aritama functions in a small one-room hut in the Plaza barrio which has been rented by the government for this purpose. The single room has a dirt floor, two doors, and one window. The furnishings consist of 15 wooden chairs covered with cowhide, seven wooden desks, a blackboard, and a map of Colombia. Color prints of several Colombian national heroes and an advertisement of a pharmaceutical firm adorn the walls. Behind the teacher's table hangs a picture of the Virgin, on an advertisement of a widely used analgesic. Two books are available for teaching purposes: a catechism and a recent (1950) general teacher's guide published by the Ministry of Public Education. Ths girls' school has its own building, a wattle-and-daub hut with a thatched roof and a cement floor, right on the main corner of the plaza. This school building is a single room of some 48 square meters, with two doors and two windows. There are 34 chairs, three benches, eight desks, and three blackboards, as well as several color prints of national heroes and Catholic saints. The teacher has no recent government textbooks but owns privately five books on orthography, church history, Colombian history, a catechism, and a general teacher's guide. In 1952 the government contributed the following items to the girls' school: two boxes of chalk, 48 pencils, 100 pens, 18 penholders, four erasers, 12 copybooks of 40 pages each, 62 sketching blocks, and one catechism. Neither of these schools has toilet facilities, bathrooms, or drinking water.

According to law the Colombian school year begins in the first week of February, and lasts through November, interrupted only by a short vacation period between the two national holidays of July 20 (Independence Day) and August 7 (Battle of Boyacá). In Aritama, however, these dates are rarely kept, and school opens or closes whenever local conditions and authorities demand it. Often it happens that the teacher's appointments have not come through or that a newly appointed teacher has not decided yet whether to accept or not, and so opening day is sometimes postponed for months. In 1950 the boys' school opened in April, one month after the girls' school had opened; in 1951 it opened late in February and closed in October; in 1952 school opened in May and closed on November 15. School hours are from 8 a.m. to 11 a.m. and from 1 p.m. to 4 p.m. each day, except Saturday afternoon. In lieu of a school bell, the bell of the nearby church is rung to announce these hours.

Schoolteachers are almost always women, generally natives of the village where they exercise their profession. They are appointed by the departmental authorities and are paid through the municipality. None of the numerous teachers we met had even a high school diploma, the educational background of most consisting of only two or three years of elementary school, followed rarely by a short course at a so-called "commercial school" (escuela de comercio) in one of the lowland towns. To qualify for a teaching post, social status, party politics, kinship, and other personal connections are all-important, completely overshadowing academic qualifications. Gaining and maintaining a teaching position is therefore not easy, and every year at the beginning of the new term there is much fear about reappointments, because of the chance of being replaced by another teacher with better connections. As a matter of fact, teachers *are* changed very frequently, not only because every change in national politics or in the personnel of the departmental government influences their position, but also because there is much jealousy and friction among candidates for any teaching position in every village. Consequently teachers belong to the local elite and occupy a high social status, and Aritama is no exception to this rule. All teachers there, present and past, were members of prominent families from the Plaza, and were very conscious of being "Spaniards." This fact causes strong resentments in the village, but it tends to give high prestige value to formal education. Many parents of lower status complain that these teachers mistreat their children or teach them useless things at school, but nevertheless there is the general feeling that getting "good" schooling depends upon the supervision and guidance of an upper-class señora. Teachers' salaries are fixed at 100 pesos a month, but are actually paid at rather irregular intervals. During our stay in the village the municipal treasury was short of funds to pay the teachers' salaries and the treasurer offered to give to each teacher a corresponding amount of bottles of rum, for resale. As the liquor factory is under state control and provides the principal revenue, similar arrangements are common even in the departmental capital. In Aritama, however, the teachers spurned this offer, because the sale of liquor could hardly be considered worthy of their high social status.

Theoretically, each school in Aritama has a kindergarten and four grades, but in practice there is no such division. The basic distinction is drawn, rather, between "backward" and "advanced" pupils, and a child's "grade" placement depends upon his behavior, his physical appearance, and the class status of his parents. Furthermore, many children, especially those of placero families, even after having passed their final examinations, do not necessarily move on to the next grade. The teacher, the child, or his parents may decide that he should repeat the same grade in order to learn the lessons in greater detail. This often happens when a teacher is replaced by a new one who is expected to teach the same subjects in a slightly different manner. After finishing school, i.e., after the second grade, many children stay on and repeat the last grade for several years. There are a number of persons who have had up to eight years of schooling by thus repeating the last grade. As a matter of fact, for many placero girls the school is a kind of social circle where "civilized behavior" is taught and practiced, and parents who do not need them at home often let their girls continue year after year.

Detailed records were available only for the girls' school, from 1945 to 1951. During this seven-year period, the total enrollment was 468 girls. Of these, 252 (53.8 per cent) dropped out during or at the end of the first school year; 193 (41.2 per cent) stayed for two years, and 18 (3.8 per cent) for three years, while only five girls (1.06 per cent) stayed for four years. In 1952, a year for which we have records of children of both sexes, 384 children of school age (between five and 14 years) were in the village, and 133 (34.6 per cent) of them were enrolled (43.6 per cent boys and 56.3 per cent girls). Lomero and placero children were about equal in number at both schools, which means that on the basis of their numbers in the community there is a much higher percentage of the placeros attending than of the lomeros. The average age of first graders was 10 years.

School attendance is sporadic because it depends on many personal factors, on the fiesta season, and on the harvesting season. The records kept by the teachers were so confused that it is impossible to gain a clear picture of attendance, but from observation we judged that the average child misses about one third of all school days. Attendance at the girls' school is at least twice as regular as at the boys' school for several reasons. In the first place, boys definitely dislike female authority, and public opinion often agrees with them. At one time, when a male teacher happened to be appointed, enrollment of boys rose sharply. In the second place, boys are often needed to work in the fields or around the house, and many parents refuse to send them to school. Girls, on the other hand, are often encouraged or even forced by their parents to attend school, as their elders believe that a few years of formal education may be of great help in their finding a good consort in later years or will enable them to procure some sort of official employment. Should a child not attend school regularly, the teacher may complain to the parents, but if they are of low social status she will not visit them or talk to them on the street. Instead she will complain to the police inspector, who will perhaps impose a fine on the child's family. Teachers know that this is against the law and try to hide the procedure, but the fact that the authorities force school attendance by fining the parents is well known in the village. A frequent excuse for not attending school is that the child's clothes have not been washed and ironed in time, and this excuse is always accepted by the teachers. Should a child be kept from attending because of urgent work in house or field, however, the teachers show considerably less patience and one of them told us: "The poor don't have any fields, so they don't need their children for work; and the rich don't need them because they have servants."

Discipline is maintained in school by stringent means. Slaps or thrashings applied with a ruler or a rod are frequent punishments. Occasionally, a child is made to kneel outside the door in the hot sun or is locked into a dark room or is obliged to have a piece of cardboard tied over his face. But ridicule and comparison with the "Indians" is by far the most common method of punishing a child. Until quite recently disobedient children were pilloried and put in stock or were forced to kneel on potsherds or pebbles while supporting a heavy stone on their heads. Several adults told us that when they were children they were locked into the empty houses of recently deceased persons as punishment for misdemeanors in school.

At the end of the school year the teachers make a short written report to the municipal director of education, stating the number of pupils, with their names, attendance records, age, weight, stature, caries, and final grades. This yearly report, to which is appended an inventory of school equipment, is then signed by the police inspector. This inspector also has to keep in contact with the municipal and departmental authorities who are responsible for the yearly appointment of teachers.

The modern government texts and the curriculum for rural schools in Colombia are well conceived and well adapted to their purpose, viz., that of imparting a basic education. They strongly emphasize practical matters, such as agriculture, reforestation, health, and nutrition. They are well printed and carefully edited in language suited to each grade level. However, the rural teachers use these texts in a very limited way. Not all own them and, of those who do, not all make use of them, either because they prefer to apply their own particular methods or because their own educational background is so insufficient that they are unable to put such textbooks to a fuller use. In Aritama the teachers select from the official curriculum only those subjects which tend to affirm local values. Thus "citizenship" (cívica), "manners" (urbanidad), the care of dress and shoes, needlework, the making of paper flowers, or the tying of ribbons are taught, while all tasks connected with agriculture, housekeeping, hygiene, or any activity which demands collaboration are ignored. Teachers are very critical of the government program and consider certain subjects quite useless or even offensive. Such government initiatives as reforestation or the establishment of kitchen gardens through rural schools are ridiculed and openly attacked.

The teachers say: "It seems that the government thinks we are a bunch of wild Indians, asking us to make our children plant trees and vegetables."

The daily subject matter depends very much on the whimsy of the individual teacher, who chooses arithmetic, geography, history, religion, citizenship, "manners," Spanish, natural history, and a number of ill-defined subjects dealing with a combination of needlework, cosmology, and hygiene. Hardly any teacher in Aritama uses the government textbooks, preferring to employ for teaching purposes a number of their own "copybooks." These copybooks have been handed down from one teacher to another, from friends and relatives, such as from aunts and nieces, and contain a more or less complete outline of subject matter arranged as questions and answers. The method of teaching consists of having the children copy, in the course of the year, all the questions and answers and making them memorize both. The teacher reads aloud a question and the children repeat it in unison at the top of their voices for 10, 20, or 50 times. The answer is read and memorized in the same way, and then some time is spent in copying these same questions and answers into individual notebooks, in exactly the same sequence and wording as is found in the teacher's copybook. The daily routine is about as follows: from 8 a.m. to 9 a.m. the children sit or walk in the schoolyard, memorizing from a copybook a certain number of questions and answers; after returning to the classroom, from 9 a.m. to 10 a.m. they recite their assignments and copy them; afterward half an hour is again spent in the yard learning more questions until class is over at 11 a.m. The same pattern is repeated in the afternoon.

To examine a child the teacher recites a question and adds the first two or three words of the answer, whereupon the child continues; a moment before the child finishes the answer, the teacher asks a new question followed by the first words of its answer, and so a monotonous stimulus-response chant is set into operation. There is no need for the child to think, the only requirement being a certain ability at rote memory. If a question is phrased in an unaccustomed manner, the child is totally unable to answer; by the same token, should a child try to phrase an answer in original words, he would be reprimanded for doing so.

The following are excerpts from the notebook of one of the teachers. On citizenship *(instrucción cívica)* it says, for example: "Monarchy is a form of government which does not exist among civilized nations." A sample question in citizenship is: "What has man been created for?" The answer: "To live in society." Under natural sciences there are the following problems. Question: "How does the rabbit reproduce itself?" Answer: "Directly." Question: "How does the bee sleep?" Answer: "Standing." Question: "What are the fins of a fish for?" Answer: "To descend, ascend, or maintain itself in a vertical position." There are many dozens of similar questions and answers on cows, pigs and sheep, taught day by day to the second graders.

During the same term Colombian history *(historia patria)* is taught. Sample questions are: "What kind of people inhabited America before Columbus?" Answer: "A people which had no knowledge of commodities." Question: "How did Bolívar die?" Answer: "Naked, as he was born."

As these notebooks have been copied and recopied for years and years, many errors have slipped into the transcriptions, and the children are taught many quite meaningless or contradictory statements, e.g., "Every action which demonstrates religion is uncivil" *(todo acto que demuestre religión es inurbano)*. During a class in geometry the teacher explained several times that a spiral was called a cone. So it said in her copybook and so the children learned it and copied it again. The question came up during final examinations and when the pupil drew a spiral on the blackboard and called it a cone, the teacher was very pleased.

The teachers themselves in their ignorance and lack of perception contribute to this confusion. After explaining that in other countries people speak different languages, such as English, French, or German, one teacher pointed out that the advantage of the Spanish language was that it could be not only spoken but also written. When lecturing on the economic geography of northern Colombia, the same teacher mentioned among the natural resources the existence of orchids (which are of no commercial value) but did not mention petroleum, coffee, or sugar cane. She also pointed out the importance of the pearl trade, although this was discontinued many years ago. When speaking of the economic importance of roads, she said that it was high time a motor road was built between two certain lowland towns, in spite of the fact that such a road had existed for the last 20 years and that she herself had often traveled on it. All this confusion arose only because she was using a copybook which had been written *before* the road had been built, *before* coffee became a major cash crop, and *before* the pearl trade had declined. One teacher, who had talked at length about microbes and who had had the children write about this theme, sent an ailing pupil home after diagnosing his trouble as "suffering from the Evil Eye." We asked another teacher what she believed exists below the ground; she answered that there is "another world peopled by green dwarfs," but added that her textbook said something else, which she did not quite remember.

July 20 is the Colombian national holiday celebrating the country's declaration of independence from Spain, and on this day all schools take part in a special program of parades, recitals, etc., in a nationwide fiesta. In Aritama the best pupil of the boys' school was chosen to recite a poem in public. The poem his teacher had taught him was an inspired eulogy of Spanish military power, describing the glorious victories at Lepanto and Pavia, yet nobody seemed to notice that this recital was rather out of place at this particular date. When we asked one of the teachers for the meaning of Independence Day, she answered that it was the day "when the slaves were freed all over the world."

At year's end we assisted at the final examination of fourth graders, in reality pupils who had attended for five or six years, and we heard the following questions. "What impelled Columbus' ships?" Answer: "The wind." Question: "How does the hen sleep?" Answer: "Standing." Question: "How does the rabbit defend itself?" Answer: "By running away." However, none of the children was able to answer our questions: "What is the capital of Colombia? Who is the Pope? Where is Venezuela?"

This sort of confusion and misinformation pervades every subject taught at school, and the teachers are certainly not aware of it. To them there are two kinds of knowledge: the empirical knowledge acquired in everyday experience and the "abstract" knowledge taught at school. These are two sets of viewpoints, two manners of seeing things, and they are not necessarily related or interdependent. The knowledge acquired at school may contradict actual experience (or vice versa), but school learning is "better" because it is "civilized" knowledge. On the other hand, as we have said above, only those subjects are selected for teaching which give expression to needs felt, to ambitions cherished, and to goals visualized as desirable. Health education, for example, is mainly oriented toward teaching the child that all physical efforts should be avoided. Great emphasis is placed upon the dangers of overexertion, explaining that movements make the muscles tired, that reading is harmful for the eyes, and that thinking "heats the head" and is likely to cause dangerous diseases.

All teachers are definitely inclined to consider the local schools as training grounds for the placero minority only, and so give little encouragement to lomero children. Favoritism and racial prejudice and discrimination, as well as social discrimination against children of poor families, are the rule. Teachers insist that children attend classes in new and clean clothes. If a child arrives barefoot or with old and mended clothes, he is scolded and word is sent to the child's family asking the parents to provide new clothes lest the child endanger the school's prestige. Ill-dressed children are ridiculed in public by teachers and by other children alike, and often this is the reason why a child will cease to attend school or why parents will refuse to enroll their children at all. New and clean clothes are the principal criterion for awarding medals or any other prizes at the end of the school year. A poorly dressed child has no chance to receive such a prize, even if he is an outstanding pupil.

Teachers encourage the girls to carry umbrellas, to use cosmetics, handbags, stockings, and costume jewelry, all of which are expensive items which only the well-to-do can afford, but the girls who do not own such paraphernalia of "civilization" are likely to be ridiculed. Children of Indian phenotype, when volunteering to answer a question, are often ridiculed by the teacher, and their knowledge is put into doubt. "You wouldn't know! You better go to the river" (i.e., to fetch water) *(Y tú, qué vas a saber? Véte al río!)*, one teacher said to an Indian girl. A woman of marked Indian features told us that when she was a schoolgirl she once produced a particularly well-done piece of needlework which was shown to a visiting school inspector. The inspector called the girl, but upon noticing her physical appearance, he said that it was a pity the teacher had "wasted her efforts on an Indian, who would never be able to take advantage of her education." Such experiences are not easily forgotten and are likely to produce deep resentments which are shared by entire families or kin groups. Placero children often molest and even beat children of Indian phenotype, and the teachers not only condone this behavior but actually approve of it with the hope that the "Indian" child will leave school.

Teachers keep in personal touch with parents of children who belong to their own social class, but will never visit a lomero family to discuss a child's school problems. In general, parents take little interest in their children's attendance or progress and seldom discuss school matters with other parents or with teachers. Many parents believe that by sending their children to school they are doing a personal favor for the government or for the teachers. As school age coincides with the years when a child could begin to take an active part in family earnings, the poorer people consider it a great sacrifice to send their children to school. Many lomero families believe that formal education is not only a loss of valuable time but also constitutes a certain danger, as they fear that their children will be spoiled by the influence of an upper-class placero teacher. On the other hand, many adult lomeros who are illiterates complain bitterly that their own parents did not send them to school and blame them for their present poverty, which they claim is due to their lack of formal education. "Because they were brutes, they wanted us to be brutes, too," they say of the older generation.

Our observations of the school system of Aritama revealed two principal problems: one, the composition of the student body, the other, the cultural effects of the teaching methods. As we have pointed out, the teachers, backed by the placeros, consider the school a "Spanish" institution in which the participation of "Indian" elements is not considered desirable. There is a strong tendency in the Plaza to monopolize the schools and to make attendance difficult and unpleasant for lomero children. The discriminatory attitude of teachers as well as of placero parents and pupils keeps many lomero families from sending their children to school, either because they cannot afford the high cost of clothes and dresses or because they resent the humiliations to which their children and they themselves will probably be exposed. The school thus increases to a marked degree the already existing intravillage tensions.

For those children who attend school, the methods employed in teaching have a far-reaching influence. In the first place, the child is systematically taught the high prestige value of good clothes and of ceremonial behavior and is made to abhor and to ridicule all manual labor and cooperative effort. Many children are thus brought into opposition to their parents, who demand collaboration and manual work. In the second place, "knowledge" is reduced to a set of ready questions and answers, beyond which there is little or nothing added or learned. The same pattern is maintained during adult life, the individual answering standard questions in a perfunctory and stereotyped way and refusing to answer an unaccustomed question because the answer might lower his prestige.

School creates, therefore, a world devoid of all reality. It teaches the children that they are well-dressed, well-fed, God-fearing and hard-working "Spaniards," who are not only equal but rather superior to all other peoples. They are taught that their village is the "heart of the world" *(el corazón del mundo),* and that the only forces bent upon destroying this paradise are the despised "Indians" and the mistrusted "government." They are taught that "work" *(trabajo)* is to be avoided, but that "employment" *(empleo)* is to be sought, as a sinecure well deserved by anyone who has attended school.

Section 7:
Language and Literacy in National Integration

Introduction to Section 7

The first selection, by Joan Rubin, examines the nature of Spanish-Guarani bilingualism in Paraguay. The author discusses the historical importance of Guarani in a social and political context but notes that those who are monolingual Guarani speakers often perceive themselves and are perceived by others with disdain. It is shown that the Ministry of Education has authorized Spanish as the only medium of instruction in schools even though the largest numbers of students speak only Guarani. The author presents data from an investigation of monolingual and bilingual students in one rural and one small urban center in which she found that as students completed higher years of schooling, proficiency in Spanish increased. Thus, although Rubin notes other factors which influence the use of Spanish, she suggests that the emphasis on instruction in Spanish by the Ministry of Education tends to encourage higher dropout and grade-repetition rates among students who are predominantly Guarani speakers.

In the second article, Erwin Epstein discusses the controversies which have developed over the use of English in the schools of Puerto Rico. The author shows that although Spanish has been the language of instruction in public schools since 1948, there is concern that in the more socially prestigious private schools, where enrollments are growing and English is the medium of instruction, Puerto Rican students are learning less Spanish while being inculcated with North American attitudes and values. Thus, as the author suggests, English ". . . is suspect to those who stress the distinctiveness of Puerto Rican culture and view independence as the only just condition, and it is extolled by those who advocate assimilation with the United States."

The author analyzes achievement scores for public and private school twelfth graders and finds that "pupils from private schools in which English is the primary language of instruction achieve appreciably higher in Spanish than pupils in public schools (where Spanish is the medium of instruction). Nevertheless, of all groups tested, pupils from private schools in which Spanish is the major language of instruction achieved the highest grades in that language."

To find out the effects on national identity of learning English, the author administered a questionnaire to ninth-grade public and private (Catholic) school pupils. His results indicate that although Catholic school pupils identify more with English, they do not view the language as a way of becoming, nor do they want to become, more North American. Public school pupils, however, are proportionately more likely to want more English taught in school and are more likely to suggest that Puerto Rico become more Americanized.

The third and fourth articles in this section are concerned with correlates of literacy and literacy training respectively. In the former, Everett Rogers and William Herzog examine the conceptual problems of functional literacy as related to indicators of modernization through the investigation of five Colombian peasant communities. Employing personal interviews, the authors found that the ability to read a short sentence in Spanish was related positively to self-defined literacy and to the number of formal years of schooling completed. The authors suggest, however, that because many individuals who were classified as functionally literate had not completed four years of schooling, much literacy learning must transpire outside the classroom. In addition, the authors report that: "Functional literacy was found to be related to mass-media exposure, to be more characteristic of children than adults, and to be associated with empathy, agricultural and home innovativeness, achievement motivation, farm size, trips to urban centers, political knowledge, and sociometric opinion leadership."

The final article, by Thomas G. Sanders, offers a description of a group method of promoting cultural awareness through literacy training that was developed by the Brazilian educator Paulo Freire. The author discusses the departure from traditional pedagogical approaches evidenced in the Freire method as illiterates engage in dialogues about their perceptions of real life situations in their own environment. Initially, the method of "conscientization" depends upon informal conversations with illiterates in order to select vocabulary which manifests a confrontation with social and political issues and which moves the learners from simple to more complex letters and sounds embedded in the language. In addition, visual aids are employed by a coordinator of the group in order to relate words to pictures and provide for self-discovery, or a ". . . realistic awareness of one's locus in nature and society. . . ." As Sanders suggests, the method ". . . regards as invalid the manipulation of education and people in order either to maintain an archaic system or to impose perspectives alien to the context. Its only ideology is a kind of humanism that affirms the freedom and capacity of the people to decide their destinies." The author points out the potentially revolutionary impact of the method and the problems which have emerged as a result of its use in Brazil and Chile.

Original Sources for Selections

Rubin, Joan. "Language and Education in Paraguay," *in* J. A. Fishman *et al.,* eds., *Language Problems of Developing Nations.* New York: John Wiley, 1968, pp. 477-488.

Epstein, Erwin H. "National Identity and the Language Issue in Puerto Rico," *Comparative Education Review,* 11 (June, 1967), pp. 133-143.

Rogers, Everett M., and William Herzog. "Functional Literacy among Colombian Peasants," *Economic Development and Cultural Change,* 14 (January, 1966), pp. 190-203.

Sanders, Thomas G. *The Paulo Freire Method: Literacy Training and Conscientización.* American Universities Field Staff: Fieldstaff Reports, West Coast South American Series Vol. XV, No. 1, 1968, 17 pp.

Language and Education in Paraguay

JOAN RUBIN

The Language Situation

According to the figures of the official census of 1950, Paraguay is the most bilingual nation in Latin America and one of the most bilingual nations in the world. In the nation as a whole in 1950, some 52 per cent of the population (three years and older) claimed to be bilingual in Spanish and the aboriginal language Guarani. In the capital itself, some 76 per cent of the population claimed to be bilingual *(Anuario Estadístico..., 1955).*[1] This bilingual character results in large part in the areas outside of the major cities of Asunción, Villarrica, Concepción, and Encarnación from the

Reproduced from *Language Problems of Developing Nations* (New York: John Wiley, 1968), pp. 477–488, by author permission.

The research for this paper was carried out in Paraguay in 1960–1961 and during the summer of 1965 and was made possible by the National Institutes of Mental Health Grant MF-11,528, The National Science Foundation Grant GS-872, and a grant from the Wenner-Gren Foundation. The author is indebted to Dr. Efraím Cardozo for calling her attention to certain historical information on language policy; she is also grateful to Ruth Krulfeld and Bernarda Erwin for editorial comments and criticism. The author worked principally in two areas, the town of Luque (population 11,000) and the rural farming area of Itapuamí (population 1,350). In addition, some research was carried out in the cities of Asunción and Concepción, and visits were made to other rural towns and farming areas.

[1] The 1962 census figures for Asunción (those for the whole country have not yet been released) seem to indicate no major change in this percentage. Of those three years and older, some 79 per cent claimed they *habitually* spoke Spanish and Guarani (República de Paraguay, *Censo... 1962, 1965).* This figure is probably somewhat higher since it can be assumed that of those who said they habitually spoke only Spanish or Guarani, some must also be able to speak Guarani or Spanish, respectively. It should be noted that exact comparability is lost because the 1950 census question asked about language ability and the 1962 census question asked about habitual language usage (cf. Lieberson, 1966, for a discussion of the need for gathering comparable linguistic data in censuses).

superimposition of Spanish in the school system. The large majority of rural Paraguayans have Guarani as their first language and are first exposed to Spanish in the classroom. Whereas one could live in the rural areas today without ever speaking Spanish, lack of knowledge of Guarani would be a real handicap. Although the reverse is true for the major cities, there are numerous occasions when lack of knowledge of Guarani would isolate a person from casual speech—for example, at even the most formal dinners after-dinner jokes are usually told in Guarani.

In this paper I shall examine how Paraguay has achieved this bilingual character and at what cost. Because the large majority of the rural population is first, and often most concentratedly, exposed to Spanish in the school system, the school system would seem to be of primary importance as a source of language learning. I shall consider how effectively the schools have performed their task.

In Paraguay, sound educational policy concerning the language of instruction would seem to be easy to establish and to implement. There are only two languages, Spanish and Guarani; everyone seems to agree that one of the major goals of the schools should be the learning of Spanish. Yet I suggest that the assumption by school authorities that students are bilingual has prevented teachers from effectively teaching the Spanish language and the rest of the curriculum.

It is unique in Latin America to find the aboriginal language given so much importance. Elsewhere in Latin America the Indian language has a secondary position; city people do not speak it at all or if they do, they may deny their linguistic ability or the aboriginal language's importance.[1] Indeed, one of the major criteria for becoming socially "white" in most Hispanic America is fluency in Spanish.[2] Insofar as I can tell, bilingualism in the rest of Latin America is a transitional stage in the process of changing from a monolingual aboriginal speaker to a monolingual Spanish or Portuguese speaker. This is in strong contrast to Paraguay, where I feel bilingualism has been and still is a permanent feature of the society. Such bilingualism presupposes that people continue to use the aboriginal language after learning Spanish. This is indeed the case. In Paraguay, the aboriginal

---

[1] According to the Mexican census of 1950, approximately 2 per cent of the population of Mexico City spoke Spanish and an aboriginal language; according to the 1960 Mexican census this percentage was reduced to 1.1 per cent; according to the Peruvian census of 1940 (none was available for 1950 and the 1961 census figures for language ability are not yet in print), approximately 10 per cent of the population of Lima spoke Spanish and the aboriginal language.

[2] The conflict presented in passing from Indian to white is illustrated by the often-cited dilemma of a Peruvian Indian who went to the coast to pass, learned Spanish, and married a chola girl (Spanish-speaking, lower-class person). Much later, some Indian friends of his appeared and to tease him insulted his wife in Quechua. He was faced with the alternative of protecting his wife and his manhood by defending himself in Quechua, and thus admitting his Indian origin, or keeping silent and maintaining his white character.

language is spoken by almost everyone. For the country as a whole some 92 per cent of the population (three years and older) was reported to know Guarani; in Asunción, the capital, 86 per cent claimed to speak Guaraní (*Anuario Estadístico . . . , 1955*).[1]

While Spanish has probably always been important for communication and business purposes in Asunción, Guarani has also played a striking role as an urban and national language. As far back as 1555 (30 years after the discovery of Paraguay) I find that the colonists had learned Guarani to such an extent that when a small group of Spanish women arrived in Asunción, the frustrated conquerors found that their habitual use of Guarani had inhibited their "speaking in Spanish to real ladies dressed in the manner God expected" (translated from Gandía, 1939, p. 132).[2] The continuing importance of Guarani during the colonial period is indicated by a report of the governor of Paraguay, who complained in a 1777 report to the Spanish crown of the difficulties the authorities had in communicating with the populace because of its monolingual character (Fernando, 1777, p. 49). Again, in 1791, Peramás noted that even from the pulpit in Asunción, the mysteries of the Catholic religion by popular preference were explained in Guarani, although he reports the audience was largely bilingual (Peramás, 1946, p. 74). The British traveler Robertson also indicated that in 1815 distinguished Paraguayans visiting him in Corrientes spoke first in Spanish but as soon as they relaxed they turned to speaking in Guarani (Robertson, 1920, p. 104).

The foregoing examples indicate that Guarani served as an important communication medium throughout the early history of Paraguay, not only for those living in the rural areas but also for the most sophisticated citizens of the capital. The importance of Guarani in the postcolonial period of the nineteenth and twentieth centuries is seen in the literature produced in Guarani by prominent Paraguayans. Among the best known were two by Narciso Colman (*Ocara Poty,* a collection of poems, and *Our Ancestors*) and a well-known epic poem, *Ñande Ypycuera.* The success of the major dramatist, Julio Correa, who wrote some 20 plays in Guarani, caused the mayor of Asunción to write a congratulatory letter noting the value of his work and its contribution to the national theater. Guarani is cited by many as the symbol of Paraguayan uniqueness. Its national function is illustrated by its use as the only language of the army during two major wars—the War of the Triple Alliance, 1865–1870, and the Chaco War, 1932–1935.

---

[1] The 1962 census figures for Asunción (República de Paraguay, *Censo . . . 1962, 1965*) indicated that these figures do not seem to have changed substantially. In Asunción, 84 per cent said they habitually spoke Guarani; in addition, some of those who habitually spoke Spanish also probably know Guarani and their ability should be added to the above percentage. See footnote 1 on p. 549 for the difficulties encountered in comparing the figures from these two censuses.

[2] The rather complex social and political reasons for the initial and continuing importance of Guarani are taken up in Rubin, *National Bilingualism in Paraguay* (The Hague: Mouton, 1968), chap. 2.

However, in spite of its continuing importance and the positive value given it by many citizens, Guarani is and has been the object of considerable disdain. Many urban Paraguayans feel that Paraguay's progress is impeded by the widespread lack of knowledge of Spanish and by the continuing use of Guarani. Monolingual speakers of Guarani are often the object of a series of pejoratives. The man who controls only Guarani is called a *guarango* (country bumpkin, boor); he is thought to be *menos inteligente* (less intelligent), *menos desarrollado* (less cultured), and *no tiene principios* (without principles). Monolingual speakers of Guarani even refer to themselves as *tavi* (stupid) because they are unable to speak Spanish. The continuing use of Guarani is often seen by literary scholars as an important factor in the dearth of Paraguayan Spanish literature. Guarani is said to *entorpecer la lengua* (dull the tongue). This fact then serves to explain Paraguayan inability to speak or write effectively in Spanish.

These negative feelings toward Guarani underlie its total rejection by the Constitutional Congress of 1870. When the representative from Paraguarí, a small town in the interior, moved that Congress members be permitted to use Guarani if they so desired, the response was a "general hilarity" and the motion "... was fought energetically by the deputies ... who requested not only that it be rejected, but also that in the future the making of such motions be forbidden. The Assembly by a two-thirds vote rejected the motion" (translated from Decoud, 1934, p. 179).

Language in Education

I have suggested that throughout Paraguayan history Guarani had an important role as a means of communication for all Paraguayans and often served as a source of group identity once independence was gained. At the same time, Spanish served as the language of government and as a vehicle for communication with other countries. Through these functions, Spanish gained prestige. Thus, although Guarani seems to have been in greater use, it was often viewed with disdain as the more primitive language. As a result educational policy has always prescribed Spanish as the only possible medium of instruction.

In establishing the school curriculum, little or no account was taken of the greater importance of Guarani as the main means of communication. The Ministry of Education seems to have assumed that Spanish was to be the official language of instruction. No concern seems to have ever been expressed for the many schoolchildren to whom Spanish was almost a foreign language. Many teachers today feel that, since in most towns some people speak Spanish, the children will have an opportunity to hear it and will automatically understand it when they hear it in school. This is, of course, an unfortunate fallacy. As I have indicated, one can get along quite successfully in the rural areas without Spanish.

Over the years the Ministry of Education has ignored the discrepancy between educational policy and linguistic reality. Teachers have tried to teach monolingual Guarani speakers to read, write, and do arithmetic in Spanish without first giving them language lessons. The ministry has expected teachers to use Spanish in the classroom as early as possible. At the same time, all of the teachers we interviewed indicated they had been given no special instruction in their normal school preparation on how to cope with the language problem.

The attitude of the ministry until very recently has been to ignore the problem. In 1812 the governmental junta advised schoolteachers to make sure that Spanish was the language of the classroom and to banish Guarani from school usage *(Instrucciones . . . , 1812)*. That this was indeed a difficult problem can be seen from the memoirs of the writer Juan Crisóstomo Centurión, born in 1840. "In school the use of Guarani in class hours was prohibited. To enforce this rule, teachers distributed to monitors bronze rings which were given to anyone found conversing in Guarani. . . . On Saturday, return of the rings was requested and each one caught with a ring was punished with four or five lashes" (translated from J. C. Centurión, 1894, p. 62). In 1894 Manuel Domínguez, head of the Ministry of Education and a man known for his interest in the progress of the school system, referred to Guarani "as a great enemy of the cultural progress of Paraguay" (Cardozo, 1959, p. 82). Whereas Domínguez clearly recognized the problem posed by the monolingual Guarani speakers, he did not recognize the discrepancy between the requirement for the Spanish instruction and the language ability of the pupils.

Even today the discrepancy goes largely unrecognized. The normal schools do not deal with the problem in their training of teachers. On the other hand, rural teachers in interviews expressed awareness of the difficulties created by monolingualism, but they did not feel it was particularly serious. Instead they indicated that the difficulty encountered was a "normal" part of teaching. In the rural areas I visited, teachers stated that, although their students could not speak Spanish, almost all of them could understand it. My classroom visits usually indicated the opposite. On a couple of occasions, I requested that a class be given in Guarani. The difference in student response was appreciable. Instead of students evidencing the apathy and lack of understanding obvious in the classes given in Spanish, student participation and interest were extremely high when the class was in Guarani.

One principal I met was aware of the language problem. She told me that she had discovered that the best student in Grade 1 of a school on the edge of town was a monolingual Guarani speaker. The child's teacher had been unaware of his ability and had discovered it only when the principal had quizzed the student.

Most teachers blame the student's inability to speak Spanish on a lack of desire to do so. Yet this hardly seems to be the case. Most students who go to school want to learn Spanish and indeed seem eager to learn everything. To test their general learning ability I spent two hours teaching 60 second-grade children three English sentences: *This is chalk. This is a pencil. This is an eraser.* On my return four years later I found children who still remembered these equivalents. Yet the very same students could not give the Spanish equivalents of these common school utensils.

In the first few grades, many teachers begin by using a limited amount of Spanish, which is gradually increased as the year progresses. Translation into Guarani is the most frequent technique used to convey the meaning of Spanish. The teacher says the sentence in Spanish, translates it into Guarani, and then asks the student to repeat in Spanish. Another technique is the memorization of poems and stories in Spanish. For many children these exercises remain completely rote during the first months or years of their education. In one rural school I found, for example, that when the first-grade teacher asked the students a question, they replied by repeating the question instead of answering it. I also found that, in order to avoid the silences which resulted from the monolinguals' lack of comprehension, the teacher called more frequently on the bilingual students, thus showing awareness of a communication problem without fully understanding it.

In addition to reliance on the translation-repetition method, some teachers forbid the use of Guarani in the classroom and at times also on the playground. This procedure, which used to be more common, has been considerably discouraged recently. Teachers have been requested to encourage use of Spanish but not to exercise sanctions against those using Guarani. In some schools teachers put monolingual and bilingual students together in the hope that the exposure will aid the monolinguals. A third procedure is to encourage the use of Spanish in the homes of students. Parents often talk about the need to use Spanish, and many make the effort when they remember. However, for many monolingual parents this is impossible, and of those who do try to speak Spanish to their children, many continue to speak Guarani to their spouses and friends, so that the exposure to Spanish is often limited.

A by-product of the insistence on Spanish in the classroom is the widespread conviction that Spanish alone is appropriate there, even among students who speak only Guarani. So strong is this feeling that when we requested the use of Guarani both teachers and students broke into laughter. Parents who are incipient or subordinate bilinguals are often inhibited in their conservations with others because they feel Spanish is the appropriate language for such a meeting.

Although there is a greater need for a good Spanish model in the rural areas than elsewhere, it is unfortunately true that rural teachers are often limited in their ability to speak Spanish and their general academic preparation. The result is that rural students are less skilled in Spanish and in their school subjects than their peers in town.

The lack of attention to the language problem resulting from the fiction that Spanish is heard by all has many serious repercussions. To mention one, students acquire Spanish very slowly. High school teachers reported that students at the seventh-grade level were often so deficient in Spanish that they could not understand instruction in that language adequately.

Most rural speakers who have had only a second- or third-grade education are not very proficient speakers of Spanish. In fact, there is a high correlation between the degree of proficiency in Spanish and the number of school years completed. The number of years of school completed is the major determinant of the linguistic skill of rural inhabitants and, indeed, a major determinant of the skill of many townspeople as well. Tables 1 and 2 use my data to illustrate this point for the rural area of Itapuamí and the rural town of Luque.[1] Several observations can be made from Table 1.

(a)   A large proportion (77 per cent) of monolingual Guarani speakers had never passed a single school grade. Almost all (92 per cent) of the monolingual speakers had passed no more than first grade.

(b)   Of those whose bilingual ability was considered incipient, the largest proportion (85 per cent) had never gone to school or had passed only the first or second grade.

Table 1. Degree of Proficiency and Number of School Years Completed for 817 Itapuamí Speakers, 10 Years and Older (in Raw Scores)

	School Years Passed								
	None	*1*	*2*	*3*	*4*	*5*	*6*	*7+*	*Total*
Monolingual[a]	143	27	13	2	–	–	–	–	185
Incipient	45	44	58	23	3	–	–	–	173
Subordinate	12	13	86	102	42	2	2	–	259
Coordinate	4	5	19	40	51	38	30	13	200

[a] The categorization of an individual's linguistic proficiency was based on subjective observation and judgment of the skill of an informant. This impressionistic information was then fitted into Diebold's (1961) useful tripartite scale of bilingualism resulting in the following categories.

1. Coordinate bilinguals—only those individuals who spoke *and* understood both languages well. Persons were included who were fluent but who had some "accent" in the second language, as well as individuals who were fluent but who made the standard sort of lexical interference error of loan translation.

2. Subordinate bilinguals—those individuals who were scored "so-so" in speaking (able to speak but not fluently) and were "good" or "so-so" in understanding.

3. Incipient bilinguals—those individuals who could not speak one of the languages but who in understanding the second language scored "so-so" or "good."

[1] Tables 1 and 2 and the comments following are from Rubin, *National Bilingualism. . . , 1968.*

(c) Of those having subordinate bilingual ability, the largest proportion (88.8 per cent) had passed only the second, third, or fourth grades.
(d) Of those whose bilingual ability was considered coordinate, the largest proportion (86 per cent) had passed the third grade or more in school.

Table 2. Degree of Proficiency and Number of School Years Completed for 272 Luque Speakers, 10 Years and Older (in Raw Scores)

		School Years Passed							
	None	*1*	*2*	*3*	*4*	*5*	*6*	*7+*	*Total*
Monolingual	3	–	–	–	1^a	–	1^a	3^a	8
Incipient	4	6	2	–	–	–	–	–	12
Subordinate	5	7	5	10	3	1	1	2	34
Coordinate	5	6	25	31	20	31	49	51	218

^{a}Foreigners whose only language was Spanish.

Several observations can be made from Table 2.

(a) The number of monolinguals does not correlate to school grade passed because in Luque five of the eight monolinguals were Spanish speakers.
(b) Of those who were incipient bilinguals, the great majority (83.3 per cent) had either not passed a single grade or had passed only the first grade.
(c) Of those who were classified as subordinate bilinguals, a small majority (64.7 per cent) had passed the first, second, or third grade. It is interesting that a larger majority had passed only the first, second, and third grades than had passed the second, third, and fourth grades (52.9 per cent). This differs from the finding for Itapuamí, where the amount of schooling relates directly to bilingual proficiency.
(d) Of those who were coordinate bilinguals the large percentage (83.4 per cent) had completed three grades or more.
(e) The opportunities for informal exposure to Spanish in Luque are much greater and would tend to make the direct effect of schooling less than in the rural areas, where informal exposure is much less.

It should be noted that other factors do play some part in the acquisition of Spanish proficiency for those whose first language is not Spanish. I found in this study that opportunities to learn Spanish outside the school were sometimes available to rural and urban inhabitants through their jobs and their army service. These opportunities usually occur in adulthood and the amount of Spanish required depends on the particular job or particular post (for example, a man stationed in Asunción would be more likely to learn Spanish than one stationed at an outpost; army officers usually address their men in Guarani).

In Paraguay, a tremendous number of schoolchildren repeat grades several times. In part, of course, such repetition is due to illness, poor attendance, or intellectual deficiency. However, I am convinced that a great part of it results from the student's inability to understand instruction given in Spanish without first having mastered that language. I feel strongly that if greater recognition were given to the student's need to learn Spanish as a foreign language and if more successful language-teaching procedures were followed, the number of grade repetitions would be drastically reduced. To illustrate the extent of this wasteful process of repetition, in Table 3 data collected at a remote rural school are compared with data from two schools in Luque.

Table 3. Rural-Urban Enrollment

Grade	Class Total			% Repeating		
	School 1[a]	School 2[b]	School 3[c]	School 1	School 2	School 3
1	185	210	177	53%	29%	19%
2	150	175	185	61	24	14
3	75	138	129	41	18	9
4	38[d]	140	173	34	19	13
5	20	65	129	20	20	10
6	25	55	89	8	9	0

[a]School 1 in Itakyry (remote rural town).
[b]School 2 in Luque (town close to Asunción). School attracts a great many rural children.
[c]School 3 in Luque (town close to Asunción). Considered to attract the better students in town.
[d]Rural schoolchildren may transfer to town for the fourth grade because many rural schools stop at the third grade.

It should not come as a surprise that Paraguay has not dealt with this problem. The choice of language to be used in a school system and the individual, social, and practical factors to be taken into account have been the subject of several seminars and studies,[1] but the issue is still to be resolved and remains a complex problem. Most educators would probably agree, however, that the child profits from having his first experience in class in his mother tongue, if at all possible.[2] In Paraguay this suggestion

[1]International Seminar on Bilingualism in Education . . . , 1965; UNESCO, *African Languages and English in Education,* 1953; UNESCO, *The Use of Vernacular Languages . . . ,* 1953; John Mac-Namara, 1966; UNESCO, *Foreign Languages . . . ,* 1963; Eugene A. Nida, 1949; Peter Wingard, 1963; John Bowers, 1966; and Robert Le Page, 1966.
[2]Eugene A. Nida, 1949; UNESCO, *The Use of Vernacular Languages . . . ,* 1953; UNESCO, *African Languages and English in Education,* 1953.

has been made repeatedly by the Guarani scholar and educator Hector De-coud. He has long tried to promote the use of Guarani as a medium of in-struction in the schools and has recommended in numerous speeches that the early grades be taught in Guarani and that the later grades be in Spanish. It is my impression that his efforts have not met with much success. Many people in Paraguay use the arguments often cited in the literature about other countries that one of the important goals of the school curriculum, the widening of the intellectual scope of the child, could not be achieved by instruction in Guarani because of its nonintellectual nature. Even those who understand Decoud's reasoning seem to feel it would be expensive and therefore impractical to create Guarani texts for the classroom.

Another solution that has often been suggested in the literature on this subject is to teach the world language (in this case Spanish) as a foreign language before beginning the regular curriculum. Some scholars argue (Bull, 1955; Le Page, 1964) that the social needs of the community should supersede those of the individual and that the teaching of the language of wider communication should begin as soon as possible. This has only re-cently been recognized in Paraguay as a possible solution. Recently the UNESCO office in Paraguay has been trying to teach Spanish as a foreign language in the first grade along with other school subjects. When I visited the program in 1965, however, it seemed to be at an impasse because of the teachers' and supervisors' lack of experience in materials preparation and the methodology of foreign-language teaching.

Summary

I have tried to present some of the educational problems of Paraguay that seem to arise from the language situation in the country. Paraguay is basi-cally a Guarani-speaking nation with a heavy incidence of Spanish-Guarani bilingualism in which each language tends to fulfill distinct functions. The roles of the two languages are such that Spanish is the language of the schools. I have suggested that such educational problems as the high drop-out rate, frequent repetition of grades, and widespread failure to achieve adequate mastery of Spanish could be dealt with more effectively if admin-istrators and teachers would plan curriculum, instructional materials, teach-ing methods, and teacher training in explicit recognition of the fact that a large segment of the population is not bilingual and that many schools, especially in rural areas, must therefore teach the children in Guarani.

References

Anuario estadístico de la República del Paraguay 1948–1953. Asunción: Ministerio de Hacienda, Dirección General de Estadística y Censos, 1955.

Bowers, John. "Language Problems and Literacy," Conference on Language Problems in Developing Nations, November 1–3, 1966.

Bull, William E. "Review of *The Use of Vernacular Languages in Education,*" *International Journal of American Linguistics,* 21 (1955), pp. 288–294.

Cardozo, Efraím. *Historiografía paraguaya.* Mexico: Instituto Panamericano de Geografía e Historia, Comisión de Historia, 1959.

Censo nacional de población y ocupación 1940. Lima, 1942.

Centurión, Juan Crisóstomo. *Memorias del Coronel Juan Crisóstomo Centurión ó sea reminiscencias históricas sobre la guerra del Paraguay.* Buenos Aires: J. A. Berra, 1894.

Decoud, Hector Francisco. *La Convención Nacional Constituyente y La Carta Magna de la República.* Buenos Aires: Talleres Gráficos Argentinos L. J. Rosso, 1934.

Diebold, A. Richard. "Incipient Bilingualism," *Language,* XXXVII (1961), pp. 97–112.

Fernando de Pinedo, Agustín. Unpublished "Informe del Gobernador del Paraguay, Agustín Fernando de Pinedo, al Rey de España sobre la Provincia del Paraguay." Asunción, January 29, 1777. [Published in *Revista del Instituto Paraguayo,* 52 (1905).]

Gandía, Enrique de. *Francisco de Alfaro y la condición social de los indios.* Buenos Aires: El Ateneo, 1939.

Garvin, Paul L., and Madeleine Mathiot. "The Urbanization of the Guarani Language: A Problem in Language and Culture," *in* Anthony F. C. Wallace, ed., *Men and Cultures.* Philadelphia, Pa.: University of Pennsylvania Press, 1960, pp. 783–790.

Gokak, V. K. *English in India: Its Present and Future.* Madras: Asia Publishing House, 1964.

Instrucciones para los maestros de escuelas por la Junta Superior Gubernativa. Asunción, February 15, 1812.

International Seminar on Bilingualism in Education, Aberystwyth, 1960. *Report.* London: H. M. Stationery Office, 1965.

Le Page, Robert B. *The National Language Question.* London: Oxford University Press, 1964.

Le Page, Robert B. "Problems to Be Faced in the Use of English as the Medium of Education in Four West Indian Territories," *in* J. A. Fishman *et al.,* eds., *Language Problems of Developing Nations.* New York: John Wiley, 1968, pp. 431–442.

Lieberson, Stanley. "Language Questions in Censuses," *Sociological Inquiry,* 36 (1966), pp. 262–279.

MacNamara, John. *Bilingualism and Primary Education: A Study of the Irish Experience.* Edinburgh: Edinburgh University Press, 1966.

Nida, Eugene A. "Approaching Reading through the Native Language," *Language Learning,* 2 (1949), pp. 16–20.

Octavo censo general de población, 8 de junio de 1960: Resumen general. Mexico City: Dirección General de Estadística.

Osterberg, Tore. *Bilingualism and the First School Language: An Educational Problem Illustrated by Results from a Swedish Dialect Area.* Umea, 1961.

Peramás, José Manuel. *La República de Platón y los guaranies.* Buenos Aires: Editores Emecé S.A. (first edition, 1791), 1946.

República del Paraguay. *Censo de Población y Vivienda 1962, Asunción.* Asunción: Ministerio de Hacienda, 1965.

Robertson, John P. *La Argentina en la época de la revolución. Cartas sobre el Paraguay:*

Robertson, John P. (Continued)
Comprendiendo la relación de una residencia de cuatro años en esa república, bajo el gobierno del Dictador Francia. Buenos Aires: Administración General Vaccaro, 1920.

Rona, José Pedro. "The Cultural and Social Status of Guarani in Paraguay," *in* William Bright, ed., *Sociolinguistics.* The Hague: Mouton, 1966, pp. 277–293.

Rubin, Joan. *National Bilingualism in Paraguay.* The Hague: Mouton, 1968.

Séptimo censo general de población, 6 de junio de 1950: Resumen. Mexico City: Dirección General de Estadística, 1953.

UNESCO. Educational Clearing House. *African Languages and English in Education.* A report of a meeting of experts on the use in education of African languages in relation to English, where English is the accepted second language, held at Jos, Nigeria, November 1952. Educational Studies and Documents, 11. Paris: 1953.

UNESCO. *The Use of Vernacular Languages in Education.* Monographs on Fundamental Education, 8. Paris: 1953.

UNESCO. *Foreign Languages in Primary Education: The Teaching of Foreign or Second Languages to Younger Children.* International Studies in Education. Paris, 1963.

Wingard, Peter. "Problems of the Media of Instruction in Some Uganda School Classes: A Preliminary Survey," *in* John Spencer, ed., *Language in Africa.* London: The Cambridge University Press, 1963.

National Identity
and the Language Issue
in Puerto Rico

ERWIN H. EPSTEIN

In 1948 Spanish was made the medium of instruction for nonlanguage subjects at all levels of the public school system in Puerto Rico; English became a special subject to be taught in all grades. During the half century prior to that time English had been the predominant language of instruction for at least some grades and/or some nonlanguage subjects.

Until 1948 the public school language program had been a center of conflict. On one side were those who felt that in conformity with the avowed objective of having Puerto Rico become a permanent part of the Union, the way to make the people American was to make them fluent in English. Fluency was to be accomplished simply by exposure to that language in the schools.[1]

The opposing view had several facets. First, it was felt that learning English would not change the attitudes of Puerto Ricans sufficiently to make the people into Americans. Merely learning English, it was argued, would not lead to an internalization of the values and norms of North Americans. Second, the principal objective of providing an adequate education to everyone could be accomplished best through the native language (Spanish) and not through English.[2] Finally, if English were used as the vehicle of

Reproduced, by permission, from *Comparative Education Review,* 11 (June, 1967), pp. 133–143.

[1] Reports of the Chavez Committee, composed of members of the United States Senate who visited Puerto Rico in 1943, express this view. See Robert Herndon Fife and Herschel F. Manuel, *The Teaching of English in Puerto Rico* (San Juan: Department of Education Press, 1951), pp. 37–38.

[2] Although English enjoys the status of an official medium, Spanish is the popular language of the island. Thus, government documents are published ordinarily in both languages; yet court proceedings and legislative debate as well as common street conversation are carried on in Spanish.

Americanization and Puerto Ricans were not to be considered full-fledged Americans until they mastered that language, it might take generations before statehood were realized.

> If the champions of statehood for Puerto Rico realized the tremendous difficulties in the way of giving all the Puerto Ricans a mastery of English comparable to that of the average citizen of the United States, they would shudder at the idea that it is an indispensable prerequisite for the admission of the Island as a State of the Union.[1]

Nationalism in Puerto Rico has long been associated with a popular demand for the use of Spanish as the official language in the schools. Since Spanish is now the official language, it might appear somewhat anomalous that the amount of English taught in the schools should continue to be an issue related to nationalism. In part, the recurrence of nationalistic feeling seems to be a reaction against continued pressure on the schools by the federal government to increase the amount of English being taught.

Federal persistence in trying to get more English in the schools is exhibited in statements like those made in 1956 by Congressman Alfred Sieminski, a member of the House Committee on Appropriations. The congressman's remarks could be construed as a threat to withdraw federal funds to education in order to force an acceleration of the program of English instruction.

> One seems to find little interest in the English language in Puerto Rico though they are United States citizens. . . . They use our money . . . yet . . . the extension of the courtesy of learning our language seems not to be there.[2]

Similarly, Congressman Adam Clayton Powell, chairman of the House Committee on Education and Labor, proposed that an intensive campaign be launched to impress upon all Puerto Ricans that they should feel proud of being citizens of the United States. It was presumed that an intensification of the teaching of English would be an integral part of that campaign.[3]

Although federal efforts to increase English instruction have remained persistent, they have also been ambivalent. However much the federal government wished to see an acceleration of English instruction in Puerto Rico, it seemed resigned to the idea that English is and will continue to be a peripheral language in the schools. Instead of withdrawing aid to force acceleration, Congress in 1959 declared English to be a *foreign* language in Puerto Rico, thereby allowing the availability of increased funds for English instruction under the National Defense Education Act. The action suggests

---

[1] Pedro Cebollero, " A Language Policy for Puerto Rico," *Revista de la Asociación de Maestros de Puerto Rico,* I (August, 1942), p. 20.

[2] *Congressional Record,* February 22, 1956, p. 3416.

[3] Miguel Salas Herrero, "Clayton Powell insta a enseñar más inglés," *El Mundo,* December 12, 1959.

that federal authorities were as committed as ever to using English as a vehicle of Americanization. But it suggests also a recognition that if Puerto Ricans were to be allowed genuine autonomy over matters of government, promotion of Americanization would have to be done far more discreetly than in the past.

The reaction of Puerto Rican nationalists to federal pressures was predictably intense. For example, Nilita Vientós Gastón, an outspoken critic of the existing language policy, charged that the insular Department of Education abetted by federal authorities was not educating Puerto Ricans, but teaching them English with the intention of depriving them of their Puerto Rican character and converting them into Americans.[1]

Such criticism had its effect on the thinking of Puerto Rican school authorities. Before 1948 the school language question centered on the public schools, but the controversy has increasingly come to revolve around the private schools, a number of which continue to teach nonlanguage subjects in English. In 1962 Cándido Oliveras, the secretary of public instruction, threatened to go so far as to withdraw accreditation of those private schools which continued using English as the medium of instruction. This threat contrasts sharply with proposals made by Congressman Powell that the public schools adopt an educational program similar to that employed by the parochial schools insofar as the latter use English as a major medium of instruction.[2]

The response of congressional leaders to the secretary's announcement was heated. Among the most pointed remarks were those of Congressman James Roosevelt.

> As long as Puerto Rico retains close ties with the United States through its Commonwealth status, and does not seek independence, I would certainly think it to be in the island's best interest to encourage rather than discourage the use of English.
>
> I am the first to recognize a desire for noninterference in Puerto Rico's internal affairs, and to avoid Federal control of education anywhere. But in this case I feel that Puerto Rico is about to embark on a path that will needlessly handicap its own citizens and drive completely the wedge of a language barrier between our peoples.[3]

It seems clear that the *batalla del idioma* has not yet subsided. Language policies continue to be influenced by partisans with purposes not entirely

---

[1] Nilita Vientós Gastón, "Otra vez el bilingüismo," *Revista del Instituto de Cultura Puertorriqueña*, 16 (July–September, 1962), pp. 9–10. For an idea of the effect that reaction against placing high priority on English had on the thinking of education authorities in Puerto Rico, see René Marqués, "Idioma, política y pedagogía," *El Mundo*, August 16, 1960.

[2] Salas Herrero, "Clayton Powell insta . . . ."

[3] *Congressional Record*, July 11, 1962, p. 13175.

pedagogical.[1] In large part these purposes derive from Puerto Rico's uncertain and highly controversial status. The Commonwealth arrangement places English in a state of limbo; it is suspect to those who stress the distinctiveness of Puerto Rican culture and view independence as the only just condition, and it is extolled by those who advocate assimilation with the United States. An uncertain political status places Puerto Rican educators in a difficult position. Supporting increased English instruction leaves them open to nationalist accusations that they follow a policy of assimilative colonialism. Limiting English further in the schools draws charges that Puerto Rican education does not go far enough to promote Americanism.

Thus, as long as the status of the island remains indefinite, it seems likely that educational policy with regard to the second language will continue to swing between two political poles. It is notable that no language policy has been safe from bitter criticism. Before 1948 almost every conceivable suggestion as to the amount of English in the schools was experimented with.[2] And even the relegation of that language to a limited subject area in the public schools did not end the controversy. Rather, the action served merely to transfer attention to the private schools.

The threat by Secretary Oliveras to withdraw accreditation from some private schools was calculated not merely as a temporary gesture to appease nationalists. It was an acknowledgment of the increasing importance of private schools in the total educational scene. In 1945–1946, enrollment in these schools constituted 4.1 per cent of the total student population; this proportion grew to 5.2 per cent in 1950–1951 and to 8.4 per cent in 1959–1960.[3] It is estimated that by 1975 the proportion will have grown to 16 per cent,[4] and predictions have run as high as an eventual 25 per cent.[5] In the San Juan metropolitan area the proportion of secondary school students in private schools is already approximately one-third.[6]

Increasing private school enrollments tend to compound the fear of some Puerto Ricans that extensive social and cultural gaps are being created in a traditionally homogeneous society. There is apprehension that the selective accessibility to and the greater amount of English instruction in the private

---

[1] For expressions of impatience with what appear to be political solutions to educational questions of language, see El Mundo, "La enseñanza del inglés," December 30, 1963.

[2] See Juan José Osuna, A History of Education in Puerto Rico (Río Piedras: University of Puerto Rico, 1949), pp. 311–342 and 377–381.

[3] Estudio del sistema educativo, Report of the Consejo Superior de Enseñanza to the Commission of Instruction of the Puerto Rican House of Representatives (Río Piedras: University of Puerto Rico, 1960), p. 334.

[4] Ibid.

[5] Robert Heifetz, "Manpower Planning: A Case Study from Puerto Rico," Comparative Education Review, VIII (June, 1964), p. 33.

[6] Beresford Hayward, "The Future of Education in Puerto Rico—Its Planning," Documento XIII, Ciclo de conferencias sobre el sistema educativo de Puerto Rico. Department of Public Instruction, Hato Rey, Puerto Rico, October 6, 1961, pp. 15–16.

schools may contribute to invidious social distinctions between the public and private educational sectors.[1] Considering the ideological implications of the school language issue, the rapidly growing enrollments in the private schools, and the fear of social dislocations arising from qualitative distinctions between public and private schools, it was almost inevitable that a concern with English instruction would shift from the public to the private sector.

In admonishing private school authorities against emphasizing English as a teaching medium, nationalists have assumed that instruction in that language tends to de-Latinize and, more specifically, deinsularize Puerto Ricans. It is assumed, in other words, that teaching more English results in learning less Spanish and, simultaneously, in Puerto Ricans losing their cultural identity. In point of fact, this view is not too dissimilar from that of the advocates of assimilation. The differences are in emphasis; the assimilationists stress the need for Americanization while treading lightly on the question of culture loss. There is a feeling generally that learning English has an appreciable effect on prevailing values and on the indigenous language. According to the general supervisor of the English Section of the Puerto Rican Department of Public Instruction,

> . . . there is room for considerable improvement in public attitudes toward the teaching of English. I would like to mention two attitudes in particular that exert a negative influence. The first is the attitude that the learning of English on the part of Puerto Rican pupils adversely affects their learning of Spanish. . . . The second is the attitude that the use of English in Puerto Rico detracts from the importance of Spanish and represents a rejection of Puerto Rican values.[2]

These assumptions as to the effects of intensive English instruction will now be examined in view of some comparative findings for the public and private schools.

Achievement in Spanish:
A Comparison of Public and Private School Pupils

In 1959 achievement tests in various subjects were administered by the Consejo Superior de Enseñanza of Puerto Rico to a sample of schoolchildren at several grade levels in both public and private schools. With regard to Spanish achievement, results for the twelfth grade were available for three types of schools: (a) urban public, (b) private, using Spanish as the major medium of instruction, and (c) private, using English as the primary instructional medium.[3]

---

[1] See Robert W. Anderson, *Party Politics in Puerto Rico* (Stanford, Calif.: Stanford University Press, 1965), p. 11.

[2] Adrian L. Hull, "The 'English Problem'," *San Juan Review,* II (June, 1965), p. 58.

[3] Consejo Superior de Enseñanza, *Estudio del sistema educativo,* pp. 254–255.

The test of Spanish achievement was broken down into several parts, including reading comprehension, grammar, vocabulary, and verbal reasoning. Table 1 shows the results of the test by type of school for each of these parts.

Table 1. Mean Scores on Spanish Achievement Test
for the Twelfth Grade, by School Type

School Type	Reading Comprehension	Grammar	Vocabulary	Verbal Reasoning
Public urban	32.3[a]	38.2[b]	18.0[c]	12.4[d]
Private in which instruction is in Spanish	41.2	46.1	above 18.0[e]	15.3
Private in which instruction is in English	40.2	46.1	18.0	13.8

Source: *Estudio del sistema educativo,* Report of the Consejo Superior de Enseñanza to the Commission of Instruction of the Puerto Rican House of Representatives (Río Piedras: University of Puerto Rico, 1960), pp. 260–263.
[a]Highest possible total score was 58. [b]Highest possible total score was 60. [c]Highest possible total score was 25. [d]Highest possible total score was 20. [e]No specific score given.

The figures in Table 1 indicate that twelfth-grade pupils from private schools in which English is used as the medium of instruction score higher on the average than twelfth-grade pupils in public schools (in which Spanish is the language of instruction) in three out of four areas of Spanish achievement. On the other hand, pupils from private schools in which Spanish is the language of instruction scored consistently higher in all areas of Spanish achievement than pupils from the other two types of schools.

Of course, factors other than media and quality of instruction are bound to affect achievement scores. It is presumed that pupils in the private schools come from homes where the conditions for learning are more favorable than conditions found in the homes of their public school age mates. Indeed, studies have indicated that the socioeconomic level of children attending private schools is appreciably higher than the level of pupils in the public schools.[1] The private school children are more likely to come from stable homes where both parents are present, where the parents have reached a higher level of education and participate to a larger extent in social and cultural activities, and where reading materials are easily accessible.[2] Under these circumstances, we would expect achievement by private school pupils to be generally higher than that by public school pupils. That children in private schools whose instruction is in English should also excel in Spanish, however, is not so expected. It is significant that public school youngsters,

[1]It is estimated that less than 10 per cent of the public school students reach the median socioeconomic level of the private school pupils. *Ibid.,* pp. 335–337, 1602–1603 and 1875–1878.
[2]*Ibid.*

whose instruction is in Spanish, have no superiority in that language over their predominantly English-taught private school peers.

Let us now examine the assumption that greater exposure to English leads to a lesser identification with Puerto Rican culture. The assumption may be examined by assessing reactions to the impact of learning English on national identity. Do proportionately more private school youngsters, as a result of usually having a greater exposure to English than their public school age mates, wish to become Americanized at the expense of their traditional Hispanic heritage? Do private school children more often than public school pupils view English as instrumental in making them more American and less Latin? Do proportionately more private school pupils than public school children desire an increase of English in the schools?

Learning English and Feelings of National Identity
PROCEDURE

To assess attitudes with regard to learning English and identifying with the national culture, a sample survey of ninth-grade public school children and of ninth-grade private school (Catholic) pupils was taken. The public school sample was acquired by separating all public schools having the ninth grade into three geographical strata—the San Juan metropolitan area, other urban areas (having over 2,500 inhabitants), and rural areas. The latter stratum consisted of 10,037 pupils, while 26,395 pupils were divided fairly evenly among the San Juan metropolitan and other urban areas.[1] A random sample of seven intermediate schools (those containing the ninth grade) was then selected from each stratum so that 21 public schools participated. One ninth-grade classroom was then selected at random from each of the 21 schools.[2] These 21 classes contained a total of 703 students.

As for obtaining a sample of ninth-grade private school students, because of the difficulty imposed by the various types of private schools (many of which act as almost completely independent systems), only the Roman Catholic among the private schools were chosen to participate in the survey. The drawback in this choice is clear. The Protestant and lay schools operate under very distinct philosophies, and the education they provide may have an effect different from that of the parochial schools. Nevertheless, the Catholic schools constitute somewhat more than half of all private schools, tend to select students from the same sectors of the

---

[1] Department of Education, *Report on Enrollment and Personnel at the End of the Sixth School Month, 1963-64*, Hato Rey, Puerto Rico, p. 45.

[2] Admittedly, a more representative sample would have been obtained by means of a selection from the population of ninth-grade classrooms rather than from schools having the ninth grade. However, this was impossible because a listing of such classrooms in general or by school did not exist, thus necessitating choosing the school prior to finding out the number of ninth-grade classes it contained.

population, and are generally believed to provide the same kind of high-quality instruction, including English instruction, as do the other private schools.[1] In other words, Catholic parochial schools, like other private schools, are very often schools for the elite. Hence, although a sampling of Catholic schools cannot be considered wholly representative, the findings should be fairly suggestive for all private schools.

Since there is, for all practical purposes, an absence of parochial ninth grades in the rural areas, the Catholic schools were placed in two strata: (a) the San Juan metropolitan area and (b) other urban areas. A random sample of six schools having the ninth grade was taken; from each, one ninth-grade class was selected randomly.[2] The sample of parochial schools drew 196 pupils from a total Catholic school ninth-grade student population of 3,804,[3] bringing the combined student samples to 899.

Reactions of schoolchildren were acquired by means of a questionnaire. Pupils responded to questions which were in Spanish and predominantly of the closed-ended type.[4]

RESULTS

The findings suggest that Catholic school pupils put more effort into and have a greater desire to learn English and they identify more strongly with that language than do public school pupils. For example, Catholic school pupils displayed a greater determination to use English after finishing school and had a stronger desire to read materials in English. They more frequently studied and made use of English and exhibited a greater desire to have, when they are grown, their own children speak that language.[5] However, the findings do not suggest that proportionately more Catholic school pupils than public school pupils wish to become more American and less Latin or that more of them regard English as a vehicle of Americanization.

When asked to respond to the probable effect on one's nationality of learning English, proportionately *fewer* Catholic school pupils felt that

---

[1]Consejo Superior de Enseñanza, *Estudio del sistema educativo*, pp. 1860–1861 *passim*.

[2]Whereas the public schools work under a 6–3–3 plan, most Catholic schools have adopted an 8–4 system. Thus, the ninth grade is found in the intermediate schools for the public sector and usually in the high schools for the Catholic sector.

[3]Department of Education, *Report on Enrollment . . .* , p. 60.

[4]For more detailed information on the sampling technique and schedules, see Erwin H. Epstein, *Value Orientation and the English Language in Puerto Rico: Attitudes toward Second-Language Learning among Ninth-Grade Pupils and Their Parents,* U.S. Office of Education, Project Number S-214, March 1966, Appendix A.

[5]*Ibid.,* pp. 188–201. Scores on English achievement tests indicate that private school pupils achieve significantly higher than do their public school peers. In tests administered by the Consejo Superior de Enseñanza of Puerto Rico, ninth-grade pupils from private schools teaching in English had a mean score of 87 (out of a maximum of 91) and those from private schools using Spanish had a mean score of 71, while urban public school ninth-grade pupils had a mean score of 55. See Consejo Superior de Enseñanza, *Estudio del sistema educativo,* pp. 252–264, and cf. Fife and Manuel, *The Teaching of English . . .* , pp. 237–238.

learning English would make them more American and less Latin or Puerto Rican. Exactly half the Catholic school pupils, in contrast to only 35 per cent of the public school students, thought that learning English would make them neither more nor less Latin American, North American, or Puerto Rican (Table 2). As for a desire to become more Americanized, the findings suggest, if anything, that fewer Catholic school than public school pupils are enthusiastic about the prospects of cultural change. The proportion of public school pupils who felt it was important for Puerto Rico to become more Americanized was twice that of Catholic school pupils (Table 3). In addition, it is noteworthy that proportionately more public school

Table 2. Effect of Learning English on Nationality,
by Public and Catholic School Pupils

Respondents	Response (%)[a]					Total	
	1	2	3	4	5	%	n
Public school pupils	13	12	25	15	35	100	(698)
Catholic school pupils	3	5	33	9	50	100	(196)

[a] I think that learning English would make me: (1) less Puerto Rican and more American; (2) less Latin and more American; (3) more American but not necessarily less Puerto Rican; (4) more Puerto Rican, more American, and less Latin; (5) neither more nor less Latin, American, or Puerto Rican.

Table 3. Desire for Cultural Change,
by Public and Catholic School Pupils

Respondents	Response (%)[a]					Total	
	1	2	3	4	5	%	n
Public school pupils	26	8	7	33	26	100	(697)
Catholic school pupils	12	5	5	52	26	100	(196)

[a] I think that it is: (1) important for Puerto Rico to become more Americanized; (2) inevitable that Puerto Rico become more Americanized regardless of whether or not it preserves its Hispanic heritage; (3) neither important for Puerto Rico to preserve its Hispanic heritage nor to become more Americanized; (4) important for Puerto Rico to conserve some of its Hispanic heritage while becoming more Americanized; (5) important for Puerto Rico to preserve its Hispanic heritage.

Table 4. Desire to Change Amount of English in School,
by Public and Catholic School Pupils

Respondents	Response (%)			Total	
	Desire for More English	Desire to Maintain Present Amount	Desire for Less English	%	n
Public school pupils	59	33	8	100	(698)
Catholic school pupils	46	48	6	100	(196)

pupils displayed a desire for having increased the amount of English taught in school (Table 4). This suggests that the greater amount of English in the Catholic schools may be more sufficient for satisfying a demand by pupils generally for that language.

Summary and Conclusion

From the beginning of American occupation in 1898, the issue of how much English to teach in the schools of Puerto Rico has plagued educators and politicians alike. For a long period, English was used often and in many ways to teach nonlanguage subjects. To both nationalists and advocates of statehood, English in the schools has been viewed as a powerful vehicle for transplanting the norms and values of North Americans to the island. To nationalists, however, instruction in that language has represented a deliberate attempt to deprive Puerto Ricans of their own national character.

With the extension of considerable political autonomy to Puerto Rico after World War II, English was excluded as a language of instruction for nonlanguage subjects in the public schools. This served to placate somewhat many Puerto Ricans who resented having to conform to federal pressures for intensive English instruction. It did not, however, resolve the issue completely. Instead, much of the attention given to the teaching of English has moved from the public to the private schools. A considerable growth in enrollments in private schools and the increasing social prestige associated with them has caused alarm among some persons with nationalist sentiments; these schools are seen as promoting social dislocations and de-Latinizing Puerto Ricans. The greater use of English in private education is viewed often as an insidious attempt to convert Puerto Ricans into Americans.

The indictment against the private schools presumes that extensive English instruction leads to a decline in the learning of Spanish and a fostering of attitudes which are incompatible with a strong insular cultural identity. Empirical evidence, however, indicates that these presumptions are highly questionable. Results of a study conducted by the Consejo Superior de Enseñanza of Puerto Rico suggest that pupils from private schools in which English is the primary language of instruction achieve appreciably higher in Spanish than pupils in public schools (where Spanish is the medium of instruction). Nevertheless, of all the groups tested, pupils from private schools in which Spanish is the major language of instruction achieved the highest grades in that language.

In addition, other findings suggest that Catholic school pupils, who are believed to resemble pupils of most other private schools in social position and in exposure to high-quality instruction (including English instruction), do not identify less with Latin or Puerto Rican culture nor do they more strongly view English as a vehicle of Americanization.

Functional Literacy
among Colombian Peasants

EVERETT M. ROGERS
WILLIAM HERZOG

> *Mass illiteracy is India's sin and shame and must be liquidated. But the literacy campaign must not end with a knowledge of the alphabet. It must go hand in hand with the spread of useful knowledge.*
>
> Mohandas Karamchand Gandhi

In spite of the widespread consensus that literacy is a key to national development, there are relatively few studies[1] in which the literacy rate of a nation is used as an explanatory variable in economic development and almost no investigations of individual literacy in relation to other variables.[2]

Reproduced, by permission, from *Economic Development and Cultural Change,* 14 (January, 1966), pp. 190-203.

The authors are teaching at Michigan State University.

Thanks are expressed to the following organizations for their financial and logistic help in conducting the present investigation: Programa Interamericano de Información Popular (PIIP), San José; Agricultural Development Council, New York; Fulbright Commission of Colombia, Bogotá; and Computer Center, Michigan State University. Special acknowledgment is made to Fred B. Waisanen, Research Director of PIIP, who suggested the measure of functional literacy utilized in the present investigation. Thanks are also due to Dr. Bradley Greenberg, Michigan State University, for his instructive comments on a previous version of this article. [E.R., W.H.]

[1] Among these studies are those of Daniel Lerner, *The Passing of Traditional Society: Modernizing the Middle East* (New York: Free Press, 1958); Hilda Hertz Golden, "Literacy and Social Change in Underdeveloped Countries," *Rural Sociology,* XX, no. 1 (March, 1955), pp. 1-7; Phillips Cutright, "National Political Development: Measurement and Analysis," *American Sociological Review,* XXVIII, no. 2 (April, 1963), pp. 153-164; Seymour Martin Lipset, *Political Man: The Social Bases of Politics* (Garden City, N.Y.: Doubleday, 1960); Dick Simpson, "The Congruence of the Political, Social and Economic Aspects of Development," *International Development Review,* VI, no. 2 (June, 1964), pp. 21-25; Arthur S. Banks and Robert Textor, *A Cross-Polity Survey* (Cambridge, Mass., MIT Press, 1963); Gabriel A. Almond and James Coleman, *The Politics of the Developing Areas* (Princeton, N.J.: Princeton University Press, 1960); and Theodore Caplow and Kurt Finsterbusch, "A Matrix of Modernization," paper presented at the American Sociological Association, Montreal, 1964.

[2] Lerner, *Passing of Traditional Society . . . ;* Daniel Lerner, "Literacy and Initiative in Village Development," *in* MIT Center for International Studies, *Rural Development Research Report* (Cambridge, Mass., 1964); Paul J. Deutschmann, "The Mass Media in an Underdeveloped Village," *Journalism Quarterly,* XL, no. 1 (Winter, 1963), pp. 27-35.

Many publications are available on *how to teach* literacy, but there is a dearth of reported research on *how to measure* literacy, its consequences, and its antecedents.

The main objectives of the present study are: (a) to examine the conceptual nature of literacy, (b) to report the use of a measure of functional literacy, and (c) to determine the correlates of functional literacy among Colombian peasants.

Data Gathering

Data related to individual levels of literacy were collected from Colombian peasants as part of a larger study carried out in five villages in the Andes mountains. A number of other reports provide greater detail on the differential characteristics of the villages.[1] Three of the communities are located in central Colombia, about an hour's drive from Bogotá, and are relatively modern in their norms; the other two, situated near the Ecuadoran border in southwestern Colombia, are relatively more traditional. All of the study sites are characterized by extremely small farms operated by subsistence farmers of mixed Indian-Spanish stock, with relatively low levels of education, low mass-media exposure, and limited economic opportunities.

Advanced students in sociology at the National University of Colombia, all of whom had had previous interviewing experience, carried out the personal interviewing in 1963–1964. A virtual census was obtained of farm operators in the five villages; 88.2 per cent of the eligible respondents were successfully interviewed. The number of farmers interviewed in each village was Pueblo Viejo, 67; San Rafael, 36; Cuatro Esquinas, 57; Nazate, 41; and La Cañada, 54 (for a total of 255 interviews).

Important differences in the attitudes and characteristics of the respondents were found which generally support the contention, based on observation, that the three central Colombian communities were quite different in norms on social change from the two southwestern Colombian communities. Most important among these differences, in terms of the present investigation, are the rates of functional literacy in the villages. For the three modern villages the rates are 27 per cent, 39 per cent, and 51 per cent for Pueblo Viejo, San Rafael, and Cuatro Esquinas, respectively. Functional literacy rates are 24 per cent and 15 per cent in the two more traditional villages.

Literacy as a Concept

Although there is little empirical research into the psychological and attitudinal changes that accompany the acquisition of the ability to read and

---

[1] Everett M. Rogers and Ralph E. Neill, *Achievement Motivation among Colombia Farmers* (East Lansing, Mich.: Michigan State University, Department of Communication, 1965); and Everett M. Rogers and Johannes C. van Es, *Opinion Leadership in Traditional and Modern Colombian Peasant Communities* (East Lansing: Michigan State University, Department of Communication, 1964).

write, speculations from quite diverse sources suggest it represents more than just a skill. Lerner, in describing his theory of modernization, stated: "Literacy is indeed the basic personal skill that underlies the whole modernizing sequence. . . . The very act of achieving distance and control over a formal language gives people access to the world of vicarious experience."[1]

Carothers,[2] a psychiatrist who studied African tribals, suggested that the spoken word has a special "magical power" for the preliterate. The ear is the principal sense-receiving organ. What is heard and what is said is more important than what is seen. The effect of literacy in such a society is to reduce the "power of the word." To see the word in written form reduces it to a passive state and physically separates symbol from referent. "By and large, however, it is clearly far more easy for words, when written, to be seen for what they are—symbols, without existence in their own right."[3]

McLuhan, building on Carothers' work, claimed that when use of one of the senses predominates, the others tend to be anesthetized. He cites hypnotism, and "audiac," the use of induced noise by dentists to remove tactility. Preliterate man is sensually anesthetized by the "intense stress on auditory organization of all experience."[4] According to McLuhan, the introduction of any new technology which brings with it a change of input to any of the senses produces an alteration of the ratio among all the senses. The introduction of literacy increases the visual input and comparatively lowers the amount of audio input producing such an alteration. This alteration of sense input serves to break the anesthetizing effect of the previously aural-dominant state.

Few empirical data are yet available to substantiate the notions of Carothers and McLuhan, nor are we provided by them with a clear definition of literacy as a concept. However, support is lent to the position that literacy is more than just a mechanical ability to read and write. Furthermore, literacy is underscored as a crucial element in the modernization process. We view this relationship as one of interdependence: literacy is necessary for modernization, but modernization, as it develops, also impels literacy forward. Thus, the arrows of relationship are mutual and reciprocal.

Literacy ⇄ Modernization

It seems clear that more research is needed on the meaning of literacy before a precise statement of its conceptual nature can be made, but that it is indeed a concept.

---

[1] Daniel Lerner, "Toward a Communication Theory of Modernization," *in* Lucian W. Pye, ed., *Communications and Political Development* (Princeton, N.J.: Princeton University Press, 1963), p. 341.

[2] J. C. Carothers, "Culture, Psychiatry, and the Written Word," *Psychiatry,* XXII, no. 4 (November, 1959), pp. 307–320.

[3] *Ibid.,* p. 311.

[4] Marshall McLuhan, *The Gutenberg Galaxy* (Toronto: University of Toronto Press, 1962), p. 24.

Measuring Literacy

One of the basic problems encountered by those concerned with the problem of illiteracy on a global scale is the lack of uniformity in the measurement of literacy. First, there is wide disparity in the age groups included in national rates of literacy. Indonesia, for example, calculates its literacy rate for persons between 13 and 45 years of age. Cuba and Malaya report literacy rates for 10 years of age and over, while Bulgaria considers people over 15 years of age.[1]

Second, a variety of competence in reading and writing is assumed by the various definitions of literacy. In the United States census, literacy is defined as having completed six grades of schooling. In the Colombia census, however, literacy is defined as people who say they can write their name. In some other national censuses, individuals are asked if they are able to read a newspaper and write a letter. UNESCO[2] reports two definitions offered by committees convened on this problem. In 1951 an Expert Committee on the Standardization of Educational Statistics suggested: "A person is literate who can with understanding both read and write a short, simple statement on his everyday life."

A Meeting of Experts on Literacy convened by UNESCO in 1962 went somewhat beyond the earlier definition to propose that:

> A person is literate when he has acquired the essential knowledge and skills which enable him to engage in all those activities in which literacy is required for effective functioning in his group and community, and whose attainments in reading, writing and arithmetic make it possible for him to continue to use these skills toward his own and the community's development and for active participation in the life of his country.
>
> In quantitative terms, the standard of attainment in functional literacy may be equated to the skills of reading, writing and arithmetic achieved after a set number of years of primary or elementary schooling.

The usual census-type, self-defined measures of literacy depend on both the honesty of the respondent and on his ability to accurately assess his own competence in reading and writing. In situations where individuals are more likely to be aware that it is not socially acceptable to be illiterate (such as in urban areas) or where they have little opportunity to utilize their once-possessed ability to read and write (as in peasant communities), self-defined literacy is likely to be relatively less accurate.

The present study, realizing the weaknesses of the self-defined literacy measures, is mainly concerned with *functional literacy,* defined as the ability to read and write adequately for carrying out the functions of the individual's role in his salient social system. This definition implies that: (a) literacy

---

[1] *World Campaign for Universal Literacy* (New York: United Nations Economic and Social Council, Document E/3771, 1963).
[2] *Ibid.,* p. 39.

is a process, i.e., it should be regarded as a continuous variable (although for some analytic purposes it is useful to treat it dichotomously); (b) functional literacy is different for different roles, i.e., the peasant in rural Colombia can probably function adequately with a lesser ability to read and write than his urban compatriot; and (c) the requirements of functional literacy change as the individual changes, i.e., if the peasant migrates to the city, then his level of literacy must rise in order for him to function with the same comparative efficiency in his urban role as he did in the rural social system.

A number of studies have attempted to secure an empirical measure of functional literacy. Goldsen and Ralis[1] asked respondents if they could write a letter. Those who responded affirmatively were then asked to demonstrate their ability by writing something on the interview schedule. Spector and others[2] developed an ingenious means of measuring functional literacy among their Ecuadoran respondents. At the close of each interview, the subject was asked if he was able to read a card which stated (in Spanish): "This concludes the interview; many thanks for your cooperation." De Young and Hunt[3] measured functional literacy among Filipino villagers by asking them, in the course of personal interviews, to read a short written selection and then answer prepared questions about it.

The present study employed a measure of functional literacy originally developed by Professor Fred Waisanen and his associates in the Programa Interamericano de Información Popular for use in a 1963 study in Guatemala and Costa Rica, and since used in Mexico, Chile, and India. A Spanish sentence was developed around six words of varying difficulty.[4] The sentence, printed on a card, was handed to the respondent in the course of the interview. His functional literacy score was the number of words which he was able to read.[5] In the present article, the measure is used mainly as a

---

[1] Rose K. Goldsen and Max Ralis, *Factors Related to Acceptance of Innovations in Bang Chan, Thailand* (Ithaca, N.Y.: Cornell University, Department of Far Eastern Studies Data Paper 25, 1957).

[2] Paul Spector *et al., Communication and Motivation in Community Development: An Experiment* (Washington: Institute for International Services, 1963).

[3] John E. de Young and Chester L. Hunt, "Communication Channels and Functional Literacy in the Philippino Barrio," in Socorro C. Espiritu and Chester L. Hunt, eds., *Social Foundations of Community Development* (Manila: R. M. Garcia Publishing House, 1964); also in the *Journal of Asian Studies*, XXII, no. 1 (November, 1962), pp. 67-77.

[4] "El *hombre movió* su *mano rapidamente* en un *ademán* de *respeto*" (The man moved his hand rapidly in a gesture of respect). A Guttman scale analysis of the measure indicated a concentration of the error-free responses at the extremes of (a) all words answered correctly (N = 74), and (b) all words answered incorrectly (N = 124). The coefficient of reproducibility is 95.5 per cent.

A detailed discussion of the development of this functional literacy measure and its correlates is Alfredo Mendez D. and F. B. Waisanen, "Some Correlates of Functional Literacy," presented at the Ninth Congress of the Inter-American Society of Psychologists, Miami, 1964.

[5] Just recently, the authors have learned of an admirably ingenious measure of functional literacy developed by Joseph Ascroft, technical manager of Marco Surveys, Nairobi, Kenya. The respondent is handed a card *upside down*, containing a short question. If he indicates that he "knows

continuous variable in order to utilize the (rather small) degree of sensitivity present, rather than as a dichotomy of functional literates and illiterates. When used as a dichotomous classification, functional literates are regarded as those who read all six words correctly.

Our results with this measure of functional literacy are encouraging but suggest need for improvement. The improved measure should be lengthened to provide greater reliability and sensitivity. Ideally, it should be based on an up-to-date Spanish word list compiled from Latin American sources. It should also be pretested in a number of Spanish-speaking countries with both urban and rural respondents to determine the breadth of its applicability.

To what extent is a respondent's self-defined literacy ability related to an objective test of that ability? Some indication of this relationship is provided by the data in Table 1, in which functional literacy scores are cross-tabulated with self-defined ability to read a newspaper. The close congruity[1] of these two measures of literacy (functional and self-defined) provides some evidence that the census type of literacy measure (self-defined) may be fairly accurate, at least in some rural areas in developing societies. Perhaps this relationship would be lower where respondents were more aware that it is not socially acceptable to be illiterate, as in more-urban and less-isolated areas. Nevertheless, 12 per cent of those who could not read one word correctly said they were able to read a newspaper, and 5 per cent of the peasants who read the entire sentence correctly said they could not read a paper.

Table 1. Relationship of Self-Defined Ability to Read a Newspaper
to Functional Literacy Scores

	Scores on Functional Literacy Measure (%)		
Self-Defined Ability to Read a Newspaper	No Words Correct (N = 117)	1-5 Words Correct (N = 63)	All 6 Words Correct (N = 75)
Able (literate)	12	81	95
Not able (illiterate)	88	19	5
Total	100	100	100

According to UNESCO standards, a minimum of four years of schooling is required to reach a level of functional literacy that can be maintained under average conditions for typical individuals. In a study of Turkish villagers,

which side is up" by turning the card, the respondent thus categorizes himself in a certain higher level of nonliteracy than if he does not turn the card. Then, a further degree of functional literacy is indicated by the respondent if he is able to read and respond to the question.

[1] Generally similar evidence was provided by de Young and Hunt, "Communication Channels and Functional Literacy . . . ," who found that 80.8 per cent of 2,688 Filipino villagers who claim to be literate could read.

Lerner[1] found that only about half (14 per cent of all respondents) of the respondents who *said* they could write a letter (29 per cent of all respondents) had completed four years of schooling. Hence, only about half of the self-defined literates were probably functionally literate in terms of the UNESCO standard.

Table 2 gives correlations between functional literacy measures and self-defined ability to write a letter, self-defined ability to read a newspaper, and years of formal education. Table 3 shows the relationship between years of schooling and rates of functional literacy for respondents in the percentage study. Only one of the respondents with a functional literacy score of zero had more than four years of education. However, numerous respondents with all six words correct had less than four years of formal schooling. Evidently, functional literacy can be learned and maintained by those with less than the UNESCO standard of four years of education.

Table 2. Correlates of Functional Literacy in Five Colombian Communities

Correlates of Functional Literacy Scores with:	Pueblo Viejo	San Rafael	Cuatro Esquinas	Nazate	La Cañada
1. Ability to write a letter	.746*	.782*	.658*	.683*	.648*
2. Ability to read a newspaper†	.809*	.782*	.734*	.756*	.666*
3. Years of formal education	.540*	.661*	.467*	.687*	.625*

*Significantly different from zero at the 1 per cent level of probability.

†The two self-defined measures of literacy, ability to write a letter and ability to read a newspaper, are highly interrelated. Intercorrelations are .835, 1.000, .919, .900, and .819, respectively, for the five communities. All of these five correlations are significantly different from zero at the 1 per cent level of probability.

Table 3. Relationship of Functional Literacy to Years of Formal Education in Five Colombian Communities

Scores on Functional Literacy Measure	Years of Formal Education* Received by Farmers (%)							
	0	1	2	3	4	5	6	7 or more
No words correct	88	28	29	24	14	0	0	11
1–5 words correct	4	48	31	21	43	38	33	0
All 6 words correct	7	24	40	56	43	62	67	89
Total	99†	100	100	101†	100	100	100	100
N =	95	46	42	33	14	13	3	9

*The dotted line dividing the table shows the level of formal education.

†These columns do not total 100 per cent due to rounding off.

---

[1] Lerner, "Literacy and Initiative . . . ."

Correlates of Literacy

If literacy acts as a key variable in the modernization process, we would expect it to be related to such variables as higher mass-media exposure, greater empathy, and more innovativeness in adopting new ideas.

MASS-MEDIA EXPOSURE

Lerner[1] found that literate Turkish villagers had much higher mass-media exposure (to radio, newspapers, and film) than illiterates. Deutschmann[2] reported similar findings in one Colombian village for radio, newspaper, movies, and books. Similar findings have been reported for Pakistan, where Rahim[3] found that literates utilized more mass-media sources than illiterates.

Lerner[4] found that for 73 self-governing countries, literacy correlated .75 with daily newspaper circulation per 1,000 population, .61 with cinema seating capacity per 1,000 population, and .82 with a composite mass-media index. He found literacy and mass-media exposure were also related at the individual level in the six Middle East countries that he studied.

A UNESCO[5] correlational analysis of mass-media consumption per capita for underdeveloped countries in Africa, Latin America, the Middle East, and South East Asia, with populations of at least 500,000, using data for the period 1957–1959, disclosed generally similar correlations with literacy (measured as the percentage of the adult population able to read and write).

All of these previous studies suffered from a similar inadequacy: a measure of functional literacy was not utilized. The present results are shown in Table 4. The highest relationships are between functional literacy and total mass-media exposure scores,[6] newspaper readership, radio listening, and magazine readership. Literacy is generally more highly related to print media exposure than to nonprint media exposure. However, support is also provided for the "centripetal effect" hypothesis:[7] literacy is related to radio exposure (although less so to TV and movie exposure), even though literacy is not necessary for exposure to nonprint media.

There are two possible reasons why the correlations (Table 4) between functional literacy and printed mass-media exposure (newspapers and magazines) are not higher. The more obvious reason might be that the *literates*

---

[1] *Ibid.*

[2] Deutschmann, "Mass Media in an Underdeveloped Society . . . ."

[3] S. A. Rahim, *Diffusion and Adoption of Agricultural Practices: A Study of Patterns of Communication, Diffusion and Adoption of Improved Agricultural Practices in a Village in East Pakistan* (Comilla: Pakistan Academy for Village Development, 1961).

[4] Lerner, "Toward a Communication Theory . . . ."

[5] *Mass Media in the Developing Countries: A UNESCO Report to the United Nations* (Paris: UNESCO, 1961), p. 17.

[6] Sten scores for radio, newspapers, magazines, movies, and TV exposure were computed separately for each community. These were summed for each individual to provide a total mass-media exposure score. Thus, each individual's score is relative to those of others in his own community.

[7] A clear statement of this hypothesis may be found in Lerner, "Literacy and Initiative . . . ."

Table 4. Relationship of Functional Literacy to Mass-Media Exposure
in Five Colombian Communities

Correlates of Functional Literacy	Correlations with Functional Literacy				
	Pueblo Viejo	San Rafael	Cuatro Esquinas	Nazate	La Cañada
1. Mass-media exposure index	.374*	.559*	.355*	.439*	.421*
2. Number of radio shows listened to in past week	.370*	.398†	.335†	.142	.388*
3. Number of newspapers read (or read to) in past week	.365*	.616*	.360*	.476*	.396*
4. Number of magazines read (or read to) in past month	.138	.562*	–.104	‡	.148
5. Number of movies seen in past year	.314†	.471*	.160	‡	.105
6. Number of TV shows seen in past year	.197	.422†	.114	‡	‡

*Significantly different from zero at the 1 per cent level of probability.
†Significantly different from zero at the 5 per cent level of probability.
‡In Nazate, none of the respondents had read a magazine (or been read to) in the past month before the interview, had seen a movie in the past year, or had seen a TV show in the past year. It was impossible for a respondent to have seen a TV show in either Nazate or La Cañada because both were outside of the range of TV stations.

are not reading to any great extent, perhaps because of cost or other limitations. A second possibility is that the *illiterates* are using the print media by having literate family members or friends read to them. This idea was suggested by Deutschmann[1] to explain his finding that some Colombian peasant illiterates had printed media exposure (for example, 48 per cent purchased newspapers), although Deutschmann's data did not allow him to test his hunch. The present data indicate that 19 per cent of the illiterates had newspapers and 6 per cent had magazines read to them. These readers provide one route around the barrier of illiteracy to print media exposure. The interview data indicate that many of these readers are children, who generally have much higher literacy rates than their parents (Table 5). In fact, the percentage of all households (in which the household head was illiterate) which had at least one literate family member was 52 per cent in Pueblo Viejo, 59 per cent in San Rafael, 84 per cent in Cuatro Esquinas, 76 per cent in Nazate, and 85 per cent in La Cañada. Thus, the number of households that do not have at least one literate family member is fairly low.

---

[1] Deutschmann, "Mass Media in an Underdeveloped Society . . . ."

Table 5. Levels of Literacy (As Reported by Farm Operator)
of Various Family Members in Five Colombian Neighborhoods

Type of Family Members	% of Family Members Literate				
	Pueblo Viejo	San Rafael	Cuatro Esquinas	Nazate	La Cañada
Farm operators*	57	53	65	37	45
Wives†	34	58	67	3	32
Children† (aged 9–19)	90	73	83	56	45
Grandparents†	100	0	0	0	0

*These are self-defined literacy rates and hence are somewhat different from the rates of functional literacy in the five communities reported previously.

†These data are reported by the farm operator for all family members, and it is necessary to assume that the household head can accurately assess and report the literacy status of his household members. In any event, this is often the usual census measure, by which one household member is asked to report the literacy status of all household members.

EMPATHY

Empathy is "the capacity to see oneself in the other fellow's situation."[1] It assumes that an important step in individual transformation from a traditional to a modern is the ability to conceive of oneself performing a different role. Lerner[2] regards literacy as a major force in unlocking this empathetic process. "With literacy people acquire more than the simple skill of reading. . . . [It] trains them to use the complicated mechanism of empathy which is needed to cope with this world." He reported data from 248 Syrian respondents which show a strong relationship between literacy and his measure of empathy; his Turkish study[3] also indicated that literate villagers had higher empathy than illiterates.

With a small sample of Hausa men, Dobb[4] found that literates were better able than illiterates to reply specifically and meaningfully to the question: "What would you like to know about the world that you do not know?"

The present measure of empathy is a five-item scale that tapped the respondent's ability to suggest actions he would take if he were president of the village council, a local extension worker, mayor of a small, nearby city, the national minister of education, and president of the republic. The correlation of empathy with functional literacy scores is shown in Table 6; all are positive, and only one is not significant.

[1] Lerner, The Passing of Traditional Society . . . .
[2] Ibid.
[3] Lerner, "Literacy and Initiative . . . ."
[4] Leonard W. Dobb, Communication in Africa (New Haven, Conn.: Yale University Press, 1961), p. 178.

Table 6. Relationship of Functional Literacy to Various Consequences
in Five Colombian Communities

	Correlations with Functional Literacy				
Correlates of Functional Literacy	Pueblo Viejo	San Rafael	Cuatro Esquinas	Nazate	La Cañada
1. Empathy scores	.437*	.568*	.143	.420*	.411*
2. Agricultural innovativeness scores	.377*	.292	.140	.485*	.196
3. Home innovativeness scores	.397*	.537*	.259	.243	.485*
4. Achievement motivation scores	.219	.285	.294*	.436*	.353†
5. Farm size (in acres)	.265†	.426*	.177	.447*	.279
6. Number of trips to urban centers	.269†	.530*	.193	.123	.255
7. Political knowledge	.480*	.595*	.341*	.292	.492*
8. Sociometric opinion leadership	.189	.422*	.221	.273	.353†

*Significantly different from zero at the 1 per cent level of probability.
†Significantly different from zero at the 5 per cent level of probability.

INNOVATIVENESS

Innovativeness[1] is the degree to which an individual adopts new ideas relatively sooner than his peers and, to that extent, breaks with traditional ideas. It is usually indexed (as in the present study) by compiling a list of recently introduced ideas and asking the respondent how many of these he has adopted and when. The relative time at which he adopts these practices, as compared to other respondents in the same village, is a measure of his innovativeness.

Lerner[2] found that literate Turkish peasants had more modern attitudes and were more likely to perceive themselves as innovators in their village. Goldsen and Ralis[3] reported that Thai literate villagers were more innovative than illiterates. Rahim[4] found that literacy was positively related to adoption of improved practices in Pakistan. Deutschmann, Mendez, and Herzog[5] found in a study of Guatemalan housewives in five villages that literates knew about and had adopted more new food and drug practices than illiterates.

---

[1] Everett M. Rogers, *Diffusion of Innovations* (New York: Free Press, 1962).

[2] Lerner, "Literacy and Initiative . . . ."

[3] Goldsen and Ralis, *Factors Related to Acceptance . . . .*

[4] Rahim, *Diffusion and Adoption . . . .*

[5] Paul J. Deutschmann, Alfredo Mendez, and William Herzog, *Adoption of New Foods and Drugs in Five Guatemalan Villages,* Programa Interamericano de Información Popular (in preparation).

The present data (Table 6) indicate positive correlations in all five communities between literacy and agricultural and home innovativeness, although only half of these relationships are significant.

ACHIEVEMENT MOTIVATION

Achievement motivation, or need for achievement, has been defined as "the desire to do well, not so much for the sake of social recognition or prestige, but to attain an inner feeling of personal accomplishment."[1] McClelland[2] claimed that achievement motivation is a cause of national economic development and modernization. Thus, we would expect achievement motivation to be related to literacy, for as Lerner and others have pointed out, literacy is *more* than just an ability to read and write; it also reflects a desire to change, to modernize. This desire is probably in part measured by achievement motivation scores.

In the present study, 19 sentence-completion statements measuring occupational achievement motivation were presented to the respondents. Ultimately, these were refined to an eight-item scale which satisfactorily measured achievement.[3] Correlations of these scores with functional literacy scores are presented in Table 6. All are positive, and three of the five are significant.

FARM SIZE

Size of farm is commonly regarded as an important measure of social status in peasant societies. Deutschmann and Fals Borda[4] found a low relationship between literacy and farm size. The present data show positive (and significant in three of the five communities) correlations between functional literacy and farm size (Table 6).

COSMOPOLITENESS

Cosmopoliteness, the degree to which an individual is oriented outside of his social system, is indexed in the present study as the number of trips per year taken by the respondents to urban centers. There are several reasons why we would expect literacy to be related to cosmopoliteness. The analyses by Lerner[5] and Golden[6] (of data where countries are the units of analysis) suggest that the relationships they found between literacy and urbanization

[1] David C. McClelland *et al.,* "The Effect of the Need for Achievement on Thematic Apperception," *in* J. W. Atkinson, ed., *Motives in Fantasy, Action and Society* (Princeton, N.J.: Van Nostrand, 1958).

[2] David C. McClelland, *The Achieving Society* (Princeton, N.J.: Van Nostrand, 1961).

[3] Detail is provided in Rogers and Neill, *Achievement Motivation . . . .*

[4] Paul J. Deutschmann and Orlando Fals Borda, *Communication and Adoption Patterns in an Andean Village* (San José, Programa Interamericano de Información Popular, 1962). Mimeo. Report.

[5] Lerner, *Passing of Traditional Society . . . .*

[6] Golden, "Literacy and Social Change . . . ."

may be due to the greater functional utility of literacy in urban life. Thus, urban orientation leads to literacy. On the other hand, literacy may cause a peasant to travel to urban centers, because the literate villager has greater awareness of the business, recreational, and other services available only in urban centers in developing countries like Colombia. In Turkey, Lerner[1] found 48 per cent of male literates traveled outside of their village at least once a week, but only 33 per cent of the illiterates.

The present data (Table 6) show functional literacy is positively related to the number of trips to urban centers in all five Colombian communities, but this relationship is significant in only two of the villages.

POLITICAL KNOWLEDGE

Political knowledge is transmitted largely through the mass media, particularly the printed media, in developing nations. Therefore, we would expect a positive relationship with literacy. However, Deutschmann[2] found no relationship between literacy and political knowledge.

The present measure of political knowledge was a five-item scale of awareness of Colombian political affairs.[3] Table 6 shows there were positive correlations between political knowledge and functional literacy in all five communities; these relationships were significant in four of the five communities.

OPINION LEADERSHIP

Opinion leadership is defined as the ability to influence informally other people's attitudes in a desired way and with a relatively high frequency. This key communication role was investigated by Stycos[4] in a rural Greek village. He found the opinion leaders were often literate priests and schoolteachers who received information from the printed media.

The measure of opinion leadership utilized in the present investigation is the number of sociometric choices received by a farmer in answer to questions[5] asked his peers regarding who they would seek for advice about agriculture, new farm ideas, health problems, marketing, and local politics.[6] Table 6 shows the positive correlations that were obtained in the five communities with mass-media exposure. Further detail is shown in Table 7,

---

[1] Lerner, "Literacy and Initiative . . . ."

[2] Deutschmann, "Mass Media in an Underdeveloped Society . . . ."

[3] A typical item was knowing who was the district representative to the national legislature.

[4] J. Mayone Stycos, "Patterns of Communication in a Rural Greek Village," *Public Opinion Quarterly*, XVI, no. 1 (Spring, 1952), pp. 59–70.

[5] Four sociometric questions were utilized in the two traditional communities and six queries were used in the three modern communities.

[6] Responses to the various sociometric questions were combined into a single score because of the high relationships found among the responses to each question (Rogers and van Es, *Opinion Leadership . . .*).

where the functional literacy of opinion leaders and "followers" in both modern and traditional villages is shown. In both types of communities, opinion leaders (the 10 per cent of respondents in each village receiving the most sociometric choices) have a higher percentage of literates than the followers, although the opinion leaders are far from 100 per cent literate.

DISCUSSION

The community-to-community differences in Tables 2, 4, 5, and 6 emphasize the importance of studying several communities in a developing country such as Colombia, where wide subcultural differences are encountered. Evidently the patterns of relationship of functional literacy to its correlates, while generally in a similar direction (either positive or negative), are subject to wide intercommunity variation. This point is also, of course, an argument for the priority of extensive replication of the present study in other developing nations, before the present conclusions are considered in any way definitive. Nevertheless, the present work clearly shows the importance of literacy as a variable in explaining various facets of modernization.

Table 7. Percentage of Functionally Literate Opinion Leaders and Followers in Modern and Traditional Colombian Communities

Opinion Leadership	Type of Community Norms	
	Modern	Traditional
Percentage of opinion leaders who are functionally literate	71	44
Percentage of opinion followers who are functionally literate	34	16
Percentage of all respondents who are functionally literate	38	19

Future Research

The present investigation is but a modest attempt to determine the correlates and, in one sense, the meaning of literacy. Future study is needed on the following topics.

(a) The *new adult literate* and how his attitudes and behavior are changed by gaining the ability to read and write. What does it mean to become literate? This type of investigation could lend itself nicely to a before-after experimental design.

(b) The cultural and ecological settings as they affect the *functions* of literacy. There is considerable difference between being illiterate in a rural village and being illiterate in a city, where literacy is needed. Golden[1] stated:

---

[1] Golden, "Literacy and Social Change . . . ."

> Though not essential to traditional agriculture and its related crafts, literacy is required for urban-industrial occupations. . . . The knowledge required for such work (traditional agriculture) can be stored in a person's memory; the principles can be transmitted verbally as part of the apprenticeship process. Since neither business documents nor accounts need be kept, and since the work requires no blueprints, reading and writing are not essential to everyday life.

(c) Literacy itself is an innovation to illiterate villagers, and we know little about *motivations* for its adoption, such as what factors draw a villager to adult literacy training. Lerner[1] found that 47 per cent of Turkish illiterate villagers said they would like to learn to read and write, and that this interest in becoming literate was inversely related with age.

(d) Little is known presently about methods of circumventing the barrier of illiteracy by means of radio, movies, or television or through the use of such oral communication systems as animation and leader-out training or through pictorial, nonverbal printed media. At least in the short range (for at least one generation), primary school education and adult literacy training cannot be effective enough to create almost complete world-wide literacy. For a considerable number of adult illiterates, ways need to be found for effective, rapid communication without reading of print.

Certain of these research leads are currently under investigation in a UNESCO-sponsored field experiment under way in Costa Rica and India, and are planned for a U.S. AID-sponsored investigation recently initiated in a Latin American, an Asian, and an African country.

Summary

Data were gathered in 1963–1964 via personal interviews from 255 peasants in five Colombian communities. Functional literacy was measured by asking each respondent to read a six-word sentence in Spanish. It appears that this functional literacy test is fairly satisfactory, but needs to be lengthened for greater sensitivity in order to distinguish degree of literacy and reliability.

High positive correlations were noted between functional literacy scores and (a) self-defined literacy and (b) years of formal education. However, some individuals said they could read a newspaper, but could not read the six-word functional literacy test, and vice versa. While numerous functional literates had less than the UNESCO standard of four years of education, only one of the functional illiterates had four years of education or more.

---

[1] Lerner, "Literacy and Initiative . . . ."

There had evidently been considerable learning of literacy among our respondents outside of the classroom.

The consequences of literacy found in the present study generally emphasize the importance of this variable in individual modernization in developing societies. Functional literacy was found to be related to mass-media exposure, to be more characteristic of children than adults, and to be associated with empathy, agricultural and home innovativeness, achievement motivation, farm size, trips to urban centers, political knowledge, and sociometric opinion leadership.

Future research should concentrate upon the new adult literate, the functions of literacy, motivations for learning to be literate, and how to circumvent the literacy barrier to communication in developing societies.

The Paulo Freire Method:
Literacy Training and Conscientización

THOMAS G. SANDERS

Latin America shares the problem of high illiteracy rates with other parts of the underdeveloped world. The exact extent of the problem is difficult to determine because people differ in how they define literacy. Brazil, for example, considers a person literate who can write his name, but the country abounds with people who can meet this requirement and still cannot read and write. Alongside unquestioned illiterates who have had no education at all, we find the category of "semiliterates," made up of individuals who have usually attended school for limited periods but who have forgotten or cannot function with what they were taught, so that in practice they neither read nor write. Thus, the estimates of illiteracy in Chile range from 15 to 30 per cent, depending on one's definition.

We rarely ask why countries should combat illiteracy because the answers seem so obvious: e.g., to raise the cultural level, to provide minimal knowledge so that the bulk of the population can undertake more-complex roles in development, and to incorporate all of the population more effectively into the structure, values, and functions of society. Until recently, at least in theory, even the most traditional groups agreed on the desirability of education, usually arguing that only when educated would the lower classes deserve to participate in political, social, and economic processes.

In Latin America today, however, literacy training has become a controversial issue. The region, long imitative of European and North American

Thomas G. Sanders, *The Paulo Freire Method* [TGS-1-'68], Fieldstaff Reports, West Coast South America Series, Vol. XV, No. 1, 1968 © by American Universities Field Staff.
[Throughout this selection, the English form of the words "concientización" and "conscientização" has been spelled "conscientization," as the author wishes. In the original, however, the word was spelled "concientización"; we have retained this spelling only in the title.—Ed.]

educational theory and techniques, has now produced an innovative method of *alfabetización* which may also represent a contribution to our understanding of social change. Its key concept of *concientización* (or *conscientização* in Portuguese) has spread from its origin in Brazil to become common usage in Spanish-speaking countries and has also recently entered the French vocabulary. Thoughtful and critical Latin Americans (as well as those linked with the maintenance of existent structures) no longer think of learning to read as acquiring a mere technical skill, but as a process implying values, forming mentalities, and leading to social and political consequences. In fact, literacy training may become revolutionary.

The chief intellectual architect of this change is an amiable Brazilian named Paulo Freire,[1] who was one of the victims of the Brazilian military coup of April 1964. Jailed for 70 days, he chose to move to Chile rather than face what seemed the probability of further preventive arrest, and he currently works quietly as an educational consultant in ICIRA, an agency of the United Nations dedicated to research and the training of personnel for the Chilean agrarian reform. The method Freire developed is sometimes called by his name, but it is also known as the "psychosocial method."

For purposes of comparison, it is worth noting that Brazil's Communist-chasing government rejected the method as "subversive" and has since tried every witch-hunting technique to efface vestiges of *conscientização* from educational programs in the country. In Chile, on the other hand, the method was officially adopted in 1965 for all government programs of literacy training.

Paulo Freire was professor of the history and philosophy of education at the University of Recife until 1964; and as early as 1947 he had become interested in adult education, especially among the illiterates who formed the majority of the population of northeast Brazil. Being a professor of pedagogy, he was, of course, familiar with the standard methods, but he felt dissatisfied with them. For one thing, they used essentially the same material for adults as for children. Furthermore, the language and situations common in the primers were drawn from urban middle-class life and bore little if any relationship to the problems and interests of the lower classes, chiefly rural, that he was trying to teach. Most fundamentally, however, Freire was concerned with the philosophical assumptions about the relative status of teacher and pupil and the psychological effect on the pupil of the existent methods. Culture was regarded as intimately linked with literacy (the word *culto* in both Portuguese and Spanish conveys a sense of polished literary elegance), and the teacher in bestowing this "culture" on the ignorant pupil intensified the sense of subordination and worthlessness that he as a member of the lower class already suffered. Thus the learning process was by its nature paternalistic, making education only one more manifestation

---

[1] Paulo Freire is currently with the World Council of Churches.

of the normal class relations of Latin America. Even more, Freire puzzled over *why* he was teaching these people to read and write: Was it to appropriate the values and assume the roles of a society that was stratified and dehumanizing? He recognized that education was attempting to make pupils adapt to a society that he, like other critical Brazilians, believed should change.

Turning his back on the textbooks, Freire began to reflect on and absorb ideas from the following three sources, from which his method was to emerge:

(a)   The language, culture, and problems of the illiterates themselves.

(b)   Philosophies of knowledge, human nature, culture, and history. The aspect of Freire's thought that I feel most guilty about neglecting for lack of space is its profound philosophical rootage; for this Brazilian, with his provincial northeastern appearance and mannerisms, has built a system of literacy training upon categories and concepts drawn from the phenomenology of Husserl, existentialists like Buber and Mounier, Marxist humanists like Schaff, the psychoanalytical theory of Fromm, and a whole range of philosophers of science and language.

(c)   The analyses of underdevelopment that began to have an impact on Latin Americans after World War II. Like many other Brazilians, Freire concluded that an older epoch of backwardness, dependence, and immobility was being replaced by one of new economic orientations, industrialization, greater national autonomy, and class mobility. Politically and culturally, a closed society was becoming more open; the traditional interpretations of such themes as democracy, popular participation, liberty, property, and authority were seeking new content. In Freire's words, "Education, therefore, in the phase of transition that we were living, became a highly important task. Its strength would derive chiefly from our capacity to incorporate ourselves into the dynamism of the epoch in transition." The trauma of change began to divide society into two groups: (1) those who did not understand the necessity of modernization and used paternalism and massification to inhibit it and (2) those eager to participate in the changes. As an educator and interpreter of this process, Paulo Freire felt that his field and function were to form a population capable of participating rationally, critically, and democratically in both the present and future of the country.

Between 1960 and 1963, Freire's reading and thinking, on the one hand, and his immersion in the life of the people and problems of Brazilian development, on the other, began to jell into a system. The principal catalyst was his participation in the Movement of Popular Culture in Recife, where such themes as nationalism, remission of profits, development, and illiteracy were discussed in groups, using visual aids to schematize the issues. So satisfactory were the results of these dialogues in awakening the consciousness of the participants that Freire decided to try the same methods with literacy training. But was it possible to transform the mentality of a rural worker, illiterate all of his life, from passive ingenuousness to critical participation at the same time that he was learning to read?

Freire distinguishes between a "magical," or unreflective, way in which man may confront the world around him and a "critical" vision of that world. He wanted to reform the illiterate's basic perspective on reality, which has usually been a profound pessimism and fatalism, by enabling him to gain awareness of his capacity to shape his environment and to acquire the means to do so. Literacy training should not immerse the pupil in his status, but rather give him the capacity to overcome it.

Why take this approach rather than the older one? Freire contends that all pedagogical methods imply a concept of man and society. There is no neutral education. Traditional theories of literacy training have tried to adjust man to a given society, while their methods treated him as an object into which superior beings poured knowledge. For Freire, however, man is not an object. Man's "ontological vocation" is to be a subject who works upon and changes the world. "If man is a being transforming the world, the educational task is different. . . . If we look on him as a person, our educational task will be more and more liberating."

Nevertheless, in Latin America the masses cannot express this destiny. To speak of humanization as the basic object of man's existence points to the presence of dehumanization, the product of centuries of exploitation, of which the prevalent illiteracy is only a manifestation. The educator facing a class of illiterates finds himself with an option: to maintain their dehumanization through what he does with them or to work toward the fulfillment of their human potential. It was precisely this problem that disturbed Freire, for he felt that the available methods gave no choice except to perpetuate attitudes of passivity and ingenuousness.

The Paulo Freire method makes of literacy training a critical, active process through which habits of resignation are overcome. The critical capacity of the pupils grows out of dialogue about meaningful situations in their life, on which they have insights to contribute. Both teacher and pupils join sympathetically in a common purpose, seeking truth about relevant problems while respecting each other's opinions. The teacher serves as the coordinator of a discussion, while the pupils become participants in a group trying to understand existence in a changing society.

As a basis for the discussions, Freire believed that he could isolate a minimal core vocabulary touching on life situations, which would also point to issues stimulating discussion and the awakening of critical consciousness.

For a Brazilian or Chilean peasant, learning to read through such sentences as "Run, Spot, run" is only alienating.

Thus the first phase of the method became a study of the context in which the illiterates lived, in order to determine the common vocabulary and the problem issues around which the process of reflection could develop. Through informal conversations, a team of educators studied the thinking, problems, and aspirations of a given community. While the Paulo Freire method assumes that themes of national importance play a role in the development of a critical mentality, it also assumes that the presentation of them should be linked to the personal, local problems of the person seeking education. The deeply contextual orientation of the method is illustrated by the fact that Freire developed different lists of words and situations for rural and urban illiterates, and even for different regions of Brazil. After his move to Chile, Freire had to begin all over again and learn the vocabulary, mentality, and problems there.

The second phase involves the selection of words from the vocabulary that have been discovered to be "most charged with existential meaning, and thus, major emotional content, but also the typical expressions of the people." Three criteria govern this choice.

The first is the capacity of the words to include the basic sounds of the language. Both Spanish and Portuguese words are based on syllables, with little variation in vocalic sounds and a minimum of consonantal combinations. Freire discovered that 16 to 20 words sufficed to cover the sounds.

The second criterion is that the vocabulary, when organized, should enable the pupil to move from simple letters and sounds to more complex ones. Experience and insight contribute to an understanding of the problems an illiterate has in learning to read and write. Because the feeling of confidence in mastering these techniques is important, difficulties should be graduated so that they can be more easily overcome: "Each success that the illiterate has in overcoming a new difficulty gives him internal satisfaction, increases his interest and learning, and gives him greater confidence in himself."

The third criterion is that words are chosen for their potential capacity to confront the social, cultural, and political reality. The words should provide mental and emotional stimulation—that is, they should suggest and mean something important. "House," for example, carries a meaning linked not only to the daily life of the family, but also to local and national housing problems. "Work" provokes a range of associations with the nature of human existence, economic functions, cooperation, and unemployment.

The lists of words in Table 1 are those that were used in two different contexts: List I was selected for use in the state of Rio de Janeiro in Brazil, a rural area satellite to a large city; List II for use in rural sections of Chile.

Table 1. Lists of Words Used for the State of Rio de Janeiro
and for Rural Sections of Chile

List I		List II	
favela	slum	*casa*	house
chuva	rain	*pala*	shovel
arado	plow	*camino*	road
terreno	plot of land	*vecino*	neighbor
comida	food	*zapato*	shoe
batuque	a popular dance with African rhythms	*escuela*	school
poço	well	*ambulancia*	ambulance
bicicleta	bicycle	*sindicato*	union
trabalho	work	*compañero*	companion
salário	salary	*radio*	radio
profissão	profession	*harina*	flour
govêrno	government	*chiquillo*	boy
mangue	swamp (also the zone of prostitution in Rio)	*yugo*	yoke
engenho	mill	*trabajo*	work
enxada	hoe	*guitarra*	guitar
tijolo	brick	*fábrica*	factory
riqueza	prosperity, wealth	*pueblo*	people

A very interesting vocabulary has also recently been developed for prisoners in Chile, including such words as *salida* (getting out), *visita* (visit), *abogado* (lawyer), and *libertad* (freedom).

Why operate with a minimal number of words rather than use a primer that can constantly supply new vocabulary and sentences? Freire believes that no primer is sufficiently contextual, and that all are paternalistic, in the sense of conveying, from outside, themes and vocabulary the authors consider significant. On the other hand, the richness of potential expansion in the word lists enables the pupils themselves to acquire a feeling of creativity and originality by making their own words and sentences. Thus the word *casa*, varied with other vowels, produces a whole family of syllables— ca, co, cu, sa, se, si, so, su—from which words like *cosa, saco, casi,* and *seco* can be derived. In the very first session, the group forms its own words and even simple sentences. To take an example that Freire often cites from Brasília, the first word used was *tijolo,* and an illiterate on the first night constructed, *tu já lê,* a slightly ungrammatical form that can be translated, "you already read." Within a few sessions the pupils have mastered sufficient syllables to express a wide vocabulary.

The third phase of the method develops teaching materials of two types. One is a set ot cards or slides which break down the words into parts for more careful analysis. The second is a set of cards of pictorial situations, related to the words, which are designed to impress on the pupil, through vision, an image of the word and also to stimulate his thinking about the situation that the word implies. In Brazil, Freire used pictures separated from the words, but in Chile he has combined the two. The pictures become the basis for dialogue, and as the examples illustrated on pages 594 and 595 indicate both the style and subjects are popular.

The actual literacy training in Brazil was preceded by at least three sessions of motivation, in which the pupil entered into his new life through an analysis of the concept of culture. In Chile, this stage has been incorporated into the literacy training itself, for it was noted that the Chilean, unlike the Brazilian who liked discussion about himself as a creative, cultural being, tended to lose interest if he did not begin to learn immediately. In Freire's method, the beginning of a critical, as opposed to a magical, outlook comes from distinguishing between nature and culture; nature is viewed as a matrix in which man lives, culture as an addition that man contributes through his own work. It is important to recognize that, for Freire, culture is not the property of the learned, something that the pupil may acquire only after he can read and write; rather, culture is something that all men have. A picture that he commonly uses shows an Indian shooting a bird with a bow and arrow and illustrates the control that even primitive men have over nature through their creations. The illiterate discovers that culture is relative; through the pictures he sees that he already has culture and a certain domination over the world itself, even though he was previously not conscious of this fact.

It is not surprising therefore that the method of Paulo Freire is usually linked with popular culture movements which emphasize the creativity of the people and seek to promote new forms among them. Popular culture collides with the imitative cultural tendencies of the Latin American upper and middle classes; and Chileans, especially, propagate a carefully cultivated myth that their country is culturally the most European in Latin America, as if a second-rate imitation were something to be proud of. What they obscure by this myth is the strong indigenous component in the lower-class culture and in popular artistic creations that bear the mark of originality. Perhaps nothing more clearly reveals the chasm between the upper and lower classes than the prevalence of this self-image of Europeanized homogeneity which supposedly distinguishes Chile from such neighbors as Peru and Bolivia.

Now the method. Figure 1, which is the initial one of a series of eight used for cultural apprehension in Chile, depicts a peasant carrying an axe with which he intends to cut down a tree. From discussing this situation,

Figure 1. Courtesy of American Universities Field Staff.

Figure 2. Courtesy of American Universities Field Staff.

casa

Figure 3. Courtesy of American Universities Field Staff.

fábrica

Figure 4. Courtesy of American Universities Field Staff.

the class realizes the existence of a world of nature and a world of culture. Through work, man alters the natural environment and creatively forms his culture. The coordinator elicits the meaning of the situation through a series of questions designed to provoke dialogue and self-discovery: What is the peasant doing? Who made the axe? What is the difference between the origin of the tree and the origin of the axe? Why does the man do what he is doing? How? The illiterate comes to understand that lack of knowledge is relative and that absolute ignorance does not exist. The mere fact of being human entails knowledge, control, and creativity.

Figure 2, which is seventh in this series, depicts a group in which a couple is performing the *cueca,* a Chilean folk dance. The class discovers that man not only creates instruments for his physical necessities, but that he creates for artistic expression as well. Man has an aesthetic sense, and the popular manifestations of culture possess as legitimate a vitality and beauty as other forms. Again the coordinator asks questions: Why are these people dancing? Who invented the dance and other similar ones that you know? Why do men create music? Can a man who composes a *cueca* be a great composer? The situation aims at indicating that a man who composes popular music is as much an artist as a famous composer.

In Figure 3, we enter the stage of literacy training itself. A class session is built around a word and a picture; and the group learns that one can symbolize a lived experience by drawing, reading, or writing it. Instead of the prosperous middle-class dwelling of the usual primer, we find a humble Chilean home and a family whose features are typical of the lower class. To the left is a somewhat shabbier house.

The literacy training involves a series of audiovisual techniques, such as repeating and recognizing the word, dissecting it into its component syllables, learning to write the letters and the word, and constructing new words from the components. The coordinator of the group guides the class in reflection and discussion on the meaning of "house," using such themes as the necessity of comfortable housing for family life, the problem of housing in the nation, the possibilities and ways of acquiring a house, types of dwellings in different regions and countries, and the problems of housing associated with urbanization. Provocative questions, such as the following, develop a critical attitude toward an everyday phenomenon: Do all Chileans have adequate houses? Where and why do they lack houses? Is the system of savings and loans sufficient for acquiring a house?

In Figure 4, we find a different situation: a factory with a sign announcing "No Jobs." The attitudes reflected on the faces of the persons probably reflect real experience for many in the class. Even though the word is directed to a rural group, all have a personal interpretation of the meaning of "factory." The questions for discussion are the following: Where are the cloth that we wear, the tools with which we work, and the paper and pencils with which we write produced? Does the factory participate in the production of our food? And the construction of our houses? Why don't people produce most of the articles they need, as they used to do? Why do countries need to industrialize? Can Chile industrialize to a greater degree? What does a country need in order to develop itself industrially? What industries have the best possibilities in our country? Does industrial expansion influence rural areas? Do rural areas contribute to the process? Can one industrialize agriculture and the production of animals?

Obviously these questions are both simple and sophisticated. The Paulo Freire method itself has no answers for them, but experience indicates that common reflection by the pupils produces considerable understanding. My own most memorable impression from visiting these classes is of the capacity of people of limited education for thoughtful analysis and logical articulation of the issues when the issues are linked to their everyday life.

The key to the successful implementation of the method is the coordinator, who does not teach but tries instead to promote self-discovery in the other participants through exploring the dimensions of the pictures. The livelier the debate, the greater the number of ideas and implications drawn and the richer and more meaningful the critical insight into the problems as well as the memory of the word. The coordinator tries to get all the members of the group to participate by directing questions to them, prolonging the discussion so that they will realize the deeper meaning of what was once for them an obvious, accepted reality. He should not give his own opinions. Like group psychotherapy, the Paulo Freire method stimulates participants to move themselves, by realistic assessment of themselves and their environment, from inauthentic interpretations of life to creative initiative.

The Paulo Freire method does not aim chiefly at literacy training, but at what is called in Brazil *conscientização* and in Chile *concientización*. The word first appeared, according to Freire, in discussions of the Higher Institute of Brazilian Studies (ISEB) in the late 1950's, but the term conveyed minimal content until Freire heard it and, realizing its implications, applied it to literacy training at about the same time as the Movement of Base Education (MEB), a system of radio schools sponsored by the Brazilian bishops, also began to use it.

Conscientization means an "awakening of consciousness," a change of mentality involving an accurate, realistic awareness of one's locus in nature and society; the capacity to analyze critically its causes and consequences, comparing it with other situations and possibilities; and action of a logical sort aimed at transformation. Psychologically it entails an awareness of one's dignity, or if we take part of the title of Freire's book, *Educação como prática da liberdade,* "the practice of freedom." Even though the stimulus to conscientization derives from interpersonal dialogue in which one discovers the meaning of humanity from encounters with other humans, an almost inevitable consequence is political participation and the formation of interest groups such as community organizations and labor unions.

Lack of consciousness is the fate of oppressed groups everywhere, and discriminatory social structures rely on this state of mind to prevent changes and challenges. The most apt parallel for North American readers is our black community, which is currently undergoing a process of conscientization. The close linkage between language and conscientization can be discerned by contrasting the subservient, fatalistic expressions of most blacks a generation ago with their present militant, confident vocabulary. Conscientization often leads to politicalization—perhaps even to violence (as we see in the United States)—when men become conscious of their rights and their lack of them.

Conscientization rests on certain value assumptions that have not received much implementation in Latin America: the equality of all men, their right to knowledge and culture, and their right to criticize their situation and act upon it. It also implies a faith in the capacity of even the illiterate to achieve a reflective outlook through self-discovery and dialogue.

Properly understood and applied, conscientization has no predictable directions. Although it does not prescribe politicalization, its content of dignity, criticism, and transformation almost inevitably leads to a quest for channels of effective action. If social dissatisfaction follows from the dialogues, it is because this is a part of the reality. Paulo Freire speaks of his method as "revolutionary." By this he primarily means a change of mentality that will inevitably have effects on the present system of class relations in Latin America, and undoubtedly will effect changes in political and economic structures as well. In this sense, the method is also "subversive"—subversive, that is, of an established and unchanging social order—but, in a play on words which Freire likes to make, he pointed out to me that while all "revolutionary" phenomena are "subversive," not all "subversive" phenomena are "revolutionary."

Both the Freire method and the concept of conscientization have attracted those who believe in its humanistic implications for the participation of the masses and also in the necessity of a rapid and decisive restructuring of society. One of its indubitable attractions is a freedom from either paternalism or outside ideologies; that is, it regards as invalid the manipulation of education and people in order either to maintain an archaic system or to impose perspectives alien to the context. Its only ideology is a kind of humanism that affirms the freedom and capacity of the people to decide their destinies. The people may choose to achieve their aims through an ideology, but the method does not presuppose that any such framework of meaning or social philosophy expresses the people's will and interests.

The Paulo Freire method first gained prominence after 1962, when Brazil, affected by the example of Cuba which had almost eliminated illiteracy through a massive campaign, was the scene of a movement by both private and public agencies eager to accomplish the same result. Paulo Freire had been conducting experiments in the Northeast which showed that his method could teach a person to read and write in six weeks, and *conscientização* was also being widely discussed among modernizing elites as a key to social and cultural development. Although the country had many of the industrial and structural symbols of economic development, it lacked the comprehension and participation in the process of the population.

In 1963, the Brazilian Ministry of Education committed itself to a literacy campaign using the method of Paulo Freire. Within eight months, training courses for coordinators were conducted in nearly every state—with 6,000 persons volunteering in the state of Guanabara alone. Students were among the most vigorous participants in the courses; it was anticipated that by 1964, 20,000 "circles of culture" would be under way, teaching and conscientizing two million people in a course lasting three months. Thus, the 40 million Brazilian illiterates would be eliminated within a few years. The revolutionary implications of the method were freely discussed and accepted, since those who participated believed that the country was in a prerevolutionary situation.

The Paulo Freire method, like many interesting ideas and events of this period, frightened many people and suffered constant attack, particularly from the influential Rio de Janeiro daily *O Globo*. The basic charge was that the method was stirring up the people, giving them ideas about changing things, and consequently fomenting subversion.

The Brazilian governmental change of 1964 had many causes, but none was more fundamental than the fear of the upper and middle classes that the country was undergoing a shift of power in which the majority of the population, the illiterate and semiliterate, would gain a voice commensurate with their numbers. By the simple expedient of forbidding illiterates to vote, half the potential electorate of the country had been disfranchised, while in many instances lack of consciousness had made possible the manipulation of those who did vote. If, then, to the modernizers, literacy training and *conscientização* represented the vehicles by which the country could move from a limited to a universal participation of the population, that is, democratization, it constituted a terror to those who enjoyed their monopoly of power. Both the middle and upper classes supported the coup from anxiety that their carefully accumulated privileges would be undercut by a proletarianization of society.

Since 1964, literacy training has continued in Brazil on a modest scale, but notably without *conscientização*. Certainly, if the Paulo Freire method has political implications, the same can be said about the present system of literacy training: it is carefully planned to check expectations and to restrict the formation of a critical perspective.

In Chile, the Paulo Freire method is now used in all governmental programs of literacy training. The Chilean experience deserves extensive treatment, for if its present momentum continues, the country will reduce its rate of illiteracy within six years to a tolerable 5 per cent.

Before 1964, literacy training was a sporadic and chiefly private endeavor. The Christian Democratic government, elected in that year, wanted to attack the problem as part of its program of promotion. As President Frei recently pointed out in an address on the state of the nation, his administration wants "to create broad forms of popular participation in the development of our community. Not only in party politics . . . but chiefly in the real expressions of our present life: those of work, neighborhood and regional life, family necessities and basic culture, and economic-social organization."

A Department of Special Planning for Education of Adults was created in mid-1965. Its director was Waldemar Cortés, a young Christian Democratic militant who had been involved in adult education for some years and was principal of a night school in Santiago. Cortés, like Freire before him, thought that both existent methods and materials needed revising, since ordinarily those used for children were simply applied to adults. "By chance," someone told him of a Brazilian in Chile named Freire, "who had some ideas on adult education." Although Cortés had never heard of the Brazilian experiments in literacy training, he discovered that Freire had worked out in detail all of his own hunches on the subject.

The problem then became that of gaining acceptance in Chile for a method considered subversive in Brazil. A number of people in the Christian Democratic party thought that the method was "radical" and even "communist." Others wanted to use literacy programs for the interests of the party. With persuasion and effort, however, Cortés managed to get the program accepted; and to counter criticism of partisanship, he chose for his chief technical team people representing a variety of political positions.

The Department of Special Planning for Education of Adults functions as the coordinator of programs that are actually carried out by other agencies. A wide variety of institutions in Chile, chiefly public but also private. have promotion as a central objective: for example, those associated with the agrarian reform, the Corporation of Agrarian Reform (CORA) and the Institute of Agrarian and Livestock Development (INDAP). CORA expropriates property and forms agricultural communities *(asentimientos)* preparatory to establishing individual ownership, while INDAP provides credit and technical assistance to small farmers; since most illiteracy is found in rural areas, these agencies are natural vehicles for bringing people together into groups. Moreover, the Chilean agrarian reform not only aims at increasing production but also at promoting the more effective functioning of neglected social groups and their integration into society. Among other agencies in close contact with illiterates are the National Health Service (which combines literacy and sanitation training), the Service of Prisons, and the Department of Popular Promotion (which encourages the formation of community organizations). Within the social vision or ideology of Christian Democracy, these institutions do not simply serve technical functions, but also try to overcome the separation between those who participate effectively in society and those who do not. The department has recently signed agreements for literacy training with certain Protestant churches, which in some isolated communities are the only institutions available.

The department develops teaching material and gives training to coordinators, who then function within the program of the other agencies. These agencies sign an agreement with the department, depositing an amount of money which is used to pay the coordinators. Originally, the program relied in part on volunteers, but, to guarantee stability, quality, and conscientiousness, stipends are now the policy. The coordinators, who are usually primary school teachers, are chosen from the local community on the recommendation of the agency involved. The department trains them in dialogue and the aims of the Paulo Freire method in a course that takes about 30 hours.

One of the most common criticisms is that the coordinators do not themselves achieve a sufficient change from their former paternalistic attitudes to internalize the spirit of the method. I myself feel, after observing several classes, that they do tend to dominate the situation too much, although this does not inhibit many fine contributions by the participants. Both Waldemar Cortés and Paulo Freire admit that this is a permanent problem. Cortés thinks that his department has improved the situation bit by bit since the program's hasty beginning in Chile. Freire believes that the method requires frankness in eliminating those who do not have the right mentality, as well as the periodic review and retraining of coordinators through careful supervision and seminars.

The Chilean program has attracted international attention in its mere two years of effective functioning; Chile recently received an award from UNESCO as one of the five nations which are most effectively overcoming the problem of illiteracy. This year the department calculates that it will have approximately 100,000 pupils and 2,000 coordinators functioning. The continuity of the program is menaced, however, by the fact that it has only a provisional status linked to the present government. Cortés would like to see a permanent division of adult education—one as fundamental, for example, as primary education—that would survive any political change in 1970.

The Department of Special Planning for Education of Adults, as its name implies, not only deals with literacy but also with a range of programs designed to enable people who have not had educational opportunities to overcome their handicap. In a recent evaluation, the department highlighted the desire of those who have become literate through the Paulo Freire method to continue their studies at higher levels.

The fact, however, that the initial stage of conscientization requires supplementation by more-advanced content suggests a problem. What kinds of things should a person learn? What attitude should the pupil take toward the material? Let us recall Paulo Freire's view that no education is neutral.

Perhaps this problem can be illustrated by referring to two quite different primers developed for the secondary level after initial literacy training. The first comes from the Movement of Base Education in Brazil and is called *Viver é Lutar* ("To Live Is to Struggle"); the second is used in the Chilean program and is called *Comunidad* ("Community"). The following are a couple of typical passages from the former: "I live and I struggle. Pedro lives and struggles. The people live and struggle. I, Pedro, and the people struggle. We struggle to live. To live is to struggle." "Pedro is disturbed and thinks. Why is our life so harsh? Why do so many children die here? Why don't the people have housing? Why don't the people learn to read? Why aren't there schools for our children? Why do the people suffer so much injustice?" (I should add that this primer was confiscated by the government of the state of Guanabara as "subversive" even before the coup.) In *Comunidad,* along with a range of useful knowledge, we find such passages as these: "So that governments can achieve the plans for collective welfare they need the support of the population. The community, therefore, ought to organize itself and unite its forces to that of government and thus be able to better its economic, social, and cultural conditions." "The struggle to elevate the level of life in the country and permit each Chilean to enjoy better conditions of life and a larger quantity of goods and essential services . . . is what is called Economic and Social Development. Chile is engaged in this great enterprise."

The differences in the two primers may be explained only in part by the two different national contexts and the fact that the former emanates from a group outside power, the other from a group participating in it. At stake are two diverging interpretations of the Latin American reality, of the relationship between integrated and marginal segments of society, and of the nature of change. Which one is correct? The Paulo Freire method does not tell us. Only those who live in the world of the illiterate understand that world and can interpret it.

Section 8:
Continuity and Change: University Students

Introduction to Section 8

Luigi Einaudi introduces this section with a discussion of the evolution of autonomy and reform in the universities of Latin America. Beginning with the historical precedents of the Córdoba movement, Einaudi demonstrates how the university entered the political arena and how the university is now becoming less politicized because of increased involvement in national life, the expansion and changes in the newly developed institutions of higher education, and the increased opportunities for graduates to become involved in careers concerned with national development. The author asserts that autonomy in the university centers on administrative and political issues rather than on economic ones and that this orientation is based on the medieval European concepts of "privileges and exemptions" as well as immunization from external societal forces. He suggests that the support for both autonomy and social and educational reform in the universities is likely to come from professional educators since only they can wed these sometimes paradoxical values.

The second article, by Kenneth Walker, compares the university reform movements in Argentina and Colombia through the application of Neil Smelser's theory of collective behavior. Tracing the historical precedents for student participation in university governance in Latin America, the author discusses the reform movement begun at the University of Córdoba and the impact of this movement on university reform in Colombia. In Argentina the "norm-oriented" movement is shown to have been broadly supported by students and to have had the advantage of a sympathetic government, which intervened to implement the radical reforms. The "value-oriented" movement in Colombia, on the other hand, is shown to have lacked widespread student support and to have been more easily diverted from its radical position. The author suggests that the reform movement in Colombia resulted in token representation by students in the university government and a consequent lack of an organizational use of subsequent action, whereas the movement in Argentina was institutionalized and students received a major role in university decision making. In his conclusion, Walker states: ". . . it would appear that where the university reform was successful, as in Argentina, it provided an important impetus toward needed reforms in the character and conduct of higher education, a defense of academic freedom against the claims of the state, and a politicizing experience for students in the democratic process. Where the movement was relatively unsuccessful, as in Colombia, student politics would appear to be more alienated from the university and society, and less responsible in its choice of means."

Robert Williamson, in the third selection, provides a profile of the National University student in Colombia. The author presents questionnaire and interview data from a sample of 610 students on a wide range of personal, social, and political phenomena. Data on student perceptions include the probability of classmates finding employment upon graduation; an appraisal of their professors, peers, and other Colombian universities; and attitudes toward student strikes, religious behavior, societal reform, world leaders, and sources of information. Data on student social activities include dating, friendship, personal preoccupations, and marriage plans. The author analyzes these dependent variables through differential responses by age, sex, class, and major. Williamson suggests that although students recognize the importance of education for upward mobility, their perceptions indicate dissatisfaction with the university environment and a general pessimism about the external socioeconomic and political environment.

In the fourth article, Kenneth Walker uses data from the study by Robert Williamson to investigate attitudes toward Cuba's Fidel Castro as an indicator of student orientation to radical change in Latin America. His results indicate that supporters of Castro are more likely to see the necessity of radical change in Colombia, more likely to perceive the future as being less happy than the present, and less likely to feel that people in general are happy in their life. Castro supporters, when compared to his opponents, view striking as effective and are less committed to the Catholic church. Walker combines church commitment with university experience, place of residence, and field of study and finds that ". . . greater exposure to the university subculture, whether by residence away from home or increased years in the university, tends to increase Castro support. This effect is greater among students in the social sciences and humanities than among those in the natural sciences; it is almost nonexistent among students with a high religious commitment who are in the natural sciences."

The fifth and sixth selections, by David Nasatir, focus on attitudes of Argentine university and nonuniversity youths. In the first article, 1,700 students were asked to provide information on job aspirations, characteristics of an ideal job, and societal responsibilities of the highly educated. The results show that Argentine university students are oriented toward vocational goals and consider their university experience as an opportunity to develop abilities which will prove beneficial to their career. University males are shown to be slightly more concerned with national goals and betterment than nonuniversity males. The major concern of both groups, with the exception of older, nonuniversity males from educated families, is their future occupations. Nasatir suggests that the university has relatively little impact on student perceptions about the social responsibilities of the highly educated since his findings indicate that such commitments appear to develop in older, nonuniverity youths as well.

In the next selection, Nasatir investigates political orientations of university and nonuniversity youths in Argentina. He asserts that university students are more concerned with politics than nonstudents and that in the case of the latter such concern varies with the level of education and the occupation of the youth's father. The author also suggests that part-time university students express a political interest more often than full-time students, although both groups are most likely to manifest differential interest in accordance with their field of study. In addition, Nasatir suggests that: "In the apolitical atmosphere which prevails in some parts of the university, political interest tends to become less common among older students; in more politicalized settings interest spreads."

The final article, by Myron Glazer, discusses professional commitments and the effects of political involvement on those commitments among students at the University of Chile. It is shown that although students from several fields of study realize the importance of ascriptive as opposed to achievement-oriented norms as influences on career opportunities, the majority think that achievement-oriented norms ought to be the primary factors influencing such opportunities. The author suggests that professional commitment is high among students and does not differ significantly when viewed from the perspective of such independent variables as sex, socioeconomic status, and religion. Instead, Glazer reports that a close relationship exists between professionalism and degree of political involvement and that in most cases this combination is characteristic of those who are willing to assume difficult urban employment but who have an aversion to accepting rural employment. Glazer concludes that ". . . political ideologies which are supportive of social change . . . can be highly functional in directing youthful energies into those channels most needed by the society."

Original Sources for Selections

Einaudi, Luigi. "University Autonomy and Academic Freedom in Latin America," *Law and Contemporary Problems,* 28 (Summer, 1963), pp. 636–646.

Walker, Kenneth N. "A Comparison of the University Reform Movements in Argentina and Colombia," *Comparative Education Review,* 10 (June, 1966), pp. 257–272.

Williamson, Robert C. "University Students in a World of Change: A Colombian Sample," *Sociology and Social Research,* 48 (July, 1964), pp. 397–413.

Walker, Kenneth N. "Determinants of Castro Support among Latin American University Students," *Social and Economic Studies,* 14 (March, 1965), pp. 88–105.

Nasatir, David. "Education and Social Change: The Argentine Case," *Sociology of Education,* 39 (Spring, 1966), pp. 167–182.

Nasatir, David. "University Experience and Political Unrest of Students in Buenos Aires," *Comparative Education Review,* 10 (June, 1966), pp. 273–281.

Glazer, Myron. "The Professional and Political Attitudes of Chilean University Students," *Comparative Education Review,* 10 (June, 1966), pp. 282–295.

University Autonomy
and Academic Freedom
in Latin America

LUIGI EINAUDI

Introduction

Latin American universities have surprisingly little in common with universities in the United States. They have their own distinctive traditions, operate in a different environment, and have functions and prerogatives not normally associated with institutions of higher learning in this country. Unlike the Constitution of the United States, which makes no reference to education, all Latin American constitutions make provision for education, sometimes at great length. The tone of higher education in the United States has, at least until recently, been set predominantly by private institutions; the opposite has been the case in Latin America ever since the founding of the first "Royal and Pontifical" universities in Peru and Mexico in 1551. In the United States, discussions of academic freedom have often centered on educational considerations, primarily in terms of the role of teachers as educators rather than as citizens, and have dealt only very secondarily with the role of students. In Latin America, freedom of instruction (*libertad de*

Reprinted, with permission, from a symposium Academic Freedom appearing in *Law and Contemporary Problems* (Vol. 28, No. 3, Summer 1963), published by the Duke University School of Law, Durham, North Carolina. Copyright 1963, by Duke University.

Luigi Einaudi: B.A. 1957, Harvard College. Ph.D. Candidate, Harvard University. Teaching Fellow and Tutor in Government, Harvard University, 1960–1961; Instructor in Government, Wesleyan University, 1961–1962; Staff Member, Social Science Department, The RAND Corporation, Santa Monica, California, since June 1962.

The author wishes to express his indebtedness to the U.S. National Student Association, which introduced him to the problems discussed here by sending him to Latin America as its representative in 1955 and 1956. The views expressed in this paper are, however, entirely those of the author. They should also not be interpreted as reflecting the views of The RAND Corporation or the official opinion or policy of any of its governmental or private research sponsors.

Unless otherwise indicated, all translations are the author's.

cátedra) has been but a small part of the controversy centering on university autonomy, which has encompassed students as much as professors, and social and political issues as well as educational ones. During the twentieth century, major questions have been raised, usually with little agreement, about the function of universities in changing societies. The issue of university autonomy has thus been combined with, and complicated further by, that of university reform.

The modern history of the Latin American university is thus largely the story of the effort to make higher education relevant to Latin America and its problems. This struggle, waged in the name of university autonomy and reform, has involved the simultaneous affirmation and rejection of past university traditions, and, since few could agree on either the needs or the means by which the universities could best fulfill them, it has also projected the university into the political arena. This in turn has created new political traditions from which most Latin American universities can today escape only with difficulty even under the best of circumstances. How and why this came about and the effect of the political role of the university on its freedom and mission are the topics of this paper.[1]

Part One

We, men of a free Republic, have just broken the last chains which in the twentieth century still bound us to monarchic and monastic domination. . . . The Universities have until now been the secular haven of the mediocre, the reward of the ignorant, a shelter for intellectual invalids, and—still worse—places in which tyranny and insensibility in all their forms can always make their voices heard. The Universities have therefore become faithful images of our decadent societies. sad spectacles of senile immobility. . . . We have rebelled against a form of administration, against a system of education, and against a concept of authority. . . . We are tired of supporting tyrants . . . and cannot be denied the right to participate in the government of our own institution.[2]

The university reform movement is normally traced to this curious mixture of education and politics infused with rebellious idealism. The students of Córdoba did in fact have serious grievances, educational and otherwise,

---

[1] The Latin American experience, particularly when contrasted with our own, has sufficient distinctiveness to justify this generalized treatment, although it will obviously not apply equally everywhere. Major exceptions will be noted.

[2] *La juventud argentina de Córdoba a los hombres libres de Sudamérica* (Manifiesto del 21 de junio de 1918). This document is reproduced in two important recent collections of documents on the university reform movement: Coordinating Secretariat of the International Student Conference (COSEC), *La reforma universitaria en América Latina* (published by COSEC, Box 36, Leiden, Holland, 1960) (also available in poor English and French editions); and Federación Universitaria de Buenos Aires (FUBA), *La reforma universitaria, 1918-1958* (Buenos Aires, 1959). An interesting commentary on the reform movement will be found in Harrison, "The Confrontation with the Political University," *in* R. N. Burr, ed., *Latin America's Nationalistic Revolutions,* Annal No. 334, pp. 74-83 (March, 1961).

and the speed with which the movement spread indicated that their feelings were shared by some of the other "free men of South America" to whom the proclamation was addressed.[1] The specific educational complaints were many: poor instruction, almost exclusive emphasis on learning by rote from obsolete texts, inadequate libraries, absence of practical training, and teaching methods "characterized by a narrow dogmatism which contributes to the insulation of the university from science and modern learning." In his message of support to the students, Alfredo Palacios commented that it was necessary to eradicate from Latin America the ideas expressed by the influential professor at the University of Unreason in Samuel Butler's *Erewhon:* "Our mission is not to help students to think for themselves.... Our duty is to make them think as we do, or at least as we find it convenient to say we think.[2]

The operational basis for the introduction of reforms was to be student participation in the administrative and policy-making organs of the university. This would enable the universities to reform themselves while remaining autonomous, that is, independent of the state, which many reformers considered hostile to their goals. Student participation in the conduct of university affairs was also considered in tune with the pace of modern ideas: the university was to be "democratized." Luis Alberto Sánchez, twice rector of the University of San Marcos, wrote later that those who see in the reform movement "a symptom of chaos or backwardness only reveal their ignorance of the history and the current needs of our Universities."[3]

The demand for drastic changes in the university system, combined with a demand for student participation which was tantamount to a vote of no confidence in the professors, amounted to an intellectual revolution. The rise of the reform movement in fact reflected more than limited educational grievances: it was also a reaction to the political and social atmosphere of the university and to the place of universities in the political order. It was a reaction to the impact of World War I, which symbolized the corruption of Europe, and the consequent need, embodied at a distance in the Russian Revolution, of finding new forms of organization and progress. In their rebellion, the students were protesting not only the conception of education as "classics for aristocrats," but that of an elite society as well. Autonomy

---

[1] The impact of the reform movement had been felt throughout Latin America by 1930. See del Mazo, "Lo que significa la Reforma," *in* COSEC, *La reforma universitaria en América Latina,* pp. 17–44.

[2] Alfredo L. Palacios, *Mensaje a la juventud iberoamericana* (1918). Palacios, unlike some of his followers, was also a respecter of intellectual freedom. Cf. his World War I support of Bertrand Russell and praise for H.G. Wells' defense of the right of Eugene Debs to appear at Harvard under the auspices of the student council. *La universidad nueva* (1925), pp. 66–67. In March 1962, at the age of 82, Palacios was still sticking to his principles and resigned as senator from Buenos Aires to protest the military coup against Frondizi.

[3] Luis Alberto Sánchez, *La universidad latinoamericana* (Guatemala, 1949), p. 15.

was a prerequisite for reform of the university, and the reform of the university was in turn the first step toward the reform of the entire society.

The reform of the university was thus linked from the outset with national politics. This was due both to the reformers themselves (Palacios is a Socialist; Sánchez is an Aprista), and to the very concept of the university which they put forth. This concept is best defined in article 143 of the 1945 Constitution of Ecuador: "The universities are autonomous . . . and will particularly attend to the study and resolution of national problems and the spread of culture among the popular classes." The best characterization of such a view of the universities is that it is a dynamic but inherently contradictory conception which explicitly makes of the university a political institution.

There are at present fewer than 100 universities in Latin America. Recent years have seen the founding of many new universities, and as indicated in the conclusion, there is something of a qualitative change taking place as a result. Nonetheless, 10 countries still have only one university: these are the smaller countries which support a single "national" or state university.[1] In other countries, those universities not supported directly by the state are mainly Catholic institutions.[2] Private secular universities are few and, with the exception of Colombia, relatively uninfluential. Although the reform movement is national in scope and universal in tone and has provided a number of themes relevant to the private universities, its main impact has been on the national universities. These are the most important as well as the most numerous, and it is to them that we now turn.

Part Two

The writings of the reform movement, an Argentine professor has recently written, contain "nothing but rebellion and protest, utopias, proclamations, and vain words."[3] Such negative sentiments, although often widely shared, have failed to prevent the adoption, in the great majority of the national universities, of the main goals of the reform movement. The implementation has been uneven, partly as a result of ambiguity in the reform movement itself, and partly because of the ease with which the reform could be adapted to serve partisan political ends.

Autonomy has been recognized, at least verbally, almost everywhere. Sometimes this recognition has been embodied in constitutional provisions,

---

[1] Costa Rica, the Dominican Republic, El Salvador, Guatemala, Haiti, Honduras, Nicaragua, Panama, Paraguay, and Uruguay. Even in some of these countries, however, there have been recent efforts to develop new specialized institutes or to establish small private universities.

[2] The most important Catholic universities are those of Chile and Peru. None was allowed in Argentina prior to 1958. One aspect of the reform movement not dealt with in this paper has been its strong anticlerical flavor.

[3] Marcos Victoria, in the prologue to Alejandro Dussant, *Crisis en la universidad argentina* (Buenos Aires, AALC, 1961), p. 8.

but it is usually to be found in the opening articles of the statutes of the university. The concept itself is deeply rooted in the Latin American university tradition, and goes back to the medieval concept of the university as a guild with special "privileges and exemptions." The statutes of most of the early colonial universities were modeled directly on those of the University of Salamanca in Spain.[1] After independence, the universities were either nationalized or closed, and it was not until after the turn of the century, and especially after the development of the reform movement, that efforts were made to reestablish effective autonomy.

The least well-established aspect of autonomy is the economic one. Few of the universities have separate endowments apart from the allotment received from the national government. In some cases, efforts have been made to make constitutional provision for the establishment of an independent source of income. These provisions have led to the earmarking of certain tax revenues automatically for the universities, so that the state could directly control neither the quantity of funds nor their use. The penury of the Latin American universities has been such, however, that they have had to be continually at the mercy of the government for increases in funds.[2]

In practice, the autonomy issue has centered on administrative and political issues. A major test of autonomy is the means of selection of the rector. If the rector, who combines the attributes of president and dean at most United States universities, is chosen internally, by the university itself, there is autonomy; otherwise not. In normal experience, of course, such a formal line is often blurred in the course of actual relations with the government, but the formal legal question of selection of the rector has assumed a central position in the public debate.

Some of the elements of this problem can be best seen by looking briefly at some of the developments in Argentina since 1945. One of Juan Perón's first actions after being elected president was to intervene in university matters by appointing his own supporters to the positions of rector and deans of faculties at the University of Buenos Aires, where much of the opposition to him had been centered. This was followed by the promulgation, in

---

[1] "Although there were often complaints of viceregal interference in the choice of rectors, or in the recommendation of candidates for degrees, the University was one of the few corporations in America that retained any degree of autonomy." Clarence H. Haring, *The Spanish Empire in America* (1947), p. 230. Cf. Julio Jiménez Rueda, *Historia jurídica de la Universidad de México,* Part I (Mexico, Facultad de Filosofía y Letras, 1955).

[2] Some indication of relative resources may be gathered by comparing receipts of the University of California in 1958–1959, $153.7 million, with the combined central government receipts of Costa Rica, Panama, and Honduras for 1959, which came to $156.7 million. For political implications, see the tragic debate in July 1960 during which the administration of the University of Havana attempted to defend itself against *fidelista* student criticisms of its shortcomings by pointing out that the University of Puerto Rico, not a notoriously wealthy institution, had 25 per cent fewer students but seven times the income. *La Universidad de la Habana hacia una nueva etapa* (1960), pp. 3–4 and *passim.*

September 1947, of a new university law.[1] According to article 1 of the law, the university was granted "technical, educational, and scientific autonomy." But after thus paying lip service to the principle of autonomy, the law provided for the naming of the rector (article 10) and full professors *(titulares)* (article 46) by the "national executive": Perón.

During the formal act of promulgation of the new law, Perón complained that the intrusion of politics into the university was "lamentable," and that the university "must be separated from politics."[2] He personally had added article 47b to the new law, stating that "full professors cannot simultaneously teach and engage in any other form of public activity." Article 47 provided that professors "cannot defend interests which may oppose, compete, or collide with those of the Nation."

The result of the new law was that only Peronist professors could teach at Argentine universities. Within three months of the original intervention, 1,250 professors had resigned, and by 1953 there had been a 90 per cent turnover. Bernardo Houssay, 1947 Nobel Prize winner, had resigned under the accusation of "incompetence."[3]

The extent of Peronist intervention and control of the universities was revealed after his overthrow. The writer of this article was allowed to participate, in October 1955, in the study carried out by a special commission of the Lonardi provisional government of the files of the Ministry of Education and its dependent organs. This study revealed the existence of a "strictly secret" administrative police organization, the "Servicio de Enlace y Coordinación," as it was euphemistically named. Receiving information from such disparate sources as the Peronist labor union, the military intelligence service, the police, both branches of the Peronist party, and a large number of informers within the universities, 48 full-time employees developed an information system which covered every phase of Argentine university life. Essential information was maintained in this office on every one of Argentina's 100,000 professors and students. The effort to control the university had led to the development of complete personal folders on 70,000 of these students and professors. These folders contained copies of personal letters, reports from informers on friendships, conversations, political beliefs, and other related information. There was abundant evidence of the use of unsubstantiated information against individuals, and the development of a system whereby the rector of the

---

[1] *Ley Universitaria, Ley 13031* of September 26, 1947, *Archivos de la Universidad de Buenos Aires,* no. 22 (July–December, 1947), pp. 421–443.

[2] *Discurso del Excelentísimo Señor Presidente de la nación, General de Brigada Juan Perón, Acto de Promulgación de la Ley Universitaria* (Universidad de Buenos Aires, Departamento de Acción Social Universitaria, 1947), pp. 20–21.

[3] Cf. Lattendorf, "Doce años de dictadura en la universidad," *in* FUBA, *La reforma universitaria,* pp. 187–195.

university could be ordered to automatically dismiss students or professors.[1]

After the fall of Perón, the universities were briefly taken over by student organizations, who carried out a "counterpurge."[2] At the end of 1957, the Aramburu government reestablished autonomy, giving the right of election of the rector to the university assembly. The political preeminence of the university meant, however, that the political storm was largely passed on into the university itself. During the elections at the University of Buenos Aires in November and December 1962, there was much heat and occasional violence. When the electoral process came to its culmination in the vote for rector, a secret ballot was called for in the assembly, since "extra-university organisms of considerable power had operated in a rather open fashion" in an attempt to influence the election.[3] The establishment of autonomy had thus done much to free the university, but it had by no means eliminated the play of politics.

Neither of these episodes is unique. Although it is unlikely that the Peronist intervention has been matched fully, there have been similar situations reported in Paraguay, the Dominican Republic, and elsewhere.[4] The recent Cuban situation is probably not very different, although as will be seen below, its dynamics were initially different.

The efforts to seize control of universities by governments have often met with failure. Batista was never able to fully control the Cuban universities. Even Perón could not prevent the students from remaining organized underground against him. One of the aspects of university autonomy which has most often stayed the hand of those interested in intervening is the retention of the medieval concept of the immunity of the university. One current formulation of this concept reads: "The university grounds are inviolable. The maintenance of order within them falls within the competence and responsibility of the university authorities."[5] This means in practice that national police and military units cannot enter the grounds without the express authorization of the rector, who is generally loath to grant it.

---

[1] I have been unable to get a printed report, if any, of the investigation. The above account is from my notes at the time.

[2] An interesting account in English is Delmas, "The Revolution in Argentina's Universities," *The Reporter* (January 12, 1956), pp. 26–30. An extremely good account of life at the University of Buenos Aires following the return of autonomy will be found in Kalman H. Silvert, "Other People's Classrooms," in *The Conflict Society: Reaction and Revolution in Latin America* (1962).

[3] *La Nación* (Buenos Aires, December 8, 1962), p. 1.

[4] The best single source, though biased from the student side, for such events, including reports on Venezuela, the Dominican Republic, Paraguay, Nicaragua and Cuba, is the RIC *Yearbook,* published by the Research and Information Commission of COSEC (see note 2, p. 610). One of the more common means used is to have young persons employed by the security departments register in the universities as students.

[5] Title I, article 6, of the Venezuelan University Law of December 5, 1958. The law is available as an appendix to the study of Foción Febres Cordero, *Autonomía universitaria* (Caracas, Universidad Central, 1959). Cordero's companion book, *Reforma universitaria* (1960), completes one professor's massively documented account of the problem in Venezuela.

This concept, meant to assist the isolation of the university from partisan pressures and politics, has actually often increased them. The key element is the respect for political and civil liberties in the country at large. When these are respected, the immunity of the university takes on little importance. But when they are not, the university becomes the haven for the opposition, which uses it as a guarantee against persecution. This use of the university may not be physical in the sense of nonstudents occupying the grounds: there is always a student group ready to pronounce itself for freedom according to the definition desired by some outside group which may offer encouragement or financial support. Two aspects of this problem should be noted. The first is that although the students are usually supporting an outside group, and sometimes initiating opposition to a government, they are usually doing so voluntarily, out of the rebelliousness of youth. They are not normally the tools in any direct sense of outside groups, although they can often be exploited. The second is that although the question of university defense of unpopular politics is easiest to understand under some form of doctrinaire dictatorship, it has relevance under most present Latin American governments. There is little consensus on political values in Latin America, partly because of the rapid process of change which is taking place. Any government thus finds itself in a position of being bitterly opposed by some group, usually originating or finding an echo in the university. The desire to put pressure on the university is thus nearly always present. It is also very difficult to draw the line between justified and unjustified interventions, especially since any intervention will be a violation of autonomy.[1]

Autonomy, one of the chief original demands of the reform movement, has often been curtailed in the name of reform. This is one of the inherent tensions and contradictions in the place of the university in society. To function properly, goes the reformist conception, the university must be autonomous. But the function of the university is not thereby exhausted: it has a role to play in society, a role which is inherent in the education it gives and in the nature of the groups it educates. "If the University Reform were only a university reform, it would do no good, since a university cannot do any good in a country sunk in misery and vassalage."[2]

One attack on autonomy in the name of reform, which failed after a prolonged and violent student-professor strike, took place in Bolivia, after the national trade union (COB), at its spring 1955 national congress, called for the "centralization in the hands of the state of the systems and plans of

---

[1] The best account of the student viewpoint is given in *The Student Struggle in South America, Report of the International Student Conference Delegation, COSEC* (1958), which is also an excellent account of the student reform movement in South America.

[2] The author of this rather extreme but clear statement is Alberto Ciria, "Los estudiantes y la política en América Latina," *in* FUBA, *La reforma universitaria, 1918-1958.*

education of the universities" because they were "creating a class hostile to the interests of the revolution."[1] This effort failed because the government bowed to the united front of opposition from the universities, and because the demand for reform, which it would otherwise have tolerated, came from outside the university.

The most striking case, however, of the destruction of autonomy in the name of reform from within the university took place in Cuba in 1960. The Córdoba manifesto had seen the participation of students in the running of the university as a means of reforming the universities without curbing their autonomy. On July 1, 1960, the student federation at the University of Havana (FEU), then presided over by Rolando Cubela, a medical student who had attained the rank of major in the Escambray, issued a long manifesto complaining that,[2]

> . . . [the] University of Havana slumbers, ineffective, sterile, bureaucratic, insensible, as though it were not a part of the Republic, like a retrograde and cursed *feudum* in the heart of the liberated land.

In terms reminiscent of the Córdoba manifesto, the FEU declared "education in our university is a fraud . . . scientific inquiry is ignored . . . libraries are notable in their absence. . . ." It condemned the "sterile memorization of single texts," placed guilt squarely on the faculty and administration, and demanded a "true university reform." To attain this end, it proposed a 17-point program, including the "expulsion of incompetent, immoral, grafting, and counter-revolutionary professors."

When the university council, on which there was no student representation, refused to meet the FEU demands, invoking the autonomy, the FEU replied that,

> . . . you are the same ones—the names do not matter—who have been running the university for 30 years, and we have now understood that to make the University Reform with you would make as much sense as to have the Agrarian Reform implemented by those who would be hurt by it. You are the great landowners of culture. . . .[3]

A new governing junta of the university, composed of four students and four professors, constituted under the threat of student violence, declared nine days later that university autonomy should "be used not as a counter-revolutionary wall, but as a vehicle to promote the unity of the government,

---

[1] For a brilliant defense of university autonomy by a revolutionary rector, see Arturo Urquidi Morales, *Labor universitaria* (Cochabamba, Bolivia, Imprenta de la Universidad, 1955), pp. 95–113.

[2] *La Universidad de la Habana hacia una nueva etapa* (1960), p. 2.

[3] *Ibid.*, pp. 21–22.

the university, and the revolution."[1] What followed was entirely reminiscent of Perón.[2]

Part Three

Student participation in the government of the university is deeply rooted in the Latin American tradition. Its origin is to be found in the thirteenth century at the universities of Bologna and Salamanca, and the development of the self-ruling *universitas magistrorum et scholarium.* The reinstitution of student (and graduate) participation was one of the chief demands of the reform movement, and although it has not been the panacea its original proponents expected, it has had an important effect on the functioning of the typical national university.[3]

To the outsider, especially at first acquaintance, this impact has been generally contrary to the development of academic freedom as it is understood elsewhere in the world. Student pressure has been weighted heavily toward such things as student participation in the naming of professors, periodic competitions for professorial chairs (no tenure), and optional class attendance. The sources of these demands, at least one of which is diametrically opposed to the United States tradition of academic freedom, must be sought in three main factors.

The first is in the position of the students of the typical Latin American university. They distinguish themselves sharply from their United States counterparts in social position, age, and self-conception. Most students in Latin America, although they may come from middle-class families, have to work to support themselves through school. Often they find full-time

---

[1] *Ibid.,* p. 30.

[2] With the slight difference that many of Perón's acts were to the chant of *"zapatillos, si; universidad, no"* (shoes yes, university no), while the student federation at the University of Havana (FEU) said it was trying to "convert the entire island into a school."

[3] The exact pattern of the integration of students into the government of the universities varies considerably. In Panama, the situation is as follows: The students are represented by their federation (UEU). The UEU's major organ, the Directorio Estudiantil, is composed of 60 members, 10 from each of the university's six faculties. This organ meets monthly and determines student policy. The academic policy of the university is determined by the Consejo General Universitario, which also elects the rector. This body is composed of approximately 110 professors and 12 students. Administrative and financial matters are dealt with by the Junta Administrativa, which has 14 members, the rector of the university, the deans of each faculty, and six students, one from each faculty, and a representative of the Ministry of Education. In addition, the university has a separate board for each faculty, made up of the professors of the faculty and two students. The total of students sitting on the governing boards of the university is thus 30. Each student has an alternate, which gives us a total of 60 students participating directly in the governing of the university. These 60 are the same 60 who sit on the directorate of the UEU. The students have taken the responsibility well, I was told by the rector in 1956, and he feels that a number of improvements are the direct result of the student intervention. Faculty and professional discussions of these matters, together with the statutes of many of the universities, will be found in *Universidades,* the publication of the Unión de Universidades de América Latina.

employment, frequently in the government bureaucracy. One of the results is that they are both older and less likely to look upon themselves as apprentices or role transients. They are simultaneously students and citizens, very much like some graduate students in the United States.[1] To this self-conception is added their political importance, and their general tendency to manifest sharp generational differences with their elders: they have yet to mature and grow indifferent to the problems which surround them.[2]

The second factor concerns the nature of the teaching staff. Although there are some notable exceptions and rapid improvements are being made almost everywhere, few teaching positions at Latin American universities are full time, and fewer still are sufficiently remunerative to enable the professor to survive without additional employment.[3] As a result teachers are often ill prepared, have little opportunity to keep up with their fields of knowledge, and often tend to regard teaching at the university as a prestigeful hobby.[4]

Finally, there is the political factor once again. This affects both students and professors. The students are fearful of indoctrination or of expulsion from the university for engaging in activities which they consider to be either defensive or proper by right. The professors are often political appointees, or fearful of being replaced by political appointees.

The students urge optional attendance to give them the opportunity to boycott poor professors and to give them the chance to go on strike without fearing expulsion. They oppose tenure so as to be able to replace poor professors, or at least have the chance to try to do so, at regular intervals.

There is universal agreement that the situation is not ideal. Judgments made of the situation depend largely on expectations of alternatives.

---

[1] Or, one might be tempted to say, some of the younger generation of Negroes in the United States. But the situation is still different. Here is an excerpt from a letter from an officer of the FUA during the struggle against Perón: "We have learned with pleasure that at International Student Conferences they spoke about student lodgings, student travel, and so on, because this shows us the high level attained [in the United States and Western Europe], but as you understand, this did not have the least bit of practical importance for us. The practical thing for us was to live hidden from the political police, to print our clandestine newspapers, to have our meetings broken up, to be expelled from the universities, to be arrested. . . ." (Letter from Gerardo Andujar.)

[2] One of the fascinating questions still to be looked at by social scientists is: What happens to the university radicals when they graduate? The reform movement as a whole has been extremely radical since its inception.

[3] Venezuela, which pays its professors on a level comparable to most United States universities, is the major exception. In Bolivia, at the time of the 1955 crisis, professors who taught six hours a week were paid $8.00 a month. In Argentina, the salary for a full-time full professor may reach as high as $500 a month, but assistants fall to as low as $20.

[4] The recent growth of research institutes in the more advanced countries, often with U.S. foundation help, should help resolve these problems in the long run. One of the reasons why national systems of higher education have not developed more fully has been the already mentioned absence of resources, often abetted by the fact that families with money could send their sons to the United States and Europe for education. In some of the smaller countries, in particular, these numbers have recently reached 15 to 25 per cent of all students.

Part Four

Several factors combine to suggest that, although tensions and conflicts will remain, there will be an increasing trend away from the political university in Latin America. One of these is the erosion of the conservative and traditional insistence that the universities should have nothing to do with national life. Reformers have thus begun to consider the problem of *how* the university can best serve the nation, rather than the emotional question of *whether* it should do so. In Argentina since 1956 and in Mexico since somewhat earlier, the idea that the university can best serve the country by providing competent professionals trained in relevant fields has been gaining ground.[1] Another element of change is to be found in the expansion of systems of higher education and the changes introduced by the founding of new private universities and research institutes. This expansion of education and improvement of research and teaching is meeting one of the major demands of the reformers and weakening the drive of students to participate in the educational process.[2] Finally, the increase in the number of institutions makes life easier for the professors also: a professor unemployable for political reasons at one university may find employment at another. There is more room to breathe. A last important factor in the depoliticization of the university is the opportunity of graduates to find jobs in new government and private agencies working on development.

But the political tradition and many of the problems which gave rise to it remain with us. University autonomy finds three kinds of supporters: those who see it as the indispensable precondition of the educational process, those who are satisfied with the university the way it is and oppose changes in the name of autonomy, and those who see autonomy as a means of obtaining a platform from which to attack the government in power. University reform similarly finds three main types of supporters: those who believe substantive educational changes are necessary within the university; those who want to increase government control over the university; and lastly those who, although weak in the university, want to strengthen their position in it as a preliminary step to social reform.

This characterization implies that there is only one group almost likely to always support both autonomy and reform: the professional educator. But it also implies that more professionals are not in themselves enough to solve the problem of the political university. That problem will be reduced to a manageable level only when some form of broad political and social consensus emerges in Latin America.

---

[1] The question was particularly raised by Risieri Frondizi while rector of the University of Buenos Aires (1957–1962). Rector Chávez at the National Autonomous University of Mexico has recently strengthened the already strong Mexican tendency in this direction. See Frondizi, "La universidad y sus misiones," *Comentario* (October–November–December, 1956), pp. 3–9 ff. (reprinted in both COSEC, *La reforma universitaria en América Latina,* and FUBA, *La reforma universitaria 1918–1958).*

[2] A number of these phenomena have already been at work in Mexico for some time.

A Comparison
of the University Reform Movements
in Argentina and Colombia

KENNETH N. WALKER

Student politics in Latin America are looked upon by many observers as something endemic to Latin American culture, personality, institutions, or all three. While it is probably true that much of the general character and frequency of student collective action can be accounted for by specific characteristics of Latin America, including relatively unstable or despotic governments in many of these societies, we now know that student political rebellion in the Western hemisphere is not restricted to the lands south of the United States, especially after the Berkeley revolt. But the political role of students in Latin America is, by and large, of more political significance in Latin than in North America, given the direct opposition by student movements to national governments on frequent occasions, and less frequently, directed toward the overthrow of governments.

There are a number of characteristics which differentiate Latin American from North American universities and colleges which may account for the disparity in the frequency and intensity of student politics between the two continents. Salient among these characteristics are the lack of a full-time faculty and the presence of student participation in university government in most Latin American universities. The university reform movement has often been pointed to as a significant force in bringing about student participation in university government, and as a factor in maintaining student political involvement at a high level. There are relatively few studies in Spanish dealing with the origins, development and consequences of the university reform movement, and almost none in English. It is generally

Reproduced, by permission, from *Comparative Education Review,* 10 (June, 1966), pp. 257–272.

known, however, that the movement began in Argentina and spread to other Latin American nations, with varying consequences for student politics and universities in the societies in which it took hold. A comparative analysis of the origins and effects of the reform movement in Argentina and another society in which the movement developed under quite different conditions, Colombia, should contribute to a deeper understanding of the present character of student politics in Latin America, especially in these two countries. This article will provide a brief historical account of those aspects of the origins of higher education in Latin America which are relevant to a discussion of more-recent student political movements, and will assess the development of the university reform movement in relationship to the characters of student politics in the two societies.

The historical antecedents of Latin American universities derive from the structure of Spanish universities of the fifteenth and sixteenth centuries, the period in which the first Latin American universities were established. The participation of students in university government was instituted in these first universities, including the election of rectors and of "catedráticos," or holders of university chairs. The proportion of student representation was reduced from that of the University of Salamanca, the Spanish university on which Latin American universities were modeled,[1] but the autonomous status of the university was retained.

> Although there were often complaints of viceregal interference in the choice of rectors, or in the recommendation of candidates for degrees, the University was one of the few corporations in America that retained any degree of autonomy.[2]

Writers on the Latin American university and the university reform movement suggest that the tradition of student participation in university government during colonial times is an important precedent for the claims made by the university reform movement in the twentieth century. However, it should be noted that at the University of San Marcos in Peru students did not participate in the election of the rector. Students were under the direct disciplinary control of the rector, who had the authority to mete out severe punishment for acts committed by students within or outside the university environs. The students' most important decision-making role appears to have been that of voting for contestants to university chairs.[3] This latter privilege was eventually withdrawn, due to the tendency of

---

[1] Gabriel del Mazo, *La reforma universitaria y la universidad latino-americana* (Resistencia: Universidad Nacional del Nordeste, 1957), pp. 77–78; Roberto Mac-Lean y Estenos, *La crisis universitaria en Hispano-América* (Mexico, D.F.: Universidad Nacional, 1956), pp. 89–92.

[2] Clarence H. Haring, *The Spanish Empire in America* (New York: Oxford University Press, 1947), p. 230.

[3] David Rubio, ed., *La Universidad de San Marcos de Lima durante la colonización española* (Madrid: Imprenta Juan Bravo, 3, 1933), pp. 47–56, 151–154, *passim;* John Tate Lanning, *Academic Culture in the Spanish Colonies* (London: Oxford University Press, 1940), pp. 44–56.

professors to ". . . succumb to the temptation to popularize and cater to the student's plebeian tastes. . . ."[1] Thus the precedent for student participation in university government is perhaps more appropriately referred to the University of Bologna, where students originally had the sole power to employ and dismiss professors.

The university was established and maintained primarily for the education of select members of the elite, and was slow to respond to intellectual and scientific currents from Europe and North America, to broaden its educational content to provide a wider and more practical content to meet the needs of new professions, or to conduct research directed to the economic and social problems of Latin American societies.[2]

Development of the University Reform Movement in Argentina

Argentina provides the setting for the first and most significant effort at university reform in Latin America. While the origin of the university reform is generally given as 1918, the date of the famous Córdoba Manifesto, its antecedents were some years earlier. As early as 1871, law students at the University of Buenos Aires mounted a university reform movement which had some effect on the structure of that university, and students of law and medicine at Buenos Aires were active in a reform movement from 1903 to 1906. In 1908 the University Federation of Buenos Aires was founded, and in the same year the first congress of American students was held, where the principle of student representation in university directive councils was proclaimed "by acclamation."

> The First International Congress of American Students accepts as an aspiration, which should be put into practice as soon as possible, the representation of students in the directive councils of university education, by means of delegates, named directly by them and renewed as frequently as possible.[3]

This principle was proclaimed subsequently in the second and third congresses of this body in 1910 and 1912, and in 1916 the University Federation of Buenos Aires sought unsuccessfully to obtain student representation in the superior council of the university.[4]

In 1918, at the University of Córdoba, what appears to have been the first large-scale attack by a Latin American student body against the university system took place. A student strike was declared, the university was closed by superior council of the university; and the Radical party government of President Hipólito Irigoyen intervened, resulting in the

---

[1] Lanning, *Academic Culture in the Spanish Colonies,* p. 56.

[2] For the state of science and medicine in the colonial period, see Lanning, *Academic Culture in the Spanish Colonies,* pp. 93–111; Haring, *The Spanish Empire in America,* pp. 238–242.

[3] As quoted by Gabriel del Mazo, *Estudiantes y gobierno universitario* (Buenos Aires: Librería "El Ateneo" Editorial, 1956), p. 25.

[4] Del Mazo, *La reforma universitaria y la universidad latino-americana,* p. 27.

institutionalization of several university reform demands as university law. The principal reforms enacted were the following: university attendance to be free and conditional only on successful completion of secondary school studies; students, professors and graduates to be represented on the governing councils of the university and of the faculty; the rector and deans of faculties to be ex officio members of the superior council of the university, and to be elected, the deans by majority vote of faculty councils, and the rector by the university assembly, composed of equal representation of students, faculty, and graduates; and professors to be free to teach and students free to attend classes without compulsion or restriction. Additional reforms were also enacted, including provision for university extension courses for the public, regulations concerning examinations, and the periodicity of the "cátedra" or chair, by which professors are subject to appointment or reappointment every six years, by election within the faculty directive councils, decided by a two-thirds vote of delegates.[1] These reforms were not enacted all at once, nor did they remain in force continually in Argentine universities from their inception, since there have been several counterreforms, in 1923, 1929–1930, 1943 and 1946, involving in some cases military occupation of the universities and the enactment of presidential decrees abrogating university statutes which embodied university reform principles.[2]

The causes and consequences of the university reform movement as these bear on a comparative analysis of the student political context in Colombia and Argentina are of major concern, since the relative success or failure of the movement has determined the character and shaped the context of contemporary student politics. It appears that the major impetus for the movement was a reaction against the archaic and oligarchic structure of the university, characterized by nepotism, and emphasis on formalism in lectures and an absence of practical training, and the domination of the university by a self-perpetuating governing council with little concern for the interests of students or lower-status professors or for the cultural needs of the nation, and with little or no support of original research, development of new fields of study or new methods of teaching.[3] The following passage from the "Córdoba Manifesto" of 1918 presents a perhaps exaggerated image of the old university, but expresses its ideological definition by reformist students.

> Up to now the universities have been the secular refuge of mediocrities, have provided a salary for the ignorant and a safe hospital for invalids, and what is worse,

---

[1] Del Mazo, *Estudiantes y gobierno,* pp. 29–73; Carlos Cossio, *La reforma universitaria* (Buenos Aires: Espasa-Calpe, S.A., 1927), pp. 119–173.

[2] Del Mazo, *Estudiantes y gobierno,* pp. 74–96.

[3] See Carlos Cossio, *La reforma universitaria,* pp. 39–86, for a characterization of the "old University."

have provided a place where all forms of tyranny and insensitivity could be taught. The universities have thus come to be faithful reflections of a decadent society, offering a sad spectacle of immobile senility. Before these closed and silent houses, wisdom passes silently or enters distorted and grotesque into the service of bureaucracy.[1]

Such conditions were probably widespread in Latin American universities, despite considerable cultural diversity among Latin American nations. A typical indictment of Latin American universities up to recent times emphasizes the discrepancy between the needs brought about by major social change and the inadequate response of the universities, which continue to prepare professionals for only a limited number of fields and to emphasize a metaphysical, speculative approach to knowledge rather than an experimental, pragmatic one concerned with social realities.[2]

Considering the apparently widespread decadence of the university in nineteenth-century Latin America, one may ask why the reform movement developed first and with such intensity in Argentina rather than elsewhere. An adequate answer to this question would require a comparative analysis of the situation in all of the Latin American nations during the latter part of the nineteenth and the early twentieth century. A partial answer, however, may be provided by a close look at the development of the movement in Argentina from the perspective of Neil Smelser's theory of collective behavior.[3] The advantage of this theoretical approach is that it provides categories for analysis in terms of the major components of social action, permitting the specification of the presence or absence of conditions which appear to be crucial for the character and outcome of collective behavioral phenomena. These conditions are defined in sufficiently abstract terms to permit the analysis of different social movements in varying social contexts, thus avoiding the difficulties for comparative analysis inherent in the natural history approach to collective behavior. The theory provides a set of determinants which, Smelser asserts, must be present for collective behavior to occur, and specifies the consequences of variations in the character of these determinants for the type of collective behavior which ensues. Two types of social movements are defined, among other types of collective behavior. These are the "norm-oriented" and the "value-oriented" movements. The first is defined as ". . . an attempt to restore, protect, modify, or create norms in the name of a generalized belief,"[4] the second as ". . . a collective attempt to restore, protect, modify, or create values in the name of a

[1] "The Argentine Youth of Córdoba to the Free Men of South America," in Federación Universitaria de Buenos Aires, *La reforma universitaria, 1918–1958* (Buenos Aires, 1959), p. 23.

[2] Mac-Lean y Estenos, *La crisis universitaria,* pp. 13–17.

[3] Neil J. Smelser, *Theory of Collective Behavior* (New York: The Free Press of Glencoe, 1963).

[4] *Ibid.,* p. 270.

generalized belief."[1] While the university reform movement had some overtones of a value-oriented movement, in its nationalist emphasis on moral and social regeneration, its major focus was on alteration of the norms governing institutions of higher education in Argentina, and later throughout Latin America. Thus the determinants of collective behavior in the form which results in a norm-oriented movement will be applied to analyze the inception of the Argentine university reform movement and to account for the less successful character of this movement in Colombia.

According to Smelser, the determinants of collective behavior are: (a) structural conduciveness, (b) structural strain, (c) growth and spread of a generalized belief, (d) precipitating factors, (e) mobilization of participants for action, and (f) the operation of social control. All of these are necessary for the development of some form of collective behavior, the first five as positive determinants and the sixth as a negative or counterdeterminant. Social control serves to prevent collective behavior or to channel it once it has begun.[2]

STRUCTURAL CONDUCIVENESS

"The most general condition of conduciveness concerns the possibility for demanding modifications of norms *without simultaneously appearing to demand a more fundamental modification of values.*"[3] The university reform movement limited its demands to modifications in university structures in the name of the need to democratize and modernize them, and in the interests of the nation as a whole. While the values appealed to as a basis for legitimatizing the demand for institutional reforms were general ones, they were held to be consistent with national values and interests, while the universities were held to be in the grip of old and outmoded values.[4]

1. "In general, the discontented must have *some* degree of access to some method of affecting the normative order."[5] The reform movement, as it turned out, had direct access to and a hospitable reception from the newly elected Radical president, Hipólito Irigoyen, who not only intervened in Córdoba University, but in other universities and institutionalized many of the demands of the movement by presidential decree. Here it should be pointed out that while universities were nominally autonomous, the national government promulgated the basic organic laws of each university. As Luigi Einaudi points out,[6] in practice the question of autonomy has

---

[1] *Ibid.,* p. 313.

[2] *Ibid.,* pp. 15–18.

[3] *Ibid.,* p. 278. (Emphasis in original.)

[4] See del Mazo, ed., *La reforma universitaria,* Vol. 1 (La Plata: Centro de los Estudiantes de Ingeniería, 1941), pp. 1–114, for documents concerning the movement in its initial, 1918 phase.

[5] Smelser, *Theory of Collective Behavior,* p. 282.

[6] Luigi Einaudi, "University Autonomy and Academic Freedom in Latin America," *Law and Contemporary Problems,* 28, no. 3 (Summer, 1963), p. 640.

centered on the means of selection of the rector, and when the university itself chooses the rector, it is considered autonomous. Students sought inclusion in the process of electing the rector, but they were not seeking autonomy, since governing councils of the universities already chose their own rectors.

The marked success of the movement in Argentina must then be attributed, to an important degree, to a sympathetic government. The Radical party had developed from a movement of middle-class elements directed against the Conservative oligarchy in the late nineteenth century, which became institutionalized in the Unión Cívica Radical party, with the goal of the secret ballot and the enfranchisement of all adult males.[1] A liberal wing of the Conservative party developed which also espoused these goals, and in 1912 it succeeded in passing the Sáenz Peña law, granting universal and secret male suffrage. Irigoyen was elected in 1916 with a majority of the popular vote, but a majority of only one in the electoral college, due in part to opposition from within his own party.[2] Thus it may be argued that without the access to a sympathetic president, the movement might have become a value-oriented one with revolutionary goals, or might have reverted to "hostile outbursts," defined as "action mobilized on the basis of a generalized belief assigning responsibility for an undesirable state of affairs to some agent."[3] Its success as a norm-oriented movement permitted its institutionalization and its symbolic value as a model for similar movements elsewhere in Latin America.

2. "Any discussion of structural conduciveness must refer also to the lack of alternative channels for expressing dissatisfaction."[4] During the early stages of the 1918 movement and later there were acts of violence and force, including seizure of various universities on occasion, and resulting in the imprisonment of students. These manifestations may be considered an aspect of the uncertainty of the effectiveness of appeals to the president, since initial reforms did not immediately grant student participation in university government, perhaps the principal change in norms sought by the movement, and thus recourse to other forms of protest were sought. The effectiveness of social control by the government and the willingness of the government to intercede and eventually to institute the demanded reforms limited the use of violence by the student movement.

3. "Like all collective outbursts, a norm-oriented movement requires a certain ability to communicate if beliefs are to be disseminated and action to be mobilized."[5] University students are especially well situated in this

---

[1] James R. Scobie, *Argentina: A City and a Nation* (New York: Oxford University Press, 1964), pp. 200–201.

[2] *Ibid.,* p. 203.

[3] Smelser, *Theory of Collective Behavior,* pp. 9, 284.

[4] *Ibid.,* p. 285.

[5] *Ibid.,* p. 286.

respect, as a collectivity with a high degree of access of members to one another, due to their joint presence at university centers. As the Córdoba Manifesto and others like it attest, Argentine university students were in full command of an impelling rhetoric to dramatize and justify demands and actions, especially to fellow students in other university centers.

STRUCTURAL STRAIN

This term is used as a general referent for words like "malintegration," "disorganization," "conflict," "anomie," and others in the literature on collective behavior referring to some kind of trouble people experience in their environment which results in one or another form of collective behavior.[1] Strain is discussed in terms of what Smelser calls the four "components of action—facilities, organization of motivation, norms and values." The most relevant components for locating strain in the environment of Argentine university students appear to be norms and values.

1. "Any disharmony between normative standards and actual social conditions can provide the basis for a movement whose objective it is to modify the norms. This is particularly true when either norms or social conditions undergo rapid change in a relatively short time."[2] The period during which the university reform developed, from about 1890 to 1918, was a period of rapid social change in Argentina, with the influx of large numbers of European immigrants, rapid urbanization, industrialization, and political conflict between the middle classes, represented by the Radical party, and the oligarchic Conservative ruling party.[3] Clearly the norms governing universities were inappropriate to these conditions, which brought pressures for modernization and democratization in all spheres of Argentine life.

2. "The rise of new values frequently creates bases for defining certain social conditions as 'evils'—social conditions which previously had passed less noticed."[4] The years preceding and during the reform witnessed the influence in political and social life of new values and ideologies. These included radicalism, socialism, anarchism, communism, especially through the influence of the Russian Revolution, and the influence of the First World War.[5] Carlos Cossio also attributes an important change in Argentine intellectual life to the 1916 visit of the Spanish philosopher Ortega y Gasset, in which he introduced to an Argentine audience neo-Kantian philosophy.[6]

---

[1] *Ibid.*, pp. 47–48.

[2] *Ibid.*, p. 288.

[3] See Scobie, *Argentina*, pp. 189-214, 275-277.

[4] Smelser, *Theory of Collective Behavior*, p. 289.

[5] See Sergio Bagú, "Como se gestó la reforma universitaria," *in* Federación Universitaria de Buenos Aires, *La reforma universitaria, 1918-1958*, pp. 28-33; Cossio, *La reforma universitaria*, pp. 102-104; del Mazo, *La reforma universitaria y la universidad latino-americana*, pp. 10-12; Einaudi, "University Autonomy," p. 638.

[6] Cossio, *La reforma universitaria*, pp. 104-107.

The influence of these values and historical events is evident in the populist democratic, anticlerical, antiimperialist, nationalist, and pacifist sentiments of the movement, although present in a diffuse and sometimes incoherent form.[1] The cumulation of these "modern" values and ideas provided ample ideological armament for judging and condemning the "old university."

GENERALIZED BELIEFS AND THE ROLE OF PRECIPITATING FACTORS

For a norm-oriented movement, the generalized belief includes a diagnosis of the forces and agents that are making for a failure of normative regulation. It also involves some sort of program—passing a law, creating a regulatory agency, scrapping an antiquated custom, etc. Those committed to the belief that adoption of this program will control, damage, or punish the responsible agent, and thus erase the source of strain [sic]. The combination of all these components results in a "cause" in the name of which the aggrieved mobilize and agitate for normative change.[2]

The Córdoba Manifesto, cited above, provides all of these elements of a generalized belief, including diagnosis, remedy, and an element not mentioned but presumably an important one for gaining broad support, that of legitimatization of the grounds for proposing the diagnosis and reforms. This latter element was put forth as an assertion of the right of inherently virtuous and as yet uncorrupted youth to play its part in university government unselfishly and wisely.

Youth lives in an ambience of heroism. It is disinterested and pure. It has not yet had time to become corrupt. It can never be mistaken in choosing its own teachers. Flattery and bribery would obtain no advantage with youth. (Córdoba Manifesto.)[3]

The remedies in the form of proposed university laws were set forth in considerable detail in messages to the minister of education.[4] It must be assumed, of course, that the generalized beliefs expressed in the Córdoba Manifesto and subsequent declarations were the result of a cumulative development, beginning at least with the first international student congress in Montevideo, and proceeding through a succession of conflicts at the University of Buenos Aires during the intervening years.[5]

1. "Precipitating factors focus the belief on a particular person, event or situation."[6] The major precipitating event which gave the movement its initial national and international impetus appears to have been the expulsion

---

[1] Tulio Halperin Donghi, *Historia de la Universidad de Buenos Aires* (Buenos Aires: Editorial Universitaria de Buenos Aires, 1962), p. 132.

[2] Smelser, *Theory of Collective Behavior*, p. 292.

[3] Federación Universitaria de Buenos Aires, *La reforma universitaria, 1918-1958*, pp. 24-25.

[4] Del Mazo, ed., *La reforma universitaria*, pp. 9-28.

[5] Halperin Donghi, *Historia de la Universidad de Buenos Aires*, pp. 106-129. Moderate success was achieved at Buenos Aires in the inclusion of all faculty members in the electoral body for faculty and university governing councils.

[6] Smelser, *Theory of Collective Behavior*, p. 294.

by indignant students of the members of the university assembly of Córdoba University from the meeting called for the installation of the rector opposed by the students. This was followed by a student strike and the closing of the university by its superior council. The events which preceded the action of the students are the following. The University of Córdoba was one of the most backward in the country, opposing intellectual currents which challenged the dogmas of the church. Although the university was secular and established by the national government, it remained in the control of a small group opposed to all reform. Tulio Halperin characterizes this group as follows:

> ... the University was in the hands of a group bound together by all sorts of ties, not only ideological or religious ones, and was disposed to avoid every change which menaced the solidity of their domination. This situation was linked to the existence of a more or less secret society—the *Corda fratres*—like that of the mysterious "Congregation" of the French Restoration, to which was imputed the goal of assuring the triumph of ideas which promoted the prosperity of those who sustained them.[1]

Student opposition to the hegemony of this group had taken the form of a series of public lectures in 1916, challenging Catholic dogma and diagnosing the ills of the university. These lectures aroused considerable public interest and strong opposition from the clergy. They were followed in 1917 by a series entitled the "popular university," with courses on public hygiene, civic virtue, penal law and political economy.[2] Student opposition gained support from the national government, which intervened in the university in April, 1918, following a student strike and the closing of the university in March. The university statutes were modified and new elections for deans and members of the university assembly were held in which all those candidates with student support won. But in the election for rector a candidate of the *Corda fratres* won, and the students reacted as described above, apparently because they felt betrayed by those they had supported for election.[3]

The experience by the students of defeat in the midst of what had appeared to be an assured victory led to the dramatic occupation of the assembly hall and to the impassioned manifesto, which together gave a symbolic significance to the movement which it had lacked previously. This may be considered an example of the "power of limited setbacks to invigorate a movement."[4] The outcome of the election for rector had the advantage for the movement of giving concrete evidence of the corrupt

[1] Halperin Donghi, *Historia de la Universidad de Buenos Aires*, p. 129.

[2] Del Mazo, ed., *La reforma universitaria*, pp. 465–467.

[3] See Halperin Donghi, *Historia de la Universidad de Buenos Aires*, pp. 130–131; del Mazo, *Estudiantes y gobierno*, pp. 34–35; Federación Universitaria de Buenos Aires, *La reforma universitaria, 1918–1958*, p. 9.

[4] Smelser, *Theory of Collective Behavior*, p. 294.

character which students had imputed to the faculty and served to legitimize their direct action, contrasting their moral superiority to that of the faculty and rector.

> The acts of violence, for which we were wholly responsible, were done in behalf of pure ideas. We stopped an anachronistic uprising, and we did so in order to raise a new spirit in these ruins. Those acts also represented the measure of our indignation in the presence of moral destitution and cunning deceit, which pretended to infiltrate itself under the guise of legality. (Córdoba Manifesto.)[1]

MOBILIZATION OF THE MOVEMENT FOR ACTION

"Characteristic of the mobilization of the norm-oriented movement is the complexity and time involved in organizing and implementing its program."[2] Smelser outlines three phases of mobilization characteristic of norm-oriented movements: "the incipient phase, the phase of enthusiastic mobilization, and the period of institutionalization and organization."[3] The incipient phase would appear to be that of the period prior to 1918, perhaps beginning as early as 1871, with the formation of the "thirteenth of December" movement by law students at the University of Buenos Aires. Reform-oriented movements or activities appear to have been sporadic in the years preceding the second decade of the twentieth century, and confined to individual faculties. The period 1903–1906 was one of student protest and strikes at Buenos Aires, culminating in reforms which made the *academias,* the term applied then to the faculties, a more integral and less autonomous part of the university and provided for greater participation of professors in university government.[4]

The period 1918 to the early 1920's represents the "phase of enthusiastic mobilization," since during this period occurred the organization of the Argentine University Federation, the Córdoba revolt, the first national congress of students (of Argentina), government intervention at Córdoba and the reform of the statutes governing Córdoba and Buenos Aires universities, providing for the participation of students in university government. Beginning in 1919 and continuing into the 1920's, the reform movement spread to other Latin American countries, with varying success in the institution of reforms. In Argentina the movement became institutionalized with the formation of university governments involving the representation of students and other reforms. The period from the 1920's up to the present may be considered the period of institutionalization and organization. There were several attempts at counterreform during this period, the most notable during Perón's rule, but these were vicissitudes of the

---

[1] Federación Universitaria de Buenos Aires, *La reforma universitaria, 1918–1958,* p. 25.
[2] Smelser, *Theory of Collective Behavior,* p. 296.
[3] *Ibid.,* p. 298.
[4] Halperin Donghi, *Historia de la Universidad de Buenos Aires,* pp. 78–122; del Mazo, *Estudiantes y gobierno,* pp. 22–28.

universities as a whole, not merely of the movement. Once the principle of direct student participation was assured, the movement became a party, winning all elections at the University of Buenos Aires up to 1961 and providing an organizational base for liberals and leftists. As Smelser states, ". . . a successful movement usually begins to focus on other, related reforms, or becomes a guardian of the normative changes it has won. . . ."[1] Clearly the university reform movement conforms to the latter alternative. Each time the basic principles of university reform were abrogated by the government, the adherents of reform struggled to reinstate them. Following Perón's overthrow in 1955, students seized the universities and carried out an orderly "counterpurge" of Peronist professors, reestablishing student involvement in university government before it was officially reinstated by the national government.[2]

SOCIAL CONTROL

This determinant is primarily that of the response of society to a movement, primarily through its political or other agencies of social control. The character of this response determines whether the movement maintains its character or becomes another type of movement.

1. "Differentiation of political from other aspects of social control makes for greater toleration of norm-oriented movements."[3] The reform movement appealed directly to the relevant political authority, that of the president, through his minister of education. There was no ambiguity concerning the locus of relevant authority, since the national government made the law concerning the institutions of higher education, and was empowered to intervene in disputes of sufficiently serious proportions.

2. "The success that a given agitation has in the political arena influences a movement's course of development."[4] The dependence of the movement's success on the fact that a newly elected Radical president had just entered office on a platform of widening democracy has been pointed out above. Although Irigoyen's government had wide popular support and could be characterized initially as democratic and modern, there were strong personalist tendencies in his rule, and although universal manhood suffrage prevailed, he was careful to insure nomination of his own supporters as candidates for office. Regarding the Radicals' orientation to the university reform movement, the Argentine historian José Luis Romero says the following:

Although the Radical government, because of its militant opposition to the

---

[1] Smelser, *Theory of Collective Behavior*, p. 306.
[2] See Nancy Delmas, "The Revolution in Argentina's Universities," *The Reporter* (January 12, 1956), pp. 26–30.
[3] Smelser, *Theory of Collective Behavior*, p. 306.
[4] *Ibid.*

oligarchy, supported the university reform movement, and consented to modify the statutes regulating the institutions of higher education, the party was nonetheless remote from the true spirit impelling the young students who sensed the revolutionary restlessness of the day.[1]

Thus it was not necessarily common ideals and principles but rather a common enemy which provided government support for the university reform movement.

Without the generally favorable response of Irigoyen, the movement might have become diverted into "hostile outbursts," or expanded into a value-oriented, revolutionary movement. In fact the movement's tactics often included what may be considered "hostile outbursts," but most characteristic was the seizure of universities, presumably to dramatize the lack of legitimacy accorded by students to university government and to insure intervention by a sympathetic government.

The Colombian Student Movement for University Reform

Colombia, like nearly all other Latin American countries, was influenced by the Argentine student movement, and took as a model many of its proposals and much of its diffuse ideology. This emulation was not successful in bringing about major reforms through direct action, however, and the reform law which was eventually promulgated in 1935 was not a direct consequence of student pressure, as in Argentina, and reveals only a moderate influence of the movement. Although the historical evidence for student political action in this period is inadequate, it would appear that the movement was not broadly supported by students and also lacked the crucial advantage of the Argentine movement in 1918, that of a sympathetic government. To place the analysis in a comparative perspective, and to seek to explain its lack of success as compared to that of the movement in Argentina, the analysis will be organized in terms of the determinants of collective behavior, as in the preceding discussion.

STRUCTURAL CONDUCIVENESS

As noted above, the possibility for demanding modification of norms without also appearing to demand a more fundamental modification of values is the most general condition of conduciveness. To assess this possibility requires a brief discussion of the origins and situation of the student movement in Colombia. It appears to have begun, at least officially, in the early 1920's. The first national student congress took place in 1923, although documents are available only for the second congress in 1924. While the documents from this meeting and the writings of Germán Arciniegas,

---

[1]José Luis Romero, *A History of Argentine Political Thought* (Stanford, Calif.: Stanford University Press, 1963), p. 223.

apparently the major spokesman of the movement, concentrate on critiques and proposals for reform similar to those put forth by the Argentine movement, several of the most active participants appear to have been involved in more radical political activity oriented toward the society at large. This suggests that the movement at this stage may have been compromised by tendencies toward a value-oriented movement. The period of the 1920's was one of considerable social change and political conflict. Colombia was much less developed economically and socially than Argentina, as reflected by the greater predominance of agriculture in the economy and the primarily rural character of the populace, and was less influenced by European events and ideologies through the mass media and trade with Europe than was Argentina. World War I and its aftermath nevertheless brought about change through the impact of new international markets, the influx of foreign capital, and, as in Argentina, the influence of revolutionary socialist doctrine.[1] With increasing urbanization and industrialization, unions were organized and labor-management conflict increased in the cities, while Indian and peasant uprisings occurred in rural areas. During this period Socialist and Communist parties were formed, largely by young intellectuals. Fluharty describes the role of the young intellectuals as follows:

> This potent brew of social ferment was ably stirred by a new generation of young intellectuals. Rejecting the old ideas regarding equality, these young men, many of whom were destined to become national political leaders, were irresistably [sic] drawn into the social fray. Gabriel Turbay, Luis Tejada, Hernández Rodríguez, and Moises Prieto organized the Communist Party. Intrigued chiefly by the doctrine of the class struggle, they actually knew little about Marx, and cared less. Others, Dios Romero and Mario Cano among them, sponsored labor syndicalism, and men like Germán Arciniegas, Armando Solano, and Juan Lozano plunged happily into the strong current of socialism running through the nation.[2]

Several of those mentioned above, including Arciniegas, Turbay and Prieto, also signed declarations presented at the second Colombian student congress, in 1924.[3] The young intellectuals' involvement in Marxist study groups contradicts Fluharty's statement that they knew or cared little for Marx. This group included Turbay and Prieto, among others.[4] The implication of these involvements in radical political and intellectual movements suggests that the university reform movement may have been invigorated by radical fervor on the one hand, while alienating potential student members on the other hand, for the same reason. While the Argentine reform movement

---

[1] Vernon Lee Fluharty, *Dance of the Millions: Military Rule and the Social Revolution in Colombia, 1930–1956* (Pittsburgh, Pa.: University of Pittsburgh Press, 1957), pp. 28–29.

[2] *Ibid.*, p. 29.

[3] Del Mazo, ed., *La reforma universitaria*, pp. 104–106.

[4] Diego Montaña Cuellar, *Colombia: País formal y país real* (Buenos Aires: Editorial Platina, 1963), p. 131.

was radical in its demands for university reform, and while it was influenced by socialist ideology and theory and by the example of the Russian Revolution as a model for the seizure of power, it nonetheless limited itself to reforms which were possible within a government dominated by the party then in power. In contrast, Conservatives dominated Colombian elections, primarily through fraud and coercion, from 1886 to 1930, when a Liberal party candidate won.[1] Thus the advent of radical left politics occurred in a period with no apparent political outlet except revolution or agitation.

Access to Methods for Affecting the Normative Order

An example of the limited access to such methods available to the reform movement at that time is provided in a message from students to the members of a German educational mission, invited to Colombia for the purpose of proposing educational reforms.[2] The message contains a comprehensive critique and set of proposals for university reform, modeled on those of the Argentine experience.[3]

Proposals for reform were made to Congress in 1925 by the German technical mission and their three Colombian university professor counterparts and included the proposal that the university ". . . should be a juridical person governed by its own legal bodies; that is, the faculty staff, the university council, the rector, and the representatives of the student body."[4] While the students may have been influential in the drafting of this proposal, it was not enacted into law, although it constituted a precedent for subsequent reform.[5]

Lack of Alternative Channels for Expressing Dissatisfaction

Short of seizing the universities by force and seeking to impose reforms, an action which would not have met with government support, the most likely channel of reform lay in influencing the government, which, as in Argentina and everywhere in Latin America, determines the constitution of public universities. On the other hand, alternative channels did exist through involvement in various left political movements and groups, as noted above, and while these were not concerned directly with university reform, they offered a base for attacking the same oligarchy which resisted reform in the universities. The influence of such involvement, which was perhaps

[1] Jesus María Henao and Gerardo Arrubla, *History of Colombia,* translated and edited by J. Fred Rippy (Chapel Hill, N.C.: The University of North Carolina Press, 1938), pp. 54–541.

[2] See Germán Arciniegas *et al.,* "Mensaje de la juventud a los miembros de la Misión Pedagógica," *in* del Mazo, ed., *La reforma universitaria,* Vol. 2, pp. 100–104.

[3] See Arciniegas, "Carta a los antiguos alumnos del Gimnasio Moderno," *in* del Mazo, ed., *La reforma universitaria,* Vol. 2, pp. 110–111.

[4] Orlando Fals Borda, "Basis for a Sociological Interpretation of Education in Colombia," *in* A. Curtis Wilgus, ed., *The Caribbean: Contemporary Colombia* (Gainesville, Fla.: University of Florida Press, 1962), p. 208.

[5] *Ibid.*

proportionately greater than that on student activists in Argentina in 1918, is evident in the declarations of the third national congress of students in 1928. In addition to goals of university reform, there were several relating to broad social reform, including "equality of life chances," the "ideological liberation of women," and the legal equality of women. Another goal was defined as "national defense, demanding the effective nationalization of petroleum and the conservation of the integrity of the national patrimony...."[1]

STRUCTURAL STRAIN

This factor was present especially in the form of new values which provided a basis for defining persisting social conditions as evil (see above discussion). But the incorporation of critiques of university structure and content with broader critiques of national life may have had the effect of weakening the impulse for university reform as such and of diverting energies of student radicals into broader and more diffuse movements, lessening the norm-oriented character of the student movement and tending to direct it toward becoming a value-oriented one.

GENERALIZED BELIEFS AND THE ROLE OF PRECIPITATING FACTORS

Generalized beliefs have been discussed above in terms of the various pronouncements of student congresses and also in the writings of Germán Arciniegas, who became to an important degree the major ideologist of the movement. What might have been a precipitating event, focusing attention on the movement and gaining militant support, occurred in the context of a broader conflict. Although details are lacking in the available account, "the university," presumably students at the National University in Bogotá, led "...a formidable movement of popular protest against a system characterized by nepotism, incapacity to deal with pressing social and economic problems enhanced by the worldwide depression, and led by a president... incapable of dealing with imperialism."[2] A law student was killed in a battle with police, the date of which event has been commemorated since as a "symbol of the struggles for the transformation of the State."[3] This event occurred during a period of widespread social discontent and revolt marked by a peasant uprising in the banana zone against the United Fruit Company, put down by the army, and numerous strikes in the cities, arising from bad working conditions, low pay, and general dislocation of the economy brought on by the depression.[4] Student activity, while significant, was part of a general social movement, or perhaps was involved in a number of interrelated movements which had in common a desire to remove

---

[1] Quoted in Montaña Cuellar, *Colombia,* p. 136.
[2] *Ibid.,* p. 137.
[3] *Ibid.*
[4] Fluharty, *Dance of the Millions,* pp. 36–41.

the oligarchy from power. A Colombian observer described the character of the social movements of the period as follows:

> With one thesis or the other . . . that of the conserving of the Liberal Party, or that of making new parties, the new generation understood that the people were obligated to battle, together, to gain their social rights, their political and their religious rights. All the revolutionary currents of the epoch . . . Socialists, Communists, syndicalists and anarchosyndicalists . . . participated in the same doctrine.[1]

The consequences of these pressures from below led to the candidacy of Olaya Herrera in behalf of a coalition government, a solution by the oligarchies of both parties to avoid revolution and to reduce pressures for major changes in the socioeconomic structure by the choice of a candidate committed to moderate reforms, with ties to both parties.[2] At least one writer credits the student movement with playing a "decisive" role in bringing about the end of Conservative rule, but he also asserts that student influence was effective for only a brief period of time.

The conclusions of observers of this period are that the young radicals did not pursue the struggle with the oligarchy, and sought neither to further the social revolution nor to continue the struggle for university reform, since their real concern was to gain entrance to the political oligarchy.

> The student leaders used the Federation of Students as a trampoline to jump into the political arena, to perform on the model of the traditional parties. They turned in the direction of bourgeois politics, offering the programs of the University Reform for the purpose of renovating the old bourgeois programs.[3]

This judgment is supported by Fluharty, although in somewhat broader terms, in reference to the young intellectuals as a group.

> The brash young men confronted the oligarchies and threw down the gauntlet. Inspired by the new ideas that came down every wind, they became the voice of Colombia's future, her nascent social conscience. For the most part, they were laughed out of the arena. The oligarchy was certain that when they had established themselves, when they had made a mark and gained a stake in the society, these young firebrands would recant. The fever would die, the innovations pall, the challenging ideas lose their validity. By and large, the oligarchy was right. . . .[4]

He goes on to discuss the liberal party leader Jorge Eliécer Gaitán as an exception to this generalization, as one who was committed to radical reform throughout his life and who never compromised his principles.[5]

---

[1] Antonio García, *Gaitán y el problema de la revolución colombiana* (Bogotá: Cooperativa de Artes Gráficas, 1955), p. 257; as quoted in Fluharty, *Dance of the Millions*, p. 40.

[2] *Ibid.*, p. 42.

[3] Montaña Cuellar, *Colombia*, pp. 137–138.

[4] Fluharty, *Dance of the Millions*, p. 29.

[5] *Ibid.*, p. 30.

The preceding discussion suggests, then, that the university reform movement was transformed into an abortive value-oriented movement, and failed
to realize the goals of either university reform or of the broader revolutionary movement in which it became involved. The explanation must take into
account several diverse factors, all related to the particular characteristics
and situation of Colombian society at that time, but generalizable in terms
of the theory of collective behavior used here. The conditions for a value-
oriented movement in Colombia during the 1920's and early 1930's were
clearly present, including the existence of large numbers of politically alienated people, an inflexible political structure, and the failure of the government to solve the problem of increasing economic misery, combined
with the capacity of the government to prevent or control hostile outbursts.[1] But a revolution was prevented by the capacity of the oligarchy to
respond sufficiently to pressure to put forward a moderate reformist candidate, and thus to remove the appearance of intransigence and inflexibility
in the face of demands for reform.[2] The Olaya Herrera regime was not sufficiently responsive, however, to prevent intensification of protest, but the
propitious occurrence of a border war with Peru in 1931 appeared to offer
a safety valve for revolutionary pressures, channeling protest into nationalist fervor and legitimatizing the imposition of martial law.[3]

Thus the student movement became diverted into a value-oriented movement which was diverted from its revolutionary course. We may here contrast the fortunes of the Colombian with those of the Argentine student
movement. The latter developed during a period of considerably less structural strain and thus was not diverted into a value-oriented movement, but
remained focused upon the explicit issue of university reform. It also had
the advantage of being allied with a middle-class political movement, in the
form of *radicalismo*, which came to power prior to the major "precipitating event" of the reform movement, and thus was in a position to accede
to the demands of the movement as a further realization of the tenets of
the Radical party's expressed concern for extension of electoral democracy.

The comments quoted above concerning the apparent readiness of Colombian student leaders to forego their radical posture, once assured of a
place within the traditional oligarchy, suggests a further contrast between
characteristics of the middle class in the two societies. One North American
observer has asserted that those who occupy middle-class positions in Colombian society are largely descendants of upper-class families and maintain a predominantly upper-class identification. This is assertedly due to the
presumed low rate of upward mobility and to the high rate of reproduction

---

[1] See Smelser, *Theory of Collective Behavior*, pp. 313–381, for a discussion of the determinants
of value-oriented movements.

[2] *Ibid.*, pp. 330–332.

[3] Fluharty, *Dance of the Millions*, p. 45.

of upper-class families, with consequent downward mobility of offspring who do not inherit sufficient wealth to maintain an upper-class style of life, and who enter middle-class status in the professions, teaching, and business, but maintain upper-class family and social contacts.[1] This thesis has been challenged by a Colombian anthropologist who asserts there is considerable social mobility, both upward and downward. He argues that there is and has been "for a long time" a "genuine" middle class, in the sense of its having derived from lower-class origins, and also that the upper-class families with downwardly mobile members are those which ascended two or three generations ago, and "have not had sufficient time to form a family tradition, to feel inextricably linked to the upper class."[2] Since neither writer offers data to support his thesis, the issue is unresolved, but nearly all observers of Colombian life have commented upon the existence of an identifiable political oligarchy based on economic power and occupying the seats of political power, both elective and appointive. The opportunity to share power with the oligarchy may be an especially compelling one in a relatively small country like Colombia, with limited access to power outside the traditional parties. Thus radical student leaders may have been more easily persuaded or encouraged to "sell out" there than in Argentina, for example, where power has been more widely dispersed, during the twentieth century at least.

A moderate university reform did come about in 1935 with the passage of the Organic Law of the National University of Colombia. With respect to the reform movement, its most important section was that referring to university government, to be exercised by a rector, a *síndico* or treasurer, a secretary general, and a directive council. The latter was composed of nine members, including the minister of national education as its president, the university rector as vice-president, and seven other members, including two representatives of the national government, one representative elected by the deans of schools and faculties of the university, two elected by the professors, and two elected by the students.[3] Student representation is thus granted in the law, but is considerably less than the one-third established in Argentina and recommended by Germán Arciniegas in the law which he proposed to the Colombian House of Representatives in 1932. He proposed a directive council, to be composed of the president, secretary, treasurer and controller of the university, the rectors of faculties, heads of university departments and representatives of each faculty, the latter to include two

---

[1] T. Lynn Smith, "Observations on the Middle Classes in Colombia," *in* Theo R. Crevenna, ed., *Materiales para el estudio de la clase media en la América Latina,* Vol. 6 (Washington, D.C.: Unión Panamericana, 1951), pp. 1–14.

[2] Gerardo Reichel-Dolmatoff, "Notas sobre la clase media en Colombia," *Notas e Informaciones en Ciencias Sociales,* 3, no. 13 (1952), p. 4.

[3] Colombia, Ministerio de Educación Nacional, *Compilación de disposiciones sobre regimen de universidades, 1888-1952* (Bogotá: Imprenta Nacional, 1953), p. 122.

each from the professors, students, and graduates of the university for each faculty. The functions of this body would have been broad and comprehensive, including the election of rector and faculty heads, and control of all matters pertaining to the organization of the university and the formulation of the educational program of the university, including matters concerning examinations, degrees, and courses of study.[1] The enacted organic law, on the other hand, while it contains similar functions for the directive council, states that the council should "approve the plans, methods of teaching, and of research and other regulations submitted to it by the academic council," a body composed of deans and directors of faculties and schools, without the representation of students or professors.[2]

The 1935 law was nevertheless a considerable move toward reform, and it did allow for student representation. But the distinct difference between the reform instituted in Colombia compared to that in Argentina lies not only in the substantive difference in the content of the reforms, but in the fact that reform in Colombia, while perhaps reflecting the influence of the student movement in some degree, was not precipitated by direct student pressure, but was rather enacted independently by a legislature dominated by a reformist Liberal party majority, elected in 1935 following the 1934 election of Liberal Alfonso López as president. Under López important reforms were instituted benefiting labor, including the right of workers to organize and strike, a minimum wage, the eight-hour day and the 40-hour week.[3] Thus university reform was a result of the shift to a reformist government, as was the Argentinean reform movement, but since it was not directly instigated by a militant student movement prepared to strongly protest the modification of its principles embodied in a body of "generalized beliefs," as had been the case in Argentina, it was unable to significantly affect the law, which granted students little more than token representation in university government.

The consequences of this difference would appear to be the following.

---

[1] Germán Arciniegas, *La universidad colombiana* (Bogotá: Imprenta Nacional, 1932), pp. 166–170.

[2] Colombia, Ministerio de Educación Nacional, *Compilación de disposiciones,* pp. 123–125. Perhaps the most significant difference between the law proposed by Arciniegas and that later enacted by Congress is the inclusion in the latter of government representatives on the directive council to the extent of three out of nine members, including the minister of education as president of the council. This would appear to considerably reduce university autonomy, placing it more directly under control by the government. This insertion of government representation within the directive council was contained in a law proposed in 1935 by a member of Congress, and which presumably influenced the drafting of the enacted law. He criticized Arciniegas' proposal of a directive council for the large number of student and former student representatives which it proposes because these representatives would lack "seriousness and permanence," but he does not attempt to justify the inclusion of government representation. Carlos García Prada, *La Universidad Nacional de Colombia y su organización* (Bogotá: Imprenta Nacional, 1935), p. 10.

[3] Fluharty, *Dance of the Millions,* p. 53.

In Argentina, the successful culmination of the university reform movement granted students a major decision-making role in university and faculty governing councils, institutionalized the movement, and established a political subculture in which student elections were significant for the actual conduct of university affairs. A party was formed (Reformista) to embody and defend the principles of university reform, providing the organizational base of subsequent movements for reform or for opposition to the government. The failure of the movement to become institutionalized in Colombia meant that collective student political action lacked a stable and persisting base, and rather tended to be discontinuous, responding to specific issues by the formation of temporary ad hoc organizations. Thus Colombian students have had considerably less direct influence on university government and policy than have their counterparts in Argentina. One would also expect that student political organizations have been less responsive to the mass of students and more easily manipulated by their leaders, since there has been a lack of the open and competitive university student party structure which has existed in Argentina. In other words, one would expect a greater tendency to oligarchy within student political organizations in Colombia, along with a tendency toward organizational instability. This last point is conjectural for the period from the 1930's to the 1950's, but recent developments would appear to support this contention.

Consequences for Contemporary Student Politics

Perhaps the major difference between the pattern of student politics in Colombia and Argentina, which bears out the contention that the relative success or failure of the university reform movement in the two societies has determined the course of subsequent political organization and activity, lies in the presence or absence of a relatively stable national federation of university students in the two nations. In Argentina, the continuing existence of the Argentine University Federation (FUA) has provided a basis for concerted political action, among and within the universities. An example is the well-organized campaign conducted against the 1955 government decree-law, which authorized private, predominantly Catholic universities to grant degrees, a right formerly permitted only to state universities.[1] The student campaign was unsuccessful, and its failure perhaps contributed to the decline of leftist representation within university government and within student councils. But the development and maintenance of the federation as an outcome of the successful university reform struggle earlier has provided a well-established structure for political conflict, as well as norms for the conduct of such conflict. In Colombia, on the other hand, there have been several attempts to form anew a national student

[1] See "La Universidad de Buenos Aires y la libertad de enseñanza," *Revista de la Universidad de Buenos Aires,* Quinta Época, 3 (1958), pp. 506–522.

federation in recent years. The present National University Federation (FUN) appears to lack legitimacy among a large proportion of students, and to be dominated by leftist student leaders oriented toward Maoist or Castroist political means and goals. Its character and ideology may be due in part to the absence of a well-institutionalized and persisting organization for national student politics in the past, leading to its being easily controlled by a minority of student radicals.[1] Students in Colombia have apparently been less ready to contest such control, in part because of the ephemeral nature of student federations in the past, and the lack of significant student participation in university government.

Thus a wide spectrum of student parties competes for office in university government in Argentina, and a much narrower spectrum in Colombia. There appears to be little representation from Catholic or non-Marxist student groups in the FUN in Colombia. In Argentina, groups reflecting a non-Marxist, "humanist" ideology have had majorities in recent elections.[2] The struggle among all ideological groups has tended to take place in the arena of the Argentine University Federation, since the fruits of victory mean significant influence within university government. In Colombia, since students lack significant representation within university government, student politics tend to be turned outward toward national and international issues, and to provide a platform for student revolutionaries.

It would appear, on balance, that in the Latin American environment, where the belief that students should participate in university government is widely held and founded to some extent on the reality of university structure, such participation may contribute to the civilizing of politics and to the development of democratic norms of political action which carry over into nonstudent life.[3] The denial of participation to students in university government does not inhibit the development of student political activism in Latin America, but may rather facilitate a more ideological, utopian political orientation among student politicians who lack the experience of pragmatic involvement in university affairs, in which authority for decision-making implies a responsibility to the university community and thus a check on the tendency toward an "ethic of ultimate ends," in Max Weber's phrase.

To conclude, it would appear that where the university reform was successful, as in Argentina, it provided an important impetus toward needed

[1] This characterization of FUN is based on a reading of Colombian newspaper accounts, and various Colombian student political publications, including *Federación Universitaria Nacional* (October, 1964), the official organ of the federation.

[2] See Mario Peralta and Ramón Gutiérrez, "Análisis comparativo de la trayectoría de los movimientos estudiantiles, Trabajo No. 1, Universidad de Buenos Aires," *CREA Boletín* (1963), pp. 5–9.

[3] See Kenneth N. Walker, "Political Socialization in Latin American Universities," paper presented at the International Seminar on the Formation of Elites in Latin America, University of Montevideo, June 6–11, 1965.

reforms in the character and conduct of higher education, a defense of academic freedom against the claims of the state, and a politicizing experience for students in the democratic process. Where the movement was relatively unsuccessful, as in Colombia, student politics would appear to be more alienated from the university and society, and less responsible in its choice of means. The different fate of the movement in these two societies was due to quite different conditions and events, differences, however, which are part of the broad historical trends in these societies and which must be taken into account if one is to interpret the character of student politics in the two nations.

University Students in a World of Change: A Colombian Sample

ROBERT C. WILLIAMSON

Introduction

The stereotype of the Latin American student both in his local environment and in the world at large has been identified by newspaper headlines and by-lines as a participant in demonstrations and strikes. A closer look would reveal a kaleidoscope of images: the starving resident of a *mesón* or *favela,* the diligent son of an upwardly mobile civil servant, the white-collar bank clerk off in the evening to the university, or even the pamphleteer setting fire to buses and streetcars. In private or religious universities he may be carrying on a family or class tradition, but in public institutions he is above all finding education the major means of mobility, and he may be regarded as a change agent in the sociopolitical sphere. Because of this confused perception, the present study attempts to assess the selected student, his background, aspirations, values, and roles in a changing society. The National University of Colombia at Bogotá was selected. It may be added that university surveys are a recent innovation for Latin America.[1] Questionnaires, attitude scales, and like instruments are gradually appearing on the Latin American scene.

Reproduced, by permission, from *Sociology and Social Research,* 48 (July, 1964), pp. 397–413.

The author is Professor of Sociology of Lehigh University, Bethlehem, Pennsylvania. The study was performed during a Fulbright lectureship at the National University of Colombia in 1961. He wishes to acknowledge his debt to the staff and students at the School of Sociology and to the various statistical agencies which played a role in the tabulation of the data. The present article is an adaptation of the author's "El estudiante colombiano y sus actitudes," *Monografías Sociológicas,* 13 (Bogotá: Universidad Nacional, 1962).

[1] Among these, Daniel Goldrich, *Radical Nationalism: The Political Orientations of Panamanian Law Students* (East Lansing, Mich.: Bureau of Social and Political Research, Michigan State

THE UNIVERSITY SETTING

In several respects Latin American universities are unique in comparison with those in some parts of the world, most notably the United States. One, there is the *autonomía* tradition by which the university enjoys a certain immunity. For example, local police authorities and army units are not permitted to enter the premises of a number of Latin American universities. This tacit, although not absolute, freedom of control from local or national authority has various political consequences. Two, following the medieval Bologna tradition, the students have considerable power in university affairs, often equal to that of the academic council. Administrative and faculty appointments may be indirectly subject to their approval. Although most of Europe abandoned this pattern of student autonomy, it lingered on in Spain and the New World in colonial and modern times. Three, there is a lack of authority and centralization combined with the proliferation of *facultades* (schools). Autonomy prevails for each *facultad* to the extent that even a central index to various *facultad* libraries is usually nonexistent. Four, both staff and students have only a marginal association with the university. A large percentage of students and professors attend on a part-time basis. This marginality is intensified by the lack of extracurricular activities and vocational or other types of advisement along with the slender financial budget of the student. Five, even more than in the United States, a university education is the major avenue of upward mobility, although there are limits as to what degree the individual may change his status. Six, the most critical aspect of the Latin American university student is his role as an opinion leader and a change agent. He has been a significant factor in toppling a number of dictatorships: Rojas Pinilla in Colombia, Jiménez in Venezuela, Vargas in Brazil, Perón in Argentina, Odría in Peru, and Lemus in El Salvador, to cite a few examples.[2]

The National University in Bogotá reflects many of these problems. Moreover, the university has been caught in disturbing social and economic events of recent Colombian history: the dictatorships of Gómez and Rojas and the more favorable but still troubled coalition government since 1958. Enjoying a pleasant physical setting in the Ciudad Universitaria and a wide program of 18 *facultades,* the National University has the country's largest student body, approximately 6,000. However, it is less prestigious than the Jesuit Universidad Javeriana and particularly the private Universidad de los Andes or the public Universidad del Valle in Cali, both of which are

University, 1961), would be representative. Other surveys, although unpublished, are E. Wight Bakke, "Students' Role in Educational, Social and Economic Development: The Cases of Colombia and Mexico"; and K. H. Silvert and Frank Bonilla, "Education and the Social Meaning of Development: A Preliminary Statement," as well as studies in progress, for example, by Rose Goldsen and Leila Sussmann.

[2] Ted Szulc, *Twilight of the Tyrants* (New York: Henry Holt and Company, 1959).

oriented toward the United States to some degree. In addition, there are a number of lesser institutions, generally with evening programs for the scores of technicians, civil servants, and schoolteachers who are on the threshold of a new middle class. In spite of the lower middle class students, the majority of schools at the National University offer programs involving day classes, consequently limiting the student to a still tighter economic base since normal employment is not possible with a day schedule.

In at least one respect the National conforms to the stereotype of Latin American universities in its yearly strike: in 1960 the rector was deemed *persona non grata;* in 1961, political problems and budgetary restrictions were suitable grounds for a five-week strike; the elections of 1962 formed the background of a still longer stoppage; and in 1963 the tenure of the mayor (June) and bus fares (August) precipitated *demostraciones.*

THE STUDY AND ITS METHODS

The purpose of the study was to determine the climate of opinion and the adjustment of the environment for a student sample of the National University. Differences were hypothesized regarding the advanced and beginning students, males and females, for social class, and for career choices.

The attempt was made to select a random sample which would be a tenth of the student body, preferably chosen from the second and fourth years. Owing to complications, about a third of the sample were volunteers from schools where randomization was not feasible. Generally the schedule was administered on a one-to-one basis but practical difficulties necessitated multiple sessions with the result that subjects occasionally failed to respond to given items. A comparison of the results of the single and multiple interviews revealed that validity apparently did not suffer except for certain items, such as family income and religious attendance, which tended to be exaggerated.[1]

DESCRIPTION OF THE SAMPLE

Of the 5,980 students at the National University, 610 (460 men and 150 women) were interviewed. While the attempt was to select 10 per cent of each *facultad,* the larger ones produced a smaller ratio of subjects than the newer *facultades,* for instance, 6.6 per cent of the School of Medicine as opposed to 29.5 per cent of the School of Education.

Nearly half (49.1 per cent) of the sample were first-year students; the remainder were advanced students, with 25.1 per cent being of the fourth year. The median age was 20.8 years; approximately 95 per cent were still single, nearly 60 per cent living at home with their family, although more than half had been reared in other parts of the country. Four fifths of the

[1] In view of the time limitations of the author's Fulbright scholarship, the survey was only introductory to the subject, namely, the general climate of students' opinions.

students described themselves as middle class; 5.4 per cent as lower or lower middle; 7.6 per cent, middle upper; and 6.7 per cent, upper. However, perhaps a fifth of the occupations listed for the fathers would appear to be lower class. The family income reported was at least a third higher than what was indicated in an earlier notarized statement (required by the registrar's office in order to determine the rate of tuition). The students reported a median family size of 6.2, or 3.4 as the median number of siblings. On the whole, the university student was from a smaller-than-average size family and he was more highly educated than his older siblings. The fact that only a fifth of the subjects worked outside their studies should not belie economic duress.

Findings
CAREERS, STUDIES, AND THE UNIVERSITY PROCESS

One of the more disturbing aspects of the student's role in developing nations is the apparent improbability of his encountering an opening in his major field—and often when his skill area is precisely what a developing nation needs. Only 46.1 per cent of the sample thought it likely that 60 per cent of their classmates would find work in their respective fields within the first year after graduation. A follow-up of the graduates of given schools of the National University indicated that this estimate was distinctly optimistic.[1]

Likewise, the approach to studies was unrealistic, particularly among the younger students. When asked to specify some of their study methods, a third of the sample could not name one. A visit to most Latin American universities finds a limited repertory of study techniques, if any at all, with libraries frequently devoid of users and with only partially filled shelves. Highly socialized approaches to study are found in the study seminars visible on the *prado* (grounds) of the university, and its neighboring cafes. An even more traditional vignette is the audible recitation of the student as he paces the length of a colonnade memorizing critical or not-so-critical sentences or paragraphs.[2]

The survey included students' reactions to the teaching staff. In view of the image of the university professor in Latin America and his marginal commitment to his institution and his discipline, the student's reaction to his teacher was a critical item. Nearly half of the respondents indicated that their professors were performing at a mediocre or less-than-adequate level. About 70 per cent preferred the full-time instructor to the part-time or "taxi professor" who uses the university as an adjunct to his more regular

---

[1] Jorge Giraldo Angel, "Universidad y oferta profesional," *Revista de Psicología,* 5 (1960), pp. 95–97.

[2] A summarization of some more remarkable study methods of Latin American students is to be found in "El estudio al exterior como sistema," *Encuestas Universitarias,* 2, no. 3 (1961).

position or who must find a number of part-time assignments in order to insure his economic survival. In ranking the characteristics important in the teacher, the highest rating (44.0 per cent) was for knowledge of the material, followed by effective lecturing (29.2 per cent) and research interests (11.9 per cent), with grading practices, relations with the students, sense of humor, and professional prestige being awarded lesser ratings.

Regarding the variations in style of given Colombian universities the subjects were asked to rank some five universities in terms of: one, the ability of the respective students, and two, the probability of finding adequate opportunities upon graduation. Regarding the former the students rated, to no one's surprise, their own institution as number one, followed by the Andes, del Valle, La Libre, a recently established leftish institution, with upper-class Javeriana in the lowest position. Significantly, placement possibilities were ranked differently: Javeriana first, followed by National, Andes, Valle, and Libre. The negative reaction to the Javeriana reflects not only the usual cross-town rivalry and anticlerical sentiment but bitterness at the supposed or genuine avenues of upper-class privilege. Regarding the rating of selected *facultades* within the National the sciences were preferred, yet philosophy and letters was rated above law and economics. There was no particular propensity to rate one's *facultad* as highest.[1]

Inescapably the students were questioned about their feelings in regard to the university strike under varying situations, as indicated in Table 1.

Table 1. Attitudes toward the University Strike
(N = 610)

The Student Strike Effectiveness	% Approving
Solving educational problems	68.5
Improving economic conditions of the students	66.6
Obtaining political objectives	25.8
Raising the prestige of the university	21.3

In view of these responses some correction might be made in the stereotype of the university student as a perennial striker. While the verbalizations of students are not necessarily valid, it would seem that for most subjects the strike was justified only when focused on the welfare of the students or of the university. However, in some instances for the student the strike

---

[1] Special factors likely played a role in certain positive judgments, as in the relatively high rating of sociology, which was undoubtedly influenced by the fact that the interviewers were from that *facultad,* and the high status assigned to humanities is hardly unrelated to the position of the arts in a country known as the "nation of poets." On literary penchant in relation to the *machismo* cult, see John P. Gillin, "Some Signposts for Policy," *in* Council on Foreign Relations, *Social Change in Latin America Today* (New York: Vintage Books, 1960), pp. 39–43.

becomes his sole means of communication when other conventional verbal processes fail to function, parenthetically, in a culture area in which poetry enjoys a brighter halo than does logic. Of course, the decision to strike is in the hands of the students' council.

RELIGIOUS BEHAVIOR

Of the sample, 76.6 per cent considered themselves as practicing Catholics, with 17.4 per cent nonactive Catholics, and the remainder divided between being agnostics and members of other faiths. In regard to attendance at mass, 63.0 per cent claimed to attend at least once a week. The religiously conditioned aspects of the subjects' belief systems were also investigated. For instance, the familiar J-curve was obtained in regard to their belief in the deity: two fifths of the students maintained they conceived of the deity as a personal Being with smaller percentages supporting more intellectualized versions. To the question "Do you believe it is possible to remain chaste until marriage?" 31.9 per cent responded "certainly"; 38.6 per cent responded "probably" or "possibly"; and 31.5 per cent, "no," with acute sex differences as revealed below. The question as to the indissolubility of the marriage bond elicited 56.4, 27.0, and 16.6 percentages, respectively. Colombia, one of the few countries of the world with no divorce provisions, remains a "double standard" country, except for a few liberated university students and other nonconformists.

SOCIOPOLITICAL IDEOLOGY

The questionnaire only touched on the gamut of the political complexion of the students. Of primary interest were the students' feelings on the general problem of reform in their country: 87.9 per cent of the sample indicated that a basic change *(un cambio radical)* was necessary in Colombia. Specifically mentioned as varieties of desirable change were: economic transformation, termination of the feudalistic class system, agrarian reform, religious liberalism, and an awakening of moral consciousness. To the accompanying question, to what degree they would participate in such changes, 86.7 per cent verbally assented to such areas as community development; education, i.e., teaching illiterates; health and medical aid; and other rural-oriented programs.

The subjects were asked to rate the programs of certain world leaders according to a continuum. The percentages of "good" or "very good" assigned to given leaders were: Kennedy, 71.3 per cent; de Gaulle, 63.4; Khrushchev, 38.5; Betancourt, 32.3; Castro, 28.6; and Franco, 20.8. Several observations are in order in regard to these findings. The support of Kennedy is noteworthy, particularly since the survey was performed only a few months after the Cuban fiasco of April, 1961. President Lleras of Colombia was not enthusiastically regarded as he was not solving the almost insolvable problems of his nation. The unfavorable attitude toward President Betancourt of Venezuela seems to be attributable to the rivalry between the two countries. Responses varied appreciably by subcultures of sex, age, and major choice. A similar question, focused on party leaders of their own country, produced similar results, with 72.2 per cent of the sample responding favorably to the assassinated (1948) charismatic Liberal leader Jorge Gaitán. The present leaders registered a maximum of 39.3 per cent favorable responses. Aside from the vibrant image of Gaitán, the past generally appeared as foreboding as the present.

The approach to the process of opinion crystallization was mainly projective: the students were asked who is most influential in the formation of the social and political ideas of their fellow students. Writers headed the list of possible sources of influence, with "much" or "considerably" constituting 63.8 per cent, followed by students (54.3 per cent), politicians and statesmen (53.1 per cent), friends (51.7 per cent), press (46.4 per cent), parents (32.5 per cent), and priests (29.2 per cent); professors seemed to be the least influential, with only 24.3 per cent listing them as a major source of opinion formation. It is understandable that the academic profession and especially the clergy were judged to be of marginal commitment as compared to students and writers. It would be valuable to know why parents were relatively high, especially since nearly half of the students were not living at home. Another unanswered question concerns the validity of the author's assumption that the perception by the respondent of his peers' processes of judgment would be related to his own. Unfortunately the limited resources of students' and interviewers' time did not permit sufficient examination of this area. The process of perception and judgment on the part of students requires more investigation.

SOCIAL LIFE AND PERSONAL ADJUSTMENT

American university students are noted for their amount of dating and social life generally. By comparison the Latin American student appears more subdued. Two fifths, or 41.9 per cent, of the sample either did not date or had no boy or girl friend (novio). An equal number reported a novio and dates. The remainder, or 18.2 per cent, had matrimonial intentions (comprometido) in regard to their novio. Regarding social life and effective bonds, the degree of deep friendships would appear restricted: the median number of intimate friends was 3.7. A quarter (25.5 per cent) of the sample stated that during the four weeks previous to the interview they had not had more than a total of three social occasions of all possible types, i.e., dates, visits with friends, parties, or visits to a cafe or bar. To be sure, these responses must be viewed with some caution because of inaccurate recall and lack of precision as to what constitutes a social occasion. Inevitably the male was markedly freer than the female in his social and sexual life.

The 25.8 per cent of the sample who reported five or more dates during the previous four weeks were almost entirely males. It could not be asked how many of the respondents had patronized bordellos; however, such patronage is considered a folkway of most single and many married males in Latin America.

A few questions were focused on the personal adjustment of the subjects. One item of a projective variety which was included was "How many of the people you know are really happy in life?" More than half of the population was estimated by 52.6 per cent of the sample to be unhappy. These results were more negative than those of a similar college sample in the United States, but less somber than those of a Central American sample.[1] Also, the Latin American samples encountered more pessimistic results from the females, whereas in the United States sample it was the male who seemed to be more threatened. Also more of the sample (32.1 per cent) thought that the world would be less happy in the future than the supporters (23.6 per cent) of the reverse position, with almost half of the sample disclaiming either position.

Regarding preoccupations of their personal life, 37.4 per cent alluded to economic problems, followed by studies, 18.0 per cent. Other problems were psychological adjustment, lack of social life or of dates, parental discipline, and housing, with 19.5 per cent asserting they had no problems. Finally, the average student planned to marry at 28.5 years and have 3.7 children, which indicates they were thinking of a later marriage but a smaller family than were their North American counterparts.[2]

Effect of Subcultures on Attitudinal Behavior

As mentioned above, the plan of the survey was not only to obtain a cross section of the complexion of opinion in the National University but to determine the range of thinking within certain subcultures. In utilizing such variables as age, sex, class, and major, certain overlappings were inevitable. For instance, women students as compared to the men were characteristically: first year, middle to upper-middle social class, and oriented toward such professions as teaching, sociology, and psychology. On the whole, these variables operated in the same direction as in the United States, with notable exceptions.

THE BEGINNING VERSUS THE ADVANCED STUDENT

The problem of resocialization in the university setting has had a lengthy

---

[1] Robert C. Williamson, "Some Variables of Middle and Lower Class in Two Central American Cities," *Social Forces,* 41 (December, 1962), pp. 195–207; and "Values and Subcultures in Mate Selection," unpublished manuscript.

[2] Rose K. Goldsen, Morris Rosenberg, Robin M. Williams, Jr., and Edward A. Suchman, *What College Students Think* (Princeton, N.J.: D. Van Nostrand Co., Inc., 1960), p. 89.

history of research.[1] Comparisons of the present samples of the first-year students with those of the advanced, largely fourth-year students favored the advanced student, namely greater availability of jobs or scholarships (p < .05).[2] The advanced-level student was more optimistic about the possibility of finding employment in his profession, which would imply acquired knowledge or established contacts about the positions he looked forward to filling. Or possibly he was reluctant to perceive a not altogether reassuring reality, even though he was currently enjoying a more solid economic base. He was more critical of his professors, especially the part-time instructors, although he acknowledged a friendlier rapport with the teaching staff than did the younger students. Religiously, he was less orthodox than the younger student: 25.0 per cent of the older students versus 15.1 per cent of the younger regarded the deity as an impersonal creative force.

On the political side, his acceptance of Castro, 35.1 per cent versus 21.7 per cent, only emphasizes the leftish political orientation that a university education implies in probably most of Latin America. Particularly the upper student was critical of his own national leaders. On the whole, he was more perceptive of what was occurring within the university. For instance, he was able to supply information about cliques and movements among the students.

MEN AND WOMEN

Although women, who constituted roughly a third of our sample, had less economic wherewithal than the men because of restricted employment possibilities, they had more affluent parents. The entrance of women into the university program is recent and is a middle-class innovation. As in the United States, the girl is more home- or marriage-oriented and less committed to the university program than the boy. He was more likely to view higher education as an avenue of upward mobility, as 55.5 per cent of the males and 38.8 per cent of the females looked forward to a higher social position than that of their parents.

Moreover, Latin American social institutions did not permit the girl to exploit the liberties accorded her male counterpart. She studied at home, whereas the male preferred a cafe or a friend's house for study purposes. She felt socially more remote from the instructional staff, although less critical in regard to their performance. She was less rejecting of the part-time instructor.

---

[1] The classical study is Theodore M. Newcomb, *Personality and Social Change* (New York: The Dryden Press, 1943). A more recent review of the literature is by Harold Webster, Mervin Freedman, and Paul Heist, "Personality Changes in College Students," *in* Nevitt Sanford, ed., *The American College* (New York: John Wiley and Sons, Inc., 1962), pp. 811–846.

[2] All differences mentioned are with a chi-square or t test (both techniques were employed, although not always for the same item) of < .05 probability of significance. Any statements that fall below or above this level will be so indicated. A complete set of tables is obtainable from the author.

As expected, the matter of religious ideology represented the most crucial variation between the sexes, with all differences at .001 level of significance. For example, 26.2 per cent of the men and only 8.2 per cent of the
women were nonpracticing Catholics. Attendance at mass and confession
all reflected this sex difference. The differential religious fervor apparently
affected perception: 0.4 per cent of the males and 18.0 per cent of the females reported that their fathers attended religious services more than once
a week. It is difficult to know whether this supposed frequency is attributable to wishful thinking or to lower interest in the questionnaire and consequently more careless responses. On the possibility of chastity until marriage, the frequencies were 39.0 and 92.6 per cent; on the indissolubility
of marriage, 69.0 and 87.1 per cent.

Politically, the girls were less informed and generally more conservative.
Kennedy was favored by 69.3 per cent of the males as opposed to 81.9 per
cent of the females. President Lleras was approved by a similar ratio, 38.3
and 51.4 per cent respectively. However, Franco was equally rejected by
each sex. Women preferred the more conservative press. Regarding sources
of opinion as perceived in their peers, the results for male and female were:
student leaders, 49.0 and 71.2; priests, 31.8 and 21.0; and writers, 61.3
and 74.0. These results would indicate that the projective type of question
reveals what the subject imputes in others more than what he regards as
true of himself. Generally the women had a more negative outlook on the
world as well as a decidedly more limited social life.

SOCIAL CLASS

As mentioned above, the students were asked to indicate in which social
class they would place themselves. However, the criterion for social class
was the reported father's occupation, that is, one, upper-lower or lower-
middle students (N = 195), whose fathers were manual workers or of lower
white-collar occupations; and two, middle to upper-middle students (N =
150), whose fathers were professionals, managers, or entrepreneurs, including a few wealthy or near-wealthy farmers. Unlike the other subcultural
analyses, the sample for social (or occupational) class included the Andes
and Javeriana students. Even so, nearly all of the lower and more than two
thirds of the upper sample were National students. Students of intermediate status, with middle white-collar fathers, were not included. Yet in
terms of the total social structure of Colombia, the two samples selected
might be regarded as two variations of the middle class.

The upper-class student showed a masculine and an age or advanced-class
bias, partly attributable to the inclusion of non-National students. In regard
to their university environment, the lowers preferred the full-time instructor (70.0 to 59.0 per cent, $p < .05$) and were more inclined to stress his research function, whereas the uppers placed more emphasis on his lecturing

ability. Only 32.1 per cent of the lowers as opposed to 52.7 per cent of the uppers described relations with the professors as cordial. Seemingly there was a more *simpático* feeling toward the professor on the part of the upper-class student. Regarding approval of the university strike, there was little difference between the two groups.

The uppers were more conventional in their religious beliefs and placed more stress on chastity before marriage. Politically, there were few significant differences, but in regard to world and national leaders there was a tendency of the lowers (not always significant) to support the more liberal candidates. In respect to opinion formation, parents were more frequently designated as a major influence by the uppers, 43.1 per cent as against 29.3 per cent for the lowers. The same preference was ascribed to newspapers (43.2 and 29.3 per cent). Presumably the upper student had more exposure to both these stimuli.

The upper student demonstrated higher organizational participation and movie attendance (both $p < .001$). He was less likely to change something if he had his life to live over (34.5 and 52.1 per cent respectively, $p < .01$) and was more inclined to view the majority of the world as happy (31.0 and 21.5 per cent).

On the whole, social class elicited a smaller number of significant differences than age or sex, and was affected itself by these subcultures. Acculturation on the college campus reduced the effects of family status.

CAREER CHOICE

Research studies have documented the significance of the choice of a major as an important conditioner of attitudes.[1] Again, the present study broke ground in this area without coming to complete fruition. The career choices were grouped arbitrarily in Group A, various *facultades* of the natural and applied sciences (N = 364); Group B, sociology, psychology, and education (N = 77); and Group C, law and economics (N = 75).[2] As 56 per cent of Group B were females and 74 per cent were first-year students, comparisons are more meaningful between Groups A and C, which were both roughly 85 per cent male and slightly over 50 per cent advanced students.

Students in the humanities and to a lesser extent those in the social sciences have been reported as having had more emotional disturbances than those in the natural or applied sciences.[3] Roe found that behavioral scientists apparently had more disturbing family relationships in childhood. These

---

[1] Cf. Carl Bereiter and Mervin B. Freedman, "Fields of Study and the People in Them," *in* Sanford, ed., *The American College*, pp. 563–596.

[2] The arbitrary breakdown was necessitated by the budgetary limits of IBM processing at the university inasmuch as three groupings had face validity. Three *facultades* (nursing, fine arts, and music) were not represented in our comparison for this reason and because their students had marginal programs.

[3] *Ibid.*, p. 571.

experiences presumably led them into the fields of human relations in contrast to the orientation toward the impersonal world of natural scientists.[1] In the present study, responses of the lawyers and economists seemed to point to some unfortunate psychological backgrounds. In any case, they were more cynical toward the status quo, which is not surprising in view of the stereotype of law and economic students as militant change agents. They perceived themselves as having a poorer standard of living than they had a few years before entering the university. They anticipated having to rely on their own efforts in securing employment, yet looked forward to the highest salaries, once established in their professions.

Table 2. Students' Perceptions of Mobility

	Natural Sciences N = 364 %	Sociology, Psychology, Education N = 77 %	Law, Economics N = 75 %
Standard of living worse than a few years ago	16.5	21.3	28.4
Necessity of depending on their own efforts in obtaining employment	58.4	54.5	69.0
Anticipation of earning $350.00 per month five years after graduation	64.8	47.1	71.7

Group C was the most critical of the instructional ability of their professors. This finding probably had no relation to the reluctance of the deans of these two *facultades* to permit the survey among their students. More likely the deans were apprehensive about leftist feelings of their students, if confronted with a survey sponsored by a "gringo" sociologist. On the whole, law and economics students regarded relations with their staff as cordial and were generally more involved in student affairs, and incidentally, in the case of law at least, were more than occasionally found in the *facultad* library.

Religious attitudes varied markedly between the three groups. On the whole, Group C was the most skeptical and Group B the least. Yet the scientists were of marginal commitment to chastity before marriage and the most defensive of the indissolubility of the marriage bond. In other terms, the natural and applied scientists represented the *machismo* cult more nearly in its classical form and were generally more traditionalistic in their religious orientation.

Politically, the law and economics students were more cynical. Approval

---

[1] Anne Roe, "A Psychological Study of Eminent Psychologists and Anthropologists and a Comparison with Biological and Physical Scientists," *Psychological Monographs,* 31, no. 2 (1953); also *The Psychology of Occupations* (New York: John Wiley and Sons, Inc., 1956), pp. 213-225.

of Kennedy was 74.6, 73.3, and 54.5 per cent respectively for Groups A, B, and C; for Castro it was 25.6, 23.3, and 44.4. The natural science students were less interested in political phenomena and were more conservative; the feminine influence in Group B operated in a similar direction. However, on a number of ideological questions such as the university strike, the differences were not significant.

Group B reported the highest number of friends, Group C the least. Whereas Group A chose "recreational" pursuits with their friends, who were predominantly from their own *facultad,* Group C described their affiliative interests as "intellectual." Although Group C reported the fewest organizational memberships they had the largest number of leadership positions. It is conceivable that the motivational outlook of Group C was ideological and manipulative. Lawyers and economists perceived only 13.5 per cent of the population to be happy as compared to the two-fifths figure of the two other groupings. Group C also looked to a later age of marriage and to a smaller number of children.

Discussion and Conclusions

In assessing the findings it is recalled that the present study was an introductory rather than the in-depth study desirable for an understanding of student universes in Latin America. Instead, the survey tapped segments of family and social relationships, reactions to the university and the political world, and an attempt was made to identify certain value orientations. The report points to findings suggestive of the climate of students' feelings and attitudes.

Despite its limitations, the study indicates some generalizations about the 610 subjects. In a number of facets the students are upwardly mobile. They look to a life markedly improved over that of their parents. Yet as compared to North American students, they have a pessimism about the world in general, and more restrained aspirations for themselves. The students' political ideologies are in the direction of change but very specific to their own subcultures, particularly length of residence in the university and whether the student is male or female. This specificity is indicated, for example, in relation to the university strike, which is differentially supported. For a minority of the students of the National the strike is not considered an acceptable form of behavior.

In regard to the university situation itself, apparently the students only dimly realized that they were among the fortunate few who had achieved a secondary education and had matriculated in an overtaxed state university albeit with the institution's limited facilities and marginally qualified teaching personnel. With their rote method of learning, if applied to a more considerable number of courses—often 20 or 24 hours of classes per week— than they would find in the North American or European university, it was doubtful if there could be any genuine maturity or adequacy in their mastery of a given curriculum or broad perspective. Yet the student did gain a perspective toward a harsh reality and a changing culture—a culture toward which he was understandably ambivalent.

Specifically, the students were asked to assess the university program and particularly the teaching personnel. Their evaluation of the instructor in view of his inadequacies seemed, if anything, generous. However, one must consider the frustrations the Latin American professor faces in teaching hours, low salary, and role ambiguity. These problems were particularly acute for the part-time instructor. The marginal service of this "taxi professor" was both cause and result of the mediocrity within the system.

This study investigated the relationships of four subcultures: age, sex, class, and career choice, as determinants of students' attitudes. Regarding the factor of age, it is not clear to what degree the resocialization process depends on age itself, on increasing contact with the university program and with student peers. Supplemental research is necessary to determine to what degree the student's differential sociopolitical idealism, accompanied by alternating pessimism, is retained after graduation. A follow-up might determine the fate of his value system in the work-a-day world.

The woman student appears to be less adequately socialized within society at large and in the university system. She has peripheral and desultory contact with the professor and has only partial knowledge of political events. Her entry into given professions such as medicine and dentistry is no better if no worse than in the United States. Her religious and social life is considerably more restrained than that of the male or of her counterpart abroad but even there, change is in the air.

Social class seems less critical a variable than some of the other subcultures. Findings in collegiate cultures of the United States point to the same direction, namely, the small portion of upper-class individuals in large state or municipal institutions blur into the lower middle class majority, or the reverse holds for the lower-class minority within the exclusive private schools.[1] Goldrich found in his Panamanian students only moderate political differences between the upper class and the middle-lower class.[2] The findings with *facultad* choice must be interpreted in view of the fact that they were derived in one university within one national culture. Some discrepancies might be found in other areas, for instance, medical students in Buenos Aires appear less religious than ours,[3] and the economics students were more traditionalistic, even though they came from lower socioeconomic

---

[1] Martin Trow, "The Campus Viewed as a Culture," *in* Hall T. Sprague, ed., *Research on College Students* (Berkeley, Calif.: The Center for Higher Education, 1960), p. 116.

[2] Goldrich, *Radical Nationalism,* also Daniel Goldrich and Edward W. Scott, "Developing Political Orientations of Panamanian Students," *Journal of Politics,* 23 (February, 1961), reprinted in Bureau of Social and Political Research, Michigan State University.

[3] Silvert and Bonilla, "Education and Development," p. 113.

backgrounds and perceived themselves as upwardly mobile.[1] Besides the possibility of international comparisons, further research might investigate in more detail the various majors and what relationship they have to value orientations.

In assessing the study from both the consideration of the cultural milieu in which the student finds himself and the goals toward which he is striving there are some fundamental questions to be raised. One, students have not clearly defined their relationship to such questions as nationalism, economic equality, or democratic processes. Inevitably the students are confronting such phenomena as *personalismo* in politics, imperfect coalition government, and the sporadic outbreak of both rural and urban political violence, in addition to severe economic dislocations. Two, it is difficult to determine the degree of the students' humanitarianism. Bakke questions the degree of idealism displayed in his Colombian and Mexican informants, namely sympathy with Indian villagers or isolated campesinos may not be as deep as asserted. In our own sample, while nearly 80 per cent offered verbally their services for community development, the responses to a program in the field elicited at most 5 per cent of the student body.

Whatever these qualifications, the survey offers a profile of the Latin American student—an individual who is inevitably confused as to his role in a changing and unpredictable society in its political, social, and economic implications, both domestic and international. Too, he is entering a society desperately in need of various skills and yet one that is only partially prepared to accept and utilize these talents. Or, in some cases an overproduction, for instance, of lawyers and economists complicates the problem (in Bogotá alone there are at least three *facultades* of both law and economics). For the newer behavioral science *facultades* like psychology and sociology there is the resistance of the more established *facultades* as well as the strong opposition the student encounters outside in his postuniversity professional quest.

Our study tends to confirm the picture of the Latin American university as being in a transitional state. The students are aware that standards have not been as high in some quarters as they should be, most notably in the instructional program itself. It is not certain when and how the students will accept the upgrading of standards which are clearly visible in several Latin American institutions. Perhaps the solution lies in the establishment of private universities such as los Andes. Even in the national universities with the almost insuperable problems of political involvement, annual or semiannual strikes, and the itinerant professor and student, improvements are inevitable. Communication is now too rapid and intricate to block out awareness of developments in other parts of the world. Although progress

---

[1] *Ibid.,* p. 116.

will not be rapid, United States universities can be useful in providing scholarships, visiting professorships, and consultancies. In this modest survey a set of verbal responses has been suggested that may be helpful in understanding the background and motivations of the Colombian student.

Determinants of Castro Support among Latin American University Students

KENNETH N. WALKER

University students have a political significance in developing nations out of proportion to their numbers, due to their future membership in the elite of their societies, as well as their active and militant participation in protest demonstrations, strikes, and sometimes violent opposition to governments. Students are not only active proponents of their own group interests, but are often the only articulate agents of protest in societies in which the masses are predominantly illiterate and politically unorganized.[1] They have been prominent in colonial struggles for independence and, in more recent times, have been decisive factors in the overturn of governments. While the revolutionary potential of students has been overrated, and while the success of their political opposition has depended in large part on the acquiescence or active support of other agencies, they often serve as political catalysts, providing leadership and ideological support for mass protest.[2]

The student as political actor has been especially prominent in Latin America. Since the early part of the century students have sought to reform

Reproduced, by permission, from *Social and Economic Studies,* 14 (March, 1965), pp. 88–105.

This paper was written as part of the Comparative National Development Project of the Institute of International Studies, University of California, Berkeley, directed by Seymour M. Lipset.

[1] "In Asia and South America, student movements have taken the political initiative because the rest of the population is sunk in exhausted indifference, and because the students, as the administrative intellectuals of the future, have a distinctive class interest of their own." Lewis Feuer, "Youth in the 60's," *The New Leader,* 64, no. 10 (1961), pp. 18–22.

[2] See the exchange between C. Wright Mills and Robert Wolfe on the relative importance of intellectuals, especially students, in revolutionary social change. C. Wright Mills, "On the New Left," *Studies on the Left,* 2, no. 1 (1960), pp. 63–72; Robert Wolfe, "Intellectuals and Social Change," *Studies on the Left,* 2, no. 3 (1962), pp. 63–68.

universities toward a broader participation in national life and a more direct concern with the needs of society. The university reform movement, which began in Argentina in 1918 or earlier and spread to other Latin American nations, defined the university as the institutional center of the nation's culture, with the task of examining and proposing solutions to the central problems of the nation.[1] The participation of students or recent graduates of universities has been notable in some of the major political reform movements in Latin America. For example, the major political parties of Venezuela developed as student political parties at the National University of Caracas, and the Aprista movement of Peru was initially led by university intellectuals. The Christian Democratic party of Chile began as a student movement at the University of Chile in Santiago. Students were instrumental in the overthrow of dictatorial governments in Cuba, Colombia and Venezuela between 1957 and 1959.[2]

Much of what has been written on Latin American student politics has focused on student involvement in events of a dramatic character, with less attention to variations in and sources of student political orientations, or to the organizational side of student politics. This has tended to create an image of the Latin American student as essentially populist, seeking change or reform by direct action, and predominantly opposed to dictatorial or oligarchial governments. While there is truth in this image, it ignores existing political cleavage within specific university populations as well as national variations in student politics. The present study will examine some factors relevant to political differentiation and cleavage, and especially those conducive to left radicalism, among students in the largest and most important university of Colombia, the National University in Bogotá. A survey of student attitudes conducted in the summer of 1961 provides data on student support for the political and social programs of a number of political leaders, among them Fidel Castro.[3]

---

[1] There are a number of sources dealing with the university reform movement, but the most comprehensive is Gabriel del Mazo, ed., *La reforma universitaria,* Vols. 1–3 (Buenos Aires, Ed. El Ateneo, 1946); a brief account in English is found in Miguel Rotblat, "The Latin American Student Movement," *New Universities Thought,* 1 (Summer, 1961), pp. 29–37. See also International Student Conference, *University Reform in Latin America* (Leiden, Netherlands: COSEC, n.d.).

[2] An excellent study in the relationship of the university to national politics in Chile is Frank Bonilla, *Students in Politics: Three Generations of Political Action in a Latin American University* (Harvard University, Ph.D. thesis, 1959). For an attempt to account for the tendency of Latin American students to take direct political action, see E. Wight Bakke, "Students on the March: The Cases of Mexico and Colombia," *Sociology of Education,* 37 (1964), pp. 200–228.

[3] The survey was conducted by Robert C. Williamson of Haverford College, who generously made the original data available to the Comparative National Development Project. Williamson's report on the survey findings is published in "El estudiante colombiano y sus actitudes," *Monografías Sociológicas,* 13 (1962). The sample consisted of 610 students from the National University (460 men and 150 women) and 159 students from three other universities in Bogotá, not included in the present study. About 10 per cent of the student population of the National University was included, representing all faculties. Students were selected randomly from official university lists,

Castro as hero or villain has been the rallying point for political conflict in a number of Latin American universities. Among other things, Castro has symbolized independence from American influence, the quick eradication of poverty and ignorance, and the total mobilization of society in the interests of rapid modernization. Thus, approval of the political program and policies of Castro in 1961 is likely to indicate a favorable attitude to radical modernization of Latin American society, and opponents of his policies are likely to include those who seek to maintain the status quo or who seek change by more moderate means, within the existing legal and political framework of society. We need not consider whether a Castro-type revolution is likely to realize the goals of rapid industrialization and increase of productivity, but rather what Castro presumably symbolized to his Latin American supporters in 1961 and earlier.

The meaning for Latin Americans of the Cuban Revolution and of Fidel Castro as its symbol goes beyond the personality of Castro or the situation in Cuba, as suggested by the following comments of North American observers:

> Fidelismo challenges the structure of the established Latin American universe, its distribution of economic, social, and political power, its accommodation with the Church, its sets of relationships between the person and the world—in short, its total self-conception.[1]

> The appeal of Fidelismo was swift and powerful. The Cuban Revolution, on its idealistic side, was a response to the very same problems plaguing every country of Latin America. Wherever there was poverty, misery, real or fancied oppression, social injustice, intellectual ferment, the lure of power, the emotions of anti-Yankeeism—and where would there not be these things?—the example of Cuba and the romantic, magnetic figure of Fidel Castro, cast their spell.[2]

> Little—indeed, surprisingly little—is new, creative, or original in the Castro movement. At bottom it is essentially the latest synthesis of elements which have been afoot in the Western Hemisphere since the opening years of the twentieth century. Yet this is precisely the appeal of *fidelismo* throughout Latin America. Fidel Castro strikes responsive chords in all countries of the Americas because his movement is composed of old and familiar elements, most of which have long been at large throughout the American Republics.[3]

---

although in a few faculties it was necessary to select students upon a voluntary basis. Interviews were conducted individually, although in some cases two or three respondents were interviewed at one time. Williamson, "El estudiante colombiano," pp. 11–12.

[1] Kalman H. Silvert, "The Island and the Continent: Latin American Development and the Challenge of Cuba," *American Universities Field Staff Reports*, 8, no. 1 (January, 1961), pp. 1–2.

[2] Herbert L. Matthews, *The Cuban Story* (New York: George Braziller, 1961), p. 195.

[3] George I. Blanksten, "Fidel Castro and Latin America," *in* Morton A. Kaplan, ed., *The Revolution in World Politics* (New York: John Wiley and Sons, 1962), p. 133. The issue of the effectiveness or appropriateness of Castro's policies for the rest of Latin America, or even Cuba, are not at issue here. The issue is rather the symbolic appeal of Castro, representing the promise of a total solution to problems of underdevelopment, social injustice, economic inequality, and United States

The question of how the students in our sample perceive Castro and the Cuban Revolution, or how they would apply Castro's policies and programs to their own nation, unfortunately cannot be answered within the present survey. Nevertheless, there is some reason to assume that Castro supporters tend to value democratic forms and processes less than the economic goals of modernization, industrialization, and equitable distribution of the national product. As K. H. Silvert states:

> There are unfortunately many reasons for youth's suspicion of democratic process in Latin America. In most countries young persons have been brought up in violence, disorder, dictatorship, and depression.... All too often in most of these countries have the words of democracy been mouthed to cover the political lecheries of wanton and egotistical dictatorship. Thus many young persons have been unable to see freedom as other than a concept debased by propagandistic misuses.[1]

Castro's own words suggest a concept of democracy which may reflect that of students who support his policies:

> A democracy is that form of government in which the majority means something, and the interests of that majority are protected; a democracy is that in which a man is assured of all his rights, not only the right to think freely, but also the right to know how to think, the right to know how to write what he thinks, the right to know· how to read what others think and say. Also the right to eat, to work, to become educated, and to mean something to your society. That is why this is real democracy, the democracy brought to you by the Cuban Revolution, by our Revolution.[2]

Castro's words in this and other speeches imply a direct correspondence of interest between the revolutionary elite and those whom the revolution purports to benefit. Thus, there is the implication that formal democratic procedures to assure the existence of legitimate opposition are unnecessary. The assumption that *fidelistas* are simply authoritarian power seekers or assuredly procommunist is unwarranted, however, as our data will suggest. Castro's supporters and opponents in Latin America are not clearly distinguishable as groups by concrete and articulate positions on political means or goals. Rather, they represent opposed *tendencies* with respect to the extent, the rate, the means, and the goals of desired change. While Castro support may have declined since 1961 among Latin American students, as a result of possible disillusionment with Castro policies or their consequences, it would appear that there has been no decline, and possibly an increase,

---

political and economic influence. See C. A. M. Hennessy, "The Roots of Cuban Nationalism," *International Affairs,* 39 (1963), pp. 345–359.

[1] Silvert, "The Island and the Continent," p. 12.

[2] Fidel Castro, "A Real Democracy," *in* Paul E. Sigmund, Jr., ed., *The Ideologies of the Developing Nations* (New York: Frederick A. Praeger, 1963), p. 267.

in support for the kind of social transformation which Castro and Cuba represented earlier. This is suggested by the continuing evidence of radical student politics in Colombia and other Latin American nations.

Before presenting data which reveal some politically relevant views of Castro supporters and opponents, a brief description of Colombian society is in order. Colombia is predominantly an agrarian society, with 50 per cent of the economically active population engaged in agriculture and only about 5 per cent in industrial manufacturing in 1959. There are great regional variations in climate, terrain and economic activity, and difficulties in transport and communication limit the development of a national economy. Colombia's dependence on coffee for foreign export earnings and the drop in its world market price in recent years have seriously limited the nation's capacity to industrialize. The population is largely rural and lower class; the middle and upper classes constitute perhaps 20 per cent of the population, and nearly 40 per cent of the population is illiterate. The proportion of the 20- to 24-year-old group which attends universities is one of the lowest in the hemisphere, about 17 per 1,000. Taking into account urbanization, industrialization, literacy, and other indicators of social and economic development, Colombia is more developed than the Central American republics and the western South American nations of Peru and Ecuador, and has been grouped with Cuba and Venezuela and below Argentina, Brazil, Chile, Uruguay, and Mexico, in terms of 1950 data, with respect to general economic and social development.[1]

Limited economic reforms have been started by the government, including an agrarian reform which is likely to have little effect on the markedly unequal distribution of land or on agricultural productivity. Recent reports of the program indicate its lack of strong support and an insufficient budget to carry it out.[2]

E. J. Hobsbawm concludes that Colombia, like most Latin American countries, ". . . contains the raw material for a social revolution both of the peasantry and of the urban poor . . ." due to the combined effect of rapid population growth, the high rate of urbanization, the low standard of living

[1] Gino Germani and Kalman Silvert, "Politics, Social Structure and Military Intervention in Latin America," *European Journal of Sociology,* 2 (1961), p. 64. Other sources for this discussion are United Nations Economic Commission for Latin America, *Economic Survey of Latin America, 1958* (Mexico: UN, ECLA, 1959); ECLA, *Analyses and Projections of Economic Development,* Vol. 3, "The Economic Development of Colombia" (Geneva: UN, Department of Economic and Social Affairs, 1957); Center of Latin American Studies, *Statistical Abstract of Latin America: 1962* (Los Angeles: University of California, 1962); and U.S. Department of Labor, Bureau of Labor Statistics, *Labor in Colombia* (Washington, 1962).

[2] See Oscar Delgado, "Revolution, Reform, Conservatism: Three Types of Agrarian Reform," *Dissent,* 9 (1962), pp. 355–356; Ernest Feder, "The Rational Implementation of Land Reform in Colombia and Its Significance for the Alliance for Progress," *América Latina,* 6 (1963), pp. 81–108; and Land Tenure Center, "Prospects for Political Stability in Colombia with Special Reference to Land Reform," *Discussion Paper,* 1 (January, 1963).

of the masses, the wide differential between middle- and lower-class living standards, and the low rate of industrialization.[1] There are a handful of political groups which profess a revolutionary ideology, but it appears that they have only a small following and offer little likelihood of leading a successful revolution.[2] Their success may depend on the extent to which they can politicalize urban workers, especially the under- and unemployed rural migrants who continue to move into the cities to escape rural violence and to find a better standard of living.

Against this background of rising expectations and increasing frustration, we should expect Castro supporters to advocate sweeping changes and to reveal a greater awareness and concern for the extent of poverty and social inequality in the country. When asked the question, "Do you believe that our country needs a radical change?" the great majority of students answered yes, but 96 per cent of the Castro supporters were in agreement as compared to 84 per cent of the Castro opponents. Table 1, which reports the kind of change desired by those who agreed on the need for change, reveals that Castro support is much less associated with radical or drastic change than one would expect. Castro supporters are somewhat more likely to mention change as such, without specification, or to indicate the desired extent of change, while Castro opponents are more likely to specify a sector within the society in which change should take place.

More subjective indicators of the relationship between Castro support and social perspectives reveal larger differences. For example, about 70 per cent of Castro supporters and only 20 per cent of Castro opponents agreed that "compared with the present, the future will be less happy." Intermediates, those who rate Castro's policies as fair, are in between, with 40 per cent pessimistic about the future. Similarly, 90 per cent of Castro's opponents respond that almost all or the majority of the people they know are happy in their lives, compared to 71 per cent of the intermediates and only 44 per cent of the pro-Castro students. It can be argued that these responses are projections of subjective personal feelings, but it seems more plausible that they derive from differing social frames of reference, with Castro supporters more pessimistic because their perspectives include a broader portion of the population and a deeper concern with its social and economic welfare.

Some evidence of the relationship between Castro support and attitudes

---

[1] E. J. Hobsbawm, "The Revolutionary Situation in Colombia," *The World Today,* 19 (1963), pp. 248–258.

[2] See Allen Young, "Revolutionary Parties in Contemporary Colombia" (Stanford University Institute of Hispanic American and Luso-Brazilian Studies, 1963), mimeo. A recent report on student politics suggests that the student left in Colombia is split among student wings of the Communist party, the MRL, and the Partido de la Revolución Socialista (PRS), "made up of dissidents from the Communist party and MRL, who claim to be the 'true followers of Marxism-Leninism.'" *Youth and Freedom,* 6, no. 3 (1964), p. 10.

Table 1. Proportion Desiring Various Types of National Change
by Degree of Support for Castro

Type of Change[a]	Support for Castro[b]					
	High		Intermediate		Low	
Change, content unspecified:						
A radical or drastic change	12%		8%		4%	
A gradual evolution	10		4		8	
Change, not necessarily gradual or radical[c]	40		39		27	
Subtotal		62%		51%		39%
Change, with content or category specified:						
Political change	7		17		20	
Economic change	4		5		9	
Social change	14		18		19	
Agrarian reform	3		0		3	
Improved public education	3		4		1	
More emphasis on religion	1		3		4	
Subtotal		32		47		56
Other, unspecified		6		2		5
Total		100%		100%		100%
		(144)		(144)		(237)

[a] This question could be answered freely, since precoded sets of answers were not provided. The categories used here were constructed on the basis of the answers obtained.

[b] Coding of "support for Castro" is based on responses to the following question:"How would you rate the economic and social programs of the following leaders?" "Very good" and "good" are coded "high"; "fair" is coded as "intermediate"; and "bad" and "very bad" are coded "low."

[c] The Spanish word *radical* as used in the original question apparently has a diffuse meaning to respondents, connoting "basic" or "fundamental" as well as "revolutionary."

toward university politics is revealed in responses to the question, "Do you consider the student strike as an effective tactic for solving academic and university problems, improving student living conditions, and increasing the prestige of the university?" A majority of students see the strike as effective for the first and second goals, but not for the third. On all three, however, a higher proportion of Castro supporters perceive the strike as effective. This is especially true with regard to academic and administrative problems, for which 81 per cent of pro-Castro students compared to 57 per cent of anti-Castro students affirm the effectiveness of strikes. These findings suggest that Castro supporters share with his opponents a willingness to support specifically student interests in a conflict with the administration or in the effort to improve student conditions but that they feel it would be quicker to use the strike in such a conflict.

The meaning of support for Castro will next be explored in terms of its relationship to support for other political leaders. First, a brief discussion of Colombian politics will provide a background for the analysis. Colombian politics still reflect the deep conflicts of the nineteenth century between the advocates and opponents of church privileges and separation of church and state, and between defenders of strong central government and of departmental autonomy. These issues no longer divide the nation, but the parties which represented the federalist, anticlerical position—the Liberals—and the centralist party of the church—the Conservatives—are still the predominant ones. The Liberal party is the party of the majority and has favored extension of the suffrage and social welfare measures, while the Conservative party has tended to be the party of privilege and reaction. However, the leaders of both parties tend to constitute an oligarchy without fundamental differences on major policy issues and are apparently opposed to the institution of major reforms, in deeds if not in words.

Rural violence between Liberals and Conservatives began during the regimes of Conservative presidents Ospina Pérez and Laureano Gómez, from 1946 to 1953. This sadistic violence in rural areas is conducted by autonomous, armed bands for whom violence and banditry have become a way of life. It was this protracted guerilla warfare which General Rojas Pinilla, who came to power by deposing Laureano Gómez, attempted to halt. Since Rojas Pinilla's overthrow in 1957, Colombia has been governed by the Frente Nacional, an arrangement by which, for a period of 16 years (until 1974), the presidency is alternated between the two parties and membership of both parties in Congress and in the presidential cabinet is equal. The purpose of this arrangement was to reduce party conflict, which had verged on civil war, and to establish the basis for a return to normal electoral procedures. It has also had the indirect effect of inhibiting reform efforts, given the impossibility of rule by a majority popular party which would reflect the interests of the impoverished masses of Colombian society.[1]

Declining support for the Frente Nacional government, and perhaps increasing alienation from the present political and social system, is evidenced by the progressive increase in abstentions from elections since 1957 and in the increase of votes going to opponents of the Frente Nacional. In the March, 1964 departmental, municipal and congressional elections, only one third of the electorate voted (everyone over 21 may vote), and opponents of the National Front received about one third of the vote.[2]

In Table 2 the relationship between attitudes toward Castro and toward other political leaders is presented. Names are ranked roughly in a left-center-right order, politically, reading from the top to the bottom of the table, but with no intention of giving a precise meaning to differences in

---

[1] See Vernon Lee Fluharty, *Dance of the Millions: Military Rule and the Social Revolution in Colombia, 1930-1956* (Pittsburgh, Pa.: University of Pittsburgh Press, 1957); John D. Martz, *Colombia: A Contemporary Political Survey* (Chapel Hill, N.C.: University of North Carolina Press, 1962); Jorge Cardenas García, *El Frente Nacional y los partidos políticos* (Tunja: Imprenta Deptal., 1958); and Mons. Germán Guzmán *et al.*, "La violencia en Colombia," Vol. 1, *Monografías Sociológicas*, 1, no. 12 (1962).

[2] *La Nueva Prensa*, 56 (1962), pp. 24, 34-35; *New York Times*, March 17, 1964.

Table 2. Proportion Who Support Various Political Leaders[a]
by Degree of Support for Castro

Support for:		Support for Castro			
		High	Intermediate	Low	Total
Nikita Khrushchev	High	69%	37%	20%	38%
	Low	7	18	56	33
Gilberto Vieira					
(leader of Colombian	High	34%	7%	3%	14%
Communist party)	Low	27	59	75	56
López Michelsen					
(leader of MRL, dissident left	High	51%	28%	12%	28%
faction of Liberal party)	Low	21	24	55	38
Romulo Betancourt	High	16%	37%	40%	32%
	Low	37	16	13	21
Lleras Camargo					
(Liberal, former	High	20%	41%	53%	42%
president, 1958–1962)	Low	49	12	8	21
John F. Kennedy	High	42%	69%	90%	72%
	Low	22	5	2	8
Ospina Pérez					
(leader of official majority	High	7%	20%	30%	20%
branch of Conservative party)	Low	76	38	35	46
Laureano Gómez					
(leader of minority faction	High	11%	15%	21%	17%
of Conservative party)	Low	70	50	50	56
Francisco Franco	High	15%	25%	22%	21%
	Low	65	49	41	50
N[b]		(133–161)	(96–131)	(201–280)	(430–569)

[a] See Table 1 for questions on which responses were based, and for categorization of responses. Because of space limitations, "intermediates" are omitted for all leaders other than Castro.

[b] Percentages of support for different leaders are computed to different bases, because those who failed to give an opinion are omitted. The bases in each of the columns take the range specified in the bottom row of the table.

rank order between adjacent leaders. It is clear from Table 2 that support for Castro is associated with support for leftist leaders and opposition to leaders representing a generally center or right position. It should also be noted, however, that support among either pro- or anti-Castro students for Vieira, leader of the Colombian Communist party, is much lower than expected, nor is there much support by any group for rightist political leaders. Kennedy is the most favored political leader among anti-Castro students, and López Michelsen and Khrushchev are most favored by pro-Castro students. The relatively high support for Kennedy and low support for Betancourt by Castro supporters, seemingly paradoxical, may be due to Kennedy's public image as a proponent of Latin American reforms and of Betancourt's image as an anti-Castro leader, although both could be identified as foes of the type of abrupt, revolutionary change symbolized by Castroism.

About one fourth of the sample are pro-Castro and one half are anti-Castro, indicating a smaller proportion of pro-Castro students than among university students in Venezuela, Peru, or Ecuador, to judge from the results of university elections in recent years, but perhaps a proportion similar to that in Chile, where the leftist coalition party (FRAP) gained about one third of the vote in recent elections for the national student federation.[1] On the other hand, the data suggest that students are somewhat more leftist than that portion of the Colombian population which voted in the 1960 elections for the lower house of the national legislature. In that election, 17 per cent of the vote was cast for *laureanistas,* or members of the Gómez faction within the Conservative party, and 17 per cent for members of the MRL, the leftist faction of the Liberal party led by López Michelsen. Our data reveal that 17 per cent of the sample of students are favorable to Gómez, but 28 per cent favor López Michelsen. The comparison is inexact but suggestive.

Catholicism

Having considered some attitudes and political preferences associated with degrees of support for Castro, we turn to an analysis of factors which may condition or determine Castro support. The major determinants of political orientation can be grouped as factors related to stratification and factors related to cultural values. Comparative analysis of voting statistics has shown that left voting is inversely related to position in the stratification hierarchy and inversely related to traditionalism, assuming a general traditional-modern continuum in terms of cultural values.[2] In the context of Latin America, one of the major institutions linked to the maintenance of traditionalism is the Catholic church. The church has tended to constitute the bulwark of traditionalist elites in most Latin American nations.[3] This alliance is not intrinsic to Catholicism as such, for, as Reinhold Niebuhr has stated, "Catholicism is at its least impressive in feudal-agrarian societies, where it frequently seeks desperately to hold on to special powers and privileges which were essential in the Middle Ages but are so no longer. Catholicism is most creative in highly developed industrial communities."[4] Further, the church is not a homogeneous entity throughout Latin America, but reveals significant variations among nations and within the clergy regarding

---

[1] *Youth and Freedom,* 6, no. 3 (1964), pp. 5–10.

[2] Seymour M. Lipset, *Political Man* (Garden City, N.Y.: Doubleday Anchor Books, 1963), pp. 230–238.

[3] See Kingsley Davis, "Political Ambivalence in Latin America," *in* Asher N. Christensen, ed., *The Evolution of Latin American Government* (New York: Henry Holt, 1951), p. 234.

[4] Reinhold Niebuhr, "Religion and Politics," *in* Peter H. Odegard, ed., *Religion and Politics* (Engelwood Cliffs, N.J.: Oceana Publications, 1960), p. 108.

support or opposition toward social reform. However, several observers have noted the predominantly conservative character of the church in Colombia and the considerable extent of its influence compared to that of the church elsewhere in Latin America. The historian Hubert Herring writes:

> Colombian churchmen, perhaps spiritually more akin to their colleagues in Spain than those in any other Latin American republic, have been impelled by the belief that Colombia is and must continue to be dedicated to the service of the true faith and that all unbelievers and heretics are enemies of the nation.[1]

The church has openly stated its support of the Conservative party, but there is evidence that this alliance may be weakening in the recent sermons of priests critical of the party's failure to carry out reforms.[2]

One would expect the committed Catholic, especially in Colombia, to be a traditionalist, both with respect to church traditions as well as to other traditional institutions of Hispanic-American culture, and to be opposed to radical social and political solutions, particularly those which propose a secular state. Weekly attendance at Mass should be a good indicator of commitment to the Catholic church, to judge from the following statement. Speaking of the tendency for Latin Americans habitually to avoid attendance at Mass, a Catholic report states: "Nominal Catholicism cannot by replaced by formal Catholicism until Mass attendance is more strictly construed for what it is: the first and most obvious index of Catholic Faith and the one for which there is no substitute."[3] This report stresses the importance of weekly Mass attendance for "profession of faith and right intention" and for instruction in the faith. Tables 3 and 4 show the relationship of church affiliation and rate of church attendance to Castro support.[4]

The data show a rather high correlation between church commitment and opposition to Castro, while support for Castro increases with decreasing commitment. This finding is not surprising in view of what has been said concerning the role and influence of the Catholic church in Latin

[1] Hubert Herring, *A History of Latin America* (New York: Alfred A. Knopf, 1955), p. 475. For other observations on the character and political involvement of the church in Colombia, see W. O. Galbraith, *Colombia, A General Survey* (London: Royal Institute of International Affairs, 1953), pp. 45–48; and J. Lloyd Mecham, *Church and State in Latin America* (Chapel Hill, N.C.: University of North Carolina Press, 1934), p. 168, *passim*.

[2] *Hispanic American Report*, 16 (1963), pp. 375–376.

[3] William J. Coleman, *Latin-American Catholicism: A Self-Evaluation* (Maryknoll, N.Y.: Maryknoll Publications, 1958), p. 32.

[4] Tables 3 and 4 reveal that 78 per cent of the respondents consider themselves practicing Catholics and that 63 per cent report weekly or more frequent attendance. These figures may seem unusually high, given the much lower rates reported by the church for the general population, but data from surveys conducted among students in other Latin American nations suggest that these figures may be fairly representative of university students generally. See Ivan Vallier, *Anglican Opportunities in South America* (New York: Columbia University, The Bureau of Applied Social Research, 1963), pp. IV–25, Table 10, reporting data from a survey conducted in Chile, Peru, and Argentina.

Table 3. Support for Castro, by Religious Affiliation[a]

	Practicing Catholic	Nonpracticing Catholic	Agnostic
Pro-Castro[b]	21%	51%	74%
Anti-Castro[a]	58	23	8
N	(436)	(99)	(23)

[a] Twelve students reported they were Protestants or members of other religions. These 12 are too few to be included in the analysis.

[b] In this and the following tables, pro-Castro students are those high on Castro support and anti-Castro students those low on Castro support.

Table 4. Support for Castro, by Frequency of Church Attendance

	Never or Almost Never	A Few Times a Year	Once or Twice a Month	Once a Week	Two or More Times a Week
Pro-Castro	58%	34%	34%	21%	12%
Anti-Castro	21	40	34	56	82
N	(69)	(45)	(92)	(297)	(60)

America, and especially in Colombia, and in view of results of research in Europe showing the link between Catholicism and conservative voting. It would appear that early socialization in the Catholic faith predisposes the devout Catholic toward an acceptance of the church's guidance in political affairs, and toward an acceptance of the social order, unless the church itself should propose the need for fundamental social change. Our data show that committed Catholics are more likely to come from homes in which fathers were also committed Catholics (nearly all mothers are reported as weekly church attenders). This suggests that committed Catholics reflect in their religious and political behavior the influence of a home environment in which Catholic rites and teachings were accorded high value. On the other hand, since not all committed Catholics are anti-Castro, and some are even pro-Castro, it must be assumed that other influences are operating which are conducive to a radical political orientation, influences which do not necessarily undermine Catholic commitment. In order to assess the extent to which Catholic commitment appears to inhibit or permit Castro support under various conditions, all subsequent tables will compare students who are low and high on Catholic commitment.

Stratification

Turning now to stratification as a determinant of Castro support, we find that, as is the case at other Latin American universities, most of the students come from middle- and upper-class families, with less than 10 per cent from lower-class backgrounds. Within the middle class, however, father's

Table 5. Proportion Favorable to Castro, by Father's Occupation
and Student's Church Commitment

Father's Occupation[a]	Low Commitment		High Commitment		Totals	
Labor, agriculture[b]	62%	(13)	25%	(28)	37%	(41)
Domestic service	12%	(8)[c]	31%	(13)	24%	(21)
Lower white-collar	40%	(45)	16%	(87)	24%	(132)
Upper white-collar	35%	(26)	19%	(48)	24%	(74)
Professional[d]	39%	(23)	20%	(46)	26%	(69)
Business	44%	(52)	19%	(72)	30%	(124)

[a] Unemployed, retired, and nonclassified are excluded.
[b] Includes only those with incomes comparable to labor.
[c] This percentage has too small a base to be reliable.
[d] Includes only those with some university education—others are classified as upper white-collar.

occupation provides an indicator of differential life style, which may be related to student's political orientations. In Table 5 support for Castro is shown by father's occupational category and also, within each category, by student's religious commitment. High commitment is measured by weekly or more frequent church attendance, and low commitment by less than weekly attendance.

Table 5 reveals that students from agricultural and labor backgrounds are most likely to support Castro, especially those with a low religious commitment. However, the differences between students from middle-class and lower-class backgrounds are not as great as those between students with a low or high religious commitment. A further analysis, using father's education and income as indicators of stratification position, reveals a similar pattern.

Our findings suggest either that the political orientations of students' families do not vary much by social strata, or else that students do not reflect the political cleavages that may exist in the larger society. Students, after all, constitute a highly selected social group, are homogeneous with respect to age, share a common social status as students, and are exposed to similar political influences within the university. These shared attributes may have a greater impact on their ideas and values than their class origins or interests. The persisting influence of religious commitment is undeniable, however, and appears to supercede socioeconomic origin as a determinant of political attitude.

University Experience

The Latin American university provides an environment conducive to the involvement of students in debate and action concerning national and international political issues. Student strikes and demonstrations are relatively frequent, and ostensibly local issues, dealing with specific university problems, often develop into broader protests against the government, the "oligarchy," imperialism, and other ideologically defined opponents. This close link between university issues and broader political concerns may be due in part to the close ties between the universities and the state, except for the few private, predominantly Catholic, universities in Latin America. Most universities are state supported and, although formally autonomous, are often exposed to considerable direct or indirect political influence. The National University of Colombia is governed by a council including representatives of the church, business associations, government, faculty and students. University reformists seek to limit council membership to faculty and students only, in addition to perhaps one government representative. Further reforms sought are greater freedom to teach and discuss, greater focus on teaching and research dealing with national problems, and improved student services. Suggesting the broader overtones of this movement, the Colombian sociologist Orlando Fals Borda writes that it is a ". . . secular expression of Colombian nationalism which finds its appropriate outlet in the university of the State."[1]

Evidence of the persisting and dramatic political activity of many, but not all, university students and of the predominantly leftist character of much of this activity in strikes and demonstrations of recent years suggests that university experience is likely both to politicalize and radicalize. For many students, university experience is conceivably a sharp break with their past, involving a transition from a relatively traditional, authoritarian family environment to one which challenges many traditional concepts and values. If these assumptions are correct, we should expect to find an increase in the proportion of left-oriented students with additional years of university experience, and to find that religious commitment should modify this influence. Table 6 provides support for this hypothesis.

Support for Castro increases up to the fourth year among students of low religious commitment, with no change between the fourth and later years. For students with high commitment, there is an increase up to the third year, but a decline thereafter. Lacking panel data, we can only infer that these changes are an effect of increased university experience. At least this is a highly plausible explanation. Furthermore, although we lack evidence of change in religious commitment over time, we may assume that some students change both their religious commitment and political orientation concurrently, bringing into congruence their religious and political views and behavior as a result of increased exposure to radicalizing and secularizing influences in the university milieu. This may account for the decline in Castro support among students in later years who are high in

---

[1] Orlando Fals Borda, "La educación en Colombia," *Monografías Sociológicas,* 11 (1962). The organic statute of the university is published in *Universidades,* 3 (1963), pp. 191–204.

Table 6. Proportion Favorable to Castro
by Year in University and Church Commitment

Church Commitment	Year in University				
	First	Second	Third	Fourth	Fifth or More
Low	33%	38%	44%	53%	52%
	(90)	(21)	(23)	(47)	(25)
High	15%	21%	30%	22%	20%
	(191)	(19)	(30)	(92)	(20)

church commitment. For their church commitment to be congruent with their political orientation, they must resist the tendency toward radicalization in the university milieu and withdraw their support from Castro.

Residence and Student Subculture

Studies of North American university students have shown that attitudes and behavior are related to membership in different student subcultures.[1] An important aspect of the subcultural environment is place of residence, since fellow residents often provide the close ties that serve to mediate and interpret the larger university experience for the individual student. A large proportion of Latin American students live at home or with relatives out of economic necessity, and this is the case for our sample of Colombian students, although university dormitories provide space for some. We would expect students living away from home to be more exposed to the political subcultures of the university, being outside the restraining influence of family tradition and authority, and more available for politicalizing activities, such as political discussions and direct involvement in student government, demonstrations and strikes. The data in fact reveal a higher proportion of pro-Castro students among those living away from home than among those living with family or relatives.

We will next consider the extent to which residence alone appears to have an effect on political orientation, controlling for year in school and religious commitment, since the less religious and the more advanced students are also the most likely to live away from home. Table 7 shows the relationships among all three factors and Castro support.

Except for the first row in the table, the results support the hypothesis that both increased university experience and residence away from family

---

[1] See Burton R. Clark and Martin Trow, "Determinants of College Student Subculture" (Center for Study of Higher Education, University of California, Berkeley, 1962); Hanan C. Selvin and Warren O. Hagstrom, "Determinants of Support for Civil Liberties," *British Journal of Sociology*, 11 (1960), pp. 51–73; and David Nasatir, "A Contextual Analysis of Academic Failure," *The School Review*, 71 (1963), pp. 290–298.

Table 7. Proportion Favorable to Castro
by Year in University, Residence, and Church Commitment

Church Commitment	Residence[a]	Year in University					
		First		Second and Third		Fourth or More	
High	Home	15%	(149)	27%	(33)	16%	(82)
	Other	12%	(41)	21%	(14)	36%	(28)
Low	Home	23%	(52)	33%	(24)	40%	(37)
	Other	46%	(53)	53%	(19)	67%	(33)

[a]Home: all those living with family or relatives. Other: those living elsewhere, including dormitories, apartments, boarding houses, and living alone or with friends.

or relatives enhance support for Castro. And the first row reveals that the reduced support for Castro among students of more-advanced status with high religious commitment, as reported in Table 6, is accounted for by those who continue to live with family or relatives. The findings suggest that residence outside the university both removes the student from traditional family influences and exposes him to politicizing experiences with fellow students. Evidence that this constitutes a socialization process is the increase of Castro support with continued years of university exposure. It is indeed likely that political discussion and debate tend to center around the significance of the Cuban Revolution, at least in its early period, and that increasing awareness of Colombian social and economic problems enhances the appeal of a revolution which appeared to offer the most successful solution to such problems.

So far in this discussion men have not been differentiated from women, who constitute one fourth of the sample, and it may appear that women students are less likely than men to respond to the politicizing influences of the university. Analysis of the data, not presented here, shows that this is true, but perhaps largely because women are more likely than men to live at home and to be high in religious commitment. When these factors are controlled, we find that women, like men, increase their support for Castro with increased years of university enrollment. Residence away from home has little or no independent effect, however, perhaps because most of the few women who live away from home are high in religious commitment. Most of these live in student dormitories, an environment which, for women at least, may sustain family religious traditions and political influences, analogous to the social control exercised in university sororities in the United States.[1]

---

[1] See Selvin and Hagstrom, "Support for Civil Liberties," for evidence that sororities apparently insulate women students from the liberalizing influence of the university.

University Career and Field of Study

The Latin American university is typically organized into relatively autonomous *facultades,* or faculties, as we shall refer to them. These are similar to professional graduate schools in the United States, since prescribed courses are restricted primarily to those within the faculty and are organized into a sequence which allows for little variation or substitution.[1] In Colombia, students must pass all courses to proceed to the next year, and failures must be made up be repeating the year, in effect. This means that students within a faculty have a higher rate of interaction than is typical for the North American undergraduate. Thus, the faculty should be an important influence in shaping the political perspectives of students. In Table 8 support for Castro is shown by field of study, for students of high and low religious commitment. Grouping of faculties is necessary because of the small samples obtained from most faculties, and in order to have sufficient numbers to control for the effect of church commitment. The grouping seeks to combine students in allied fields. Economics, mathematics, and statistics were combined on the assumption that the three share a mathematical orientation, and because statistics is primarily taught as an applied field.

As Table 8 indicates, the different fields of study vary considerably in the proportion of their students supporting Castro. This is especially true for students with a low religious commitment, among whom the social science and humanities students are much more likely to support Castro than those in the natural sciences. Among the religiously committed, the relationship between field of study and Castro support is relatively minor, attesting to the insulating effect of religious commitment.

There are a number of possible explanations for the pattern of Castro support within the various *facultades.* Clearly, the social sciences are concerned with a different subject matter, dealing with society and human values to a greater extent than the natural sciences. This suggests that students of the social sciences and humanities are more likely to be confronted in their classes by the severe social problems facing Colombian society and may therefore be more likely to direct their attention to these matters. This explanation is plausible, but there are a number of difficulties inherent in it. There is, for example, little or no evidence that professors in the National University have a Marxist orientation. Economics, for example, which in some countries is a field of study with an excessive amount of ideology, tends to be taught in combination with business administration.[2]

---

[1] For a general description of the structure and characteristics of Latin American education, see Robert J. Havighurst, "Latin American and North American Higher Education," *Comparative Education Review,* 4 (1961), pp. 174–182. See also John Harrison, "The Confrontation with the Political University," *The Annals of the American Academy of Political and Social Science,* 334 (1961), pp. 74–83.

[2] John M. Hunter, *Emerging Colombia* (Washington, D.C.: Public Affairs Press, 1962), p. 55.

Table 8. Proportion Favorable to Castro
by Field of Study and Church Commitment

Field of Study	Church Commitment		
	Low	High	Total
Law	63% (24)	19% (26)	40% (50)
Economics, mathematics, statistics	60% (15)	39% (23)	47% (38)
Sociology, psychology, education	55% (20)	11% (54)	23% (74)
Humanities, fine arts	47% (17)	20% (20)	32% (37)
Architecture, engineering	41% (49)	23% (79)	30% (128)
Medical fields[a]	35% (20)	14% (92)	18% (112)
Medicine	33% (30)	24% (21)	29% (51)
Agronomy, geology	22% (23)	12% (24)	17% (47)

[a]Pharmacy, dentistry, veterinary medicine, and nursing.

It may be, therefore, that pro-Castro students are recruited to the social sciences and humanities in disproportionate numbers, and that the influence of fellow students is more important than course contents in forming a critical perspective toward society, including support for radical programs of social reform.

An alternative explanation for the findings in Table 8 is economic. The survey data include questions about students' perceptions of the income they would obtain five years after graduation and about their expectation of people in their field finding jobs during the first year after graduation. One could hypothesize that a relatively low level of income expectation and doubts about one's career chances should be associated with a greater propensity toward radicalism. However, analysis of the data gives ambiguous results. When individual faculties are ranked by the proportion in each expecting to earn only 2,500 pesos ($250 U.S.) or less a month five years after graduation, six social science and humanities fields and two natural science fields are at or above the median, while eight natural science fields and only one social science field are below the median. Yet, correlation between the above rankings and the rank order of faculties according to their proportion of pro-Castro students is approximately zero (-.04), due largely to some wide discrepancies in a few fields between level of income expectation and Castro support.

There is a positive, if relatively low, correlation (.33) between the rank orders of faculties by their proportion pro-Castro and by the proportions who expect that 40 per cent or fewer of the graduates within their faculties will find jobs during the first year after graduation. Since this is not necessarily an estimate of the individual's own chances, it suggests that there may be a group response to career opportunities, so that a generally low estimate of employability for the field as a whole may tend to influence the propensity toward radicalism.

This interpretation fits into other recent discussions of student radicalism, in which emphasis is placed on the dissatisfactions of students who receive a modern education in underdeveloped societies not yet ready to utilize modern skills or to accept secular values and orientations.[1] The situation is somewhat different in Colombia, where agronomists, for example, who are in a "modern" field, can find ample employment opportunities among the large landholding corporations. Similarly, fields like medicine, pharmacy, and dentistry are oriented toward private practice among the urban middle and upper classes, a relatively affluent clientele. The above fields have relatively low proportions of pro-Castro students. Thus, it may be the relative utilization of skills and not their "traditional" or "modern" character which is crucial in determining the degree to which students in different disciplines desire a radical transformation of their society. Radical students are likely to be those least able to apply their competence, and these tend to be students in fields concerned with the social order and its structure. These students are most predisposed to favor rapid modernization, which would hopefully realize their images of the ideal society as well as give them a greater hand in its direction.[2]

Thus far the evidence supports the argument that cultural factors are more significant than stratification or economic factors in accounting for Castro support. We have shown above the influence of year in school, residence, and field of study. In Tables 9 and 10 the influences of year in school and residence are shown separately within broad categories of natural and applied science on the one hand, and humanities and social science on the other, in order to indicate the cumulative effect of the major explanatory variables. These tables support the previous findings that greater exposure to the university subculture, whether by residence away from home or increased years in the university, tends to increase Castro support. This effect is greater among students in the social sciences and humanities than among those in the natural sciences; it is almost nonexistent among students with a high religious commitment who are in the natural sciences. When the variables of field of study, religious commitment, residence, and year in school are considered simultaneously, support for Castro is nearly unanimous among students in the most "radicalizing" contexts. Among those living away from home, in the fourth to sixth years at the university,

[1] See Edward Shils, "The Intellectual in the Political Development of the New States," *in* John Kautsky, ed., *Political Change in Underdeveloped Countries* (New York: John Wiley, 1962), pp. 195–234; John Kautsky, "An Essay in the Politics of Development," *in* Kautsky, *ibid.,* pp. 3–122, especially pp. 44–49.

[2] The tendency of Japanese students in the humanities and social sciences to be more politically active and leftist than students in the physical sciences, due partly to their differential opportunities stemming from an oversupply of humanities and an undersupply of science students, is discussed in Michiya Shimboru, "Zengakuren: A Japanese Case Study of a Student Political Movement," *Sociology of Education,* 37 (1964), pp. 229–253.

Table 9. Proportion Favorable to Castro
by Field of Study, Year in the University, and Church Commitment

Year in University	High Commitment		Low Commitment	
	Natural Sciences [a]	Social Sciences [b]	Natural Sciences [a]	Social Sciences [b]
First to third	17% (135)	16% (93)	26% (66)	49% (57)
Fourth to sixth	18% (79)	30% (27)	45% (51)	76% (17)

[a] Medicine, pharmacy, nursing, dentistry, engineering and architecture, agronomy, and geology.
[b] Economics, sociology, education, psychology, mathematics and statistics, law, fine arts, and humanities.

Table 10. Proportion Favorable to Castro
by Field of Study, Place of Residence, and Church Commitment

Place of Residence	High Commitment		Low Commitment	
	Natural Sciences [a]	Social Sciences [a]	Natural Sciences [a]	Social Sciences [a]
Home	17% (168)	17% (87)	23% (64)	44% (41)
Other	20% (46)	24% (33)	49% (51)	72% (31)

[a] The categorization of fields is the same as in Table 9.

in the social sciences or humanities, and low in church attendance, about 90 per cent are Castro supporters. The number of students (nine) on which this percentage is based is too small to be reliable, but the cumulative effects of field of study, residence, year in school, and church commitment are apparent.

These findings may be contrasted to those based on surveys of political attitudes among college and university students in the United States. Studies of attitudes toward civil liberties, democratic institutions, and general tolerance indicate that university exposure increases support for these values and institutions, but that relatively little change occurs in students' party support or attitudes toward economic reforms.[1] The present study lacks data on democratic values or civil libertarianism, but it does show the marked selective influence of the university upon the political orientations of students.

Summary and Conclusion

Our findings support the generalization that increased exposure to a politically active milieu, within academic fields which confront problems

---

[1] For a survey of American studies emphasizing the apparent lack of ideological change as an effect of college and university experience, see Alex S. Edelstein, "Since Bennington: Evidence of Change in Student Political Behavior," *Public Opinion Quarterly*, 26 (1962), pp. 564–577.

inherent in the social structure, increases favorable attitudes of students toward a political figure who symbolizes a radical reordering of the society. A major argument in this analysis, supported by the data, is that students who have a high commitment to the Catholic church are least likely to respond to the ideological influences in the university, apparently because deep commitment to the church is inconsistent with support for radical or revolutionary change, being rather linked with the acceptance of traditional perspectives.

Education and Social Change:
The Argentine Case

DAVID NASATIR

Social change, economic development, and political unrest are terms commonly associated with underdeveloped nations. Until recently, however, relatively little attention has been given to the partially developed nations—those on the periphery of world power. Highly urbanized, relatively industrialized and self-consciously modernizing, Argentina is such a nation. Composed almost entirely of European immigrants and their children, it presents a sharp contrast to the common stereotype of the Latin American society. Yet Argentina, too, is a country in the midst of a profound process of change. It has only recently emerged from a period of totalitarian rule; there have been four changes of government in the last 10 years, and even now the country is wracked by serious political and economic problems.

The Perón regime (and its overthrow) accelerated the process of change in Argentina; traditional activities of ranching and farming are being supplemented, increasingly, by activities more characteristic of urban and industrial life. A prerequisite for these changes is the availability of highly trained and competent individuals prepared to enter key positions in government and industry. However, inherited family position does not guarantee technical competence. Thus a characteristic of the change process is

Reproduced, by permission, from *Sociology of Education,* 39 (Spring, 1966), pp. 167–182.

Revised version of a paper delivered at the annual meetings of the American Sociological Association, September 1965.

The author is from the University of California at Los Angeles.

Acknowledgment is gratefully given to the Comparative National Development Project of the Institute for International Studies, University of California, Berkeley, for aid in the analytic phases of the study upon which this paper is based.

an increase in the importance of the schools for the production of modernizing elites.

Technical competence is necessary for the fulfillment of strategic roles in any society, and especially in a society which is consciously attempting to direct the nature of the changes taking place within its boundaries. But competence alone is not enough. A distinct set of attitudes concerning the desirability of performing such roles and of the general responsibilities inherent in elite positions is also necessary. Although it has been suggested that urban life in itself might produce such attitudes, it is commonly assumed that formal education is even more central to their development.

> . . . [the school class] is an agency through which individual personalities are trained to be motivationally and technically adequate . . . [in] the performance of adult roles. It is not the sole such agency. . . . But, in the period extending from entry into the first grade until entry into the labor force or marriage, the school class may be regarded as the focal socializing agency.[1]

As in many parts of the world, recent and extensive changes in Argentina have made much of the expertise of the older generation obsolete, producing a rapid advancement of youths to positions of great importance. Clearly, this is a trend that will continue. In order to illustrate more clearly the role played by higher education in the development of attitudes conducive to social change, a study of almost 1,700 youths was undertaken. University students and nonuniversity youths in various parts of Argentina were asked about their job aspirations, the manner in which they would characterize an ideal job, and their opinions concerning the responsibilities of educated members of the society at large.

Although national enrollment figures were not available, informed local observers claimed that the approximately 60,000 students enrolled in the 10 faculties of the University of Buenos Aires constituted the majority of students in the Argentine nation. A random sample of approximately equal size was drawn from each of the 10 faculties, giving a total of 639 students from the University of Buenos Aires.[2]

In order to define the universe for sampling, the voters' registration for each faculty was employed. Since it is necessary to vote in student elections in order to take exams and to obtain credit for courses, these lists are very complete. In order to be included in the list of registered student voters it is necessary to be formally inscribed as a student in the faculty and to have completed at least one course during the period prior to the election during which the list was to be used. For this reason, there was a systematic

---

[1] Talcott Parsons, "The School Class as a Social System: Some of Its Functions in American Society," *Harvard Educational Review*, XXIX (Fall, 1959), p. 297.

[2] Disparities in the sizes of the faculties should be kept in mind when considering the overall figures from the University of Buenos Aires. Responses from the different faculties vary considerably.

tendency to include older and more-advanced students and exclude those who were just starting their university careers. At the same time the lists tended to exclude students who, although registered in the faculty, had not yet begun to take courses, as well as those who had partially or completely abandoned them.

Quota sampling techniques, adjusting the quotas to the sex, age, and social-class parameters of the University of Buenos Aires, were used in selecting students from the Catholic University of Buenos Aires and four provincial state universities. A total of 393 additional students was thus incorporated in the sample. In Buenos Aires and two of the provincial capitals, quota sampling techniques were also employed to select a total of 634 additional youths of college age for interviewing. These "nonuniversity" youths came from families similar to those of the university students but they had never enrolled at any time in any institution of higher education.

As a first step in the examination of the attitudes of Argentine youths, attention was focused upon their view of university education. Access to the Argentine university is relatively free, yet many middle-class youths who might qualify for admission go to work instead. Therefore it is important to understand the manner in which university education itself is seen by youths as different perspectives on the university may account for differences regarding the responsibilities attributed to members of an educated elite.

After a series of questions concerning the importance of several different reasons for which young people might elect to go to the university, respondents were asked to choose which reason they considered to be *most* important. In contrast to data on American students reported by Rose Goldsen,[1] Argentine youths appeared to be preoccupied with vocational concerns. Data in Table 1 show that 36 per cent of 2,975 university students in Goldsen's sample claimed the most important ideal that colleges or universities ought to emphasize was the provision of vocational training and the development of skills and techniques directly applicable to careers. The same percentage of Argentine youths chose this alternative (i.e., to receive professional training) as being the most important reason for going to the university.[2] In addition, however, another 25 per cent felt that the most important reason for going to the university was simply to obtain a license to work—professional degrees such as doctor or lawyer, architect or engineer. Differences in the response patterns may also be due to the absence of a liberal arts college in the structure of the Argentine university. Of the

---

[1] Rose K. Goldsen, Morris Rosenberg, Robin Williams, and Edward Suchman, *What College Students Think* (Princeton, N.J.: D. Van Nostrand and Company, Inc., 1960), p. 7.

[2] Of a random subsample of the 33,982 college seniors responding in James Davis' study, *Great Aspirations,* 32 per cent gave a similar answer. J. A. Davis, *Great Aspirations: The Graduate School Plans of American College Seniors* (Chicago, Ill.: Aldine Publishing Co., 1964), p. 9, Table 1.3b.

American students, 35 per cent felt that the provision of a basic general education and the appreciation of ideas should be the most important goal that the ideal college or university ought to emphasize,[1] but only 12 per cent of the Argentine youths felt that the most important reason for going to college was to obtain a basic education and the appreciation of ideas. And while a bare 3 per cent of the American students felt the development of knowledge and interest in community and world problems should be considered highly important as the goal of the ideal college or university, 17 per cent of the Argentine youths felt that this was the most important reason for going to the university.

What is really of interest here, however, is not the differences between Argentine youths and their American counterparts, but the differences between Argentine students and their nonuniversity peers. In general, the nonuniversity youths view the attainment of a title permitting one to work as the most important reason for going to college. Since in most cases (between 62 and 68 per cent of the nonuniversity sample) these nonuniversity youths are already employed, it is easy to see why they have not elected to go on in higher education. Although university students also take a more vocational than academic view of the purposes of a college education, they see the university as providing an opportunity for the development of abilities directly applicable to a career. This view contrasts with that of nonstudents, who see university education as a device to provide the formal title which permits one to practice a profession.

Different views about the importance of vocational training are offset by some consensus regarding the university's role in developing knowledge about the society. Table 1 reveals only slight differences between students and nonstudents regarding their assessment of the importance of a college education in developing knowledge and interest in community and national problems. The data suggest that important self-selective processes operate in the recruitment of students to the university. These processes, however, do not appear to produce systematic differences in the impressions of the university's role in the development of civic interest held by students and nonstudents.

Turning now to the anticipations of Argentine youths (shown in Table 2), respondents were asked which aspect of their future lives they expected to be most important to them. Fifty-one per cent of all the respondents claimed the most important aspect of their future lives would be their careers, occupations or professional lives. This was true (with one exception) of students and nonstudents alike. The one exception, the capital of Chaco Province, might be attributed to a strong local interest in fine arts. Businessmen in Resistencia have invested a great deal in the purchase of contemporary and

[1]Goldsen, Rosenberg, Williams, and Suchman, *What College Students Think;* cf. 67 per cent of the Davis sample (Davis, *Great Aspirations*).

Table 1. Most Important Reason for Going to College

| | University Students | | | | | | | Nonuniversity Youths | | | |
	U.S.ᵃ	Buenos Aires	Catholic	Mendoza	Córdoba	Rosario	Resistencia	Buenos Aires	Rosario	Resistencia	Totalᵇ
Obtain professional training and develop abilities directly applicable to career	36%	43%	32%	47%	41%	38%	43%	27%	20%	17%	36%
Develop capacity to deal with different kinds of people	17	3	5	7	3	0	1	5	3	2	3%
Obtain a basic education and appreciation of ideas	35	11	20	12	8	11	11	13	11	8	12%
Develop knowledge and interest in community and national problems	3	16	18	12	24	21	25	14	16	31	17%
Contribute to development of moral capacity and ethical standards	8	3	9	12	3	7	5	5	8	4	5%
Obtain connections with people who will be important for future activitiesᶜ	—	1	2	0	0	0	2	3	3	2	2%
Obtain a licence to practice	—	23	12	3	17	21	13	33	37	31	25%
Do not know/no answer	—	0	1	8	3	2	0	0	1	6	1%
Number of cases (100%)ᵈ	(2,975)	(638)	(99)	(75)	(63)	(100)	(56)	(491)	(91)	(52)	(1,695)

ᵃPercentage of 2,975 American students at 11 colleges and universities ranking each as a most important goal to be emphasized in an ideal college or university. Adapted from Goldsen, Rosenberg, Williams, and Suchman, *What College Students Think* (New York: D. Van Nostrand, 1960), Table 1-1.
ᵇ Excluding U.S.
ᶜ In this and following tables, a dash (—) indicates question was not asked of American students.
ᵈ In this and following tables, some percentages may not add to 100 due to rounding off.

classical works of art. Modern statues (rather than monuments) are prominently displayed in the streets and homes of the city. One mark of prestige in this community is owning a key to the architectural landmark for the region. This modern building serves as a clubhouse for members of the local elite and contains within it an extraordinary collection of local, national, and international art. It is not surprising, therefore, that many business-oriented nonstudents of Resistencia choose art, literature, and music as the most important aspects of their future lives. But the students preparing for the professions in this city are much like other students throughout the nation.

It is interesting to note that a comparable question asked by Goldsen[1] showed family relationships were far and away the first choice of American students when identifying activities they expected would give them the most satisfaction in their lives. In Argentina family relationships come in a poor fourth after a concern for career, activities directed towards national betterment, and relationships with friends.

The importance of careers as a central preoccupation of students becomes clearer if the analysis is restricted to a consideration of the 1,118 males in the sample. A look at Table 3 shows that among men even personal activities fall quickly into the background with respect to the anticipated importance of career and working for the national betterment. Differences between students and nonstudents are slight, but there is some suggestion that the students are more concerned with national betterment and less preoccupied with their jobs than are the nonstudents. Sixteen per cent of the students rank working for the national welfare as of primary importance, compared to 10 per cent of the nonstudents; 54 per cent of the students compared to 59 per cent of the nonstudents claim the most important aspect of their futures will be their occupations or professional lives.

Is a concern for national betterment a product of the university experience or are the small differences observed due to factors such as the age of the respondent and the simple process of maturation? Or are they due, perhaps, to the kind of family from which the respondent comes? Re-examination of Table 3 provides some answers to these questions. Here we see that these factors are of little importance among university students. Being connected with the university tends to erase differences that might be attributed, generally, to processes of maturation or antecedent characteristics such as those indicated by the degree of father's education. Almost no differences exist between those under 22 and those older, between those whose fathers are ex-university people and those whose fathers were never connected with the university. Young and old, from educated families and uneducated families, they tend to share a belief in what is important. Of

---

[1] Goldsen, Rosenberg, Williams, and Suchman, *What College Students Think*, p. 24.

Table 2. Most Important Aspects of Future Life

	University Students							Nonuniversity Youths			
	U.S.[a]	Buenos Aires	Catholic	Mendoza	Córdoba	Rosario	Resistencia	Buenos Aires	Rosario	Resistencia	Total
Art, literature or music	—	5%	5%	0	6%	6%	2%	6%	4%	46%	5%
Career, occupation, professional life	28%	54	34	59%	52	41	50	54	45	15	51%
Family	55	7	11	3	6	2	13	10	10	8	8%
Social life	—	11	8	7	10	12	7	14	18	4	12%
Leisure-time recreational activities	5	0	0	0	0	1	0	2	2	2	1%
Religious beliefs or activities	4	1	3	3	0	1	0	1	0	15	1%
Activities directed toward national betterment	1	13	27	8	6	15	16	8	3	6	12%
Participation in community affairs	1	3	2	0	6	3	4	3	5	2	3%
Do not know/no answer	—	5	9	21	13	19	9	2	12	0	7%
Number of cases (100%)	(2,975)	(638)	(99)	(75)	(63)	(100)	(56)	(491)	(91)	(52)	(1,695)

[a] Adapted from Goldsen, Rosenberg, Williams, and Suchman, *What College Students Think*, Table 2-1.

Table 3. Most Important Aspect of Future Life (Male Students Only)

	Nonuniversity Father		University-Educated Father		Total Students	Grand Total
	Under 22	22 or Older	Under 22	22 or Older		
Civic work	3%	5%	1%	3%	3%	4%
National betterment	17	17	16	15	16	14%
Religion	1	1	3	2	1	1%
Free time	1	0	1	0	0	1%
Friends and social life	5	7	6	11	7	8%
Family	4	6	2	7	5	5%
Professional life	52	55	54	52	54	56%
Art, literature, etc.	7	5	4	4	5	5%
Do not know	3	2	1	3	2	1%
No answer	9	3	12	4	6	4%
Number of cases (100%)	(165)	(280)	(106)	(113)	(664)	(1,118)

Most Important Aspect of Future Life (Male Nonstudents Only)

	Nonuniversity Father		University-Educated Father		Total Nonstudents
	Under 22	22 or Older	Under 22	22 or Older	
Civic work	2%	6%	4%	10%	4%
National betterment	10	7	13	15	10%
Religion	1	1	4	0	1%
Free time	2	5	0	10	3%
Friends and social life	10	7	11	15	9%
Family	6	6	6	5	6%
Professional life	63	56	55	35	59%
Art, literature, etc.	5	7	9	5	6%
Do not know	2	0	0	0	1%
No answer	0	5	0	5	2%
Number of cases (100%)	(252)	(127)	(55)	(20)	(454)

these men 52 to 55 per cent see their careers as the most important aspect of their future lives; about 16 per cent of them selected activities related to national betterment as being of prime importance.

When attention is turned to the youths who have not enrolled in any university, a different picture emerges. Antecedent factors (as well as maturation) appear to influence their feelings about the most important aspect of their future lives. Among those from homes where the father was never connected with the university, there is an overriding sense of the importance of future jobs. This importance becomes tempered somewhat with increasing age of the respondent. While 63 per cent of the respondents under 22 years of age indicated that jobs would be the most important characteristic of their future lives, 56 per cent of the older respondents from nonuniversity homes made this selection. Greater differences may be observed among those from families where the father was once associated with the university; a difference of 20 percentage points occurs between the younger and the older groups of nonuniversity respondents. Preoccupation with the future job appears to drop off rather than increase with age as the students become more involved in the working world. But there is no concomitant increase in commitment to problems of national welfare. Future occupation is apparently the overriding concern for students and nonstudents alike. The unique exception here is found among older, nonuniversity youths from educated homes. Far more of them choose leisure and personal friendships as the most important aspect of their future lives than do respondents from any other group. These youths are, perhaps, the representatives of the traditional aristocratic class. The future, for them, holds few uncertainties in the realm of occupations.

But what does work mean to the youth of Argentina? Does contact with the university affect this idea? In order to find out, respondents were asked what they considered to be the most important characteristic of an ideal job. Their responses are presented in Table 4. Like their American counterparts,[1] the Argentines selected the provision of an opportunity to use special aptitudes and abilities as being by far the most important.

Slight differences are observable between students and nonstudents in the smaller provincial capitals, but they become quite pronounced in the large metropolitan areas of Buenos Aires and Rosario. In each case, the desire for an opportunity to use special abilities is more frequently expressed by students than by nonstudents. Also, more students appear to be willing to take risks when considering security as an important characteristic of an ideal job. Nonstudents, especially in more rural areas, appear much more concerned with problems of security. In the three areas where comparisons are available, they rank security as the most important characteristic of an ideal job more frequently than do their student colleagues.

Finally, and perhaps most important, in every case students rank the opportunity to work for the good of the country as being of greater importance as a characteristic of an ideal job than do nonstudent respondents. This suggests that a desire to be of service is more pronounced among those with greater potential for entering into the strategic positions in the process of Argentine development. The question remains, however, whether this desire may be developed in the university environment, even though it is not considered to be an important aspect of college life either by students or nonstudents (Table 1).

[1] Goldsen, Rosenberg, Williams, and Suchman, *What College Students Think*, p. 27.

Table 4. Most Important Characteristic of an Ideal Job

	University Students							Nonuniversity Youths			
	U.S.[a]	Buenos Aires	Catholic	Mendoza	Córdoba	Rosario	Resistencia	Buenos Aires	Rosario	Resistencia	Total
Permits use of special aptitudes and abilities	27%	7%	22%	15%	30%	30%	20%	18%	18%	19%	25%
Permits creativity and originality	10	32	8	7	13	6	5	7	8	6	7%
Allows direction of others	4	1	3	3	2	1	0	2	1	2	1%
Allows helping of others	10	9	9	45	14	14	7	6	3	4	10%
Allows working for the good of the country	–	13	22	7	14	15	23	10	4	8	13%
Allows earning a lot of money	10	1	3	0	5	0	0	6	5	13	3%
Allows a secure and stable future	24	10	10	5	5	9	9	17	20	23	12%
Allows gaining prestige	2	0	4	0	2	1	4	1	2	0	1%
Allows getting things done the way I want them	–	2	3	0	2	2	0	2	2	0	2%
Allows being faithful to ideals	–	15	12	5	10	16	21	10	10	13	13%
Allows complying with parents' wishes	–	0	2	0	5	3	2	4	8	2	3%
Allows having good working companions	7	1	3	0	3	2	0	1	1	2	1%
Allows working alone without supervisor or subordinate	3	8	5	0	6	11	2	16	13	6	10%
Number of cases (100%)	(2,975)	(638)	(99)	(75)	(63)	(100)	(56)	(491)	(91)	(52)	(1,695)

[a] Adapted from Goldsen, Rosenberg, Williams, and Suchman, *What College Students Think*, Table 2–3, p. 27.

Table 5. Characteristics of an Ideal Job (Male Students Only)

	Nonuniversity Father		University Father		University Total	Grand Total
	Under 22	22 or Older	Under 22	22 or Older		
Faithful to ideals	13%	12%	12%	13%	12%	11%
Make people do things the right way	2	2	0	3	2	2%
Prestige	0	1	2	4	1	1%
Security	15	10	13	8	11	14%
Make money	1	2	3	1	2	3%
Good of country	18	17	16	11	16	14%
Aid others	14	7	11	12	10	8%
Lead people	2	2	0	2	2	2%
Creative	4	9	10	9	8	8%
Special abilities	24	30	23	27	27	23%
Other and no answer	8	10	9	12	10	15%
Number of cases (100%)	(165)	(280)	(106)	(113)	(664)	(1,118)

Characteristics of an Ideal Job (Male Nonstudents Only)

	Nonuniversity Father		University Father		Total Nonstudents
	Under 22	22 or Older	Under 22	22 or Older	
Faithful to ideals	8%	9%	15%	25%	10%
Make people do things the right way	0	4	2	0	2%
Prestige	2	0	0	5	1%
Security	16	21	20	0	17%
Make money	6	6	0	5	5%
Good of country	11	10	13	15	11%
Aid others	3	4	9	5	4%
Lead people	2	2	2	0	2%
Creative	6	6	11	25	8%
Special abilities	18	16	20	15	18%
Other and no answer	29	23	9	5	24%
Number of cases (100%)	(252)	(127)	(55)	(20)	(454)

If attention is restricted once again to the male respondents in the sample, it is easier to separate antecedent influences and those which may be attributed to the university experience. In Table 5 we see that antecedent characteristics are of some importance. For example, the opportunity to be creative in a job is more often cited as being of primary importance by the children of university-educated fathers (whether or not they themselves are students). The effects of age are noticeable only among the nonuniversity youths from educated families; the older respondents select creativity as an important criterion more frequently (25 per cent) than do the younger members in this category (11 per cent). But the nonuniversity sons of university-educated fathers in general are much more concerned with the question of creativity in a job than are the nonuniversity youths from nonuniversity families (of which only 6 per cent selected creativity as the most important characteristic of an ideal job). A similar difference is observable among the university students, although in a much smaller magnitude. These differences suggest that the university experience itself tends to reduce the impact of factors such as father's education, and even the process of aging itself; only 4 per cent of the younger students chose creativity and 9 per cent of the older ones did so. As students mature, their background characteristics become less important.

A similar phenomenon may be observed in other areas that students consider to be important for an ideal job. When the desire to be faithful to one's ideals is examined, for example, almost no variation is observed among students, whether young or old, from educated families or from families where the father has not been connected with the university; about 12 per cent of all these students claimed that the opportunity to be faithful to their ideals is of primary importance among the characteristics of an ideal job. Nonuniversity youths from uneducated families are less prone to select this characteristic of an ideal job, about 8 or 9 per cent of them doing so, while 15 per cent of the younger nonuniversity youths from educated families chose fidelity to ideals as being important. It is only among that group of nonuniversity youths who are over 22 years of age and whose fathers were associated with the university at one time that as many as 25 per cent of the respondents chose fidelity to ideals as being of prime importance. This group chose fidelity to ideals with the same frequency that they chose being creative as a prime characteristic of an ideal job. Here, again, this appears to be a response pattern more characteristic of those assured a position in the traditional order. In general, however, contact with the university appears to counteract the effects of aging that appear among nonstudents.

Finally, when we look at the role played by the university in developing a commitment to working for the good of the country, no simple, systematic pattern emerges. A slightly higher percentage of students tended to single out the opportunity for working for the good of the country as being of primary importance in an ideal job, 16 per cent of them claiming it is the most important characteristic; 11 per cent of the nonstudents made this claim. There are no readily detectable patterns of fluctuation in this evaluation due to the age of the respondent or his background with a highly educated father. The range among university students who chose this as the first alternative is from 11 to 18 per cent. The lowest frequency among them came from the older sons of university-educated fathers. In contrast, among the nonuniversity youths, where the range is from 10 to 15 per cent, the least interested in working for the good of the country are the older youths from nonuniversity homes, while the most interested are the older youths from homes where the father was connected with the university at one time. This is consistent with the pattern of "noblesse oblige" which might be expected for those not pursuing higher education and coming from cultivated homes. This is also the group most concerned with being faithful to their ideals; it will be recalled that 25 per cent of them selected fidelity to ideals as the most important characteristic of an ideal job in comparison to 8 per cent of the young, nonuniversity youths from uneducated homes. In fact, this is twice the percentage of students in general, among whom only slight variations can be observed as a function of age or father's education.

But ideal characteristics and real jobs are often disparate. What do Argentine youths see as their probable future? Table 6 presents the distribution of responses to a question on realistic expectations regarding occupation within five years' time, regardless of desires or preferences. The students see themselves going into the professions, and in Argentina this has traditionally been a prerequisite for obtaining positions within any of the large decision-making agencies of the society. Nonstudents expect to go into some aspect of business.

The accusation has often been made that many Latin Americans feel the attainment of a position or privilege is sufficient justification for taking advantage of that position for personal gain. When Argentine youths were asked about their agreement with a statement that people with more education should use it to better society even at the cost of personal sacrifice, they refuted the accusation, at least verbally. Table 7 shows almost all respondents were in agreement with the statement presented above, although there was considerable variation in the degree of that agreement.

Little difference can be observed between nonstudents and students of the University of Buenos Aires, where 37 and 35 per cent, respectively, take a strong position of agreement with this proposition. Differences are more pronounced, however, in other regions of the country, where a higher proportion of students take a strong position of agreement than do the nonstudents. There is a tendency for an increasing percentage of students to take a strong position of agreement in smaller provincial capitals and in those less industrialized. In the heavily industrialized federal capital and the auto production center of Córdoba, the proportions of students willing to take a position of strong agreement are the smallest. In the smallest and the least industrialized of the capitals, Resistencia, the proportion is relatively high. The 16 per cent of the students from the Catholic University

Table 6. "Realistic" Job Expectations in Five Years' Time

	University Students						Nonuniversity Youths			
	Buenos Aires	Catholic	Mendoza	Córdoba	Rosario	Resistencia	Buenos Aires	Rosario	Resistencia	Total
Professional	83%	57%	77%	65%	63%	74%	22%	14%	27%	63%
Managerial	1	3	1	2	4	1	15	19	12	6%
Business owner	2	18	0	3	2	2	7	8	0	8%
Self-employed	1	3	0	2	5	1	19	15	17	9%
Skilled laborer	0	0	0	0	0	0	2	3	2	1%
Unskilled laborer	0	0	0	0	0	0	0	0	2	0%
Teacher	5	3	4	10	20	10	6	7	12	7%
Employee	2	6	1	3	4	0	11	10	8	1%
Housewife	2	3	0	3	2	2	8	14	12	3%
Do not know/no answer	4	7	16	13	2	10	9	10	10	2%
Number of cases (100%)	(638)	(99)	(75)	(63)	(100)	(56)	(491)	(91)	(52)	(1,695)

Table 7. People with More Education Should Apply It to the Betterment of Society Even at the Cost of Personal Sacrifice

	University Students						Nonuniversity Youths			
	Buenos Aires	Catholic	Mendoza	Córdoba	Rosario	Resistencia	Buenos Aires	Rosario	Resistencia	Total
Strongly agree	35%	61%	52%	43%	54%	55%	37%	35%	46%	40%
Agree	59	38	33	52	46	36	56	60	48	53%
Disagree	5	1	9	2	0	5	6	4	6	5%
Strongly disagree	0	0	0	2	0	1	1	0	0	0%
Do not know/no answer	0	0	5	2	0	3	1	0	0	1%
Number of cases (100%)	(638)	(99)	(75)	(63)	(100)	(56)	(491)	(91)	(52)	(1,695)

who agree strongly with the above proposition can be understood best, perhaps, in light of the ideological differences between the Catholic University and its national counterpart. The former represents, in many ways, the traditional agricultural aristocracy of Argentina while the latter is more closely linked with modernizing and industrializing forces and has a concomitant secular emphasis.

It is still not clear whether the differences observed so far are, in any way, attributable to the university and its impact upon youth. When we look at Table 8 and the responses of university students to the statement, "People with more education should apply it to the betterment of society even at the cost of personal sacrifice," we still see only slight fluctuations. About 43 per cent of all students strongly agree with this statement. When we turn to the responses of the nonuniversity youths, however, considerable variation can be observed, and it appears that this variation is due largely to the process of maturation rather than to differences in family backgrounds. Twenty-nine per cent of the young nonuniversity youths from uneducated families strongly agree to this statement and 35 per cent of those from educated families do so. But among the youths from families where the father has not been connected with the university, there is a difference of 20 percentage points between the younger and the older groups. Twenty-nine per cent of the former agree strongly with the statement about the responsibility of the educated to work for the betterment of society even at the cost of personal sacrifice; 50 per cent of those over 22, who are not students and whose fathers were not connected with the university, make this claim. While 35 per cent of the younger group who have university fathers are in agreement, 45 per cent of the older group checked the "strongly agree" response.

Apparently the process of self-selection which leads youths to the university in the first place, rather than the impact of the university, produces the relatively uniform level of agreement among students regarding the social responsibility of an educated elite. For example, it is easily seen that the young university students (regardless of their fathers' education) are more frequently in agreement with the statement about the responsibilities of the educated than are the young nonstudents (regardless of their fathers' education). But it is also apparent that the older nonuniversity youths are at least as frequently committed to this ideal as are the students. Commitment is, apparently, as frequently developed in the society at large as within the university proper.

In summary, the data presented in this paper suggest that contemporary Argentine youths, although similar in many ways to their North American counterparts, are far more vocationally oriented. Exposure to the university in urban, industrial settings appears to produce young professionals consciously moving toward positions of strategic importance in

Table 8. Responsibility of the Intellectual to Society (Male Students Only)

	Nonuniversity Father		University Father			Grand Total
	Under 22	22 or Older	Under 22	22 or Older	Total	
Strongly agree	44%	43%	41%	44%	43%	40%
Agree	50	52	53	51	52	54%
Disagree	4	4	5	4	4	4%
Strongly disagree	0	0	0	1	0	0%
Do not know	1	0	1	0	0	1%
No answer	2	1	1	0	1	1%
Number of cases (100%)	(165)	(280)	(106)	(113)	(664)	(1,118)

Responsibility of the Intellectual to Society (Male Nonstudents Only)

	Nonuniversity Father		University Father		Total
	Under 22	22 or Older	Under 22	22 or Older	
Strongly agree	29%	50%	25%	45%	36%
Agree	64	43	56	55	57%
Disagree	5	6	7	0	6%
Strongly disagree	1	1	0	0	1%
Do not know	1	1	0	0	1%
No answer	0	0	1	0	0%
Number of cases (100%)	(252)	(127)	(55)	(20)	(454)

the development of their nation. Yet they are secular, pragmatic, and much less frequently committed to the ideal of personal sacrifice than their more rural counterparts. Furthermore, such commitment appears to develop outside the university rather than within it.

Thus, the role played by the university in the creation of elites for the processes of economic development and social change is neither simple nor clear cut. It would appear that many of the differences observed among the students are due to processes which occur in the larger society as well; as time passes, nonstudents come to resemble students in certain areas of attitude and belief while becoming increasingly different in others. In order to understand the process whereby university education affects the attitudes and beliefs of maturing young adults, it is necessary to reconsider the nature of the university context itself. More refined analyses of data from the study described here are now being undertaken in an attempt to specify more completely the social contexts in which students are immersed.[1] It is

[1] See D. Nasatir, "University Experience and Political Interest of Students in Buenos Aires," *Comparative Education Review,* 10 (June, 1966), pp. 273–281. [This article immediately follows, pp. 701–712, this volume. Ed.]

hoped that such refinements may illuminate the process whereby commitment to public service among university students may be developed.

University Experience and Political Unrest of Students in Buenos Aires

DAVID NASATIR

It is known that higher education has numerous effects on the lives of those who partake of it: expanding their knowledge, modifying their tastes, preparing them for occupations, and introducing their mates. Its role in developing and shaping their political beliefs is not known, although in recent years this has been a topic of increasing theoretical and empirical interest.[1] In his work, *Political Man,* S. M. Lipset claims:

> Education presumably broadens man's outlook, enables him to understand the needs for norms of tolerance, restrains him from adhering to extremist doctrines and increases his capacity to make rational electoral decisions.[2]

Yet in her book, *What College Students Think,* Rose K. Goldsen gives evidence for increasing conservatism throughout the college years.[3] In contrast to the above, Philip E. Jacob, after an extensive review of the available evidence, has concluded that higher education probably has little or no effect on attitudes and values.[4] And Peter I. Rose has suggested that it is quite possible that each of the above conclusions may be true—under certain

Reproduced, by permission, from *Comparative Education Review,* 10 (June, 1966), pp. 273–281.

[1] See, for example, Nevitt Sanford, ed., *The American College: A Psychological and Social Interpretation of the Higher Learning* (New York: Wiley, 1962); see also Alex S. Edelstein, "Since Bennington: Evidence of Change in Student Political Behavior," *Public Opinion Quarterly,* XXVI (Winter, 1962), pp. 564–577.

[2] Seymour M. Lipset, *Political Man* (Garden City, N.Y.: Doubleday, 1960), p. 56.

[3] Rose K. Goldsen *et al., What College Students Think* (Princeton, N.J.: Van Nostrand, 1960), p. 123.

[4] Philip E. Jacob, *Changing Values in College: An Exploratory Study of the Impact of College Teaching* (New York: Harper and Brothers, 1957).

conditions.[1] This article is an attempt to illuminate some of those conditions.

Rose Goldsen has stated, ". . . if young people are exposed for four years to institutional norms and values in the very milieu in which they are explicit and authoritative, they will become socialized to the predominant values of that milieu and will come to acknowledge their legitimacy."[2] Thus, to the extent that the norms of the university differ from those of the society at large, systematic differences should be observable among the values and norms of students and nonstudents. These differences should be observable, as well, among the students themselves to the extent that the milieus in which they play out their roles as students differ.

A simple test of the impact of university life can be devised, then, by comparing the responses of students and nonstudents to questions indicative of deeper normative orientations. To the extent that there are systematic differences in the contexts of their everyday lives, we may expect differences in their responses to such questions. Similarly, to the extent that there are important differences within the larger student context, there should also be differences in the responses of students from these subcontexts.

University students throughout the world have a political significance out of proportion to their numbers. They constitute the future elite of their societies and frequently have an image of that future at variance with their daily experiences. This is especially true, perhaps, in developing nations, where students have more opportunity to come in contact with new ideas and products as well as greater skills in articulating feelings of deprivation and demands for change. One area in which the impact of university life should be most evident, therefore, is that of political interest. For whatever else it might be, bringing about large-scale change, like the preservation of the status quo, is an eminently political task. It may be expected, therefore, that an interest in politics will be more widespread among students than among other youthful members of the population.

But elite potential and cosmopolitanism are not the monopoly of students alone. The children of elite families are exposed to factors at home which might well produce similar contacts and skills. And it is, of course, precisely these children who are also most likely to be students. Therefore, before attributing a special politicalizing impact to the university, it is necessary to examine the manner in which political interest is manifested by youth in general and to determine whether such interest is especially associated with highly politicalized subcultures among students.

In order to illustrate more clearly the role played by the university in developing an interest in politics, a study of some 1,600 Argentine youths was

[1] Peter I. Rose, "The Myth of Unanimity: Student Opinions on Critical Issues," *Sociology of Education,* 37 (Winter, 1963), pp. 129–149.

[2] Goldsen *et al., What College Students Think,* p. 198.

undertaken. Argentina presents many interesting contrasts to the United States which facilitate such a study. It is relatively easy to locate groups of young middle-class Argentines who do not attend institutions of higher education as well as children of manual laborers who do.[1] Comparisons of a kind not possible in the United States (where it is quite difficult to locate youths from middle-class families who have not been associated with some institution of higher education at one time or another) can thus be made in an effort to distinguish the effects of higher education from those of social class and family background.

In order to simplify the analysis somewhat, the following discussion will be based only upon the responses from 630 students of the University of Buenos Aires and 489 nonuniversity youths from the metropolitan area that constitutes greater Buenos Aires. Random samples of approximately equal size were drawn from the lists of eligible voters in each of the 10 faculties (professional schools) which constitute the university.[2] In order to be included in the lists it is necessary to be formally registered as a student in the particular school and to have finished at least one course during the electoral period prior to the one in which the list is to be employed.

Nonuniversity youths were selected according to a quota sampling technique. Interviewers were sent throughout the greater metropolitan area of Buenos Aires with instructions to obtain interviews from subjects between 18 and 25 years of age who had never had any contact with any university (including those who had started but not finished even the first course). Examination of the university census provided an estimate of the age, sex, and social-class distribution of the students and these parameters were used in constructing the remaining quotas for the nonuniversity youths.

That some differences in political interest do exist between groups of university students and nonuniversity youths comes as no surprise. Table 1 shows rather clearly what might have been expected all along; students respond more often than nonstudents in that they sometimes or even frequently get as excited about something that happens in politics as about

---

[1] According to a study by Otis Dudley Duncan and Robert W. Hodge, "Education and Occupational Mobility: A Regression Analysis," *American Journal of Sociology*, LXVIII (May, 1963):

"The data are consistent with the supposition that education was becoming a more important determinant of occupational status, in terms of both its net influence apart from level of origin and its role as a variable intervening between origin and destination," p. 644.

In contrast to the situation in the United States, see Sugiyama Iutaka, "Mobilidade social e oportunidades educacionais em Buenos Aires e Montevidéu, uma análise comparativa (1)," *América Latina*, VI: "Formal education in these cities does not appear to be as important a route to higher social status as might on other grounds have been expected," p. 39. See also Table 11A, p. 36, "Buenos Aires, nivel educacional do entrevistado em relação ao nivel educacional do país, e ao seu status relativo."

[2] It is important to note that differences in the enrollment among the various schools are very great, and, since the samples taken from each faculty were of about equal size, it is not proper to generalize about the entire student population of the University of Buenos Aires without giving proper weight to these differences. This has not been done here and the reader is warned accordingly.

Table 1. More Students Frequently Interested in Politics Than Nonstudents:
Answers to the Question, "Do You Ever Get as Excited about Something That
Happens in Politics as about Something That Happens in Personal Life?"

	Frequently	Sometimes	Never	No Answer	Total
University students[a]	38%	48%	13%	—	(630)[b]
Nonuniversity youths[a]	26%	41%	32%	—	(489)

[a] University of Buenos Aires and nonuniversity youths from Buenos Aires.
[b] Number in parentheses indicates size of sample from which percentages were computed.

something that happens in their personal life. While only 13 per cent of the
students say that they never develop such an interest, a complete lack of
interest is characteristic of 32 per cent of the nonstudents. In fact, nonstudents more often respond that they *never* get excited about politics
than that they *frequently* do. Students, in contrast, claim frequent interest
almost three times as often as they claim complete lack of interest.[1]

These differences are not simply differences in subjective orientations
but are also reflected in the behavior of the two groups. Tables 2 and 3 reveal the same type of relationship between university attendance and talking about politics with friends as was observed in Table 1. In Table 2, 45
per cent of the students claim that they frequently talk politics with their
friends in contrast to 26 per cent of the nonstudents claiming such activity.
Where only 4 per cent of the students say that they never talk politics with
their friends, 22 per cent of the nonstudents may be considered relatively
apolitical.[2]

A final indicator of political interest can be obtained from analysis of
the role played by the students and the nonstudents in political discussions.
Table 3 shows that almost one-fifth more (69 per cent) of the students
claim that they intervene in political discussions rather than listen in comparison with the 50 per cent of nonuniversity youths making such a claim.
No matter what indicators are used, students are clearly more interested
in politics. The question is, of course, why do such differences exist? Are
they due to differences in family background? Differences in the values of
youths who select the university rather than the market place? Or are they,
in fact, due to the impact that the university experience has upon those
that participate in it?

That some part of the difference between students and nonstudents may
be attributed to differences in family background is to be expected. Just

[1] This is consistent with data presented by S. M. Lipset, *Political Man,* on political apathy.
[2] It should be noted that this is a very relative apathy. At the most politicized of the 11 North
American campuses reported on in the Goldsen book, 54 per cent of the students said no to the
question, "Do you ever get as worked up about something that happens in politics as something
that happens in personal life?" (*What College Students Think,* appendix 13, p. 218).

Table 2. More Students Frequently Talk Politics Than Nonstudents: Answers
to the Question, "Do You Often Talk Politics with Your Friends?"

	Frequently	Sometimes	Rarely	Never	No Answer	Total
University students	45%	38%	12%	4%	—	(630)
Nonuniversity youths	26%	34%	19%	22%	—	(489)

Table 3. More Students Usually Talk in Political Discussions Than Nonstudents:
Answers to the Question, "In These Conversations Do You Usually
Intervene or Listen?"

	Intervene	Listen	No Answer	Total
University students	69%	29%	19%	(630)
Nonuniversity youths	50%	38%	11%	(489)

Table 4. Father's Occupation Is Positively Related to Interest in Politics

Father's Occupation	Interest in Politics			
	Frequently	Sometimes	Never	Total
Unspecialized workers up to foreman	30%	40%	30%	(258)
Technicians and managers	30%	52%	17%	(208)
Professionals and owners of businesses	35%	45%	20%	(653)

what that difference is, however, is not clear. Many studies in the United
States have demonstrated the political apathy of working-class families,
but there is a reasonable doubt that this same pattern might hold in a society only recently emerged from a totalitarian regime characterized by its
emphasis upon creating political consciousness in the working classes. Table
4 shows that, to some degree, the expectation that children of manual
workers would manifest interest in political matters with less frequency
than children from middle-class and professional homes is verified. While
70 per cent of the workers' children claim that they get excited about politics sometimes or even frequently, 82 per cent of the children of technicians and managers and 80 per cent of the children of professionals and
owners of businesses express such an interest. What is important here is not
the existence of such a relationship between father's occupation and child's
level of political interest, but that the differences between students and
nonstudents persist.

Table 5 shows that in each category of father's occupation, there is still
a consistent tendency for students to express excitement about political
events more often than nonstudents. This difference is brought about in a

Table 5. More Students Frequently Interested in Politics Than Nonstudents
Even When Controlling for Father's Occupation

| | | Interest in Politics | | | |
Father's Occupation	Education	Frequently	Sometimes	Never	Total
Unspecialized	University	42%	43%	16%	(113)
up to foreman	Nonuniversity	24%	40%	45%	(145)
Technicians and	University	34%	53%	11%	(123)
managers	Nonuniversity	24%	51%	26%	(85)
Professionals and	University	39%	48%	13%	(393)
business owners	Nonuniversity	29%	41%	30%	(260)

Table 6. Father's Education Accounts for Much of the Variation
between Students and Nonstudents

| | | Interest in Politics | | | |
Father's Education	Education	Frequently	Sometimes	Never	Total
Primary	University	37%	46%	15%	(336)
	Nonuniversity	21%	39%	40%	(225)
Secondary	University	38%	50%	11%	(204)
	Nonuniversity	26%	46%	27%	(147)
University	University	39%	49%	12%	(181)
	Nonuniversity	42%	46%	12%	(85)

rather interesting way. Rather than a consistent increase in political interest
for both groups as higher statuses of father's occupation are examined (as
marginal frequencies presented in Table 4 might suggest), a differential
sensitivity to political interest can be observed. That is, a marked influence
of father's occupational status can be seen in the case of the political interest of the nonstudents but diverse family backgrounds appear to have
only a slight influence upon the level of political interest of the university
students. The students express a generally high level of political interest
regardless of the occupations of their fathers, but such interest is more likely
to be found among the nonstudents who are not from the homes of un-
specialized workers and foremen, although even youths from middle-class
homes, if they are not affiliated with the university, are less likely to get as
excited about politics as are university students.

Although father's occupation is a well-established indicator of family
life style, there are always some problems associated with accurate characterization of occupational titles into analytical categories. It is surprising,
therefore, that when the more clearly defined variable of father's education
is substituted as an indicator of family values, the above relationship changes

fundamentally. Table 6 shows that the relationship we have come to expect between students and nonstudents continues to hold true for children of fathers with only a primary school education. While 83 per cent of the students claim that they frequently or sometimes get excited about political matters, only 60 per cent of nonstudents make such a claim. Although the percentage of students excited about politics remains relatively stable regardless of the educational level of the student's father, a sharp increase in political interest is associated with increasing level of father's education for nonstudents. The effect is so pronounced that among the children of university-educated fathers, the original relationship between the interest in politics of students and the lack of interest associated with nonstudents has essentially disappeared; both groups express their interest with almost equal probability.

Thus it is reasonable to conclude that a considerable part of the differences observable between the population of students and that of nonstudents, with respect to political interest at least, is due to factors antecedent to the university experience. The differences in political interest are associated with the level of education and the type of occupation engaged in by the youth's father.

But the similarity of students and nonstudents from educated families in fact says little about the politicalizing process of the university experience. We still do not know if the university imparts an interest in political events that is separate from such an interest which may normally develop in young adults as they take on the full responsibilities of citizenship. It is necessary to focus upon dynamic factors to probe the adequacy of dynamic formulations.

It is reasonable to assume that some change will be manifested on the part of both students and nonstudents simply due to their changing age roles in the society. However, an examination of Table 7 reveals very slight relationships, not regular, and not nearly of the magnitude that one might expect to be associated with a fundamental social process.

There are, however, many kinds of students. If, as other research would lead us to believe,[1] some part of the university's impact is transmitted through informal primary associations, such effects should be more pronounced for those in some way more "integrated" into university life.

But what is university life? The university is not a homogeneous entity. It is entirely possible that the differences among the various faculties are greater than the similarities, at least with respect to the process of political socialization. A look at Table 8, in which the degree of political interest has been tabulated for the students of each faculty, reveals the truth of this

---

[1] See, for example, "A Contextual Analysis of Academic Failure," by D. Nasatir, in *The School Review,* LXXI (April, 1963).

Table 7. Age Is Not Strongly Related to Political Interest
Either for Students or Nonstudents

	University Students Interest in Politics					Nonuniversity Youths Interest in Politics			
Age	Frequently	Sometimes	Never	N.A.[a]	Total	Frequently	Sometimes	Never	Total
17[b]	–	–	–	–	(1)	–	–	–	(1)
18–19	43%	41%	14%	2%	(44)	28%	34%	37%	(220)
20–21	38%	51%	11%	1%	(180)	22%	50%	27%	(127)
22–23	36%	48%	11%	–	(157)	21%	47%	32%	(77)
24–25	37%	55%	8%	–	(105)	33%	40%	27%	(63)
26–27	43%	43%	14%	–	(56)	–	–	–	(1)
28–29	28%	51%	20%	–	(35)				
30–35	49%	31%	20%	–	(45)				
36[c]	14%	56%	28%	–	(7)				

[a]N.A.: no answer. [b]Seventeen or less. [c]Thirty-six or more.

Table 8. Political Interest Varies from Faculty to Faculty

	Interest in Politics				
Faculty	Frequently	Sometimes	Never	No Answer	Total
Law	55%	35%	10%	0%	(63)
Economics	45%	41%	12%	2%	(65)
Architecture	44%	44%	12%	0%	(64)
Exact sciences	41%	37%	22%	0%	(68)
Agronomy and veterinary	40%	37%	13%	0%	(68)
Medicine	38%	40%	22%	0%	(65)
Pharmacy	28%	52%	19%	1%	(68)
Philosophy and letters	26%	65%	9%	0%	(67)
Engineering	21%	62%	17%	0%	(63)
Dentistry	17%	59%	24%	0%	(41)

supposition. Although the variation among faculties in the proportion of students responding that they never become very interested in political matters is considerable, the variation in the proportion claiming that they frequently develop such an interest is even greater. A first glance might lead to the conclusion that such variations are due entirely to the subject matter of the various faculties. The law school presents the highest proportion of politically interested students (55 per cent claiming that they frequently become interested in political matters) while dentistry presents the lowest (17 per cent making such a claim). Some suspicion is immediately cast upon this hypothesis, however, when the relatively high position of architecture is noted (44 per cent of the responses claim a frequent interest in political matters) and contrasted with the relatively low position of philosophy and letters (where only 26 per cent claim a frequent interest). An alternative hypothesis which might be entertained at this point

Table 9. Time Spent in the Faculty Is Related to Political Interest

	Interest in Politics				
Time in Faculty	Frequently	Sometimes	Never	No Answer	Total
Less than 5 hours/day	43%	44%	14%	–	(441)
5 hours/day or more	27%	57%	16%	1%	(180)

derives from the variable time demands made by each faculty rather than the content of its courses. Table 9 shows that there is, indeed, some relation between the amount of time spent in the faculty each day and the degree of interest manifested in politics. Where 43 per cent of the students in the faculty spending less than five hours per day claim a frequent interest, 27 per cent of the students spending more than five hours per day express such an interest. The decrease in interest is associated with an increase in contact with the university; but a drop in interest is contrary to expectations based on a theory that the university experience, in and of itself, has a politicalizing effect. It is entirely possible, of course, that this effect is due to an unequal distribution of contexts with respect to political interest. It may be that a special process of adult socialization does take place here, but that the majority of the daily activities of the students most involved in university life are carried out in contexts with relatively low political interest.

The data presented in Table 10 provide a test of the above hypothesis. A rough classification has been made of the various careers that exist in the 10 faculties of the University of Buenos Aires. Those departments with a percentage of students expressing frequent political interest above the mean level of such interest for all students were classified as high level of interest contexts. Similarly, in those departments where the percentage of students expressing frequent interest was below the mean level for all students the classification was that of a low-interest context. In addition, students were classified by the average number of hours per day that they reported spending in their faculty.

The most suggestive aspect of Table 10 derives precisely from the above division. Although the observed decrease in interest might have been expected in contexts characterized by their low level of political interest (i.e., students more involved in the context would be more like the contextual characteristic in their political interest), the hypothesis of contextual influence is weakened somewhat by the decrease in political interest associated with involvement even in high-interest contexts. While 51 per cent of the students in the high-interest context less than five hours per day claim a frequent interest in political matters, 34 per cent of those in the faculty more than five hours per day make such a claim.

Table 10. Political Interest Is Not Awakened by a Highly Politicalized Context

		Interest in Politics				
Context	Time in Context	Frequently	Sometimes	Never	No Answer	Total
Low level of interest	Less than 5 hours/day	28%	54%	16%	–	(158)
	5 hours/day or more	22%	62%	15%	–	(110)
High level of interest	Less than 5 hours/day	51%	40%	10%	–	(294)
	5 hours/day or more	34%	52%	16%	–	(70)

The data presented up to this point cast some doubt upon hypotheses of adult socialization in the university situation, at least in regard to the development of political interest. All of the tests employed, however, have ignored the most essential aspect in any process—change over time. Table 11 presents a final test of the socialization hypothesis by comparing students at various levels within their careers, in high-interest and low-interest contexts, while taking into account the amount of time these students spend, on the average, in those contexts.

An examination of these data fails to reveal a pattern of steadily increasing political interest over the years, even for those students spending proportionately larger amounts of time in high-interest contexts. A marked curvilinearity is to be observed instead. A steady increase in the proportion interested over the first four years is followed by a marked dropping off among the most advanced students.

A slightly different pattern may be seen for the students spending less than five hours per day in the same type of high-interest context. Interest becomes more widespread sooner, and fails to drop off with approaching termination of the university career.

In contrast to the full-time students, the part-time students develop their interests while integrated into the larger social context. The interests thus developed are, presumably, consonant with their other activities. Full-time students at the last stages of their academic careers, on the other hand, are faced with a special problem of impending status transition. Data are not yet available to test the supposition that political interest is once again widely manifest among such students upon their successful transitions to the status of full-time, nonstudent professionals.

In summary, a slight increase may be observed in the proportion of students in high-interest contexts who are frequently interested in politics when progressively more advanced students are considered. This is true

Table 11. Political Interest Does Not Develop over Time
Even with Insertion in Highly Politicized Contexts

Amount of Interest	Part-Time Students				Full-Time Students			
	Frequently	Sometimes	Never	Total	Frequently	Sometimes	Never	Total
Low								
1st year	50%	20%	30%	(10)	–	–	–	(03)
2nd year	34%	46%	18%	(35)	30%	50%	10%	(10)
3rd year	20%	58%	20%	(30)	18%	66%	16%	(38)
4th year	35%	56%	09%	(34)	28%	52%	21%	(29)
5th & 6th yrs.	25%	75%	00%	(12)	–	–	–	(04)
High								
1st year	42%	58%	00%	(24)	–	–	–	(03)
2nd year	44%	49%	07%	(55)	31%	46%	23%	(13)
3rd year	56%	37%	06%	(80)	35%	50%	15%	(20)
4th year	52%	35%	15%	(55)	54%	36%	09%	(11)
5th & 6th yrs.	50%	30%	18%	(65)	28%	56%	17%	(18)
Thesis	53%	47%	00%	(15)	–	–	–	(05)

both for part-time and full-time students although more pronounced among
the former. If first- and second-year students are compared to all others,
the proportion claiming a frequent interest in politics rises from 31 per
cent to 35 per cent among the full-time students and from 43 per cent to
51 per cent among their part-time colleagues.

Examination of the responses for students in low-interest contexts reveals the opposite effect: political interest becomes less widespread as students progress through the university. Thirty seven per cent of the students
in the first two years of study in low-interest contexts claim a frequent interest in politics. The level for more-advanced students, however, drops to
24 per cent. A similar phenomenon is observable among the full-time students in the low-interest contexts, i.e., the frequent expression of political
interest drops from 31 per cent to 21 per cent.

The socializing impact of the university may be observed most clearly
in Table 12. As we have seen, the initial degree of interest varies between
students and nonstudents and among the students themselves; there are
also differences between more-advanced students and the newcomers, as
there are among older and younger nonstudents. But the magnitude and
direction of the changes appear quite systematic.

In general, full-time students express a high degree of political interest
less frequently than do the part-time students. But all students become, in
time, more like the context in which their studies are carried out. Since,
as Glaucio Soares has pointed out,[1] it is the small proportion of activists

[1] G. Soares, "The Active Few: A Study of Student Political Ideology and Participation in Developing Countries," *Comparative Education Review*, 10 (June, 1966).

Table 12. Changes in Political Interest

	Percentage Expressing Frequent Interest in Politics			
	Young[a]		*Old*	
Nonstudents	28	(221)[b]	24	(268)
Students				
Low-interest contexts[c]				
Part-time[d]	37	(45)	24	(76)
Full-time	31	(13)	21	(71)
High-interest contexts				
Part-time	43	(79)	51	(215)
Full-time	31	(16)	35	(54)

[a]"Young" is less than 20 or not yet a third-year student. "Old" is 20 or over or third-year student or more advanced.

[b]Numbers in parentheses are bases of percentages.

[c]Low-interest contexts have a mean score on the political-interest factor less than 0.00. High-interest contexts have a mean score equal to or greater than 0.00. (The mean of the factor score is 0.0; the standard deviation is 1.0.)

[d]Part-time students are on campus less than four hours per day. Full-time students are on campus four or more hours per day.

that creates an image of the university as a political hotbed, it is worthwhile noting that political interests can also decay in the university; it is, in part, a question of the nature of the student environment. It is even possible, as shown in Table 12, for political interest among older students to be less common than would have been expected had they not entered the university.

In conclusion, attention is drawn to the heterogeneous character of the large university, not only in the United States, as Rose points out,[1] but in Buenos Aires as well. Consequently, in order to examine the impact of the university experience, some finer breakdowns are necessary. In the analysis of political interest presented here, we have seen that when this is done, the university experience may be observed to have multiple and even opposite effects. Thus, it has been shown how changes do take place in the political interests of students. In the apolitical atmosphere which prevails in some parts of the university, political interest tends to become less common among older students; in more politicized settings interest spreads. As in many other areas, an understanding of the context in which students spend their time and develop their conceptions of the world is vital to an understanding of the impact of a university education.[2]

[1]P. I. Rose, "The Myth of Unanimity."

[2]Acknowledgment is gratefully given for support obtained from the Comparative National Development Project of the Institute of International Studies, University of California, Berkeley, directed by Seymour M. Lipset; and from the Committee on Research of the Los Angeles Division of the Academic Senate of the University of California.

The Professional and Political Attitudes of Chilean University Students

MYRON GLAZER

The need of developing societies for highly trained professionals is well documented by economists, sociologists, and other social scientists. Recent writings on a number of developing countries emphasize the importance of expanding the educational recruitment base, building new professional groups, improving the quality of teaching, and staffing rural positions. The writers generally assert, furthermore, that professional commitment is of prime importance in developing areas for the assumption is made that this commitment will result in motivation to spur economic and social development, and the consequences of this commitment, then, will be positive in meeting and solving the most pressing problems facing these countries.[1]

It has been stated, moreover, that student involvement with other activities, especially political ones, can only draw student energies away from their trainee role and undermine their professional identification. Such

Reproduced, by permission, from *Comparative Education Review,* 10 (June, 1966), pp. 282–295.

I am deeply indebted to the Inter-University Study of Labor Problems in Economic Development and the Industrial Relations Section of Princeton University for providing the time and facilities for the preparation of this article. Professor Frederick H. Harbison has been an enthusiastic advocate of the Chilean project from its inception and I am pleased to acknowledge his essential support. Wilbert E. Moore and Melvin M. Tumin have been my most important teachers and I am ever aware of how significant they have been to me. Mr. Terry Lichtash and Penina M. Glazer contributed, as always, editorial assistance and moral encouragement. The Henry L. and Grace Doherty Foundation and the Center for International Studies of Princeton University supported my 15 months of travel and research in Latin America. [M.G.]

[1] The writings of the members of the Inter-University Study of Labor Problems in Economic Development have especially emphasized the need for high-level manpower. See, for example, Frederick Harbison and Charles A. Myers, *Education, Manpower, and Economic Growth* (New York: McGraw-Hill Book Company, 1964).

criticism has often been leveled especially against students in Latin American countries.[1]

It was to investigate the validity of such broad assumptions that I conducted a research project in one developing country, Chile.[2] This paper will be directed toward an analysis of the extent and nature of professional commitment among Chilean university students, the positive and negative effects of political involvement on such commitment, and its consequences for the process of modernization.

Several criteria were considered before selecting Chile as the country in which to conduct the empirical research. Chile has long been in the process of economic development, beset by many problems, and torn by controversy concerning alternative solutions. Many of its schools, nevertheless, enjoy the reputation of training very competent professionals, whose work has been highly esteemed in their own nation, as well as in international organizations and foreign countries.

Chilean university students, furthermore, have traditionally been socially concerned and politically active as spokesmen for the most underprivileged in the society, although the extent of their involvement has fluctuated during different periods in Chilean history. Prior sociological research has shown that university students had been an especially active and effective political force during the 1920's and 1930's.[3] In more recent years, university students seemed to be moving toward a greater preoccupation with local university issues and toward lesser involvement in national affairs. The year prior to the presidential election of September 1964 seemed to provide an excellent opportunity in which to observe and study student activities and attitudes during a period of greatly heightened national tension, in which candidates of conservative, center-left, and extreme-left positions vied for the nation's highest elective office.

Data Collection Procedure

To gather data several approaches were utilized. Contemporary Chilean newspaper and journal articles, as well as scholarly and government sources, were used to secure a picture of the official and popular thinking on educational problems in general, and the student role in particular. Persons well acquainted with Chilean education, including social scientists, university professors, professional practitioners, and current university students,

---

[1] See R. P. Atcon, "The Latin American University," *Die Deutsche Universitätszeitung* (February, 1962), pp. 7–49; J. P. Harrison, "The Role of the Intellectual in Fomenting Change: The University," *in* J. J. Tepaske and S. N. Fisher, eds., *Explosive Forces in Latin America* (Columbus, Ohio: Ohio State University Press, 1964).

[2] M. Glazer, "The Professional and Political Attitudes of Chilean University Students." Ph.D. thesis, Princeton University, 1965.

[3] Frank Bonilla, "Students in Politics: Three Generations of Political Action in a Latin-American University." Ph.D. thesis, Harvard University, 1959.

were relied on as informants. Finally, a lengthy interview schedule, completed and tested during the first few months after my arrival in Chile in September 1963, was utilized to obtain the attitudes of a representative sample of university students.

The 24-page interview schedule included several major sections: family and educational background, professional training experiences and attitudes, political background and experiences, and political attitudes. The professional part of the schedule was strongly influenced by the approaches utilized in recent studies of United States graduate education.[1] The political questions were constructed almost entirely on the basis of my observations of Chilean national life and of the intense political struggles which characterized the country in late 1963–1964. The schedule was pretested and was discussed at great length with Chileans from different professions and of all political persuasions to ensure that our queries focused on those matters held to be most relevant by local observers.

The actual interviews were conducted with students in four schools of the University of Chile in Santiago, the largest and most important university in the country. The schools from which the sample was drawn are training students in fields which are essential for national development and include medicine, engineering, secondary school teaching, and physics.[2] My aim was to interview approximately 100 students in each of the schools,[3]

---

[1] The questionnaire of James A. Davis and his colleagues was especially important. Also see R. K. Merton, G. G. Reader, P. L. Kendall, *The Student Physician* (Cambridge, Mass.: Harvard University Press, 1957); H. S. Becker and J. Carper, "The Elements of Identification with an Occupation," *American Sociological Review,* 23 (February, 1958), pp. 50–56; I. H. Simpson, "Patterns of Socialization into Professions: The Case of Student Nurses," paper presented at the meetings of the American Sociological Association, August, 1960. The questionnaire appears in M. Glazer, "Attitudes of Chilean University Students," Appendix II.

[2] The goal was to choose schools in traditional fields (medicine, engineering, and teaching) and in a new one (physics). Another basis of selection was to compare schools of high prestige (medicine and engineering) and those of lower prestige (teaching and physics) in the general society. A third aim was to include schools that are oriented toward working with people and thus with social issues (medicine and teaching) and ones that are oriented toward technical and scientific achievements (engineering and physics). A final goal was to select schools that were reputed to be very politicized and left wing (teaching and medicine), a school that was somewhat more conservative (engineering), and one that was apolitical (physics). The plan to interview in a fifth school, which is training students for new careers in public administration, had to be abandoned when first my wife and then I were bedridden for five weeks each with hepatitis.

[3] This number, of course, represented a different percentage of the total student body because of the variation in enrollment in the different schools. Thus, in engineering, with almost 1,500 students, our sample represented about 6 per cent of the students. In medicine, which had 1,225 students, it represented about 8 per cent. History had approximately 250 students and the number interviewed there was somewhat less than 40 per cent. In physics 75 per cent were sampled. The high dropout rate in history resulted in a total population of less than 35 students in certain years. To ensure an adequate sample, the decision was made to combine the second and third years for the midpoint, and the fourth and fifth years for the final point. In engineering and medicine the problem of sufficient numbers did not arise. However, the six-year curriculum in both cases led to the decision to combine the final two years in order to reduce the gap between the mid and final points. This, we felt, would have been too great had we simply sampled from the first, third and sixth years.

and 35 names were drawn at random from those enrolled in each of the first, middle, and final years of their courses of study.[1] However, the pressure of time and the great difficulty in locating some of the students forced us to accept a minimum of 30 in each of the years selected.[2]

Degree of Professional Commitment

Among those questions bearing on professional attitudes, there were several which attempted to elicit: (a) the means which students would employ to achieve professional success, (b) the types of job characteristics most important to them, and (c) their desire to implement their professional knowledge.

THE MEANS

In determining the means which students regarded as necessary for the attainment of their goals, we focused on several aspects: how the students define the realities of advancement in Chilean professional life, what they believe this situation ought to be, and, finally, how students would choose for themselves in a conflict situation.

We first listed six characteristics on an ascription-achievement continuum ranging from social position of family to professional ability. The students were asked to rate, in order of importance, the three characteristics which, in their opinion, were currently most important in obtaining a desirable position in their professions.

Their responses indicate that students are very much aware of the great contemporary significance of such features as family background, personal contacts, and political affiliations in influencing career opportunities. Although there are important variations by school, a very substantial number of the total group rate these as more potent than achievement-oriented

---

[1] This was true in all cases, except the final years in medicine. There, the students are divided and assigned to different teaching hospitals throughout the city, and our random sample was drawn from only one hospital. From conversations with informants we could not determine any differences among the students assigned to the different hospitals.

[2] In general, excellent cooperation in both engineering and medicine resulted in our completing over 90 per cent of our stratified random sample in those schools. Far greater difficulty arose in the School of History. Not only was it an extremely challenging task to track down respective respondents because many did not regularly attend class, but also lists of students, up to date and easy to acquire in the other schools, did not accurately reflect actual enrollment in history. The greatest modification of the sampling design occurred in the School of Physics. Since total enrollment consisted of only 40 students, we had planned to interview them all. Serious political difficulty, however, necessitated an end to our work after 30 students had been interviewed. It was my impression, however, derived from informal discussions with students and professors at the school, that there were no outstanding differences among the 10 students whom we had not interviewed. This observation was confirmed when we reported our initial findings to our informants in the school. For a full discussion of the problems encountered, see my article, "Field Work in a Hostile Environment: A Chapter in the Sociology of Social Research," in *Comparative Education Review*, 10 (June, 1966).

Table 1. Actual Factors Necessary to Obtain a Good Position (by School)

School	All Achievement	Primarily Achievement	Primarily Ascriptive	All Ascriptive	Does Not Know	Total
Engineering	5	37	45	7		94
	(5)*	(39)	(48)	(7)		(100)
History	6	25	36	27		94
	(6)	(27)	(38)	(29)		(100)
Physics	13	12	3		2	30
	(43)	(40)	(10)		(7)	(100)
Medicine	19	48	29	1	2	99
	(19)	(48)	(29)	(1)	(2)	(99)

*Numbers in parentheses are percentages. Percentages may not add up to 100 due to rounding off.

Table 2. Factors That Should Be Necessary to Obtain a Good Position (by School)

School	All Achievement	Primarily Achievement	Primarily Ascriptive	All Ascriptive	R	Total
Engineering	51	34	9	—	—	94
	(54)*	(36)	(10)	—	—	(100)
History	57	32	5	—	—	94
	(60)	(34)	(5)	—	—	(99)
Physics	26	3	1	—	—	30
	(87)	(10)	(3)	—	—	(100)
Medicine	78	18	2	—	1	99
	(79)	(18)	(2)	—	(1)	(100)

*Numbers in parentheses are percentages. Percentages may not add up to 100 due to rounding off.

criteria of professional ability, grades, and recommendations of one's professors (Table 1).

After the students indicated which factors they felt were actually important in obtaining a good position, they were asked what they thought such factors ought to be (Table 2). Their responses readily demonstrate that there is a marked difference between the students' conceptions of what is and of what should be. In every school the vast majority of the students have stated that the achievement-oriented characteristics should be the determining, or at least predominating, factors in influencing students' future career opportunities. The students, then, strongly reject the ascriptive factors, so characteristic of a traditional society, in favor of universalistic norms of evaluation.

The respondents were subsequently asked how they would choose in the following situation in order to test more fully their attitudes in this area:

Two professors have asked you to serve as an assistant and you can only accept one of these positions.

Professor "A" is very highly thought of as an expert in his field and you are certain that you will be able to learn a great deal from him. However, he has very few contacts which would be of help to you in getting a job after graduation.

Table 3. Which Professor Would You Work with?(by School)

School	Definitely "A"	Probably "A"	Definitely "B"	Probably "B"	Other	Total
Engineering	45	31	3	15	–	94
	(48)*	(33)	(3)	(16)		(100)
History	64	20	4	6	–	94
	(68)	(21)	(4)	(6)		(99)
Physics	21	6	–	2	1	30
	(70)	(20)		(7)	(3)	(100)
Medicine	58	33	–	8	–	99
	(59)	(33)		(8)		(100)

*Numbers in parentheses are percentages, which may not add up to 100 due to rounding off.

Professor "B" is also a competent professional. Even though you do not have as high regard for his ability, you know that he has many contacts that will be of great help to you when you begin to look for a job.

Which position would you choose?

The overwhelming majority of the students in every school and every year respond that they would like to work with Professor "A" (Table 3). Thus, when asked to project themselves into a future conflict situation, their responses again are consistently away from the customary paths of interaction in the society and indicative of a high degree of professional commitment.

"SYMBOLIC" VERSUS "INSTRUMENTAL" ORIENTATIONS

Students were also asked to select the two characteristics of a future job most important to them. The factors listed ranged from good income and high prestige to the opportunity to serve the community (Table 4). The responses in all the schools focus most heavily on the opportunity for professional growth (56–77 per cent). Strong emphasis is also given to the importance of service to the community, especially by student doctors (63 per cent) and teachers (49 per cent). Furthermore, little significance is given by the students to income or prestige, with the exception of the engineers who place strong emphasis on the former (38 per cent).

To test more specifically the range of attitudes to the "symbolic" versus "instrumental" orientation to task performances, we asked the students to choose between the following positions:

You have just graduated and have been offered two jobs.

Job "A" is a very distinguished position, especially for a person of your age. However, there will be very little opportunity to apply the most modern methods you have learned in your education.

Job "B" is a job of much less prestige, but you will have the opportunity to use directly your professional knowledge and the opportunity to improve your skills.

Which would you choose?

Table 4. Two Most Important Characteristics of a Job (by School)

School	Political Liberty	Social Prestige	Income	Gain Professional Recognition	Perfect Skills	Help People	Other	R	T
Engineering	35	16	36	10	53	38	–	–	94 (2)
	(37)*	(17)	(38)	(11)	(56)	(40)			199
History	30	5	20	14	73	46	–	–	94 (2)
	(32)	(5)	(21)	(15)	(77)	(49)			199
Physics	13	3	7	2	21	11	3	–	30 (2)
	(43)	(10)	(23)	(7)	(70)	(37)	(10)		200
Medicine	26	10	11	11	73	62	4	1	99 (2)
	(26)	(10)	(11)	(11)	(74)	(63)	(4)	(1)	200

*Numbers in parentheses are percentages.

Although some engineers (19 per cent) and teachers (13 per cent) show a preference for the more "symbolic" position, the overwhelming majority of the students select the more "instrumental" path[1] (Table 5).

Table 5. Accept Job Which Has More Prestige or Allows Use of Training?
(by School)

School	Prestige		Training		R	Total
	Definitely	Probably	Definitely	Probably		
Engineering	5	13	39	37	–	94
	(5)*	(14)	(41)	(39)		(99)
History	5	8	61	19	1	94
	(5)	(8)	(65)	(20)	(1)	(99)
Physics	1	1	20	7	1	30
	(3)	(3)	(67)	(23)	(3)	(99)
Medicine	3	2	71	21	1	99
	(3)	(2)	(72)	(21)	(1)	(99)

*Numbers in parentheses are percentages, which do not add up to 100 due to rounding off.

To specify consistency of response, and possible explanatory variables influencing degree of professionalism, we have constructed a scale combining the three last questions utilized above.[2] The results emphasize the

[1] E. Wight Bakke believes that the student "image" in Mexico and Colombia is still "confused." Students have not yet "digested" the two major components of a professional as a person who has prestige and contacts or as a person who is concerned with the implementation of knowledge. There is a very strong movement toward identification with the latter, however. "Students on the March: The Cases of Mexico and Colombia," *Sociology of Education*, 37 (Spring, 1964), pp. 214–215.

[2] A simple point scale allocated four points to those who definitely chose the more instrumental job, two points to those who probably would make this decision, and zero points to those who definitely or probably would choose the job offering great social prestige. Similarly, students were awarded two points for any one or four points for choosing any two of the following: opportunity to increase professional knowledge, to gain professional recognition, or to work directly with people to improve their life situations. Zero points were given in each case where students

Table 6. Position on Professional Scale (by School)

School	High Professional	Mid Professional	Low Professional	Total
Engineering	31 (33)*	21 (22)	42 (45)	94 (100)
History	54 (57)	22 (24)	18 (19)	94 (100)
Physics	20 (67)	3 (10)	7 (23)	30 (100)
Medicine	62 (63)	21 (21)	16 (16)	99 (100)

*Numbers in parentheses are percentages.

heavy concentration of students in the high professional category (Table 6). In attempting to specify who are the students who are high, medium, or low on the scale of professional commitment, we found that background variables of sex, socioeconomic status, religion, and secondary school do not offer any explanation. In all schools professional attitudes seem to be most correlated with the important variable of degree of political involvement.

Degree of Political Involvement

In the training of young professionals experiences in the informal structure of the university have an importance beyond the formal socialization that each student undergoes. Some students join or sympathize with political groups which may be affiliated with national parties and whose activities are often directed toward influencing both national and university events. Others, less involved, attend lectures and speeches and participate in the ubiquitous political discussions which characterize university life in many developing societies. In periods of political crisis this latter group rallies to the call of the political activists and provides the mass base for strikes, demonstrations, and other manifestations of student discontent. A third group of students is alienated from any form of political activity and rejects the importance of such participation. Emphasizing nonmembership and freedom from all "deals" or compromise, some see themselves as independent critics of the social order while others, uninformed or disinterested, have no political position that can be measured.

To place the students politically, categories were devised, dividing them into three groups. In the first, or activist, segment are those who stated that they were leaders, members, or sympathizers completely in accord with a particular university political group. In the second, or weak political, category are those students who sympathize with one group but who have

chose social prestige, income or political freedom as primary job characteristics. In the final question students definitely deciding to work with the more competent professor were given four points, those probably working with him were allocated two points, and those who did not want to work with him zero points. On the basis of this scoring procedure 12 points were the maximum which any student could secure. Those with this total and their peers who achieved 10 points were rated as high professionals. Students with eight points were placed in the medium professional category and those with six or less in the low category.

Table 7. Position on Professional Scale by Position on Political-Critical Scale

	High Professional	Mid Professional	Low Professional	Total
Activist	56 (64)*	20 (22)	12 (13)	88 (99)
Weak	79 (52)	27 (18)	45 (30)	151 (100)
None	32 (41)	20 (26)	26 (33)	78 (100)

*Numbers in parentheses are percentages, which may not add up to 100 due to rounding off.

strong reservations either about it or about the usefulness of any type of political involvement. Also in this category are those who did not state that they sympathize with any group, but who voiced a distinct preference for one of the national parties and who voted for its affiliate in the university election. Members of the final category include those students who claim no political affiliation, who define themselves as having no interest in politics, and who show no consistent voting pattern.

The Relationship between Professional Commitment and Political Involvement

Table 7 indicates the high correlation between degree of professionalism and degree of political involvement. Thus, 64 per cent of the activists are to be found in the high professional category and only 13 per cent are in the low professional group. In contrast, while 41 per cent of the nonpolitically active students are also highly professional, fully 33 per cent are in the low professional category.

These results challenge the widely asserted view that political activism is a direct impediment to professional modernization.[1] The implication of this position is that, were Latin American university students less politically active, they would almost inevitably devote their energies to professional concerns, which, in turn, would accelerate development of their countries. The Chilean evidence strongly questions the existence of the polarization. Rather, political and social ideology seems to give strong impetus to the rejection of the remnants of traditional society and to increase the desire for change and modernization. Among these students, there is often a direct marriage between their political and professional goals.

Important areas of role conflict do, nevertheless, exist. One frequent source of such tension involves strikes within the university. How do students who are both highly political *and* highly professional resolve the conflict over the strike situation? Are they more or less likely to support the strike, even when it means interference with the intake of important professional knowledge?[2]

[1] See R. P. Atcon, "The Latin American University"; and J. P. Harrison, "The Role of the Intellectual."

[2] The question posed to the students was: There is a probability of a student strike in your faculty for what you consider to be a justifiable reason. You are an officer on the Centro de Alumnos

Table 8. Would You Vote to Strike? (by Position on Policial-Critical Scale
and Position on Professional Scale)

Professional	Political-Critical	Definitely Yes	Probably Yes	No	R	Total
High	Activist	38 (68)*	11 (20)	6 (11)	1 (2)	56 (101)
	Weak	24 (30)	36 (46)	18 (23)	1 (1)	79 (100)
	None	10 (31)	12 (38)	10 (31)		32 (100)
Medium	Activist	10 (50)	7 (35)	3 (15)		20 (100)
	Weak	8 (30)	15 (56)	4 (15)		27 (101)
	None	5 (25)	10 (50)	4 (20)	1 (5)	20 (100)
Low	Activist	5 (42)	5 (42)	2 (17)		12 (101)
	Weak	13 (29)	15 (33)	16 (36)	1 (2)	45 (100)
	None	6 (23)	13 (50)	7 (27)		26 (100)

*Numbers in parentheses are percentages, which may not add up to 100 due to rounding off.

Table 8 clearly shows that among all professional categories, the political activists are most definitely in favor of the strike and least numerous in the "no" category. It is especially notable that among the high professionals, the percentage of definite responses among the activists (68 per cent) is more than double the combined percentage of students in the other two groupings (30 per cent and 31 per cent). Degree of political activism, therefore, appears to be a vital intervening variable influencing students' attitudes in favor of the relative significance of the strike.

The strike is a key mechanism used by Latin American students attempting to influence university and national policy. Their concerns were crystallized in, and given direct impetus by, the University Reform Movement of 1918. Beginning in Argentina, it spread to all Latin American countries with varying degrees of intensity. In Chile, historical circumstances limited the effectiveness of the reform movement. Nevertheless, Chilean students are very much influenced by the reformist tradition, and the strike can be best understood as their most effective weapon, both facilitating and inhibiting legitimate improvement of the university.

Though our earlier findings have indicated that the two student roles tend to be complementary, the response to the question of a strike demonstrates that there are important areas of potential role conflict. This often extends beyond the strike issue and can have consequences for the student's concept of the primary purpose of his entire university education, especially in times of heightened national political tensions. To test students' attitudes further, the following problem was posed.

and can have an important voice in the decision to strike or not. At the same time you are involved in several interesting and important courses in which you are receiving valuable professional training. You would vote (a) definitely to strike, (b) probably to strike, (c) probably not to strike, or (d) definitely not to strike.

Table 9. Technical Competence ("A") versus Basic Social Changes ("B")
(by Position on Political-Critical Scale)

Political-Critical	Competence		Changes				
	Definitely "A"	More "A" Than "B"	Definitely "B"	More "B" Than "A"	Neither	Other	Total
Active	20 (23)*	29 (33)	12 (14)	21 (24)	2 (2)	4 (5)	88 (101)
Weak	50 (33)	52 (34)	10 (7)	30 (20)	6 (4)	3 (3)	151 (101)
None	32 (41)	30 (38)	2 (3)	7 (9)	2 (3)	5 (6)	78 (100)

*Numbers in parentheses are percentages, which may not add up to 100 due to rounding off.

"A" says that the most important factor for the development of Chile is to have well-trained and prepared people. Therefore, the major responsibility of the student is to devote the majority of his time to learning the materials in his field and only a minimum of time to other activities.

"B" says that Chile needs basic social changes before it can bring about any other changes effectively. He believes that the student has a responsibility to devote a good part of his time to political activities, even if this reduces somewhat the amount of time he can spend on his studies.

With whom do you agree?

Our results strongly support our previous findings. Chilean students, generally, see the intake of technical knowledge as the primary rationale of university study.

Yet differences, again, arise among those with varying degrees of political involvement (Table 9). Although a majority of activists in all schools (56 per cent) chose the central importance of professional concerns, this group is still less committed to the professional choice than the weakly political (67 per cent) or nonpolitical (79 per cent) groups. Conversely, the activists are most convinced of the need for basic social change (38 per cent).

These responses confirm our previous findings in regard to the strike. Although we found a high correlation between high professional commitment and political activism, and while both orientations are geared toward the central importance of modernization of the social system, conflict does at times arise over the most effective means for the attainment of social and economic change and how students may best effect this change.

Implications for Economic Development

The burden of the discussion in this section will be upon an exploration of the following questions.

(a) Which students are willing to engage in pioneering activities with the urban poor and in rural areas?

(b) Which students are willing to accept positions which will increase the stature and teaching level in the university?

(c) Are students susceptible to foreign employment?

THE MEDICAL STUDENT

There is an active concern in Chile with extending professional services to the urban slum dweller and to the rural poor. One attempt to develop such services occurred during our stay. This was a major summer program involving 82 fourth-, fifth-, and sixth-year students from the School of Medicine. The site was Chiloé, one of the most primitive and rural provinces. The 30-day trip was sponsored jointly by the School of Medicine and the National Health Service in order to give the students "an integrated vision of the medical reality that they would have to face upon the completion of their studies."[1]

In this environment students experienced a completely different set of circumstances from those in the medical school. In addition to the vaccination program carried out, students were exposed to one of the major causes of mortality, infant diarrhea. The neophyte physicians introduced basic concepts about the necessity of washing hands with soap and water, gave lessons on what to do in areas where soap was not available, and generally supplied very fundamental information.

In servicing these consumers, medical students encountered a whole new set of problems. In addition to the stark medical needs, they learned that providing service often involves the ability to justify treatment and educate prospective patients about their needs. Students had discussions with community leaders, public meetings, and showings of films to indicate the importance of vaccinations, which are, of course, taken for granted in the more metropolitan and developed areas of the country.[2] This kind of experience so well points up some of the concerns of the medical students. One of our keenest informants said:

> In hospital training we are given careful instruction on how to speak to patients, to instruct them on medicinal, psychological and diet remedies. We might well tell them to take their blender and make a banana and milk combination, etc. What good does this type of instruction do for people who never heard of a blender and have neither bananas nor milk?

As a result of their involvement with the realities of contemporary Chilean society, many other medical students also indicated to us that their training does not sufficiently emphasize or prepare them to face and solve their country's major medical problems. Excessive emphasis on specialization has the contrary impact. Thus amidst new exposure and changing concepts

---

[1] *El Mercurio,* January 18, 1964.

[2] Similar changes also seem to be occurring in other Latin American countries. E. Wight Bakke reports that in Mexico and Colombia, the concept of the university as a servant of the people has been growing. "In both countries the medical students spend a substantial portion of their final year carrying medical service to a particular village which lacks such service." There have been attempts, supported by the medical students, to include other students in this type of program, "Students on the March," pp. 213–214.

of what a medical education is all about, the whole training program has been called into serious question. For example, a medical school delegate to the FECH, the student federation, has summarized the results of three conferences involving medical students. The underlying theme of his statement is the necessity for an integrated and dynamic approach to medical education. What is needed, he argues, is a thorough realization of what Chile is, a rejection of the wisdom of the past, and of overzealous borrowing from the practices of the medical professions in highly developed countries.[1]

This significant stream of criticism and social consciousness among the students is by no means the total picture. Most resist positions in small towns with primitive medical facilities or with marginal consumers in the large cities. Youthful idealism is not sufficient in a social structure in which the highest rewards still lie in specialization, work in large Santiago hospitals, and a private practice geared to middle- and upper-class urban dwellers. Thus, a great tension exists between the current road to high prestige and professional success, and what is idealistically recognized as an important social problem, but thus far given only sporadic attention. In essence the combination of high specialization and the current distribution of rewards produces a situation in which the excellence of medical training does not result in the alleviation of basic national health problems.

THE HISTORY STUDENTS

Student decisions as to future professional tasks, institutional positions, and locations are central not only to personal, but also to national development. To gain further insight, we asked the history (teaching) students about a variety of future employment situations. The student teachers place the highest positive evaluation on public secondary school positions in a middle-class urban area. The next most desirable positions are in the university, although it is well known that such jobs are very difficult to obtain.

Although there are no secondary schools in the *callampa* slums, these prospective teachers were asked how they would evaluate such a position were it available to them. There is no greater contrast in Chilean society than that between the *callampa* and the solid middle-class neighborhood. As in most centers of rapid population growth, there are extraordinary differences between those who are well-to-do and relatively secure and the newcomers who arrive from the countryside without wealth, education, or personal contacts and who live on the edge of the community in tumbledown dwellings made from scraps of wood, cardboard, and other readily available material.

---

[1] J. Raffo, "Problemas de la enseñanza," *Cuadernos Médico-Sociales,* 4 (December, 1963), especially p. 38.

Table 10. History Students' Willingness to Work in a Public School in a *Callampa*
(by Position on Political-Critical Scale and Position on Professional Scale)

Professional	Political-Critical	Yes	No	R	Total
High	Active	21 (78)*	6 (22)		27 (100)
	Weak	12 (63)	6 (32)	1 (5)	19 (100)
	None	5 (63)	3 (38)		8 (101)
Medium	Active	7 (70)	3 (30)		10 (100)
	Weak	3 (38)	5 (63)		8 (101)
	None	2 (50)	2 (50)		4 (100)
Low	Active	3 (50)	3 (50)		6 (100)
	Weak	2 (33)	4 (67)		6 (100)
	None	1 (17)	5 (83)		6 (100)

*Numbers in parentheses are percentages, which may not add up to 100 due to rounding off.

In view of the contrasts it is very impressive that a large number of students consider working in such depressed areas (56 per cent). Variation in decision making is somewhat clarified when the students are divided by their degree of professionalism and political activism (Table 10). Not only is it the activists in every professional group who are most willing to work in a *callampa,* but it is also the activists within the high professional group (78 per cent) who are most affirmative and those in the low professional category (50 per cent) who are least so. It is also important to stress that the other students in the high professional group are more willing to accept such employment (63 per cent) than are students in almost any category. High professionalism, therefore, is a key characteristic among those willing to pioneer in new and difficult types of urban employment and becomes even more potent when combined with high political involvement.

When our focus shifts to attitudes toward working in the countryside, we find that degree of political activity becomes an inhibiting variable. Now it is the most active who are among the least willing to accept rural employment among all the professional categories. High professionalism is therefore neutralized by high political involvement (Table 11). The most politically active students are most willing to accept difficult employment if it permits them to remain close to the hub of national events but least willing to accept it when it entails living in rural areas.

THE ENGINEERING STUDENTS

The engineering students, who more often emphasize their interest in prestige and financial rewards than do their peers in the other schools, are also less unwilling to accept rural positions. For them, these activities do not involve great sacrifice. Financial rewards upon graduation are more abundant

Table 11. History Students' Willingness to Work in a Public School in a Rural Area
(by Position on Political-Critical Scale and Position on Professional Scale)

Professional	Political-Critical	Yes	No	R	Total
High	Active	14 (52)*	13 (48)		27 (100)
	Weak	13 (68)	5 (26)	1 (5)	19 (99)
	None	6 (75)	2 (25)		8 (100)
Medium	Active	4 (40)	6 (60)		10 (100)
	Weak	6 (75)	2 (25)		8 (100)
	None	2 (50)	2 (50)		4 (100)
Low	Active	3 (50)	3 (50)		6 (100)
	Weak	3 (50)	3 (50)		6 (100)
	None	2 (33)	4 (67)		6 (100)

*Numbers in parentheses are percentages, which may not add up to 100 due to rounding off.

outside the large cities, as are more challenging opportunities for professional growth. The ambitious engineering graduate need have less fear of
rural "exile" than his teaching or medical school peers. Many engineers see
this type of employment as an initiation into highly desired entrepreneurial
or administrative positions in the major cities, which they hope to obtain
at the peak of their careers. In this sense there is less conflict between the
engineering students' goal of professional advancement and the needs of
national development.

This entrepreneurial and managerial orientation is highly indicative of,
and may be highly functional in, the transitional stage of industrialization.
Engineers believe that their skills enable them to move into a great variety
of positions, instead of merely preparing them for highly specialized work.[1]
Although this is also true, to some extent, of industrialized nations, the
overwhelming emphasis on entrepreneurial and managerial goals is much
more characteristic of a society which has not yet reached the point at
which specially trained administrators capture high-level business and government positions. This entrepreneurial and management-oriented spirit
can be functional in a society in which large sectors of the country are still
vastly untapped by business enterprise or controlled by backward and monopolistic firms.

There are also very serious dysfunctional aspects of this attitude, which
have been described by Fischer in his discussion of Asian professionals. The
goal of administrative employment has not resulted in efficient bureaucracy
but often has culminated in waste of much valuable talent.

---

[1] Engineering students frequently point to the fact that the president of Chile from 1958–1964
was an engineer by training and that his entire first cabinet was made up of engineers.

For example, engineers, chemists, and economists prefer to be administrators while leaving complex technical tasks to individuals who have had little specialized training. Surveys made of activities of elites in Thailand, Burma, Indonesia, and India indicate that in some fields as many as 60% of those trained are not using their skills or the specialized knowledge which university training has given them.[1]

Another significant difference between engineering and all other students is the pronounced lack of enthusiasm for university positions by the former. Pay and prestige differentials, of greater importance to engineering than other students, distinguish industrial and government from university opportunities and place the university in a poorly competitive position. We did, however, have very extensive contacts with one planning center in the University of Chile. This group is staffed by highly competent young engineers, who emphasize the central role of economic factors in influencing the attainment of technical goals. The great significance of this group lies in its ability to recruit some of the most able graduating students. Although the impact has not yet been sufficient to affect general student evaluation on university positions, some change is under way. The cycle of the best engineers going only to better paying industrial and government positions, reinforcing the low prestige of full-time university positions and undermining the quality of teaching, is slowly being challenged.

THE SCIENCE STUDENTS

In contrast to the responses of the engineers are those of the physics students. For them, a university position is the only one consistently rated very highly. No other institution commands a comparable degree of loyalty and even the prestigious international organizations are only mildly attractive. In Chile, however, the situation for scientists is extremely difficult. The profession is not old and established like teaching and also suffers from low prestige and salaries. It is unformed and disadvantaged in the competition for good students, jobs, and appreciation of its contribution. While there is superficial recognition of the need for training people in the basic sciences, there is at the same time a strong feeling in powerful quarters that Chile cannot yet afford to support scientists working, for example, in experimental or theoretical physics. When the country is ready to use such skills, it is argued, it will be able to acquire the necessary researchers.

Dedijer's discussion on the difficulties facing science in certain types of developing countries is pertinent here. Where there is little effort to modify industrial products because of near-monopolistic practices, innovative contributions are little solicited.[2] Research is then almost always pure,

---

[1] J. Fischer, "The University Student in South and Southeast Asia," *Minerva*, II (Autumn, 1963), p. 52.
[2] S. Dedijer, "Underdeveloped Science in Underdeveloped Countries," *Minerva*, II (Autumn, 1963), p. 79.

"simply because its results are never demanded or used by their native agriculture or industry."

Thus, on the one hand, Chilean newspaper articles discuss in laudatory terms the creation of an institute of science to give degrees in physics, mathematics, biology, and chemistry to fill a large gap in manpower needs.[1] At the same time, the floundering institute has its budget cut annually, is forbidden to buy equipment needed for a recently formed research group, is limited to no more than 15 students per year and is in every way discouraged by university authorities, who show little concern that the entire institute may be stillborn.[2]

The contrast which clearly emerges between newspaper publicity and reality is reflective of many education issues. From reading the papers and following the forums, commissions, and planning sessions held, one gets the distinct impression of tremendous public concern and action. A closer look at the situation reveals that enthusiasm on a surface level far exceeds the willingness to accept and carry out the structural changes necessary to achieve the stated goals. Powerful people in the university can then deplore the poor training of mathematics and science in the secondary schools, which results in large part from inadequate training of high school teachers. Yet, they simultaneously refuse to accept fully that in order to improve teacher training, Chile must attract scientists to the university who are well educated and deeply involved in their specialties. Chileans who have gone to the United States and England to obtain Ph.D.'s in mathematics, physical science, or biology find it difficult to remain in their country to train future professionals when they are denied the support necessary to work in their fields of specialization. Ironically, under these conditions the best-trained and most professionally committed young scientists may be precisely those who are most driven to foreign employment.

FOREIGN EMPLOYMENT

Many of the science students define foreign employment as an opportunity for gaining greater professional competence. For others, it is a guarantee of professional positions, no matter what the situation is in their own country. Indeed, this tendency to look favorably upon employment in other countries is widespread among the other students as well (Table 12). In this

---

[1] Within a period of only a few months in late 1963 and early 1964, a rash of articles appeared heralding the importance of basic research. These also spoke approvingly of the university's initiating study in scientific investigation and a physics course for secondary school teachers. For example, see *El Mercurio,* October 29, 1963, November 30, 1963, and January 21, 1964.

[2] These observations derive from lengthy conversations with members of the institute's staff; these scientists are an impressive group from the standpoint of education background, commitment to their work, and desire to remain in their country. Confirmation of their statements came from enlightening discussions with persons knowledgeable of the thinking of officials in the highest university councils.

Table 12. Do You Want to Work in a Foreign Country after Graduation?
(by School)

School	Yes	No	Undecided	Total
Engineering	47 (50)*	27 (29)	20 (21)	94 (100)
History	55 (58)	20 (21)	19 (20)	94 (99)
Physics	19 (63)	6 (20)	5 (17)	30 (100)
Medicine	38 (38)	32 (32)	29 (29)	99 (99)

*Numbers in parentheses are percentages, which may not add up to 100 due to rounding off.

situation, the variables of political involvement and professional commitment offer no explanation, nor did any of the others we tested.

There is considerable public concern about the exodus of high-talent manpower, and criticism is severe of those who succumb to the temptation of foreign employment. Many proposals have been put forth to counteract the trend.[1] Some students, nevertheless, consider opportunities for personal and professional advancement more important than a commitment to the solution of national problems. For them, the alternatives are simple. For others, who are more dedicated to national development, the decision is replete with conflict. It is a dilemma which young professionals face with increasing frequency. Dedijer sums up this situation very clearly and his discussion appears applicable in Chile even for those young professionls who have not studied abroad.

> The reluctance of the highly trained young scientist from an underdeveloped country to return to his own country upon completion of his training is not simply attributable to deficient patriotism or enslavement to the money bags and fleshpots of the advanced countries. In many cases it is motivated, at least, in part, and in some cases it is entirely motivated by the knowledge that it is difficult to do good research in their own countries. Not only is equipment and financial provision incomparably poorer than it is in the advanced countries, but scientific administration is usually far more bureaucratic and antipathetic to the needs of scientists for freedom from petty controls.[2]

Conclusion

The evidence collected from our study of students at the University of Chile in Santiago shows a high degree of professional commitment among student doctors, engineers, physicists and history teachers. This should not, however, compel an automatic assumption that such commitment has only positive implications for Chilean economic and social development. For those students who are very committed to high quality professional

---

[1] *El Mercurio*, October 14, 1963; October 18, 1963; and May 23, 1964. Emigration of trained professionals also plagues highly industrialized societies. See *Time* (February 21, 1964), p. 46.

[2] S. Dedijer, "Underdeveloped Science," p. 68.

performance, the attractions of working conditions in the advanced countries or in international organizations are very frequently irresistible. This is particularly true in science—where jobs in Chile are scarce, where facilities for advanced research are limited, and where few opportunities exist for postgraduate specialization. Similarly, in medicine, students are well trained, are ambitious to specialize and are often undermotivated to deal with the primitive health problems which beset much of rural Chile.

It becomes quite evident, then, that qualitative professional training is in itself not sufficient for solving the manpower shortages from which Chile is suffering. As is the case with many Latin American countries, the greatest problems exist in building new professional groups and motivating members of the traditional professions to work with low-income groups in urban and rural areas, where professional services are desperately needed but are virtually nonexistent. In such situations a special kind of professional identification is demanded. Professionals are needed who are not only technically competent but also aware of their country's problems and motivated to assist in their solution.

We maintain, furthermore, that political involvement can, at times, serve to support directly the type of professional commitment most geared to solve the society's most urgent problems. The Chilean evidence indicates, for example, that there is a marked difference in students' willingness to pioneer by practicing their professions in remote geographical areas and with those urban groups who have hitherto been excluded from the market for professional services. Attempts to explain the divergent student orientations by the use of such variables as sex, socioeconomic background, and religion were unsuccessful. Our results indicate that the most potent variable is the degree of political involvement exhibited by the student. In contemporary Chile this type of involvement most often consists of an identification with the reformist or revolutionary national political parties. Our evidence strongly leads to the conclusion that political ideologies which are supportive of social change, which emphasize the importance of modifying or drastically altering the social order, which reject the current distribution of rewards, which deny the innate inferiority of the economically underprivileged, which advocate the broadening of the society's opportunity structures, and which emphasize the responsibility of youths to engage in this process as part of their student roles can be highly functional in directing youthful energies into those channels most needed by the society.

On the other hand, our investigation also indicates that in certain situations political involvement does conflict with the trainee role and can have negative results. Under certain conditions political activity and affiliation can inhibit the propensity to pioneer professional services where there is a conflict between the needs of the political and professional roles. Moreover, in other instances it can directly interfere with the intake of professional knowledge by drawing off too much of the students' time and energy into political activities.

We believe that, although these results are limited by time and space factors, they give further evidence to the complexity of the student role. There is an urgent need for further research before broad and often questionable generalizations are made about the degree of student professional commitment, its possible contribution to national development, and its relationship to political activism.